TAKING SIDES

Clashing Views on Controversial

Issues in Cognitive Science

Clashing Views on Controversial

Issues in Cognitive Science

Selected, Edited, and with Introductions by

Marion Mason
Bloomsburg University

McGraw-Hill/Dushkin
A Division of The McGraw-Hill Companies

Photo Acknowledgment
Cover image: M. Freeman/PhotoLink/Getty Images

Cover Art Acknowledgment
by Maggie Lytle

Manufactured in the United States of America

First edition

1234567890DOCDOC0987654

0-07-295328-4
ISSN: 1548-7555

Printed on Recycled Paper

Preface

Cognitive science is one of the fastest growing and most influential areas of science in the twenty-first century. Coming together as an interdisciplinary approach involving anthropology, artificial intelligence (AI), computer science and mathematics, linguistics, neuroscience and brain science, philosophy, and psychology, the influence of cognitive science research is felt in almost every major area of life. While most cognitive science research is conducted in specialized laboratories and clinics, researchers are being called upon by those traditionally outside academic circles, such as the legal system to explore memory for crime details, the military to explore robotic and mind-controlled vehicles and weaponry, health care providers to explore the effects of brain trauma and treatment, and educators to explore the best ways to teach and learn.

This scientific quest to understand human thinking and to imitate thinking artificially with computer software, however, is not without controversy. One of the basic principles cherished by scientific culture is the practice of sharing research findings and theoretical explorations with the rest of the scientific community. Often such sharing takes place at conferences and through books and journal articles. The goal is to create a body of scholarship that either confirms or rejects particular findings or conclusions. This practice also adds a level of accountability, knowing that the scientific community will scrutinize all published research. As this review and replication process takes place, the theories and models are refined, reworked, and when ready, applied to real-world situations. The selections in this volume are samples of this most important scientific dialogue.

The issues in this volume are divided into six major parts: mind and brain, concepts, memory, language, intelligence, and reasoning and intuition. Each of the six part openers provides several Internet sites you can browse to learn more about the six areas. The entire book consists of 36 readings comprised of 18 debating pairs of articles. Each of the 18 issues features an introduction that sets the stage for the two selections. The introduction provides an overview of the new terms, theories, and each side's position. Each issue also has a postscript that will summarize the debate and suggest other views on the topic as well as additional readings. These issues are complex and multifaceted; thus, it is important to keep an open mind while reading an entire entry. It is important to read the introduction, each selection, and the postscript before coming to your own conclusions. The introductions and postscripts cannot possibly cover every angle in the controversies, and you are encouraged to come up with your own analysis and critique. You may also suggest new ways of conducting similar research or new applications for the future.

Acknowledgments There are many individuals who, in their own way, have contributed to this effort. My graduate school mentors at The Ohio

State University, especially my advisor, Dr. John Gibbs, gave me the foundation upon which to build an understanding of cognitive science. Among the strongest influences in my personal development are the many students who have passed through my cognitive psychology course at Bloomsburg University. More than anyone else, they keep me motivated as a researcher and challenged as a professor. The librarians and student assistants at Andruss Library helped in many ways during this process. My editor, Ted Knight, and the staff at McGraw-Hill/Dushkin have provided excellent support throughout this entire process. My gratitude goes to my colleagues in the psychology department, particularly Winona Cochran for her support as my department chair, Steven Cohen and Alex Poplawsky for their advice on statistical arguments, and Eileen Astor-Stetson and Jim Dalton for their much appreciated moral support and encouragement. Thanks to Holly for helping locate articles and for her continued friendship. Many thanks go to the Thursday Night Supper Club at Chez Jean who keep me sane. More than anyone else, however, my deepest gratitude goes to my husband, J. Stan Mason, for his never-ending support, for his appreciation for my passions and dreams, and on a more practical level, for his willingness to take over the household chores in order to give me the time to complete this project.

Contents In Brief

Contents

Preface v
Volume Introduction xv

PART 1 MIND AND BRAIN 1

Issue 1. Are Mind and Brain the Same? 2

YES: Paul C. L. Tang, from "A Review Essay: Recent Literature on Cognitive Science," *Social Science Journal* (1999) *4*

NO: Jon Mills, from "Five Dangers of Materialism," *Genetic, Social & General Psychology Monographs* (February 2002) *10*

Philosophy professor Paul C. L. Tang explains the argument that anything usually attributed to the mind is only brain activity by describing the position of Paul Churchland, a leader in the field of cognitive science. Researcher Jon Mills points out five dangers of dismissing a concept of mind, such as the elimination of free will and a sense of self, and instead proposes a psychic holism.

Issue 2. Do Children Develop Theories about Other People s Minds? 22

YES: Henry M. Wellman, David Cross, and Julanne Watson, from "Meta-Analysis of Theory-of-Mind Development: The Truth about False Belief," *Child Development* (2001) *24*

NO: Brian J. Scholl and Alan M. Leslie, from "Minds, Modules, and Meta-Analysis," *Child Development* (2001) *34*

Senior research scientist Henry Wellman and his colleagues, David Cross and Julanne Watson, present a meta-analysis revealing support for their belief that stage-related conceptual changes bring about an understanding of theory-of-mind in small children. Cognitive researchers Brian Scholl and Alan Leslie argue that the data do not support conceptual change but rather the development of innate specific skills that lead to children's understanding of theory-of-mind.

Issue 3. Is Mindfulness a Cognitive Style? 46

YES: Robert J. Sternberg, from "Images of Mindfulness," *Journal of Social Issues* (2000) *48*

NO: Ellen J. Langer and Mihnea Moldoveanu, from "The Construct of Mindfulness," *Journal of Social Issues* (2000) *60*

American Psychological Association president Robert Sternberg makes the case that the concept of mindfulness would be enhanced by association with the area of cognitive styles. Psychology professors Ellen Langer and Mihnea Moldoveanu find Sternberg's cognitive style category inadequate and much too restrictive for the concept of mindfulness.

NO: Fernand Gobet, from "Chunk Hierarchies and Retrieval Structures: Comments on Saariluoma and Laine," *Scandinavian Journal of Psychology* (2001) *141*

Cognitive scientists Pertti Saariluoma and Tei Laine present the case that through computer simulation they can demonstrate that associations made between frequent types of chess pieces and the colors of the pieces were the most salient aspects in novices learning chess patterns. Professor of intelligence systems Fernand Gobet argues that Saariluoma and Laine have not properly modeled human memory, and with a more competent computer simulation it is clear that proximity or location is the most salient feature in remembering chess patterns.

Issue 8. Is Imagination Inflation Imaginary? 154

YES: Kathy Pezdek and Rebecca M. Eddy, from "Imagination Inflation: A Statistical Artifact of Regression Toward the Mean," *Memory & Cognition* (2001) *156*

NO: Maryanne Garry, Stefanie Sharman, Kimberley A. Wade, Maree J. Hunt, and Peter J. Smith, from "Imagination Inflation Is a Fact, Not an Artifact: A Reply to Pezdek and Eddy," *Memory & Cognition* (2001) *164*

Professors of psychology Kathy Pezdek and Rebecca Eddy demonstrate through analysis and replication of a primary investigation that false memories are not being planted through imagination, but rather the researchers have been fooled by the statistical principle of regression toward the mean. Researchers and lecturers Maryanne Garry, Stefanie Sharman, Kimberley Wade, Maree Hunt, and Peter Smith argue that Pezdek and Eddy have performed inappropriate statistical analyses, and the proper treatment of the data further demonstrates the phenomenon of imagination inflation.

Issue 9. Is Adult Memory for Childhood Abuse Unreliable? 178

YES: Peter A. Ornstein, Stephen J. Ceci, and Elizabeth F. Loftus, from "Adult Recollections of Childhood Abuse: Cognitive and Developmental Perspectives," *Psychology, Public Policy, and Law* (1998) *180*

NO: Judith L. Alpert, Laura S. Brown, and Christine A. Courtois, from "Comment on Ornstein, Ceci, and Loftus (1998): Adult Recollections of Childhood Abuse," *Psychology, Public Policy, and Law* (1998) *193*

Professors of psychology and law Peter Ornstein, Stephen Ceci, and Elizabeth Loftus question the accuracy of adult memories for child abuse by explaining the many delicate and malleable features of human memory that can create false memories. Law professor Judith Alpert and clinical psychologists Laura Brown and Christine Courtois respond by challenging the memory researchers' understanding of trauma research and psychotherapy, and by accusing them of undermining the healing process of abuse victims.

PART 4 LANGUAGE 211

Issue 10. Is Context Stronger Than Frequency? 212

YES: **Charles Martin, Hoang Vu, George Kellas, and Kimberly Metcalf**, from "Strength of Discourse Context as a Determinant of the Subordinate Bias Effect," *The Quarterly Journal of Experimental Psychology* (1999) *214*

NO: **Keith Rayner, Katherine S. Binder, and Susan A. Duffy**, from "Contextual Strength and the Subordinate Bias Effect: Comment on Martin, Vu, Kellas, and Metcalf," *The Quarterly Journal of Experimental Psychology* (1999) *226*

Psychology professors Charles Martin, Hoang Vu, George Kellas, and Kimberly Metcalf demonstrate that human memory retrieval is influenced most by context when selectively searching for the meaning of ambiguous words. Cognitive researchers Keith Rayner, Katherine Binder, and Susan Duffy argue that when appropriate stimuli are used, research results indicate that memory retrieval is influenced most by the order in which possible meanings are retrieved when trying to find the intended meaning of ambiguous words.

Issue 11. Is Stuttering Isolated from Lexical Retrieval? 238

YES: **Ann Packman, Mark Onslow, Tanya Coombes, and Angela Goodwin**, from "Stuttering and Lexical Retrieval," *Clinical Linguistics & Phonetics* (2001) *240*

NO: **James Au-Yeung and Peter Howell**, from "Non-Word Reading, Lexical Retrieval and Stuttering: Comments on Packman, Onslow, Coombes and Goodwin," *Clinical Linguistics & Phonetics* (2002) *247*

Senior researchers Ann Packman and Mark Onslow, along with their research assistants Tanya Coombes and Angela Goodwin, demonstrate that stuttering occurs even when there is no lexical or meaningful content connected to the spoken words. Computational linguist James Au-Yeung and professor of experimental psychology Peter Howell argue that the study by Packman, et al. is so full of flaws that it explains very little about stuttering.

Issue 12. Can Computer Models Explain Language Disorders? 256

YES: **William Frawley**, from "Control and Cross-Domain Mental Computation: Evidence from Language Breakdown," *Computational Intelligence* (2002) *258*

NO: **B. Chandrasekaran**, from "Reach Exceeds Grasp: Comments on Frawley's 'Control and Cross-Domain Mental Computation: Evidence from Language Breakdown,'" *Computational Intelligence* (2002) *264*

Professor of linguistics and cognitive science William Frawley proposes that some language disorders are actually breakdowns in the control mechanisms of the brain, similar to the control breakdowns found in computational models. Senior research scientist B. Chandrasekaran believes Frawley has made the mistake of taking the brain-as-computer analogy as fact, and thus his conjectured arguments are of little value.

Volume Introduction

Researchers in the field of cognitive science are dedicated to understanding all the many facets of what most people call *thinking*. One way to view cognitive science is to think of it as the study of the way we come to *know* something. We use the word *know* all the time. We might say, "I know this is my car" or "I know I'm forgetting something," but just how does this process work? Your cognitive skills are hard at work as you read these printed words. At this very moment you are engaging in a vastly complex and fully integrated set of processes, and yet you are making sense out of these spots of ink with ease. The quest to understand these kinds of processes is at the heart of the science of cognition.

One of the first steps in understanding cognition is to analyze the simultaneous processes that are taking place when we are thinking. Whether working with humans, animals, or computer software, cognitive scientists are exploring how entities take in information from the environment, store it temporarily or permanently, work with it, sometimes transform it into something new, and relate it back to the environment in appropriate ways. Cognitive scientists use scientific methods to test hypotheses, theories, and models in this effort to understand thinking. As you read through this volume, you will find many research investigations exploring several aspects of thinking, including conceptual understanding, memory processes, language processing, intelligence, reasoning, and intuition.

If you choose to browse a book about cognitive science or surf the Web for resources, you will quickly find that this relatively new area of study is interdisciplinary. An Internet search of various cognitive science organizations and graduate school programs will reveal that the most common disciplines involved in cognitive science are (in alphabetical order) anthropology, artificial intelligence (AI), computer science and mathematics, education, information science and technology, linguistics, neuroscience and brain science, philosophy, and psychology. Each issue in this volume involves several of these disciplines.

A Bit of History

Another strategy for exploring cognitive science is to consider its history and evolution. The term *artificial intelligence* is said to have first been used in an official capacity at a gathering at Dartmouth College in 1956, while the term *cognitive science* is attributed to Longuet-Higgins in 1973 (Scheerer, 1988). The Cognitive Science Society was formed in 1977, and soon afterward the journal *Cognitive Science* was launched (Von Eckardt, 1995). Many historians trace the foundational ideas and events that were critical to the later development of cognitive science to the 1950s, while tracing the formal, organizational history of this interdisciplinary field to the 1970s. When considering the foundational events of the 1950s, from which cognitive science sprang, most accounts begin with the influential fields of psychology and artificial intelligence.

The effect of the cognitive revolution on American psychology was dramatic in terms of its influence on the discipline. It also cleared the way for psychology to contribute to the new field of cognitive science. American psychologists of the 1930s and 1940s were primarily behaviorists with little use for anything cognitive. An example of just how anti-cognitive the sentiment was comes from *The Logic of Modern Psychology*, written by Rutgers University Psychology Professor Carroll Pratt in 1939. Regarding the concept of *mind*, Dr. Pratt writes, "for all scientific intents and purposes the concept has already outlived its usefulness" and "in scientific circles its death will not be mourned" (page 26). By the 1950s, however, American psychology was undergoing radical changes. Behaviorism faced numerous challenges, such as questions regarding the generalizability of research on nonhuman species to human behavior. Another area of contention was behaviorism's inability to explain the development and use of language. Noam Chomsky was among the first to assert that behavioral principles could not account for language development.

While this dissatisfaction with behaviorism shifted attention to the cognitive aspects of human existence, it did not provide a way of modeling or conceptualizing cognition. For that, according to Hunt and Ellis (2004), cognitive psychology adopted the computer science model of information processing. This gave cognitive psychologists an analogy to explore, new vocabulary terms and principles to work with, and many new hypotheses to investigate. Suddenly there were many new and important issues to resolve, such as what might be the equivalent of computer-based symbol processing in human thinking, or what mechanisms the brain might use to permanently store data. In addition to the adoption of the information processing model, psychologists began publishing important works on attention, imagery or imagination, short-term memory, and memory organization. All these factors led American Psychological Association President Donald Hebb, in his Presidential Address of 1960, to describe the *revolutionary* return to the study of mental processes and cognition to the once behavioral American psychology (Hunt and Ellis, 2004).

Early work in artificial intelligence focused on the analogy of computer hardware as a human brain. According to Scheerer (1988), John von Neumann, the mathematician who designed the first computer, deliberately tried to mimic the human nervous system in his theory and design, even to the point of using biological terminology for computer parts and functions. Eventually the focus shifted from computer hardware–as–brain to software-as-brain. Scheerer divides the development of artificial intelligence into two phases. The first phase focused on methods of information processing, such as the particular mathematical procedures or algorithms used in problem-solving programs. The current phase emphasizes knowledge structures or ways of organizing information, with one of the goals being to imitate the ways humans organize information. For example, when programming software to imitate human brain information storage, should the programmer place information in lists and then program in procedures for searching the lists? Should the programmer build hierarchies of information like decision trees? These questions are focused on *data structures,* a term referring to the way the data are organized.

Another current area of controversy that touches computer science, artificial intelligence, cognitive psychology, and philosophy is the notion of computer consciousness. This issue stems from pondering just how far the computer-as-brain analogy can go. This is sometimes referred to as *strong artificial intelligence* or *strong AI.* Will the computer systems of the future imitate the human brain to the point that they will develop a sense of self? A sense of humor? A moral conscience? These are hotly debated topics in cognitive science.

An Interdisciplinary Nature

All of the disciplines that make up cognitive science are exploring the mind-as-brain and brain-as-computer models, and information is continually flowing between the disciplines. When researchers in artificial intelligence are working with computer scientists to design software programs that simulate human thinking, there must be a way to symbolically represent something that is outside of the computer. For example, imagine that a cognitive scientist is working to have the computer software understand the concept of a cat. There must be a way to *represent* a cat within the computer using language the software can process, such as alphabetic or numerical symbols. Psychologists often use the term *mental representation* in the same way in reference to the human brain rather than a computer. When you think of a cat and all the corresponding associations, you are using mental representations. Neuroscientists look for evidence of mental representations at work when observing and evaluating brain functioning. By using the latest brain scanning technologies, such as computerized axial tomography (CAT scans) and positron emission transaxial tomography (PET scans), neuroscientists can observe healthy brains in action. To return to our example, a scientist could observe your brain in action as you recall everything you can think of about cats. When designing computer software, artificial intelligence must be built in to provide a way to connect such information, such as the letters *c, a,* and *t,* and the word *cat,* and the image of a cat. These software connections or bonds are created using mathematical relationships.

The picture is not complete, however, as it is not enough to have only the representations and their various connections. Whether we are considering human interaction or artificial intelligence programs designed to communicate, there must be the ability to transform these representations into a language. Returning to the cat example, when the computer software finds the combination of letters *c-a-t,* what type of response is desired? Should the software find the sounds of the three letters and produce a sound file that attempts to pronounce *cat* like an English-speaking human would? There is still much to learn regarding the development of language. Researchers in linguistics provide much of the needed insight into the symbolic transformations that take place in private thinking and in dialogue. By observing the way humans talk and think, especially when thinking aloud, cognitive psychologists and linguists can then develop theories as to how we organize and store the mental representations that comprise our memories. When computer scientists and artificial intelligence researchers design a software program to imitate human thinking, they must have a plan as to what types of data structures they will use to imitate human memory.

The cat example we have been working with is rather simple. Suppose the goal was to develop human-like robots for space exploration, military operations, or high-risk construction situations. Cultural anthropologists will quickly remind us of the influence of culture and environment on cognition. They offer insight as to what aspects of mental processing seem common to all people and what aspects are unique to certain cultures. Philosophers, particularly those who specialize in philosophy of science or philosophy of mind, explore the broad implications, ethical considerations, and societal effects of various methods, theories, models, and hypotheses. What would life be like if there were human-like robots with fully functioning cognition? Would they have a conscience? Would they be under human command? Is such a world even possible? Would it be desirable? These philosophical and ethical components are a key part of cognitive science.

Finally, the fields of education and information science and technology are often among the first to apply current research in cognitive science to educational and industrial settings. How might these human-like software programs be useful in education? If cognitive scientists can imitate human thinking, can they imitate conditions like mental retardation and autism? And if they can imitate those conditions, can they figure out how to improve the lives of those with such conditions? Could corporations or governments send out robots to teach children in areas of the world where teachers are not available? There are a seemingly infinite number of possibilities for the use of cognitive science breakthroughs in all areas of major industry—particularly in manufacturing, banking and finance, health care, and military operations.

This interdisciplinary approach to cognitive science, while appreciated by many, is not without controversy. One point of tension stems from the equity, or rather the lack of equity, among the various disciplines. Eckart Scheerer, in his 1988 article *Towards a History of Cognitive Science,* states, "the various component disciplines of cognitive science should resist their complete domination by the AI movement." Another point of disagreement involves the current state of cognitive science. The debate continues over whether the area has evolved into a unified discipline, or is simply the gathering of several related disciplines (for more on this see Gardner, 1985/1987, Scheerer, 1998, and Von Eckardt, 1995).

Core Issues Under Debate

In this volume, you will find debates over mind/brain duality, concept formation, memory functions, language processing, types of intelligence, reasoning skills, and the validity of intuition. It will become apparent as you read through each section that while the debates are focused on these important topics, they are also focused on issues of research methods, specific theoretical models, and the application of research findings. There is a funny irony in the fact that the study of cognition is about how we come to *know* something, and many of these debates focus on how scientists come to know their findings are accurate, how theorists come to know that their own model is the best, and how scientists and practitioners know how to best apply their findings.

Research Debates

The general public relies on scientists to follow objective empirical methods when engaged in research. While it may seem like a straightforward process, there are many questions that arise during the planning and conducting of the research as well as in the interpretation of the findings. Some of the issues in this volume are debates over the wisdom of particular methodological decisions.

Who Are the Participants?

The participants will respond to the particular tasks or questions put before them, and in essence they will produce the data. It is most important to consider any of the participants' characteristics that may influence the results. For example, if the research question is based on novice memory for chess, then it is important to find out how much chess experience each participant has. To investigate novice memory for chess, the researcher, quite obviously, needs participants with no chess experience. The researchers might also want to *match* the participants in other areas to eliminate extraneous influences. For example, when conducting memory research, the investigator may want to match participants for similar levels of education, intelligence, or even age.

Another aspect to consider is just how many participants are or should be involved. In some case studies, there are often only two or three participants. That situation may occur because the researcher is focused on subjects with very specific conditions, such as adults with brain trauma causing a particular type of aphasia or speech loss. In that case, there may be only a few participants available. Even though the reason behind the small sample is clear, the question of *generalizability* arises. Can researchers honestly generalize their findings to the general public, which is to say that they understand how everyone remembers words by studying three people with aphasia? Going to the other extreme, some researchers have used a method called *meta-analysis,* which involves combining numerous studies over many years. This allows for literally thousands of participants. If a finding is consistent for ten or twenty thousand adults, does that make it indisputable?

Even in this case, it is still debatable as to whether the results should be given near-factual status.

Many times in cognitive science research, the participants are computer software programs, and the question of matching is again important. Any inherent differences in the programs may be the source of differences in the results. If there is only one software program imitating human or animal processing, and that software is given several different tasks to complete, the question of generalizability still remains. Just how similar is that program to human or animal mental processing? On the one hand, when programming a computer to simulate a human cognitive process, the programmer must account for all steps. Unlike humans who might say, "I used my intuition" or "I just got lucky," the programmer cannot insert the command "intuition" and be done with it. On the other hand, just because programmers are attempting to create concrete software language commands to simulate attention or memory models, the question remains as to how close these models are to the actual human process.

Are the Methodology and Analyses Sound?

One of the first steps in research is to clarify the variables under investigation and determine how they will be measured. This requires the development of an *operational definition* for each variable. For example, suppose a researcher wanted to know if college students learn things better in the morning or the afternoon. It is necessary to operationally define learning. In this case, the researcher may define learning as accurately remembering visually encoded information for seven days. Participants may be asked to read a story and return in seven days for a quiz over the details in the story, with some participants reading the story in the morning and the others in the afternoon. As you consider the studies described in this book, it will be important to pay attention to the variables under consideration and the exact way they are operationalized. For example, how do researchers operationalize and measure intuition, mindfulness, or wisdom? And, to follow up on that question, is it even possible to study something as abstract as wisdom or intuition in the laboratory?

It is also important to consider whether the measurement tools chosen, which could be questionnaires, skills tests, or open-ended questions, appear to be measuring the intended variables. For example, suppose a cognitive scientist is attempting to find the differences in processing time for frequent and unusual meanings of words using homonyms, which are words that have several meanings. The researcher may assume that when considering the word *screen,* the most frequent association is with a movie screen. While the researcher is assuming the task is measuring retrieval of word meanings, the truth may be that cultural background and geographic location are being measured as well. It might be that the common meaning for *screen* in Massachusetts might be movie screen while the common meaning for *screen* in Florida might be a window or door screen. If "movie screen" is the correct response, according to the researcher, then most participants from the southern United States may answer incorrectly and be judged to have poor memory retrieval, when in reality the task is flawed.

Choosing the methodological design and statistical analyses can bring numerous decision points and much room for judgment and debate. For example, when studying the effects of birth order on various cognitive processes, is it better to study the same children over several years, which is a *longitudinal study,* or is it better to survey many firstborns and lastborns at one point in time, which would be a *cross-sectional study.* Each design has its benefits and its deficits. As you read through this volume you will find debates over design as well as debates over statistical analyses. It is very important to pay attention to how data are generated and exactly what they reference.

Theoretical Debates

Research doesn't happen in a vacuum without context. Ideally research and theory should go hand-in-hand, each influencing the other at every step. The reality is that sometimes the research or the theory can get far ahead or separated from the other. Cognitive science has often been accused of being *data-driven,* which means many studies are conducted to see what the results might be without any theory guiding the research design or without offering an interpretation of the findings. Several of the issues presented in this volume are focused on theoretical debates.

Is the Theory Sound?

While the notion of what makes a theory good or useful might be debatable in itself, it is important to consider the characteristics of the theories presented. A theory should provide insight on a large scale, whereas a hypothesis is usually quite specific. Theories are often broad and abstract; however, they should also be testable so that researchers can confirm, discount, or modify the theory. As you read through the various theoretical debates, consider the amount of background research given to demonstrate the power of the theory. Many scientists would also say that theories should be *parsimonious* (that is, they should offer the simplest reasoning or explanation).

All scientists, including cognitive scientists, should strive to keep in mind that a theory is just that—a theory and not a fact. In some cases, scientists can be guilty of giving a theory so much power that they ignore evidence that would discount the theory. We must be willing to give up our favorite theory when it has been rejected and thus finished serving its purpose. For example, consider the issue of usefulness when reading the many issues in this volume focused on the brain-as-computer model. It is important to consider what aspects of this model are supported with evidence, and on the other hand, how aspects of this model may be limited or even inappropriate for some cognitive research.

Is the Theoretical Debate a Classic?

There are some theoretical debates that have been discussed for many years. One example of such a debate is the *nature vs. nurture* debate. This important issue considers just how much humans are influenced by their nature or the inherited aspects of development and how much influence comes from our nurture or the environment. You will find the nature vs. nurture debate in several of the issues in this volume, particularly in the section on intelligence.

Another set of theoretical debates found in this volume focus on the essence of cognitive development. For many years, psychologists have looked to the stage-based theory of Jean Piaget to provide the basic foundational theoretical structure of children's cognitive development. His theory asserts that children move through patterns or stages of thinking that progress from basic habits and reflexes, to a focus on the use of symbols and imagination, to literal, concrete thinking, and eventually to develop logical and abstract cognitive skills. As you read through the debates in this volume, you will find some authors supporting this Piagetian theory while others attempt to discount it. Some of the authors support innate abilities with characteristics different from Piagetian theory, while others reject the notion of stages completely.

Finally, as you read through these specific debates, you will find many views on the nature of memory. Our memories provide the foundation for most of our cognitive abilities. The issue of how we store enormous amounts of information, and retrieve it when needed, or experience retrieval problems (what we often call forgetting), is still quite mysterious. We rely on memory for all aspects of language, education, and learning. The debates over memory processes include various theories of overall and specific parts of memory, such as short-term memory and expert memory. These debates also raise questions of the appropriateness of the brain-as-computer analogy and the generalizability of software research in explaining human memory.

Debates over Application

Along with debates over research design and theoretical models, you will find debates over the appropriate applications of the research findings. A primary motivator for most research is the desire to eventually apply the findings to real-world problems or needs. Most of the issues in this volume have relevance to real-world issues, and you will find issues of appropriate application to be the core of several of the debates.

Are the Findings of High Quality and Appropriate?

There are several points to keep in mind when considering the appropriateness of moving from research findings to assertions in real-world situations. Among the most important of those points is the accuracy and strength of the findings. Is there a body of research supporting these findings, and are the studies involved considered to be of high quality? It is important to consider the participants, research design, and theoretical foundations when assessing the quality of the research. Were the research findings strong and robust, or statistically significant but weak? For example, while well-constructed research indicates that human memory can rather easily be swayed and tricked, it is important to be careful in how those findings are applied to various real-world situations. Some would argue that while those findings are sound and accurate, when applied to victims' memory of sexual abuse, one must consider the impact of trauma on memory more so than basic memory functioning.

Can the Findings Be Implemented?

The application of some research, while important, may not be realistically feasible based on any number of obstacles, such as high cost and limited resources. For example, there is a great deal of research demonstrating that children's learning is enhanced when there are relatively few students per teacher. Unfortunately most school districts cannot afford to hire enough teachers to fully implement those findings.

Should the Findings Be Implemented?

Perhaps the most important question to be considered is how much research, and of what quality, is required before acting in high-risk or sensitive areas? In this volume, you will be asked to consider controversies in which the application of flawed or inappropriate results could have devastating effects. Here are some examples: Can children repress sexual abuse experiences until they are adults, and then bring legal charges against those perpetrators? Should nurses be able to make health care choices based on their intuition rather than medical references and evidence? What would happen on the societal level if cognitive scientists felt certain that large families produce lower-IQ children? How drastically would public education change if teachers taught for wisdom, or followed constructivist methods, or banned IQ tests as flawed measurements?

Conclusions

One of the most important aspects of the scientific approach is the expectation that investigations will be published so that all others can read, evaluate, criticize, and attempt to replicate research. This process allows independent scientists to confirm, refute, and modify theories and models. The debates covered in this volume are examples of the scientific approach at work. As you read through the issues in this volume, keep in mind that it is critical that scientists have these discussions in order to produce the most accurate research, theory, and application as possible.

Also keep in mind that while the authors may present two sides to the topic at hand, these are complex issues with many facets and nuances. In some cases, it may be that truly one side is right and one is wrong, but chances are the truth is much more complex than simply right or wrong. You may find in some debates it appears that each side has partial truth and partial error. In other cases, it may seem that the authors are not asking the right questions or are not using the most appropriate method in order to answer their research question. Try to consider all the possibilities when reading both sides of each issue, and try to withhold judgment until you have read the introduction, both selections, and the postscript.

Cognitive science influences almost every area of life. As you read through this volume, you will find that these debates are important in education, health care, the legal system, the financial network, government and the military, and business and industry. While some of these issues may seem specialized and remote, keep in mind that the results of these studies and similar ones are often applied in real-world settings. Cognitive science needs this debate and dialogue in order to produce the most accurate research possible.

References

Gardner, H. (1985/1987). *The Mind's New Science: A History of the Cognitive Revolution, with Epilogue: Cognitive Science After 1984*. New York: Basic Books.

Hunt, R. R., and Ellis, H. C. (2004). *Fundamentals of Cognitive Psychology,* Seventh Edition. Boston: McGraw-Hill.

Pratt, C. C. (1939). *The Logic of Modern Psychology*. New York: MacMillan Company.

Scheerer, E. (1988). Toward a history of cognitive science. *International Social Science Journal, 40*(1), 7–19.

Thagard, P. (2002). Cognitive Science. *The Stanford Encyclopedia of Philosophy (Winter 2002 Edition),* http://plato.stanford.edu/archives/win2002/entries/cognitive-science.

Von Eckardt, B. (1995). *What Is Cognitive Science?* Cambridge, MA: MIT Press.

On the Internet . . .

Here you will find the Stanford Encyclopedia of Philosophy entry for cognitive science. It provides a good history and overview of the discipline.

http://plato.stanford.edu/entries/cognitive-science/

This Serendip site, sponsored by Bryn Mawr College, will give you a great background on the mind-brain dilemma within philosophy.

http://serendip.brynmawr.edu/Mind/Table.html

The Alliance for Lifelong Learning offers a well-rounded introduction to cognitive science.

http://www.allianceforlifelonglearning.org/er/tree.jsp?c=220

At Cogweb, sponsored by the University of California at Los Angeles, you can find links to many cognitive science resources, including information on mind-brain and theories-of-mind.

http://cogweb.ucla.edu/CogSci/index.html

PART 1

Mind and Brain

Most of us use the words mind *and* brain *synonymously to refer to anything mental. Cognitive scientists pay close attention to how these two words are used. Within cognitive science, which is often interdisciplinary and includes philosophers, psychologists, neuroscientists, and computer scientists, there is much debate over the function and purpose of the mind and brain and over how we develop the notion that we have a mind, and in individual, private mind separate from the minds of others. In Part 1, you will be introduced to these concepts and controversies.*

- Are Mind and Brain the Same?
- Do Children Develop Theories about Other People's Minds?
- Is Mindfulness a Cognitive Style?

ISSUE 1

Are Mind and Brain the Same?

YES: Paul C. L. Tang, from "A Review Essay: Recent Literature on Cognitive Science," *Social Science Journal* (1999)

NO: Jon Mills, from "Five Dangers of Materialism," *Genetic, Social & General Psychology Monographs* (February 2002)

ISSUE SUMMARY

YES: Philosophy professor Paul C. L. Tang explains the argument that anything usually attributed to the mind is only brain activity by describing the position of Paul Churchland, a leader in the field of cognitive science.

NO: Researcher Jon Mills points out five dangers of dismissing a concept of mind, such as the elimination of free will and a sense of self, and instead proposes a psychic holism.

Do you think your sense of *self* is something different or separate from your body? For much of recorded history, that question was considered the domain of philosophers and theologians. When psychology was established as the science of mental activities and behaviors, those questions about the existence and workings of the mind, and how the mind related to the brain and the rest of the body, were critical. A quick look at the history of psychology will reveal how this debate has evolved.

As each theory or heuristic in psychology grew in popularity, a different view of the mind/body and mind/brain dilemma emerged. Freud focused much of his work on the mind, particularly the unconscious. Following the popularity of Psychoanalytic Theory came Behaviorism. Under the influence of Watson and Skinner, the field of psychology turned totally to the physical, measurable aspects of behavior. At that point in time the concept of the mind had no place in psychology. Then, in the late 1950s, psychology experienced the Cognitive Revolution. Suddenly, it was acceptable to discuss some less behavioral aspects of human life such as memory, language development, reasoning, and cognitive development. The debate between dualism (two separate parts, mind and brain) and monism (one unified part, and in this case, brain only) began to rage again.

Today this mind/brain issue is passionately debated by the psychologists, computer scientists, neuroscientists, and philosophers who make up the new interdisciplinary field of cognitive science. Many cognitive scientists assume a monistic position that everything once thought to be mental is actually nothing more than brain activity. This is the focus of the first selection, the position of Paul Churchland as explored by Tang. Neuroscientists are learning a great deal about how the brain activates and controls the processes of chemically storing memories and initiating emotions. Another area of support for this position comes from the complex *mental* work being done by computers. Could it be that our brains operate in the same way as high-powered computers?

There are philosophers and psychologists who react against this monist position, arguing that the concept of mind is useful and even necessary. In the second selection, Mills explores the dangers of discarding the concept or theory of mind. Mills uses some philosophical terms that may be new to you. One of those terms is *ontology,* which refers to a specific way of explaining the existence of something. Mills argues that reducing everything mental to brain activity takes away any possibility of an ontology of consciousness—it rejects any way of conceptualizing consciousness as something with its own unique existence and properties. Mills uses the term *teleology* when discussing free will. Teleology refers to actions or thoughts that have a purpose and that are designed to reach an end state. Mills believes that rejecting the concept of mind reduces human beings to behavioral objects, totally controlled by outside forces, and lacking any free will. Could it be that discounting the mind is a step backwards for the field of psychology?

In the first selection, professor Paul Tang will explore the arguments of Paul Churchland in support of the perspective that all mental processes are simply the experience of brain activity. The second selection summarizes the counterargument of researcher Jon Mills. He points out the dangers in this line of reasoning and provides an alternative with his notion of psychic holism. Consider these arguments carefully as you try to determine your personal position.

Paul C. L. Tang  **YES**

A Review Essay: Recent Literature on Cognitive Science

. . . Paul Churchland is a very distinguished analytic philosopher, philosopher of science, and philosopher of cognitive science. He is a leading proponent of the philosophical doctrine of *eliminative materialism,* which claims, among other things, that mental processes or mental states (e.g., believing) as traditionally conceived do not exist. He maintains that advances in the neurosciences and artificial intelligence hold the key to understanding cognition. Churchland is widely regarded as a leader in the fields of philosophy of mind (also called "philosophical psychology"), philosophy of science, epistemology, philosophy of perception, and philosophy of cognitive science. Moreover, he is also a leading defender of the philosophical doctrine of scientific realism, which, on one common definition, claims that our scientific theories give us a literally true account of the world, especially of the unobservable world. In his book, *Matter and Consciousness,* several philosophical themes have emerged, some of them controversial.

Eliminative Materialism

The French philosopher, René Descartes (1596–1650), often called "The Father of Modern Philosophy," posed the metaphysical mind/body problem in its sharpest form. Descartes asked: What do human beings have that material objects do not have that allows human beings to cognize, to learn languages, and to learn mathematics? He argued that human beings must have an immaterial, non-spatial mind over and above a material, spatially located brain that inanimate objects and lower life forms do not have. Descartes called this mind "mental substance," the essence of which is thinking. Mental substance, Descartes argued, is to be contrasted with material substance, the essence of which is extension, the occupying of space. These two, radically distinct substances are the basis of Descartes' metaphysical dualism. (For Descartes, there was also a third substance, viz., Divine Substance or God.) These substances have necessary existence and need nothing else for their existence. For Descartes, the separation of material substance from mental substance meant that science (that deals with material substance) would

From *Social Science Journal,* Issue 4, vol. 36, 1999, pp. 675–685.

never have to come into conflict with religion (that deals with mental substance, or spirit, or soul). Nevertheless, a problem immediately arose as to the nature of the causal interaction between an immaterial, non-spatial mind and a material, spatial body. Descartes held that this interaction occurred in the pineal gland, but this answer simply postpones the problem rather than solving it. To this day, there is no generally received answer to this mind/body problem from philosophers, or psychologists, or neuroscientists.

Although few scholars would hold Descartes' theory of substance dualism today, there are, nevertheless, many varieties of contemporary dualism. . . .

[One of] these dualistic theories, *reductive materialism,* more often called "the identity theory," holds that mental states are physical states of the brain. An even more popular materialist theory is *functionalism,* which holds that the defining feature of any type of mental state is the set of causal relations it bears to environmental effects on the body; to other types of mental states; and to bodily behavior. So pain, for example, typically results from bodily injury; causes annoyance and distress; and causes wincing, blanching and the nursing of the injured area. Any state that plays exactly the same functional role is a pain, according to functionalism. A third type of materialism is *eliminative materialism,* which holds that our theory of mental states is impoverished, if not simply incorrect. For eliminative materialists, there are no mental states, only brain states.

Eliminative materialism is the philosophical theory of mind/brain that Churchland holds. He argues that it is a position well supported by advances in the neurosciences. . . . [A]dditional support for eliminative materialism is gained by studying cases of brain damage, degeneration, and disequilibrium. For example, lesions to the connections between the secondary visual cortex and the secondary auditory cortex of the left hemisphere may result in the inability to identify perceived colors, whereas lesions to the secondary auditory cortex of the left hemisphere results in the more drastic effect of total and permanent loss of speech comprehension, whereas bilateral damage to the hippocampus results in the inability to lay down new memories.

Nevertheless, eliminative materialists, such as Churchland, must still account for the phenomenon of introspection and the "qualitative feel" of our alleged mental states. The eliminative materialist must account for the difference we claim to perceive between pain, for example, and our understanding of a mathematical problem or our believing or knowing a fact. A strong case can be made that these latter phenomena are best explained under some dualist theory of mind/brain.

Scientific Realism

The argument from introspection in favor of a dualism of mind/brain is a serious problem for Churchland. He responds to it by invoking a robust scientific realism, which is, basically, the position that our scientific theories give us a literally true account of the world. Moreover, Churchland claims that, if our scientific theories are successful at explaining and predicting phenomena, then we have very good reason to believe that the entities that the theories postulate really exist, even if they are not directly sense perceivable. For example, the Standard Model Theory of Matter claims that electrons, protons, quarks and other subatomic entities exist even if we do not directly perceive them with our five senses. As Churchland argues, when we experience a warm summer day as 70° Fahrenheit, what we are experiencing is the mean kinetic energy of the air molecules, which is about 6.2×10^{-21} joules, whether we realize it or not. For heat is mean kinetic energy of molecules. And if we don't perceive it that way, we can learn to do so.

Realism is important for Churchland, for it allows him to formulate a response to the argument from introspection, the strongest argument against the eliminative materialism that Churchland embraces. Churchland argues that, with suitable training and knowledge, one can eventually introspect directly his or her own brain states. This claim, if successfully argued both conceptually and empirically, would undercut the dualist position that one introspects one's mental states that exist over and above the brain. But this leads to one of the most controversial of Churchland's theses, for he would then claim that eventually we could directly introspect such brain states as spiking frequencies in specific neural pathways and dopamine levels in the limbic system, as based on a realist account of our most current and successful neurophysiological theories.

To support this controversial claim—concerning direct introspection of our brain states—Churchland asks us to consider the case of the musical prodigy who, at a very early age, can distinguish between for example, sound pitches. Very soon, with more training and study, he can distinguish between different instruments of the orchestra and as he matures into a talented young conductor, he can distinguish when instruments in an orchestra are playing in tune and when they are not. And so on. Churchland then analogizes with the introspection of brain states. He claims that we will have to learn the conceptual framework of a matured neuroscience if we are to introspect brain states directly and that we will have to practice its non-inferential application. Eventually we will reach the stage analogous to that of the mature conductor who can now directly experience phenomena that he could not experience at an earlier stage of his development. Churchland holds that the amount of self-apprehension gained by such direct introspection of brain states will be more than worth the effort of the training and study. . . .

Neural Nets

As an eliminative materialist, Churchland is quick to use parallel distributive processing (PDP) or neural nets from artificial intelligence (AI) research as a model of cognitive processes. Such digital computers function solely as symbol manipulators and it is unclear whether any symbol manipulator—whether computer or human being—can ever possess intentionality, the state of having meanings that point to, or are about features of the world. Typically, intentionality is said to be "the mark of the mental." The philosopher John Searle argues that mere symbol manipulators cannot have semantics or meanings and thus intentionality. Thus, on the computational model of conscious intelligence that Churchland holds, Searle argues that a brain that simply manipulates symbols cannot account for people having meanings that are about the world. But as many philosophers hold, a dualist theory of mind/brain can. Meanings (or propositions) are just the objects of mental states.

Searle uses his famous "Chinese Room Argument" (of which there are several versions) to argue his case. Suppose Searle himself is the central processing unit (CPU) of a digital computer and understands no Chinese at all. If Searle is given rules of syntax, he can string together Chinese characters and output them in such a way that a person fluent in Chinese could read the outputted string of symbols, understand, and respond. But, he, Searle, cannot so respond even though as a CPU he gives the appearance of knowing what the symbols mean. Searle argues that the meaning of the symbols have intentionality, that they are about the world and hence the Chinese speaker can understand and respond appropriately to the output sentence in a way that Searle as a mere symbol manipulator cannot. So brains or computers, which can only manipulate symbols according to a program, cannot have intentionality. Intentionality can be had only by objects that have a conscious mind, such as the Chinese speaker. Searle claims that his argument will hold independently of technological advances, however great, in computer design. Searle's argument presents a serious challenge to Churchland's eliminative materialism and the associated view that the material brain is just a neurocomputer.

Churchland counters Searle's argument with his own "luminous room argument." Churchland asks us to imagine a small, closed off room that is literally dark. The occupant in this room is the scientist James Clerk Maxwell, who claims that light is nothing other than electromagnetic waves. Maxwell shakes a bar magnet that produces such waves. An outside critic points out that the room is completely dark, so light could not possibly be electromagnetic waves. Churchland says that all Maxwell needs to do is claim that the room is indeed lit, albeit at a grade too poor to be detected. All that is needed for visible light is that the electromagnetic waves be speeded up to produce visible light. Similarly with Searle's argument, claims Churchland. All that is needed is that the syntax of a language be sufficiently complex in order for us to detect the meaning and thus the intentionality of symbol manipulation. . . .

The Brain as the Engine of Reason and the Seat of the Soul

Churchland's *Matter and Consciousness* is introductory and repays close study. He gives a balanced view of all sides of a topic. However, in *The Engine of Reason, the Seat of the Soul,* Churchland takes a firm stand on his own position of eliminative materialism and his other positions as well. For example, he argues strongly that the neurosciences and AI research have recently contributed, and will continue to contribute to a greater understanding of the brain and of cognitive processes. In addition, contrary to what many philosophers and theologians have held over the years, there is no "mind" or "spirit" or "soul" over and above the brain. The brain is the self.

This Churchlandian position runs counter to the classical position known as "mind/body dualism." The mind is the origin of thought ("the engine of reason") as well as "the seat of the soul." For Descartes, the mind causally interacts with the brain, although this interaction is difficult to explain. Modern dualists have not been successful either, and this problem has led many philosophers, psychologists and cognitive scientists in general (who may be neuroanatomists, neurochemists, AI researchers, scientifically trained philosophers) to argue for materialism, the view that denies there is such an entity called "the mind" and claims that there is only one entity, the material brain.

Moreover, Churchland argues that all cognitive processes can be explained entirely in terms of the brain. This revolutionary treatment of cognition and ultimately of the self will also result in reconceptions of consciousness, philosophy, science, society, language, politics and art. Finally, the technology that could arise from this neural net approach to brain function could have important medical and legal consequences, claims Churchland.

As discussed previously, Churchland specifically holds the position of eliminative materialism, a position he claims is also supported by studies on brain damaged and brain lesioned patients or on, for example, Alzheimer's patients. Postmortem examinations of the brains of Alzheimer's victims reveal material plaques and tangles throughout the fine web of synaptic connections of the neurons of the brain that embodies all of one's cognitive skills and capacities for recognition.

Moreover, Churchland is impressed with the tremendous advances in the neurosciences and in AI research that allows for the modeling of brain processes. These advances allow cognitive scientists to represent brain function as massively parallel distributive processing (PDP) of recurrent neural nets that carry out vector to vector transformations or vector completions (see below). This new model (perhaps theory) of human cognitive brain processes will effect, Churchland claims, a revolution in our understanding of the self, of consciousness, of all cognitive processes, of science, of art, and of much else besides. Churchland's book, *The Engine of Reason, the Seat of the Soul* is intended to convey the possibilities and excitement of this revolution. . . .

Consciousness

[In his work,] Churchland deals with the fascinating but difficult puzzle of consciousness. This phenomenon seems unique to human beings and beyond scientific and purely physical explanation. Traditionally, philosophers have argued that the phenomenon is basically a subjective occurrence, accessible only to the creature that has it. Churchland argues against this classical view.

Churchland begins by reviewing a number of similar arguments for the classical view advanced by such philosophers as Gottfried Leibniz (1646–1716) and the contemporary philosophers Thomas Nagel, John Searle, and Frank Jackson. Nagel's argument is perhaps the most familiar and was advanced in his seminal paper, "What Is [It] Like to Be a Bat?" Nagel argues that no matter how much one might know about the neuroanatomy of a bat's brain and the neurophysiology of a bat's sensory apparatus, one will never know "what it would be like" to have the bat's sensory experience. Even if scientists could track the neuroactivation patterns, one would never know what they are like from the unique perspective of the creature that possesses them; that is, their intrinsic character as felt experiences would still be unknown to us. A purely physical science of the brain, Nagel and others argue, does have a limit on the capacity of understanding as it reaches the subjective character of the contents of one's consciousness.

Churchland responds by arguing that Nagel fails to make a distinction between how one knows something and the thing known. Churchland argues that the existence of a unique first-person epistemological access to a conscious phenomenon does not entail that the phenomenon is nonphysical in character. For example, the difference between X's knowledge of her facial blush and Y's knowledge of X's facial blush lies not in the thing known but rather in the manner of knowing it. The blush itself is a physical entity.

Churchland then proposes seven provisional criteria of adequacy that a neuroscientific theory of consciousness must try to reconstruct. Consciousness (1) involves short-term memory; (2) is independent of sensory inputs; (3) displays steerable attention; (4) has the capacity for alternative interpretations of complex or ambiguous facts; (5) disappears in deep sleep; (6) reappears in dreaming; (7) holds the contents of several basic sensory modalities within a single, unified experience. . . .

Concluding Remarks

Churchland's position that all cognitive processes and the phenomenon of consciousness can be reduced to brain processes representable as a testable theory of recurrent neural nets is a powerful and carefully argued position. He is at pains to warn the reader several times that he may be wrong. Indeed, there will continue to be strong arguments raised against his position and it is too soon to say whether his approach will triumph. . . .

References

Churchland, P. M. (1995). *The Engine of Reason, the Seat of the Soul: A Philosophical Journey into the Brain.* Cambridge, MA: MIT Press.

Churchland, P. M. (1988). *Matter and Consciousness.* Cambridge, MA: MIT Press.

Searle, J. (1980). Minds, Brains, and Programs. *Behavioral and Brain Sciences 3:* 417–424.

Searle, J. (1984). *Minds, Brains, and Science.* Cambridge, MA: Harvard University Press.

Searle, J. (1992). *The Rediscovery of the Mind.* Cambridge, MA: MIT Press.

Jon Mills  NO

Five Dangers of Materialism

Contemporary theories in cognitive science and the philosophy of mind lend burgeoning support to the materialist position regarding the mind–body problem. That is, naturalism, physicalism, and material monism are the preferred theories that explain the relationship between mental processes and physical brain states. Although dualist and spiritualist approaches offer counter-arguments to materialism (Vendler, 1994; Warner, 1994), the preponderance of current research in the philosophical, natural, and social sciences concludes that mental states are nothing but physical states (Armstrong, 1968; Bickle, 1998; Churchland, 1981; Dennett, 1991; Dretske, 1995; Searle, 1994). From these accounts, mind *is* brain.

Throughout this article, I highlight five central dangers associated with materialism that ultimately result in (a) the displacement of an ontology of consciousness, (b) a simplistic and fallacious view of causality, (c) the loss of free will, (d) renunciation of the self, and (e) questionable judgments concerning social valuation practices. I attempt to demonstrate that the physicalist position eliminates the possibility of free agency and fails to adequately account for psychic holism.

The Spectrum of Materialism

. . . One thing is clear about materialism: It is a reaction against and rejection of Cartesian dualism that posits a non-extended "thinking substance" associated with an immaterial mind (Descartes, 1641/1984). It is worth noting, however, that there are many forms of dualism, including the Platonic distinction between appearance and reality; Kant's separation of phenomena from noumena; the ontological distinctions between being and essence; the dialectically opposed forces and manifestations of consciousness; and the epistemological chasms between the knowing subject and object. It is not my intention to defend ontological dualism, but to show that materialist conceptions of mind pose many problems for those trying to understand the complex psychological, psychosocial, and ontological configurations that constitute the human condition.

Rather than explicate the multitude of materialist positions ranging from identity theories (Armstrong, 1968; Lewis, 1966; Place, 1956),

From GENETICS, SOCIAL AND GENERAL PSYCHOLOGY MOMOGRAPHS, February 2002, pp. 5–23.

functionalism (Levin, 1986; Putnam, 1967; Smart, 1962; Sober, 1985), supervenience (Teller, 1983), eliminativism (Churchland, 1981; Stich, 1994), and representationalism (Dretske, 1988, 1995; Fodor, 1987, 1998), to anomalous monism (Davidson, 1980), I refer collectively to the materialist position, which includes the following characteristics as operationally defined:

1. *Physical reductionism,* which holds that (a) all mental states are simply physical states in the brain; there is nothing "over and above" biological–neurochemical–physiological structures, processes, and evolutionary pressures; (b) all mental events, properties, and processes arise out of physical preconditions whereby (c) the organism is conceived of as a matter–energy system composed solely of active material properties or substances reified through material-efficient causal attributions.
2. *Naturalism,* as I define it, (a) is the belief that all knowledge comes from physical conditions governed by natural causal laws based on an empirical epistemology; (b) supports realism, which is often (but not always) incompatible with a priori truths or transcendental idealist positions; (c) is a form of positivism, in that truth claims about reality are quantifiable facts that can be directly observed, measured, or verified within systematic science relying on experience, experimentation, and rational methods of inquiry; (d) is anti-supernaturalistic, anti-theological, and anti-metaphysical (despite its metaphysical consequences); (e) is pro-scientific—that is, all natural phenomena are adequately explained, or in principle can be explained, through scientific methodology; and (f) displays tendencies toward non-teleological, non-anthropomorphic, and non-animistic explanations.

If materialism is going to make such ontological assertions, then it must be able to coherently defend its own self-imposed assumptions without begging the question. If we are going to properly understand the question of mind, we must ferret out the philosophical, humanistic, and ethical implications of the materialist project and expose the conundrums it generates. I attempt to show that psychic holism becomes an alternative paradigm to the materialist position and more successfully addresses the multifaceted domains of mental processes, personal experience, and discourse surrounding mind–body dependence without succumbing to a reductive metaphysics.

The Naturalistic Fallacy

Freud (1900) admonished us to "avoid the temptation to determine psychical locality in any anatomical fashion" (p. 536), insisting that the mind should not be reduced to "anatomical, chemical or physiological" properties (1916–1917, p. 21). Materialists, on the other hand, are dogmatic in their insistence that all mental events can ultimately be reduced to physical events or brain states in the organism. Thus, physical reductionism is the sine qua non of materialism. Teller (1983) summarized this position nicely: "Everything . . . is at bottom physical." In other words, there is no mind, only brain. One might ask materialists, "How do you know that?" To justify their claims, they inevitably rely on science, empirical psychology, the bare appeal to sensible and tangible experience, and/or naturalized or evolutionary accounts of epistemology (see Quine, 1969; Vollmer, 1975; Wuketits, 1990). Science has its legitimate status; however, it must first establish a coherent criterion for truth. To fall back on the very criterion that it must set out to prove simply begs the question and envelops materialist justifications in circularity.

. . . Putnam (1983) charged that naturalized epistemology presupposes a metaphysical realism and a correspondence theory of truth in that truth corresponds to the "facts." He ultimately argued that this notion is incoherent, whereby "truth" is relevant to one's scheme of describing and explaining physical phenomena, hence embedded in a social language practice that determines how truth is to be defined and measured. This metaphysical assumption postulates a set of "ultimate" objects that are "absolute" and can be "objectively" measured, hence are "real," essentially aiming to revive the whole failed enterprise of the realism–anti-realism debate. . . .

The Destruction of an Ontology of Consciousness

Materialist conceptions of mind are highly problematic for several reasons. First, the individual is reduced to physical substance alone, which gives rise to an organismic and, in some cases, mechanistic view of the human being. By reducing the psyche to matter, materialism displaces an ontology of consciousness. That is, there is no distinct ontological status to mental events; psychic processes and properties are merely physical properties within a functional system that constitutes the organism. The transcendental properties of the mental are reduced to atomic and subatomic particles within a closed system of energetics constituted through quantum mechanics. In this sense, mind does not direct consciousness or action, *matter* does. In short, the human being is reduced to a thing—a reified biological machine engineered by evolution and stimulated by the environment.

This approach can lead to a very dehumanizing account of the individual. The intrinsic uniqueness of individuality, personality, and the phenomenology of psychical experience collapses in reductionism. By making the human being merely an organism, one has stripped the uniquely personal and idiosyncratic dimensions of selfhood down to biology. Although this ideology has its rudiments in natural science and evolutionary biology, from this standpoint consciousness does not exist; that is, consciousness, intentionality, the phenomenal experience, qualia, the "aboutness" or "what it's like" to experience something and to live are reduced to changes in brain states engulfed in a language describing physical processes alone. Within this context, all conscious experience and behavior constitute a functional (and at times mechanical) operation that is organized within a systemic structure. The meaning of being human and the existential questions and dilemmas that populate mental life are abandoned to sterile scientific depictions of animate organic matter. Although materialist theories vary in conceptual depth and locution, in the end there is no metaphysical mind, only physical–energetic substance.

Simplicity and Causal Fallacies

Materialism ultimately rests on a simplistic view of causality—a view that is inherently biased and conforms to the empirical positivist tradition—namely, psychic reality is that which is directly observable, measurable, and quantifiable, thus constituted as fact. We owe this view to the law of parsimony, or Ockham's razor. The virtue of simplicity is intended to be in the service of economy; that is, anything intelligible can be explained in material terms. Abstract theories of complexity and ambiguity are less economical and do not neatly "fit" into ordinary belief systems; therefore, simplicity is preferred to complexity. However, the simplest explanation is not necessarily the most accurate. This position has been applied in the following way: "If one cannot observe it or measure it, it does not exist." In my view, the value of simplicity has been abused here. There is no value in reducing the human being to a thing. While the value of parsimony is appropriate for various types of social, professional, and pragmatic discourse, this view sacrifices the qualitative aspect of what it is like to be human. Cognitive science today is content with explaining consciousness as experiential changes in brain states that can in part be observed, measured, and quantifiably verified. Observation is one thing, but the generalized claim "That is all there is!" is epistemically problematic. This positivistic account presupposes a "God's eye" view of reality and thus makes a sweeping metaphysical judgment.

Materialism fallaciously posits that if psychic events are realized physically, then their tenets are proved. At the very least, materialists are obliged to take an agnostic position with regard to an ontology of consciousness. Just because one cannot directly observe or measure conscious phenomena does not mean that neurophysiology is all there is. As previously mentioned, this is a naturalistic or reductive fallacy. The very idea of the mental is that it is something that is not tangible, it is literally *no-thing,* hence psychical. This is not to deny the interdependence and interpenetration of mind and body: While physical processes and properties are necessary conditions of mind, they are far from being sufficient conditions to produce mind. Mind is embodied or instantiated physically, but by virtue of its transcendental and elusive functions and properties, it cannot be spatially localized or dissected. Most materialists want to eliminate this stance as a viable possibility and hold allegiance to a simple economy—that which is *real* is something that is tangible. This fixation with making metaphysical and epistemic pronouncements based on tangible evidence in the service of economy jeopardizes the integrity of psychical reality.

Another pitfall of the materialist position is the simplistic notion of causality as physical reduction. Thus, materialism relies on the interaction of two primary causal attributions: (a) physical causation and (b) environmental determinism. This position insists that the human being is, in Aristotelian terminology, the conglomeration of material and efficient causes: Mind is caused by the matter or physical substance it is made of and is causally affected by the material forces that constitute the flux of environmental events. This is the case for the most unrefined materialist positions ranging from the type–type identity theory to the more sophisticated functional monist approaches. It boils down to (a) the physical causing all mental events, thus instituting force and motion that bring about effects; and (b) environmental contingencies that cause the organism to respond to a stimulus prior to the effect in time. This is the theoretical foundation of most materialist theories as well as American behaviorism, which espouses the stimulus–response paradigm of psychological processes. In other words, some stimulus (whether internal or external) precedes a response (changes in brain states, neurochemical networks and patterns of activity, or behavioral output due to environmental variables), thereby causing physiological, cognitive, and behavioral changes in the organism. . . .

Loss of Freedom

Reliance on material and efficient causal explanations, the over-valuation of simplicity à la Ockham's razor, and consequently, physical reductionism, completely eliminate any possibility of free will. From this standpoint, the human being is not free. This position is summarized by the exclusion thesis, which posits that human beings have no properties or mental powers that no object or physical system can possess (Graham, 1993). Thus, if free will is a mental process or property, and no physical system is free, then we do not possess free choice and are consequently not free. This simplicity denies the possibility of final causal determinants and transcendental teleology characteristic of free agents. *Agent* is defined here as a subject who is telic, purposeful, and self-directed via choices and deliberation in judgments constituting self-conscious activity. Therefore, thoughts, volitional intentions, and behaviors are the activities of the will: Freedom is ultimately defined as the ability to choose or *be* otherwise. Freedom, however, is not merely restricted to choice; it also encompasses the structural organization of the individual doing the choosing, namely the agent. In short, agency, free will, intentionality, and final causality (e.g., choosing the grounds for the sake of which to behave) are problematic for the materialist, for physical matter is caused rather than freely causal. . . .

Death of the Self

One of the most disturbing consequences of the materialist position is that the notion of the self dissolves. In the spirit of Nietzsche, "The Self is Dead!" and materialism killed it. Essentially, this view of the self is commensurate with a Buddhist or Humean view—there is no self, only sensations and impressions impinging on the senses in a fleeting moment. For Hume, there is no "I" directing mentation. There is only the theater of the mind where thoughts are cast by natural laws and where self-reflection is only second-order perception. The self is merely an illusion. Thus, free will and any sense of personal identity are non-existent. In Dennett's (1991) words, we "*spin* a self," or as Skinner would contend, we are only operantly conditioned to believe in a self. The "I" is just a social construction or invention of language: We are a collection of dynamic mental properties and perceptions in flux, that's all.

Whether one conceives of the self in the tradition of Descartes's *cogito* as the "I" that resides behind the cognizer; the Kantian transcendental unity of apperception as the nominal, enduring, unified unifier; Hegel's notion of subjective spirit (*Geist*); Sartre's notion of the self as radical freedom; or the Freudian ego (*Ich*) as a self-directed synthesizing agent, the distinctive *psychical* processes and properties of consciousness—not to mention the unconscious—are dismissed from the materialist framework. While a physical system can be dynamically organized and functionally sophisticated, in the end, the organism—not the self—is doing the thinking and behaving. Materialists would contend, however, that the organism *is* the self. But it is precisely this definitional issue that becomes problematic. The notion of the self plays a great role in human value practices and should not be conceived merely as a physical entity. We cannot simply reduce human experience, personal identity, character formation, and selfhood to atoms and sub-atomic particles without losing the integrity of freedom and an ontologically transcendental self.

Furthermore, materialism offers very little comfort for those looking for the possibility of a personal afterlife. Not only are free will and the self eliminated, but materialism is consequentially a fundamental atheism. Spiritual transcendence of the soul or personality, and the possibility of an afterlife are not tenable within the materialist framework. If the mind or psyche is nothing more than its material substrate (merely active particles), then the substance ceases to exist upon its physical death. The soul as psychical substance could not exist in disembodied form, hence death of the organism is death of the soul. As Graham (1993) told us, if "the soul is something mental and the soul survives bodily death, whereas the brain fails to survive, then there is no such thing as a soul" (p. 129). Unless there were some miraculous means by which to reconstitute brain-matter, the soul would not exist. It would be virtually impossible to rebuild and reconnect the millions of neural pathways destroyed by physical decay, such as in the case of brain trauma or dementia. And if this were possible, such as in some *Star Trek* episode, the question of sustained personal identity would remain equivocal. By definition, reconstituted matter would no longer be identical to itself. A duplicated self would not be the same self. For materialists, all natural phenomena eventually pass out of existence and return to an eternal, primordial, material ground in an eternal transformation of matter, so wave "good bye" to a personal afterlife. Simply put, spiritualism, supernaturalism, immaterialism, disembodiment, transcendentalism, and any appeal to mystical experience, revelation, or faith are untenable hypotheses. . . .

Value Judgments Concerning Social Practices

Because materialism is overidentified with a scientific epistemology, there is a tacit prejudice that the human being is a biological machine that one can control, predict, and manipulate. Science and medicine have provided and continue to provide humanity with knowledge and technology that drastically improve the quality of life, but there is an inherent danger in the tendency to view the human being as nothing more than a biological organism. Within this context, there is a medicalization or objectification of the human subject. The hazard in this treatment of the subject as an object is that it may lead to social, political, and scientific practices that fail to account for the dynamic psychological complexity of mental life and the existential human needs inherent in conscious experience. This biased naturalistic view may condone various professional practices in medicine, psychiatry, and the social sciences. We have already seen how the medical model of psychiatry has usurped psychological approaches to the treatment of certain types of mental illnesses. For example, Prozac is preferred over psychotherapy as the salient mode of intervention for depression—assuming that all forms of depression have a biological correlate that is confused with etiology, hence all forms are physically caused. This is simply erroneous. The danger of such medical practices is that people get the message that all they need to do is take a pill and they will be happy. Physical interventions and psychopharmacological treatments may be appropriate for some medical or psychiatric conditions, but certainly not all. Such objectification of the human being may potentially justify myriad ethically dubious practices (e.g., fetal tissue research, euthanasia, physician-assisted suicide, genetic and human cloning). The reduction of the phenomenology of consciousness could further lead to an invalidation of uniquely subjective, lived, existential experience. The human being is not just an organism to be manipulated by science; rather a person is to be acknowledged and valued. The medicalization of and clinical depiction of the human being seem to lack a degree of empathy, concernful solicitude, and careful insight into the array of human experiences that cannot be reduced or explained away with technical jargon or physicalistic nomenclature. . . .

Another potentially dehumanizing aspect of the materialist agenda is that it advocates a change in linguistic communication practices that emphasize physical description. For example, Paul Churchland (1981) proposed that we adopt a new language to describe brain states rather than conscious experiences. This was proposed earlier by Smart (1962), who stated "it would make sense to talk of an experience in terms appropriate to physical processes" (p. 173). Why? Why do we need a conceptual and social change in language and communication practices? How would it be pragmatic and useful for people to communicate their complex cognitive, emotive, and psychological experiences in physically descriptive language? How could doing so facilitate arriving at a more accurate picture of inner reality? Instead of saying, "I love you," we would say, "My neurons are firing in sector 14.2 of my left frontal lobe." Is love really like a heatwave (see Levin, 1986)? Churchland (1981) even went so far as to propose that we eliminate current social language practices and replace them with an alternative language that would require monumental social and educational changes, not to mention experimental surgery on human beings. He suggested we could "construct a new system of verbal communication entirely distinct from natural language" (p. 220). Such a proposal would require massive changes in the way the world thinks, communicates, and operates. In addition, he proposed placing a "transducer for implantation at some site in the brain" (p. 221).

To me this is clearly an unethical proposal and probably motivated by the need to generate controversy in the service of personal narcissism, ideology, or both. Experimentation on humans?—as if everyone would be a willing participant. The ramifications of such a practice would completely alter the way people think, talk, and perceive reality; thus personality, identity, and one's sense of self would be radically mutated. In essence, people would no longer be who they previously were: It would be tantamount to turning people into machines. . . .

Toward Psychic Holism

Throughout this article, I have attempted to delineate five dangers of materialism characteristic of the naturalistic and physically reductive paradigms within the cognitive sciences and the philosophy of mind today. Perhaps the main motive of materialism is simply this: If you say all mental events are just physical events, then you do not have a mystery—the mind–body conundrum is solved. Searle (1994) summarized this position: "The famous mind–body problem . . . has a simple solution . . . Here it is: mental phenomena are caused by neurophysiological processes in the brain and are themselves features of the brain" (p. 277). This is reductionism at its finest.

The claim that the mind is nothing but the brain is a dogmatic assertion that attributes ontological primacy to physical states over mental processes and properties. In short, the materialist holds a fallacious and simplistic view of causality, denies free agency of the self, and increasingly portrays the human being as a clinical object. The ethical implications of such approaches in medical and social–political practices may potentially threaten the integrity of individuality and collective identity, which may further lead to an invalidation and/or empathic impasse regarding human difference and understanding.

Furthermore, within this context, the transcendental features of psychic reality—emotive, aesthetic, spiritual, moral, and religious experience—are trivialized. Not only is the quality of the lived experience truncated, but materialism consequently neglects the function and role the concept of self assumes for human value. The value and concept of our sense of self serve a fundamental structural and functional role in identity, ethical responsibility, and self-representation. The transcendental qualities of experience and selfhood are in danger of becoming displaced if we are to view the human condition solely from naturalistic paradigms. While the boon of materialism is scientific, medical, technological, and consequently social advancement, the bane is the demise of the self as a complex integrated whole. . . .

References

Armstrong, D. M. (1968). *A materialist theory of mind.* London: Routledge & Kegan Paul.

Bickle, J. (1998). *Psychoneural reduction: The new wave.* Cambridge, MA: Bradford Books/MIT Press.

Churchland, P. M. (1981). Eliminative materialism and the propositional attitudes. *The Journal of Philosophy, 78,* 67–90.

Davidson, D. (1980). *Essays on actions and events.* Oxford, UK: Clarendon Press.

Dennett, D. C. (1991). *Consciousness explained.* Boston: Little, Brown.

Descartes, R. (1984). *Meditations on first philosophy.* In J. Cottingham, R. Stoothoff, & D. Murdoch (Trans.), *The philosophical writings of Descartes* (Vol. 2, pp. 1–62). New York: Cambridge University Press. (Original work published in 1641).

Dretske, F. (1988). *Explaining behavior: Reasons in a world of causes.* Cambridge, MA: MIT Press.

Dretske, F. (1995). *Naturalizing the mind.* Cambridge, MA: Bradford Books/MIT Press.

Fodor, J. (1987). *Psychosemantics: The problem of meaning in the philosophy of mind.* Cambridge, MA: Bradford Books/MIT Press.

Fodor, J. (1998). *In critical condition: Polemical essays on cognitive science and the philosophy of mind.* Cambridge, MA: Bradford Books/MIT Press.

Freud, S. (1900). *The interpretation of dreams.* In James Strachey (Ed. & Trans.), *The standard edition of the complete psychological works of Sigmund Freud* (Vol. 5). London: Hogarth Press.

Freud, S. (1916–1917). *Introductory lectures on psycho-analysis.* In J. Strachey (Ed. & Trans.), *The standard edition of the complete psychological works of Sigmund Freud* (Vol. 15). London: Hogarth Press.

Graham, G. (1993). *Philosophy of mind: An introduction.* Oxford, UK: Blackwell.

Levin, J. (1986). Could love be like a heatwave? Physicalism and the subjective character of experience. *Philosophical Studies, 49*(2), 245–261.

Lewis, D. (1966). An argument for the identity theory. *Journal of Philosophy, 63,* 17–25.

Place, U. T. (1956). Is consciousness a brain process? *The British Journal of Psychology, 47,* 42–51.

Putnam, H. (1967). Psychological predicates. In W. H. Capitan & D. D. Merrill (Eds.), *Art, mind, and religion* (pp. 156–170). Pittsburgh: University of Pittsburgh Press.

Putnam, H. (1983). Why reason can't be naturalized. In P. K. Moser & A. Vandernat (Eds.), *Human knowledge* (pp. 355–365). Oxford, UK: Oxford University Press.

Quine, W. V. (1969). Epistemology naturalized. In *Ontological relativity and other essays.* New York: Columbia University Press.

Searle, J. (1994). What's wrong with the philosophy of mind? In R. Warner & T. Szubka (Eds.), *The mind-body problem* (pp. 290–311). Oxford, UK: Blackwell.

Smart, J. J. C. (1962). Sensations and brain processes. In V. C. Chappell (Ed.), *The Philosophy of mind* (pp. 19–36). Englewood Cliffs, NJ: Prentice-Hall.

Sober, E. (1985). Putting the function back into functionalism. *Synthese, 64*(2), 165–193.

Stich, S. P. (1994). What is a theory of mental representation? In R. Warner & T. Szubka (Eds.), *The mind-body problem* (pp. 321–341). Oxford, UK: Blackwell.

Teller, P. (1983). A poor man's guide to supervenience and determination. *Southern Journal of Philosophy, 22*(Supplement), 147.

Vendler, Z. (1994). The ineffable soul. In R. Warner & T. Szubka (Eds.), *The mind-body problem* (pp. 197–214). Oxford, UK: Blackwell.

Vollmer, G. (1975). *Evolutionary epistemology.* Stuttgart, Germany: Hirzel.

Warner, R. (1994). In defense of dualism. In R. Warner & T. Szubka (Eds.), *The mind-body problem* (pp. 215–229). Oxford, UK: Blackwell.

Wuketits, F. (1990). *Evolutionary epistemology.* New York: SUNY Press.

POSTSCRIPT

Are Mind and Brain the Same?

The fields of psychology and cognitive science continue to debate the mind/brain or mind/body issue. Churchland believes that mental processes do not exist as anything separate or different from the brain. What we once called mental processes are only brain activities. He draws upon the work of neuroscientists and computer scientists working in artificial intelligence to support his view that even though we intuitively believe we have an existence separate from our bodies, we are fooled by sophisticated brain processes. Churchland favors a scientific approach that focuses on verifiable evidence, namely brain research and computer modeling of brain activities.

Mills points out the dangers of the eliminative materialism of Churchland. The five dangers he describes are: (1) the rejection of the unique and separate existence of consciousness, (2) the simplistic view that psychological attributes are directly linked to physical structures, and thus all mental activities are caused by physical structures, (3) the elimination of any possibility of free will, (4) the loss of any sense of self, and (5) the degradation of human beings as biological machines and the resulting change in social values. Mills believes we should strive for a psychic holism that acknowledges our emotional, aesthetic, spiritual, religious, and moral experiences.

In many instances, the mind/body issue is presented in a way that makes the reader feel as if one has to be totally on one side or the other. Mills accuses those who hold the materialism view of being dogmatic in their assumption that there is only brain activity and nothing more. While the debate may be presented this way, it is not the only approach. A well-known leader in the fields of multiple intelligences and education, Howard Gardner recently wrote an essay for *The Chronicle of Higher Education* on this topic. Gardner prefers to think of a continuum of ways of understanding, spanning from physics and biology to ethics and religion. He states, "In essence, there is no gulf between behavior and soul; nor is there a need to insist that science and philosophy have nothing to say to each other. At each point on the continuum, a somewhat different blend of disciplines and intellectual tools must be drawn upon" (Gardner, 2001).

The mind/body debate raises many important foundational issues that move us to the core of psychology and cognitive science, both historically and currently. Historically, psychology has been viewed as both a natural science and a social science. Currently, the field of psychology includes many different and unique areas, such as behavioral neuroscience and cognitive therapy. Some have predicted that such a variation in viewpoints will cause psychology to fracture, with some moving to the natural sciences, others to cognitive science, and still others moving to the philosophy. What do you think about that possibility?

The mind/body debate leads us to think about the relationship between the areas that make up cognitive science. Should we strive to map the human psyche in much the same way as a chemical periodic table? Should we strive to build machines that would fully imitate the human brain? Should we strive to understand human nature and our core self? Should we try to do all these? How might we best move forward in all these areas? The mind/body debate will likely continue for a long time to come, and our response to it will shape the cognitive science of the future.

Suggested Readings

L. Brothers, *Mistaken Identity: The Mind-Brain Problem Reconsidered* (Albany, NY: Suny Series in Science, Technology, and Society, 2002).

A. Clark, *Being There: Putting Brain, Body, and World Together Again* (Cambridge, MA: MIT Press, 1998).

H. Gardner, "The Philosophy-Science Continuum," *The Chronicle of Higher Education* (Volume 47, Issue 26, March 9, 2001).

J. Horgan, *The Undiscovered Mind: How the Human Brain Defies Replication, Medication, and Explanation* (Westport, CT: Touchstone Books, 2000).

J. W. Richards (Editor), *Are We Spiritual Machines: Ray Kurzweil vs. the Critics of Strong Artificial Intelligence* (Seattle: Discovery Institute, 2002).

ISSUE 2

Do Children Develop Theories about Other People's Minds?

YES: Henry M. Wellman, David Cross, and Julanne Watson, from "Meta-Analysis of Theory-of-Mind Development: The Truth about False Belief," *Child Development* (2001)

NO: Brian J. Scholl and Alan M. Leslie, from "Minds, Modules, and Meta-Analysis," *Child Development* (2001)

ISSUE SUMMARY

YES: Senior research scientist Henry Wellman and his colleagues, David Cross and Julanne Watson, present a meta-analysis revealing support for their belief that stage-related conceptual changes bring about an understanding of theory-of-mind in small children.

NO: Cognitive researchers Brian Scholl and Alan Leslie argue that the data do not support conceptual change but rather the development of innate specific skills that lead to children's understanding of theory-of-mind.

Since the 1980s, cognitive scientists have been interested in how children first come to realize that every person engages in private cognitions, and then realize that they can predict and potentially influence other people's thoughts. Trying to see the world from someone else's perspective isn't always an easy task, and it can be particularly difficult for small children. The research area of *Theory-of-Mind* seeks to understand how children first develop a theory for predicting other people's thoughts.

One of the most popular ways to assess early theory-of-mind development is to present a child with a false-belief task. Wimmer and Perner (1983) demonstrated the usefulness of the false-belief task in what has now become a classic study in this field. Wellman, Cross, and Watson, the authors of the first selection, summarize the false-belief task this way:

> Maxi puts his chocolate in the kitchen cupboard and leaves the room to play. While he is away (and cannot see) his mother moves the

> chocolate from the cupboard to a drawer. Maxi returns. Where will he look for his chocolate? (page 655)

The child who has not developed a theory-of-mind will expect Maxi to look in the drawer for his chocolate because that is where the chocolate really is. The child who has developed a theory-of-mind will realize that Maxi has a false belief regarding the location of the chocolate that will lead the character to look in the cupboard, which is counter to the real situation.

The issue debated in the two selections is primarily about which theories best explain the current research findings. Wellman, Cross, and Watson believe that when a child reaches age three or four a conceptual change occurs, stemming from the movement into a new stage that allows the child to understand the false-belief situation. In a sense, children develop their own theory of the workings of other people's minds, and thus it is sometimes called the "theory-theory" because it is a theory about children's developing theories of other's minds.

Scholl and Leslie are approaching the false-belief data from a different theoretical perspective called the "early competence" model. They believe that the skills needed to pass the false-belief task are very specific to this task (rather than coming out of a general stage advancement), innate (rather than conceptual or stage based), and modular. Unlike a sweeping stage-based developmental approach, Scholl and Leslie believe the development of theory-of-mind comes as modules or components become activated. The important module in this case is the Theory-of-Mind Mechanism/Selection Processing (ToMM/SP) component. Scholl and Leslie assert that:

> . . . in the false-belief task, in order to compute the content of the protagonist's belief about the location of the target object (a job for ToMM), the child must first inhibit ToMM's initial response based on the target's salient actual location (a job for SP). (page 697)

When considering the results of the meta-analysis provided by Wellman, et al., Scholl and Leslie believe that the ToMM/SP provides a stronger interpretation of the data.

In the following selections, the false-belief task is scrutinized through the meta-analysis conducted by Wellman, et al., involving 77 research reports and articles that included 178 separate studies, 591 conditions, and more than 4,000 children. In the first selection, Wellman and his colleagues present the results of the meta-analysis and their conclusion that the results can best be explained by a conceptual change or stage model. In the second selection, Scholl and Leslie make the case that children have innate and specific skills that, when biologically mature, allow the child to understand the false-belief task.

Henry M. Wellman, David Cross, and Julanne Watson

Meta-Analysis of Theory-of-Mind Development: The Truth about False Belief

Introduction

"Theory of mind" has become an important theoretical construct and the topic of considerable research effort. Theory of mind describes one approach to a larger topic: everyday or folk psychology—the construal of persons as psychological beings, interactors, and selves. The phrase, theory of mind, emphasizes that everyday psychology involves seeing oneself and others in terms of mental states—the desires, emotions, beliefs, intentions, and other inner experiences that result in and are manifested in human action. Furthermore, everyday understanding of people in these terms is thought to have a notable coherence. Because actors have certain desires and relevant beliefs, they engage in intentional acts, the success and failure of which result in various emotional reactions. Whether or in what sense everyday psychology is theorylike is a matter of contention (see, e.g., Gopnik & Wellman, 1994; Nelson, Plesa, & Henseler, 1998). Regardless, the phrase, theory of mind, highlights two essential features of everyday psychology: its coherence and mentalism.

How, when, and in what manner does an everyday theory of mind arise? This question has generated much current research with children. The question has been investigated using a variety of tasks and studies that focus on various conceptions within the child's developing understanding, for example, conceptions of desires, emotions, beliefs, belief–desire reasoning, or psychological explanation, among others (see, e.g., Astington, 1993; Flavell & Miller, 1998; Wellman, 1990). From the earliest research, however, a central focus has been on children's understanding of belief, especially false belief. Why? Mental-state understanding requires realizing that such states may reflect reality and may be manifest in overt behavior, but are nonetheless internal and mental, and thus distinct from real-world events, situations, or behaviors. A child's understanding that a person has a false belief—one whose content contradicts reality—provides compelling evidence for appreciating this distinction between mind and world (see, e.g., Dennett, 1979).

A now classic false-belief task presents a child with the following scenario (Wimmer & Perner, 1983): Maxi puts his chocolate in the kitchen cupboard and leaves the room to play. While he is away (and cannot see) his mother moves the chocolate from the cupboard to a drawer. Maxi returns. Where will he look for his chocolate, in the drawer or in the cupboard? Four- and 5-year-olds often pass such tasks, judging that Maxi will search in the cupboard although the chocolate really is in the drawer. These correct answers provide evidence that the child knows that Maxi's actions depend on his beliefs rather than simply the real situation itself, because belief and reality diverge. Many younger children, typically 3-year-olds, fail such tasks. Instead of answering randomly, younger children often make a specific false-belief error—they assert that Maxi will look for the chocolate in the drawer to which it was moved. . . .

False-belief performance has come to serve as a marker for mentalistic understanding of persons more generally. Thus, in research on individual differences in young children's social cognition, false-belief performances are used as a major outcome measure to assess the influence of early family conversations (Dunn, Brown, Slomkowski, Tesla, & Youngblade, 1991), engagement in pretend play (Youngblade & Dunn, 1995), or family structure (Hughes & Dunn, 1998; Perner, Ruffman, & Leekam, 1994) on development of mentalistic understandings. False-belief understanding has also become a major tool for research with developmentally delayed individuals. The theory-of-mind hypothesis for autism, in particular, claims that the severe social disconnectedness evident in even high-functioning individuals with autism is due to an impairment in their ability to construe persons in terms of their inner mental lives (see, e.g., Baron-Cohen, 1995). False-belief performances provided an initial empirical test of this claim in that high-functioning children with autism who are able to reason competently about physical phenomena often fail false-belief tasks, whereas Down syndrome and other delayed populations of equivalent mental age often do not (e.g., Baron-Cohen, Leslie, & Frith, 1985; for more comprehensive findings and comparisons, see Happe, 1995; Yirimiya, Erel, Shaked, & Solomonica-Levi, 1998).

For various reasons, therefore, a considerable body of research has accumulated, which employ an increasing variety of false-belief tasks that focus on attempting to demonstrate and explain false-belief errors, as well as relate performance on false-belief tasks to other conceptions, tasks, and competencies. Theory-of-mind research goes well beyond this task and these data; nonetheless false-belief tasks have a central place in current social-cognitive research (see Flavell & Miller, 1998), much as conservation tasks once were focal for understanding cognitive development and for testing Piaget's findings and theorizing. For the case of false belief, just as in the conservation literature, the initial accounts, the initial tasks, and especially the claims of conceptual change have all been vigorously challenged.

In particular, research on false belief instantiates a basic conundrum in the study of cognitive development. Performance on any cognitive task reflects at least two factors: conceptual understanding required to solve the problem ("competence") and other non-focal cognitive skills (e.g., ability to remember the key information, focus attention, comprehend, and answer various questions) required to access and express understanding ("performance"). The last 25 years of cognitive development research have produced a plethora of early competence studies and accounts essentially showing that on various tasks young children fail not because they lack the conceptual competence, but rather because the testing situation was too demanding or confusing. This research has had several desirable results: undeniable underestimations of young children's knowledge have been exposed; information-processing analyses of how children arrive at their answers and responses, and not just what answers or responses they make, have flourished; and domain-general accounts of cognitive competence have yielded to more precise domain-specific understandings of children's conceptions and skills. At the same time, however, accepted demonstrations of conceptual change have largely disappeared. This is curious inasmuch as the interplay between cognitive change and stability is the cornerstone of all major theories of cognitive development. Yet each proposed developmental change (e.g., Piaget's conservation competence, Carey's proposed shift from naive psychology to naive biology, false-belief understandings) has seemingly evaporated in the mist of task variations showing enhanced performance in still younger children.

Conceivably, conceptual change may indeed be rare. The contemporary re-emergence of strongly nativist perspectives on cognitive development both contributes to and derives from this possibility (e.g., Spelke, 1994). On the other hand, genuine conceptual changes may be obscured by current emphasis on early competence and task simplifications, making it difficult to comprehend the bigger picture amidst the haze of accumulating results from numerous task variations. A comprehensive analysis of the voluminous and varied false-belief research provides an important contemporary opportunity to examine this basic issue.

Empirically, an increasing number of researchers now claim that the original false-belief tasks are unnecessarily difficult and that 3-year-olds can evidence improved, even above-chance, false-belief reasoning if the tasks are suitably revised (e.g., Siegal & Beattie, 1991; Sullivan & Winner, 1993). Not only the correct estimation of 3-year-olds is at issue, but more importantly, basic developmental trends. Some authors now claim that 3-year-olds, and much younger children as well, understand belief and false belief (e.g., Chandler, Fritz, & Hala, 1989; Fodor, 1992). False-belief competence, assessed correctly, is thus predicted to be high even in young children. Other authors (e.g., Robinson & Mitchell, 1995) claim that many 3-year-olds fail false-belief tasks but claim many 4- and 5-year-olds do as well. "The most striking thing about the age trends was the lack of them. . . . Quite simply, it has become fashionable to claim that there is a sharp age trend, but in fact there is not" (Mitchell, 1996, pp. 137–138).

These issues, controversies, and theories, along with the increasing amount of empirical findings, mandate a careful review. . . .

Method

. . . [O]ur analyses encompassed 77 reports or articles including 178 separate studies and 591 conditions. . . .

[A] large majority of false-belief research was examined, representative of both published and unpublished false-belief studies in the field as of January 1998. The analyses of the data provided by these studies proceeded in several stages. In each, different subsets of the total data were used, as clarified in [a different section].

Coding

Each condition included in the analyses was coded for the dependent variable (proportion of correct responses to the false-belief question) and for a variety of features constituting the following independent variables:

1. Year of publication.
2. Mean age and number of participants in a condition.
3. Percentage of participants passing control questions, and percentage dropped from the research.
4. Country of participants: for example, the United States, United Kingdom, Austria, Japan, and so forth.
5. Type of task: Three levels of task type, which distinguished locations versus contents versus identity tasks (as described earlier).
6. Nature of the protagonist: Five levels that described the protagonist as a puppet or doll; a pictured character; a videotaped person; or a real person present in, or absent from, the current situation. Protagonists who were real, present persons were then also coded as either the self or another person.
7. Nature of the target object: Four levels that described the target object as a real object (e.g., chocolate), a toy, a pictured object, or a videotaped object.
8. Real presence of the target object: Two levels denoting whether, at the time the false-belief question was asked, the target object was real and present (e.g., chocolate was in the drawer) or not (e.g., Maxi's chocolate was used up and thus now absent).
9. Motive for the transformation: Two levels capturing whether the key transformation (e.g., the change of location) was done to explicitly trick the protagonist (deception), or for some other reason including for no explicit reason at all.
10. Participation in the transformation: Three levels describing whether the child initially helped to set up the task props, engaged in actively making the key transformation, or only passively observed the events.
11. Salience of the protagonist's mental state: Four levels describing whether the mental state had to be inferred from the character's simple absence during the key transformation, whether the

character's absence was emphasized and explicitly noted, whether the false-belief experience was demonstrated initially on the children themselves, . . . or whether the character's mental state was explicitly stated (e.g., the child was told "Maxi thinks it is in the cupboard") or pictured in some fashion (e.g., via a thought bubble).

12. Type of question: Four levels denoting whether the false-belief question was phrased in terms of where the protagonist would look (or some other belief-dependent action the character might take), what he'd think or believe, what he'd say, or what he'd know.
13. Temporal marker: Two levels capturing whether the false-belief question explicitly mentioned the time frame involved ("When Maxi comes back, which place will he look in first?") or not. . . .

Discussion

Development

The basic finding in this study is the presence of a substantial effect for age in every analysis. Correct performance significantly increases with increasing age; in some cases, correct performance increases from chance to above chance, but in most cases it increases from below chance to above chance. Such findings clearly support the initial claims of substantial development during these preschool years, and contradict recent suspicions that developmental change is nonexistent (Mitchell, 1996) or is confined to only a few standard tasks that are unusually demanding (Chandler et al., 1989).

"Noneffects"

Many potentially relevant variables (e.g., nature of the protagonist, nature of the target object, type of question, and type of task) systematically failed to affect children's age-related performances. These results confirm those of several individual studies that have failed to find differences for these variables. However, detecting a lack of differences when comparing small samples of 12 to 20 children is problematic. In contrast, because our meta-analysis encompassed 350 to 500 different conditions representing more than 4,000 children, it is certainly powerful enough to detect differences on these variables, if they existed.

The null findings of this study have important methodological implications. Knowing that valid and comparable assessments of false-belief performance are uninfluenced by a variety of task specifics, experimenters can confidently vary their tasks over an extended set of possibilities for ease of presentation and to achieve other experimental contrasts. More crucially, this lack of effects is of theoretical importance as well. That children's false-belief judgments are systematically unrelated to such task variations increases the likelihood that their judgments reflect robust, deep-seated conceptions of human action, rather than task-specific responses provoked by the special features of one set of materials or questions. Specifically, the irrelevance of these task and procedural variations increases the likelihood that children's performance is systematically dependent on the one thing that does not vary, namely their conception of belief states.

For adults, the task variations mentioned above are conceptually equivalent or irrelevant; it is a substantive finding that young children treat them as equivalent as well. Consider the notion of belief that is targeted by standard false-belief tasks. The beliefs involved are determined by informational access—whether or not Maxi saw the chocolate being moved—but should be uninfluenced by irrelevant individual differences in the target protagonists, such as their age, gender, and their real life presence versus video or storybook nature (Miller, 2000). The meta-analytic findings show that even young children appropriately understand the irrelevance of several protagonist differences for an understanding of belief.

Early Competence versus Conceptual Change

As noted in the Introduction, our findings speak to an important divide between two general accounts of young children's poor false-belief performance. One account argues for conceptual change, that is, developmental changes in performance on false-belief tasks reflect genuine changes in children's conceptions of persons. A contrasting account argues for early competence, that is, even young children have the necessary conception; their poor task performances reflect instead information-processing limits, unnecessarily demanding tasks, or confusing questions. . . .

Empirical confirmation of early competence accounts requires that there be some version of the target task that indeed demonstrates enhanced performance by young children, when task limitations have been eliminated or reduced. Our findings show that several task manipulations do increase young children's performance: framing the task in terms of explicit deception or trickery, involving the child in actively making the key transformations, and highlighting the salience of the protagonist's mental state or reducing the salience of the contrasting real-world state of affairs, all help young children to perform better.

Early competence accounts require more than just improved performance, however. First, such accounts require that relevant task manipulations differentially enhance young children's performance. This requirement derives from the essential claim that such task factors mask early competence, thereby artifactually producing apparent developmental differences on the target tasks. Second, such accounts require demonstrations of above-chance performance. . . . Third, demonstrations of above-chance performance must extend beyond children at an intermediate, transitional age. If children at an intermediate age are aided, but younger children still genuinely fail the task, then the timing of a developmental change, but not its absence versus presence, may be at issue. Thus, for early competence accounts, task variations should interact with performance in a specific developmental pattern.

None of these three pieces of evidence for an early competence view were sustained in the meta-analysis: older children as well as younger children were aided by certain task manipulations; no set of manipulations boosted younger children's performance to above chance; and only one variable, presence or absence of temporal marking in the test question, interacted with age, but not in an early competence pattern. Even a combined-effects model, statistically assembling the most powerful package of helpful task manipulations, failed to produce above-chance performance in the youngest children and failed to interactively change the shape of the basic developmental pattern of performance across these years. It is important to note that the finding of an interaction between age and temporal marking demonstrates that the meta-analysis was able to detect interactions in the data, if they were present. . . .

With regard to a general contrast between conceptual change and early competence accounts, then, the meta-analysis suggests that an important conceptual change in children's understanding of persons is taking place between the ages of 2½ and 5 years. . . .

Chandler's and Leslie's Accounts

Recall that Chandler (1988; Chandler et al., 1989) proposed that early competence at false-belief judgments is masked by unnecessarily demanding features of the standard tasks. In contrast to standard tasks, Chandler argued, tasks framed in terms of explicit deception, which enlist the child in concocting the deceptive circumstances and minimize verbal demands by having the child point or nonverbally arrange props, would better reveal young children's early competence. In their research, tasks employing these features have been found to enhance young children's performance (e.g., Chandler et al., 1989; Hala, Chandler, & Fritz, 1991), although in other studies this has not been the case (e.g., Sodian et al., 1991). The meta-analysis showed that these features—especially deception and active participation—indeed aid performance. The pattern of findings for these factors, however, failed to fit an early competence model more specifically. To reiterate, these task manipulations, although helpful, do not alter the shape of the general developmental trajectory and do not raise the youngest children's performance to systematically above-chance performance.

Leslie also proposed a specific early competence account (e.g., Leslie & Roth, 1993; Roth & Leslie, 1998) in which understanding persons' mental attitudes or states, such as the "belief that X is so," is the result of a special Theory-of-Mind Mechanism (ToMM) that is activated early in development. Performance in any task situation, however, depends not simply on ToMM but also on a Selection Processor (SP) that can limit the application of ToMM in any specific case. According to this account, standard false-belief tasks place large demands on SP and hence mask, rather than reveal, young children's Theory-of-Mind competence. In contrast, nonstandard tasks can reduce these demands thereby revealing early ToMM competence. Thus, Leslie (Leslie & Roth, 1993, p. 99) notes approvingly that "three-year-olds do succeed on some non-standard false-belief tasks" (see, e.g., Mitchell & Lacohee, 1991; Roth & Leslie, 1998; Wellman & Bartsch, 1988). The arguments above against early competence accounts more generally apply to Leslie's specific account; manipulations of the type that

Leslie endorses do aid performance, but across numerous studies in the meta-analysis such manipulations did not systematically produce an early competence pattern of results. . . .

Conclusions

The current meta-analysis organizes the available findings on false-belief understanding—a sizable accomplishment, given that the voluminous accumulating findings had begun to seem contradictory and interpretively intractable. It is now clear that across studies, when organized systematically, the results are largely robust, orderly, and consistent. Theoretically, once the findings are clarified, several competing accounts of false-belief performance can be evaluated. In particular, early competence accounts that claim apparent developments during the ages of 3 to 5 years are solely the products of overly difficult tasks masking young children's essentially correct understanding of belief are not substantiated in several key regards.

The meta-analysis also argues against proposals that an understanding of belief, including false belief, is the culture-specific product of socialization within literate, individualistic Anglo-European cultures (Lillard, 1998). A mentalistic understanding of persons that includes a sense of their internal representations—their beliefs—is widespread. Although children may acquire such conceptions sooner or later depending on the cultural communities and language systems in which they are reared, young children in Europe, North America, South America, East Asia, Australia, and Africa, and from nonschooled "traditional" as well as literate "modern" cultures, all acquire these insights on roughly the same developmental trajectory. . . .

Methodologically, these results inform us about several task variations that are essentially equivalent. This frees investigators to use a specific task instantiation because it is easier for them to administer than others (e.g., using puppets versus people as the target character) or because it best fits their theoretical purposes (e.g., for some purposes an unexpected-contents task may most closely parallel a target-contrast task, whereas for other purposes a change-of-locations task may do so). . . .

Equally important methodologically, the meta-analysis underwrites the increasingly common practice of using false-belief tasks as a marker of theory-of-mind understanding in other types of research, such as research on individual differences in early social cognition (e.g., Hughes & Dunn, 1998) and on impaired or delayed social cognition with autistic individuals (e.g., Baron-Cohen, 1995). False-belief tasks demonstrably provide a robust measure of an important early development. Nevertheless, several cautions are necessary. (1) False-belief tasks measure only one narrow aspect of social cognitive development; therefore, use of a battery of social cognition tasks would be best for many studies. (2) Individual differences can take several forms: Some individual difference dimensions (perhaps shyness) can differentiate individuals across the lifespan; other differences emerge only within a particular window of development and thus reflect an individual's speed of attaining a common developmental milestone. False-belief measures fall into the latter category, and their nature needs to be carefully considered in research on individual differences. (3) To be useful in individual-differences research a measure needs to be a valid representative of the proposed construct, and must have certain psychometric properties. Critically, reliability and unreliability of measurement place limits on the assessment of interrelation among variables of interest. The meta-analysis suggests that, within its developmental window of usefulness, false-belief measures are reliable. To reiterate, the meta-analysis includes 52 reports of children's consistency of responding across equivalent false-belief tasks. On average, consistency, or proportion of agreement, was .84; that is, 84% of the time children's first false-belief response was matched in their second response. . . .

Finally, under the heading of methodological implications, it seems to us that the meta-analysis should lay to rest a great many questions about how task modifications enhance performance, thereby reducing the volume of studies designed simply to assess such questions. In general, the accumulation of 591 conditions includes task variations of sufficient scope to obviate the need for still one more variation. There will always be defensible exceptions to this caveat. For example, it might be of some use to empirically assess, within the scope of a single study, the effects of a false-belief task that includes all four performance-enhancing features outlined earlier. For the most part, however, researchers should turn to looking at the important theoretical questions that are outstanding, such as what mechanisms account for the developmental changes now clearly evident in children's understanding of belief and of the mind. The results of the meta-analysis, summarizing 591 false-belief conditions, can facilitate such theoretically driven research on still broader issues in the field. . . .

References

Astington, J. W. (1993). *The child's discovery of the mind.* Cambridge, MA: Harvard University Press.

Baron-Cohen, S. (1995). *Mindblindness: An essay on autism and theory of mind.* Cambridge, MA: MIT Press.

Baron-Cohen, S., Leslie, A. M., & Frith, U. (1985). Does the autistic child have a "theory of mind?" *Cognition, 21,* 37–46.

Chandler, M. (1988). Doubt and developing theories of mind. In J. Astington, P. Harris, & D. Olson (Eds.), *Developing theories of mind.* New York: Cambridge University Press.

Chandler, M., Fritz, A. S., & Hala, S. (1989). Small scale deceit: Deception as a marker of 2-, 3-, and 4-year-olds early theories of mind. *Child Development, 60,* 1263–1277.

Dennett, D. C. (1979). *Brainstorms.* Hassocks, Sussex: Harvester.

Dunn, J., Brown, J., Slomkowski, C., Tesla, C., & Youngblade, L. (1991). Young children's understanding of other people's feelings and beliefs: Individual differences and their antecedents. *Child Development, 62,* 1352–1366.

Flavell, J. H., & Miller, P. H. (1998). Social cognition. In D. Kuhn & R. Siegler (Vol. Eds.), W. Damon (Series Ed.), *Handbook of child psychology: Vol. 2. Cognition, perception, and language* (pp. 851–898). New York: Wiley.

Fodor, J. A. (1992). A theory of the child's theory of mind. *Cognition,* 44, 283–296.

Gopnik, A., & Wellman, H. M. (1994). The theory theory. In L. Hirschfeld & S. Gelman (Eds.), *Domain specificity in cognition and culture* (pp. 257–293). New York: Cambridge University Press.

Hala, S., Chandler, M., & Fritz, A. S. (1991). Fledgling theories of mind: Deception as a marker of 3-year-olds' understanding of false belief. *Child Development, 62,* 83–97.

Happe, F. G. E. (1995). The role of age and verbal ability in the theory of mind task performance of subjects with autism. *Child Development, 66,* 843–855.

Hughes, C., & Dunn, J. (1998). Understanding and emotion: Longitudinal associations with mental-state talk between young friends. *Developmental Psychology, 34,* 1026–1037.

Leslie, A. M., & Roth, D. (1993). What autism teaches us about meta-representation. In S. Baron-Cohen, H. Tager-Flusberg, & D. Cohen (Eds.), *Understanding other minds: Perspectives from autism* (pp. 83–111). Oxford, U.K.: Oxford University Press.

Lillard, A. (1998). Ethnopsychologies: Cultural variations in theories of mind. *Psychological Bulletin, 123,* 3–32.

Miller, S. A. (2000). Children's understanding of preexisting differences in knowledge and belief. *Developmental Review, 20,* 227–282.

Mitchell, P. (1996). *Acquiring a conception of mind: A review of psychological research and theory.* Hove, U.K.: Psychology Press.

Mitchell, P., & Lacohee, H. (1991). Children's early understanding of false belief. *Cognition, 39,* 107–127.

Nelson, K., Plesa, D., & Henseler, S. (1998). Children's theory of mind: An experiential interpretation. *Human Development, 41,* 7–29.

Perner, J., Ruffman, T., & Leekam, S. R. (1994). Theory of mind is contagious: You catch it from your sibs. *Child Development, 65,* 1228–1238.

Robinson, E. J., & Mitchell, P. (1995). Masking children's early understanding of the representational mind: Backwards explanation versus prediction. *Child Development, 66,* 1022–1039.

Roth, D., & Leslie, A. (1998). Solving belief problems: Toward a task analysis. *Cognition, 66,* 1–31.

Siegal, M., & Beattie, K. (1991). Where to look first for children's understanding of false beliefs. *Cognition, 38,* 1–12.

Sodian, B., Taylor, C., Harris, P. L., & Perner, J. (1991). Early deception and the child's theory of mind. *Child Development, 62,* 468–483.

Spelke, E. S. (1994). Initial knowledge: Six suggestions. *Cognition, 50,* 431–445.

Sullivan, K., & Winner, E. (1993). Three-year-old's understanding of mental states: The influence of trickery. *Journal of Experimental Child Psychology, 56,* 135–148.

Wellman, H. M. (1990). *The child's theory of mind.* Cambridge, MA: MIT Press, A Bradford Book.

Wellman, H. M., & Bartsch, K. (1988). Young children's reasoning about beliefs. *Cognition, 30,* 239–277.

Yirimiya, N., Erel, O., Shaked, M., & Solomonica-Levi, D. (1998). Meta-analyses comparing theory of mind abilities of individuals with autism, individuals with mental retardation, and normally developing individuals. *Psychological Bulletin, 124,* 283–307.

Youngblade, L. M., & Dunn, J. (1995). Individual differences in young children's pretend play with mother and sibling: Links to relationships and understanding of other people's feelings and beliefs. *Child Development, 66,* 1472–1492.

Brian J. Scholl and Alan M. Leslie

Minds, Modules, and Meta-Analysis

Wellman and colleagues' meta-analysis of performance on the false-belief task is methodologically useful, but it does not lead to any theoretical progress concerning the nature of the mechanisms that underlie the existence and development of "theory of mind." In particular, the results of this meta-analysis are perfectly compatible with "early competence" accounts that posit a specific, innate, and possibly modular basis for theory of mind. The arguments presented by Wellman and colleagues against such views stem not from their meta-analytic data, but from mistaken assumptions regarding the requirements of such theories (e.g., that there exist manipulations that improve performance only, or to a greater degree, in young children). Contrary to what Wellman and colleagues claim, their meta-analysis, while consistent with conceptual change, does not lend any new support for such theories.

Introduction

Many aspects of human behavior are the result of internal mental states such as beliefs and desires. Furthermore, as is well known, even young children perceive, interpret, predict, and explain the behavior of others in terms of their underlying mental states. The acquisition of such abilities—collectively referred to as a "theory of mind"—is early, universal (except in certain clinical populations), seemingly effortless, and largely dissociable from more general intellectual development. In adults, the exercise of such abilities is often irresistible and seemingly instantaneous. One hallmark of a mature theory of mind is the ability to reason about false beliefs: One can often successfully reason about true beliefs simply by considering the world itself as a proxy, but this heuristic fails in the case of false beliefs. As such, successful reasoning about false beliefs is a sufficient (although not necessary) criterion for the existence of a theory of mind (e.g., Dennett, 1978). It is precisely this ability that is tapped by the "false-belief task," wherein a child must infer that a protagonist will look for a target object where he mistakenly believes it to be, rather than looking in its actual location (Baron-Cohen, Leslie, & Frith, 1985; Wimmer & Perner, 1983; for a description and review, see Wellman, Cross, & Watson, 2001).

Of course, solving a false-belief problem also requires several other abilities that are not theory of mind specific, and the existence of theory of mind in young children is also indicated by many other types of experiment (see Bloom & German, 2000). Still, given the degree to which this single task has dominated developmental research on theory of mind, the meta-analysis conducted by Wellman and colleagues (2001) is extremely welcome. Furthermore, we agree that this analysis is methodologically useful: for example, it identifies several factors that, thus far, appear to play no substantive role in false-belief performance; it might be more permissible for future studies to ignore such variables (but see our final comment later). Aside from these methodological morals, however, this analysis, with one exception, does not lead to any theoretical progress concerning the nature of the mechanisms that underlie the existence and development of theory of mind. The one exception is that the meta-analysis confirms an important role for "executive processes" in false-belief performance, a finding that should encourage the "early competence" theorist. In any case, the results of this meta-analysis are perfectly compatible with early competence accounts that posit a specific, innate, and possibly modular basis for theory of mind.

In the remainder of this commentary, we discuss one such modular theory, and show how the arguments proffered by Wellman and colleagues against such views stem not from their meta-analytic data, but from mistaken assumptions about the requirements of such theories. We conclude by highlighting some of the general issues raised by this meta-analysis that actually favor modular theories over theories that invoke conceptual change.

The Modular Basis of Theory of Mind

One early competence theory of theory of mind is the Theory-of-Mind Mechanism/Selection Processing (ToMM/SP) model proposed by Leslie and colleagues (e.g., German & Leslie, 2000, 2001; Leslie, 1987, 1994, 2000a, 2000b; Leslie & Polizzi, 1998; Leslie & Roth, 1993; Leslie & Thaiss, 1992; Roth & Leslie, 1998; Scholl & Leslie, 1999; Surian & Leslie, 1999). The essence of this model is that theory of mind has a specific, innate basis. Each part of this claim is crucial. First, theory of mind has a *specific* innate basis in that the essential character of theory of mind is determined by specialized mechanisms deploying specialized representations that do not apply to other cognitive domains, and that can, therefore, be selectively impaired. In the limit, the origin of theory of mind may be a cognitive module (for a recent discussion of the relation of modules to development, see Scholl & Leslie, 1999). This contrasts with the "theory-theory," in which the processes underlying theory of mind are simply general processes of theory or knowledge formation (i.e., general induction), and are presumed to be the same as those employed in scientific reasoning (e.g., Gopnik & Meltzoff, 1997; Gopnik & Wellman, 1994).[1]

Second, theory of mind has a specific *innate* basis in that the essential character of theory of mind—including the concepts of belief, desire, and pretense—is part of our genetic endowment, which are triggered by appropriate environmental factors, much as, for example, is puberty. In Wellman's terminology, that is what makes this view a type of early competence theory. However, it is worth noting the possibility that the concept belief is triggered relatively late, around 4 years of age, rather than early, around 3. This is entirely consistent with our general view, just as it is consistent with the theory-theory view that the child discovers the representational theory of belief early rather than late. The controversies remain, even if the ages are different.

Finally, the ToMM/SP model's claim is not that the entirety of theory of mind is modular, but rather that theory of mind has a specific innate *basis*. That is, this theory is intended primarily to capture the origin of theory of mind abilities, and not the full range of mature activities that may employ them. Clearly the totality of theory of mind is not modular, any more than the totality of perception is modular. In each case the interesting question is whether a significant part of such a capacity has a modular origin. This appears to be the case with "early vision" (see Pylyshyn, 1999), and it seems equally likely in the case of "early theory of mind." Consistent with this modular view, theory of mind acquisition is universal and follows a consistent timetable, and the interpretation of people in terms of their underlying mental states appears to be fast and irresistible. In addition, theory of mind ability is subject to specific neuropsychological impairments (e.g., Baron-Cohen et al., 1985; Langdon & Coltheart, 1999), is resistant to others (Varley & Siegal, 2000), and recruits specific brain structures (Frith & Frith, 1999).

The ToMM/SP theory has two parts. The first, ToMM, is essentially a module that spontaneously and postperceptually processes behaviors that are attended, and computes the mental states that contributed to them. In doing so, it imparts an innate concept, belief, which is thereby available to a child long before other abstract concepts are acquired via general theory construction. Leslie and Thaiss (1992) introduced the idea that ToMM by itself has limited powers that need to be supplemented in certain situations if the child is to select the correct content for mental states; in particular, if the child is to select the correct content of beliefs that are false. They dubbed this supplemental processing, Selection Processing (SP). SP was conceived to be a general executive process required in many situations to inhibit salient but unwanted responses. . . . The theoretical idea behind the ToMM/SP model is that ToMM automatically attributes beliefs with contents that are true. This default or best-guess strategy is thought to reflect the fact that a person's beliefs *ought* to be true and, indeed, typically *are* true. The strategy thus represents an optimal design for default attributions that should have been favored in the evolution of ToMM and that plausibly form the initial state of this cognitive mechanism. However, it does so at the cost of producing a prepotent response, which, in false-belief situations, needs to be inhibited. Thus, in the false-belief task, in order to compute the content of the protagonist's belief about the location of the target object (a job for ToMM), the child must first inhibit ToMM's initial response based on the target's salient actual location (a job for SP). Recently, Leslie and Polizzi (1998) have published two distinct models that develop the ToMM/SP theory in greater detail.

The ToMM/SP model has given rise to the following theory of normal and abnormal development. ToMM is thought to be specifically impaired in autism (Baron-Cohen, 1995, 2000; Frith, Morton, & Leslie, 1991; Happé, 1995; Leslie, 1987, 1991, 1992); for this reason autistic individuals fail the false-belief task despite intact selection processing. By contrast, normally developing 3-year-olds have an intact ToMM, but fail the false-belief task because of immature selection processing. The critical aspect of this difference is that autistic individuals have an impairment that is specific to theory of mind, whereas 3-year-olds have a domain-general impairment of inhibitory control. Experimentally, this contrast has been supported by demonstrations that autistic individuals, but not 3-year-olds, easily pass exact analogues to the false-belief task that do not employ theory of mind (e.g., false photographs and maps); whereas 3-year-olds, but not autistic individuals, can be aided in false-belief tasks by manipulations that decrease the need for inhibition (for a summary of these experiments, see Leslie, 2000b). As Roth and Leslie (1998) recognize, subtly different versions of this general thesis are possible. For example, selection processing may itself come in different "Flavors" depending on the task (e.g., ToMM may have its own on-board selection processing rather than drawing on a selection-processing resource that is entirely general across domains).

Wellman and colleagues (2001) lump the ToMM/SP theory in with several other variants of what they call early competence theories, and maintain that the results of their meta-analysis are "completely inconsistent" with such views. We completely disagree. In fact, for the reasons discussed in the next sections, the results of the meta-analysis are entirely consistent with both early competence views and conceptual change accounts.

Modular Views Do Not Require Above-Chance Performance in Young Children

Wellman and colleagues argue that in order to confirm early competence theories, some task manipulations must be found that yield above-chance performance on the false-belief task for even young children. Since such performance was not observed in the meta-analysis, even in the best-effects model, Wellman et al. take early competence models to be disconfirmed. We agree that above-chance performance at young ages would tend to support early competence models. However, the inverse is simply not true. In fact, from an early competence viewpoint, there are many reasons why young children might still fail, despite being given a package of helpful task manipulations. We highlight two such reasons.

First, it might simply be the case that the particular task manipulations considered in the meta-analysis did not sufficiently attenuate the need for inhibition by immature selection processing. Moreover, inhibitory control may not be the only limiting performance factor; future research may well uncover new such factors. There may even be no combination of manipulations that makes the task easy enough for 3-year-olds to perform above chance. Even if this is the case, unless one is simply going to *define* the concept belief as the passing of a given task and thus trivialize a serious empirical issue, the 3-year-old may still have the concept. As Bloom and German (2000) stress, the false-belief task is intrinsically difficult for a host of reasons (many not specific to theory of mind), and reasoning about false beliefs is much harder than, for example, simply recognizing that beliefs can be false. It is for this reason that passing a standard false-belief task is sufficient *but not necessary* for demonstrating that a child has the concept belief.

Second, even when only theory of mind-specific factors are considered, it is still not the case under a modular theory that theory of mind competence be in place from birth, any more than puberty (or mature visual processing) must be in place from birth. The ToMM module itself may still require environmental triggering and tuning to mature. Furthermore, there is nothing in the notion of modularity that prevents even matured modules from learning and developing. Modularity is primarily defined in terms of restrictions on informational access (see Fodor, 1983), and it is perfectly consistent with this idea that the processes inside the module develop on the basis of their limited input (Scholl & Leslie, 1999). In sum, modular theories are in no way "antidevelopmental," as Wellman has claimed in the past (Gopnik & Wellman, 1994, p. 283). This is a common misconception and a source of unnecessary heat in many discussions. Modules are distinguished by how they develop, not by the fact that they don't develop. Although there is more we could say, the above two reasons suffice to establish that modular early competence theories impose no requirement that extremely young children be able to pass false-belief tasks at above-chance levels.

Modular Views Do Not Require That Task Manipulations Help Only Young Children

Wellman and colleagues (2001, p. 672) also impose the following requirement on early competence theories: there must be some task manipulations that improve performance on the false-belief task *only* in younger children, or at least provide *more* improvement in younger than in older children: "this requirement derives from the essential claim that . . . task factors mask *early* competence, thereby artifactually producing apparent *developmental* differences on the target tasks." Actually, we believe that changes in performance factors constitute *genuine* developmental effects, not just artifacts, and we strenuously resist the attempt of Wellman and colleagues to equate development exclusively with conceptual change. In the meta-analysis, several factors were found to improve performance—for example, having the actual target object absent (or at least not visible) at the test. Presumably, such manipulations improve performance by facilitating inhibition of the actual location of the target object (the true belief), thus reducing the load on selection processing. (For other recent demonstrations of such effects, see Carlson, Moses, & Hix, 1998; Leslie & Polizzi,

1998; Roth & Leslie, 1998; Surian & Leslie, 1999.) Wellman and colleagues stress, however, that none of these factors interacted in the allegedly required way with age; rather, they improved performance at all ages.

We agree that improvements only in young children might be required by some extreme versions of early competence theories, but we also think such theories are obvious strawmen. In the ToMM/SP theory (which Wellman and colleagues explicitly cast as an early competence theory), this requirement clearly does not apply. At any age at which at least some children are failing the false-belief task, various manipulations should improve performance by facilitating inhibition of the actual location of the target object. Moreover, the more likely disparity would involve greater improvement in older children, who enjoy more matured selection processing, and therefore require less facilitation of inhibition to pass the false-belief task. To make this concrete: suppose that passing some version of the false-belief task requires that 10 units of inhibition be exerted via selection processing. Children at age 3,0 can by themselves muster only 5 units of inhibition, whereas children at age 3,6 can supply 7 units, and children at 3,11 can supply 9 units. Now suppose that some task manipulation is introduced that reduces the demand for inhibition by 2 to 3 units. Clearly, on this model, it is the older children who will reap the largest benefit until ceiling effects kick in. Far more complex models of the interaction between competence, performance, and age are of course possible. These possibilities will have to be investigated by seeking to actually quantify executive functioning and other performance factors. Further serious open-minded research is very much required.

The selection-processing model predicts not only that older children will tend to be helped more (aside from ceiling effects) for a fixed amount of help with inhibitory processing; it also predicts that the ability to solve false-belief tasks will continue to increase right through age 5 and beyond. Thus, the fact that 4-year-olds show better-than-chance performance is not to be read as "they have reached the end of the line developmentally" as fans of conceptual change would believe. . . . Finally, Leslie and Polizzi (1998) and Cassidy (1998) showed that 4-year-olds perform above chance in the standard false-belief task only as long as the protagonist's desire is to approach the target object. If, instead, the desire is to avoid the object, the 4-year-olds show a 3-year-old level of performance, with fewer than 40% passing. The conclusion that Leslie and Polizzi drew from this striking finding is not that 4-year-olds lack the concept belief; instead, they argued that a false-belief + avoidance-desire task demands much more complex inhibitory control.

In sum, early competence views do not require targeted improvement only in younger children, and if anything, they predict the opposite pattern of results. There clearly are developmental processes in theory-of-mind and false-belief reasoning that go beyond 4-year-old success on standard tasks and that have nothing to do with conceptual change. These developments can all be given a detailed account within a modular early competence theory.

Conclusion: Why Favor a Modular Theory of Theory of Mind over Conceptual Change?

In both of the arguments discussed above, the alleged theoretical implications of Wellman et al.'s meta-analysis stem not from their data, but rather from mistaken theoretical assumptions. When these assumptions are dispatched, we find that the results of the meta-analysis are perfectly compatible with at least one view labeled by Wellman et al. as an "early competence" theory. Their meta-analysis of the false-belief task may be methodologically useful, but it does not lead to any theoretical progress concerning the nature of the mechanisms that underlie the existence and development of theory of mind.

Still, this meta-analysis does highlight some useful comparisons between modular theories of theory of mind and the conceptual change view favored by Wellman and colleagues. According to this competing view, theory of mind development involves a fundamental change in how children conceive of people and their behavior. Prior to age 4, children fail the false-belief task because they have no concept of belief; after age 4, when this concept is acquired, they pass the false-belief task. The content of this concept—which is typically thought to embody a bona fide theory of belief (e.g., Gopnik & Meltzoff, 1997; Gopnik & Wellman, 1994; Perner, 1995)—does not simply mature in the child, but is learned from scratch (or nearly so) via interaction with the environment. Furthermore, the processes that drive this acquisition are considered to be completely general; in fact, they are thought to be the same processes involved in theory construction in science (e.g., Gopnik & Meltzoff, 1997; Gopnik & Wellman, 1994). (For extensive discussions on why such views are misguided, see Carey & Spelke, 1996; Leslie, 2000a; Stich & Nichols, 1998.) As Wellman and colleagues stress, this theory is consistent with the results of the meta-analysis. We agree, of course, but this conclusion was virtually preordained, since the only pattern of results inconsistent with conceptual change is one wherein children's performance on these tasks does not improve with age (which, of course, it does). Given the expected robust effect of age in all of the meta-analytic results, no pattern of effects regarding the many other variables could disconfirm the conceptual change view.

This point highlights an important contrast between modular theories and theory-theories. Both views are consistent with the universality of theory of mind acquisition; its consistent timetable; the fast, effortless, and often irresistible computation of the mental states underlying behavior, and so forth.[2] The modular theory *must* predict these features, however, whereas the conceptual change theory is also equally consistent with nonuniversal acquisition, a wildly variable timetable, effortful and voluntary operation, and so forth. Ironically, this makes the ToMM/SP model a stronger *theory* than the theory-theory. To highlight this excessive flexibility in conceptual change stories, consider the strongest prediction that Wellman et al. are able to muster on their behalf in the context of the meta-analysis: "performance on [the false-belief task and related tasks] must change from incorrect to systematically above-chance judgments with age." In other words, this view makes the single daring prediction that children should get better as they get older! Surely, however, a meta-analysis was not required to uncover the truth of such development, which is perhaps the single prediction that is common to all theories of theory of mind!

Wellman et al. conclude "the meta-analysis suggests that an important conceptual change is taking place between the ages of 2½ and 5 years in children's understanding of persons" (p. 673). We disagree: what it demonstrates is just what we knew all along—that there is an important change that takes place between these ages regarding the ability to compute the mental states that underlie behavior. The burning question is what is driving this change. We have argued here that Wellman et al.'s meta-analysis is silent on such issues, that at least one early competence view is perfectly consistent with the outcome of the meta-analysis, and that several other factors favor modular theories of theory of mind over theories that appeal to an unconstrained notion of conceptual change.

Finally, the meta-analysis conducted by Wellman et al. will undoubtedly attract a great deal of attention, and may well be appealed to as an authoritative statement on certain methodological issues in theory of mind. It would be tragic, however, if readers take away from it the conclusion that "the meta-analysis should lay to rest a great many questions about how task modifications enhance performance," and that research on false-belief performance can now be safely abandoned. . . . Should we really believe that such tough and important questions could possibly be laid to rest with a simple meta-analysis? Of course not! We conclude our commentary then with a plea to workers in this area to avoid such intellectual complacency and to continue, and indeed redouble, their efforts to understand the neurocognitive basis of theory of mind and its development. . . .

Notes

1. It has been suggested to us that some theory-theorists might be happy with the idea that theory of mind rests on a modular basis, which then provides a specialized database for general "theorizing" processes to work on. If so, there would be little disagreement between us. However, this type of view is not consistent with the idea of "theories all the way down"—an idea that Wellman and others have advanced. It is crucial to distinguish mechanisms that may be theorylike from knowledge of something that really is a theory (see Leslie, 2000a for an extended discussion on this point).
2. This is not to say that conceptual change stories are necessarily consistent with all aspects of theory of mind development. For example, the specialized nature of theory of mind, which is highlighted by the many studies involving autistic individuals (see Baron-Cohen, 2000), is naturally explained by modular theories, but sharply contrasts with the supposed domain-general nature of the cognitive processes underlying conceptual change.

References

Baron-Cohen, S. (1995). *Mindblindness: An essay on autism and theory of mind.* Cambridge, MA: MIT Press.

Baron-Cohen, S. (2000). Theory of mind and autism: A fifteen year review. In H. Tager-Flusberg, D. Cohen, & S. Baron-Cohen (Eds.), *Understanding other minds: Perspectives from autism and developmental cognitive neuroscience.* Oxford, U.K.: Oxford University Press.

Baron-Cohen, S., Leslie, A. M., & Frith, U. (1985). Does the autistic child have a 'theory of mind'? *Cognition, 21,* 37–46.

Bloom, P., & German, T. (2000). Two reasons to abandon the false belief task as a test of theory of mind. *Cognition, 77,* B25–B31.

Carey, S., & Spelke, E. (1996). Science and core knowledge. *Philosophy of Science, 63,* 515–533.

Carlson, S. M., Moses, L. J., & Hix, H. R. (1998). The role of inhibitory processes in young children's difficulties with deception and false belief. *Child Development, 69,* 672–691.

Cassidy, K. W. (1998). Three- and four-year-old children's ability to use desire- and belief-based reasoning. *Cognition, 66,* B1–B11.

Dennett, D. (1978). Beliefs about beliefs. *Behavioral and Brain Sciences, 1,* 568–570.

Fodor, J. A. (1983). *The modularity of mind.* Cambridge, MA: MIT Press.

Frith, C. D., & Frith, U. (1999). Interacting minds—A biological basis. *Science, 286,* 1692–1695.

Frith, U., Morton, J., & Leslie, A. M. (1991). The cognitive basis of a biological disorder: Autism. *Trends in Neurosciences, 14,* 433–438.

German, T., & Leslie, A. (2000). Attending to and learning about mental states. In P. Mitchell & K. Riggs (Eds.), *Children's reasoning and the mind* (pp. 229–252). Hove, U.K.: Psychology Press.

German, T. P., & Leslie, A. M. (2001). Children's inferences from *knowing* to *pretending* and *believing. British Journal of Developmental Psychology, 19,* 59–83.

Gopnik, A., & Meltzoff, A. (1997). *Words, thoughts, and theories.* Cambridge, MA: MIT Press.

Gopnik, A., & Wellman, H. (1994). The theory theory. In L. Hirschfield & S. Gelman (Eds.), *Mapping the mind: Domain specificity in cognition and culture* (pp. 257–293). New York: Cambridge University Press.

Happé, F. G. (1995). *Autism: An introduction to psychological theory.* Cambridge, MA: Harvard University Press.

Langdon, R., & Coltheart, M. (1999). Mentalising, schizotypy, and schizophrenia. *Cognition, 71,* 43–71.

Leslie, A. M. (1987). Pretense and representation: The origins of "theory of mind." *Psychological Review, 94,* 412–426.

Leslie, A. M. (1991). The theory of mind impairment in autism: Evidence for a modular mechanism of development? In A. Whiten (Ed.), *Natural theories of mind: Evolution, development and simulation of everyday mindreading* (pp. 63–78). Oxford, U.K.: Blackwell.

Leslie, A. M. (1992). Pretense, autism, and the "theory of mind" module. *Current Directions in Psychological Science, 1,* 18–21.

Leslie, A. M. (1994). Pretending and believing: Issues in the theory of ToMM. *Cognition, 50,* 211–238.

Leslie, A. M. (2000a). How to acquire a 'representational theory of mind.' In D. Sperber (Ed.), *Metarepresentations: A multidisciplinary perspective* (pp. 197–223). Oxford, U.K.: Oxford University Press.

Leslie, A. M. (2000b). 'Theory of mind' as a mechanism of selective attention. In M. Gazzaniga (Ed.), *The new cognitive neurosciences, 2nd edition* (pp. 1235–1247). Cambridge, MA: MIT Press.

Leslie, A. M., & Polizzi, P. (1998). Inhibitory processing in the false belief task: Two conjectures. *Developmental Science, 1*, 247–254.

Leslie, A. M., & Roth, D. (1993). What autism teaches us about metarepresentation. In S. Baron-Cohen, H. Tager-Flusberg, & D. Cohen (Eds.), *Understanding other minds: Perspectives from autism* (pp. 83–111). Oxford, U.K.: Oxford University Press.

Leslie, A. M., & Thaiss, L. (1992). Domain specificity in conceptual development: Neuropsychological evidence from autism. *Cognition, 43*, 225–251.

Perner, J. (1995). The many faces of belief: Reflections on Fodor's and the child's theory of mind. *Cognition, 57*, 241–269.

Perner, J., & Wimmer, H. (1985). "John thinks that Mary thinks that . . .": Attribution of second-order false beliefs by 5- to 10-year-old children. *Journal of Experimental Child Psychology, 39*, 437–471.

Pylyshyn, Z. W. (1999). Is vision continuous with cognition? The case for cognitive impenetrability of visual perception. *Behavioral and Brain Sciences, 22*, 341–423.

Roth, D., & Leslie, A. M. (1998). Solving belief problems: Toward a task analysis. *Cognition, 66*, 1–31.

Scholl, B. J., & Leslie, A. M. (1999). Modularity, development, and 'theory of mind'. *Mind and Language, 14*, 131–153.

Stich, S., & Nichols, S. (1998). Theory-theory to the max. *Mind and Language, 13*, 421–449.

Surian, L., & Leslie, A. (1999). Competence and performance in false belief understanding: A comparison of autistic and three-year-old children. *British Journal of Developmental Psychology, 17*, 141–155.

Varley, R., & Siegal, M. (2000). Evidence for cognition without grammar from causal reasoning and 'theory of mind' in an agrammatic aphasic patient. *Current Biology, 10*, 723–726.

Wellman, H. M., Cross, D., & Watson, J. (2001). Meta-analysis of theory-of-mind development: The truth about false belief. *Child Development, 72*, 655–684.

Wimmer, H., & Perner, J. (1983). Beliefs about beliefs: Representation and constraining function of wrong beliefs in young children's understanding of deception. *Cognition, 13*, 103–128.

POSTSCRIPT

Do Children Develop Theories about Other People's Minds?

Wellman, Cross, and Watson make the case that the results of their meta-analysis support a conceptual change or stage theory of the development of children's theory-of-mind. A conceptual or stage theory suggests that when a child moves into a new cognitive stage, a general advancement can be seen in many areas. When comparing the results of 591 task and condition variations, such as the specific wording of questions, Wellman, et al. found that the variations made little difference in the child's ability to pass the false-belief task. It appears that a general cognitive advancement has taken place. They charge that if the early competence model was at work, "task variations should interact with performance in a specific developmental pattern" (page 672). Rather than a pattern of gradual performance improvement, Wellman, et al. believe the data reflect the movement to a new conceptual stage, and that influences performance across the many task variations.

Scholl and Leslie view the results of the meta-analysis as fully supporting the early competence model. Rather than looking for a general cognitive stage progression that allows children to understand a theory of mind, Scholl and Leslie are looking for very specific components or modules that are innate. These various modules are waiting for the right point in maturity to activate, much in the same way hormones wait for activation to begin puberty. Once the right modules are mature or activated, the child can pass the false-belief task. The Theory of Mind Mechanism (ToMM), once mature, allows a child to compute mental states. The Selection Processing (SP) chooses the appropriate response when questioned regarding what the main character thinks and the observing child thinks.

While this debate is focused on theory-of-mind, it reflects a much larger issue within the field of cognitive development. For many years, the work of Jean Piaget has served as the standard theory of children's cognitive development. Piaget's work focused on children's stages, or patterns of thinking, and on the transitional periods of new skill development that would facilitate the movement to the next, more advanced stage. While numerous critics of Piaget's work have emerged, the general idea of stage development has been dominant for many years.

In an ideal situation, research and theory would work hand-in-hand in an effort to find the truth. Research would present data, and theory would attempt to explain it in the best way. Then theory would generate hypotheses for further research. When data are consistent, the theory is supported, and when data are inconsistent, the theory is modified or discarded. It can be a difficult task for scientists to put aside their preference for a particular theory in order to consider data from other perspectives. Did either side convince you of their interpretation of the data, or do you view both interpretations as possibilities?

Suggested Readings

Bloom, P., and German, T. "Two reasons to abandon the false belief task as a test of theory of mind," (*Cognition*, 2000).

Butterworth, G., Harris, P., and Wellman, H. (Editors). *Perspectives on the Child's Theory of Mind* (New York: Oxford University Press, 1997).

Carpenter, M., Call, J., and Tomasello, M. "A new false belief test for 36-month-olds," *British Journal of Developmental Psychology* (September 2002).

Legerstee, M. *Infants' Sense of People: Precursors to a Theory of Mind* (New York: Cambridge University Press, 2004).

Repacholi, B., and Slaughter, V. *Individual Differences in Theory of Mind: Implications for Typical and Atypical Development* (New York: Psychology Press, 2003).

ISSUE 3

Is Mindfulness a Cognitive Style?

YES: Robert J. Sternberg, from "Images of Mindfulness," *Journal of Social Issues* (2000)

NO: Ellen J. Langer and Mihnea Moldoveanu, from "The Construct of Mindfulness," *Journal of Social Issues* (2000)

ISSUE SUMMARY

YES: American Psychological Association president Robert Sternberg makes the case that the concept of mindfulness would be enhanced by association with the area of cognitive styles.

NO: Psychology professors Ellen Langer and Mihnea Moldoveanu find Sternberg's cognitive style category inadequate and much too restrictive for the concept of mindfulness.

Ellen Langer, co-author of the second selection, brought a new area of research into public awareness in 1989 with the publication of her book *Mindfulness*. The earliest research on mindfulness, dating back to the 1970s, was conducted in health care and therapeutic areas. Numerous studies found that increased mindfulness brought about an increased sense of control, which often leads to less stress and better overall health. Since that early research, the concept has been applied to numerous areas, including business management and employee satisfaction, teaching and learning styles, political theory, psychotherapy, and spirituality.

While much as been written on the topic, and an instrument is under development to measure mindfulness, even Langer agrees that the concept is hard to define. In the second selection she states, "Mindfulness is not an easy concept to define but can be best understood as the process of drawing novel distinctions" (page 1). Mindfulness, with its focus on novel distinctions, brings about subjective feelings of involvement with the environment. The opposite, or mindlessness, involves the application of typical, well-learned routines and thinking habits. Mindlessness could be characterized as automatic or routine thinking, whereas mindfulness, according to Langer, involves an openness and sensitivity to multiple perspectives and different contexts. Mindfulness creates a sense of being fully aware of one's present surroundings.

The debate highlighted in these two articles is not over the existence of mindfulness, or even the value of mindfulness, but rather on how to approach and categorize it. Sternberg's view, presented in the first selection, is that mindfulness would gain more attention if it were related to another psychological construct. He describes the downward spiral of some areas of study because they were isolated from standard psychological theory. He believes that if the concept of mindfulness were viewed as belonging to an area of psychology, then more social scientists would be interested in it and willing to explore it. In his attempt to figure out what area should adopt it, Sternberg compares mindfulness to cognitive abilities, personality traits, and cognitive styles. His conclusion is that mindfulness/mindlessness should be regarded as a cognitive style.

Langer and Moldoveanu disagree with Sternberg's analysis and his conclusion. They argue that a key aspect of any cognitive process is the ability to reduce the process to an algorithm. Algorithms are formulas or step-by-step procedures that lead to the solution of a problem, such as the procedure used to solve a long division problem or the steps one takes to save a word processing document on a hard drive. Algorithms are often used in artificial intelligence programs to mimic human information processing. Langer and Moldoveanu believe that the essence of mindfulness is the ability to think in novel ways, or non-algorithmic ways, thus the construct cannot be seen as a cognitive style.

Langer and Moldoveanu expand their argument beyond cognitive styles to the entire field of cognitive science. They state, "the phenomenon of mindfulness also has implications for the ways in which we view and represent the mind and its connection to the brain" (page 5). Here they discuss several problems with the mind-as-computer model. One problem is that scientists have not built computers sophisticated enough to empirically test the mind-as-computer model in a satisfactory way. Another problem is that the mind-as-computer metaphor has become so standard and common that cognitive scientists assume that all cognition is algorithm-based, and thus most do not consider any possibility of non-algorithm–based processing, such as mindfulness.

In the first article, Sternberg compares mindfulness to several areas of psychology and determines that it would be best for construct to be associated with cognitive styles. Langer, who is considered the original expert on the topic, and Moldoveanu not only disagree with Sternberg's conclusion, but also with his attempt to force mindfulness to fit into an existing structure.

Robert J. Sternberg

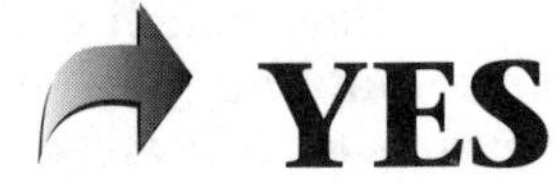

Images of Mindfulness

. . . Yesterday I woke up, trudged to the kitchen, and as usual, I took out the regular coffee for myself and the espresso for my wife. I made our separate kinds of coffee, at which point I realized that my wife's coffee would be cold by the time she got to drink it: She had left the day before for Venezuela and would not be back for a week. The week before it was I who had been on a trip abroad, attending a professional conference. The first morning—the day of my presentation—I whipped out my portable electric razor, wanting to look good for my talk. The battery had discharged and so I needed to recharge it. Unlike some mindless people, I even had remembered to bring my worldwide electrical converter. That was the good news. The bad news was that I had forgotten the cord, so that although I had the razor and the converter, I had no cord to connect the razor to the converter and hence to an electrical socket.

Is there really anyone in the whole world who cannot relate to Ellen Langer's (1989, 1997) construct of *mindlessness* and its complement, *mindfulness*? I doubt it. Whether it is the cup of coffee with no one to drink it, or the razor discharged so that no one can use it, we all act at times in ways that are so mindless that we find ourselves astounded. The constructs of mindlessness and mindfulness are intriguing because they seem so much a part of our lives.

When I speak of "mindfulness," I define mindfulness in this article via Langer's (1997) definition, as containing components of (a) openness to novelty; (b) alertness to distinction; (c) sensitivity to different contexts; (d) implicit, if not explicit, awareness of multiple perspectives; and (e) orientation in the present. Mindfulness thus is a many-sided, or heterogeneous, construct. "Mindlessness" is the lack of these attributes. But how should mindfulness (in contrast to mindlessness) be understood?

Although Langer (1989, 1997) tends to view mindfulness in relative isolation from the literatures on cognitive abilities, personality, and cognitive styles (see review in Ferrari & Sternberg, 1998), the construct might attract more attention from scholars in these fields if they believed the construct "belonged" to one field or another. At the same time, it is precisely this narrow compartmentalization of fields from which the construct of mindfulness helps us escape. But which field does it belong to, if any? Or does it belong to more than one field? Answering this question is made somewhat more challenging by the heterogeneous components of mindfulness.

My main goal in this article is to relate mindfulness to a variety of kinds of constructs in the psychological literature. This goal is important because mindfulness has stood in relative isolation from much of the psychological literature. We would understand mindfulness better if we understood the relation between this construct and other constructs in the literature.

Is Mindfulness a Cognitive Ability?

A cognitive ability can be viewed as a latent source of cognitive skill and usually also is viewed as a source of individual differences in such skills. Cognitive abilities are most often identified by (a) the existence of systematic and relatively stable individual differences, usually through factor analysis or related techniques, or (b) the identification of a unique processing component that accounts for differences in performance of a given individual on various tasks or task variants (Sternberg, 1977). In other words, the ability is a source of variation among either persons, stimulus conditions, or both. At this time, a scale for the measurement of mindfulness has been constructed only recently and is not yet construct-validated, so it is not possible to say whether the construct will meet these conditions. However, openness to novelty; sensitivity to different contexts; implicit, if not explicit, awareness of multiple perspectives; alertness to distinction; and orientation in the present sound related to, although not necessarily identical to, cognitive abilities.

Starting with Theories of Abilities

When one looks at current theories of abilities, mindfulness seems to bear some correspondence. The most thorough taxonomy, at least from a psychometric perspective, is that of Carroll (1993). Carroll conducted an exhaustive review and reanalysis of more than 460 data sets in the factor-analytic literature. These data sets all used covariation-correlation information in order to obtain factor structures underlying the scores comprising the data sets. The assumption is that the factors underlying the scores represent latent mental abilities. The classes of abilities he identified included (a) general abilities (e.g., fluid ability and crystallized abilities); (b) reasoning abilities (e.g., verbal reasoning and syllogistic reasoning); (c) abilities in the domain of language behavior (e.g., verbal comprehension and spelling ability); (d) memory abilities (e.g., associative memory and memory span); (e) visual perception abilities (e.g., perceptual speed and closure speed); (f) auditory perception abilities (e.g., pitch discrimination and auditory closure); (g) number facility (no more specific abilities were identified); (h) mental speed abilities (e.g., general mental speed and simple reaction time); (i) abilities in producing and retrieving words, ideas, and figural creations (e.g., ideational fluency and word fluency); (j) sensory abilities (e.g., auditory hearing threshold and visual acuity); (k) attention and concentration abilities (e.g., attention and concentration, and carefulness and attention to detail); and (l) abilities pertaining to interpersonal behavior (e.g., interpretation of facial expressions and gestures). . . .

The set of cognitive abilities that mindfulness is most reminiscent of is (k), including attention and concentration abilities. Carroll notes that he has found very few factor-analytic studies addressed to attentional abilities, so his analysis is not on the firmest of ground. Because of the possible overlap with mindfulness, it is perhaps worth specifying in further detail some of the 21 factors Carroll identified in this subset of cognitive abilities. The factors are not explicitly named and not all are adequately described. The tests loading on these factors are described in Carroll (1993, p. 549). Examples of such tests are concentration tests, carefulness tests (such as number checking, filing, and checking copy), time-sharing letter tasks, tests of oral and written directions, reverse reading, tests requiring parallel information processing, tracing-precision tasks, and freedom from distractibility. . . .

Other theories also might be queried for overlap with the mindfulness construct. Gardner (1983, 1998) speaks of linguistic intelligence, logical-mathematical intelligence, spatial intelligence, musical intelligence, naturalist intelligence, interpersonal intelligence, intrapersonal intelligence, and most recently, existential intelligence. None of these intelligences seems to overlap much with the mindfulness construct.

Another way to examine the overlap between mindfulness and abilities is to consider the components of mindfulness and examine their interrelations to various abilities—thus one starts with mindfulness rather than with other theories.

Starting with Aspects of Mindfulness

Openness to Novelty

The relationship of openness to novelty to conventional theories of intelligence would seem to be through what Cattell (1971) and Horn (1994) have referred to as "fluid abilities." These are the abilities used to reason with relatively novel kinds of stimuli. They are measured, for example, by the geometric matrix problems found in the Raven (1965) Progressive Matrices or the various kinds of geometric reasoning tests (including matrices) found in the Cattell and Cattell (1957) Test of *g*—Culture Fair (with the "Culture Fair" label almost certainly a misnomer). More recent theories of intelligence (e.g., Raaheim, 1974; Sternberg, 1985, 1997a) have also stressed the importance of coping with relative novelty for intelligence.

In our own work, my colleagues and I have measured one of the aspects of mindfulness as defined by Langer, openness to novelty, or something similar to it, in a variety of ways. We typically have used maximum-performance rather than typical-performance tests because of our belief that typical-performance measures are somewhat more susceptible to demand characteristics. We have used both convergent and divergent tasks. Consider each in turn as elucidating measurement operations that may help capture this important aspect of mindfulness.

One kind of convergent task is called a conceptual-projection task (Sternberg, 1981, 1982; Tetewsky & Sternberg, 1986). In one instantiation of the task, participants are presented with a description of the color of an object in the present day and in the year 3000. The description in each case can be either pictorial—a green dot or a blue dot—or verbal—one of four color words, namely, *green, blue, grue, bleen.* An object was defined as green if it appeared physically green both in the present and in the year 3000. An object was defined as blue if it appeared physically blue both in the present and in the year 3000. An object was defined as grue if it appeared physically green in the present but physically blue in the year 3000 (i.e., it appeared physically green until the year 3000 and physically blue thereafter). And an object was defined as bleen if it appeared physically blue in the present but physically green in the year 3000 (i.e., it appeared physically blue until the year 3000 and physically green thereafter). The terminology was based on Goodman (1955).

The participant's task was to describe the object in the year 3000. If the given description of the year 3000 was a pictorial one, the participant had to indicate the correct verbal description of the object; if the given description for the year 3000 was a verbal one, the participant had to indicate the correct physical description of the object. There were always three answer choices.

Performance on this task was decomposed into elementary information-processing components. Perhaps the most interesting finding was the identification of the component that measured something similar or identical to what Langer calls *openness to novelty.* This component was measured in two ways: through the amount of time it took a person to switch from the conventional green-blue type of thinking to the unconventional grue-bleen type of thinking, and back again, and through the error rate for this process. Some people find it relatively comfortable and easy to switch back and forth; others find it extremely difficult. They can think well in conventional ways but have a great deal of difficulty adopting unconventional or novel ways of thinking. . . .

Other investigators also have been interested in the relation of openness to novelty to various kinds of mental abilities. Perhaps the most relevant theoretical and empirical work is actually that done on infants by Fagan (1992), Lewis and Brooks-Gunn (1981), and others (see Bornstein, 1989, for a review). This work has shown that infants with a greater preference for novelty when they reach later childhood score better on IQ tests than do infants with a lesser preference for novelty. The researchers typically use habituation and dishabituation paradigms in order to establish this point.

This research represented something of a turning point in work on infant intelligence. Prior to this work, sensorimotor tests such as those found in the Bayley (1969) Scales and such as would be consistent with Piaget's (1972) theory of intellectual development had been used to measure infant intelligence. But these tests had failed to show any consistent correlations with IQ later in childhood (Sternberg, Grigorenko, & Bundy, 1998).

Alertness to Distinction

Alertness to distinction ((b) above) is measured at the perceptual level by certain tests of perceptual speed (in which often one has to indicate which of a set of geometric or other objects differs in some minute detail from other objects in a list) and at the conceptual level by certain tests of inductive reasoning (in which often one has to say which of several objects does not belong with the others in a list). In the classificatory induction task, the difference is conceptual, whereas in the perceptual-speed task it is perceptual. Both perceptual speed and inductive reasoning are fairly standard elements in conventional psychometric theories of intelligence (e.g., Carroll, 1993; Thurstone, 1938).

Alertness to conceptual distinction also has played an important role in the componential subtheory of the triarchic theory of human intelligence (Sternberg, 1985, 1997a). When components are applied to relatively familiar tasks, they are involved in analytical thinking. Some of the mental processes involved in analytical thinking, beyond analysis, are comparing and contrasting and making judgments of how things are the same and different. . . .

Sensitivity to Different Contexts

Sensitivity to different contexts, another aspect of mindfulness according to Langer, is in some ways a difficult construct to pin down, as it is not clear that it is a characteristic that a person will show that is generalizable across all contexts. Because the problems found on conventional intelligence tests tend to be rather decontextualized, I would doubt that they would provide any valid measure of the construct of sensitivity to different contexts. . . .

In our own work, my colleagues and I have measured sensitivity to context through the assessment of tacit knowledge as it applies in contexts that one encounters in one's daily life. These contexts can be exquisitely detailed, and the right course of action may depend on minor variations in the details of the context (Sternberg et al., 2000; Sternberg, Wagner, Williams, & Horvath, 1995). We have done an extended series of studies in which we have compared people's practical intelligence in the context of their work to their academic intelligence in the context of a typical conventional test of intelligence. The design of these studies is different from that of, say, Ceci and Bronfenbrenner (1985). We were not looking at the identical task administered under different conditions. Our design also was different from that of, say, Nuñes and her colleagues (1994) or Lave and her colleagues (1984), in that we did not look at roughly isomorphic tasks administered under different conditions. Rather, we tried to construct tests that would be as relevant as possible for predicting performance in practical, as opposed to academic, settings.

In this series of studies with business managers, academic psychologists, elementary school teachers, salespeople, college students, military leaders, and others, we repeatedly have found that scores on tests of practical intelligence typically do not correlate with scores on tests of academic intelligence. When they do correlate significantly, they may correlate positive or negatively. But scores on these tests predict performance in real-world settings as well as or better than do tests of academic intelligence (see Sternberg et al., 1995).

Thus it appears that people are very sensitive to context. Their performance in one context may be very different from their performance in another context. A theorist of general intelligence might view this result as problematic. But from the perspective of mindfulness, the result is not problematic at all. People should treat tasks differently in different contexts. If one has a decision to make, there is no reason to believe that one's decision will or should be the same if the decision is unimportant as opposed to if one's life depends on it. Thus, one might be willing to invest a sum of money in a risky stock if the money represents a sum that is not important to one's well-being. But one is (or at least should be!) less likely to invest the same sum of money in that risky stock if one's whole retirement fund depends on it.

Awareness of Multiple Perspectives

Awareness of multiple perspectives has been studied by some cognitive-developmental psychologists under the rubric of dialectical thinking. Some of these psychologists have argued that the ability to think dialectically constitutes a fifth stage of thinking beyond that specified by the four stages in Piaget's model of intellectual development. These psychologists even have argued that such thinking is the hallmark of wisdom (Birren & Fisher, 1990; Labouvie-Vief, 1990; Pascual-Leone, 1990; Riegel, 1973; Sternberg, 1998a, 1999). It also has been argued that dialectical thinking can serve as a basis for teaching and learning psychology and other disciplines (Sternberg, 1998b).

According to this view, dialectical thinking would develop at some point after the end of formal operations, perhaps in the college years. It is then a critical attribute for success in higher order thinking. People who do not learn to think dialectically—to see things from different and often opposing points of view—may be good formal-operational thinkers, but they will never go beyond formal operations. They will be locked in a logical mode of thinking that often does not adequately serve in solving the problems that life dishes out.

Orientation in the Present

Orientation in the present is perhaps the most elusive of the elements of mindfulness specified by Langer. One certainly can see its relevance to the mindfulness construct. Presumably people who are paying attention to their present surroundings are behaving in a more mindful fashion than those who are not. For example, those pedestrians in dangerous cities who pay more attention to their immediate surroundings and signs of danger in these immediate surroundings presumably are less at risk than those who amble along mindlessly, failing to heed the danger signals around them. This aspect of mindfulness seems to be the most problematic, since a future orientation, as exhibited by delay of gratification, might be more adaptive for many kinds of tasks (Mischel, 1973). . . .

To conclude, mindfulness seems to bear considerable overlap with cognitive abilities and intelligence, broadly defined (Carroll, 1993; Sternberg, 1985). Nevertheless, I think that the mindfulness construct—whatever its overlap with constructs of cognitive abilities or intelligence—makes at least two valuable additions. First, the particular conjunction of attributes specified for mindfulness is not specified by any theory of intelligence. Whether these attributes in fact will be found to cohere psychometrically remains an empirical question, but at a theoretical level, the construct seems at least somewhat distinct from existing ability constructs. Second, the mindfulness construct may be more useful when conceived of in state rather than in trait terms. People may differ in their average levels of mindfulness, but perhaps the standard deviation in a person's mindfulness is a more interesting construct than is the mean. To the extent that this state can be measured successfully, such measurement will be a valuable contribution to our understanding of people's interactions with the contexts in which they live.

Is Mindfulness a Personality Trait?

Mindfulness might be a personality trait rather than a cognitive ability. It might be useful to consider a well-regarded trait theory of personality and to inquire as to whether mindfulness resembles any of the traits proposed. Here mindfulness is considered as a whole rather than in terms of its parts because the available research does not enable one to pinpoint its aspects as clearly for personality as for cognition.

The most popular trait theory today is probably the big-five theory (Costa & McCrae, 1992a, 1992b; Digman, 1990; Goldberg, 1993; McCrae & John, 1992; Peabody & Goldberg, 1989). Although there are certainly other theories, big-five theory has gained such overwhelming comparative acceptance that I will limit my discussion to this theory alone. This theory of personality recognizes the frequent recurrence of five personality traits across studies (especially factor-analytic studies) and even across theorists. The big-five traits were first proposed by Warren Norman (1963) but since have been championed by many others.

Although different investigators sometimes have given the big five different names, they generally have agreed on five key characteristics as a useful way to organize and describe individual differences in personality. The following descriptions represent the five traits:

1. *Neuroticism*—characterized by nervousness, emotional instability, moodiness, tension, irritability, and frequent tendency to worry.

2. *Extraversion*—characterized by sociability, expansiveness, liveliness, an orientation toward having fun, and an interest in other people.
3. *Openness to experience*—characterized by imagination, intelligence, and aesthetic sensitivity, as well as openness to new kinds of experiences.
4. *Agreeableness*—characterized by a pleasant disposition, a charitable nature, empathy toward others, and friendliness.
5. *Conscientiousness*—characterized by reliability, hard work, punctuality, and a concern about doing things right.

Mindfulness seems potentially related to openness to experience. There is almost certainly some overlap. Moreover, research suggests that openness to experience itself is correlated with cognitive abilities (McCrae, 1996). So it would seem potentially fruitful to pursue the relation between the two constructs. Mindfulness also may bear some relation to conscientiousness. Studies are needed that correlate mindfulness with these traits to see if indeed there is a relation.

Is Mindfulness a Cognitive Style?

The scale Ellen Langer is developing for measuring mindfulness/mindlessness is a typical-performance one (whereby one describes patterns of behavior rather than exhibiting those patterns of behavior), so that whatever mindfulness may be, it is being measured in a way that more typically characterizes personality or cognitive styles than cognitive abilities. Again, mindfulness is considered as a whole rather than in its components because the available research does not enable us adequately to pinpoint its components.

Styles are preferred ways of using one's cognitive abilities (Sternberg, 1997b). That is, they represent not abilities per se, but how people like to employ their abilities in their daily lives. Styles can be of different kinds: thinking styles, learning styles, teaching styles, cognitive styles. Langer's mindfulness/mindlessness construct most resembles what are called "cognitive styles," so those are the attributes that will be reviewed here. These styles, like mindfulness, involve a preferred way of viewing the world in general and specific problems in particular.

Some of the main cognitive styles are identified by Carroll (1993, p. 554). They include

1. *field independence versus field dependence*, which is the extent to which one perceives things independently of their backgrounds (field independence) versus dependently upon their backgrounds (field dependence);
2. *scanning*, which is the extent to which one scans stimuli extensively versus intensively;
3. *breadth of categorizing*, which is a consistent preference for broad inclusiveness in categories as opposed to narrow exclusiveness;
4. *cognitive complexity versus simplicity*, which is the extent to which one structures the world in a complex versus a simple way;

5. *reflexivity versus impulsivity,* which is the extent to which one thinks carefully before one acts as opposed to acting impulsively;
6. *leveling versus sharpening,* which is the extent to which one tends to blur similar memories (leveling) or to remember things as very distinct and as less similar than they actually are (sharpening);
7. *constricted versus flexible control,* which is the extent to which one is susceptible to distraction and cognitive interference;
8. *tolerance for incongruous or unrealistic experiences,* which is the extent to which one is willing to accept perceptions that are at [variation] with conventional expectations.

The mindfulness/mindlessness distinction seems to fit well into this kind of a framework at the same time that it does not seem identical to any of the existing cognitive styles. Thus, Langer's may be one additional cognitive style, arguably, one of the more important ones. Should this be the case, then there is an important caveat to be observed.

The traditional cognitive-styles movement was very active in the 1960s and early 1970s and seemed to provide a fruitful way of integrating the study of personality with the study of cognition. Mindfulness/mindlessness seems to be in this same tradition of being at the interface between personality and cognition. But the cognitive-styles movement hit a dead end, perhaps for several reasons (Sternberg & Grigorenko, 1997). Indeed, a review written more than 20 years ago by Goldstein and Blackman (1978) covers most of the cognitive styles that are still considered contemporary. What happened?

First, the styles referred to specific attributes and seemed neither to derive from any general theory of personality or cognition nor to lead to any general theory of personality or cognition. The cognitive-styles literature thus remained isolated from the rest of psychology and eventually contracted. Second, the measures of cognitive styles never quite lived up to their promise. Most particularly, they did not always correspond well to the construct, and multiple measures of a given construct sometimes did not correspond so well even with each other. Third, it was not clear just how generalizable the cognitive styles were—whether they were a generalized characteristic of a person or more situationally based. In fact, traditional cognitive styles have characteristics both of traits and of states. Fourth and perhaps most importantly, the styles came to be seen as too similar to abilities. Although the original idea was that styles, unlike abilities, are neither good nor bad in themselves, this original idea did not hold. For example, field independence and reflexivity seemed clearly better than field dependence and impulsivity. Furthermore, empirical studies showed the former to be associated with good performance and the latter to be associated with bad performance. For example, field independence proved to be essentially identical to spatial ability (MacLeod, Jackson, & Palmer, 1986). With styles being so closely related to abilities, it became less clear why the field needed a separate construct of styles.

Mindfulness/mindlessness seems to be in this tradition of cognitive styles as well. For the most part, mindfulness seems to be better than mindlessness. Langer (1989, 1997) certainly presents the constructs in this way. At the same time, one might argue that she overstates the case. For example, with motor activities, concentrating hard on the activity and attending carefully to it (e.g., a tennis serve, a golf shot) is more likely to impair performance of the activity than to help it. As another example, it is sometimes better to filter out certain aspects of the environment if they are disturbing but one cannot do anything about them. Thus, suppose one has a disagreeable colleague at work and that colleague shows no signs either [of] becoming more agreeable or of leaving. If one does not want to leave one's job over such a disagreeable colleague, one might be best off ignoring the colleague as much as possible—that is, not being mindful of the colleague at all if one concludes there is nothing to be done. Test anxiety is yet another case of a person's being overly mindful of something over which he or she has no control, and of thereby damaging his or her performance on that something (a test) as a result.

Conclusion

Mindfulness has shown itself to be a useful construct in understanding a variety of behavior. But its relations to other constructs in cognitive, social, and personality psychology have not yet been fully explored. The goal of this article is to explore some of these interrelations.

Mindfulness/mindlessness probably is more similar to cognitive styles than it is to cognitive abilities or personality traits. Mindfulness/mindlessness possesses many of the same characteristics as do cognitive styles but appears to be identical to none of the styles that have been proposed in the past. Mindfulness, like cognitive styles, is at the interface between cognition and personality. It also has yet to be integrated into larger theories of cognition and personality. It can lend itself to typical- or maximum-performance measurement. It has characteristics both of a state and of a trait. And one pole is likely to be superior to the other pole under most, but not all, circumstances. Strong psychological measurements still need to be developed for mindfulness/mindlessness, as is the case even today for cognitive styles proposed long ago.

References

Bayley, N. (1969). *Manual for the Bayley Scales of infant development.* New York: The Psychological Corporation.

Birren, J., & Fisher, L. M. (1990). The elements of wisdom: Overview and integration. In R. J. Sternberg (Ed.), *Wisdom* (pp. 317–332). New York: Cambridge University Press.

Bornstein, M. H. (1989). Stability in early mental development: From attention and information processing in infancy to language and cognition in childhood. In M. H. Bornstein & N. A. Krasnegor (Eds.), *Stability and continuity in mental development: Behavioral and biological perspectives* (pp. 147–170). Hillsdale, NJ: Erlbaum.

Carroll, J. B. (1993). *Human cognitive abilities: A survey of factor-analytic studies.* New York: Cambridge University Press.

Cattell, R. B. (1971). *Abilities: Their structure, growth, and action.* Boston: Houghton-Mifflin.

Cattell, R. B., & Cattell, A. K. S. (1957). *The IPAT Culture Fair Intelligence Scales.* Champaign, IL: Institute for Personality and Ability Testing.

Ceci, S. J., & Bronfenbrenner, U. (1985). Don't forget to take the cupcakes out of the oven: Strategic time-monitoring, prospective memory, and context. *Child Development, 56,* 175–190.

Costa, P. T., & McCrae, R. R. (1992a). "Four ways five factors are not basic": Reply. *Personality and Individual Differences, 13,* 861–865.

Costa, P. T., & McCrae, R. R. (1992b). Four ways five factors are basic. *Personality and Individual Differences, 13,* 653–665.

Digman, J. M. (1990). Personality structure: Emergence of the five-factor model. *Annual Review of Psychology, 41,* 417–440.

Fagan, J. F., III. (1992). Intelligence: A theoretical viewpoint. *Current Directions in Psychological Science, 1,* 82–86.

Ferrari, M., & Sternberg, R. J. (1998). The development of mental abilities and styles. In W. Damon (Series Ed.) & D. Kuhn & R. S. Siegler (Vol. Eds.), *Handbook of child psychology* (Vol. 2, pp. 899–946). New York: Wiley

Gardner, H. (1983). *Frames of mind: The theory of multiple intelligences.* New York: Basic Books.

Gardner, H. (1998). A multiplicity of intelligences. *Scientific American Presents, 9,* 18–23.

Goldberg, L. R. (1993). The structure of phenotypic personality traits. *American Psychologist, 48,* 26–34.

Goldstein, K. M., & Blackman, S. (1978). *Cognitive style.* New York: Wiley.

Goodman, N. (1955). *Fact, fiction, and forecast.* Cambridge, MA: Harvard University Press.

Horn, J. L. (1994). Fluid and crystallized abilities, theory of. In R. J. Sternberg (Ed.), *Encyclopedia of human intelligence* (Vol. 1, pp. 443–451). New York: Macmillan.

Labouvie-Vief, G. (1990). Wisdom as integrated thought: Historical and developmental perspectives. In R. J. Sternberg (Ed.), *Wisdom* (pp. 52–83). New York: Cambridge University Press.

Langer, E. J. (1989). *Mindfulness.* Reading, MA: Addison-Wesley.

Langer, E. J. (1997). *The power of mindful learning.* Reading, MA: Addison-Wesley.

Lave, J., Murtaugh, M., & de la Roche, O. (1984). The dialectic of arithmetic in grocery shopping. In B. Rogoff & J. Lave (Eds.), *Everyday cognition: Its development in social context* (pp. 67–94). Cambridge, MA: Harvard University Press.

Lewis, M., & Brooks-Gunn, J. (1981). Visual attention at three months as a predictor of cognitive functioning at two years of age. *Intelligence, 5,* 131–140.

MacLeod, C. M., Jackson, R. A., & Palmer, J. (1986). On the relation between spatial ability and field dependence. *Intelligence, 10,* 141–151.

McCrae, R. R. (1996). Social consequences of experiential openness. *Psychological Bulletin, 120,* 323–337.

McCrae, R. R., & John, O. (1992). An introduction to the five-factor model and its applications. *Journal of Personality, 60,* 175–215.

Mischel, W. (1973). Toward a social learning reconceptualization of personality. *Psychological Review, 80,* 252–283.

Norman, W. T. (1963). Toward an adequate taxonomy of personality attributes: Replicated factor structure in peer nomination personality ratings. *Journal of Abnormal and Social Psychology, 66,* 574–583.

Nuñes, T. (1994). Street intelligence. In R. J. Sternberg (Ed.), *Encyclopedia of human intelligence* (Vol. 1, pp. 1045–1049). New York: Macmillan.

Pascual-Leone, J. (1990). An essay on wisdom toward organismic processes that make it possible. In R. J. Sternberg (Ed.), *Widsom: Its nature, origins, and development* (pp. 244–278). New York: Cambridge University Press.

Peabody, D., & Goldberg, L. R. (1989). Some determinants of factor structures from personality-trait descriptors. *Journal of Personality and Social Psychology, 57*, 552–567.
Piaget, J. (1972). *The psychology of intelligence*. Totowa, NJ: Littlefield Adams.
Raaheim, K. (1974). *Problem solving and intelligence*. Oslo, Norway: Universitetsforlaget.
Raven, J. C. (1965). *Progressive matrices*. New York: The Psychological Corporation.
Riegel, K. F. (1973). Dialectical operations: The final period of cognitive development. *Human Development, 16*, 346–370.
Sternberg, R. J. (1977). *Intelligence, information processing, and analogical reasoning: The componential analysis of human abilities*. Hillsdale, NJ: Erlbaum.
Sternberg, R. J. (1981). Intelligence and nonentrenchment. *Journal of Educational Psychology, 73*, 1–16.
Sternberg, R. J. (1982). Natural, unnatural, and supernatural concepts. *Cognitive Psychology, 14*, 451–488.
Sternberg, R. J. (1985). *Beyond IQ: A triarchic theory of human abilities*. New York: Cambridge University Press.
Sternberg, R. J. (1997a). *Successful intelligence*. New York: Plume.
Sternberg, R. J. (1997b). *Thinking styles*. New York: Cambridge University Press.
Sternberg, R. J. (1998a). A balance theory of wisdom. *Review of General Psychology, 2*, 347–365.
Sternberg, R. J. (1998b). The dialectic as a tool for teaching psychology. *Teaching of Psychology, 25*, 177–180.
Sternberg, R. J. (1999). A dialectical basis for understanding the study of cognition. In R. J. Sternberg (Ed.), *The nature of cognition*. Cambridge, MA: MIT Press.
Sternberg, R. J., Forsythe, G. B., Hedlund, J., Horvath, J., Wagner, R. K., Williams, W. M., Snook, S., & Grigorenko, E. L. (2000). *Practical intelligence in everyday life*. New York: Cambridge University Press.
Sternberg, R. J., & Grigorenko, E. L. (1997). Are cognitive styles still in style? *American Psychologist, 52*, 700–712.
Sternberg, R. J., Grigorenko, E. L., & Bundy, D. A. (1998). The predictive value of IQ. Manuscript submitted for publication.
Sternberg, R. J., Wagner, R. K., Williams, W. M., & Horvath, J. (1995). Testing common sense. *American Psychologist, 50*, 912–917.
Tetewsky, S. J., & Sternberg, R. J. (1986). Conceptual and lexical determinants of nonentrenched thinking. *Journal of Memory and Language, 25*, 202–225.
Thurstone, L. L. (1938). *Primary mental abilities*. Chicago: University of Chicago Press.

Ellen J. Langer and Mihnea Moldoveanu

NO

The Construct of Mindfulness

. . . Although the concept of mindfulness overlaps with many other constructs in psychology . . . , it also offers some unique perspectives on how to investigate psychological processes. The concept of mindfulness and the related concept of mindlessness were introduced to social psychology more than 2 decades ago. They have been applied to many diverse areas, including psychopathology, developmental psychology, education research, political theory, and communication processes, to name a few.

Definition of Constructs

Mindfulness is not an easy concept to define but can be best understood as the process of drawing novel distinctions. It does not matter whether what is noticed is important or trivial, as long as it is new to the viewer. Actively drawing these distinctions keeps us situated in the present. It also makes us more aware of the context and perspective of our actions than if we rely upon distinctions and categories drawn in the past. Under this latter situation, rules and routines are more likely to govern our behavior, irrespective of the current circumstances, and this can be construed as mindless behavior. The process of drawing novel distinctions can lead to a number of diverse consequences, including (1) a greater sensitivity to one's environment, (2) more openness to new information, (3) the creation of new categories for structuring perception, and (4) enhanced awareness of multiple perspectives in problem solving. The subjective "feel" of mindfulness is that of a heightened state of involvement and wakefulness or being in the present. This subjective state is the inherent common thread that ties together the extremely diverse observable consequences for the viewer. Mindfulness is not a cold cognitive process. When one is actively drawing novel distinctions, the whole individual is involved.

Brief History of Research

Research on the differences that emanate from mindful versus mindless behavior began in 1974, and the results have been both wide-ranging and of great practical concern. Early work focused on looking at basic characteristics

From *Journal of Social Issues,* Spring 2000, pp. 1–9.

of mindfulness (e.g., Chanowitz & Langer, 1981; Langer, Blank, & Chanowitz, 1978). Studies with relevance to social issues fall into three major categories: health, business, and education.

Studies of health ramifications were among the earliest studies of mindfulness. These focused upon aging and the issue of control. Perceived control has been shown to have very positive effects on stress reduction and health (e.g., Geer, Davison, & Gatchel, 1970; Langer, Janis, & Wolfer, 1975). It is the perception of control, rather than any objectively viewed control, that is the significant variable. Interestingly, when a person behaves mindlessly, the perception of control is not possible. Therefore, we conducted several investigations (e.g., Alexander, Langer, Newman, Chandler, & Davies, 1989; Langer, Beck, Janoff-Bulman, & Timko, 1984) to see if mindfulness in elderly populations could be increased with positive effects.We found that this could be accomplished with relatively simple manipulations, for example, having more control over one's schedule and taking care of plans. Mindful treatments had dramatic effects: They decreased adverse health symptoms such as arthritis pain and alcoholism and increased longevity (see Langer, 1989, for a more detailed review of this work and further examples of the effect of mindfulness on health).

Those in the business world have been eager to utilize techniques that increase mindfulness in workers and managers. Studies of mindfulness in a business context have shown that increases in mindfulness are associated with increased creativity and decreased burnout (e.g., Langer, Heffernan, & Kiester, 1988). A study by Park conducted with businessmen in Korea found an increase in productivity as well (Park, 1990). We anticipate that increased mindfulness will be shown to decrease accidents as well, particularly when new technology is introduced. For example, when many of us learned to drive, we were told to pump the brakes slowly while trying to stop on a slippery surface. With the advent of antilock brakes, however, the more appropriate response is to firmly press the brakes down and hold them there. Thus, accidents that could be prevented in the past by our learned behavior can now be caused by the same behavior. This is an example of mindlessness that can easily occur in everyday life as well as the workplace.

Education is an area that often seems to abound in mindlessness. Many educational ramifications of mindfulness are reviewed in *The Power of Mindful Learning* (Langer, 1997). Whether intending to learn an academic subject, a new sport, or how to play a musical instrument, we often call upon mind-sets that hamper rather than help us to learn. For example, many of us believe that we should learn the *basics* of a task so well that they become second nature to us. Having mindlessly accepted this information, it rarely occurs to us to question who determined what the basics are. Surely, if women and men engage in the same sport, the differences in their bodies should result in differences in how to play the game, for example. Once we learn the basics mindlessly so that we no longer have to think about them, we are not in a position to vary them readily as we get more information about the task.

But there are relatively simple ways of reducing mindlessness in learning. Several studies more fully described in Langer (1997) explored the ramification of inducing mindful learning. In one study (Langer & Piper, 1987), mindfulness was encouraged by introducing information about objects in a conditional way, using language like "could be," rather than the more traditional, absolute way ("is," "can only be"), which was defined as the mindless condition. Participants in the mindful conditions were better able to use the objects creatively when the need for a novel use of the object arose. In subsequent studies this work was extended to the introduction of text in the same conditional manner. Here, the language that was used consisted of expressions such as "could be," "perhaps," "from one perspective." Similar benefits accrued from the mindfulness treatments in these studies (e.g., Langer, Hatem, Joss, & Howell, 1989).

Attentional processes have been assumed to be central to learning. These have also been illuminated by mindfulness research. In one study (Langer, 1997) I asked both students and teachers what they meant by *paying attention*. Interestingly, both groups believed that this meant to "hold the image still as if focusing a camera." The problem, however, is that if one follows this instruction, it is very difficult to stay attentive. In contrast, in studies with children, college students and the elderly, (Langer & Bodner, 1997; Langer, Carson, & Shih, 2001; Levy & Langer, 2001), we found that if people are instructed to vary the stimulus, that is, to mindfully notice new things about it, then attention improves. Moreover, such mindful attention also results in a greater liking for the task and improved memory.

Other mindful manipulations in the educational context have involved asking students to make material more meaningful for themselves, compared to groups asked to memorize it (Lieberman & Langer, 1997). The meaningful group retained the information better and was able to utilize it in more creative ways in essays. Adding perspective taking also elicits better performance (Lieberman & Langer, 1997). Consider the difference between introducing a history lesson as "Here are the three reasons for the Civil War" versus "Here are three reasons for the Civil War from the perspective of. . . ." The former presents the information as a closed package; the latter invites further consideration of how the information might vary from still other perspectives. Almost all of the facts most of us learned in school were taught to us in a perspective-free way that encourages mindless use of the information because it does not occur to us to question it again. In contrast, information presented in the mindful, perspective-taking condition was learned better by high school students, even though they had to deal with more information. Clearly, mindful teaching practices can have a pronounced effect on student learning.

Other areas currently being investigated through a mindfulness lens include decision making (see Langer, 1994, for a theoretical review), evaluation, meditation and Eastern religious practices, and emotion. The work described in the current issue further demonstrates the breadth of application possibilities of this construct, ranging from interaction with computers to understanding of mental retardation.

Mindfulness, Cognition, and Computers

The question of how mindfulness relates to intelligence, cognitive abilities and cognitive styles is considered in the [preceding "yes" article] by Robert Sternberg. He concludes that although there is some overlap with other types of cognitive processes, and it is most like the construct of cognitive style, the concept of mindfulness has some unique properties. We are not in complete agreement with his conclusion that mindfulness is most like a cognitive style because, in our view, a style is not expected to change over time and through different circumstances, whereas the essence of mindfulness is change.

We prefer to consider the problem of the relation between mindfulness and other types of cognitive processes in terms of whether something is reducible to an algorithm for processing information. Having a particular cognitive style cannot be mindful, by definition, because it is precisely the sensitivity to the novel and, therefore, unexpected (i.e., nonalgorithmic) that is one of the key components of mindfulness. The French philosopher Giles Deleuze captured part of the spirit of mindfulness when he wrote, "To the answer embedded in every question, answer with a question from a different answer" (Deleuze & Guattari, 1980).

The algorithmic aspects of problem-solving behavior have been extensively addressed by the literature on cognition and problem solving (Newell, 1990) and this has had a major effect on cognitive psychology. Paradoxically, although this early work established a whole new approach to the mapping of cognitive processes, it also limited the scope of what a mind-mapping venture could look like.

The Simon-Newell paradigm (Newell, 1990) is based on what has been called the mind-as-computer metaphor (Gigerenzer & Goldstein, 1996). The central tenet of this metaphor is that mental processes are nothing more than algorithmic processes, or processes that can be simulated by general-purpose computational devices, such as a digital computer. This central tenet is, by definition, irrefutable, because it contains a set of cognitive commitments that we commonly use to refer to a problem. According to this view, solving large arrays of linear equations is a legitimate problem and an adequate topic for the study of mental processes because the answer is computable by a finite algorithm working on a finite-state computational device. Inventing a new topology for a space-time—as Einstein did—would not be a legitimate problem for this view (or would be considered an ill-posed problem) because it is not susceptible to formulation as the input to a finite-state computational device. Thus, the cognitive abilities scholar cannot account for acts of creation of new concepts, even something like the general theory of relativity, that have become new paradigms in their fields. In contrast, the student of mindfulness focuses often on those particular cognitive processes that defy immediate algorithmic representation.

The phenomenon of mindfulness also has implications for the ways in which we view and represent the mind and its connection to the brain. The "cognitive revolution" has relied, as previously noted, on models of the human mind based on the image of a computer or a generalized computational device. Most investigators in this area (e.g., Churchland, 1987) have sought to explain mental processes by reduction to computational or algorithmic processes that can be modeled using sophisticated computer science representations. This reduction has recently been extended to explaining mental phenomena in terms of neurobiological processes taking place in the brain (e.g., Churchland, 1987), which can themselves be represented in computational terms. An epistemological problem, however, is that these metaphorical devices cannot be transcended or refuted by empirical means because the organizing metaphors have never been explicitly made subject to empirical investigation. All that investigations based on the mind-as-computer metaphor can tell us is whether our problem-solving processes deviate from the normative precepts that make up the metaphor in question. Thus, we are not informed about the possibly nonalgorithmic processes by which people come to solve the practical problems that cognitive scientists expect them to solve by algorithmic means.

Mindfulness theorists are not alone in positing the importance of nonalgorithmic factors in problem solving. Logician Kurt Godel wrote eloquently about the incompleteness of any non-self-contradictory logic system (see Putnam, 1985). Because of this, we as a society are still trying, with little success, to build robots that can navigate their way around a relatively uncrowded room and can resolve problems like catching a ball that a child can resolve while riding a bicycle, carrying on a conversation, and listening to his favorite tune on the radio. We believe that the time to investigate the nonalgorithmic dimensions of thinking is ripe, and the phenomena of mindful engagement can provide a portal to these relatively unexplored dimensions. . . .

References

Alexander, C., Langer, E. J., Newman, R., Chandler, H., & Davies, J. (1989). Aging, mindfulness and meditation. *Journal of Personality and Social Psychology, 57,* 950–964.

Chanowitz, B., & Langer, E. J. (1981). Premature cognitive commitments. *Journal of Personality and Social Psychology, 41,* 1051–1063.

Churchland, P. (1987). *Matter and consciousness: An introduction to the philosophy of mind.* Cambridge, MA: MIT Press.

Deleuze, G., & Guattari, F. (1980). *Capitalism and schizophrenia.* Cambridge, MA: MIT Press.

Geer, J. H., Davison, G. C., & Gatchel, R. (1970). Reduction of stress in humans through non-veridical perceived control of aversive stimuli. *Journal of Personality and Social Psychology, 16,* 731–738.

Gigerenzer, G., & Goldstein, D. (1996). Mind as computer: Birth of a metaphor. *Creativity Research Journal, 9*(2–3).

Langer, E. J. (1989). *Mindfulness.* Reading, MA: Addison-Wesley.

Langer, E. J. (1994). The illusion of calculated decisions. In R. Schank and E. Langer (Eds.), *Beliefs, reasoning and decision making*. Hillsdale, NJ: Erlbaum.

Langer, E. J. (1997). *The power of mindful learning*. Reading, MA: Addison Wesley.

Langer, E. J., Beck, P., Janoff-Bulman, R., & Timko, C. (1984). The relationship between cognitive deprivation and longevity in senile and non-senile elderly populations. *Academic Psychology Bulletin, 6*, 211–226.

Langer, E. J., Blank, A., & Chanowitz, B. (1978). The mindlessness of ostensibly thoughtful action: The role of "placebic" information in interpersonal interactions. *Journal of Personality and Social Psychology, 36*, 635–642.

Langer, E. J., & Bodner, T. (1995). *Mindfulness and attention*. Unpublished manuscript, Harvard University, Cambridge, MA.

Langer, E. J., Carson, S., & Shih, M. (2001). Sit still and pay attention? *Journal of Adult Development, 8*, 183–188.

Langer, E. J., Hatem, M., Joss, J., & Howell, M. (1989). Conditional teaching and mindful learning: The role of uncertainty in education. *Creativity Research Journal, 2*, 139–159.

Langer, E. J., Heffernan, D., & Kiester, M. (1988). *Reducing burnout in an institutional setting: An experimental investigation*. Unpublished manuscript, Harvard University, Cambridge, MA.

Langer, E., Janis, I., & Wolfer, J. A. (1975). Reduction of psychological stress in surgical patients. *Journal of Experimental Social Psychology, 11*, 155–165.

Langer, E. J., & Piper, A. (1987). The prevention of mindlessness. *Journal of Personality and Social Psychology, 53*, 280–287.

Levy, B., & Langer, E. J. (1997). Improving attention in old age. *Journal of Adult Development, 8*, 189–192.

Lieberman, M., & Langer, E. J. (1997). Mindfulness in the process of learning. In E. J. Langer (Ed.), *The power of mindful learning*. Reading, MA: Addison Wesley.

Newell, A. (1990). *Unified theories of cognition*. Cambridge, MA: Harvard University Press.

Putnam, H. (1985). Reflexive reflections. *Erkenntnis, 35*(1).

Park, K.-r. (1990). *An experimental study of theory-based team building intervention: A case of Korean work groups*. Unpublished doctoral dissertation, Harvard University, Cambridge, MA.

POSTSCRIPT

Is Mindfulness a Cognitive Style?

Sternberg finds that mindfulness is not adequately related to cognitive abilities or personality traits. His view is that while there is a great deal of overlap, mindfulness has some unique attributes that stand outside these traditional areas. In Sternberg's view, mindfulness is more accurately portrayed as a state rather than a trait. Traits are usually thought of as life-long personal characteristics, while states are more temporal and often related to certain situations, contexts, or environments. For example, a college student might have the trait of shyness, and that individual might be in a state of anxiety because she has to give a speech in a public speaking class.

Based on his analysis, Sternberg finds that mindfulness, as portrayed by Langer, is most closely related to cognitive styles. These styles reflect the ways people prefer to process information and engage in problem solving. For example, the cognitive style of reflexivity and impulsivity describes why some people read slowly and reflectively (reflexivity) and others read quickly for the main points (impulsivity). This style reflects one's preferred speed of processing. Cognitive styles are contextual in that the environment determines which of the two styles is preferred. For example, when reading important information for a test, a reflexive mode may be best, but when driving an impulsive glance at a billboard is better (and safer!). Sternberg views Langer's concepts of mindfulness and mindlessness in a similar way. There are contexts in which mindfulness is important, such as in artistic endeavors, and there are times when mindlessness is actually better, as in filtering out annoying noise.

Langer and Moldoveanu strongly disagree with Sternberg's assessment. They find the notion of any cognitive ability, based on an algorithmic model, too restrictive and counter to the basic essence of mindfulness. In their view, mindfulness is primarily the engaged awareness of one's present surroundings, and the continual search for novel and creative aspects of any situation. The creative nature of mindfulness is, in their view, the opposite of the predetermined formulaic nature of algorithms and the mind-as-computer-using-algorithms model.

At a superficial level, all three of these authors seem to desire to elevate the status of mindfulness among social scientists, and to encourage more research into this fascinating topic. Yet, while these two articles were written to address the same topic, and Langer and Moldoveanu wrote specifically in response to Sternberg's article, at a deeper level they are arguing different points. Sternberg's aim is to explore mindfulness as a psychological construct similar to cognitive abilities, personality traits, and cognitive styles. He may be guilty of the very charge Langer and Moldoveanu leveled at those who assume the mind-as-computer metaphor to be fact. He is taking the template or structure defined by each of those areas of study and trying each one on mindfulness.

On the other hand, Sternberg's goal is to bring more attention and research to the topic of mindfulness, and he believes that associating it with an accepted area of study is the way to do that. After he makes his case that mindfulness/mindlessness has characteristics most closely associated with a cognitive style, he describes the decline in research on cognitive styles. Sternberg may be warning Langer and Moldoveanu that the construct of mindfulness is in danger of the same neglect. Sternberg says that cognitive styles were never associated with a general psychological theory, their assessment instruments were not accurate, and they were never well defined. There was confusion over how generalizable and how unique (from abilities) cognitive styles are. Sternberg is hoping to give more life to the concept of mindfulness by guiding the construct down a different path.

There are many important points made in this debate. What do you think of Langer and Moldoveanu's criticism of the strength of the mind-as-computer metaphor? Do you think Sternberg has a better plan for the longevity and vitality of mindfulness as a research concept?

Suggested Readings

Langer, E. *Mindfulness* (Boulder, CO: Perseus Publishing; second printing, April 1990).

Langer, E. *The Power of Mindful Learning* (Reading, MA: Addison Wesley, 1997).

McQuaid, J., and Carmona, P. *Peaceful Mind: Using Mindfulness and Cognitive Behavioral Psychology to Overcome Depression* (Oakland, CA: New Harbinger Publications, April 2004).

Sternberg, R. *Thinking Styles* (New York: Cambridge University Press, 1999).

Sternberg, R., and Zhang, L. (Editors). *Perspectives on Thinking, Learning, and Cognitive Styles (The Educational Psychology Series)* (Mahwah, NJ: Lawrence Erlbaum, April 2001).

On the Internet . . .

This Web site, sponsored by Educarer, gives an informative overview of infant brain development and conceptual understanding.

`http://www.educarer.org/brain.htm`

The American Psychological Association Division for Developmental Psychology provides many helpful links to laboratories, journals, and organizations focused on infant cognitive development.

`http://classweb.gmu.edu/awinsler/div7/links.shtml`

The Psi Cafe provides a wealth of background information on children's cognitive development as well as many useful links.

`http://www.psy.pdx.edu/PsiCafe/Areas/Developmental/CogDev-Child/index.htm`

The last issue in this section focuses on people with aphasia and how their disorder may offer insight into conceptual development. The National Aphasia Association offers a good overview of the condition and many helpful links.

`http://www.aphasia.org/`

PART 2

Concepts

One of the first considerations in understanding the ways infants and children deal with so much new information, or in programming artificial intelligence software to store and manipulate unfathomably large data sets, is how the data are, or should be, organized. Research with children shows that they begin by attempting to place bits of data into basic conceptual groupings. For example, one of the first groupings children learn is "boy things" and "girl things." In this section we explore the ways infants begin to form concepts, and what aspects of conceptual data are most important.

ISSUE 4

Are We Overestimating Infants' Math Ability?

YES: Leslie B. Cohen and Kathryn S. Marks, from "How Infants Process Addition and Subtraction Events," *Developmental Science* (2002)

NO: Karen Wynn, from "Do Infants Have Numerical Expectations or Just Perceptual Preferences?" *Developmental Science* (2002)

ISSUE SUMMARY

YES: Professor of psychology Leslie Cohen and his research associate Kathryn Marks make the case that infants prefer to stare longer, and thus respond more, to familiar situations as compared to novel ones, and that this has been mistaken for numerical understanding.

NO: Psychologist and researcher Karen Wynn argues that her assumptions are sound, and that infants are capable of calculating the outcomes of very basic addition and subtraction problems.

In 1992 *Nature* published the amazing research of scientist Karen Wynn demonstrating that five-month-old human infants are able to add and subtract. Wynn had five-month-old babies watch the following scenario: a doll is placed on a stage, a cover is placed in front of the stage, a hand holding another doll goes behind the stage, and then the hand leaves empty. This is an addition design (one doll on stage plus the one added). Babies were shown varying outcomes when the stage cover was removed. In some trials, babies would see two dolls on the stage, while in other trials they would see either one doll or three dolls. Wynn monitored babies' eye movements and found that babies looked longer at the incorrect outcomes (one or three dolls) than the correct outcome (one doll). She also found the same to be true in subtraction scenarios. When the trial began with two dolls on the stage, the screen covered the front, and an empty hand appeared, went behind the screen and left with one doll, babies looked longer at the incorrect response of two dolls than the correct outcome of one doll.

Wynn's research is not only remarkable in its suggestion that infants have an innate sense of number, her research is also noteworthy because the findings are inconsistent with standard cognitive developmental theory. Much of the early research in cognitive development rested on the influential theoretical foundation proposed by Jean Piaget (1896–1980). His theory details four stages of cognitive development that begin with basic sensory and motor learning and culminate in sophisticated logical and abstract reasoning. Piaget's theory is often labeled *constructionist* or *structuralist* because he assumed that each stage or skill served as the foundation upon which any new stage or skill would be built. His conclusions regarding numerical understanding were that such processes would be built on the foundation of a basic use of symbols, which develops for most children between the ages of 18 to 24 months.

While Piaget's work has greatly influenced numerous areas of study in psychology and education, his theory and research are not without criticism. As other researchers began to replicate and extend Piaget's research, some began to speculate that the reason Piaget found such limited cognitive processing in children less than 18 months old was that he relied on the children's linguistic and motor skills. Today, researchers use different methodologies that rely on simple responses, such as Wynn's scenario that measures eye movement. It is also common to monitor changes in heart rate or sucking patterns. From these behavioral responses, researchers can make assumptions about an infant's cognitive processing (Papalia, D., Olds, S., and Feldman, R. (2004). *Human Development,* 9th Edition. Boston: McGraw-Hill).

Not only has Piaget's research methodology been challenged, his constructionist theory has been criticized as well. Often when a scientist accepts a particular theoretical point of view as the correct or best available option, that perspective influences that scientist's research methodology. Much of Piaget's work, influenced by his constructionist view, focused on how one skill leads to another, or the opposite, measuring a skill in continually younger children to find its beginnings. Wynn's research comes out of a different theoretical viewpoint called *nativism.* This view proposes that many skills, including numerical sensitivity, are innate in humans. Rather than searching for Piagetian-type building blocks, Wynn's research assumes that infants have these innate abilities and seeks to find ways for preverbal infants to demonstrate their skills.

In the first selection, Cohen and Marks attempt to show that Wynn overestimated infants' numerical understanding. They attempt to replicate Wynn's results, and they offer alternative interpretations of the data. In the second selection, Wynn responds to Cohen and Marks by giving her concerns with their research and defending her original assumptions. As you read these two articles, pay attention to the details of each experiment. Often subtle differences in a procedure can bring great differences in results. Also pay attention to the role of theory in design of the experiments as well as the interpretations of the findings.

Leslie B. Cohen and Kathryn S. Marks

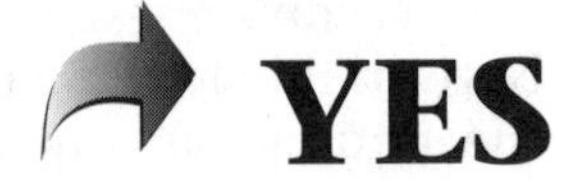

How Infants Process Addition and Subtraction Events

Learning the number system and how to manipulate it is one of the most difficult tasks a young child encounters; it is a slow and laborious process taking years to complete (for example, Fuson, 1988). Children study mathematics from their earliest school days to high school graduation and beyond. However, like most areas of psychology, there are multiple perspectives on this topic. Three major views on the development of numerical competence can be distinguished. The empiricist view argues that children learn about numbers by observing numerical transformations and noting the consistencies between events (Kitcher, 1984). Piaget's constructionist view argues that the number concept is built from previously existing sensorimotor intelligence (Piaget, 1941/1952). In contrast, a more recent nativist view argues that sensitivity to number is innate and even young infants possess strikingly mature reasoning abilities in the numerical domain (Wynn, 1992b, 1992c). . . .

In what has become a frequently cited paper, Wynn (1992a) argued that infants as young as 5 months of age 'are able to *calculate* the precise results of simple arithmetical operations' (p. 750, emphasis added). In her first set of experiments, Wynn showed infants a large stage on which various objects were inserted and removed. In the 1 + 1 condition, infants saw a doll placed on the stage. A screen then rotated up to occlude the middle of the stage. Infants then saw a second doll placed behind the screen. When the screen rotated back down, infants saw one of two outcomes. In the arithmetically possible event, there were two dolls standing on the stage. In the arithmetically impossible event, there was only one doll standing on the stage. A similar course of events took place in the 2 – 1 condition. Initially two dolls were placed on the stage one at a time. After the screen rose to occlude the dolls, a hand entered and removed one of the dolls. At the end of the trial, either one (arithmetically possible event) or two dolls (arithmetically impossible event) were present on the stage. Wynn found that infants looked significantly longer at the impossible outcome than at the possible outcome. In a separate experiment (Wynn, 1992a, Experiment 3), she showed infants 1 + 1 = 2 or 3. As with the original experiment, she found that infants looked significantly longer at the impossible outcome of 3. She argued that this was evidence that infants were actually predicting the precise outcome of the event, rather than relying on simpler mechanisms such as directionality.

Based on the results of her experiments, Wynn (1995a, 1995b) has argued that infants are not only sensitive to number, they are able to manipulate small numerosities. In the course of her work, Wynn has made three major claims about infants' abilities. The first is that infants understand the numerical value of small collections of objects. Number is abstracted over varying perceptual details (Wynn, 1992a, 1995b, 1996). Second, and related to the first, is that infants' knowledge is general and can be applied to varying items and different modalities (for example, Starkey *et al.*, 1990). Third, she claimed that infants are able to reason at the ordinal level and compute the result of simple arithmetic problems (i.e. add and subtract).

In contrast to Wynn's innate, domain-specific, numerical approach, Simon (1997, 1998) has argued that a non-numerical, domain-general set of competencies can account for the data Wynn (1992a) presented. One is memory and discrimination. Another is the ability to individuate a small set of items. The third is object permanence, and the fourth is the ability to represent objects in terms of spatio-temporal characteristics (Simon, 1998).

Both Simon and Wynn have made predictions regarding what infants should do in the Wynn task. In fact, both approaches make the assumption that infants will compare sets of items based upon a one to one correspondence between the sets and will respond more (i.e. look longer) at arithmetically impossible events than at arithmetically possible events. However, there are other possible reasons why infants may respond more to the impossible events than to the possible events in the Wynn task.

One possibility is that infants understand that when material is added, the outcome should be more, or less in the case of subtraction, but they don't know how much more or less. This 'directional' explanation would be consistent with a rudimentary understanding of the ordinal property of numbers, an assumption made by Simon as well. Reasoning at this level would involve comparing the final outcome to the initial display based upon the relative amount of material. As long as the outcome is consistent with the direction of transformation, i.e. greater than or less than, the infants should look less than when the direction of transformation is violated. As we noted earlier, Wynn (1992a) presented some preliminary evidence (Exp. 3) that infants are doing more than making an ordinal transformation; but . . . there may be another explanation for her results. In any case, it seems reasonable at least to consider this directional hypothesis.

Another possible explanation, one that has not been addressed before in the context of infant addition and subtraction, is that the infants are simply responding more to familiar than to novel displays. That familiarity may be based upon either the number of objects in the display, or as Clearfied and Mix (1999a, 1999b) and Feigenson and Spelke (1998) have proposed, the overall quantity created by the objects. Since the 1960s theorists have proposed that organisms are most interested in an intermediate, optimal level of stimulation (e.g. Berlyne, 1963; Hunt, 1965; McCall & Kagan, 1967). According to Berlyne, for example, that level of stimulation is based upon the overall novelty, complexity and incongruity of the display. Several experiments in the 1960s and 1970s demonstrated that indeed young infants often responded more to a familiar stimulus than to a novel stimulus. In fact, recently Roder, Bushnell and Sasseville (2000) reported another example of 4½-month-old infants having a familiarity preference, prior to a novelty preference.

These results regarding infants' preferences for familiarity and novelty have been summarized in the three-dimensional model presented by Hunter and Ames (1988). According to this model, with repeated presentations of a stimulus, infants should display a familiarity preference prior to a novelty preference. Furthermore, the extent of this familiarity preference should depend upon the age of the infant, with younger infants showing a greater familiarity preference than older infants, and the complexity of the stimulus or event, with more complex events producing greater familiarity preferences than simple events.

Based upon this type of model, one might well predict that the Wynn task could be producing familiarity preferences. The infants are relatively young, approximately 5 months of age. The task is quite complex, with noises, multiple objects and a hand moving in and out, and both a screen and a Venetian blind going up and down. Furthermore, the infants have not been habituated to any of the events so they would be expected to be in an early stage of processing the objects, a stage when a familiarity preference is likely to occur. It is also the case that in the addition event they receive many more exposures to the single object (the incorrect result) than to the two objects (the correct result) whereas in the subtraction event they receive many more exposures to the two objects (the incorrect result) than to the single object (the correct result). Therefore, based upon the model provided by Hunter and Ames, the conditions would seem optimal for infants to look longer at the impossible event, not because it is impossible, but because it is more familiar. . . .

General Discussion

Three experiments were conducted to evaluate Wynn's (1992a) claim that 5-month-old infants can add and subtract. Experiment 1 was designed to test three competing hypotheses concerning why infants would look longer at the incorrect number (1 test item) in the addition problem and (2 test items) in the subtraction problem. One hypothesis was that infants were actually adding and subtracting. A second hypothesis was that they were responding at an ordinal level to more versus fewer items. A third hypothesis was that the infants were simply demonstrating a greater response to the familiar test display. It should be noted that either of the last two alternatives could be accomplished by attending to the overall quantity of objects rather than the exact number of objects as suggested by Clearfield and Mix (1999a, 1999b).

The results of Experiment 1 did not support any of the three hypotheses independently. However, the results were consistent with two possible dual-process explanations. One explanation posited that infants could, in fact, add and subtract, but that their tendency to look longer at the incorrect number was superimposed on a tendency to look longer when there were more items on the stage. The other hypothesis was that infants were responding more to a familiar outcome, but that this preference for familiarity also was superimposed on a tendency to look longer when there were more items on the stage.

Experiment 2 tested whether, in fact, infants would look longer when more items were on the stage. In Experiment 2, infants were given only the test items from Experiment 1 without any prior warm-up, familiarization or addition and subtraction experience. Evidence was found (overall and particularly on the second block of test trials) for a linear increase in looking as the number of items in the stage increased.

In Experiment 3 infants were familiarized with either 1 item or 2 items before encountering each test event. Thus, their experience was similar to that of Experiment 1, except that there was no warm-up period and no hand added or subtracted any items. Nevertheless, in most respects their behavior mirrored that of infants in Experiment 1. As both the analyses of individual experiments and the direct comparison of Experiment 1 with Experiment 3 indicated, in both experiments infants familiarized with 1 item looked longer at 1 item than at 2 items in the test, whereas infants familiarized with 2 items looked longer at 2 items than at 1 item in the test. There was also a tendency in both experiments for infants to look longer the more test items there were to look at. Thus, Experiment 3 provided support for the familiarity plus more items hypothesis over the addition-subtraction plus more items hypothesis.

One consistent difference between Experiment 1 and Experiment 3 was also found. Infants looked considerably longer overall in Experiment 3 than in Experiment 1. Although the reason for this difference in looking time is unclear, the nature of the events themselves may help to explain it. In Experiment 1, infants saw items placed on a stage, and a hand enter and leave the stage. These actions took approximately 20 seconds in the addition condition and 23 seconds in the subtraction condition. During the majority of this time, infants were looking at the stage. In contrast, in the third experiment none of these actions took place. Infants saw an item on a stage for approximately 2 seconds, the screen rotate up, and the screen rotate down. The entire sequence of events took approximately 10 seconds. Assuming that there is a maximum amount of time infants will look at any event, the shorter procedure in Experiment 3 gave infants more time to process the end of the event, possibly resulting in longer looking times. In any case, despite the overall difference in looking times and the physical differences between Experiments 1 and 3, since type of experiment did not interact with the main findings of a familiarity preference and a longer looking with more items preference, these two preferences should be considered viable explanations for the results in Experiment 1. The present results also raise the distinct possibility that other studies using the Wynn procedure, including Wynn's original experiment, that have found apparent evidence for addition and subtraction, may merely have found evidence for a familiarity preference.

These experiments are not the only ones that have contradicted Wynn's (1992a) assertion that young infants can add and subtract. In another recent report, Wakeley, Rivera and Langer (2000) attempted to replicate Wynn's studies with a more controlled procedure. They found that infants did not look longer at the impossible events in the addition or the subtraction conditions. Based on their findings, they argued that infants' ability to compute the outcome of arithmetic problems is fragile and inconsistent at best.

In response to this counter-argument, Wynn (2000) reported a number of studies that have replicated the original results using that procedure as well as modified procedures. In addition, Wynn discussed three potential methodological differences that may have affected Wakeley *et al.*'s results. The first two relate to infant attentiveness to the events. The final one relates to subject exclusion due to fussiness. The controls used in our procedure (i.e. presenters being blind to the participant during trials) more closely matched those of Wakeley *et al.*, yet we did find the same differences (i.e. looking longer at 1 item in the addition condition and longer at 2 items in the subtraction condition) reported by Wynn (2000). Thus, it seems that these methodological differences cannot account for the null results found by Wakeley *et al.*

Why, then, did we find differences when Wakely *et al.* did not? According to our predictions, infants should have shown a familiarity preference, just as they did in previously published studies. We are not certain. One potential difference between our Experiment 1 and the Wakeley *et al.* study is the length of the intertrial interval. In Wynn (2000) and in our procedure, as soon as the stage was reset, a new trial began. On average, the intertrial interval was less than 6 seconds with a standard deviation of 1 second. In contrast, Wakeley, Rivera and Langer used a consistent 10 s intertrial interval. Allowing more time to elapse between trials may have made it more difficult for infants to become sufficiently familiar with the 1 object. The lack of a comparable subtraction condition also makes comparison between the two studies difficult.

Perhaps Wakeley *et al.* are correct that the evidence for infant addition and subtraction is fragile and inconsistent. However, no matter how carefully a study is done, it is difficult to mount a convincing challenge against previously reported evidence when one fails to find a significant difference. In essence it amounts to trying to prove the null hypothesis. That difficulty is compounded when, as Wynn (2000) correctly points out, several other studies have replicated her results. In fact, we did so in Experiment 1. The problem with Wynn's explanation is that we also replicated her results in our Experiment 3, an experiment in which no addition or subtraction was involved. It is much more difficult to counter a challenge when a set of experiments first replicate the results in question and then show that those results can be accounted for by a different, and in this case simpler, set of reasons.

The other studies reported by Wynn (2000) that have replicated her results all tested infants on 1 and 2 items after a 1 + 1 event or a 2 – 1 event. To our knowledge, no previous study has included controls for a possible familiarity preference. The one that may come closest was reported recently by Uller, Carey, Huntley-Fenner and Klatt (1999). They argued they were testing an 'Object-file' model versus an 'Integer-symbol' model. But from our point of view they may also have been varying the familiarity of the objects during their test trials. In their experiments they showed infants 1 + 1 = 1 or 2 when the items were either placed on the stage first (object first condition) or the screen was placed on the stage first and the objects were dropped behind the screen (screen first condition). In the object first condition infants had more of an opportunity to build up a familiarity preference for one, the incorrect number. It is not surprising, then, that in their first two experiments Uller *et al.* (1999) found 8-month-old infants responding more to the impossible event (or from our point of view the familiar event) only in the object first condition. In contrast, in Experiment 3, 10-month-old infants responded to the impossible event even in the screen first condition. Perhaps, as suggested by Hunter and Ames (1988), older infants need less familiarization time with the objects before showing a familiarity preference.

Uller *et al.*'s final experiment is more difficult to interpret from a familiarity preference point of view. In this experiment two separate small screens were used instead of a single large screen. In contrast to the first experiments, 8-month-old infants in the screen first condition now looked longer at 1 item than at 2 items in the test. One could make the argument that with two small screens and one object dropped behind each screen during familiarization, the infants may have treated the familiarization period as two examples with 1 object rather than as a single example with 2 objects. Perhaps that produced enough familiarization with 1 object for 8-month-old infants to respond more during the test to 1 object than to 2 objects. Admittedly, this interpretation of Uller *et al.*'s Experiment 4 is highly speculative. But the interpretation could easily be tested by running a subtraction condition as well as an addition condition. When two screens are used, we would expect 8-month-olds to have more 'trouble' with subtraction than with addition. If the infants are becoming more familiarized with one object in the two screen condition, they should tend to prefer one object in the test, which would be the 'impossible' result in an addition problem, but the 'possible' result in a subtraction problem.

It is clear that future research should follow Uller *et al.*'s example by testing older infants and considering possible developmental changes in the processes underlying how infants treat these events. An important question is whether infants progress from a simple preference for familiarity to more sophisticated approaches, such as the directional (i.e. ordinal) one, and proceed to true addition and subtraction. Feigenson (1999) tested infants ranging from 12 to 18 months of age in a discrimination learning task involving the ordinal relationship between numbers. She found that infants in this age range were capable of learning the correct rule (look at the bigger number or look at the smaller number). Hauser, Feigenson, Carey and Mastro (1999) also found similar results using 10-month-olds in a procedure where they searched to retrieve either one or two cookies. This evidence suggests that by 10 months of age, infants may be able to reason about the events using the more complex, directional method. The studies by Uller *et al.* (1999) also seem to suggest certain changes in processing by 10 months of age.

In conjunction with the issue of infant addition and subtraction, we believe that the experiments presented here raise a more general and important issue. One should be cautious about attributing sophisticated cognitive processes to young infants when simpler processes will suffice. The fact that infants, particularly younger infants, sometimes prefer familiarity in these tasks is not an accident or fluke. Familiarity preferences have been reported repeatedly since the early 1970s (e.g. Greenberg, Uzgiris & Hunt, 1970; Rose, Gottfried, Mellow-Carminar & Bridger, 1982; Wetherford & Cohen, 1973). As we mentioned previously, Hunter and Ames (1988) provide an excellent summary of this older literature. In addition, recent studies are also beginning to report the same familiarity effect with 4- and 5-month-old infants in tasks similar to those used in addition-subtraction studies. Bogartz, Shinskey and Schilling (2000) and Schilling (2000) both found that in object permanence tasks, in which one object repeatedly appeared and disappeared behind an occluder, 5-month-old infants, for a time, also preferred familiar events. Cashon and Cohen (2000) reported the same effect with 8-month-old infants in an animated version of the events. The point is that under some circumstances, familiarity preferences are real, even predictable. Studies that rely on assessing infant visual preferences without first habituating infants should add appropriate controls to rule out familiarity preferences as a possible explanation. Even studies that do habituate infants to a criterion but include non-habituators along with habituators should make certain their findings do not result from the non-habituators who may still have a lingering familiarity preference (e.g. Cashon & Cohen, 2000; Roder *et al.*, 2000).

Based upon the evidence presented in the present three experiments, Wynn's (2000) claims notwithstanding, we believe it is still an open question as to whether 5-month-old infants can actually add or subtract. [The] evidence is still in dispute. When certain abilities are attributed to young infants, simpler mechanisms can sometimes account for the data. Clearly, further research is needed to delineate infants' understanding of quantity and their development of numerical knowledge. Until that research reveals convincing evidence of infants' numerical competence, we believe caution and parsimony are the best principles to follow when trying to understand the development of infants' abilities.

References

Berlyne, D. E. (1963). Motivational problems raised by exploratory and epistemic behavior. In S. Koch (Ed.), *Psychology: A study of a science. Vol. 5. The process areas, the person, and some applied fields: Their place in psychology and in science* (pp. 284–364). New York: McGraw-Hill.

Bogartz, R. S., Shinskey, J. L., & Schilling, T. H. (2000). Object permanence in five-and-a-half-month-old infants? *Infancy,* 1, 403–428.
Cashon, C. H., & Cohen, L. B. (2000). Eight-month-old infants' perception of possible and impossible events. *Infancy,* 1, 429–446.
Clearfield, M. W., & Mix, K. S. (1999a, April). Infants use contour length—not number—to discriminate small visual sets. Poster presented at the biennial meeting of the Society for Research in Child Development, Albuquerque, NM.
Clearfield, M. W., & Mix, K. S. (1999b). Number versus contour length in infants' discrimination of small visual sets. *Psychological Science,* 10, 408–411.
Feigenson, L. (1999, April). An anticipatory-looking paradigm for examining infants' ordinal knowledge. Poster presented at the biennial meeting of the Society for Research in Child Development, Albuquerque, NM.
Feigenson, L., & Spelke, E. (1998, April). Numerical knowledge in infancy: the number/mass distinction. Poster presented at the biennial meeting of the International Conference on Infant Studies, Atlanta, GA.
Fuson, K. C. (1988). *Children's counting and concepts of number.* New York: Springer-Verlag.
Greenberg, A., Uzgiris, I. C., & Hunt, J. McV. (1970). Attentional preference and experience: III. Visual familiarity and looking time. *Journal of Genetic Psychology,* 117, 123–135.
Hauser, M., Feigenson, L., Carey, S., & Mastro, R. (1999, April). Non-linguistic number knowledge: evidence of ordinal representations in human infants and rhesus macaques. Poster presented at the biennial meeting of the Society for Research in Child Development, Albuquerque, NM.
Hunt, J. McV. (1965). Intrinsic motivation and its role in psychological development. *Nebraska Symposium on Motivation,* 14, 189–282.
Hunter, M. A., & Ames, E. W. (1988). A multifactor model of infant preferences for novel and familiar stimuli. In C. Rovee-Collier & L. P. Lipsitt (Eds.), *Advances in infancy research* (Vol. 5, pp. 69–95). Norwood, NJ: Ablex.
Kitcher, P. (1984). *The nature of mathematical knowledge.* Oxford: Oxford University Press.
McCall, R. B., & Kagan, J. (1967). Stimulus-schema discrepancy and attention in the infant. *Journal of Experimental Child Psychology,* 5, 381–390.
Piaget, J. (1941/1952). *The child's conception of number.* London: Routledge & Kegan.
Roder, B. J., Bushnell, E. W., & Sasseville, A. M. (2000). Infants' preferences for familiarity and novelty during the course of visual processing. *Infancy,* 1, 491–507.
Rose, S., Gottfried, A. W., Mellow-Carminar, P., & Bridger, W. H. (1982). Familiarity and novelty preferences in infant recognition memory: implications for information processing. *Developmental Psychology,* 18, 704–713.
Schilling, T. H. (2000). Infants' looking at possible and impossible screen rotations: the role of familiarization. *Infancy,* 1, 389–402.
Simon, T. J. (1997). Reconceptualizing the origins of number knowledge: a 'non-numerical' account. *Cognitive Development,* 12, 349–372.
Simon, T. J. (1998). Computational evidence for the foundations of numerical competence. *Developmental Science,* 1, 71–78.
Starkey, P., Spelke, E. S., & Gelman, R. (1990). Numerical abstraction by human infants. *Cognition,* 36, 97–127.
Uller, C., Carey, S., Huntley-Fenner, G., & Klatt, L. (1999). What representations might underlie infant numerical knowledge? *Cognitive Development,* 14, 1–36.
Wakeley, A., Rivera, S., & Langer, J. (2000). Can young infants add and subtract? *Child Development,* 71, 1525–1534.
Wetherford, M. J., & Cohen, L. B. (1973). Developmental changes in infant visual preferences for novelty and familiarity. *Child Development,* 44, 416–424.

Wynn, K. (1992a). Addition and subtraction by human infants. *Nature,* 358, 749–750.
Wynn, K. (1992b). Evidence against empiricist accounts of the origins of numerical knowledge. *Mind and Language,* 7, 315–332.
Wynn, K. (1992c). Issues concerning a nativist theory of numerical knowledge. *Mind and Language,* 7, 367–381.
Wynn, K. (1995a). Infants possess a system of numerical knowledge. *Current Directions in Psychological Science,* 4, 172–177.
Wynn, K. (1995b). Origins of numerical knowledge. *Mathematical Cognition,* 1, 35–60.
Wynn, K. (1996). Infants' individuation and enumeration of actions. *Psychological Science,* 7, 164–169.
Wynn, K. (2000). Findings of addition and subtraction in infants are robust and consistent: reply to Wakeley, Rivera, and Langer. *Child Development,* 71, 1535–1536.

NO 

Karen Wynn

Do Infants Have Numerical Expectations or Just Perceptual Preferences?

Why do infants respond as they do in 'numerical reasoning' experiments? In Wynn (1992), when shown a '1 + 1' addition event, 5-month-old infants looked longer at incorrect outcomes of 1 and 3 than at the correct outcome of 2. When shown a '2 – 1' subtraction event, they looked longer at an incorrect outcome of 2 than at a correct outcome of 1. These results were interpreted within the framework of expectancy-violation: infants were computing the outcomes of these events, expecting a '2' outcome to a '1 + 1' event and a '1' outcome to a '2 – 1' event, and hence looking longer at the incorrect outcomes because they were unexpected.

Cohen and Marks present data from three experiments that, they suggest, support an alternative explanation for infants' performance. In their first experiment, 5-month-old infants saw either a series of '1 + 1' events or a series of '2 – 1' events, each with four different outcomes shown, of 0, 1, 2 or 3 objects. In both series, they showed longest looking, not to the three impossible outcomes over the one possible one, but to the outcome display identical to the initial display (i.e. to 1 object in the 1 + 1 series, to 2 objects in the 2 – 1 series) over the outcomes differing from the initial display. In the second experiment, when simply presented with displays containing 0, 1, 2 or 3 items, infants showed a preference for larger set sizes over smaller ones. In the third experiment, infants were presented with 'number-change' events (in which they were shown either 1 or 2 objects subsequently hidden by a screen; when the screen was removed, either 0, 1, 2 or 3 items were revealed); here, infants again looked longer at the (possible) outcome in which the number revealed was the same as that in the initial display, than they did when the number (impossibly) changed.

Cohen and Marks argue that these results suggest that infants in the original Wynn (1992) experiments were not showing preference (as evidenced by longer looking times) for the impossibility of the outcome, but for familiarity (as when, for example, 1 + 1 appeared to result in 1 object) or for a larger number (accounting for infants' longer looking to 3 over 2 following a '1 + 1' event). However, there are reasons to doubt this conclusion.

Cohen and Marks Do Not Replicate the *Findings* of Wynn (1992)

First, in Cohen and Marks' Experiment 1 (in which infants were presented with '1 + 1' and '2 – 1' events), they found the pattern of results obtained in Wynn (1992)—a pattern of longer looking to 1 over 2 in the addition group and to 2 over 1 in the subtraction group, *in the first block of test trials only.* In Wynn's experiments (and in replications of these experiments by other researchers: Koechlin, Dehaene & Mehler, 1997; Simon, Hespos & Rochat, 1995; Uller, Carey, Huntley-Fenner & Klatt, 1999), this pattern was obtained across all test blocks taken together as a whole, and was evident at the end of the experiment as well as at the beginning.

Second, in Wynn (1992), when shown a '1 + 1' addition that resulted in an outcome of either 2 or 3, infants looked significantly longer at the (impossible) outcome of 3 over 2; this preference was statistically significant across all test blocks taken together as a whole. But Cohen and Marks' group of '1 + 1' addition infants did not look significantly longer at an outcome of 3 over 2 at all, either in the first block, the second block, or across the two blocks taken together. In the first block, infants did look longer at 3 than at 2, but this was not significant. In the second block, infants showed the reverse (but again non-significant) pattern of preference, looking longer at 2 than at 3.

Cohen and Marks Do Not Replicate the *Methods* of Wynn (1992)

These failures to replicate Wynn's overall patterns of results suggest that Cohen and Marks' experiments are not tapping some of the cognitive processes operative in Wynn's and others' experiments. This may be due to the fact that Cohen and Marks employed significant methodological deviations from the original Wynn (1992) study. In Wynn's experiments, infants were presented with just *two different outcomes* of the operation (either addition or subtraction) shown to them—and infants received *three repetitions of each outcome,* for a total of six test trials alternating between the correct and the incorrect outcome (in counterbalanced order). Cohen and Marks used a quite different design. In all of their experiments, they presented each infant with four distinct outcomes rather than two, each repeated twice, for a total of eight test trials.

We know that small physical alterations to an experiment can strongly affect infants' performance; for just one example, consider Hespos and Baillargeon's (2001) elegant and painstaking examination of infants' reasoning about occlusion versus containment. Young infants failed to make correct inferences about an object A that was placed inside another object B, but reasoned correctly about A when the very same object B served as an occluder rather than a container, by placing the to-be-hidden object *behind* it rather than *inside* it. Thus, even subtle changes can profoundly influence infants' performance. Cohen and Marks' significantly different methods, combined with their failure to replicate Wynn's original results, make comparison of their results with Wynn's difficult at best. It also weakens their argument: showing that processes (such as a preference for familiarity, preference for a larger number, etc.) are operative in one experimental situation is not sufficient as evidence that they are operative in other situations (e.g. the Wynn 1992 experiments). Their failure to replicate in itself shows that some processes are operative in the Wynn (1992) paradigm that are not being revealed in Cohen and Marks' paradigm.

Two speculations on the reason for the different results obtained by Cohen and Marks (I keep this brief as, given the absence of personal communications between Cohen and Marks and myself regarding our procedures, stimuli and set-up, there are no doubt many unknown differences between their experiments and mine, any of which may have contributed to the difference in results):

1. Providing 5-month-old infants with many different test outcomes (four in Cohen and Marks' experiment, as opposed to two in Wynn's original study), may increase infants' attention to the perceptual features of, and perceptual differences between, test trials—differences which are superficially evident and therefore easier to process—over the conceptual differences between them (detection of which requires inferential processes, which may be the first to suffer under conditions of information overload).
2. In a paradigm in which the majority of test trials depict impossible outcomes (75% of trials in Cohen and Marks' Experiments 1 and 3, as opposed to just half of trials in standard violation-of-expectation experiments such as Wynn's 1992 ones; that is, *triple the ratio* of impossible to possible events), infants may quickly learn to 'expect the unexpected', or that any outcome is 'possible' in this experimental context. This modification may therefore actually invalidate an expectancy-violation paradigm. (It would have been helpful if Cohen and Marks had data showing that some genuine violation of infants' expectations is detectable with this method.)

These two concerns raise the question, What would infants have done if shown, as in Wynn's experiments, only two different outcomes, one possible, one impossible? Using a between-subjects design, Cohen and Marks could have compared infants' looking to the same four outcomes of 0, 1, 2 and 3 objects. Such a design would have allowed more meaningful comparison of their results with those of the Wynn (1992) studies.

Cohen and Marks' Data Do Not Support Their Explanation

Cohen and Marks argue that in Wynn's (1992) study, infants looked longer at an outcome of 3 over an outcome of 2 to a '1 + 1' event due to a general preference for larger numbers, not due to having generated an expectation that the outcome should be 2. They offer as data supporting this argument the fact that, in their own Experiment 2 in which infants were simply presented with different numbers of objects to look at (without any prior operation rendering some of these 'possible', others 'impossible'), they found a trend for infants to give longer looks to larger set-size displays. However, this trend occurred in the second block of test trials only. *In their first block, infants actually looked longer at 2 than 3.* But in Wynn's experiment, infants showed a preference for 3 over 2 from the very beginning of the test trials. Moreover, to the extent that Cohen and Marks' infants looked longer at (albeit not significantly) a '1 + 1 = 3' outcome than a '1 + 1 = 2' outcome in their Experiment 1, they showed this preference in the *first* block of test trials only, not the second! Given Cohen and Marks' data that infants' preference for larger numbers does not emerge until *after* their first four test trials, such a preference cannot account for infants' non-significant preference for 3 in block 1 of Cohen and Marks' Experiment 1; nor can it account for infants' preference for 3 over 2 in the early trials of Wynn's study. In sum, Cohen and Marks' evidence actually suggests that to account for infants' preference for the impossible outcome of 3 over 2 in Wynn's (1992) study, one must appeal, *not to a preference for larger numbers, but to something else*; for one possibility, to an expectation on the part of infants for the correct *number* of objects.

Conclusions

To present a compelling alternative explanation for infants' performance, it is not enough to merely show that some processes that might, in theory, account for infants' performance (such as preference for familiarity or preference for larger sets over smaller) are operative at some points in some experimental conditions. One must show that such processes are operative at the *same* points and in the *same* conditions where infants' performance, the performance to be explained, is obtained. And, of course, the data presented in support of the alternative account should support the account, not undermine it. In both these respects, Cohen and Marks' alternative account is wanting.

References

Hespos, S. J., & Baillargeon, R. (2001). Infants' knowledge about occlusion and containment events: a surprising discrepancy. *Psychological Science,* 12, 140–147.

Koechlin, E., Dehaene, S., & Mehler, J. (1997). Numerical transformations in five-month-old human infants. *Mathematical Cognition,* 3, 89–104.

Simon, T. J., Hespos, S. J., & Rochat, P. (1995). Do infants understand simple arithmetic? A replication of Wynn (1992). *Cognitive Development,* 10, 253–269.

Uller, C., Carey, S., Huntley-Fenner, G., & Klatt, L. (1999). What representations might underlie infant numerical knowledge? *Cognitive Development,* 14, 1–36.

Wynn, K. (1992). Addition and subtraction by human infants. *Nature,* 358, 749–750.

Wynn, K. (1995). Origins of numerical knowledge. *Mathematical Cognition,* 1, 35–60.

POSTSCRIPT

Are We Overestimating Infants' Math Ability?

How should researchers interpret these findings that in some situations infants will consistently look longer at the wrong outcome in the Wynn task? Which are reasonable conclusions, and which have gone beyond the boundaries of reasonable assumptions? These questions are at the heart of the debate over infants' numerical understanding. Through a series of experiments, Cohen and Marks found that they could not fully replicate Wynn's results from her 1992 study. Based on their findings, Cohen and Marks hypothesize that infants choose to look longer at the more familiar situation. They believe that "caution and parsimony are the best principles to follow" when interpreting their results (page 200). Wynn counters Cohen and Marks by pointing out the ways they deviated from her original experimental method, and thus concludes that they were measuring different cognitive processes. Wynn suggests that Cohen and Marks test their familiarity hypothesis directly rather than indirectly while trying to undermine her research paradigm.

This debate provides several examples of the complicating factors that make this type of research difficult to conduct. Just how far can a researcher go in varying a methodology before the changes bring all the results into question? Cohen and Marks felt that the variations they introduced were justified, while Wynn argued that even subtle changes bring all the results into question. The intricacies of the design are then magnified by the influence of theoretical assumptions and interpretations. Are the researchers here looking for basic building blocks (the constructionist view), such as awareness of the direction of more or less, or are they looking for ways to allow infants to demonstrate their innate abilities (the nativist view)? Not only can a set of theoretical assumptions shape methodological designs and interpretations, they can also keep researchers from considering data from other areas. For example, researchers in the area of information processing have found in their research that, rather than focusing on the familiar, infants tend to habituate and give less attention to the familiar (Papalia, Olds, and Feldman, 2004).

While researchers are busy trying to understand infant cognitive development, there are parents, grandparents, babysitters, and daycare teachers who want to know what they can do to help infants develop in the healthiest way. Based on what you've read here, do you have any suggestions for them? If it is true that five-month-old infants can calculate the outcomes for very basic addition and subtraction, how might that change infants' toys or programs for television or a computer? It is important to remember that the study of infant cognition is more than an academic exercise. There are many important applications to [be] made from sound research.

Suggested Readings

Brannon, E. M. "The Development of Ordinal Numerical Knowledge in Infancy," *Cognition* (April 2002).

Cohen, L. B., and Cashon, C. H. "Infant Perception and Cognition," *Handbook of Psychology: Developmental Psychology* (Hoboken, NJ: Wiley & Sons, 2003).

Rakison, D. H., and Oakes, L. M. (Editors). *Early Category and Concept Development: Making Sense of the Blooming, Buzzing Confusion* (New York: Oxford University Press, 2004).

Wynn, K., Bloom, P., and Chiang, W. "Enumeration of Collective Entities by 5-Month-Old Infants," *Cognition* (April 2002).

ISSUE 5

Can Infants Develop Abstract Concepts?

YES: Jean M. Mandler, from "Perceptual and Conceptual Processes in Infancy," *Journal of Cognition and Development* (2000)

NO: Eleanor J. Gibson, from "Commentary on Perceptual and Conceptual Processes in Infancy," *Journal of Cognition and Development* (2000)

ISSUE SUMMARY

YES: Research professor of cognitive science Jean Mandler provides evidence to show that, counter to traditional cognitive developmental theory, infants are capable of abstract conceptual processing.

NO: National Medal of Science recipient Eleanor Gibson questions the assumptions Mandler makes regarding preverbal infants and presents her own view that perceptual development leads children into conceptual processing.

Cognitive scientists are eager to understand complex cognition for many reasons. Once it is understood how we process information using higher-order cognitive skills, the potential exists to develop artificial intelligence computer software to do such thinking. The potential also exists to find methods of treatment or rehabilitation for those who have never developed or lost their abilities to perform complex cognitive tasks. One strategy for trying to understand complex cognition is to trace the development of infant cognition from its simplest form to the most complex adult thinking. There are some major obstacles to work around when attempting to understand infant cognition, however, that can make this research tenuous. Researchers often observe participants' cognitive processes by analyzing what they say or write, and an infant can do neither of these. Infants are not yet verbal, nor do they have enough fine motor control to write or press a button, and depending on how young they are, they may not yet be able to point accurately. Through clever research designs, some cognitive scientists believe they have found ways infants can demonstrate what they know, which then allows scientists to make less tenuous assumptions.

One example of a clever research design is used by Carolyn Rovee-Collier in demonstrating the existence of infant memory. In her laboratory, she created a situation in which an infant is placed in a crib, over which hangs a mobile. A ribbon is carefully tied to the infant's leg, with the other end of the ribbon tied to the mobile. Infants in this situation learn very quickly that by kicking their leg, the mobile will move. Most infants enjoy watching the brightly colored mobile move, and they will keep kicking in order to keep it moving. The memory test comes when the infants are returned to the laboratory after several days. Rovee-Collier has demonstrated that infants as young as 3 months old will remember the situation for up to 3 days and begin kicking as soon as they are placed in the crib (Gulya, M., Rossi-George, A., and Rovee-Collier, C. (2002). Dissipation of retroactive interference in human infants. *Journal of Experimental Psychology: Animal Behavior Processes, 28(2),* pp. 151–162). What makes her technique so clever is that she has found a way for preverbal infants to demonstrate their use of a cognitive process (memory) by engaging in physical movement that is well within their control (deliberate kicking).

In the first selection by Jean Mandler, other clever research designs are described that allow infants to show remarkable understanding. Mandler and her research team create situations in which infants as young as 9 months old are given opportunities to make choices and imitate simple movements. For example, Mandler will use toys to show an infant a scenario in which a dog is getting a drink out of a cup and a car is giving a child a ride. She will then switch the dog for a bird and the car for a bus. The infant can choose to imitate by giving the bird or the bus a drink; however, most infants choose the bird. The infant could choose to have the bird give the child a ride, but most choose the bus for that.

Based on these and other similar observations, Mandler suggests that infants develop conceptual groups or categories of things, and more specifically, the categories of furniture, animals, plants, and vehicles. She finds it significant that these categories are based on the function or what these items do, rather than how they look. To support her theory, she points out that while infants may assume a dog and a cat are similar because they have so many features in common, infants in her experiments gave drinks to animals that were quite distinct from the original toy dog, including fish and birds. She also found that while infants would place the toy child on a bus for a ride, after seeing the car give the child a ride, infants also placed the child on a forklift and a motorcycle for a ride. Based on her research, she finds the abstract qualities of function to be the organizing factor rather than the perceptual features of how the items look.

In the first selection, Mandler presents evidence to support her view that perceptual and conceptual abilities develop separately, and that conceptual abstract abilities are present in young infants. Gibson, in the second selection, questions several assumptions made by Mandler and presents her reasons in support of perceptual skills developing first and later leading to conceptual understanding when the child is older.

Jean M. Mandler

Perceptual and Conceptual Processes in Infancy

Conceptual Categories Are Used for the First Inductive Inferences

All categorization results in something less particular than a given instance, whether it be perceptually or conceptually realized. The main difference for purposes of inductive inference seems to be the notion of kind. Since the pioneering work of Carey (1985) and Gelman and her colleagues (e.g., Gelman & Markman, 1986) we have known that preschool children make inductions on the basis of conceptual kind rather than on the basis of physical similarity. These studies taught children a fact about an object, and then they were asked to decide the categorical range over which the taught property is valid. At least from 2½ years of age, children use conceptual class membership to constrain their inductions, and they do so in preference to perceptual similarity between training and test exemplars (Gelman & Coley, 1990).

Until recently, however, there was no information on inductive inferences in younger children, particularly in the infancy period. Does inductive generalization originally begin on the basis of perceptual salience or do even infants use more principled bases for their generalizations? McDonough and I have been investigating how infants go about making generalizations about the characteristic properties of objects. Some of the questions we have asked are the following: When infants observe that a dog eats or sleeps, how far do they generalize such behavior—only to other dogs, to all animals, or to all objects? That is, do category boundaries constrain their inductions, and if so, how broad are these categories? How much of a role does physical similarity play? For example, will infants generalize a bird eating to an airplane eating? Or will infants constrain their inductions to the animal class but be more likely to generalize eating from a dog to a similar-looking mammal than from a dog to a fish?

The traditional empiricist doctrine of induction, exemplified in modern times by Quine (1977), is that the first inferences are based not on conceptual kinds but instead on raw perceptual similarity. Quine posited that infants and young children use an innate animal sense of similarity to make their first generalizations because they do not yet have any concepts at their disposal. Keil (1991) dubbed this the doctrine of original sim: Before children develop theories about the world, they can only be influenced by similarity of appearance. The more two things look like each other, the more likely it is the infant will generalize the properties of one to the other. In this kind of view, upon seeing the family dog eat, the infant comes to expect that other dogs eat as well. The generalization happens because a category of dogs can be formed on the basis of the innate sense of similarity. With experience, the infant observes cats eat, birds eat, and various other animals eat, and eventually (perhaps with the help of language) makes the more difficult inference that all animals—even though they do not look alike—eat.

There are a number of difficulties with this view of the foundations of inductive inference. First, it implies that a global category of animal already exists. Otherwise the infant might infer that all objects eat: Without an animal category boundary there is no stop rule. To be sure, the infant has negative evidence, never having seen cars or chairs eat, but in all likelihood the infant has never seen turtles or elephants eat either. At best there might be a perceptual similarity gradient around the objects initially observed to eat, but this would surely map very imperfectly onto such a diverse domain as animals. Second, as I have noted throughout this article, this approach does not tell us how anything conceptual ever emerges. Indeed, as Keil (1991) pointed out, no one espousing the traditional view has shown how generalization on the basis of physical appearance gets replaced by more theory-based generalization. As we will see in the studies of induction described next, we cannot leave the infant in a state in which he or she has perceptual categories of different levels of generality (but no concepts) and still be able to explain why one level of categorization is used for induction and not the other.

Given that infants' early conceptual categories seem to be little influenced by surface perceptual similarity, McDonough and I predicted that the first inductions would not be so determined either. The technique we use to study this issue is to model actions with little models of animals and vehicles and see if infants imitate the actions afterward on different exemplars from these domains. We chose this technique because infants are more likely to imitate actions that make sense to them than actions they find odd (Killen & Uzgiris, 1981; O'Connell & Gerard, 1985). In the first set of experiments (Mandler & McDonough, 1996), we studied 14-month-olds and modeled actions appropriate either to the animal domain or to the vehicle domain. We modeled giving a dog a drink from a cup or sleeping in a bed, and we modeled turning a key against a car door or a car giving a child a ride. Following each modeling, a generalization test was given. The modeled item was put away and a different animal and vehicle were brought out and put on either side of the prop that had been used (e.g., the cup). We measured which object, if either, the infants used to imitate what they had seen modeled.

We assessed the role of perceptual similarity by using animals and vehicles that we judged to be either physically similar or dissimilar to the modeled objects. Thus, when we used a dog for modeling, half the infants received an animal similar to the dog for the generalization test (a cat or a rabbit) paired with a vehicle. The other half of the infants received an animal dissimilar to the dog (a bird or a fish) paired with a vehicle. When a car was used for modeling, half of the infants received a similar vehicle (a truck or a bus) paired with an animal for their generalization test. The other half received a dissimilar vehicle (a motorcycle or an airplane) paired with an animal. In this way we could test the breadth of the generalizations the infants made. That is, we tested whether infants generalize from a dog to a cat or a rabbit more frequently than to a bird, fish, or vehicle; and whether they generalize more from a car to a truck or bus than to a motorcycle, airplane, or animal.

The results were straightforward. The infants strongly preferred to perform the actions on the exemplars from the appropriate domain (67%) and rarely crossed the appropriate domain boundary (11%). As long as the test exemplar was from the same category, it did not matter whether it looked like the dog they had seen or not—they were just as likely to imitate giving a drink to a cat, rabbit, fish, or bird, and, after seeing a car being keyed, to key a truck, bus, motorcycle, or airplane. Thus, there was no effect of the physical similarity or dissimilarity of the exemplars within a domain on generalization. It is also of interest that the infants generalized keying to airplanes, given that the only vehicles they are likely to have seen keys used with are cars. Their domain-wide generalization suggests overgeneralization that in some instances, such as fish drinking, will later need correction.

We replicated this experiment using highly atypical exemplars (e.g., an armadillo and a forklift) so we could be sure the infants had not seen the particular exemplars before (Mandler & McDonough, 1996). The same pattern of results was found (72% appropriate vs. 13% inappropriate). We then used a more difficult test. We modeled the actions on both the correct and incorrect exemplars. For example, we modeled turning a key against the car door but also modeled turning the key against the dog's side. This is a stringent test because our modeling of the actions on inappropriate exemplars essentially tells infants that in this game it is okay to do odd things. The results, however, were very similar to those obtained before; there was only a slightly greater tendency to use the inappropriate object that we had just modeled for them. So even when encouraged to imitate inappropriate properties, relatively few babies did so.

We have also extended the generalized imitation method to 9- and 11-month-olds (McDonough & Mandler, 1998). We had to use a somewhat simpler technique, but again the data mirrored the results of the first two experiments already described. Fewer of the 9-month-olds imitated than older infants, however. We cannot be sure, therefore, whether 9-month-olds are at the lower age limit for this kind of inductive generalization, or whether at this young age imitation of complex events is too difficult to provide a viable technique to examine any such generalizations that are taking place.

In more recent work we studied domain-neutral ("accidental") properties along with a set of the domain-specific properties studied earlier (Mandler & McDonough, 1998). In addition to the properties of drinking and being keyed, we modeled going into a building and being washed. The patterns of generalization were quite different for domain-neutral and domain-specific properties: 14-month-olds generalized across domain boundaries in the case of going into a building but did not generalize drinking and keying across domains. Both this and the previous result of refusing to imitate modeled behavior when it is inappropriate are important because they demonstrate that infants are not merely treating our little models as toys, but are treating them representationally. If they were considering the situation merely a game of "follow the experimenter," then they should behave the same way toward domain-specific and domain-neutral properties, but they do not. Instead they treat the objects and actions appropriately.

I stress the representational response of infants in the age range of 9 to 14 months because it is such convincing evidence of conceptual functioning. It is usually assumed that infants this age have not yet formed a representational capacity, using the term *representation* here not merely as conceptual knowledge but in the more traditional sense of using one object to stand for another. Because of Piaget's theory and also because of DeLoache's (1989) work showing the great difficulties 2-year-olds have in using scale models (and photographs) as representations of other objects, it is usually assumed that this is a late-developing capacity. However, we know that by around 18 months infants begin to use one object to stand for another in symbolic play (McCune-Nicolich, 1981). In addition, DeLoache showed that although 2-year-olds have trouble using a photograph to help them find an object hidden in a depicted room, they can nevertheless use the photograph to help them hide something in the room (DeLoache & Burns, 1994). Thus, the representational capacity is multiplex and appears to undergo considerable development; our imitation data indicate that its roots are present even in the first year.

We have recently completed a series of experiments investigating whether there are any generalizations that are restricted to the basic level. The first of these is reported in Mandler and McDonough (1998). We investigated artifact properties such as that beds are used for sleeping and cups are used for drinking, and natural kind properties such as that dogs eat bones and flowers are to be smelled. We found that 14-month-olds overgeneralize these properties. For example, when we demonstrate giving a little model of a person a drink from a tea cup and then give the person to the infant along with a coffee mug and a frying pan, they are as likely to choose the frying pan as the mug to imitate drinking. It is as if they are conceptualizing these utensils as containers and have not yet narrowed them down to their common social uses. Similarly, they are as likely to put a little person to sleep in a bathtub as in a bed, to smell a tree as a flower, and to feed a bone to a bird as to a dog. Even at 20 months, infants are still making some of the same overgeneralizations. They have begun to narrow the artifact characteristics appropriately, but are still overgeneralizing the natural kind characteristics (presumably because of fewer interactions with animals and plants than with artifacts). We have since replicated these findings with other properties and shown that the overgeneralizations made do not extend beyond domain boundaries; for example, 14-month-olds use a toothbrush to groom hair but not a spoon, and they hammer with a wrench but not a cup (Mandler & McDonough, 1999). Needless to say, we do not conclude that young children cannot restrict inductions to subcategories in either natural kind or artifact domains. Indeed, we assume that one of the functions of the names that parents use with children is to teach them that there are smaller categories than the domain level that are important and that constrain some kinds of properties. Nevertheless, it appears that before the onset of language, the earliest inductive inferences tend to be remarkably broad.

Overall, these induction data are consistent with our previous categorization findings. Thus, our findings from the object examination task, the sequential touching task, and the generalized imitation task converge on the conclusion that infants initially form broad, relatively undifferentiated concepts of animals, vehicles, furniture, and plants (with some evidence that artifacts become differentiated earlier than animals and plants, including earlier correct assignment of basic-level properties; Mandler & McDonough, 1999). Furthermore, these tasks all indicate that these domain-level concepts are not organized around individual features or overall perceptual appearance, but rather around some (possibly quite primitive) notion of kind.

In addition, these data tell us something very important about the way infants form associations. They indicate that property association and generalization are controlled not by the common features of objects or by the perceptual appearance of the objects that infants have actually observed, but instead are organized by the concepts infants have formed. In the initial stages the boundaries of these concepts are very broad. The world has been divided into a few global domains of different kinds of things. The meaning of these broad classes, such as animals or vehicles, does not arise from commonality of physical features. Babies do learn at least some of these features, of course; indeed, they must learn them to identify an object as a member of a particular category. In terms of meaning, however, it appears that infants observe the events in which animals and vehicles take part and use their interpretation of the events to conceptualize what sort of thing an animal or a vehicle is. Animals are things that move themselves and act on other things; vehicles are things that give animals rides. The most important aspect of this meaning creation is that it is the meaning of the class as a whole that determines what gets associated with what, not just the individual objects or features of objects actually experienced. So, for example, drinking is associated with self-movers and with containers, not just with the dogs one has seen drink or the cups one has drunk from. Note that this view does not claim that no associations between dogs and drinking or cups and drinking are formed—only that initially the associations are broader than that.

Thus, even though infants must use various physical features to tell animals such as dogs and cats apart, they do not rely on them when they are construing the meaning of an event or even when generalizing from it. When we model an event with a dog and give infants a choice between another dog and a cat or another dog and a rabbit to use for their imitations, they are as apt to choose the cat or the rabbit as the dog (Mandler & McDonough, 1998). They do not give a drink to a Flying Tiger airplane in spite of its prominent mouth. They use a key on forklifts and airplanes, associations that, of course, they have never observed. Infants presumably have not seen people sleeping in bathtubs or drinking from frying pans either, yet they generalize broadly to these pieces of furniture and containers. All of these phenomena provide evidence that associations are not controlled by individual features or objects but instead by object kind.

I assume that from an early age infants pick out features such as eyes, mouths, wheels, and windows. Some such features are necessary to recognize a new little exemplar as a member of a class. However, eyes and mouths have become associated with animate things moving and wheels and windows have become associated with inanimate things moving, and so these features can be used to identify these objects even when they are not engaging in their customary activities. In the typical real-world case, infants see a familiar object with various features engaging in animate activities. In our imitation task, the infants see only the features and must infer the relevant concepts. (Although our modeling provides relevant information, it does so only for the modeled objects, not the generalization objects.)

Why should we not say, then, as did Haith and Benson (1998), that because physical features are required to recognize an exemplar as a member of a category, it is those features that define the category? These investigators suggested that infants form a category first on the basis of physical features, and then they infer other characteristics as a result of the categorization. Given the great difficulties adults have forming disjunctive categories (Bruner et al., 1956), it seems unlikely that infants could do so by aggregating over the highly varied features found in superordinate categories (e.g., legs or fins or wings, fur or feathers or scales, etc.). This has been the major argument for why superordinate categories should be late developing—they do not have common features (Rosch & Mervis, 1975; Smith & Medin, 1981). The hypothesis also does not fit well with infants' lack of attention to many physical features or with the need for attention to detail that such an analytic attitude would require, as exemplified by the basic-level induction data just described (Mandler & McDonough, 1998). If an infant categorizes a cup, for example, solely or even primarily on the basis of its physical features, why do these features not control the associations of drinking with it? If an infant categorizes a car on the basis of four wheels, doors, and windows, why do these features not control the associations with keying? I agree with the importance of commonalities, but at the level of superordinate categories these are difficult to find insofar as physical features are concerned. Instead, the commonalities seem to reside in how exemplars behave within the context of events. The commonalities I have talked about, such as animate or inanimate motion, self-motion or caused motion, interactions with objects from a distance or being acted on by others, do characterize superordinate domains and should make it relatively easy to do global categorization. Once the global category has been formed, then different kinds of limbs or facial features can be associated with it.

I stress, however, that this point of view does not deny that perceptual similarity can influence the likelihood of making a generalization, particularly when making inferences within conceptual domains (e.g., Gelman & O'Reilley, 1988). Even adults often have little information to differentiate one animal species from another except physical appearance. To the extent that is so, they must rely on perceptual similarity and dissimilarity to regulate their inferences. However, they use differences in perceptual appearance to distinguish one kind from another, which is not the same as asserting that associations or generalizations are made on the basis of these differences.

Conclusions

I have argued for the necessity of distinguishing between conceptual and perceptual categories. Some such distinction is necessary because both kinds of categorization occur in young infants. Infants certainly do make use of similarity of appearance in forming perceptual categories and do so with ease and from an early age. However, infants also form conceptual categories at least by 7 months of age and do so in a way that largely ignores surface similarity. I would characterize the bases of the earliest concepts as theory-like, in that a small set of abstract distinctions is being used to define animals, vehicles, plants, and furniture as different kinds. I call these distinctions *defining* because they are necessary and sufficient for the simple inferences that infants make: What something looks like does not matter as much as whether it has these characteristics. These characteristics are more abstract than perceptual features. For example, even though motion can be considered a perceptual feature, what that motion actually looks like is not included in the notion of self-motion or the role of agent. These notions are themselves no longer perceptual (unless one wants to say that all mental processes are perceptual). Interestingly, the characteristics that seem to act like necessary and sufficient conditions for the infant may do so because the conceptual base is so meager. If the only way an infant conceptualizes an animal is as a self-mover, then if something cannot move by itself, how could it be an animal? This is undoubtedly something of an exaggeration, but it does suggest how concepts might be built up around a core that acts like a definition in spite of the more variable accretions of later experience that temper and qualify the initial formulation. The result would be the kind of radial categories built around core notions that typify adult cognition (Lakoff, 1987).

Even in this approach, perceptual information is fundamental. If I am correct that the earliest concept of animal is something like a self-mover that interacts with other objects from a distance, the underlying bases for these notions are information given by the perceptual system. In addition, infants must use perceptual appearance to identify an object as a member of a given conceptual class. . . .

It is for reasons such as these that I have argued for the necessity of differentiating perceptual and conceptual similarity in concept formation. At least in the early stages of development when the basis of the human conceptual system is being laid down, there is evidence that perceptual similarity is not much used in its formation. It is being used for perceptual categorization, but that is different from conceptual categorization, which depends on other kinds of information than what objects look like. There are several ways in which this difference manifests itself in the infancy period and, at least to some extent, throughout life.

First, perceptual categories work on different kinds of information than conceptual categories. . . .

Second, perceptual categories contain more detailed information (at least in infancy) than do conceptual categories. . . .

Third, much of the information in perceptual categories is inaccessible, whereas the contents of concepts are accessible for purposes of thought, problem solving, recall, and so on. . . .

Fourth, there is a different course of acquisition for the two kinds of categories. . . .

Last and most important, perceptual and conceptual categories serve different functions. Perceptual categorization is used for recognition and object identification. Conceptual categories, on the other hand, are used to control inductive generalization (and for other kinds of thought as well). . . .

Our developmental exploration has shown that beginning early in infancy more than one kind of categorization occurs. Given their different functions, reliance on different kinds of information, different degrees of selectivity in the information that is used, probable differences in accessibility, and different developmental time courses, it would seem wise not to assume that categorization is categorization is categorization. At the very least we must distinguish between perceptual categorization, which automatically computes perceptual similarity, and conceptual categorization, which rests on determining meaning. I have speculated that meaning in turn rests on what objects do, not what they look like. . . .

References

Bruner, J. S., Goodnow, J. J., & Austin, G. A. (1956). *A study of thinking.* New York: Wiley.

Carey, S. (1985). *Conceptual change in childhood.* Cambridge, MA: MIT Press.

DeLoache, J. S. (1989). Young children's understanding of the correspondence between a scale model and a larger space. *Cognitive Development, 4,* 121–139.

DeLoache, J. S., & Burns, N. M. (1994). Early understanding of the representational function of pictures. *Cognition, 52,* 83–110.

Gelman, S. A., & Coley, J. D. (1990). The importance of knowing a dodo is a bird: Categories and inferences in 2-year-old children. *Developmental Psychology, 26,* 796–804.

Gelman, S. A., & Markman, E. M. (1986). Categories and induction in young children. *Cognition, 23,* 183–209.

Gelman, S. A., & O'Reilley, A. W. (1988). Children's inductive inferences within superordinate categories: The role of language and category structure. *Child Development, 59,* 876–887.

Haith, M. M., & Benson, J. B. (1998). Infant cognition. In W. Damon (Series Ed.) & D. Kuhn & R. Siegler (Vol. Eds.), *Handbook of child psychology: Vol. 2. Cognition, perception, and language* (5th ed.). New York: Wiley.

Keil, F. C. (1991). The emergence of theoretical beliefs as constraints on concepts. In S. Carey & R. Gelman (Eds.), *The epigenesis of mind*. Hillsdale, NJ: Lawrence Erlbaum Associates, Inc.

Killen, M., & Uzgiris, I. C. (1981). Imitation of actions with objects: The role of social meaning. *Journal of Genetic Psychology, 138,* 219–229.

Lakoff, G. (1987). *Women, fire, and dangerous things*. Chicago: University of Chicago Press.

Mandler, J. M., & McDonough, L. (1996). Drinking and driving don't mix: Inductive generalization in infancy. *Cognition, 59,* 307–335.

Mandler, J. M., & McDonough, L. (1998). Studies in inductive inference in infancy. *Cognitive Psychology, 37,* 60–96.

Mandler, J. M., & McDonough, L. (1999). *Advancing downward to the basic level.* Manuscript submitted for publication.

McCune-Nicolich, L. (1981). Toward symbolic functioning: Structure of early use of pretend games and potential parallels with language. *Child Development, 52,* 785–797.

McDonough, L., & Mandler, J. M. (1998). Inductive generalization in 9- and 11-month-olds. *Developmental Science, 1,* 227–232.

O'Connell, B. G., & Gerard, A. B. (1985). Scripts and scraps: The development of sequential understanding. *Child Development, 56,* 671–681.

Quine, W. V. (1977). Natural kinds. In S. P. Schwartz (Ed.), *Naming, necessity, and natural kinds*. Ithaca, NY: Cornell University Press.

Rosch, E., & Mervis, C. B. (1975). Family resemblances: Studies in the internal structure of categories. *Cognitive Psychology, 7,* 573–605.

Smith, E. E., & Medin, D. L. (1981). *Categories and concepts*. Cambridge, MA: Harvard University Press.

NO 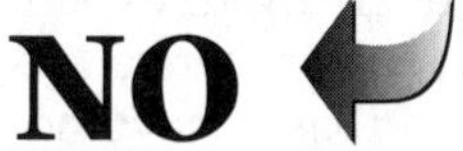

Eleanor J. Gibson

Commentary on Perceptual and Conceptual Processes in Infancy

I am honored to have the opportunity to comment on Jean Mandler's feature article about perceptual and conceptual processes in infancy. Her knowledge of the increasingly popular field of infant cognition is comprehensive, and her proposal to distinguish two types of categorization, perceptual and conceptual, is novel and interesting. I begin with a brief characterization of Mandler's theoretical position, go on to the ideas she presents in her feature article and some criticisms of them, and finally state my own position with regard to the relation between perception and conceptualization. This relation is of interest to both of us, and because her view is structural and mine functional, they are in strong contrast to one another.

Mandler is an enthusiastic and prolific contributor to present-day cognitive psychology of infancy. I characterize her view as structuralist, dwelling principally on mental content; as more akin to rationalism than to information processing; and as firmly based on the notion that perception is founded on a representation of whatever is perceived. The representation is a kind of mediator between information about the world and what is perceived, so perception itself is already a construction. Perception is basic, nevertheless, to the formation of categories of things and to concept formation.

Mandler discards the traditional notion that children progress developmentally from categorizing a set of objects as all looking alike to categorizing the set conceptually as the same kind of things. She believes that conceptual categorization begins early in life and "does not consist of adding conceptual information onto perceptual categories." It is, rather, conceptually based from the outset. The persistent difficulty of explaining how abstract concepts develop from earlier categories based on physical appearance vanishes, she believes, if it is recognized that there are two different processes of categorization from the start.

Perceptual categorization occurs as a result of passive exposure to visual stimuli and is concerned with the physical appearance of things. In content, it is a perceptual schema constructed via a computing process.

From *Journal of Cognition and Development,* vol. 1, February 2000, pp. 43–48.

Mandler illustrates the reality of this type of category, referring to experiments with infants as young as 3 months who learned to categorize pictures of, for example, dogs versus cats or horses versus zebras. I have not the slightest doubt that results such as these are genuine. Research over the past two decades has demonstrated convincingly that infants' powers of discrimination are astonishingly good and that they detect common information and invariants over contextual differences. However, these laboratory demonstrations of perceptual categories are a far cry from the scenes and events that constitute the daily circumstances of a young infant's life. For one thing, infants' experiences are always multimodal. They hear, feel, and smell as well as see what is going on around them. They have been hearing voices and feeling gravity and proprioceptive changes even before birth. Any event after birth, such as being picked up by a caretaker and spoken to, produces multimodal information of many kinds. In my opinion, what is perceived is a unified event, most certainly not a visual representation of an object. Indeed, vision is not necessarily the most prominent source of information, as it is immature in the first few months and may be reliably informative only when carried by motion. Motions occur over time, as indeed all events do. Exposure to a static scene, visual alone, is highly unusual in a baby's life.

Perceptual categories serve to identify objects, Mandler says, evidently primarily visually. She accepts the reality of perceptual categories, but distrusts the notion that these begin as basic-level categories and then move up the ladder to superordinate ones. What is meant by basic level? Apparently, specific instances of classes such as dogs or articles of furniture, with superordinate categories such as animals or household articles developing later in a sort of hierarchy. She maintains, rather, that categorization begins at a more global, domain level, such as animals or vehicles. Such categorization is more than a perceptual category that merely identifies objects. I share her distrust of the basic categories and the hierarchical development of structural relations between objects. However, the static, content-only character of her description of what is learned seems to be missing something vital. Where is action in all of this? What is the baby doing?

Conceptual categorization dealing with domains begins in infancy, in Mandler's opinion. It is not based on physical appearance, but on what things do. Commonality within the domain or category depends on the object's role in an event. Conceptual categories provide meanings (unlike perceptual categories). They do not simply add conceptual information to perceptual categories, but depend on "attentive, conscious analysis" of what is perceived. Conceptual processing is presumably abstract, and infants may organize domains around goal-directed activities in which objects are involved. I like this, except that we are soon back to representational content because, we are told, the results of perceptual analysis are in the form of image schemas. Image schemas are relational and are abstracted from events in which objects take place. Motion and paths characterizing events may be the object of perceptual analysis. For example, the concept of animal may be founded on analysis of biological motions. This is a good example.

I know from my own research that infants distinguish between rigid (inanimate) motion and elastic (animate) motion as early as 3 months of age. The difference is specified by two types of temporally invariant information. These temporal invariants are relational and abstract. I think it takes more than the discrimination of a difference to get to meaning, however. The image schemas represent "biological motion, self-motion, and contingent motion," but does that provide the meaning? Mandler says that it is "these redescriptions that give objects meaning." These ideas are more dynamic than standard structuralist ones, I must in fairness point out. Babies discover the kinds of things that animals or vehicles are by observing the events in which they take part. Commonalties reside in "how exemplars behave within the context of events" (p. 28). So far so good; is that the meaning?

Mandler describes many of her own experiments as illustrations of her point, but I have trouble understanding their relevance. In her research, typically, infants are simply presented with toys and not with events, and they presumably do not need to discover any common physical features. Indeed, she argues that perceptual categories need not developmentally precede conceptual ones. The physical features may be very different within a category, and some in her experiments must be quite foreign to an infant's experience. How does an infant determine that a toy tractor or fork-lift is the same "kind" as a toy car? By finding that they play the same role in events, evidently, but wouldn't one have to witness the events, at least?

I cite again Mandler's point that meaning is about what objects do, not what they look like, because I intend to talk about meaning, too. To explain how my thoughts on the issue differ, I begin with my view of perception, go on to its part in development and learning, and then to its role in the development of concepts. (These ideas are stated in more detail in E. J. Gibson & A. D. Pick, 2003.)

Perception is an active process of obtaining information from the environment. Even infants search for information about what is going on, what things are, and especially what they are good for—in other words, what they afford. Perception and action are reciprocal; perception obtains information for action, and action, in turn, informs perception. Action extends the reach, extends the view, and via proprioception provides information for what the perceiver is doing (information about oneself). Knowledge of an action and its consequences is vital for cognition, certainly as vital as knowing about the physical appearances of things.

Perception is not only active, it is directed and intentional. Information from the world does not simply fall on the helpless infant like rain on the ground, but is sought for; we listen, we do not just hear; we look, do not just see. By 4 to 5 months, babies are reaching for things, touching and mouthing them. Mandler's perceptual schema, on the contrary, is said to be "domain-specific, mandatory," and "not accessible to consciousness" (p. 7). I offer an example of intentional perceiving. Perception, being intentional, is embedded in a task. Consider the task of steering. Steering begins early in life as orienting to sounds and aiming toward moving objects, restricted at first to the eyes and head, positioning them to hear and look; it soon proceeds to the arms and the hands, and eventually to the whole body when locomotion begins. The active orienting and steering action is underwritten by perception from the start. It will be noted that the underwriting is multimodal, combining information from looking and listening with proprioceptive information from the perceiver's own body–kinesthetic information from the muscles turning the head, limbs and torso, and information from vestibular organs that keep one's place in the surroundings, about "where I am" and "where I am going." Even orienting is goal directed.

Perception is not only active and intentional, it is meaningful. What in fact do we perceive? Visual or acoustic or proprioceptive information? Certainly not. What is perceived is an event, relating a happening, place, or thing in the world to the perceiver herself or himself. This relation is referred to as an *affordance,* a term coined by J. J. Gibson (1979; see also E. J. Gibson & A. D. Pick, 2003). It refers to an organism–environment relation, one that defines a fit (or lack of it) between the two. A mouse walking toward a wall detects a small hole in the wall; the mouse perceives the hole to be large enough to squeeze through, an organism–environment fit. When the consequences of a perception–action cycle are observed, perceptual learning occurs. Perceiving the affordance is meaningful. An affordance frequently defines a user relation, based on information that some happening or resource offered by the environment can be beneficial, acted on, or used by the perceiver. What is perceived may be an object, but almost certainly an object embedded in an event. An infant lying in his or her crib, listening to and watching a door opening, may detect the consequent footsteps and appearance of a caretaker, a very meaningful event for an infant. All of this goes on over time and is anything but static.

Meanings are learned and rest on information about some event in the world and at the same time information about the perceiver, what he or she is doing, and what his or her state is. Here, I believe, is the origin of meaning, via perceptual learning of affordances in the course of development. Perception is educable; information comes to specify an affordance, in a process of differentiation and selection (E. J. Gibson & A. D. Pick, 2003). It seems likely that all perceived affordances are learned, starting very early. I cite an instructive example from the laboratory.

An experiment by van der Meer, van der Weel, and Lee (1995) with infants younger than 1 month of age found evidence of learned control of a limb movement following an experimental intervention. A weight was strapped to one of the infant's wrists, and the infant turned on one side so that only the hand on that side could be viewed when raised. Infants quickly learned to raise a weighted limb only when the hand could be viewed. When a mirror was positioned to make viewing possible on that side, the hand that could be viewed in the mirror was raised. The sight of the infant's own hand, raised intentionally, produced useful consequences. Not only could the infants feel themselves controlling the action; when the hand appeared, it provided a unique standard for comparisons of size, shape, locus, and movement with any features of the layout such as the crib frame, a toy, or the room structure. This experiment demonstrates that a neonate can learn to control a limb movement to produce interesting and useful consequences, for instance information about the effects of occlusion during movement of the limb and size constancy. There is good reason to suppose that such actions occur frequently and spontaneously. In this simple action something meaningful is learned about oneself and the world.

Now, what about conceptualization? I illustrate my view with two examples of very abstract concepts that are based on perceptual learning. The first is agency. Both the earlier examples (steering and raising a weighted limb) are examples of the development of a concept of *agency,* controlling a self-produced action that is a means to a goal or that provides needed information about features of the world. In both cases, the consequences are important in relation to the perceiver and actor, and detection of this relation is possible because both proprioceptive and exteroceptive information are produced, perceived in relation to one another. Relations are abstract per se, so detecting one is an instance of perceptual learning of something abstract. As infants discover their ability to control events in diverse situations, the perceived relation is generalized, resulting in a concept of agency. Relational information has specified the affordance of control, and it is generalizable over a broad category of self-produced events.

My second example, *animacy,* is also a very broad category. It is specified in many ways, some of which are readily perceptible to young infants. Perhaps responsiveness in a caretaker is most immediately informative. When infants cry, coo, or make gestures such as smiling or grimacing, the caretaker acts, responding to the infant's sounds and gestures. These events can be very different from one another, but all are characterized by the same affordance, response to one's own actions. Other information specifying animacy such as type of motion (nonrigid, deforming motion like that of a face breaking into a smile or speaking) and spontaneity of movement are gradually assimilated into a very broad concept through perceptual learning and generalization based on common specification of affordances.

Categorization is, thus, based on perception and perceptual learning of affordances, which are meaningful, relational, and necessarily abstract. I do not, therefore, see a need for separating perceptual from conceptual categories. My argument rests here, and I await the response.

References

Gibson, E. J., & Pick, A. D. (2003). *An ecological approach to perceptual learning and development.* New York: Oxford University Press.

Gibson, J. J. (1979). *The ecological approach to visual perception.* Boston: Houghton Mifflin.

van der Meer, A. H. L., van der Weel, F. A., & Lee, D. N. (1995). The functional significance of arm movements in neonates. *Science, 267,* 693–695.

POSTSCRIPT

Can Infants Develop Abstract Concepts?

In the first selection, Mandler is suggesting that infants develop perceptual abilities separately from conceptual abilities, and that conceptual abstract abilities are apparent in infants as young as 9 months old. Mandler's findings are particularly interesting in that several of the toy items represented objects the infants had never seen before, such as forklifts. Her conclusions are that infants place items in conceptual categories based on what they do, rather than perceptual categories based on how things look. The primary categories used in Mandler's research are furniture, vehicles, animals, and plants.

Gibson, in the second selection, does not find the results of Mandler's research to be farfetched or odd, but her interpretation of the infants' behaviors is quite different from Mandler's. Gibson believes that perceptual abilities develop first and later lead a child to create conceptually based meaningful categories. Perception, in Gibson's view, is the active process of observing the environment in order to better understand and know how to interact. The more one interacts with the environment, the better one understands or perceives the way items in the environment work. Perception is not static and one dimensional, as in looking at a picture. Perception is the awareness, with all one's sensory abilities, of an event that unfolds over time. Gibson makes the case that perception is not void of meaning. Perceiving an event, such as the refrigerator door being open, something taken out, and quickly baby has her favorite applesauce, is quite meaningful. As the infant observes these meaningful events, Gibson believes that perception will lead to conceptual development.

Mandler's suggestion that infants are capable of any type of abstract thinking is counter to traditional cognitive developmental psychology. According to the most well-known and influential researcher in this field, Jean Piaget, infants are focused on the sensory information that is continually coming from the environment as well as movement, including both their own body movement and the sensation of being moved. According to standard Piagetian theory, babies' perceptual exploration leads to the next stage of cognitive development, usually between 18 and 24 months of age, when babies begin to form basic concepts. Many of these early basic concepts are based on appearance. According to Piaget, children must progress to this fourth and highest stage, Formal Operations, before abstract thinking is apparent. For most children, this doesn't occur until approximately 11 years old. Mandler's suggestion that abstract conceptual reasoning may be apparent at 11 months old is striking when compared to the traditional theory.

The debate here is not over the accuracy of the findings in infant research, but rather over how they should be interpreted. It is so easy to attribute more meaning than what is actually indicated by a behavior, particularly in a preverbal or non-verbal being. For example, if you've had a pet, such as a dog, that responds to your voice you may start to think that the dog cognitively understands your words. If you look at your dog and say, in your dog-loving voice, "You're the best dog," chances are your dog will wag its tail, maybe lick your hand, and in general get excited and active. Before you attribute great cognitive skills to your dog, consider that if you say, in your dog-loving voice, "You are the most stupid, ugly dog," chances are your dog will still wag its tail and lick your hand. Scientists must be careful in the assumptions they make, particularly when language is absent from the analysis.

Suggested Readings

Cohen, D. *How the Child's Mind Develops* (New York: Routledge, 2001).

Lacerda, F. J., von Hofsten, C., and Heimann, M. (Editors), *Emerging Cognitive Abilities in Early Infancy* (Mahwah, NJ: Lawrence Erlbaum, 2000).

Rakison, D. H., and Oakes, L. M. (Editors), *Early Category and Concept Development* (New York: Oxford Press, 2003).

Scholnick, E. K., Gelman, S., Miller, P. H., and Nelson, K. (Editors), *Conceptual Development: Piaget's Legacy* (Mahwah, NJ: Lawrence Erlbaum, 1999).

Stein, N. L., Rabinowitz, M., and Bauer, P. J. (Editors), *Representation, Memory, and Development: Essays in Honor of Jean Mandler* (Mahwah, NJ: Lawrence Erlbaum, 2002).

ISSUE 6

Is Sensory Information the Strongest Part of a Stored Concept?

YES: Helen Bird, David Howard, and Sue Franklin, from "Why Is a Verb Like an Inanimate Object? Grammatical Category and Semantic Category Deficits," *Brain and Language* (2000)

NO: Kevin Shapiro and Alfonso Caramazza, from "Sometimes a Noun Is Just a Noun: Comments on Bird, Howard, and Franklin," *Brain and Language* (2001)

ISSUE SUMMARY

YES: Researchers and lecturers Helen Bird, David Howard, and Sue Franklin present research consistent with a new model of knowledge representation that emphasizes sensory and functional categories.

NO: Linguistic researchers Kevin Shapiro and Alfonso Caramazza provide numerous challenges to the new model and caution against a search for one explanatory model.

Cognitive scientists often work with people who have had a brain injury to better understand cognitive functions and deficits, particularly when investigating language processing. Obviously researchers cannot damage a healthy human brain in order to study the corresponding deficits. They can, however, study the thinking and behaviors of those who have experienced brain trauma. When brain cells have been damaged such that they cannot function, the damaged tissue is referred to as a lesion. The purpose of these types of studies is to relate patients' intact abilities to the parts of the brain that are healthy and any deficits to the parts of the brain with lesions.

By studying people who have aphasia, the inability to process or use words due to a brain lesion, cognitive scientists can learn more about the ways healthy people store and process language. We turn mental representations or thoughts into verbal behaviors so easily and quickly that we are unaware of the complex transformations that take place in our brain. For example, suppose you see your friend wearing a new red shirt and you want to express how much you like it. You must match that mental representation with the appropriate words retrieved from long-term memory, arrange the words in the appropriate grammatical order, and then take action to speak the words, "I really like that red shirt." In order to find the appropriate words among all the many words in your long-term memory, you must follow an organizational scheme that is based on conceptual groupings.

People who have aphasia have lost their ability to communicate with words due to some kind of brain damage. An individual with fluent aphasia will speak words without knowing what they mean, and often use words incorrectly and in the wrong context. Fluent aphasia can be categorized as "lexical spared, semantic deficit." In this case the brain damage spared the ability to retrieve the word (lexical aspect) from memory; however, the damage has caused the loss or inability to retrieve the meaning (semantic aspect) of the word. Individuals who have the opposite situation—that is, they know what they want to say, the concept is in their mind, but they can't come up with the right words—are suffering from motor aphasia, which is also called ataxic, expressive, or Broca's aphasia. There are many other types of aphasia, such as anomic, which is the inability to name objects, and syntactic, which is the inability to use proper grammar.

By observing the types of language communication various patients with aphasia can produce, and by relating the abilities and inabilities to the type of brain lesions in each patient, cognitive scientists have proposed several theories regarding how our brains store various types of knowledge. These are often called models of knowledge representation. Bird, Howard, and Franklin explain that the more accepted model is that our brains store semantic category-specific information, such as whether a word refers to an object, animal, or plant, separately from grammatical category-specific information, such as the way a verb implies action or connection with the other words in a sentence. Referring back to the example of the shirt, this model suggests you have stored the meaning (semantic category) of the word *shirt* as clothing worn on the upper part of the body as something separate from your understanding of the word *shirt* as a noun (grammatical category). This would be consistent with observed behaviors in patients with fluent aphasia, who would know the word *shirt* but not know what it means and use it inappropriately, and those with motor or non-fluent aphasia, who would know the concept of shirt and try to express that concept but cannot remember the actual word *shirt*.

In the following selections, Bird, et al., make the case that the data thought to indicate grammatical category-specific information have been misinterpreted. They propose that all data are stored in semantic categories, with the primary distinctions being the amount of sensory information or imageability and the amount of function or action associated with the item. In the second selection, Shapiro and Caramazza attempt to discredit the primary tenets of this new model and warn against trying to explain all types of aphasia with one grand theory.

Helen Bird, David Howard, and Sue Franklin

Why Is a Verb Like an Inanimate Object?

. . . Neuropsychological research has paid much attention in recent years to apparent dissociations in the categories of words which can be selectively impaired or spared after brain damage. There are two main bodies of literature: one investigates deficits specific to grammatical word classes, such as for function versus content words (see Pulvermuller, 1992, pp. 191–192, for a good summary), or for classes within the content word domain, such as for nouns and verbs, summarized in Berndt, Mitchum, Haendiges, and Sandson (1997). The second describes impairments for specific semantic categories, such as animals versus inanimate objects (Hart, Berndt, and Caramazza, 1985; Hillis & Caramazza, 1991; and see Caramazza, 1998, and Grossman, 1998, for summaries of semantic category deficits). Within both of these areas, the question arises as to whether true category-specific deficits occur or whether the phenomenon can be explained by other confounding variables. In both cases this question has not been satisfactorily resolved: evidence has been presented which supports both explanations.

A number of psycholinguistic variables have been shown to affect word retrieval in aphasia. Low frequency words are generally more difficult to retrieve than high frequency (Ellis, Miller, & Sin, 1983; Howard, Patterson, Franklin, Morton, & Orchard-Lisle, 1984; Kay & Ellis, 1987), although a reverse frequency effect has also been reported (Marshall, Pring, Robson, & Chiat, 1998.) Similarly, the number of phonemes or syllables in a word can affect retrieval, with either longer words being harder (Howard et al., 1984) or easier (Best, 1995) to retrieve. Imageability (the case with which a word produces a mental image) is necessarily correlated with concreteness, but they are not exactly the same thing. Items rated lower in imageability (and hence usually more abstract) are less well retrieved in aphasia (Franklin, Howard, & Patterson, 1995; Nickels & Howard, 1995), but again the reverse effect has been reported both in semantic dementia (Breedin, Saffran, & Coslett, 1994) and aphasia (Marshall, Chiat, Robson, & Pring, 1996).

This paper draws strands of both grammatical and semantic category deficits together in a study of a small case series and suggests that the same

From *Brain and Language,* vol. 72, no. 3, May 2000, pp. 246–256, 300–301, 304.

phenomenon might account for both types of category effects in aphasia. We make two main assertions. The first is that many reported "grammatical class-specific deficits" are not truly class specific, but the result of the confounding of class with imageability. The second assertion is that "true" word class-specific deficits are in fact due to differences in the distributions of semantic feature types, analogous with the favored explanation of semantic category deficits. We suggest that pictureable objects have a greater weighting of sensory features compared with actions, which are primarily motor and functional. Thus, in general, concrete nouns have more perceptual features, and verbs (as well as abstract nouns) more functional.

Semantic Category-Specific Deficits

. . . Category-specific semantic deficits have been explained in various ways. One proposal is that the semantic store might be categorically organized, with (at least partially) separate meaning representations for categories, such as animals, fruit, and vegetables (Hart et al., 1985). A second suggestion is that animate and inanimate items may differ because of differences in the proportions of shared features. McRae, de Sa, and Seidenberg (1997) argue that animate items have greater clustering of semantic features: for example, many animals share the same features of eyes, ears, nose, fur, four legs, and so on. Thus there is much overlap, and the retrieval of a single item might be impeded by having so many similar semantic competitors. A third explanation is that the semantic representations of animals and man-made items differ primarily in terms of the weighting of sensory and functional information contained in their representations, such that the semantics of animals, birds, fruit, and vegetables is heavily based on the senses, particularly vision (Warrington & Shallice, 1984), while for artifacts function is more important. . . .

Grammatical Category-Specific Deficits

The aphasia literature abounds with cases of patients who apparently find retrieval of verbs more difficult than that of nouns (Caramazza & Hillis, 1991; Jonkers & Bastiaanse, 1998; Zingeser & Berndt, 1988; Orpwood & Warrington, 1995; Rapp & Caramazza, 1998). Many of these patients are nonfluent and agrammatic (Zingeser & Berndt, 1990; Miceli, Silveri, Villa, & Caramazza, 1984). Fluent anomic patients are reported to be impaired in the retrieval of nouns, but in most cases their verb retrieval is not formally tested (Kay & Ellis, 1987). The spontaneous speech of fluent anomic patients often lacks nouns, but seems to have sufficient verbs to allow grammatical speech production. It has been demonstrated that an inability to produce anything but high frequency words would result in this pattern (Marshall, 1977; Bird, Lambon Ralph, Patterson, & Hodges, 2000). In studies comparing noun and verb production in single word naming, frequency and length are normally controlled, but not imageability (Hillis & Caramazza, 1995; Miozzo, Soardi, & Cappa, 1994; Berndt et al., 1997; Bastiaanse &

Jonkers, 1998). It can be assumed that all items used in confrontation naming must necessarily be quite highly imageable, but this does not mean that items are equally imageable. We will return to this problem later. . . .

Why a Verb Is Like an Inanimate Object

In a survey of neuroanatomical correlates of category-specific disorders, Gainotti et al. (1995) suggest that different categories of knowledge might be located at specific brain areas linked with the perceptual and motor brain mechanisms needed to acquire these concepts. They find that patients reported to have a verb deficit tend to have lesions involving anterosuperior portions of the left temporal lobe and the inferoposterior parts of the left frontal lobe, whereas deficits in the production of nouns correlate with lesions of the lateral and inferior parts of the temporal lobe which extend toward the posterior association areas. They refer to the Geschwind (1967) model suggesting that sensory semantic information might converge in posterior association areas and that this is why object names are impaired with such lesions. Similarly, action names, for which semantic representations must depend greatly on motor schemata, suffer when more anterior portions of the brain are lesioned. Gainotti et al. (1995) suggest therefore that the differing features of the semantic representations of verbs and nouns lie behind their differential impairment found in brain damage and that this correlates with areas of the brain known to be associated with motor and sensory functions.

The Gainotti et al. (1995) survey of deficits for living and nonliving categories shows quite a consistent pattern of lesions also involving the inferior part of the temporal lobes in cases of impairment of living things (but IW, the Lambon Ralph et al. (1998) patient is an exception). There is, therefore, an area of the brain which is affected both in deficits of noun production (with spared verbs) and semantic deficits for living things, which suggests that both phenomena can be explained by damage to part of the semantic system which "may play a critical role in processing, storing and retrieving the semantic representations of these semantic categories" (Gainotti et al., 1995, pp. 259–260). Category-specific disorders for inanimate items correlate with lesions involving frontoparietal areas, which correspond with somatosensory and motor functions. We have already seen that verb deficits too are associated with more frontal lesions. Deficits for inanimate objects, such as tools, are often associated with a corresponding deficit for body parts. The most important semantic feature of tools and body parts is surely what one does with them: body parts particularly involve movement and tools involved manipulation and use (a functional rather than sensory weighting). In other words, their actions and how they are acted upon are the most salient parts of their meaning. Herein lies the similarity of verbal function and semantic content of verbs and man-made items and body parts. It should be no surprise, therefore, that similar areas of cortex should be associated with these items and that patients for whom naming of inanimate objects is spared relative to animates should also have action naming spared relative to objects in general.

The first section of this paper describes an attempt to model semantic space in terms of sensory and functional feature representations. Representations of "animate nouns," "inanimate nouns," and "verbs" are produced simply by varying the distributions of these types of features. Four models are presented, with differences in design and in the assumptions of the actual ratio of sensory to functional features. Each is tested by selectively damaging feature types, and the resulting patterns of deficits in word naming are described. We demonstrate that the same basic predictions arise from each of these models: deficits for inanimate objects should be accompanied by poor verb naming, and sparing of verb naming should co-occur with sparing of the production of inanimate objects relative to living things.

We go on to investigate these predictions in two patient groups, "verb deficit" and "verb spared." First we examine the robustness of the noun–verb effects using abstract as well as pictureable items. These results suggest that many apparent verb deficits are in fact due to imageability effects: when imageability is controlled, performance on nouns and verbs is equal. Then we compare the patient groups' performance in naming animate and inanimate nouns, to demonstrate that the "verb spared" group are indeed worse at naming animate nouns. Finally we test these patients on definition production and show that, as predicted, the "verb spared, inanimate spared" group suffer a deficit for sensory feature knowledge. We will conclude that this sensory feature deficit is the cause of both their animacy effect and the grammatical class effect shown in picture naming. . . .

Further investigation of three verb deficit and three verb spared patients showed that their grammatical class deficit was not present when tested on more abstract items. Verb deficit patients performed poorly on these abstract nouns and verbs, as they have strong imageability effects, which, we believe, are the reason for their apparent verb deficit. This is because, in a picture naming test, verbs are rated less imageable than nouns, and control cannot be achieved for imageability in such a test. Verb spared patients, however, were not spared at verbs because of a reverse imageability effect. Their impairment for naming concrete nouns was due to damage to sensory features in semantic representations. Thus they were better at naming inanimate objects, which do not depend as heavily on sensory information as do animates, and for the same reason they were better at naming verbs.

Confirmation of their sensory feature deficit came from the task requiring definitions to be produced to a list of animals and inanimate objects controlled for imageability. The verb deficit patients gave impoverished definitions, but the quality of their definitions was equal for animates and inanimates, and they seemed to produce the features which were most salient (more sensory for animals, but more functional for objects). In contrast, the verb spared patients gave much poorer quality definitions for animals, and this was because they suffered a significant lack of sensory information across all items. We conclude that the pattern of spared verbs and spared inanimates shown by the verb spared group was due to damage to sensory features in semantics. The verb deficit patients did not have functional feature damage, but their pattern of deficits was the result of a raised threshold, so that a greater number of total features needed to be activated in order to access word forms. . . . We suggest, therefore, that imageability, while correlated with sensory features, is more a measure of semantic richness, and the more semantic richness associated with a word, the more likely it is to be produced on demand (while all other variables are held constant). While the verb deficit patients presented here did not have specific functional feature damage, our models suggest that verb deficit patients will exist which do and that these patients should show a reverse animacy effect. . . .

We believe these data point to a single cause for the relative difficulties in retrieval of both grammatical and semantic categories for the patients assessed here. We have proposed the inanimate/animate distinction is in part due to weighting of functional and sensory information and in part due to the semantic representations of animate items having features with a greater tendency to overlap or "cluster." If our assertion is true, this entails that supposed "grammatical class" effects arise at the level of semantics and not at a lexical level. . . .

Semantic category deficits have been generally assumed to arise at the level of semantics: we propose that grammatical category deficits arise at the same level. Apparent verb deficits need to be scrutinized in more detail and in better controlled conditions, before a simple imageability effect can be eliminated: we would even go as far as to claim that true "verb deficits" do not exist, when imageability differences between verbs and nouns are taken into account. We have shown that it is possible (though rare) for noun production to be differentially impaired compared with that of verbs, but only for the most concrete items. This assertion, however, also carries a caveat: there are insufficient (if any) verbs which are as highly imageable as the kinds of nouns that are impaired in these patients, so that controlled testing is rendered impossible. The coincidence of poor pictureable noun naming relative to verbs, poor naming of animate nouns relative to inanimates, and poor production of sensory information in definitions relative to functional points to an impairment of the sensory features of semantic representations relative to functional features. This is in agreement with a model of distributed semantics over a large area of the cortex, which in the case of the multitude of so-called "verb deficit" patients might have suffered physically widespread (though varying in depth) damage. In the case of verb spared patients, we suggest that the unusual nature of their impairment might be due to damage to a relatively discrete area of the semantic cortex which deals specifically with sensory semantic information.

References

Bastiaanse, R., & Jonkers, R. (1998). Verb retrieval in action naming and spontaneous speech in agrammatic and anomic aphasia. *Aphasiology, 12,* 951–969.

Berndt, R. S., Mitchum, C. C., Haerdiges, A. N., & Sandson, J. (1997). Verb retrieval in aphasia: 1. Characterizing single word impairments. *Brain and Language, 56,* 68–106.

Best, W. (1995). A reverse length effect in dysphasic naming: When elephant is easier than ant. *Cortex, 31.*

Bird, H., Lambon Ralph, M. A., Patterson, K., & Hodges, J. (2000). The rise and fall of frequency and imageability: how the progression of semantic dementia impacts on noun and verb production in the Cookie Theft description. *Brain & Language,* doi:10.1006/brln.2000.2293.

Breedin, S. D., Saffran, E. M., & Coslett, H. B. (1991). Reversal of the concreteness effect in a patient with semantic dementia. *Cognitive Neuropsychology, 11,* 617–660.

Caramazza, A. (1998). The interpretation of semantic category-specific deficits: What do they reveal about the organization of conceptual knowledge in the brain? *Neurocase, 4,* 265–272.

Caramazza, A., & Hillis, A. E. (1991). Lexical organization of nouns and verbs in the brain. *Nature, 349,* 788–790.

Ellis, A. W., Miller, D., & Sin, G. (1983). Wernicke's aphasia and normal language processing: a case study in cognitive neuropsychology. *Cognition, 15,* 111–144.

Franklin, S., Howard, D., & Patterson, K. (1995). Abstract word anomia. *Cognitive Neuropsychology, 12,* 519–566.

Gainotti, G., Silveri, M. C., Daniele, A., & Giustolisit, L. (1995). Neuroanatomical correlates of category specific semantic disorders: a critical survey. *Memory, 3,* 247–264.

Geschwind, N. (1967). The varieties of naming errors. *Cortex, 3,* 97–112.

Grossman, M. (1998). Not all words are created equal: Category specific deficits in central nervous system disease. *Neurology, 50,* 324–325.

Hart, J. Jr., Berndt, R. S., & Caramazza, A. (1985). Category-specific naming deficit following cerebral infarction. *Nature, 316,* 439–440.

Hillis, A. E., & Caramazza, A. (1991). Category-specific naming and comprehension impairment: A double dissociation. *Brain, 114,* 2081–2094.

Hillis, A. E., & Caramazza, A. (1995). Representation of grammatical categories of words in the brain. *Journal of Cognitive Neuroscience, 7,* 396–407.

Howard, D., Patterson, K., Franklin, S., Morton, J., & Orchard Lisle, V. (1984). Variability and consistency in picture naming by aphasic patients. In E. Rose (Ed.), *Advances in neurology*. Vol. 42. *Progress in aphasiology*. New York: Raven Press. Pp. 263–276.

Jonkers, R., & Bastiaanse, R. (1998). How selective are selective word class deficits? Two case studies of action and object naming. *Aphasiology, 12,* 215–256.

Kay, J., & Ellis, A. W. (1987). A cognitive neuropsychological case study of anomia: Implications for psychological models of word retrieval. *Brain, 110,* 613–629.

Lambon Ralph, M. A., Howard, D., Nightingale. G., & Ellis. A. W. (1998). Are living and non living category specific deficits causally linked to impaired perceptual or associative knowledge? Evidence from a category specific double dissociation. *Neurocase, 4,* 311–338.

Marshall, J., Chiat, S., Robson, J., & Pring, T. (1996). Calling a salad a federation: An investigation of semantic jargon. Part 2 Verbs. *Journal of Neurolinguistics, 9,* 251–260.

Marshall, J., Pring, T., Robson, J., & Chiat, S. (1998). When ottoman is easier than chair: An inverse frequency effect in jargon aphasia? *Brain and Language, 65,* 78–81.

Marshall, J. C. (1977). Disorders in the expression of language. In J. Morton & J. C. Marshall (Eds.), *Psycholinguistics series*. London: Elek Science.

Miceli, G., Silveri, M. C., Villa, G., & Caramazza, A. (1984). On the basis for the agrammatic's difficulty in producing main verbs. *Contex, 20,* 297–220.

Miozzo, A., Soardi. M., & Cappa, S. F. (1991). Pure anomia with spared action naming due to a left temporal lesion. *Neuropsychologia, 32,* 1101–1109.

Nickels, L., & Howard, D. (1995). Aphasic naming. What matters? *Neuropsychologia, 33,* 1281–1303.

Orpwood, L., & Warrington, E. K. (1995). Word specific impairments in naming and spelling but not in reading. *Cortex, 31,* 239–265.

Pulvermuller. F. (1992). Constituents of a neurological theory of language. *Concepts in Neuroscience, 3,* 157–200.

Rapp, B., & Caramazza, A. (1998). A case of selective difficulty in writing verbs. *Neurocase, 4,* 127–140.

Warrington, E. K., & Shallice, T. (1984). Category specific semantic impairments. *Brain, 107,* 829–854.

Zingeser, L. B., & Berndt, R. S. (1988). Grammatical class and context effect in a case of pure anomia: Implications for models of language production. *Cognitive Neuropsychology, 64,* 475–516.

Zingeser, L. B., & Berndt, R. S. (1990). Retrieval of nouns and verbs in agrammatism and anomia. *Brain and Language, 39,* 14–32.

NO 

Kevin Shapiro and Alfonso Caramazza

Sometimes a Noun Is Just a Noun: Comments on Bird, Howard, and Franklin

. . . Among the hallmarks of clinical neuropsychology are category-specific deficits, in which patients are unable to name or reason about particular categories of words (nouns, verbs, or function words) or objects (animals, artifacts, or foods) while knowledge about other, unaffected categories is broadly intact. When the category in question corresponds to a set of related objects, it seems only reasonable to assume that naming difficulties arise at the level of meaning or semantics, prior to the stages in lexical access at which information about word form and syntactic function becomes available. By contrast, there is more controversy as to the level(s) at which deficits restricted to categories relevant only in the domain of language, like nouns and verbs, might originate.

Bates, Chen, Tzeng, Li, and Opie (1991) have distinguished three broad classes of explanations for observed dissociations between noun and verb processing: grammatical explanations, semantic-conceptual explanations, and lexical explanations. The first group of hypotheses is centered around the correlation, observed in many patients with so-called agrammatic or Broca's aphasia, between an inability to produce fluent speech and a specific difficulty in retrieving main verbs (Miceli, Silveri, Villa, & Caramazza, 1984). Many models of speech production assume that verbs play a crucial role in syntactic processing, specifying which noun arguments can occur in a sentence and how they are arranged (Bock, 1987; Garrett, 1988). Consequently, it is possible that a breakdown in processing the argument structures of sentences in agrammatism can lead to observed deficits in retrieving main verbs or vice versa (Saffran, 1982). Such "grammatical" explanations for category-specific deficits may yield important insights into patterns of verb production in nonfluent patients, but generally they are not equipped to account for selective noun deficits or naming deficits in fluent aphasic patients.

Semantic-conceptual explanations for grammatical category-specific deficits hinge upon the different sorts of meaning associated with nouns

From *Brain and Language,* February, 2001, pp. 202–212.

and verbs—that is, the idea that nouns prototypically refer to concrete objects, while prototypical verbs express reportable actions. Accounts in this class essentially reduce grammatical categories to semantic categories, assuming that mental representations of most nouns are localized in brain regions that also subserve the processing of more general semantic knowledge about concrete properties of objects—possibly in regions that have input from "sensory association" areas, like the inferior temporal lobe. By the same token, representations of verbs should be subserved by regions important for knowledge about actions, perhaps somewhere in the frontal cortex near motor/premotor areas. Grammatical class-specific deficits, which may not really be based on grammatical class at all, arise by dint of focal damage to these patches of neural tissue (Damasio & Tranel, 1993).

Last, there is a class of explanations which posit that lexical representations for words include features that specify their form class, or grammatical category, separate from features relating to phonology or semantics. Grammatical category information relating to nouns and verbs may be stored in different cortical areas, which can be damaged selectively following stroke or other trauma (Miceli et al., 1984, 1988; Caramazza & Hillis, 1991; Hillis & Caramazza, 1995). Lexical explanations of this sort do not depend on an association of grammatical class-specific deficits with either global syntactic difficulties (as with grammatical explanations) or problems with certain semantic categories of words (as with semantic-conceptual explanations). As a consequence, certain lexical explanations appear to be best equipped to explain cases of category-specific deficits in which the patients are fluent, or have apparently intact semantic knowledge, or both. Nevertheless, the difficulty of accounting for some such deficits by reference to semantics has not dissuaded many researchers from suggesting that all deficits that seem to be specific to one grammatical category are in fact based in the semantic system.

Bird, Howard, and Franklin (2000) propose a two-pronged semantic-conceptual account that attributes verb deficits and noun deficits to two distinct mechanisms. In fact, they regard the former as largely illusory: What appear to be deficits in verb production are not class-specific but rather are epiphenomena of the lower imageability of verbs, on average, compared to concrete nouns. Presumably, if we were to devise a naming test in which noun and verb targets were matched for imageability (as well as frequency, length, and other relevant factors), we should never find a patient significantly better at naming the nouns: as Bird and colleagues write, "we would even go so far as to claim that true 'verb deficits' do not exist, when imageability differences between verbs and nouns are taken into account" (p. 304). This claim is ostensibly corroborated by the naming performance of three "verb deficit" patients described in the article (IB, JM, and TJ), whose difficulties at producing verbs relative to nouns in confrontational picture-naming tasks are not replicated in other tasks, such as naming to definition, where noun and verb targets are matched for imageability.

Observed deficits in noun production, by contrast, are said to arise from differences in the distribution of semantic feature types. According to this explanation, the naming of nouns representing concrete objects relies more heavily on sensory features than the naming of actions, whose semantic representations are more heavily weighted with functional features. Within the category of nouns, living things depend more heavily on sensory features than do nonliving things. Therefore, damage to areas of the brain where primarily sensory features are encoded should adversely affect the naming of concrete nouns, and especially animate concrete nouns, while verb production should appear to be spared in comparison. In support of such a model, the authors present data from three "verb spared" patients (JS, ML, and NT), who are described as being impaired at naming living things compared to nonliving things and at retrieving sensory information about target items in a definition task.

The main theoretical assumptions behind the semantic-conceptual hypothesis put forward by Bird and colleagues are (1) that conceptual knowledge is organized in the brain in a way that distinguishes between information derived from the senses (vision, audition, olfaction, etc.), on the one hand, and functional information, on the other; and (2) that certain classes of concepts (e.g., living things and artifacts) rely more heavily on one type of information than the other. These two assumptions lie at the core of a family of related accounts, collectively dubbed the sensory/functional theory (SFT) by Caramazza and Shelton (1998), that were originally proposed to account for differences in the abilities of some aphasic patients to name living compared to nonliving things (Allport, 1985; Gainotti & Silveri, 1996; Hart & Gordon, 1992; Shallice, 1988; Silveri & Gainotti, 1988; Warrington & McCarthy, 1983, 1987; Warrington & Shallice, 1984). According to the variant proposed by Bird and colleagues, which we will call the "extended sensory/functional theory" (ESFT) for ease of reference, animates are regarded as the most prototypical (i.e., highly sensory-loaded) nouns. Therefore, any deficit in noun naming compared to verb naming should be accompanied by relatively greater difficulties naming living items compared to nonliving items.

In order to determine whether this and other predictions of the ESFT are likely to be correct, we need to examine more closely the theory's three basic tenets. The first concerns the architecture of the cognitive system: The ESFT assumes that the distribution of sensory and functional information is such that representations of living things include a much higher proportion of sensory information than do representations of nonliving things. These in turn must include more sensory information than do representation of actions. This assumption is obviously shared by other versions of the SFT, though a crucial problem in comparing various formulations of the model is that there is a good deal of ambiguity in what kind of information counts as functional. Bird and coworkers seem to understand the latter to include knowledge about the function of an object as well as other nonsensory information (for instance, where something is found). As we shall see, however, other authors have defined functional features more strictly (e.g., Farah & McClelland, 1991).

Second, the ESFT necessarily presupposes that the distribution of conceptual knowledge described above is adequate to account for observed differences in the recognition and naming of living things and nonliving things by aphasic patients. Difficulties retrieving names of living things should be traceable to damaged representation of sensory features, while damage to functional features should result in a relatively greater inability to name nonliving things. Conversely, patients with deficits in naming living things should present with problems reasoning about sensory features even of nonliving things, and likewise patients with inanimate naming deficits should have impaired functional knowledge about living things (whatever this might mean). These are, again, claims entailed by the original SFT.

The third assumption, unique to the ESFT, is that the same distribution of conceptual knowledge can account for observed deficits in producing concrete nouns. Since the conceptual representations of both living and nonliving things, which correspond to nouns, include a greater proportion of sensory information than do representations of actions, which correspond to verbs, damage to sensory features should have the effect of making nouns in general relatively more difficult to name than verbs.

It is our intention here to show that each of these three pillars of the ESFT is fundamentally unsound and that as a consequence this hypothesis about the nature of semantic and grammatical category deficits is unsupportable. In doing so, we hope also to draw attention to the pitfalls of drawing sweeping inferences about the organization of lexical and conceptual knowledge from patterns of weakly associated deficits.

Let us begin by asking whether there is evidence to support the contention that conceptual representations of living things include a greater proportion of sensory information than do representations of nonliving things. Farah and McClelland (1991) sought empirical support for this claim, which had been presented purely as conjecture in earlier versions of the SFT (Warrington & McCarthy, 1983, 1987; Warrington & Shallice, 1984), by asking normal subjects to underline visual and functional descriptors in written definitions of living and nonliving things. In apparent agreement with the predictions of the theory, Farah and McClelland found that the ratio of visual to functional properties underlined by their subjects was much higher for living things (7.7:1) than for nonliving things (1.4:1).

However, as Caramazza and Shelton (1998) have observed, the utility of this result is seriously compromised by the actual instructions given to subjects in the study. Specifically, functional features were defined as "words describing what the item does or what it is for" (p. 342), a definition that accords with a strict understanding of function but is virtually inapplicable to features of living beings. Caramazza and Shelton argue that this instruction therefore contains a built-in category bias inasmuch as it excludes many important nonsensory features of animals, like where they are found, what they eat, or whether they are friendly to humans. When Caramazza and Shelton attempted to repeat Farah and McClelland's study, with instructions to underline all nonsensory features (rather than just those pertaining strictly to function), they obtained ratios of sensory to nonsensory properties of 2.9:2.5 for living things and 2.2:2.3 for nonliving things.

Indeed, studies subsequent to Farah and McClelland (1991) that have utilized a more realistic assessment of nonsensory knowledge have uniformly found little difference in the ratios of sensory to nonsensory features for living and nonliving items (McRae, de Sa, & Seidenberg, 1997; Hodges, Patterson, Graham, & Dawson, 1996). Moreover, at least two studies have shown that when subjects are asked to generate spontaneous lists of features for given words, they produce nearly as many functional features (by Farah and McClelland's definition) as sensory features for both living things and nonliving things (Garrard, Lambon Ralph, Hodges, & Patterson, 2001; McRae & Cree, 2002). . . .

Apparently, then, empirical tests have so far failed to corroborate the assumptions of the ESFT (and related theories) with regard to the semantic features of living and nonliving things. On the other hand, even if we disregard the available evidence and simply imagine that the distribution of semantic features conforms to the theory, it is not clear that the ESFT can account *in principle* for the core features of semantic category-specific deficits.

As we mentioned above, the ESFT predicts that patients with impaired sensory knowledge should also be impaired in tasks that require knowledge about living things. As it turns out, this is not always the case: two articles, by Coltheart et al. (1998) and Lambon Ralph, Howard, Nightingale, and Ellis (1998), have shown that at least some patients with difficulties in processing visual attributes of objects do *not* also show evidence of impaired knowledge of living things. Moreover, several recent studies have described patients with category-specific deficits for living things who are equally impaired with visual and functional attributes of living things and equally unimpaired with both attribute types of nonliving things (Laiacona, Barbarotto, & Capitani, 1993; Laiacona, Capitani, & Barbarotto, 1997; Caramazza & Shelton, 1998). This result is inconsistent with the claim that the deficit for living things results from damage to sensory knowledge. . . .

The ESFT does not fare any better when we consider whether it is adequate to explain all observed grammatical category specific deficits or at least specific deficits in noun processing. To be sure, there are some cases where such deficits may in fact be attributable to semantic factors, as Bird and colleagues postulate. One case in point is DM, described by Breedin, Saffran, and Coslett (1994), who presented with a clear "reverse concreteness effect": DM performed poorly on tests of semantic knowledge that relied on an ability to identify perceptual properties of objects, an impairment that might account for his superiority at producing abstract over concrete words and even perhaps an advantage for verbs over nouns. Patient RG, reported by Marshall and coworkers (Marshall, Chiat, Robson, & Pring, 1996b; Marshall, Pring, Chiat, & Robson, 1996a), showed similar difficulties with perceptual features of nouns coupled with an overall advantage for naming verbs compared to nouns.

At the same time, there are numerous reports in the literature of patients whose deficits in noun or verb production cannot readily be accommodated by the ESFT or indeed by any semantic-conceptual explanation of grammatical category-specific deficits, including the imageability account of verb deficits offered by Bird and colleagues. Perhaps the most striking examples in this vein are descriptions of patients with grammatical category-specific deficits restricted to only one modality of output (Caramazza & Hillis, 1991; Hillis & Caramazza, 1995; Rapp & Caramazza, 1997, 1998). The fact that these patients were all able to produce verbs in either written or spoken form, but not both, suggests that the locus of the grammatical class effect in these cases is at the lexical, not the semantic, level. . . .

We have seen that the three fundamental claims of the ESFT do not hold up to careful scrutiny. First, the assumption that representations of living things are more heavily freighted with sensory features than are those of artifacts does not have any reliable empirical grounding, calling into question the entire enterprise of modeling semantic and grammatical category-specific deficits in terms of the differential distribution of sensory and functional features. Even if we were to ignore this problem, however, we would still be faced with the fact that the ESFT incorrectly predicts associations between deficits in processing sensory features and living things or functional features and nonliving things. Finally, there are numerous cases of patients with grammatical category-specific deficits that defy explanation under semantic-conceptual models, including one patient with noun and verb deficits restricted to different modalities and another whose problems with nouns extend to words with no discernible semantic content. All of this suggests that the ESFT is not a particularly useful model for considering grammatical (or semantic) category-specific deficits.

This is not to say that semantic-conceptual explanations in general, and sensory/functional theories in particular, have no place in accounting for deficits in noun or verb naming. It is possible that a similar hypothesis might explain *some* cases of grammatical category specific deficits (if not, perhaps, those cases described in the paper). It would appear, however, that Bird and colleagues do not confine themselves to this limited claim:

> We believe that these data point to a single cause for the relative difficulties in retrieval of both grammatical and semantic categories *for the patients assessed here*. We have proposed the [sic] inanimate/animate distinction is in part due to weighting of functional and sensory information and in part due to the semantic representations of animate items' [sic] having features with a greater tendency to overlap or 'cluster.' If our assertion is true, *this entails that supposed 'grammatical class' effects arise at the level of semantics and not at a lexical level.* (p. 301; emphasis added)

Unfortunately, the authors do not offer us any clue as to how they might justify the logical leap from accounting for the constellation of deficits observed in their patients to proposing that "supposed" grammatical class effects arise at the level of semantics in other patients described in the literature, many of whom present with markedly different patterns of impairment. As an alternative, we suggest the possibility, indeed the probability, that there is no single account adequate to explain all instances of noun and verb deficits in aphasia. Rather, it is likely that deficits in some patients [like DM (Breedin et al., 1994) and RG (Marshall et al., 1996a, 1996b)] may arise at the semantic-conceptual level, while for others [like JR (Shapiro et al., 2000) and EBA (Hillis & Caramazza, 1995)] impairments in retrieving nouns and verbs may be more truly categorical in nature. Still other patients may present with verb retrieval deficits that stem from problems in constructing sentences. We are apt only to confuse matters by trying to shoehorn the diverse range of phenomena described as category-specific deficits into one explanatory rubric.

References

Allport, D. (1985). Distributed memory, modular subsystems and dysphasia. In S. Newman & R. Epstein (Eds.), *Current perspectives in dysphasia*. Edinburgh, UK: Churchill–Livingstone.

Bates, E., Chen, S., Tzeng, O., Li, P., & Opie, M. (1991). The noun–verb problem in Chinese. *Brain and Language, 41,* 203–233.

Bird, H., Howard, D., & Franklin, S. (2000). Why is a verb like an inanimate object? Grammatical category and semantic category deficits. *Brain and Language, 72,* 246–309.

Bock, K. (1987). An effect of the accessibility of word forms on sentence structures. *Journal of Memory and Language, 26,* 119–137.

Breedin, S., Saffran, E., & Coslett, H. (1994). Reversal of the concreteness effect in a patient with semantic dementia. *Cognitive Neuropsychology, 11,* 617–660.

Caramazza, A., & Hillis, A. (1991). Lexical organization of nouns and verbs in the brain. *Nature, 349,* 788–790.

Caramazza, A., & Shelton, J. (1998). Domain-specific knowledge systems in the brain: The animate-inanimate distinction. *Journal of Cognitive Neuroscience, 10,* 1–34.

Coltheart, M., Ingris, L., Cupples, L., Michie, P., Bates, A., & Budd, B. (1998). A semantic subsystem specific to the storage of information about the visual attributes of animate and inanimate objects. *Neurocase, 4,* 353–370.

Damasio, A., & Tranel, D. (1993). Nouns and verbs are retrieved with differently distributed neural systems. *Proceedings of the National Academy of Sciences of the United States of America, 90,* 4957–4960.

Farah, M., & McClelland, J. (1991). A computational model of semantic memory impairment: Modality specificity and emergent category specificity. *Journal of Experimental Psychology: General, 120,* 339–357.

Gainotti, G., & Silveri, M. (1996). Cognitive and anatomical locus of lesion in a patient with a category-specific semantic impairment for living beings. *Cognitive Neuropsychology, 13,* 357–389.

Garrard, P., Lambon Ralph, M., Hodges, J., & Patterson, K. (2001). Prototypicality, distinctiveness and intercorrelation: Analyses of the semantic attributes of living and nonliving concepts. *Cognitive Neuropsychology, 18,* 125–174.

Garrett, M. (1988). Processes in language production. In F. Newmeyer et al. (Eds.), *Language: Psychological and biological aspects. Linguistics: The Cambridge survey,* Vol. 3. Cambridge, UK: Cambridge Univ. Press.

Hillis, A., & Caramazza, A. (1995). Representation of grammatical categories of words in the brain. *Journal of Cognitive Neuroscience, 7,* 396–407.

Hodges, J., Patterson, K., Graham, N., & Dawson, K. (1996). Naming and knowing in dementia of Alzheimer's type. *Brain and Language, 54,* 302–325.

Laiacona, M., Barbarotto, R., & Capitani, E. (1993). Perceptual and associative knowledge in category specific impairment of semantic memory: A study of two cases. *Cortex, 29,* 727–740.

Laiacona, M., Capitani, E., & Barbarotto, R. (1997). Semantic category dissociations: A longitudinal study of two cases. *Cortex, 33,* 441–461.

Lambon Ralph, M., Howard, D., Nightingale, G., & Ellis, A. (1998). Are living and non-living category-specific deficits causally linked to impaired perceptual or associative knowledge? Evidence from a category-specific double dissociation. *Neurocase, 4,* 311–338.

Marshall, J., Chiat, S., Robson, J., & Pring, T. (1996b). Calling a salad a federation: An investigation of semantic jargon. Part 2—Verbs. *Journal of Neurolinguistics, 9,* 251–260.

Marshall, J., Pring, T., Chiat, S., & Robson, J. (1996a). Calling a salad a federation: An investigation of semantic jargon. Part 1—Nouns. *Journal of Neurolinguistics, 9,* 237–250.

McRae, K., & Cree, G. (2002). Factors underlying category-specific semantic deficits. In E. Forde & G. Humphreys (Eds.), *Category specificity in brain and mind.* East Sussex, UK: Psychology Press.

McRae, K., de Sa, V., & Seidenberg, M. (1997). On the nature and scope of featural representations for word meaning. *Journal of Experimental Psychology: General, 126,* 99–130.

Miceli, G., Silveri, M., Villa, G., & Caramazza, A. (1984). On the basis for the agrammatic's difficulty in producing main verbs. *Cortex, 20,* 207–220.

Miceli, G., Silveri, M., Nocentini, U., & Caramazza, A. (1988). Patterns of dissociation in comprehension and production of nouns and verbs. *Aphasiology, 2,* 351–358.

Rapp, B., & Caramazza, A. (1997). The modality-specific organization of grammatical categories: Evidence from impaired spoken and written sentence production. *Brain and Language, 56,* 248–286.

Rapp, B., & Caramazza, A. (1998). A case of selective difficulty in writing verbs. *Neurocase, 4,* 127–140.

Saffran, E. (1982). Neuropsychological approaches to the study of language. *British Journal of Psychology, 73,* 317–337.

Shallice, T. (1988). Specialisation within the semantic system. *Cognitive Neuropsychology, 5,* 133–142.

Shapiro, K., Shelton, J., & Caramazza, A. (2000). Grammatical class in lexical production and morphological processing: Evidence from a case of fluent aphasia. *Cognitive Neuropsychology, 17,* 665–682.

Silveri, M., & Gainotti, G. (1988). Interaction between vision and language in category-specific impairment. *Cognitive Neuropsychology, 5,* 677–709.

Warrington, E., & McCarthy, R. (1983). Category specific access dysphasia. *Brain, 106,* 859–878.

Warrington, E., & McCarthy, R. (1987). Categories of knowledge: Further fractionations of an attempted integration. *Brain, 110,* 1273–1296.

Warrington, E., & Shallice, T. (1984). Category specific semantic impairments. *Brain, 107,* 829–854.

POSTSCRIPT

Is Sensory Information the Strongest Part of a Stored Concept?

In the first selection, Bird, Howard, and Franklin make the case that an explanation other than the standard semantic/grammatical model could account for the behaviors of patients with aphasia. Based on their observations of three verb-deficit and three verb-spared patients, Bird, et al., believe that the suggested grammatical category doesn't exist. They suggest that the behaviors others thought indicated grammatical categories actually indicate an organizational scheme based on imageability and function. Imageability is similar to concreteness, and refers to the sensory information attached to a concept. For example, if asked to imagine "shirt," you could most likely do that with ease. If asked to imagine "democracy," you may have some difficulty. Certainly you know a great deal of information about democracy that you could talk about, but to find a mental image of it would be hard because it doesn't have much sensory information associated with it. Bird, et al., propose that we organize all knowledge by semantic categories, and that within the subcategories or classes of semantic information, some knowledge groups are organized by sensory information or imageability, and some are organized by function, action, or procedure.

Shapiro and Caramazza do not find value in the new model proposed by Bird, et al., and in the second selection they systematically critique the model's three primary assumptions. The extended sensory/functional theory proposed by Bird, et al., assumes that (1) stored information for living things includes more sensory information than that stored for non-living things, (2) the model can explain and predict the abilities of aphasic patients in recognizing and naming living and non-living things, and (3) the model can explain and predict the abilities of aphasic patients in recognizing and naming nouns. Shapiro and Caramazza present research evidence to demonstrate the inaccuracy and inadequacy of the model by attacking each of the three primary tenets. They find no evidence for the first assumption regarding sensory information, and they find that the model proposed by Bird, et al., does not predict patients' abilities. Shapiro and Caramazza conclude by chiding Bird, et al., for thinking that one model could account for all the complexities of cognitive processing and cognitive deficits.

The issues debated here are difficult on many levels. To understand any discussion of the finer points of neuropsychology, brain functioning, or language processing, one must immerse in a new vocabulary. For the individual without much background in these areas, the articles present many new vocabulary words. These issues are also difficult because the data often come from small numbers of participants with similar but not identical situations. Students in experimental methodology courses are taught to control all independent and extraneous variables, and also to match the participants as closely as possible so that variance in the dependent variable can be explained. In the types of studies discussed in this issue, the researchers do not have the luxury of such control. There are only small numbers of patients with particular types of aphasia available. If a researcher wants to have 6 or 8 patients in an experiment, it may not be possible to match patients on sex, age, previous educational level, or other important variables. In fact, the most important variable of all, the precise type of brain lesion and the extent of the damage, may be not identical across all the participants.

This issue reminds us of the complexity of the human brain and the many cognitive skills it takes for us to think and to speak our thoughts. As you ponder these selections and what you have learned, you can also appreciate the many cognitive systems all working together, which allow you to store, transform, and produce mental representations.

Suggested Readings

Forde, E., and Humphreys, G. (Editors), *Category Specificity in Brain and Mind (Brain Damage, Behaviour and Cognition)* (New York: Psychology Press, 2003).

Gentner, D., and Goldin-Meadow, S. (Editors), *Language in Mind: Advances in the Study of Language and Thought* (Cambridge, MA: MIT Press, 2003).

Hillis, A. (Editor), *The Handbook of Adult Language Disorders: Integrating Cognitive Neuropsychology, Neurology, and Rehabilitation* (New York: Psychology Press, 2001).

Jackendoff, R. *Foundations of Language: Brain, Meaning, Grammar, Evolution* (New York: Oxford Press, 2002).

Nickels, L. (Editor), *Cognitive Neuropsychological Approaches to Spoken Word Production: Special Issue of Aphasiology (Macquarie Monographs in Cognitive Science)* (New York: Psychology Press, 2002).

On the Internet . . .

The Exploratorium sponsors a most informative Web site that explains much of what we know of memory functions.

http://www.exploratorium.edu/memory/index.html

The Memory Page will help you improve your memory through the use of mnemonics and other tricks.

http://www.thememorypage.net/

The Memory Debate Archives contains many key articles in the continuing debate of the possibility and accuracy of repressed or recovered memories, including news articles, legal cases, and academic articles.

http://www.tmdarchives.org/

The American Psychological Association, in its Public Affairs section, offers a question & answer section on memories of childhood abuse.

http://www.apa.org/pubinfo/mem.html?CFID=2748609&CFTOKEN=46298232

PART 3

Memory

We are all aware of our ability to remember and, sometimes, to forget information. Cognitive scientists are very interested in how we store information in our brains and how we retrieve it. Scientists are also interested in those cases when we can't remember something that we should know, when we can't forget something we would like to forget, and when we are certain we remember something that, in reality, we did not experience. In these issues we will explore how memories are formed and how we may be fooled by our recollections.

ISSUE 7

Is Novice Memory Based on Associations?

YES: Pertti Saariluoma and Tei Laine, from "Novice Construction of Chess Memory," *Scandinavian Journal of Psychology* (2001)

NO: Fernand Gobet, from "Chunk Hierarchies and Retrieval Structures: Comments on Saariluoma and Laine," *Scandinavian Journal of Psychology* (2001)

ISSUE SUMMARY

YES: Cognitive scientists Pertti Saariluoma and Tei Laine present the case that through computer simulation they can demonstrate that associations made between frequent types of chess pieces and the colors of the pieces were the most salient aspects in novices learning chess patterns.

NO: Professor of intelligence systems Fernand Gobet argues that Saariluoma and Laine have not properly modeled human memory, and with a more competent computer simulation, it is clear that proximity or location is the most salient feature in remembering chess patterns.

As the titles of the two selections indicate, the debated topic is the development of novice memory for chess patterns. What isn't clear from the titles is that the primary evidence for the debate comes from computer simulations. Why are computer simulations of interest when we can observe real human beings learning? The answer lies in the fact that while it is obvious that we learn new things all the time, we are less aware of the actual steps we take in learning. In building a computer simulation of the learning process, the cognitive scientists must make sure every step is accurately portrayed. They do not have the luxury of programming in "then make a lucky guess" or "then use your intuition." Computer simulations, when successful, provide hypotheses and insights into the detailed process of learning, storing information, and retrieving it when needed.

The researchers featured in this debate are both interested in the differences in memory skills of novice and expert chess players. Saariluoma and Laine gave two participants, known by their initials NT and MQ, the task of learning 500 chess positions as might be found in the middle of a game. Chess involves two sets of pieces placed on each side of an 8 × 8 checkered board. Each player begins with 16 pieces consisting of 8 pawns, 2 rooks, 2 knights, 2 bishops, 1 queen, and 1 king. Each piece has its own starting point, and each type of piece can move only in its designated way. For example, bishops can only move diagonally and rooks can only move up and down or sideways. Saariluoma and Laine found that both novices learned the positions faster for the first 100 to 150 positions, and then the speed of learning declined. This is referred to as a negatively accelerating learning curve because the learning speed decreases after a short period of time, and it continues to decrease even more as new information is learned. Saariluoma and Laine also tested NT and MQ by asking them to remember random patterns in which the chess pieces were placed on the board in any way, contrary to the rules of the game. They found a slow but steady rise in memory for random positions.

In trying to understand this pattern of negative acceleration in the learning curve for true game positions and a linear increase in learning for random positions, Saariluoma and Laine tried to simulate this situation with computer software. Their database, which serves as long-term memory, began with an entry for every type of chess piece (12 different pieces) on each spot on the board (64 locations) for a total of 768 pieces of information. They used two different simulation models, with each one following a different set of learning rules that are known as chunking heuristics. The *random neighborhood heuristic* starts by picking a piece at random, and then considers any adjacent pieces when "learning" or recording a pattern. The *correlation heuristic* starts with the most frequently seen piece, and then looks for "correlated" pieces. Correlations or associations are made between pieces that match in color, type, and proximity. Saariluoma and Laine trained the computer program by testing the growth of the databases (i.e., the learned patterns stored in long-term memory) after exposure to the same 500 patterns seen by NT and MQ. Based on the way the databases grew, the researchers came to several conclusions. They believe that NT and MQ learned more by associating type and color than by proximity, they used more memory capacity than would be available in their working memory, and thus they must have retrieved information directly from long-term memory, and that knowledge structures do not need to be hierarchical. It is the last point that Gobet, in the second selection, is most concerned about.

In the first selection, Saariluoma and Laine demonstrate through computer simulation of human learning of chess patterns that associations made between frequent types of pieces and the colors of the pieces were the most salient aspects in remembering chess patterns. In the second selection, Gobet argues that Saariluoma and Laine did not program their software with the appropriate hierarchical structure, and further demonstrates through another computer simulation that proximity or location is the most salient feature in remembering chess patterns.

Pertti Saariluoma and Tei Laine

Novice Construction of Chess Memory

Introduction

The rise of constructivist thinking within the cognitive psychology of learning makes it necessary to investigate knowledge modification and its theoretical explanations. They are not only important in laboratory psychology but they also have a wide applicability from social psychology to clinical and educational thinking (on constructivism see e.g., Prawat, 1996; Resnick, 1987). Indeed, constructivism is clearly becoming one of the major theoretical alternatives for any psychologists interested in practical problems. One important problem domain in which knowledge construction has specific importance is undoubtedly expertise research.

Experts' ability to process task-specific materials seems astonishing. The ease with which they are able to remember relevant information may appear supernormal (Saariluoma, 1989, 1995). It is possible to hear expert chess players arguing without a chess set about games, which were played a long time ago. These discussions certainly say nothing to novices, though each word used by disputing masters is familiar to them. Unlike the masters, novices cannot recollect a long-past game or construct an image of it. Their memories are in some sense inferior to the masters', though they can remember everyday things equally well.

Experts' superior task-specific memory was brought to the awareness of psychologists by Djakov, Petrovsky and Rudik (1926), and especially de Groot (1965, 1966). In the mid-sixties it was also observed that the memory differences between expert and novice chess players were not due to the superior general memory abilities of the experts but to task-specific training (Lemmens and Jongman, unpublished research, see Vicente and de Groot, 1990). In this crucial experiment skilled players were clearly better than less skilled in remembering real game positions after a short presentation of three to seven seconds, but did not maintain their superiority when they had to remember random positions (Chase & Simon, 1973; Chi, 1978; Lemmens & Jongman, unpublished; Saariluoma, 1985). It was argued that the reason for the superiority of skilled chess players lies in

From *Scandinavian Journal of Psychology,* April 2001, pp. 137–146.

their ability to use previously learned chess specific patterns in chunking game positions. They are unable to do this as rapidly when faced with random positions (Chase & Simon, 1973; de Groot, 1966; Lories, 1987; Saariluoma, 1989). The above finding has proven to be not solely a feature of chess, but has been observed in many task environments. . . .

The phenomenon of chess experts' superior memory has thus become one of the cornerstones of cognitive skills research (Chase & Simon, 1973; Gobet & Simon, 1996; Holding, 1985; Newell & Rosenbloom, 1981; Newell & Simon, 1972; Rosenbloom & Newell, 1987). Consequently, it is logical to start asking further questions about the nature of chunking. The more we understand about chunks the better we can understand the acquisition of higher cognitive skills, and this is why it is necessary to go into details of chunking mechanisms to clarify all the unclear points in the argumentation.

One could argue that the research into chess players' memories is relevant only when top-level skills are considered. When the basic skills training is focused on people that have far less than ten years' experience in the field, it should be interesting to investigate what are the major properties relevant to early learning in chess. The first hours of chess training are similar to any basic course in some symbolic subject matter. Therefore, it would be good to pay more attention to these early stages of information processing. An important shift in the direction of early learning was made by Fisk and Lloyd (1988), when they studied the acquisition of skilled visual search in chess using absolute novices. Fisk and Lloyd's (1988) study showed that skill develops very rapidly at first, but later the speed of learning decreases substantially. By studying a later stage of skill development, they could not have made this observation (see also Newell & Rosenbloom, 1981, and Rosenbloom & Newell, 1987 for parallel findings in different task environments). If a similar pattern of skill development to the one concerning the reaction time results of Fisk and Lloyd (1988) can also be found in chess-recall tasks, it might explain why the development of skilled memory takes so much time. Though it is easy to achieve one level, each new step takes more and more effort.

To help resolve the problems above, two students with only very elementary knowledge of chess were asked to study hundreds of chess positions ten to twenty minutes a day for four to six months in order to recall the positions as well as they could. The development of their recall was tested several times during this period. The aim was to determine the form of the learning curve for a later simulation analysis. This study is in fact an extension of Ericsson and Harris's study (1990) in which a novice chess player studied chess positions for about 50 hours and improved her performance in recalling game positions. Our objective is totally different from Ericsson and Harris's. They wanted to make a distinction between superior memory performance and expert knowledge of the task domain, and investigated whether a total dissociation between memory performance and expertise exists in chess, as corresponding evidence has been found earlier in the case of mental calculation (Ericsson & Harris, 1990). Ericsson and Harris's novice subject achieved a chess master's level of memory performance in recalling game positions, but the developed skill did not transfer to random positions. Thus their result was that memory performance of chess experts can be achieved through systematic training, although there might be some qualitative differences in what pieces trained novices and experts retrieve in test sessions.

By using computer simulation we wished to study the nature of chunking mechanisms in early learning. Chase and Simon (1973) suggested that a number of chess-specific relations, such as colour, kind, threat, defence and proximity are important in chunk construction. Here, we are interested in an even more simple factor. This is general associativity, which basically means correlation between instants. If the pieces of the same colour and type that commonly co-occur are used in building new chunks (following the idea that general associativity is important), one should get the most suitable simulation outcome by chunking pieces which are highly correlated. . . .

Method

Subjects

Two graduate psychology students participated in the experiment. One was a woman, NT, who has played only a few games of chess in her life and had no real interest in chess. The second subject was a man, MQ, with the same background, who had played chess a little more frequently, but had neither chess ambitions nor qualifications. Neither of the subjects had ever been to a chess club or participated in a chess competition. Both of the subjects were thus absolute novices.

Task and Procedure

NT was the first subject. She was asked to study five hundred middle-game positions from a book of combinations. She studied four to five positions for approximately fifteen minutes a day. When studying the positions she put the pieces on the board according to the illustration and tried to learn the location of each piece. She concentrated, however, only on the patterns and did not study the moves at all. She was tested five times: before the experiment began, and after 110, 250, 365, and 500 positions. Her involvement in the whole experiment lasted about four months.

The experiment involving MQ was carried out a few months after the end of the experiment with NT. This second experiment took six months, as MQ wanted to spend more time per position than NT. He also studied five hundred middle-game positions from a book of middle-game combinations and his method of study was similar to NT's. It was possible to test MQ somewhat more frequently than NT. His recall was tested eight times: at the beginning, and after 30, 60, 175, 220, 270, 350, and 500 studied positions. The irregularities in testing intervals were due to certain practical problems involved in carrying out these long running experiments, such as study examinations, Christmas holidays, etc. Each test consisted of a standard memory experiment (de Groot, 1965). Subjects were shown ten game and ten random positions, with 18 to 28 pieces in each. The presentation time was five seconds per position and the presentation order was random. The positions presented in the various testing sessions were always different. The test positions were made by using chess print transfers which were then photographed as slides, and these were subsequently shown using a slide projector. The subjects sat at a distance of 150 cm from the display. The size of chess boards displayed was 40 × 40 cm.

Results and Discussion

. . . The effect of learning is clear. The subjects were able to increase their percentage of recalled pieces from roughly fifteen to somewhere between forty to fifty percent, which was a rise of 25–35 percentage points. In recalling random positions the effect was, however, substantially smaller, averaging about five percentage points. The learning curve profile was very much the same for both subjects. The greatest increase in recall percentages was shown when studying the first hundred to one hundred and fifty positions. The increase was far slower from two hundred positions onwards. There was also some improvement in recalling random positions, but the profile is very different from the game positions, the increase being more linear throughout the whole learning period.

The learning curves of NT and MQ have a standard form. They are like many other learning curves, first very steep with a sharp improvement in learning. However, after a short period of time the speed of learning decreases and the gain in performance level becomes smaller per training unit (Fisk & Lloyd, 1988; Newell & Rosenbloom, 1981; Rosenbloom & Newell, 1987). This kind of curve can also be called negatively accelerating or logarithmic.

The main problem with the learning curve is how it should be interpreted. What are the precise mechanisms which can explain it? Normally, one single phenomenon does not suffice, but learning is rather a combination of several factors. To investigate the combination of relevant phenomena we decided to build a learning simulation model. This is apparently the most effective way to investigate how relevant factors combine to produce the observed outcome. . . .

Simulative Analyses

Simulation is one way to sophisticate the analysis of experimental results. It can be criticized, because the outcome of any simulation is ambiguous. Furthermore, simulation cannot really prove anything, because there are normally alternative ways of reaching the same outcome (Anderson, 1976). Nevertheless, simulation models are logically consistent and are capable of realizing the processes, which are suggested. Therefore, they often provide a better way to explicate theoretical analyses than mere speculation, because they provide a better safeguard against errors than intuitions.

. . . [We] had four main goals for our simulations. Firstly, we were interested in whether the *incremental increase in chunk size* explains the negative acceleration of learning curves. . . . The present results would suggest that the chunks grow piece by piece. As the number of chunks containing five items is much larger than the number of items containing three, learning is slower when all the chunks that are five items long must be learnt to improve performance. Chase and Simon (1973) observed that skilled chess players do not necessarily recall more chunks than novices, but the size of their chunks is larger. This result has been confirmed by Charness (1989) in an elegant study in which he asked a subject from an experiment he had performed ten years earlier to carry out the original experiments again. As his subject had been able to raise his level of skill from novice to master during this time, it was possible to compare his current chunk sizes with the original sizes. The conclusion was very clear. Chunk size increases with the level of skill. Moreover, the increase is not an absolute phenomenon, but instead takes place incrementally. Good players do not learn new and longer chunks at any one time, rather their chunks slowly lengthen and their recall improves (Chase & Simon, 1973; Newell & Simon, 1972). This is also the way chunk learning is assumed to occur in some theories of cognitive skills (Newell & Rosenbloom, 1981; Rosenbloom & Newell, 1987). Thus, although empirical evidence for this model can be found in the literature, it is still good to make a simulation to test the explanation.

The second problem concerns the nature of *inter-piece relations in a chunk*. Chase and Simon (1973) found five chess-specific relations which were related to the probability of two successive pieces belonging to one chunk. These relations were *kind (i.e.* two successive pieces are of the same type, e.g. bishops), *colour* (they are the same colour), *threat* (one threatens the other), *defence* (one defends the other) and finally *proximity* (they are located in adjacent squares). The more of these relations there are between two pieces, the smaller the inter-piece interval in recall. . . .

The third problem concerns *working memory (WM) size*. There are several different assumptions concerning the working memory. Miller (1956) suggested his famous five to nine chunks, Simon (1974) discussed working memory with four chunks. Ericsson and Kintsch (1995) suggested even larger retrieval structures. Here we are interested in beginners' performance and it would be logical to think that working memory size would be closer to short-term working memory sizes. However, to get a clearer idea we decided to vary the WM size to see which size gives the best fit to the real data.

Finally, we want to investigate, whether one must necessarily use unified and hierarchic memory representations in constructing simulation models of recalling chess positions. Charness (1976) and Saariluoma (1989) have all collected evidence that systematically supports the idea that chess players must construct some kind of a retrieval structure in their long-term memory. This means that subjects have some pieces of knowledge in their immediate working memory and the rest of task-relevant information is stored into long-term memory (Ericsson & Kintsch, 1995;

Gobet & Simon, 1996; de Groot & Gobet, 1996; Richman, Staszewski & Simon, 1995). The problem is the accurate form of memory information, which has mostly been investigated by using simulation.

In the mainstream symbolic simulation model the idea has been to use a hierarchical structure (Richman, *et al.,* 1995). This monolithic approach is a serious alternative, but it need not be the only plausible model. There are alternative simulation approaches (Laine, *et al.,* 1998). One may simulate chess results with neural models or use heterarchic models. The latter do not presuppose a multilayer unified structure, but it assumes that retrieval structure is formed by a set of parallel and non-integrated patterns. Here, we are interested in investigating this alternative, and therefore, we have constructed a model, in which the retrieval structure is not discrimination net but a set of patterns activated by the presentation of the stimulus. In this kind of model the contents of the patterns themselves cause the integration but no direct links combining patterns are required.

Structure and Functioning of the Simulation Program

Two versions of computer simulation programs accomplishing different chunking mechanisms were built to model the chunk construction strategies of novice chess players in the experiments described above. The models were programmed in the object-oriented language Java. . . . The systems were only designed to predict the development of the learning curve of an inexperienced chess player due to accumulation of new chess chunks in the memory when his or her recall of unfamiliar chess positions is tested regularly during the learning phase.

Learning and Recall

In the beginning the simulation systems have 768 chunks in the long-term memory (LTM), which represent every possible one-piece chunk that can be formed, i.e. every piece type (12) on each location (64) on the board. So it was assumed that the subject can superficially recognize single isolated pieces wherever they are situated on the board. Of course, it would be absurd to think that subjects could not have information about single objects such as chess pieces in some location of visual space, when looking at them.

The systems form new chunks in the LTM from every shown study position. The size of chunks stored in the LTM increases due to the systems' experience; in the beginning chunks of two pieces are constructed, but later on the systems memorize larger chunks as they add new pieces to existing chunks. Thus, the models are able to construct chunks of different sizes parallelly depending on what chunks they have learnt earlier. The growth of the chunks' sizes is interpreted as the construction of more complex retrieval structures, as in Chase and Ericsson's model (1982) implemented in Richman *et al.*'s EPAM IV simulation (Richman *et al.,* 1995). In the case of our experiment this means that smaller chunks are combined to form more complex and bigger chunks that are further stored and retrieved as one entity. The retrieval structures are not hierarchical, though.

The retrieval process is guided by an association based recognition. Simulation systems do not examine the chess positions as a whole but process them one chunk at a time, starting with a specific or random piece on the board. In the test phase the systems first build a proper chunk of the pieces in a test position, and then look for a corresponding chunk in the LTM. The models do not reconstruct positions on empty boards like in Simon and Gilmartin (1973), but try to cover the pieces on the board with corresponding chunks in the LTM if they are found. If the chunk cannot be found, the systems try a chunk which is one piece smaller or a totally new chunk, otherwise they add the chunk to the STM and mark the corresponding pieces on the board as recalled. Finally the recall score is calculated as a percentage of pieces explained by chunks in the STM of all the pieces in the position.

The number of chunks learnt from one position and used in recalling one position is limited by the capacity of the working memory. Overlapping chunks are not constructed from a single position. Pieces or chunks that are not seen in the learning phase are never memorized or retrieved, so the models make no commission errors. Once the models have learnt something, they never forget it, nor do they retrieve any incomplete or wrong chunk from the memory. The models do not learn any chunks from the test positions, either. Unlike Simon's and Gilmartin's (1973) EPAM-based learner, the systems can find a chunk in the memory independent of the piece around which it is built, so the chunk is identified by all the pieces in it and no duplicates of the chunks are stored. Simon's and Gilmartin's (1973) chunks were identified by the focal pieces around which the chunks were built, so if several chunks consisted of the same pieces but the focal piece had been a different one, multiple copies of the chunk are memorized.

Chunking Heuristics

The first version of the simulation uses a **random neighbourhood heuristic.** In the learning phase and in the recall phase the system always processes the chess positions in random order, and it starts building a chunk from a random piece (a focal piece). When expanding a chunk to its neighbours the system proceeds in a random direction. It should be noted that only the pieces in adjacent locations can form a chunk. The pieces that do not have any immediate neighbours can only form a one piece chunk.

The other simulation model uses a **correlation heuristic** when constructing chunks. Its decision about which pieces belong to a chunk is in this way of thinking based on the frequency of co-occurrence and the similarity of those pieces. Thus it makes very similar assumption to the classic associationism. The system chooses the most commonly seen piece as a focal piece around which it tries to form a chunk. Next it calculates correlation measures between this focal piece and all other pieces on the board. In addition to the similarity—colour and type—of pieces the system takes into account the proximity (distance determined by squares between the pieces) when calculating the measures. The first two factors have an equal weight, the proximity contributes to correlation measure by a factor calculated as an Euclidean distance of the two pieces. So two black Knights in neighbouring squares gather more mutual correlation than a black Knight and a white Knight or two different types of pieces with the same colour, or two same type of pieces in squares on different sides of the board. The system adds to the chunk the piece with the highest correlation measure with the focal piece, and further expands the chunk to the piece with the highest correlation with this newly added piece. . . .

Simulation

The simulation models were tested in similar conditions to those of subjects MQ and NT. The models were taught 500 chess positions and the recall of unfamiliar game and random positions was requested with the same intervals as MQs, in the beginning, and after 30, 60, 175, 220, 270, 350 and 500 studied positions. Every test session consisted of ten game and ten random positions. The random positions were permutations of the real chess positions used in the tests. They included the same number and type of pieces, only in different locations. . . .

General Discussion

The empirical results are very clear. A negatively accelerating learning curve was found. In this chess is similar to many other symbolic and motor skills (Newell & Rosenbloom, 1981). The first steps in acquiring any skill are the quickest. In that period one learns the most basic but also the most common aspects of the target domain. In chess this means the familiar chunks, such as castling or standard pawn chains. In random positions the absence of such regularities makes it impossible to find equally common piece configurations, and chunking is much less effective. Later in skill development, while the number of pieces in a chunk increases, the number of combinatorial alternatives also increases exponentially. Consequently, it is logical that the increase in the number of recalled pieces decreases respectively.

By computer simulation we investigated various possibilities to interpret this empirical data. Of course, simulation has several weaknesses as a method. It is far from unambiguous, because it is possible to construct several different types of models in order to investigate possible interpretations of data. The formal dimensions of thinking are mostly better controlled by using modelling than by relying on mere intuition. Therefore, simulation, though having undeniably speculative sides, can be beneficial.

Our model can simulate many of the standard experimental results, such as random and game difference, but it can also model some new issues, which are informative with respect to chess skill and the nature of early skill acquisition. The first problem is whether the learning curve would be negatively accelerating and whether this phenomenon is related to the incremental growth of memory chunks. The answer to both questions is affirmative. Our model produces a learning curve of correct shape, and the most natural explanation to this is the incremental growth of chunks. The problem to resolve is the problem of the combinatorial increase in the number of needed chunks. One must get a sufficient number of chunks of size three to cover twelve piece locations when working memory size is 4. However, to cover twenty locations demands an exponentially growing number of chunks and thus the learning curve is negatively accelerating.

The second question concerned the nature of associative links. When proximity is compared with frequency-based associations, the latter provides much better fit. It would be interesting to know whether frequency-based associations have some role in expert recall as well. The long history of associative thinking naturally suggests that this general associativity might have some role in chess recall as well.

The third problem was working memory size. Again, the model showed good predictive fit with the empirical results, and indeed it seems to be the case that with the increase of skill one must assume [a] larger number of chunks than short-term WM capacity. This means that chess players construct some type of a retrieval structure in their long-term working memory (Ericsson & Kintsch, 1995; Richman, *et al.,* 1995). This assumption is the most natural one considering the interference results in chess psychology (Charness, 1976; Lane & Robertson, 1979; Saariluoma, 1989).

Finally, our simulation provides evidence the hierarchy is not the only alternative to construct retrieval structures. It is also possible to assume that a retrieval structure is formed by a set of independent chunks. This kind of retrieval structures are heterarchic and thus somewhat different from the ones postulated by Ericsson and Kintsch (1995), Richman, *et al.* (1995). The consistency is achieved here by virtue of the contents of chunks. One chunk is different from [another], because it is differently located and has different pieces. Each recalled chunk is located on its own location independently of all other chunks. Consequently, one needs not necessarily postulate a hierarchy but rather a set of independently located chunks, which contents makes them an integrated whole. However, this problem deserves more research.

Going back to the most global issue, one can argue that chunking is one form of knowledge construction. As is well known, the major contemporary global learning theory is constructivism. It is the predominant way of thinking both in clinical and in social and educational psychology (Prawat, 1996; Resnick, 1987). The crucial theoretical problem in this way of thinking is the notion of construction itself. What it means, in concrete terms, is that people construct their own knowledge bases. The simulation of early learning provides one alternative. One of its dimensions is a frequency-based construction of associative and prelinguistic patterns.

References

Anderson, J. R. (1976). Language, memory and thought. Hillsdale, N.J.: Lawrence Erlbaum Associates.

Charness, N. (1976). Memory for chess positions: Resistance to interference. *Journal of Experimental Psychology: Human Learning and Memory, 2,* 641–653.

Charness, N. (1989). Expertise in chess and bridge. In D. Klahr and K. Kotovsky (Eds.), Complex Information Processing: The Impact of Herbert A. Simon. Hillsdale, N.J.: Erlbaum.

Chase, W. G., & Simon, H. A. (1973). The mind's eye in chess. In W. G. Chase (Ed.), *Visual Information Processing.* Academic Press: New York.

Chi, M. T. H. (1978). Knowledge structures and memory development. In R. Siegler (Ed.), *Children's Thinking: What Develops?* Hillsdale: N.J.: Erlbaum, 73–96.

Djakov, I. N., Petrovsky, N. B., & Rudik, P. A. (1926). Psihologia Shakhmatnoi Igry. (Chess psychology). Moscow: Avtorov.

Ericsson, K. A., & Harris, M. S. (1990). Expert chess memory without chess knowledge. A training study. Poster presentation at the 31st Annual Meeting of the Psychonomics Society, New Orleans.

Ericsson, K. A., & Kintsch, W. (1995). Long-term working memory. *Psychological Review, 102,* 211–245.

Fisk, A. W., & Lloyd, S. J. (1988). The role of stimulus to rule consistency in learning rapid application of spatial rules. *Human Factors, 30,* 35–49.

Gobet, F., & Simon, H. A. (1996). Recall of random and distorted chess positions: Implications for the theory of expertise. *Memory & Cognition, 24,* 493–503.

de Groot, A. D. (1965). Thought and choice in chess. The Hague: Mouton.

de Groot, A. D. (1966). Perception and memory versus thought: Some old ideas and recent findings. In B. Kleinmuntz (Ed.), *Problem solving: Research, Methods and Theory.* New York: Wiley.

de Groot, A., & Gobet, F. (1996). Perception and Memory in Chess. Studies in the Heuristics of the Professional Eye. Van Gorcum.

Holding, D. H. (1985). The Psychology of Chess Skill. Hillsdale, N.J.: Erlbaum.

Laine, T., Hyötyniemi, H., & Saariluoma, P. (1998). Foundations of simulative theorzing. In: H. Prade (Ed.), *The Proceedings of the 13th European Conference on Artificial Intelligence, ECAI 98.* London: Wiley & Sons Ltd.

Lories, G. (1987). Recall of random and non random chess positions in strong and weak chess players. *Psychologica Belgica, 27,* 153–159.

Miller, G. E. (1956). The magical number seven plus or minus two: Some limits on our capacity for processing information. *Psychological Review, 63,* 81–97.

Newell, A., & Rosenbloom, P. (1981). Mechanisms of skill acquisition and law of practise. In J. R. Anderson (Ed.), *Cognitive Skills and Their Acquisition.* Hillsdale, N.J.: Erlbaum.

Newell, A., & Simon, H. A. (1972). Human Problem Solving. Englewood Cliffs, N.J.: Prentice-Hall.

Prawat, R. (1996). Constructivism, Modern and Postmodern. *Educational Psychologist, 31,* 215–225.

Resnick, L. B. (1987). Learning in school and out. *Educational Researcher,* December.

Richman, H. B., Staszewski, J. J., & Simon, H. A. (1995). Simulation of expert memory using EPAM IV. *Psychological Review,* Vol. 102, No. 2.

Rosenbloom, P., & Newell, A. (1987). Learning by chunking: A production system model of practise. In D. Klahr, P. Langley and R. Neches (Ed.), *Production System Models of Learning and Development.* Cambridge, Mass.: MIT Press.

Saariluoma, P. (1985). Chess players' search for the task relevant cues. *Memory & Cognition, 13,* 385–391.
Saariluoma, P. (1989). Chess players' recall of auditorily presented chess positions. *European Journal of Cognitive Psychology, 1,* 309–320.
Saariluoma, P. (1995). *Chess players, thinking.* London: Routledge.
Simon, H. A. (1974). How big is a chunk? *Science, 183,* 129–138.
Simon, H. A., & Gilmartin, K. (1973). A Simulation of memory for chess positions. *Cognitive Psychology, 5,* 29–46.
Vicente, K. J., & de Groot, A. D. (1990). The memory recall paradigm: Straightening out the historical record. *American Psychologist, 45,* 285–287.

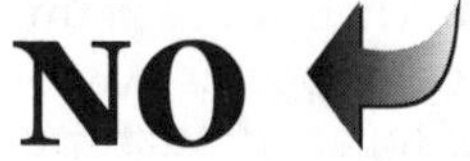

NO

Fernand Gobet

Chunk Hierarchies and Retrieval Structures: Comments on Saariluoma and Laine

Saariluoma and Laine present interesting data on early learning in skill acquisition, and explore computational mechanisms allowing such learning. They also make the theoretical proposal that chunks have a flat organisation that can be used as a retrieval structure, which contrasts with the hierarchical organisation typically used for that purpose in cognitive psychology.

In this paper, I first comment on Saariluoma and Laine's experimental results and on their modelling experiments. I then discuss their theoretical proposal of a flat organisation of chunks, and compare it with the organisation used by CHREST [Chunk Hierarchy and REtrieval STructures], a computational theory of chess expertise (de Groot & Gobet, 1996; Gobet, 1993; Gobet & Simon, 1996b; 2000). Simulations with CHREST of the data presented by Saariluoma and Laine will be used to illustrate some of the differences between the two approaches.

The Experimental Data

While a great deal is known about learning in simple tasks (especially perceptual learning, cf. Shiffrin, 1996) and about expertise in general, relatively little is known about learning at the early stages of expertise. With chess, there is little more about this topic than the experiments carried out by Ericsson and Harris (1990) and Fisk and Lloyd (1988). Therefore, the experiment described by Saariluoma and Laine, where two subjects were trained to improve their memory for briefly-presented chess positions, represents a welcome addition to the literature.

Two main results may be singled out from this experiment. First, with game positions, both subjects improved rapidly at the beginning, and then increasingly more slowly, a curve that is captured by logarithmic or power functions. Second, both subjects showed a slight increase in the

From *Scandinavian Journal of Psychology,* April 2001, pp. 149–155.

recall of random positions. Both results are predicted by theories explaining expertise by the regular acquisition of chunks (for the power law of learning, see Newell & Rosenbloom, 1981; for the use of logarithmic functions describing chunking-based learning and for the recall of random positions, see Gobet & Simon, 1996a, 1996b).

Although these data are interesting, it is a pity that Saariluoma and Laine do not give more details about strategies, errors, or type of chunks replaced by the subjects, as was for example done in Chase and Ericsson's (1982) seminal research on digit-span memory. Indeed, Ericsson and Harris's (1990) sister study on training a novice in recalling chess positions would at least suggest that Saariluoma and Laine's subjects did use some kind of explicit strategy during the learning phase. Information about how well the positions in the training set were learnt would have been of interest as well. Such details would have given more diagnostic power to the data, in particular with respect to modelling. Another slight problem with the data is that both subjects had some knowledge of chess at the beginning of the experiment, which probably inflates the estimate of their recall performance. . . .

As noted above, both subjects improved their recall performance with random positions. Indeed, it is of special interest that Saariluoma and Laine used random positions in their experiment, as recent work has shown that these positions do not simply constitute a control task, as was thought for a long time, but are highly discriminative for theories of expertise. It is well known that Chase and Simon (1973a; 1973b) found that skill effects disappear with briefly-presented random positions, a result that led to an intriguing situation. On the one hand, this finding has often been heralded as one of the most robust phenomena in expertise research (e.g., Ericsson & Kintsch, 1995; Gobet, 1993; Holding, 1985; Saariluoma, 1995). On the other hand, some issues did not fit the puzzle quite so well. For example, Chase and Simon found that "even in the randomised boards, players are noticing the same kinds of structures as those they perceive in the coherent positions, even though these structures occur rarely in randomised boards" (1973b, p. 232), which seems to suggest some kind of skill effect. The presence of adventitious chunks in random positions has been noted by several authors (Chase & Simon, 1973a; 1973b; Saariluoma, 1984, 1989; Simon & Barenfeld, 1973).

It is only recently that the riddle was solved. Gobet and Simon (1996a), combining the result of all published studies they could find on the recall of random chess positions, showed that there is a reliable skill effect, albeit a small one. This effect, however, was not significant in most individual experiments, due to their lack of statistical power. Gobet and Simon (1996a, 1996b) also showed that the chunking theory (Chase & Simon, 1973a, 1973b; Simon & Gilmartin, 1973) and related models predict such a (slight) skill superiority in random positions, because the presence of a large database of chunks makes it more likely to find at least a few chunks in a random position. More recently, Gobet and Simon (2000) showed that CHREST makes accurate quantitative predictions on the recall of random positions, with presentation times spanning from one second to one minute. The skill effect with random positions is theoretically important, because it is difficult to explain with theories based on high-level concepts, such as the theories proposed by Cooke *et al.* (1993) and by Holding (1985). Here, I certainly agree with Saariluoma and Laine that chunks play a key role in chess expertise, and probably in most other kinds of expertise.

The Computer Simulations

In their simulations, Saariluoma and Laine contrast two chunking heuristics. First, a heuristic where chunks are built around a focal piece, using adjacent pieces (random neighbourhood heuristic). Second, a heuristic based on the frequency of co-occurrence and similarity of pieces, which is not constrained by spatial proximity (correlation heuristic). The correlation heuristic fits the data reasonably well. However, a surprising feature of the simulations is that, with both game and random positions, the random neighbourhood heuristic actually gets worse as it learns additional chunks. It is not really clear from the description of the heuristics given by Saariluoma and Laine why this should be so. It is also unclear why the two versions differ at the beginning of the experiment, when no learning has taken place.

As noted by Saariluoma and Laine, the correlation heuristic learns in a way reminiscent of neural nets. A consequence is that it makes predictions about the kind of chunks learnt that differ from the predictions of the random neighbourhood heuristic as well as of the chunking theory and CHREST, which emphasise spatial proximity in learning. What kinds of chunks chess players really learn could be tested in experiments where, for example, the type of chunks acquired by either method were flashed for a few seconds on a computer screen, and recall performance was assessed.

Saariluoma and Laine's goal was not really to run cognitive simulations, but to compare two learning methods. Even so, in order to understand chunking in general, it is worth mentioning some features of their simulations which do not match the empirical data. Contrary to the human data (Chi, 1978) there is no overlap between chunks. Nor does the program make any errors. Finally, the assumption that the program starts with a chunk for each combination of piece and square (a total of 768 chunks) leads to a recall which is too high with random positions at the beginning of learning. While it is probably true that novices can distinguish different kinds of pieces on different squares, as argued by Saariluoma and Laine, it is unlikely that they can memorise them—which is what the program is doing. . . .

Chunk Hierarchies and Retrieval Structures

The main theoretical contribution of Saariluoma and Laine's paper is their discussion of the organisation of chunks and its relation to retrieval structures. Models in the EPAM family organise chunks as a hierarchy, which develops dynamically as a function of learning (see Feigenbaum & Simon, 1984, or de Groot & Gobet, 1996, for details on the learning algorithms). By contrast, Saariluoma and Laine propose a flat, modular organisation, which is similar to that used by most production systems (Newell & Simon, 1972). Both representations are plausible (as are many others), and it is unclear whether current empirical data can discriminate between them.

The next step taken by Saariluoma and Laine is intriguing, however. They first define retrieval structure as meaning that "subjects have some pieces of knowledge in their immediate working memory and the rest of task-relevant information is stored into long-term memory [. . .]" (p. 140). They then propose that "[the] retrieval structure is formed by a set of parallel and non-integrated patterns" and that "the contents of the patterns themselves cause the integration but no direct links combining patterns are required" (Saariluoma and Laine, 2001, p. 140). Before commenting on this proposal, it is necessary to briefly review how the concept of retrieval structure has been used in recent research.

Retrieval structures have enjoyed great popularity in recent years as a means of accounting for (expert) memory in various domains. However, one difficulty with this concept is that different authors use it with different meanings. Chase and Ericsson (1982), who originated the term, give the following definition: "A retrieval structure is a long-term memory structure for indexing material in long-term memory. It can be used to store and order information, but is more versatile because it can allow direct retrieval of any identifiable location. A good example of a retrieval structure is the mnemonic system known as the Method of Loci [. . .]" (p. 17). Note the importance given to storing information, not only to retrieving it. Chase and Ericsson also emphasise the hierarchical structure of retrieval structures and the fact that it takes a massive amount of practice to learn them.

Ericsson and Kintsch (1995) use a similar definition: Retrieval structures are "a set of retrieval cues [that] are organized in a stable structure" (Ericsson & Kintsch, 1995, p. 216; see also their Fig. 1). They also stress that, in addition to retrieval structures, "knowledge-based associations relating units of encoded information to each other along with patterns and schemas [. . .]" (p. 221) are necessary for expert memory.

Kintsch (1998, p. 74) proposes a model where "knowledge is represented as a network of propositions. Such a network is called a *knowledge net.* The nodes of the net are propositions, schemas, frames, scripts, production rules [. . .]". Retrieval structures are defined within this framework: "[. . .] most nodes in a knowledge network are connected with powerful, stable links—retrieval structures—to other nodes in the net that can be brought into working memory" (p. 74). Kintsch's definition is more encompassing than Ericsson and Kintsch's (1995), since it includes patterns and schemas, which are clearly treated separately by Ericsson and Kintsch from cue-based retrieval (retrieval structures), although the two types of encoding are supposed to interact (compare Fig. 4 of Ericsson & Kintsch, 1995, with Fig. 7.2 of Kintsch, 1998).

Like Chase and Ericsson (1982), Richman, Staszewski and Simon (1995) as well as Gobet and Simon (1996c; 2000), who work in the EPAM tradition, emphasise that retrieval structures can store information swiftly and they have a hierarchical organisation. For them, the key aspect of a retrieval structure is that it contains slots (variables) that allow values to be encoded rapidly. They distinguish between structures acquired *explicitly* to meet the demands of the task (retrieval structure in the strict sense), for example by the subjects trained in the digit-span task, and structures acquired *implicitly* in the acquisition of expert knowledge, for example by chess players. They call the latter structures "templates." Both types of retrieval structure have been implemented as computer programs simulating expert memory in the digit-span task and in chess respectively. Note that these authors do not consider an index to long-term memory (LTM) such as the EPAM discrimination net as a retrieval structure, because it lacks the property of allowing rapid encoding. In this respect, their use of the term is consistent with that of Chase and Ericsson (1982, p. 16–17).

As can be seen, Saariluoma and Laine's definition is clearly new: it does not include the ideas of rapid storage, of hierarchical organisation, and of linked nodes, present in all the sources just mentioned. In a sense, it is even less restrictive than Kintsch's (1998) definition, which still provided structure through the links connecting nodes in semantic memory. As noted by Saariluoma and Laine, it is probably too early to evaluate their framework, as more detail about the psychological mechanisms allowing information to be learnt and retrieved are lacking. Perhaps the lack of a hierarchical structure is debatable, since, as we have just seen, it has often been emphasised in the literature on expertise. In addition, the results of Freyhof, Gruber and Ziegler (1992), who asked chess players to partition positions at various levels of granularity, would seem to support a hierarchical organisation.

Obviously, verbal arguments will not settle the question. Saariluoma and Laine present computer simulations, and it is incumbent on theorists defending a different point of view to offer such simulations as well. Fortunately, the template theory (Gobet & Simon, 1996c; 2000) is implemented as a program, called CHREST, which incorporates both the idea of a hierarchical organisation of chunks and the concept of retrieval structure. It is therefore possible to compare it in detail to the theoretical ideas advanced by Saariluoma and Laine.

CHREST: A Computational Theory of Chess Expertise

CHREST (de Groot & Gobet, 1996; Gobet, 1993; Gobet & Simon, 1996b; 2000) is a computational theory of expert chess perception, memory and learning. It is inspired by Simon and Barenfeld's (1969) and Simon and Gilmartin's (1973) programs of perception and memory in chess. CHREST consists of a short-term memory (STM), limited to four items, of a discrimination net, and of mechanisms directing eye movements and managing memory. It acquires chunks (symbols denoting patterns of pieces on the board) by growing a discrimination net when scanning positions from a database of chess games. The discrimination net provides a structure in which chunks are organised hierarchically.

Some of the large chunks evolve into more complex data structures, called templates, which contain a core (similar to chunks) and variable slots, where the information can be rapidly stored. Templates are essentially schemata; the originality of CHREST is in providing mechanisms on how schemata can be learnt, how they relate to perceptual information, and in providing estimates of the time it takes to encode information into schemata. A version of CHREST plays (weak) chess by pure pattern recognition, where recognised patterns elicit potential moves (Gobet & Jansen, 1994).

Eye movements play an important role in CHREST, as they determine the focus of attention, and attention in turn determines what will be learnt. Six mechanisms potentially direct eye movements (de Groot & Gobet, p. 233–236): (a) LTM information; (b) perceptual salience; (c) lines of force (attack and defence); (d) random square in peripheral vision; (e) random piece in peripheral vision; and (f) heuristics aimed at gaining information from a part of the display that has not been fixated yet. Given that some of these mechanisms are not specific to chess, Saariluoma and Laine's (p. 144) statement that "the major simulation models . . . have an important presupposition: they use only chess specific relations, and these are their only heuristics (Simon & Gilmartin, 1973; de Groot & Gobet, 1996)" is simply incorrect.

The program accounts for a large amount of data, including the role of presentation time in the recall of game and random positions (Gobet & Simon, 2000), the effect of mirror-image modification of the board (Gobet & Simon, 1996b), eye movements during the first 5 seconds of the presentation of a position (de Groot & Gobet, 1996), and the recall of multiple boards (Gobet, 1993). Although most of the simulations have been done with the aim of explaining skilled behaviour, it seems worthwhile to see how well CHREST accounts for the data collected by Saariluoma and Laine on early learning. In fact, it turns out that CHREST does this rather well.

Methods

These simulations use the same version of CHREST as discussed by Gobet and Simon (2000); no parameter was altered in order to fit the data. The only difference was that eye-movement heuristics based on relations of defence and attack were disabled (see Saariluoma & Laine, p. 140). To facilitate the comparison with Saariluoma and Laine's simulations, I followed their methodology: same database of positions; 500 positions in the learning set; tests after the study of 30, 60, 175, 220, 270, 350 and 500 positions; 10 game and 10 random test positions, presented for 5 seconds each; 20 independent runs. The only differences were as follows. First, advantage was taken of the fact that CHREST possesses detailed time parameters to carry out fine-grained simulations of the two human subjects, who studied each position for different amounts of time on average (roughly 3 minutes for NT and 5 minutes for MQ). One version of CHREST was allowed 3 minutes per position (CHREST-3), and another 5 minutes (CHREST-5). Second, the program started with zero chunks, but with some knowledge of the board and the pieces. With the recall tests at the beginning of the experiment, it was assumed that CHREST could memorise location, colour and type of piece in three different chunks, yielding a recall of one piece (cf. Gobet & Simon, 1996b). Third, only one estimate of STM capacity was used (three chunks). In previous simulations, Gobet (1998) varied STM capacity with the recall of random positions and found that this capacity gave a good fit to human performance. In addition, STM capacity has been estimated as about three items in domains other than chess (e.g., Zhang & Simon, 1985). Interestingly, this capacity is close to that which gives the best results in Saariluoma and Laine's simulations (four).

Results

. . . CHREST-3 and CHREST-5 account for the human data very well with game positions and reasonably well with random positions. Both human subjects do better at the beginning of the experiment than CHREST, which may be explained either by both having played some chess before the experiment or by a poor calibration of CHREST. . . . Interestingly, the human data for the recall of random positions are not well captured by either function; Saariluoma and Laine propose a linear function to describe learning with the random positions, although a stepwise function would perhaps offer a better fit. The sudden jump present with both human subjects may indicate a change in strategy (Delaney, Reder, Staszewski & Ritter, 1998). . . .

Comparison with Saariluoma and Laine's Approach

In this section, CHREST will be evaluated with respect to the four points addressed by Saariluoma and Laine in their introduction and in their discussion. I will mostly limit the comparison to their correlation heuristic, as their random neighbourhood heuristic does not fit the human data very well.

First, the characteristics of the learning curve. Both CHREST and the correlation heuristic learn in a way that fits a negatively accelerating learning curve such as a power law or a logarithmic function. The human data supports such a learning curve with game positions, but not with random positions. Second, the nature of associative links. Saariluoma and Laine note that the heuristic based on frequency fits the data better than that based on proximity. CHREST, which learns in a way that emphasises spatial proximity, does not support this conclusion, as it fits the human data at least as well as the correlation heuristic. Obviously, frequency is also important with CHREST, since patterns that recur often in the training set are learnt faster than rare patterns. However, frequency is modulated by proximity in a way that is not achieved by the correlation heuristic. As seen above, CHREST learns chunks that reflect the properties found in human chunks. This is interesting in that relations of adjacency, colour, defence, and, more rarely, attack can be acquired with a learning algorithm that heeds only proximity (i.e., non-chess-specific information), assuming that the learning environment consists of coherent material. It is unclear whether the correlation heuristic produces such a result. At any rate, Saariluoma and Laine's claim about the superiority of the frequency heuristic is premature.

Third, the size of working memory. Previous simulations with CHREST have shown that a short-term memory capacity of three matches the human data well (Gobet, 1998; Gobet & Simon, 2000), which is close to the number that gives the best fit in Saariluoma and Laine's simulations. CHREST is also consistent with their view that chess players construct retrieval structures to expand working memory—templates play that role. Finally, the question of hierarchy in retrieval structures. As noted above, Saariluoma and Laine's definition of retrieval structures would include the discrimination net used by CHREST and is therefore more inclusive than that of Simon, Richman, Staszewski and Gobet. The idea of a flat organisation of chunks is of interest, although it is unclear whether current data could discriminate between this kind of organisation and a hierarchical organisation.

Conclusion

Several points of disagreement, some important, have been uncovered in this paper. Some relate to methodological differences. For example, I prefer using richer data, including errors and information about chunks, as well as convergent evidence from various experiments, to evaluate computer models, while Saariluoma and Laine prefer comparing several learning methods on a single set of data (see Hyötyniemi & Saariluoma, 1998, or Laine, Hyötyniemi & Saariluoma, 1998, for a connectionist learning algorithm). Others are more substantial, for example my view that the hierarchical organisation of retrieval structures is critical, compared with Saariluoma and Laine's emphasis on a flat organisation, and my disagreement that their simulations are diagnostic of the superiority of frequency-based chunking over proximity-based chunking.

Although I have emphasised the differences between our approaches in this paper, it should be noted that they also share several similarities. In particular, there is clear agreement about the importance of chunking, the necessity of investigating retrieval structures, the strength of modelling for studying human cognition, and the need for theories of learning, including constructivist theories, to be formulated clearly and precisely, if possible as computer programs. It is unfortunately all too often the case that key concepts in psychology, such as "schema" and, as was shown here, "retrieval structure," evolve multiple meanings due to the flexibility offered by informal theorising. Even if they diverge on several points, our approaches to modelling at least offer the rigour necessary for elucidating these concepts. . . .

References

Chase, W. G. & Ericsson, K. A. (1982). Skill and working memory. In G. H. Bower (Ed.), *The psychology of learning and motivation* (Vol. 16). New York: Academic Press.

Chase, W. G. & Simon, H. A. (1973a). Perception in chess. *Cognitive Psychology, 4,* 55–81.

Chase, W. G. & Simon, H. A. (1973b). The mind's eye in chess. In W. G. Chase (Ed.), *Visual information processing.* New York: Academic Press.

Chi, M. T. H. (1978). Knowledge structures and memory development. In R. S. Siegler (Ed.), *Children's thinking: What develops?* Hillsdale, N.J.: Erlbaum.

Cooke, N. J., Atlas, R. S., Lane, D. M. & Berger, R. C. (1993). Role of high-level knowledge in memory for chess positions. *American Journal of Psychology, 106,* 321–351.

de Groot, A. D. & Gobet, F. (1996). *Perception and memory in chess. Heuristics of the professional eye.* Assen: Van Gorcum.

Delaney, P. F., Reder, L. M., Staszewski, J. J. & Ritter, F. E. (1998). The strategy specific nature of improvement: The power law applies by strategy within task. *Psychological Science, 9,* 1–8.

Ericsson, K. A. & Harris, M. S. (1990). Expert chess memory without chess knowledge. A training study. *Paper presented at the 31st Annual Meeting of the Psychonomic Society,* New Orleans, LA.

Ericsson, K. A. & Kintsch, W. (1995). Long-term working memory. *Psychological Review, 102,* 211–245.

Feigenbaum, E. A. & Simon, H. A. (1984). EPAM-like models of recognition and learning. *Cognitive Science, 8,* 305–336.

Fisk, A. W. & Lloyd, S. J. (1988). The role of stimulus to rule consistency in learning rapid application of spatial rules. *Human Factors, 30,* 35–49.

Freyhoff, H., Gruber, H. & Ziegler, A. (1992). Expertise and hierarchical knowledge representation in chess. *Psychological Research, 54,* 32–37.

Gobet, F. (1993). A computer model of chess memory. *Proceedings of 15th Annual Meeting of the Cognitive Science Society* (pp. 463–468). Hillsdale, NJ: Erlbaum.

Gobet, F. (1998). Memory for the meaningless: How chunks help. *Proceedings of the 20th Meeting of the Cognitive Science Society* (pp. 398–403). Mahwah, NJ: Erlbaum.

Gobet, F. & Jansen, P. (1994). Towards a chess program based on a model of human memory. In H. J. van den Herik, I. S. Herschberg, & J. E. Uiterwijk (Eds.), *Advances in Computer Chess 7.* Maastricht: University of Limburg Press.

Gobet, F. & Simon, H. A. (1996a). Recall of rapidly presented random chess positions is a function of skill. *Psychonomic Bulletin & Review, 3,* 159–163.

Gobet, F. & Simon, H. A. (1996b). Recall of random and distorted positions: Implications for the theory of expertise. *Memory & Cognition, 24,* 493–503.

Gobet, F. & Simon, H. A. (1996c). Templates in chess memory: A mechanism for recalling several boards. *Cognitive Psychology, 31,* 1–40.

Gobet, F. & Simon, H. A. (1998). Expert chess memory: Revisiting the chunking hypothesis. *Memory, 6,* 225–255.

Gobet, F. & Simon, H. A. (2000). Five seconds or sixty? Presentation time in expert memory. *Cognitive Science, 24,* 651–682.

Holding, D. H. (1985). *The psychology of chess skill.* Hillsdale, NJ: Erlbaum.

Hyötyniemi, H. & Saariluoma, P. (1998). Simulating chess players' recall: How many chunks and what kind can they be? *Proceedings of the Second European Conference on Cognitive Modelling* (p. 195–196). Nottingham: University Press.

Kintsch, W. (1998). *Comprehension. A paradigm for cognition.* Cambridge, UK: Cambridge University Press.

Laine, T., Hyötyniemi, H. & Saariluoma, P. (1998). Foundations of simulative theorizing. *Proceedings of the 13th European Conference on Artificial Intelligence* (p. 109–113). London: Wiley.

Newell, A. & Rosenbloom, P. S. (1981). Mechanisms of skill acquisition and law of practice. In J. R. Anderson (Ed.), *Cognitive skill and their acquisition.* Hillsdale, NJ: Lawrence Erlbaum.

Richman, H. B., Staszewski, J. J. & Simon, H. A. (1995). Simulation of expert memory with EPAM IV. *Psychological Review, 102,* 305–330.

Saariluoma, P. (1984). *Coding problem spaces in chess: A psychological study.* Turku: Societas Scientiarum Fennica.

Saariluoma, P. (1989). Chess players' recall of auditorily presented chess positions. *European Journal of Cognitive Psychology, 1,* 309–320.

Saariluoma, P. (1995). *Chess players' thinking.* London: Routledge.

Saariluoma, P. & Laine, T. (2001). Novice construction of chess memory. *Scandinavian Journal of Psychology, 42,* 137–146.

Shiffrin, R. M. (1996). Laboratory experimentation on the genesis of expertise. In K. A. Ericsson (Ed.), *The road to excellence.* Mahwah, NJ: Erlbaum.

Simon, H. A. & Barenfeld, M. (1969). Information processing analysis of perceptual processes in problem solving. *Psychological Review, 76,* 473–483.

Simon, H. A. & Gilmartin, K. J. (1973). A simulation of memory for chess positions. *Cognitive Psychology, 5,* 29–46.

Zhang, G. & Simon, H. A. (1985). STM capacity for Chinese words and idioms: Chunking and acoustical loop hypothesis. *Memory and Cognition, 13,* 193–201.

POSTSCRIPT

Is Novice Memory Based on Associations?

It has been well established that when experts are working with information in their domain of expertise, they process information faster and remember more and larger chunks or patterns of information. It is also well established that experts demonstrate mundane memory skills when tested outside their area of expertise. In order to better understand expert memory, Saariluoma and Laine explored the development of expertise by observing how absolute novices learn to recognize chess patterns. They developed a computer model to simulate the memory performances of two participants, NT and MQ. The researchers had to make several decisions in designing the model, including what characteristics of the arrangement of chess pieces the software program should notice, such as the pieces adjacent to the target or focal piece, the color, and the type of piece. Saariluoma and Laine made the decision to use a non-hierarchical or heterarchical structure for their model. After training the software model, they found that associations, or to use their term *correlations*, made between frequent types of pieces and the colors of the pieces were the most salient aspects in remembering chess patterns.

In the second selection, Gobet argues that a hierarchical system is essential. When designing a software program to imitate human thinking, the programmer must decide if any pieces of information or heuristics have more weight or value. For example, when playing chess the ultimate goal is to capture the other player's king. Therefore, an important rule or heuristic when given a middle-of-the-game board is to locate your king and any immediate threats to your king. If this were a competition in which players were given a chessboard with the game already in progress, one can imagine a coach telling his player, "Remember, the first thing you need to do is look for your king and assess the threats." In a hierarchical structure or model, there are some heuristics, like the "locate king/threats" heuristic that are more valuable or are given a higher priority. In a heterarchical model (Saariluoma and Laine's term) or a flat organizational model (Gobet's term) all the pieces of data and heuristics are of equal value, parallel and non-integrated. Gobet's CHREST software, which stands for Chunk Hierarchy and REtrieval STructures, utilizes a hierarchical model. When Gobet used CHREST to simulate the performance of NT and MQ, he found that proximity or location is the most salient feature in remembering chess patterns.

As removed from reality as this computer modeling might seem, it is consistent with one of the latest trends in education, which is *constructivism*. Developing out of the work of Jerome Bruner, a constructivist approach is most concerned with the way students are constructing or building their individual knowledge bases. As a teaching technique, the goal is to have students integrate new knowledge with their current understanding by keeping them engaged in problem solving and personal discovery. This approach to learning is quite different from a behavioral approach, emphasizing reinforcements and punishments such as extra credit and lost recess time, or an information-processing approach, emphasizing memorization and permanent storage of information. A constructivist approach to learning fits well with computer simulations of learning because both the human being and the software program are trying to construct or build databases and rules for putting data together in meaningful ways.

Suggested Readings

Gobet, F., Lane, P. C. R., and Croker, S. "Chunking mechanisms in human learning," *Trends in Cognitive Sciences,* 5(6), (2001):236–243.

Golledge, R. G. (Editor), *Wayfinding Behavior: Cognitive Mapping and Other Spatial Processes* (Baltimore, MD: Johns Hopkins University Press, 1999).

Saariluoma, P. Chess and content-oriented psychology of thinking. *Psicologica,* 22(1), (2001):143–164.

Saariluoma, P. *Chess Players' Thinking: A Cognitive Psychological Approach* (New York: Routledge, 1995).

Waters, A., Gobet, F., and Leyden, G. "Visuospatial abilities of chess players," *British Journal of Psychology,* 93(4), (2002):557–565.

ISSUE 8

Is Imagination Inflation Imaginary?

YES: Kathy Pezdek and Rebecca M. Eddy, from "Imagination Inflation: A Statistical Artifact of Regression Toward the Mean," *Memory & Cognition* (2001)

NO: Maryanne Garry, Stefanie Sharman, Kimberley A. Wade, Maree J. Hunt, and Peter J. Smith, from "Imagination Inflation Is a Fact, Not an Artifact: A Reply to Pezdek and Eddy," *Memory & Cognition* (2001)

ISSUE SUMMARY

YES: Professors of psychology Kathy Pezdek and Rebecca Eddy demonstrate through analysis and replication of a primary investigation that false memories are not being planted through imagination, but rather the researchers have been fooled by the statistical principle of regression toward the mean.

NO: Researchers and lecturers Maryanne Garry, Stefanie Sharman, Kimberley Wade, Maree Hunt, and Peter Smith argue that Pezdek and Eddy have performed inappropriate statistical analyses, and the proper treatment of the data further demonstrates the phenomenon of imagination inflation.

The question of the existence and characteristics of imagination inflation is quite important to both researchers and practitioners. Memory researchers are continually trying to understand the many ways in which our memories are less than perfect, including the ways our memories can be fooled into accepting that a false or never-occurring event actually happened. Understanding this process is extremely critical in cases of eyewitness testimony in legal situations. Could it be that police officers, investigators, lawyers, and others can actually lead a client to sincerely believe something happened in a certain way when the reality is different? Can interview techniques and suggestive statements actually alter someone's memory? These important questions are at the heart of this discussion of imagination inflation, which is the increased confidence that a never-occurring event actually occurred after simply imagining it.

This issue also highlights the importance of choosing and interpreting appropriate statistical procedures in any scientific endeavor. Scientists rely on the objectivity of their measurements, methodologies, and statistical analyses to keep their findings free of personal bias and influence. Unfortunately in some cases, it is not clear as to which statistical analysis is truly the best. Sometimes the results can be interpreted in several different ways, and it is not clear what the "truth" of the situation is. Often scientists will seek the assistance of a specialist in statistics, psychometrics, mathematics, or experimental methodology to help with these research dilemmas.

Much of this debate is focused on the statistical phenomenon of regression toward the mean. This regression is most likely to occur when engaging a non-random sample of participants and when using two imperfectly correlated measures. At first glance, one might think, "Most measures are not perfectly correlated, but shouldn't all scientists collect data from random samples?" and the answer, ideally, is "Yes." The problem occurs when we deliberately choose a biased sample or when we think we have collected data from a random sample, but in reality we have not.

In the first selection, Pezdek and Eddy perform an experiment similar to that of Garry et. al. to prove their claim that imagination inflation is imaginary, and that Garry et. al.'s results were nothing but a regression toward the mean. In the second selection, Garry et. al. defend their original findings and assert that their data prove that imagination inflation does exist, and they cite several examples of how the experiment by Pezdek and Eddy fails to prove otherwise.

Kathy Pezdek and
Rebecca M. Eddy

Imagination Inflation: A Statistical Artifact of Regression Toward the Mean

> Regression toward the mean is an artifact that as easily fools statistical experts as lay people. The universal phenomenon of regression toward the mean is just as universally misunderstood. Regression toward the mean is a very subtle phenomenon and easy to miss. (Campbell & Kenny, 1999, p. xiii)

This study addresses the conditions under which false autobiographical events are likely to be planted in memory and the potential role of regression toward the mean in interpreting some of the research findings on this topic. In a number of studies, it has been reported that it is possible to plant false events in memory. For example, Loftus and Pickrell (1995) had 24 volunteers suggest to an offspring or younger sibling that he or she had been lost in a mall while shopping when he or she was about 5 years old. Six of the 24 subjects reported either full or partial memory for the false event. Similarly, Hyman, Husband, and Billings (1995) asked college students about their memory for numerous true events and two false events. The percentage of subjects who recalled the false events as real was 20% in Experiment 1 and 25% in Experiment 2. And Ceci, Huffman, Smith and Loftus (1996) read preschool children a list of true and false events and asked them to "think real hard about each" event and "try to remember if it really happened." In the initial session, 44% of the children 3–4 years of age and 25% of the children 5–6 years of age remembered at least one of the false events.

On the other hand, there are clear constraints on the conditions under which false events can be planted in memory (see Pezdek & Hinz, 2002, for a review of these constraints). Pezdek and Roe (1997), for example, reported that although entirely new false events can be planted in children's memory, it is relatively more difficult to suggestively plant a memory for a touch to the body that did not occur than to suggestively change a memory for a touch that did occur. Also, Pezdek, Finger, and Hodge (1997) reported that plausible false events are more likely to be planted in memory than implausible false events. In the second experiment in this study, 20 confederate experimenters read descriptions of one true event and two false events to a younger sibling or close relative. One false event described the relative's being lost in a mall while shopping (the plausible event); the other false event described the relative's receiving a rectal enema (the implausible event). More subjects recalled the false event that involved being lost ($n = 3$) than the false event that involved the enema ($n = 0$). Similar results were reported with 5- to 7-year-old and 9- to 12-year-old children by Pezdek and Hodge (1999).

Recently, Garry, Manning, Loftus, and Sherman (1996) investigated the possibility that childhood events could be suggestively planted in memory by having subjects simply think about the to-be-planted event once. This procedure, called imagination inflation, assesses the extent to which people's confidence that an event occurred in childhood was increased after imagining the event. In the study by Garry et al. (1996), young adults completed a Life Events Inventory (LEI), in which they rated the likelihood that each of 40 events had happened to them before the age of 10 on a scale from 1 (*definitely did not happen*) to 8 (*definitely did happen*); we call these *likelihood ratings*. The list included 8 target events. Two weeks after completing the LEI, the subjects were asked to imagine 4 target events; the other 4 target events served as not-imagined control events. After imagining the events, the subjects completed the LEI a second time. . . . The major finding was that the majority of scores did not change from Time 1 to Time 2. However, when scores did change, positive change scores were more likely to occur than were negative ones. The authors stated that "imagining a self-reported counterfactual event increased confidence that the event did happen" (p. 213). In summarizing the results of this experiment and several others using the imagination inflation paradigm, Garry and Polaschek (2000) concluded that "a growing body of literature shows that imagining contrary-to-truth experiences can change memory" (p. 6). Furthermore, "when people think about or imagine a false event, entire false memories can be implanted. Imagination inflation can occur even when there is no overt social pressure, and when hypothetical events are imagined only briefly" (p. 6).

This study was motivated by concerns about an alternative interpretation of the findings of Garry et al. (1996). Two results in their study suggested that perhaps their findings could be explained as simply a case of regression toward the mean. First, for events initially rated 1–4, likelihood ratings increased for both imagined and not-imagined events. Although there were more imagined events (34%) for which ratings increased from Time 1 to Time 2 than not-imagined events (25%; significance tests of this difference could not be conducted, since individual subjects contributed different numbers of events to each condition), nonetheless this finding suggested that regression toward the mean might explain the upward shift in scores that occurred in both conditions. Second, we recently obtained from the authors their findings regarding the events initially rated 5–8 (C. G. Manning, personal communication, May 19, 1999). . . . When scores did change from Time 1 to Time 2 for these events, 44% decreased (32 of 73), only 16% increased (12 of 73), and this pattern of results was consistent for both imagined and not-imagined events. These findings are exactly what would be predicted by regression toward the mean: When gathering data on the same measurement scale twice, scores below the mean tend to increase, and scores above the mean tend to decrease. . . .

The procedure used in this experiment was similar to the imagination inflation procedure utilized by Garry et al. (1996) and subsequently revised by Garry, Manning, and Loftus (1997). We were primarily interested in the statistical analysis of the ratings of all target events, not just those initially rated as not likely to have occurred. In addition, to provide a specific test of whether the results of Garry et al. (1996) reflect suggested changes in the underlying memories, we included older adults (mean age = 76 years), as well as younger adults (mean age = 21 years), in this study. If the results of Garry et al. (1996) reflect the extent to which false autobiographical events are suggestively planted in memory, the change in likelihood ratings from Time 1 to Time 2 would be expected to be greater for older adults than for younger adults. This prediction follows from the finding of Cohen and Faulkner (1989) that older adults are more suggestible than younger adults.

If the imagination inflation procedure does assess the extent to which false events are planted in memory, several predictions would follow. First, mean likelihood ratings for all imagined target events, not just for those initially rated 1–4, would increase from Time 1 to Time 2. Second, the change in likelihood ratings from Time 1 to Time 2 would significantly interact with the imagination condition, so that ratings for imagined events would change more than ratings for events not imagined. Third, the time × imagination condition × age interaction would be significant, so that the change in likelihood ratings from Time 1 to Time 2 in the imagined condition would be greater for older than for younger adults. On the other hand, if the results simply reflect regression toward the mean, then (1) likelihood ratings for events initially rated 1–4 would be more likely to increase and likelihood ratings for events initially rated 5–8 would be more likely to decrease from Time 1 to Time 2, (2) the change in scores from Time 1 to Time 2 would not interact with imagination condition, and (3) none of the effects involving the imagination condition would interact with age.

Method

Subjects and Design

Seventy-five subjects completed all the phases of Experiment 1. The subjects included one group of 32 older adults (age, $M = 75.66$ years, $SD = 6.18$) and one group of 43 younger adults (age, $M = 20.93$ years, $SD = 3.58$). The younger adults were students in an introductory psychology class at a local community college and received course credit for participating in the experiment. The older adults were recruited from a local senior citizens community center, and each older adult received $10 for his or her participation.

Materials

During the first experimental session, all the subjects completed a 19-item LEI similar to the instrument used by Garry et al. (1996). Whereas Garry et al. (1996) used a 40-item LEI, we used the 20-item LEI utilized by Garry et al. (1997), with one item deleted because it did not translate across cultures. It was also necessary to modify some events in the LEI to indicate more culturally appropriate descriptions of events (e.g., "Shook hands with the Prime Minister" was changed to "Shook hands with the Governor"). . . . Four of these were target events, and 15 were nontarget events. In the Garry et al. (1996) study, 4 target events were imagined, and 4 target events were not imagined per subject. In the interest of time, in this study, the subjects imagined 2 of the 4 target events, and the other 2 target events were not imagined. Three of the 4 target events used in this study were target events from the Garry et al. (1996) study. The assignment of target events to the imagined and non-imagined conditions was counterbalanced across subjects, as was the order of presentation, so that each target item was assigned to the imagined and not-imagined conditions equally often.

Procedure

The procedures used were similar to those in Garry et al. (1996). All the subjects participated in small groups in two phases of the experiment. During the first phase, each subject completed the 19-item LEI with no time limit. The subjects rated how likely it was that each event happened to them before the age of 10 by circling the corresponding number on a scale from 1 (*definitely did not happen*) to 8 (*definitely did happen*). This dependent measure will be called the *likelihood ratings*. A standard vocabulary test was administered after the first LEI was completed. After completing the first phase, the subjects were dismissed and instructed to return 2 weeks later.

In the second phase of the study, the subjects were instructed to imagine two of the four target events. During the imagination sequence, the experimenter instructed the subjects to imagine that each of two target childhood events had happened to them before the age of 10 and to respond in writing to four questions about the imagined scenario. The questions were included to aid in the imagining of the physical details of each event. As each target event was presented, the subjects were instructed as follows:

> I am interested in how elaborately people can imagine events that they may have experienced in their life. I am going to ask you to imagine each of two events. As I read you a description of each event, I am going to ask you to picture the event in your memory in as much detail as possible. I will speak slowly and give you as much time as you need to develop a clear image of the event in your mind. It will help you to form a complete mental picture if you include familiar places, people, and objects in

> your image. Feel free to close your eyes while you form your image or to look at a neutral focal point in this room. On the sheet in front of you, please write your answer to each of the questions that I ask you.

Each subject was allowed 3–5 min to imagine each event and to write down the description.

After completing the imagination sequence, the subjects completed the LEI a second time. The LEI in the second session was identical to the LEI in the first session, with the same instructions given both times. The subjects were allowed unlimited time to complete the inventory and were debriefed after all materials had been collected. The timing of the imagination sequences and the administration of the second LEI followed the procedures of Garry et al. (1996). . . .

Discussion

. . . The major findings in the study by Garry et al. (1996) were replicated in this experiment, suggesting that when the data from both studies were analyzed similarly, the same results occurred; ratings for events initially rated 1–4 were more likely to increase than to decrease. Although these findings were interpreted by Garry et al. (1996) as evidence that imagining the specific target events results in increased confidence that the events are part of one's autobiography, an alternative interpretation exists. The alternative interpretation is that the change in ratings from Time 1 to Time 2 is a statistical artifact of regression toward the mean. Garry and Polaschek (2000) briefly considered this interpretation but concluded that it was "easily dismissed" (p. 9). Several additional analyses were included in this experiment specifically to assess the role of regression toward the mean in accounting for the results of Garry et al. (1996). The two interpretations can be differentiated on the basis of four specific predictions.

First, if the imagination inflation procedure assesses the extent to which events are planted in one's autobiographical memory, mean likelihood ratings for all imagined target events, not just for those initially rated 1–4, would increase from Time 1 to Time 2. . . . In this experiment, as well as in that of Garry et al. (1996), although the mean likelihood ratings for events initially rated 1–4 increased from Time 1 to Time 2, the mean likelihood ratings for events initially rated 5–8 decreased from Time 1 to Time 2. Furthermore, shifts in likelihood ratings toward the mean were not only more frequent . . . but also of a larger mean magnitude than were shifts in likelihood ratings away from the mean, and this trend was similar for the imagined target events, for the target events not imagined, and for the nontarget events. These results support the interpretation that the change in likelihood ratings from Time 1 to Time 2 occurred as a result of regression toward the mean.

Second, if the imagination inflation procedure assesses the extent to which events are planted in one's autobiographical memory, the change in likelihood ratings from Time 1 to Time 2 will significantly interact with imagination condition, so that ratings for imagined events would change more than ratings for events not imagined. This prediction could not be tested in the study by Garry et al. (1996) because an ANOVA was not reported on those data. The ANOVA conducted on the data in this experiment resulted in a nonsignificant interaction of time with the imagination condition ($F < 1$). Furthermore, for target events initially rated 1–4, when large rating increases of more than 3 points did occur from Time 1 to Time 2, they were more likely to occur for events that were not imagined (65% of positive change scores for events not imagined) than for events that were imagined (49% of positive change scores for imagined target events). Again, these results suggest that the change in likelihood ratings from Time 1 to Time 2 occurred as a result of regression toward the mean and does not reflect a change in memory as a result of imagining the target events.

Third, if the imagination inflation procedure assesses the extent to which events are suggestively planted in one's autobiographical memory, the change in likelihood ratings from Time 1 to Time 2 would be greater for older adults than for younger adults. This prediction follows from the finding of Cohen and Faulkner (1989) that older adults are more suggestible than younger adults. This experiment included older (M age = 75.66 years) and younger (M age = 20.93 years) adults to specifically test this prediction. None of the effects involving age significantly affected the likelihood ratings. This result supports the interpretation that the change in likelihood ratings from Time 1 to Time 2 does not reflect a suggestive change in memory as a result of imagining the target events.

Fourth, the strongest test of whether the results from the imagination inflation paradigm result from the planting of the imagined event in memory or from regression toward the mean is provided in the analysis of the mean residual differences, $y - y'$, in the imagine condition. That is, if imagination inflation accounts for the results, then for events initially rated below the mean in the imagine condition, the mean difference between y, the actual obtained Time 2 LEI score, and y', the Time 2 LEI score predicted by the equation $Z_{y'} = (r_{xy})(Z_x)$ should be significantly greater than zero. . . . For each of the four target events, the mean residual difference was not statistically significant. It is clear that for the imagined events that were initially rated as unlikely to have occurred in one's childhood, beyond the effect of regression toward the mean, there is no consistent variance in the change in LEI scores from Time 1 to Time 2, that can be accounted for by any other factors. This analysis of the data provides the strongest statistical basis for concluding that regression toward the mean, and not imagination inflation, accounts for the obtained results.

Because the procedure used in this study did not exactly replicate that of Garry et al. (1996), it might be argued that this study simply presents a failure to replicate Garry et al.'s (1996) results, owing to these methodological differences. There were several procedural differences between the two studies (e.g., the use of 4 vs. 8 target events, the use of 15 vs. 32 filler events, and the use of no cover story vs. a cover story at the beginning of the second administration of the LEI). Many of these methodological differences, in fact, reflect procedures introduced by Garry et al. (1997) in a study subsequent to their 1996 experiment. However, the important point in this study is that *the findings of Garry et al. (1996) were replicated* when the results were analyzed as in Garry et al. (1996). . . . What is new here is the pattern of results for the events initially rated 5–8. . . . Again, there is a similar pattern of results in both studies. Also, the similar pattern of results with the target events and the non-target events in this study suggests that the findings in this study are not item-specific effects. Thus, the present results cannot be attributed to procedural differences between this study and that of Garry et al. (1996). Despite the procedural differences between the two studies, similar results were obtained when similar analyses were conducted.

It might also be argued that imagination inflation is supposed to occur for events that are originally rated as unlikely rather than likely to have occurred. According to this argument, imagining highly probable events could lead to planting new details in memory that conflict with details for related events already stored in memory. As a consequence, likelihood ratings would be reduced by imagining these highly probable events. This argument is not compelling, given that the increase in likelihood ratings from Time 1 to time 2 for events initially rated low and the decrease in likelihood ratings from Time 1 to Time 2 for events initially rated high occurred for the imagined target events and the target events not imagined, as well as for the nontarget events. Thus, the results do not appear to be attributable to the cognitive process of imagining the target events.

It is evident from previous research that under some conditions, false events can be suggestively planted in memory (Hyman et al., 1995; Loftus & Pickrell, 1995; Pezdek et al., 1997; Pezdek & Roe, 1997). However, from the results of this experiment, along with those of Garry et al. (1996), it is clear that the act of thinking about or imagining a false event is not sufficient to plant that false event in memory. In the imagination inflation paradigm, the change in likelihood ratings from Time 1 to Time 2 for imagined events is accounted for by regression toward the mean, and not by a change in memory that results from imagining these events. Extensions of this research are needed to test whether there are only conditions under which imagination inflation for autobiographical memories does occur, above and beyond the effects of regression toward the mean. . . .

Psychologists are currently debating the extent to which false events can be suggestively planted in memory (see Pezdek & Banks, 1996, for a review). Although it is evident that some false events can be planted in memory under some conditions, it is not yet clear what the full range of these conditions is. From the results of this study, it is clear that one act of imagining a fictitious childhood event *does not* alone increase people's confidence that the event happened to them. When people simply think about or imagine a false event, this does not result in the false event's being implanted in memory. What may appear to be imagination inflation is actually a case of statistical regression toward the mean.

References

Campbell, D. T., & Kenny, D. A. (1999). *A primer on regression artifacts.* New York: Guilford.

Ceci, S. J., Huffman, M. L. C., Smith, E., & Loftus, E. F. (1996). Repeatedly thinking about a non-event: Source misattribution among preschoolers. In K. P. Pezdek & W. P. Banks (Eds.), *The recovered memory/false memory debate* (pp. 225–244). San Diego: Academic Press.

Cohen, G., & Faulkner, D. (1989). Age differences in source forgetting: Effects on reality monitoring and on eyewitness testimony. *Psychology & Aging, 4,* 10–17.

Garry, M., Manning, C. G., & Loftus, E. F. (1997, July). *A cognitive whodunit: Thinking about an event can make you think it happened to you.* Paper presented at the meeting of the Society for Applied Research in Memory and Cognition, Toronto.

Garry, M., Manning, C. G., Loftus, E. F., & Sherman, S. J. (1996). Imagination inflation; Imagining a childhood event inflates confidence that it occurred. *Psychonomic Bulletin & Review, 3,* 208–214.

Garry, M., & Polaschek, D. L. L. (2000). Imagination and memory. *Current Directions in Psychological Science, 9,* 6–10.

Hyman, I. E., Husband, T. H., & Billings, F. J. (1995). False memories of childhood experiences. *Applied Cognitive Psychology, 9,* 181–197.

Loftus, E. F., & Pickrell, J. E. (1995). The formation of false memories. *Psychiatric Annals, 25,* 720–725.

Pezdek, K., & Banks, W. P. (Eds.) (1996). *The recovered memory false memory debate.* San Diego: Academic Press.

Pezdek, K., Finger, K., & Hodge, D. (1997). Planting false childhood memories: The role of event plausibility. *Psychological Science, 8,* 437–441.

Pezdek, K., & Hinz, T. (2002). The construction of false events in memory. In H. Westcott, G. Davies, & R. Bull (Eds.), *Children's testimony: A handbook of psychological research and forensic practice.* London: Wiley.

Pezdek, K., & Hodge, D. (1999). Planting false childhood memories: The role of event plausibility. *Child Development, 70,* 887–895.

Pezdek, K., & Roe, C. (1997). The suggestibility of children's memory for being touched: Planting, erasing and changing memories. *Law & Human Behavior, 21,* 95–106.

Maryanne Garry, et al.

Imagination Inflation Is a Fact, Not an Artifact: A Reply to Pezdek and Eddy

> A Western traveler encountering an Oriental philosopher asks him to describe the nature of the world:
> "It is a great ball resting on the flat back of the world turtle."
> "Ah yes, but what does the world turtle stand on?"
> "On the back of a still larger turtle."
> "Yes, but what does he stand on?"
> "A very perceptive question. But it's no use, mister; it's turtles all the way down." (Sagan, 1979, p. 293)

Like Pezdek and Eddy (2001), we begin our reply with an instructive quote. This well-known parable, here told by Carl Sagan, illustrates the dangers of building an argument by stacking faulty thinking on top of faulty thinking. Although Pezdek and Eddy do raise some valid points, in the end their criticisms of imagination inflation are a turret of turtles.

Let us begin with their very first sentence. Contrary to Pezdek and Eddy's claims, their paper does not address "the conditions under which false autobiographical events are likely to be planted in memory" (p. 707). Imagination inflation is not about implanting memories. Pezdek and Eddy still continue to assert that it is, even though we have stressed this point with them before (Garry & Loftus, 2000). Imagination inflation is an increase in confidence that a fictional or hypothetical event that was merely imagined was actually experienced. This point is not trivial, because other imagination inflation researchers have been careful to distinguish between imagination inflation and an implanted memory. For instance, in two different papers, Heaps and Nash (1999, in press) described imagination inflation variously—and accurately—as a change in subjective likelihood; a false belief about the past; or a mechanism by which "imagination can serve to raise subsequent likelihood judgments" (Heaps & Nash, 2001). Mazzoni (2001) has clearly captured the difference between confidence that an event actually happened and a memory for that event. We are all confident, they note, that

From MEMORY AND COGNITION, July 2001, pp. 719–729.

our births occurred as our mothers have explained them to us, although we do not actually have memories for them.

When we change people's confidence that an event might have happened to them, have we affected their memory? We think the answer is yes, because we have changed the way they think about and report their past. But is that an implanted memory? No, because the imagination inflation effect does not meet the criteria others have proposed for implanting a false memory. Take Hyman and colleagues' (Hyman & Kleinknecht, 1999; Hyman & Loftus, 1998) proposal that implanting false memories involves three conditions. First, subjects must accept that the event is plausible. Second, they must construct details about the false event that include an image plus a narrative. Finally, subjects must misattribute the source of that information, wrongly ascribing the mental information to genuine experience rather than to their own imagination. Increased confidence that the target event did happen—the definition of imagination inflation—meets the first criterion, but there is no evidence that it meets the remaining two. Of course, this is not to say that some subjects who participate in an imagination inflation experiment do not develop false memories about the events they imagine, but our aim has been to examine only the change in confidence.

The title of the original paper, "Imagination Inflation: Imagining a Childhood Event Inflates Confidence That It Occurred" (Garry, Manning, Loftus, & Sherman, 1996), makes the definition of imagination inflation clear, and so does quoting Garry and Polaschek (2000) more accurately than Pezdek and Eddy did. Pezdek and Eddy wrote:

> In summarizing the results of this experiment and several others using the imagination inflation paradigm, Garry and Polaschek (2000) concluded that "a growing body of literature shows that imagining contrary-to-truth experiences can change memory" (p. 6). Furthermore, "when people think about or imagine a false event, entire false memories can be implanted. Imagination inflation can occur even when there is no overt social pressure, and when hypothetical events are imagined only briefly." (p. 708–709)

While Garry and Polaschek's (2000) review paper focused on imagination inflation, it did so in the context of a larger review on imagination and memory. In that larger context, the few specific lines Pezdek and Eddy quoted from the Garry and Polaschek abstract make sense. Thus, when the Garry and Polaschek abstract foreshadows that "when people think about or imagine a false event, entire false memories can be implanted," it refers to the opening section of the Garry and Polaschek paper, which reviews what we might call the "Lost in the Mall" genre of studies: Loftus (1993), Loftus and Pickrell (1995), and Hyman and Pentland (1996). Later on in the paper, when the focus is on imagination inflation, Garry and Polaschek refer only to the "effect of imagination on memory" (p. 7) and even define imagination inflation rather tightly as the "confidence-boosting effect of imagination" (p. 7).

Now that we know what effect we are talking about, let us turn to the heart of Pezdek and Eddy's argument. Put bluntly, they assert that Garry et al.'s (1996) results might not show any confidence-inflating effect of imagination at all. Instead, Pezdek and Eddy say these "findings could be explained as simply a case of regression toward the mean" (p. 709; hereafter RTM). Pezdek and Eddy put forth a number of arguments as evidence of their claim, but we believe each argument is flawed. Below we summarize Pezdek and Eddy's experiment, review their four predictions, and examine the strength of their arguments in light of the evidence. First, however, we begin with a basic overview of RTM.

Regression to the Mean: The (Very) Short Course

Every time researchers measure some construct, they unwittingly drag some error into their measurement. Take, for instance, the case each of us might face when administering an Introductory Psychology exam. There are students for whom error depresses their score, and students for whom error inflates their score. So what is the conscientious college professor to do? Suppose you gave the exam again, to the whole class. Of course, you would give a parallel form of the exam, but it would not be perfectly correlated with the first exam. What might happen? The end result would be that some students would find that their retest scores increased, while others would find that their scores decreased. The mean, however, would stay the same, as would the standard deviation and the shape of the distribution in general. With each retest students would change and test scores would change, as long as tests were not perfectly correlated. In short, with subsequent tests, error would be shuffled around differently. The shuffling around would tend to work so that scores farther away from the mean moved closer to the mean on a retest. Instead of referring to this shuffling around under the curve by a tedious name such as "shuffling around under the curve," we call it RTM. . . .

Pezdek and Eddy's Predictions

Pezdek and Eddy hypothesize that if imagination inflation is a real effect, we should expect to see the following pattern of results.

1. The residuals between actual posttest scores and RTM-adjusted (predicted) posttest scores should be greater than zero.
2. There should be a test occasion × condition interaction.
3. All mean likelihood ratings should increase from the pre- to post-test, not just those initially rated as 1–4.
4. There should be a time × imagination × age interaction.

Below we examine the logic behind each prediction, the data on which Pezdek and Eddy rely, and the various conclusions that can be responsibly drawn.

1A. The Prediction: Actual versus RTM-Adjusted Residuals Should Be Greater Than Zero

Pezdek and Eddy argue that if imagination inflation is a real effect, posttest confidence for imagined events will be above and beyond the increase in confidence produced by RTM alone. To analyze their data according to this hypothesis, they did the following analysis.

First, they found the correlation between pretest and posttest scores for not imagined (control) target events, and used the correlation to estimate the effects of RTM. In other words, they constructed a regression line to predict the change in posttest confidence scores that are attributable only to RTM. Second, Pezdek and Eddy used this regression line to predict the posttest scores for the imagined events, again assuming that only RTM was responsible for changing these scores. Finally, they compared the predicted imagined posttest scores with the obtained imagined posttest scores to produce residual scores. Where the residuals are positive, there is undoubtedly an effect over and above RTM. However, what does it mean when the residuals are not different from zero? Pezdek and Eddy argue that it means imagination has no effect, and that imagination inflation is nothing more than RTM disguised as imagination inflation. But they are wrong.

1B. The Turtle: Their Analysis Does Not Work

Contrary to Pezdek and Eddy's claim, their residualized change scores analysis is not a strong statistical basis for drawing any conclusion. There are two broad problems with the attempt to predict—and then correct for—RTM using residualized change scores. The first is a general problem: Several researchers have noted that the method is fraught with difficulties (Campbell & Kenny, 1999; Rogosa, Brandt, & Zimowski, 1982; Rogosa & Willet, 1985). In the end, Campbell and Kenny recommend that if the purpose of the research is to examine causes of change, then "it is inadvisable ever to use residualized change scores or estimated true scores" (p. 99). The second problem is specific to imagination inflation: Pezdek and Eddy's use of residualized change scores just does not work. Because this article is about imagination inflation in particular, let us concentrate on the second problem. We shall see that their formula actually *fails* to detect imagination inflation in some circumstances. Below, we illustrate this problematic situation.

Hypothetical Situation: Failing to Detect Imagination Inflation

Suppose we give a sample of people the same test on two different occasions. If there is no intervening treatment, no measurement error, and no other behavioral change among our subjects, then each person's pretest score and posttest score should be the same. In other words, pretest and posttest scores would be perfectly correlated (r = 1), as in Figure 1. However, a more realistic scenario is that our measurements will include some error, and/or some of our subjects' behavior will change over time. Therefore,

Figure 1

Perfect correlation line, imagination inflation line, and regression line.

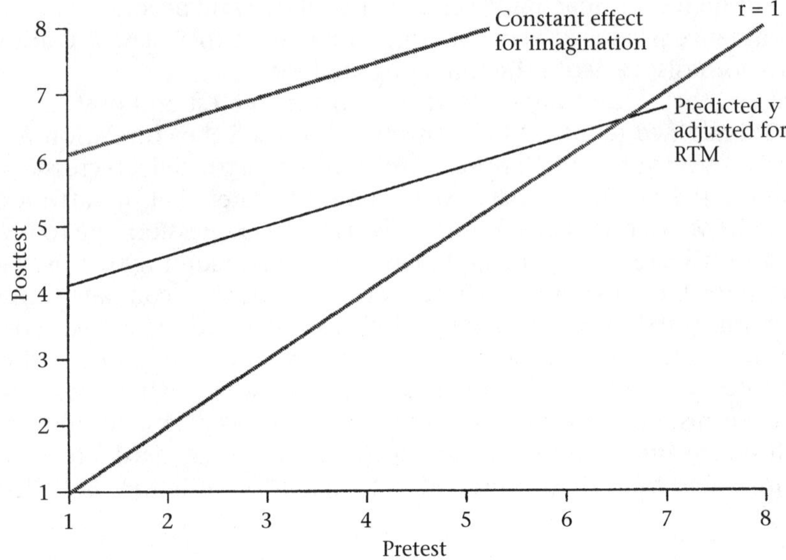

we actually expect a shift away from the perfect correlation line and toward the mean. Figure 1 shows how the predicted *y* line shifts toward the mean. The amount of regression can be estimated by looking at the distance between the perfect correlation line and this predicted line (Campbell & Kenny, 1999).

Suppose we now assume, in this hypothetical example, that imagination inflation has a consistent and genuine effect on confidence. Indeed, such an effect is Pezdek and Eddy's fundamental thesis, that imagination should increase all scores by the same amount, not just low scores. Such a constant effect would produce a parallel line above the predicted *y* line. Let us consider the first of Pezdek and Eddy's recommended analyses, that a test occasion × imagination condition interaction is evidence of imagination inflation. In our hypothetical example, there will be a significant interaction. Now let us consider the second—and what Pezdek and Eddy claim is their most sensitive technique—the residualized change scores analysis. What will this analysis find? It will never be able to find the effect, because it is unable to detect imagination inflation when the shape of the distributions does not change from pretest to posttest. . . . In short, no matter how large the effect size, the technique touted by Pezdek and Eddy as very sensitive to RTM is *insensitive* to imagination inflation if imagination inflation is a homogenous effect.

In sum, Pezdek and Eddy claim that their residual analysis "provides the strongest statistical basis for concluding that regression to the mean—not imagination inflation" (p. 715)—caused their results. However, we have demonstrated that when the shape of the distribution does not change from pretest to posttest, the analysis will not actually detect an effect.

2A. The Prediction: There Should Be a Test Occasion and Condition Interaction

According to Pezdek and Eddy, the mean change in confidence ratings for imagined events should be greater than the mean change for not imagined events, from pretest to posttest. A lack of interaction would signify no effect over and above RTM.

2B. The Turtle: An ANOVA Is Not Always the Best Way to Go

In some ways, the interaction between test occasion and imagination condition is intuitively appealing. Indeed, the difference between the imagined and not imagined change scores is what is evaluated in the interaction term: When it is different from zero, there is an interaction. However, the extent to which the analysis of variance (ANO A) reveals an interaction depends not only on whether there is an interaction, but on other factors as well. It matters, for example, to what extent the data meet the ANO A assumptions. When some assumptions are violated, the ANO A will not reveal an effect that is there, but when other assumptions are violated, it might signal an effect that is not really there. For example, if the data are not normally distributed, the ANO A will be less able to fit a model to the data, and it may not be sensitive to an effect should one exist. In imagination inflation research, target events are deliberately constructed so that the majority of subjects rate them low at pretest; thus, the data are skewed. Outliers pose an additional problem, as does a change in variance between pre- and posttest and across event(s). If the variance changes dramatically, the ANO A copes by fitting a common, interpolated variance. If, for instance, one set of measurements has a large variance and the other has a small variance, the ANO A assumes a moderate variance overall. This moderate assumption causes the ANO A to assume a lower variance than is true in one of the subsets, which might produce false significance for effects in these parts of the data. In addition, it will assume a higher variance than is true in the other subset, which might fail to detect genuine effects found in the other parts of the data. . . .

The problem, as we see it, is to find the right combination of design, measures, and analytical technique to detect the influence of imagination. On that count, the papers by Garry et al. (1996), Heaps and Nash (1999), and Pezdek and Eddy all fall short, and future research on imagination inflation should look at ways to increase the size of the effect, modify the method, and come up with better ways of analyzing the data.

3A. The Prediction: All Mean Likelihood Ratings Should Increase from the Pretest to Posttest

If imagination inflation is a real effect, all mean confidence ratings for imagined events, including those rated 5–8, should inflate from pretest to posttest.

3B. The Turtle: There Is No Basis for the Prediction

To address this third prediction, Pezdek and Eddy analyze their data in several different ways. First, for each critical event, they split the data into two groups, based on pretest responses. Events that were initially rated 1–4 were put into one group, and events initially rated 5–8 were put into the other. For the sake of simplicity, let us refer to these two groups as the *low* and *high* pretest groups, respectively. Then, for each event in each group, Pezdek and Eddy calculated the percentage of subjects whose confidence increased, decreased, or stayed the same from the pretest to posttest Life Events Inventory (LEI). Within each group, they collapsed these change scores across all subjects and all events and classified them according to whether the event was imagined or not imagined. This analysis is what Garry et al. (1996) did, but they confined their analysis to low events, explaining that the purpose of their study was to examine what happens when people imagine an unlikely event, not recall a likely one.

Pezdek and Eddy's analysis of their data, and the comparable analysis of the Garry et al. (1996) data can be summarized into three broad findings.

Finding 1: For Low Pretest Events, Ratings Increased for Both Imagined and Not Imagined Events

Garry et al. (1996) found that for low events, confidence ratings inflated when they were imagined and when they were not imagined; 34% of imagined events showed increased confidence, and 25% of not imagined events showed increased confidence. Pezdek and Eddy found a similar pattern in their data. . . .

We are heartened to see that Pezdek and Eddy's findings contribute to the growing list of those who have replicated imagination inflation (Heaps & Nash, 1999; Paddock et al., 1998; Paddock et al., 1999).

Finding 2: For High Pretest Events, Ratings Were More Likely to Decrease Than Do Anything Else

. . . Both Garry et al. (1996) and Pezdek and Eddy found that when high pretest events were imagined, confidence tended to decrease, or stay the same. How are we to make sense of these results? Pezdek and Eddy make sense of them by saying "these findings are exactly what would be predicted by regression toward the mean" (p. 709). It is true that RTM predicts that high scores should move closer to the mean on retesting (as should low scores). . . .

If we assume that imagination inflates confidence that the low, "probably didn't happen" events did happen, what should be the effect of imagination on confidence for the high, "probably did happen" end of the scale? We might make a number of predictions. On the one hand, Read and Lindsay (2000) have shown that when people think about genuine events, they remember more about them over time. On the basis of their research, we might expect that if high pretest confidence events indicate recall of genuine experiences, imagining these events will cause subjects to become even more confident about them than about high pretest events that are not imagined. On the other hand, it might well be the case that imagining counterfactual details about genuine experiences ultimately makes subjects less confident about what is real and what is imagined. The issue of how imagining "probably did happen" events affects memory for those events is a question worthy of study in its own right, and it is unlikely to be answered by post hoc analysis and speculation. As matters stand now, we have no idea what might be the effect of imagining events that subjects believe were probably genuine experiences. Pezdek and Eddy's assertion that if imagination inflation is a real effect, it should affect confidence about events no matter what their pretest ratings, is untenable given how little we know about the effects of imagination on memory. . . .

Finding 3: Items Tend to Move toward the Mean at Posttest

Pezdek and Eddy examined their data according to the following rationale: "If regression toward the mean is operative in the imagination inflation paradigm, it should be evidenced with the nontarget events, as well as with the target events" (p. 711). On this point, we have no dispute with Pezdek and Eddy. . . .

Finding 4: Only the Low Pretest Group Showed Inflation

We were also heartened to see that Pezdek and Eddy replicated another of Garry et al.'s (1996) findings. That is, when low events were treated as cases, there was more inflation (the percentage of positive change) for imagined events than for not imagined events. It is interesting to note that even though Pezdek and Eddy used fewer critical items—and thus had fewer degrees of freedom in their *t* test—they still showed imagination inflation. . . .

4A. The Prediction: There Should Be an Age and Imagination Interaction

On the basis of G. Cohen and Faulkner's (1989) finding that older adults perform more poorly than younger adults at distinguishing between externally and internally generated information (watched vs. imagined events), Pezdek and Eddy claim that if imagination inflation is a real effect, there should be an age × imagination interaction when one compares the effects of imagination on college aged and on older adults. However, if RTM is behind imagination inflation, there will be no interaction, because RTM will affect both age groups equally.

4B. The Turtle: Pezdek and Eddy Failed to Consider Other Mechanisms

Although Pezdek and Eddy describe their prediction in a couple of sentences, we think it is worth more than a brief overview. There is nothing wrong with this prediction per se, but in focusing on the source-monitoring explanation (Johnson, Hashtroudi, & Lindsay, 1993), Pezdek and Eddy have failed to take into account other equally likely explanations, such as a familiarity-based explanation. Imagination inflation can also occur if the familiarity of an event is misattributed to the actual occurrence of the event rather than the imagining of the event. . . .

Pezdek and Eddy failed to take plausibility into account when they included "Found a $10 bill in a parking lot" as one of only two critical events imagined by half of the subjects. Their college subjects (mean age, 20.9 years) probably believed that finding a $10 bill in the parking lot in 1988 (when these subjects were approximately 10 years old) was quite plausible. However, consider the situation for the older adults (mean age, 75.7 years). Finding a $10 bill in 1933 (when the older subjects were approximately 10) would be the equivalent of finding nearly $120 today according to the Bureau of Labor Statistics' Consumer Price Index (2000). Finding such a significant sum of money is not very plausible at all, particularly during the Great Depression. A second plausibility problem caused by using the "$10 bill" event is the frequency with which subjects might have been in a parking lot. When the college students were 10 years old, there were approximately 137 million cars in the United States (Bureau of the Census, 1988). However, when the older adults were 10, there were only about 1 million cars, and—presumably—not as great a need for somewhere to park them (Bureau of the Census, 1934). Thus, we may conclude that Pezdek and Eddy's older adults might have found the idea of being in a parking lot as a child to be a rather unusual event. The conjunction of these two situations—finding the equivalent of $120 and finding it in a parking lot—would be even less likely than either one alone.

In short, we believe that the 50% of older subjects who imagined finding a $10 bill in a parking lot may well have found the experience implausible, and/or difficult to imagine. These factors might have offset any tendency of these older subjects for increased source confusion (which by itself might have caused more imagination inflation), resulting in no effect for age on imagination inflation. Therefore, Pezdek and Eddy's claim that no age × imagination interaction shows that imagination inflation is nothing more than RTM is premature. . . .

Final Comments

We have illustrated several shortcomings in Pezdek and Eddy's paper. These shortcomings range from the relatively minor instances of misrepresenting what imagination inflation is and what others have said about it, to major problems with their predictions. Perhaps the most important problem in their arguments is the lack of appreciation that comparisons between control and experimental conditions are used to adjust for a variety of possible factors, including RTM. Still, we believe that Pezdek and Eddy have made a contribution to the research on the effects of imagination and memory, in much the same way as McCloskey and Zaragoza (1985) did for misinformation research (Loftus, Miller, & Burns, 1978). McCloskey and Zaragoza attempted to demonstrate that there was no evidence that misleading postevent information had an effect on memory. Although they did not claim that previous evidence of postevent memory distortion was simply RTM disguised as an effect, they did claim something similar: that the standard forced-choice memory test Loftus and colleagues used biased subjects to respond in such a way as to give the appearance of an effect. Later, Belli (1989) showed that McCloskey and Zaragoza's modified test was actually insensitive to memory impairment. In many ways, McCloskey and Zaragoza's most important contribution was to spark renewed interest in the area, the end result being that this new research advanced our knowledge of how postevent suggestions affect memory (Abeles & Morton, 1999; Belli, 1989; Frost, 2000; Lindsay, 1990; Loftus & Hoffman, 1989; Zaragoza & Lane, 1998; Zaragoza & McCloskey, 1989). What we discovered grew quickly, and by leaps and bounds. We are grateful to Pezdek and Eddy for providing researchers with a similar opportunity to discover the ways in which imagination can influence our sense of ourselves and our past. Let us hope our research advances faster than a turtle does.

References

Abeles, P., & Morton, J. (1999). Avoiding misinformation: Reinstating target modality. *Quarterly Journal of Experimental Psychology, 52A,* 581–592.

Belli, R. F. (1989). Influences of misleading postevent information: Misinformation interference and acceptance. *Journal of Experimental Psychology: General, 118,* 72–85.

Bureau of the Census, S Department of Commerce (1934). *Statistical Abstracts of the United States* (57th ed.). Washington, DC: Government Printing Office.

Bureau of the Census, S Department of Commerce (1988). *Statistical Abstracts of the United States* (108th ed.). Washington, DC: Government Printing Office.

Campbell, D. T., & Kenny, D. A. (1999). *A primer on regression artifacts.* New York: Guilford.

Cohen, G., & Faulkner, D. (1989). Age differences in source forgetting: Effects on reality monitoring and on eyewitness testimony. *Psychology & Aging, 4,* 10–17.

Frost, P. (2000). The quality of false memory over time: Is memory for misinformation "remembered" or "known"? *Psychonomic Bulletin & Review, 7,* 531–536.

Garry, M., & Loftus, E. F. (2000, March). *Imagination inflation is not a statistical artifact.* Paper presented at the meeting of the American Psychology-Law Society, New Orleans.

Garry, M., Manning, C. G., Loftus, E. F., & Sherman, S. J. (1996). Imagination inflation: Imagining a childhood event inflates confidence that it occurred. *Psychonomic Bulletin & Review, 3,* 208–214.

Garry, M., & Polaschek, D. L. L. (2000). Imagination and memory. *Current Directions in Psychological Science, 9,* 6–10.

Heaps, C., & Nash, M. (1999). Individual differences in imagination inflation. *Psychonomic Bulletin & Review, 6,* 313–318.

Heaps, C., & Nash, M. (2001). Comparing recollective experience in true and false autobiographical memories. *Journal of Experimental Psychology: Learning, Memory, & Cognition, 27,* 920–930.

Hyman, I. E., Jr., & Kleinknecht, E. E. (1999). False childhood memories. In L. M. Williams & . L. Banyard (Eds.), *Trauma and memory* (pp. 178–188). Thousand Oaks, CA: Sage.

Hyman, I. E., Jr., & Loftus, E. F. (1998). Errors in autobiographical memory. *Clinical Psychology: General, 117,* 371–376.

Hyman, I. E., Jr., & Pentland, J. (1996). The role of mental imagery in the creation of false childhood memories. *Journal of Memory & Language, 35,* 101–117.

Johnson, M. K., Hashtroudi, S., & Lindsay, D. S. (1993). Source monitoring. *Psychological Bulletin, 114,* 3–28.

Lindsay, D. S. (1990). Misleading suggestions can impair eyewitnesses' ability to remember event details. *Journal of Experimental Psychology: Learning, Memory, & Cognition, 16,* 1077–1083.

Loftus, E. F. (1993). The reality of repressed memories. *American Psychologist, 48,* 518–537.

Loftus, E. F., & Hoffman, H. G. (1989). Misinformation and memory: The creation of new memories. *Journal of Experimental Psychology: General, 118,* 100–104.

Loftus, E. F., Miller, D. G., & Burns, H. J. (1978). Semantic integration of verbal information into a visual memory. *Journal of Experimental Psychology: Human Learning & Memory, 4,* 19–31.

Loftus, E. F., & Pickrell, J. E. (1995). The formation of false memories. *Psychiatric Annals, 25,* 720–725.

Mazzoni, G. (2001, June). *Time course in the development of false beliefs and memories after imagination.* Paper presented at the meeting of the Society for Applied Research in Memory and Cognition, Kingston, ON.

McCloskey, M., & Zaragoza, M. (1985). Misleading postevent information and memory for events: Arguments and evidence against memory impairment hypotheses. *Journal of Experimental Psychology: General, 114,* 1–16.

Paddock, J. R., Joseph, A. L., Chan, F. M., Terranova, S., Manning, C., & Loftus, E. F. (1998). When guided visualization procedures may backfire: Imagination inflation and predicting individual differences in suggestibility. *Applied Cognitive Psychology, 12,* S63–S75.

Paddock, J. R., Noel, M., Terranova, S., Eber, H. W., Manning, C. G., & Loftus, E. F. (1999). Imagination inflation and the perils of guided visualization. *Journal of Psychology, 133,* 581–595.

Pezdek, K., & Eddy, R. M. (2001). Imagination inflation: A statistical artifact of regression toward the mean. *Memory & Cognition, 29,* 707–718.

Read, J. D., & Lindsay, D. S. (2000). "Amnesia" for summer camps and high school graduation: Memory work increase reports of prior periods of remembering less. *Journal of Traumatic Stress, 13,* 129–147.

Rogosa, D., Brandt, D., & Zimowski, M. (1982). A growth curve approach to the measurement of change. *Psychological Bulletin, 92,* 726–748.

Rogosa, D. R., & Willett, J. B. (1985). nderstanding correlates of change by modeling individual differences in growth. *Psychometrika, 50,* 203–228.

Sagan, C. (1979). *Broca's brain: Reflections on the romance of science.* New York: Random House.

Zaragoza, M. S., & Lane, S. M. (1998). Processing resources and eyewitness suggestibility. *Legal & Criminological Psychology, 3,* 305–320.

Zaragoza, M. S., & McCloskey, M. (1989). Misleading postevent information and the memory impairment hypothesis: Comment on Belli and reply to Tversky and Tuchin. *Journal of Experimental Psychology: General, 118,* 92–99.

POSTSCRIPT

Is Imagination Inflation Imaginary?

In the first selection, Pezdek and Eddy conducted a partial replication of an earlier study by Garry, Sharman, Wade, Hunt, and Smith in order to test the hypothesis that the research team did not find imagination inflation, but rather regression toward the mean. Pezdek and Eddy asked adults to rate a series of events according to how likely it was these events occurred during the individual's childhood using a Likert scale from 1, meaning it definitely did not happen, to 8, meaning it definitely did happen. Then they asked each participant to imagine an event that did not happen. At a later time the participants again rated the likelihood of the same series of events. Results indicated that rather than false memories being planted, which would be indicated by only increasing scores on the Likert scale, all the scores moved toward the mean. The lower scores drifted up, and the higher scores drifted down toward the middle scores. Further, Pezdek and Eddy found that the larger increases in certainty that a false event occurred were associated with the non-imagined events rather than the imagined ones.

Garry, et al., go to great lengths to refute each of the claims in the first selection. First they demonstrate that what Pezdek and Eddy claim to be their most powerful test, analysis of the residual change scores from pretest to posttest, is actually insensitive to imagination inflation scores. Garry, et al., claim that the use of the statistical procedure known as ANOVA, or analysis of variance, was a poor choice because it will not reveal whether confidence in the occurrence of imagined-but-never-occurring items is greater than confidence in the non-imagined-never-occurring items. Garry, et al., point out that little is known as to the influence of imagining an event that probably occurred, and they question the assertions made by Pezdek and Eddy that imagination inflation should increase the confidence scores in such a case. Finally, Garry, et al., question the appropriateness of the items used for the older adults, comparing the situation of "finding a $10.00 bill when 10 years old" for a college student, who was likely to be ten year.s old in the late 1980s, and an older adult, who would have been ten years old in the 1930s. Their conclusion is that Pezdek and Eddy were wrong on numerous accounts, and that in fact their findings were consistent with notion of imagination inflation.

As a college professor in psychology, I occasionally get asked, "Why do I need to know so much about statistics? All I want to do is help people." This debate brings to light several of the answers to this question. Scientists are human beings with emotions, opinions, biases and sometimes prejudices, and because of our humanity we cannot simply give our opinion about a topic. We must provide evidence gathered ethically and objectively through research. Our research evidence is then given to practitioners to apply to their clients' situations. Statistical procedures can be complex and may involve areas of uncertainty that require the scientist to make decisions in somewhat ambiguous situations. Practitioners need some basic training in statistical analysis in order to interpret the evidence passed on to them through journals and conferences, and they need the ability to determine whether the statistical judgments made in ambiguous situations are sound.

Suggested Readings

Dowdy, S., Wearden, S., and Chilko, D. *Statistics for Research* (New York: John Wiley and Sons, 2004).

Keppel, G., and Wickens, T. *Design and Analysis: A Researcher's Handbook* (Upper Saddle River, NJ: Prentice-Hall, 2003).

Pezdek, K., and Hinz, T. "The construction of false events in memory." In H. Westcott, G. Davies, and R. Bull (Editors), *Children's testimony: A Handbook of Psychological Research and Forensic Practice* (New York: Wiley, 2002).

Pezdek, K., and Taylor, J. "Memory for traumatic events." In M. L. Eisen, G. S. Goodman, and J. A. Quas (Editors), *Memory and Suggestibility in the Forensic Interview* (Mahwah, NJ: Lawrence Erlbaum and Associates, 2002).

Whitfied, C., Silberg, J., and Fink, P. (Editors), *Misinformation Concerning Child Sexual Abuse and Adult Survivors* (Binghamton, NY: Haworth, 2002).

ISSUE 9

Is Adult Memory for Childhood Abuse Unreliable?

YES: Peter A. Ornstein, Stephen J. Ceci, and Elizabeth F. Loftus, from "Adult Recollections of Childhood Abuse: Cognitive and Developmental Perspectives," *Psychology, Public Policy, and Law* (1998)

NO: Judith L. Alpert, Laura S. Brown, and Christine A. Courtois, from "Comment on Ornstein, Ceci, and Loftus (1998): Adult Recollections of Childhood Abuse," *Psychology, Public Policy, and Law* (1998)

ISSUE SUMMARY

YES: Professors of psychology and law Peter Ornstein, Stephen Ceci, and Elizabeth Loftus question the accuracy of adult memories for child abuse by explaining the many delicate and malleable features of human memory that can create false memories.

NO: Law professor Judith Alpert and clinical psychologists Laura Brown and Christine Courtois respond by challenging the memory researchers' understanding of trauma research and psychotherapy, and by accusing them of undermining the healing process of abuse victims.

The debate illustrated in this section is among the most interesting and the most painful. Many professionals, including clinicians and psychologists, lawyers and judges, and law enforcement and forensic investigators, are struggling with the immensely important task of determining who is lying, who is sincerely confused, and who is telling the truth in legal cases. While the need to determine the truth is important in every case, it is particularly important in cases involving crimes of a sexual nature in which there are often no witnesses. It is the word of the accused against the word of the victim. Cognitive scientists have joined in this discussion by offering research findings on how human memory works, when it tends to be accurate, and how and when it can be fooled.

According to the Rape, Abuse, & Incest National Network (RAINN; www.rainn.org), the number of sexual crimes, while declining is some cases, is still staggering. RAINN reports that one out of every six American women, or about 17%, have been the victim of an attempted or completed rape. This crime is perpetrated against men as well, with data indicating that approximately 3% of American men have been victims. Statistics regarding the attempted or completed rape of children are often shielded because of the confidentiality issues involved; however, RAINN estimates that approximately 44% of all rape victims are under age 18, and of that 15% are under age 12. These sobering statistics are painful and inflammatory. American citizens want to bring these perpetrators to justice.

Cognitive scientists have known for some time that our memories are often delicate and can decay or be swayed over time. In his article titled "The Seven Sins of Memory," Daniel Schacter of Harvard University summarizes the fallible aspects of human memory (Schacter, D. L. 1999. The Seven Sins of Memory: Insights from Psychology and Cognitive Neuroscience. *American Psychologist, 54(3)*, 182–203). The seven problems are:

- Transience: Memory is susceptible to gradual forgetting, and with that our memories for facts and events typically become less accurate over time.
- Absent-mindedness: We can fail to encode routine things, such as where we put our car keys, or our retrieval may be incomplete, such as when we forget to do something.
- Blocking: Even when a fact or event has been encoded deeply and has not been lost, it may sometimes be temporarily inaccessible, and we just can't seem to remember the information.
- Misattribution: Particular pieces of information may be misattributed to an incorrect time, person, event, or concept.
- Suggestibility: We have a tendency to incorporate information provided by others when trying to recall something.
- Bias: Memory encoding and retrieval are highly dependent on, and influenced by, preexisting knowledge, beliefs, mood, and emotional state.
- Persistence: We experience persistence when we continue to remember something we would rather forget.

In the first selection, Ornstein, Ceci, and Loftus are concerned about the possibility that innocent people have been sent to prison based on an alleged victim's false memories. In particular, they are most concerned about the validity of memories that first surface years after the event occurred and while the individual is in therapy. Ornstein, et al., conclude that based on a review of memory research, professionals should be quite skeptical of adult memories of childhood abuse. In the second selection, Alpert, Brown, and Courtois show that, as memory researchers, Ornstein, et al., do not have an understanding of human traumatization and memory for emotional events. Alpert, et al., assert that the researchers are guilty of selecting literature to prove their points, and that in doing so they contribute to the gross misunderstanding and continued pain of victims of abuse.

Peter A. Ornstein, Stephen J. Ceci, and Elizabeth F. Loftus

Adult Recollections of Childhood Abuse: Cognitive and Developmental Perspectives

Increasingly during the 1980s, the specters of two equally awful phenomena arose. Genuine sexual victimization became more and more visible, and many victims were not believed when they came forward. A separate but also painful problem is the realization that innocent people have been accused of these crimes, with attendant devastation for themselves and their families.

An understanding of these two types of life-shattering phenomena requires a consideration of the operation of memory. Of special importance are issues such as the extent to which delayed reports of traumatic experiences are taken (by the self and others) to be accurate and believable reflections of reality and the degree to which memory is malleable and can come to be distorted over time. In this regard, experiences involving victimization can be arrayed along a continuum. At one extreme, there is the type of case in which a victim has sustained enduring memory for a traumatic experience that is independently corroborated. At the other extreme, there is the situation in which an individual has no memory at all for having been victimized, and there is no corroboration. Between these two extremes are a variety of cases in which different types of partial memory are reported, with or without corroboration. . . .

A Framework for Examining Memory

A person's ability to remember events involves the execution of a complex set of processes on information to which he or she is exposed. These cognitive activities are often discussed by cognitive and developmental psychologists in terms of the flow of information within the memory system. A consensus view in the field would hold that at a minimum, memory involves the encoding of information into some type of storage system from which it may be subsequently retrieved and reported. . . .

Consistent with this emphasis on encoding, storage, and retrieval, Loftus and Davies (1984) suggested that remembering was determined by

From PSYCHOLOGY, PUBLIC POLICY AND LAW, December 1998, pp. 1025–1051.

such factors as the organization and quality of the initial representation of the event to be recalled, the individual's prior knowledge of that event, the delay interval between storage and subsequent retrieval, the type of cue or prompt used to elicit recall, and the events that take place in the interval prior to recall testing. In a similar fashion, Ornstein and his colleagues (Ornstein, Larus, & Clubb, 1991; see also Ornstein, 1995) have discussed remembering in terms of the following four general themes about memory performance: (a) Not everything gets into memory; (b) what gets into memory may vary in strength; (c) the status of information in memory changes; and (d) retrieval is not perfect (i.e., not all that endures gets retrieved). . . .

Theme 1: Not Everything Gets into Memory

It is important to emphasize at the outset that not all "problems" of remembering are due to failures to retrieve stored information. Indeed, some experiences may not be remembered because they were not entered into memory in the first place. The human cognitive system is quite limited, and some incoming information must be selected for attention and further processing, whereas other information is essentially excluded. . . .

A number of factors influence the encoding of information in memory, perhaps the most important of which is having the necessary prior knowledge to understand and interpret what is being experienced. A great deal of research suggests that what an individual already knows and the expectations that are created by this knowledge can severely influence how he or she monitors the world, how events are interpreted and, hence, how incoming information is coded and placed in memory (Bjorklund, 1985; Chi, 1978; Chi & Ceci, 1987; Ornstein & Naus, 1985). . . .

Theme 2: What Gets into Memory May Vary in Strength

Assuming that information about an experience is encoded and entered into long-term memory, several factors may influence the strength and organization of the resulting trace in memory. Moreover, strong traces may be readily retrieved, even in response to minimal cues and prompts, whereas weak traces may be more difficult to recover and may require greater levels of "support." The research literature suggests several basic factors that have the potential to affect the strength of traces in memory: the amount of exposure to a particular event (both in terms of the length of exposure and the number of repetitions), the age of the individual, and the salience of the event (with highly salient experiences surviving longer that less salient ones). . . .

Theme 3: The Status of Information in Memory Changes

Given that information about an event has been stored, the status of the memory trace can be altered during the course of the interval between the actual experience and a report of it (see Brainerd & Ornstein, 1991; Ornstein, Gordon, & Baker-Ward, 1992). The passage of time, as well as a variety of intervening experiences, can influence strongly the strength and organization of stored information. In this regard, it is quite possible that professional interactions with therapists may alter clients' reports of the events being discussed (see Lindsay & Read, 1994). Moreover, the impact of these encounters and discussions will likely increase as a function of increase in the delay interval, as the memory trace undergoes decay. . . .

Theme 4: Retrieval Is Not Perfect

The final step in remembering involves the retrieval of information in storage. Not everything in memory can be retrieved all of the time. Putting aside the issue of whether the basic memory representations have been altered or not, it still is the case that the contents of the memory system are not always retrievable. A variety of cognitive and social factors can have an impact on an individual's ability to gain access to previously acquired information or even to attempt to do so. . . .

It must also be recognized that what a person "remembers" and reports may not always be retrieved from memory storage. Indeed, particularly after long delays during which time the details of events may have faded, the gaps may be filled in by constructive processes at retrieval. Thus, recall may be determined by the recovery of some stored information in combination with the logical construction of what might have taken place. Indeed, recall at a delay may be more profitably viewed as a mixture of reproduction and reconstruction, with the latter process often being unconscious. It must also be recognized that social forces (e.g., fear of embarrassment) may operate under some conditions to lead an individual to elect not to report publicly what has been retrieved from memory. . . .

A Developmental Perspective

A developmental orientation is implicit in any discussion of the flow of information within the memory system. As suggested, age-related differences in prior knowledge, in the strength and organization of underlying representations, in the time course of forgetting, and in fundamental information processing skills all have important implications for what can be remembered. . . .

Understanding and Encoding

At the most fundamental level, one cannot retrieve a memory of an event unless it was adequately encoded and stored in memory in the first place. As suggested above, prior knowledge about the events being experienced is essential for successful encoding and memory storage, and an implication of the literature is that a child who does not understand what is happening to him or her will have little basis for subsequently remembering what was experienced. For example, when the targets of abuse are young enough to have almost no knowledge of sexuality, they will be unable to interpret what has happened, and their memory may not be very accurate. Although children as young as 2 and 3 years of age will clearly understand that something is wrong if they experience physical pain associated with anal or vaginal penetration, when they experience "milder" forms of abuse (e.g., frequent "accidental" touching of private parts) they may not even be aware that they are being abused. . . .

Developmental Changes and Cognitive Reorganization

Even when experiences are understood and encoded in memory, what is remembered later depends upon many factors. Age-related changes in the strength and organization of the underlying representations, as well as developmental differences in the time course of forgetting and the level of support required for recall are all critical determinants of what can be remembered. The influence of these factors, moreover, is exacerbated as the "delay interval" and is extended from days to months to years, which is obviously the case in discussions of adults' abilities to remember early experiences. Further, the dramatic cognitive reorganization that takes place with development from infancy and early childhood to the adult years is so complete that it becomes difficult to approach the task of remembering from the same cognitive perspective that was operative when the events to be remembered were originally experienced. . . . It is thus unlikely that an event that was encoded using an infant's or young child's perceptual-motor schemes can be retrieved using adult inferential schemes that were not available to the infant at the time of encoding. . . .

In general, on the basis of an assessment of the total corpus of the developmental literature, there is scant evidence for the claim that an adult can gain access to the contents of children's perceptual encodings and can then recode them using more mature interpretive schemes, though such recodings may occur under special circumstances. Differences in the organization of adult and 2-year-old minds make it difficult for the former to gain access to the cognitive products of the latter. The same mental schemes used by an immature cognitive system to encode an event are needed to later retrieve the original encoding of the event. To repeat, it is hard to imagine how an event that requires semantic interpretation can be recalled in adulthood if the event was not semantically interpreted at the time of encoding. Thus, there is reason to be skeptical of claims that adults can retrieve memories of early events that are laden with current adult meaning. . . .

Infantile Amnesia

The developmental analysis presented here relates directly to the well-documented phenomenon of infantile or childhood amnesia, that is, the general "poverty" of adult recollections of the first several years of life.

Freud (1905/1953) identified the phenomenon in some of his earliest writings: "What I have in mind is the peculiar amnesia which . . . hides the earliest beginnings of the childhood up to their sixth or eighth year" (p. 174). Subsequent investigators would say that Freud's suggestion about the 6th year misses the mark. Indeed, most studies of childhood amnesia suggest that the earliest recollections of adults are not generally of experiences taking place before the age of about 3 or 4 (Kihlstrom & Harackiewicz, 1982; Pillemar & White, 1989). For example, Winograd and Killinger (1983) have reported that few of their participants who were younger than 3 at the time of the Kennedy assassination were able to recall any information about where they were when they heard the news. . . .

Suggestibility and Distortions of Memory

A central feature of the framework introduced above is that memory representations are not static but rather are subject to considerable change over time. Details may be lost and information in storage may be modified so as to increase its consistency vis-à-vis underlying knowledge. Moreover, for a variety of reasons, exposure to postevent information, either prior to retrieval or at the time of questioning, has the potential to result in changes in the contents of memory, or at least in participants' reports of what is remembered. . . .

The Influence of Postevent Misleading Information

. . . A great deal of research illustrating that memory can become skewed when people assimilate new data makes use of a simple variation on the traditional retroactive interference paradigm. Participants first witness a complex event, such as a simulated violent crime or an automobile accident. Subsequently, half of the participants receive new misleading information about the event, whereas the others do not get any misinformation. Finally, all participants attempt to recall the original event. Consider, for example, a study in which participants saw a simulated traffic accident and then received one of two types of written information about the accident. Some participants were misled about what they had seen (e.g., a stop sign was referred to as a yield sign), whereas the others did not receive misleading information. Later, when asked whether they originally saw a stop or a yield sign, those participants who had been given the incorrect information (yield sign) tended to choose it on the recognition test (Loftus, 1979).

By now, this basic finding has been replicated in a wide range of experiments involving a broad variety of materials (see Loftus, 1982), with the result being that the memory performance of participants who were exposed to misleading postevent information was routinely inferior to that of individuals who had not been presented with such information. Indeed, people have recalled nonexistent broken glass and tape recorders, a clean-shaven man as having a mustache, straight hair as curly, stop signs as yield signs, hammers as screwdrivers, and even something as large and conspicuous as a barn in a bucolic scene that contained no buildings at all. In short, misleading postevent information can alter a person's recollection in a powerful, even predictable, manner. In some experiments, moreover, the deficits in recollection following receipt of misinformation have been dramatic, with performance differences as large as 30% or 40% being observed. . . .

Developmental Changes in Suggestibility

Recent research suggests that young children may be disproportionately vulnerable to suggestive influences (see Ceci & Bruck, 1993, for a review). For example, studies of the misinformation effect with children of different ages (e.g., Ceci, Ross, & Toglia, 1987; see also Ceci & Bruck, 1993) indicate that preschoolers are usually more susceptible to the influences of misleading postevent information than are older children and adults. Moreover, in an extension of this paradigm to a pediatric examination setting in which an inoculation was administered, Bruck, Ceci, Francoeur, and Barr (1995) found that 5-year-olds' reports could be influenced by the provision of misleading postevent suggestions. Feedback that was pain affirming (i.e., that the shot hurt), pain denying (i.e., that the shot did not hurt), or neutral did not affect the children's reports after 1 week of the amount of pain experienced or the degree to which they had cried. However, pain-affirming and pain-neutral feedback, as well as other misleading information about certain actions of the physician and an assistant that were given approximately 1 year after the check-up, did have a substantial effect on the children's reports. Most importantly, in this study misleading information influenced children's delayed accounts about salient actions that involved their bodies under stressful circumstances. After a 1-year delay and four suggestive interviews, 32% of the children who had erroneously been told that the doctor was a woman reported that he was indeed a woman.

Research with other paradigms documents further the vulnerability of young children to suggestion. Recent work shows that merely repeating erroneous suggestions over time can have a massive influence on what children report. In a series of studies, Ceci and his colleagues (Ceci, 1993; Ceci, Huffman, Smith, & Loftus, 1994) questioned parents about events that had and had not happened to their children within the previous 12 months. The children were then interviewed individually and asked to make judgments about (individually determined) real and fictitious events. For each child, the events were read aloud along with instructions to "think real hard about each one of them . . . try to remember if it really happened" (Ceci, Huffman, et al., 1994, p. 394). The participants were asked for these judgments on 7 to 10 separate occasions, with the final assessment taking place 10 weeks after the first session. The findings indicated that the preschool participants almost always recalled the true events correctly but that they were inaccurate between 25% and 44% of the time in their judgments of the false events. Moreover, in their final narratives, the children frequently described the false events with vivid detail, so much so that professionals (e.g., clinical and developmental psychologists) could not differentiate accurately between descriptions of the experienced and false events. . . .

Can Traumatic Memories Be Changed?

In contrast to this account of the malleability of memory, there are some who argue that traumatic events leave some sort of indelible fixation in mind. For example, Terr (1988, p. 103) indicated that "traumatic events create lasting visual images[,] . . . burned-in visual impressions," and Kantor (1980, p. 163) stated that such "memory imprints are indelible, they do not erase—a therapy that tries to alter them will be uneconomical." These assertions, however, fail to recognize evidence that memories even of life's most traumatic experiences can be quite malleable. For example, Neisser and Harsch (1992) examined adults' recollections of how they heard the news of the 1986 explosion of the space shuttle Challenger. The participants were questioned on the morning after the explosion, and again nearly 3 years later. Most individuals described their memories as "vivid," but none of them was entirely correct, and over one third were "wildly inaccurate." One participant, for example, was on the telephone having a business discussion when her best friend interrupted the call with the news. Later she would remember that she heard the news in class, and at first thought it was a joke. She later walked into a TV lounge and saw the news and then reacted to the disaster. Warren and Swartwood's (1992) research on children's recollections of the Challenger disaster has documented similar distortions in memory. . . .

Is It Possible to "Inject" a Complete Memory for Something That Never Happened?

A growing literature now suggests that it is relatively easy to create pseudomemories, at least in some individuals. Recent studies, for example, suggest that the use of hypnosis can lead to the establishment of pseudomemories for events that never happened. In one study, Laurence and Perry (1983) instructed participants to "relive" a recent night, and a suggestion was implanted that they had heard some loud noises and had awakened. Nearly half the participants accepted the suggestion and stated after hypnosis that the suggested event had actually taken place. . . .

In addition, Loftus and Pickrell (1995) tried to convince 24 individuals (ages 18 to 53) that they had been lost for an extended period of time, that they had been crying or scared, and that they had been eventually rescued by an elderly person and reunited with their families. The participants thought that they were participating in a study of "the kinds of things you may be able to remember from your childhood" (p. 721). They were given a brief description of four events (three true and one false "lost" event) that supposedly occurred while the participant and family members were together. These research participants were then asked to write about these events in detail and were interviewed about the events on two subsequent occasions, after delays of 1 and 2 weeks. The results indicated that of the

24 participants, 75% said that they couldn't remember the false event. The remaining participants, however, developed a complete or partial false memory for the suggested experience. These false memories were described in fewer words and were rated as less clear than the true memories. Nonetheless, despite these differences between the true and false memories, it was still the case that sometimes the false memories were described in quite a bit of detail and were embraced with a fair degree of confidence. . . .

Source Monitoring

As the above discussions of memory and suggestibility imply, accurate remembering involves the ability to make distinctions among various types of information in memory. For example, when attempting to remember a particular instance of a frequently occurring activity (e.g., a visit to the doctor for a routine check-up), it is essential to differentiate between memory for the specified instance on the one hand and generic knowledge of the class of activities on the other hand. It is also necessary to distinguish between the "target," or to-be-remembered, information and other information to which one has been exposed, and the treatment of suggestibility illustrates how difficult this differentiation process can be. Indeed, one interpretation of the basic misinformation effect is that it reflects a failure to monitor accurately the sources of available information. . . .

Distinguishing between Reality and Fantasy

Suppose that a child is asked to perform certain actions (e.g., touch his or her ear), but merely to imagine carrying out other actions (e.g., touch his or her nose). Later, the child is asked to decide which actions had been actually performed and which had been only imagined. As implied above, this task requires the ability to monitor the multiple origins or sources of memory. Sometimes, as in this example, it is essential to discriminate between an external source (doing something) and an internal source (thinking about or imagining doing something); at other times, it is necessary to distinguish between two internal sources (e.g., memories resulting from what one said vs. what one thought) or between two external sources (e.g., memories of what was said or done by one person versus what was said or done by another). Source monitoring makes use of "typical" differences between different sources of memories. For example, compared with imagined events, observations of actual events typically tend to be more vivid and have less information about cognitive operations (e.g., inferences). In addition, real events tend to be retrieved more easily (see Johnson et al., 1993; Lindsay & Read, 1994). . . .

Outside of the classical work on animism by Piagetians, the topic of reality monitoring did not receive empirical scrutiny until the 1970s, when a number of studies converged on the view that young children were, in fact, able to reliably distinguish reality and fantasy (J. H. Flavell, E. Flavell, & Green, 1987; Morrison & Gardner, 1978; Taylor & Howell, 1973). Morrison and Gardner reported the results of a "triad sorting task" in which children ages 5–12 were instructed to put two fantasy figures (e.g., dragon and elf) together and to exclude one that is real (e.g., frog). They found that even 5-year-olds were quite aware of this distinction, although accuracy did increase with age, as did explicit fantasy-based explanations (i.e., stating that "they are both fake"). Similarly, the 5-year-old children were quite adept at sorting pictures into piles of real and pretend figures, although they made more errors than the 12-year-olds.

Harris, Brown, Marriott, Whittall, and Harmer's (1991) findings modified these conclusions in important ways. As in the above studies, preschool children showed a firm grasp of the distinction between fantasy and reality, with most correctly stating that imagined ghosts, monsters, and witches were not real. However, when the children were told to imagine a pretend character that was sitting in a box, many of them, over a period of time, began to act as though the pretend character was real. For example, half of the children in one study were told that the pretend character was a rabbit and half were told that it was a monster. After this instruction, all the children agreed that it was a pretend character and that the box was empty. The experimenter then said she had to leave the room for a few minutes, but a third of the children who had been told that there was a pretend monster in the box would simply not let her leave the room. None of the other children acted this way. Upon the experimenter's return, almost half of the children in both age groups said they wondered if perhaps there was an imaginary creature in the box. Further questioning uncovered some magical and unrealistic thinking. Although almost all of the children admitted to pretense before the experimenter's departure, 25% of the children now thought that pretend creatures could become real. These data are illuminating because they show the fragile distinctions of children's fantasy–reality boundaries, as measured in earlier studies. When situations and questioning become more intense, children appear to easily give up distinctions between what is real and what is only imagined. In this study, despite the fact that the children were repeatedly assured that the creatures were imagined, it seems that a procedure that was only mildly suggestive succeeded in breaking down their shaky differentiations within a short period of time.

Distinguishing between Perception and Imagination

Consistent with young children's fragile ability to distinguish between concrete fantasy and reality figures, there is some evidence that they have difficulty differentiating between what they experienced through perception and what they only imagined they experienced. Johnson and her colleagues have been at the forefront of this area of research for a decade (see Johnson, 1991 for a review; Foley & Johnson, 1985; Lindsay, Johnson, & Kwon, 1991; Suengas & Johnson, 1988). In the most embellished model, called MEM, for the "Multiple-Entry Modular Memory" system, recollection is based on the interplay of two subsystems, one that is the repository of perceptual processing and the other that contains the contents of reflective processing.

The perceptual system records and stores the contents of perceptual processes such as seeing and hearing, whereas the reflective system records psychologically generated information such as imagining, thinking, and speculating. Without going into the theoretical nuances of the various MEM subsystems, suffice it to say that developmental differences about reality–fantasy monitoring could reflect the earlier functional capability of the perceptual subsystems, and the later development of the reflective systems. At issue is whether these subsystems are developmentally invariant or whether they unfold over a prolonged period of development (Lindsay et al., 1991). . . .

Implications

The reader may ask why it is important that we assay this literature? There are several reasons. In some of the cases of "repressed memory," the clients themselves are young children (Ceci & Bruck, 1995). Moreover, in the therapeutic context with adults, an aim is to recall childhood experiences, and if these experiences have been contaminated in ways documented here, then the memory reports themselves are also contaminated. Further, the same mechanisms described in these studies could be played out in adult therapy, as, for example, with repeated visually guided imagery inductions (see Lindsay & Read, 1994).

Although this brief review does not include many cognitive variables that could conceivably lead to developmental differences in suggestibility (e.g., age-related changes in inferential skills, abstract reasoning abilities, perspective taking, and metacognitive skills), it does describe those that have received the most attention of researchers in the field of suggestibility. Taken together, this research indicates that there are nontrivial sources of suggestion that can lead children and adults to mistakenly believe that they experienced events that they either merely imagined or had suggested to them by an interviewer. Although such forms of suggestibility may be more common when the memory is peripheral or nonsalient, it is also the case they can be found even for highly salient, central events such as injuries, genital exams, and inoculations. . . .

Conclusions and Concerns

Suggestibility effects can and have been found for all types of events, including ones that involve a person's body, that are sexual and painful, and that entail loss of control. Perhaps it is somewhat harder to alter a report about an event when it is salient, persistent, painful, sexual, and well understood, and we certainly need additional research to document the extent to which this is the case. Moreover, . . . , we are still a long way from predicting which individuals are most prone to the deleterious influence of suggestive techniques. Further, the existing evidence leads us to conclude that at least part of the false reporting that has been described in the scientific literature is the result of cognitive mechanisms but that part of it also reflects the operation of social factors. Finally, the available evidence makes clear that individuals who have been exposed to repeated suggestive techniques over long periods of time sometimes provide highly detailed and coherent narratives that happen to be false. When this occurs, it is quite difficult for professionals to detect the falsehood in the absence of external corroboration.

For all of these reasons, we have grave concerns about the "memory work" methods for retrieving abuse memories that are advocated by some clinicians. These included guided imagery, sexualized dream interpretation, body work, hypnotic regression, and more. One source for such recommended tactics is a popular book on repressed memories by Fredrickson (1992). This book has been referred to as "a textbook for memory invention" and a "lethal" one at that (Pendergrast, 1995, p. 69). The book encourages women to believe that they were abused as infants by several perpetrators:

> How old do you think you were when you were first abused? Write down the very first number that pops into your head, no matter how improbable it seems to you. . . . Does it seem too young to be true? I assure you it is not. (pp. 59–66)

The "imagistic" work advocated by Frederickson (1992) is especially problematic. Under the guidance of a therapist, the patient is supposed to close her eyes, relax, breathe deeply, and try to picture some kind of abuse. "If nothing surfaces, wait and then give your best guess in answer to the questions. . . . If you feel resistance or skepticism, try to go past it" (pp. 109–112). Afterward, the therapist is supposed to follow up with questions that can fill in any blanks. The prescriptions go on to tell readers that this is an exercise in imagination, in picturing what might have happened. Ultimately, sadly, such imaginations can turn into a tragic reality, providing a real-world analogue for the kinds of pseudomemories created in the experimental research that we have reviewed.

References

Bjorklund, D. F. (1985). The role of conceptual knowledge in the development of organization in children's memory. In C. J. Brainerd & M. Pressley (Eds.), *Basic processes in memory development* (pp. 103–142). New York: Springer-Verlag.

Brainerd, C. J., & Ornstein, P. A. (1991). Children's memory for witnessed events: The developmental backdrop. In J. L. Doris (Ed.), *The suggestibility of children's recollections* (pp. 10–20). Washington, DC: American Psychological Association.

Bruck, M., Ceci, S. J., Francoeur, E., & Barr, R. J. (1995). "I hardly cried when I got my shot!": Influencing children's reports about a visit to the pediatrician. *Child Development, 66*, 193–208.

Ceci, S. J. (1993, August). *Master lecture.* Presented at the 101st Annual Convention of the American Psychological Association, Toronto, Ontario, Canada.

Ceci, S. J., & Bruck, M. (1993). The suggestibility of the child witness: A historical review and synthesis. *Psychological Bulletin, 113*, 403–439.

Ceci, S. J., & Bruck, M. (1995). *Jeopardy in the courtroom: A scientific analysis of children's testimony.* Washington, DC: American Psychological Association.

Ceci, S. J., Huffman, M. L. C., Smith, E., & Loftus, E. F. (1994). Repeatedly thinking about a non-event: Source misattributions among preschoolers. *Consciousness and Cognition, 3,* 388–407.

Ceci, S. J., Ross, D. F., & Toglia, M. P. (1987). Suggestibility of children's memory: Psycholegal implications. *Journal of Experimental Psychology: General, 116,* 38–49.

Chi, M. T. H. (1978). Knowledge structures and memory development. In R. S. Siegler (Ed.), *Children's thinking: What develops?* (pp. 73–96). Hillsdale, NJ: Erlbaum.

Chi, M. T. H., & Ceci, S. J. (1987). Content knowledge: Its role, representation, and restructuring in memory development. In H. W. Reese (Ed.), *Advances in child development and behavior* (Vol. 20, pp. 91–142). New York: Academic Press.

Flavell, J. H., Flavell, E., & Green, F. L. (1987). Young children's knowledge about the apparent–real and pretend–real distinctions. *Developmental Psychology, 23,* 816–822.

Foley, M. A., & Johnson, M. K. (1985). Confusions between memories for performed and imagined actions. *Child Development, 56,* 1145–1155.

Fredrickson, R. (1992). *Repressed memories: A journey to recovery from sexual abuse.* New York: Simon & Schuster.

Freud, S. (1953). Three essays on the theory of sexuality. In J. Strachey (Ed.), *The standard edition of the complete psychological works of Sigmund Freud* (Vol. 7, pp. 135–243). London: Hogarth Press. (Original work published 1905)

Harris, P., Brown, E., Marriott, C., Whittall, S., & Harmer, S. (1991). Monsters, ghosts and witches: Testing the limits of the fantasy–reality distinction in young children. *British Journal of Developmental Psychology, 9,* 105–123.

Johnson, M. K. (1991). Reality monitoring: Evidence from confabulation in organic brain disease patients. In G. Prigatano & Schacter (Eds.), *Awareness of deficit after brain injury* (pp. 124–140). New York: Oxford University Press.

Johnson, M. K., Hashtroudi, S., & Lindsay, D. S. (1993). Source monitoring. *Psychological Bulletin, 114,* 3–28.

Kantor, D. (1980). Critical identity image. In J. K. Pearce & L. J. Friedman (Eds.), *Family therapy: Combining psychodynamic and family systems approaches* (pp. 137–167). New York: Grune & Stratton.

Kihlstrom, J. F., & Harackiewicz, J. M. (1982). The earliest recollection: A new survey. *Journal of Personality, 50,* 134–148.

Laurence, J. R., & Perry, C. (1983). Hypnotically created memory among highly hypnotizable subjects. *Science, 222,* 523–524.

Lindsay, D. S., Johnson, M. K., & Kwon, P. (1991). Developmental changes in memory source monitoring. *Journal of Experimental Child Psychology, 52,* 1–22.

Lindsay, D. S., & Read, J. D. (1994). Psychotherapy and memories of childhood sexual abuse: A cognitive perspective. *Applied Cognitive Psychology, 8,* 281–338.

Loftus, E. F. (1979). *Eyewitness testimony.* Cambridge, MA: Harvard University Press.

Loftus, E. F. (1982). Memory and its distortions. In A. G. Kraut (Ed.), *G. Stanley Hall lectures* (pp. 119–154). Washington, DC: American Psychological Association.

Loftus, E. F., & Davies, G. M. (1984). Distortions in the memory of children. *Journal of Social Issues, 40,* 51–67.

Loftus, E. F., & Pickrell, J. E. (1995). The formation of false memories. *Psychiatric Annals, 25,* 720–725.

Morrison, P., & Gardner, H. (1978). Dragons and dinosaurs: The child's capacity to differentiate fantasy from reality. *Child Development, 49,* 642–648.

Neisser, U., & Harsch, N. (1992). Phantom flashbulbs: False recollections of hearing the news about Challenger. In E. Winograd & U. Neisser (Eds.), *Affects and accuracy in recall* (pp. 9–31). Cambridge, MA: Cambridge University Press.

Ornstein, P. A. (1995). Children's long-term retention of salient personal experiences. *Journal of Traumatic Stress, 8,* 581–605.

Ornstein, P. A., Gordon, B. N., & Baker-Ward, L. E. (1992). Children's memory for salient events: Implications for testimony. In M. L. Howe, C. J. Brainerd, & V. F. Reyna (Eds.), *Development of long-term retention* (pp. 135–158). New York: Academic Press.

Ornstein, P. A., Larus, D. M., & Clubb, P. A. (1991). Understanding children's testimony: Implications of research on the development of memory. In R. Vasta (Ed.), *Annals of child development* (Vol. 8, pp. 145–176). London, England: Jessica Kingsley.

Ornstein, P. A., & Naus, M. J. (1985). Effects of the knowledge base on children's memory strategies. In H. W. Reese (Ed.), *Advances in child development and behavior* (Vol. 19, pp. 113–148). Orlando, FL: Academic Press.

Pendergrast, M. (1995). *Victims of memory: Incest accusations and shattered lives.* Hinesburg, VT: Upper Access.

Pillemar, D. B., & White, S. H. (1989). Childhood events recalled by children and adults. In H. W. Reese (Ed.), *Advances in child development and behavior* (Vol. 21, pp. 297–340). New York: Academic Press.

Suengas, A. G., & Johnson, M. K. (1988). Qualitative effects of rehearsal on memories for perceived and imagined events. *Journal of Experimental Psychology: General, 103,* 377–389.

Taylor, R., & Howell, M. (1973). The ability of 3-, 4-, and 5-year-olds to distinguish fantasy from reality. *Journal of Genetic Psychology, 122,* 315–318.

Terr, L. (1988). What happens to early memories of trauma? A study of 20 children under age five at the time of documented traumatic events. *Journal of the American Academy of Child and Adolescent Psychiatry, 27,* 96–104.

Warren, A. R., & Swartwood, J. N. (1992). Developmental issues in flashbulb memory research: Children recall the Challenger event. In E. Winograd & U. Neisser (Eds.), *Affect and accuracy in recall* (pp. 95–120). Cambridge, England: Cambridge University Press.

Winograd, E., & Killinger, W. A., Jr. (1983). Relating age at encoding in early childhood to adult recall: Development of flashbulb memories. *Journal of Experimental Psychology: General, 112,* 413–422.

NO

Judith L. Alpert, Laura S. Brown, and Christine A. Courtois

Comment on Ornstein, Ceci, and Loftus (1998): Adult Recollections of Childhood Abuse

We welcome Ornstein, Ceci, and Loftus's (1998) article: "Adult Recollections of Childhood Abuse: Cognitive and Development Perspectives." Our response to the article involves a summary of points of agreement and a more expanded critique regarding points of disagreement and observations.

Points of Agreement

Within this working group report, the reviews of the literature on trauma and child sexual abuse by Alpert, Brown, and Courtois and the literature on memory by Ornstein, Ceci, and Loftus have a number of points of agreement:

1. Real occurrences of sexual abuse and false allegations of sexual abuse are serious and potentially life-shattering for victims. . . .
2. Memory is not perfect. . . .
3. Remembering is facilitated by retrieval cues, contextual support, and the reexperiencing of affect similar to that which occurred at the time of an event. . . .
4. Some people are suggestible under certain conditions. . . .
5. Psychotherapy can be substandard, as can research. . . .
6. When a report or memory of sexual abuse arises for the first time in therapy, a neutral and exploratory stance on the part of the therapist should be maintained. . . .

Points of Disagreement

We have four main points of disagreement with Ornstein et al.'s (1998) article, including (a) the selective review of the memory literature, (b) the lack of attention to methodological issues, (c) the selective interpretation of the literature and the resultant drawing of implications, and (d) a serious misunderstanding of some of the concepts under discussion.

1. The Selective Review of the Memory Literature

The review of the memory literature presented by Ornstein et al. (1998) was selective and contained serious omissions. An uninformed reader of this article may come away from it believing that significant agreement exists among memory experts on the various points reviewed and emphasized by these authors. In fact, and to the contrary, disagreement does exist in the memory research field on many of the points presented in Ornstein et al.'s (1998) article. For example, a large body of literature focuses on the relative accuracy of memory and contradicts some of what is reported (e.g., Christianson, 1984; Heuer & Reisberg, 1992; Reisberg, Heuer, McLean, & O'Shaughnessy, 1988; Yuille & Cutshall, 1986). This literature receives little or no mention. Further, as summarized, the included studies are presented as overly conclusive, as though they have little chance of modification even if and when further investigations are undertaken. Methodological problems and limitations are ignored even though they seriously compromise the generalizability of many of the studies presented.

Ornstein et al. (1998) took another overly conclusive position regarding the memory capabilities of children. The review, from our perspective, presented a negative assessment of children's capabilities and seemed to suggest that almost nothing can be remembered with any accuracy from childhood as a result of developmental shifts in cognitive processing. The research presented can be interpreted to support the position that children are highly suggestible and that if they are interviewed more than one time they will almost inevitably give unreliable reports, no matter what the circumstance. There is more to the story. The studies reviewed here are designed with the intent to mislead children. The results, grounded on some laboratory studies based on the responses of very young children who were repeatedly asked questions by interviewers who presuppose the truth of the suggested material, may not be generalizable to all children who report sexual abuse or to adults who remember abuse in childhood.

Relevant studies from the memory literature that disconfirm this negative assessment of children's capabilities were either discounted or absent from Ornstein et al.'s (1998) article. For example, work by Goodman and her associates most approximated the trauma associated with sexual abuse. These researchers conducted innovative experimental studies on children that attempted to use many features common to cases of alleged sexual abuse (Goodman & Aman, 1990; Goodman, Hirschman, Hepps, & Rudy, 1991; Goodman, Quas, Batterman-Faunce, Riddleberger, & Kuhn, 1994; Goodman & Reed, 1986; Goodman, Rudy, Bottoms, & Aman, 1990; Rudy, Goodman, Nicholas, & Moan, 1991). In one set of studies, for example, children interacted with a stranger in an unfamiliar setting in which there were play sequences, some of which involved nonsexual touch and many of which differentiated being a passive witness from being an active participant. They also differentiated between the type of postevent misinformation suggested (e.g., whether misleading suggestions focused on central actions or minor details). Memory performance was assessed at a later time by free narrative recall of the play sequence at first and then by a series of specific questions, some of which were inaccurate. The latter sometimes directly addressed abuse-related issues such as sexual touch (e.g., "He took your clothes off, didn't he?"). In general, these as well as other studies that utilize real-life stressful events (e.g., King & Yuille, 1987) indicate, as Goodman, Aman, and Hirschman (1987) stated

> [Children's] suggestibility is greater for characteristics of the room in which an event occurred than for actions that took place or the physical characteristics of the 'culprit'. . . . Across these studies children never made up false stories of abuse even when asked questions that might foster such reports. (p. 690)

Second, the application of research on the malleability and suggestibility of normal memory to the current memory debate has been questioned by some memory researchers (see Hammond, 1995, for a review). Such application is believed to result in an extreme position with little, if any, empirical substantiation and the potential for a misinformation effect. In Ornstein et al.'s (1998) article, there is little, if any, consideration of either the controversy within the memory research field nor the research that challenges the position the authors put forth. Related to this point, although the article includes an excellent review of the malleability of normal memory, there is little consideration of traumatic or emotional memory. Such consideration is particularly important because a large body of evidence exists to suggest that, in contrast to normal memories, emotional (and, hence, traumatic) memories are encoded differently (e.g., Bower, 1981; Cahill, Prins, Weber, & McGaugh, 1994; Christianson, 1992; Horowitz & Reidbord, 1992; Joseph, 1996; LeDoux, 1992, 1994; McGaugh, 1992; Nilsson & Archer, 1992; Pitman, 1994; Saporta & van der Kolk, 1992; van der Kolk & Saporta, 1991). Emotional memories have been described as detailed and accurate (Yuille & Cutshall, 1989) and not prone to error (Christianson, 1992; Reisberg & Heuer, 1992). Although the relationship between emotion and memory is believed to be complex, suggestibility in emotional memories has consistently been lacking. Actual victims and witnesses of crime resist information provided by the media and the investigators (Cutshall & Yuille, 1992; Yuille & Cutshall, 1986). Further, a review of research on traumatic memories indicates the relative accuracy and persistence of traumatic memories as compared to more ordinary ones (Koss, Tromp, & Tharan, 1994). The affect and memory literature is important and most relevant to the topic of memory for trauma, and its omission in Ornstein et al.'s (1998) article is most significant.

Third, little attention was given to the many contributing factors to the misinformation effect and the ongoing debate in the memory literature about these factors (e.g., Loftus & Hoffman, 1989). The focus of the review was on research measuring misinformation suggestibility, which focuses on cognitive factors (e.g., type of postevent misinformation, encoding status) affecting suggestibility. Ornstein et al. (1998), in general, omitted studies concerned with social factors that affect suggestibility and/or that assist or impede the retention of memory (Goodman et al., 1994; Tessler & Nelson, 1994). As Brown (1995) pointed out, psychotherapy is mainly a social interaction. Also, there is minimization of the fact that memory commission errors are relatively easy to create and the magnitude of the misinformation effect substantial if the focus is on peripheral details or if there was not encoding of the original event. Those studies that varied the type of postevent misinformation (Christiansen & Ochalek, 1983; Reisberg, Sculler, & Karbo, 1993) consistently showed that the greater portion of the variance of the misinformation effect is limited to details that are peripheral and irrelevant to the central actions.

Fourth, other disagreements in the memory research field regarding the findings of the suggestibility literature were not mentioned. For example, Spanos and McLean (1986) reported that many so-called pseudomemories in suggestibility experiments with highly hypnotizable adults are simply reporting biases, artifacts of the participants' desires to please the experimenter. The extent to which this holds true in the children's suggestibility literature is unclear, but it is an alternative hypothesis not noted by Ornstein et al. (1998).

Fifth, confirmatory bias is also evident in Ornstein et al.'s (1998) use or misuse of examples from psychotherapy. The article gives the impression, unsupported by research, that most clinicians working with adults who allege abuse conduct treatment that is suggestive, leading, and almost exclusively focused on the retrieval of memory to the exclusion of other therapeutic tasks. For example, the statement is made that the task of some therapeutic orientations is the "hunt for the missing memory" (p. 1025). We suggest that this position is due to the misapplication and overgeneralization of material from the lay literature for abuse survivors to all psychotherapists, whatever their level of training and technique. We know of no professional program in psychology that specifically trains graduate students in such a therapeutic strategy nor any mainstream approach to treatment to have this approach as a focus. . . .

[S]everal recent studies of psychotherapist approaches (Poole, Lindsay, Memon, & Bull, 1995; Waltz, 1994; Yapko, 1994) have found that the retrieval of memories in therapy where abuse is reported or suspected is not the primary focus of the treatment for the majority of therapists, although, as reported by Poole et al., a constellation of beliefs and practices suggestive of a focus on memory recovery was found in a minority of the therapists they surveyed. Yapko found, however, that some therapists held erroneous beliefs about the nature of memory, memory retrieval, and hypnosis that he speculated could lead to suggestive practices in therapy. As of yet, the generalizability of these findings awaits replication across more broad-based and representative samples. . . .

2. Methodological Concerns

During the first 90 years of the scientific study of memory, the focus was largely on laboratory-based investigations of serial learning tasks (e.g., memory for nonsense syllables and word lists) that shifted to the study of everyday memory. Since the mid-1970s, another shift has occurred as memory science has increasingly become an applied science. Eyewitness reports of crimes was the first major area of application, and the second was delayed memory of childhood trauma. The study of memory for normal events (everyday memory) is a new science (Cohen, 1989). The application of this literature to psychotherapy is newer still, less than 3 years old. As of yet, no laboratory studies of memory suggestibility in psychotherapy exist that have been conducted by contemporary memory scientists (Brown, 1995).

Given that the application of this literature to psychotherapy is most recent, problems with ecological validity are the norm. In general, most of the data on children's memory come from laboratory studies of word lists, stories, and pictures, which do not resemble the real-life and potentially traumatic experience of sexual abuse. Also, laboratory studies on suggestibility with normal, nontraumatized college students have been applied to the work of psychotherapy with traumatized patients who suffer from posttraumatic stress disorder (PTSD). The operating assumption seems to be that such findings from the laboratory have wholesale application and generalizability to a clinical population and, more specifically, to those patients diagnosed with and being treated for posttraumatic syndromes. The most ecologically valid studies (those by Goodman and her research group) are omitted; in fact, these studies do not support the suggestibility hypothesis and instead support the notion that children are not highly suggestible in traumatic circumstances and that they have better recall when good interpersonal support is available at the time of the event or sometime soon after. As we discussed in our article (Alpert et al., 1998), such support is least available to the incestuously abused child, a factor that might well be associated with self-protective dissociation/amnesia, especially when abuse is repetitive and occurs with strong injunctions and/or threats for secrecy. . . .

It may be that memory for trauma and memory for nontraumatic events follow different rules as some research suggests. One example involves encoding. The interpretation of the reviewed memory literature seems to indicate that having prior knowledge to understand and interpret what is experienced influences encoding, such that a child who does not understand what is happening has little basis for remembering. The statement ignores the fact that affect and sensory experiences are aspects of a child's prior knowledge. Clinical experience and data contradict the notion that specific prior knowledge of sexual abuse is necessary for the encoding in memory of such abuse. Even when a young child does not have a full understanding of sexual abuse or language to describe it, the experience may encode differently than memory for nontraumatic events and may be experienced in sensorimotor or somatosensory ways (Fisler, Vardi, & van der Kolk, 1994; Joseph, 1996; Saporta & van der Kolk, 1992; van der Kolk, 1984, 1987, 1988, 1995; van der Kolk & Saporta, 1993; van der Kolk & van der Hart, 1991).

It seems that the memory literature focuses on cognitive recall whereas the trauma literature attends more to noncognitive expressions of abuse memory. Ornstein et al. (1998) ignore research that suggests that experiences encoded prior to the onset of speech can be accurately retrieved cognitively and verbally at a later stage of maturation. The trauma literature indicates that trauma and the ensuing psychic shock change the neurochemistry and neurophysiology of an individual (at the time and later) and hence have the potential to disrupt the individual's physical maturation and psychosexual development, as we indicated in our article. Traumatic recall may occur nonverbally by means of affective, sensory, and behavioral manifestations, such as play, startle responses, flashbacks, obsessions, and compulsions.

As another example, the research on normal memory suggests that the amount of exposure to a particular event and, specifically, the length of exposure and the number of repetitions will have the potential to strengthen traces in memory and therefore, potentially, be more readily retrieved (Crowder, 1976). Research findings seem to differ when the focus is on traumatic memory. In the trauma literature, it is consistently reported that repeated abuse may be less likely to be retrieved, especially in children in a captive/dependent circumstance (Freyd, 1994; Herman, 1992a, 1992b; Terr, 1988, 1990, 1991), and that the intensity of emotion, betrayal, social context, and other variables of the trauma, including the type of trauma, affect encoding retention, and later recall (Briere & Conte, 1993; Elliott, 1994; Fisler et al., 1994; Freyd, 1994; Goodman et al., 1994; Herman & Schatzow, 1987).

A third example involves memory over time. The memory research indicates that the passage of time is associated with increased difficulty in recall, whereas the trauma literature, in general, indicates that memories associated with repeated abuse, war trauma, and other major traumatizations may vacillate, return over time, and, in fact, never go away (Alpert, 1995; Herman, 1992a, 1992b; Horowitz, 1986; van der Kolk, 1984, 1987), a circumstance documented in the diagnostic criteria for PTSD (American Psychiatric Association, 1980, 1987, 1994). The study of war trauma, for example, has documented that some veterans cannot forget; rather than suffering from memory loss, they suffer from repeated intrusions of traumatic memory, as Herman's (1992b) review indicates. On the other hand, other veterans have been found to have only spotty memory for well-corroborated traumatic events. Also, these memories may return in ways unlike the return of nontraumatic material and memory, for example, in flashbacks and in skewed reactions to cues that in normal circumstances would be neutral rather than eliciting and triggering (Horowitz, 1986; van der Kolk, 1987). These are increasingly understood by researchers and clinicians as the product of the dissociated affect and knowledge of the traumatic material which reemerges with associated intense affect (Spiegel & Cardena, 1991). Finally, Kihlstrom and Harackiewicz (1982) suggest another explanation derived from their study of adults' early childhood memories: "Unpleasant and traumatic memories were especially susceptible to change, shifting toward the neutral and/or trivial on the second trial-suggesting selectivity in the service of avoidance." Thus, memory for traumatic events may be different from memory for normal events.

An alternative hypothesis is that memory for ordinary events and memory for traumatic occurrences follow similar rules in ways that are not yet adequately investigated or acknowledged. Conclusions of the sort that "It is thus unlikely that an event that was encoded using an infant's or young child's perceptual-motor schemes can be retrieved using adult inferential schemes that were not available to the infant at the time of encoding" (Ornstein et al., 1998, p. 1032) seem closed and premature. A recent study of two children by Hewitt (1994) documents later verbal description of abuse that occurred preverbally, a phenomenon also reported by Burgess, Hartmann, and Baker (1994) and by Terr (1988, 1990). Also, recent preliminary studies by van der Kolk and his colleagues (e.g., van der Kolk et al., 1994) have documented that memory described by adult victims of many types of trauma are organized in sensory modalities. These findings offer preliminary research substantiation to clinical observations and reports concerning flashbacks and other sensorimotor manifestations of trauma-related materials. . . .

Although the literature discussed in the article may be empirical, it is not all experimental, and methodological deficiencies are not discussed. Random sampling and the use of comparison groups, for example, are not consistently used. A frequently quoted study (Loftus, Coan, & Pickrell, 1996), for instance, is often referred to as "proof" that pseudomemories can be created. This study, quasi-experimental in design, is based on 5 participants, ages 8 to 42, who were told by a trusted adult, all of whom were Loftus's undergraduate students, that they were lost in a shopping mall (or comparable place) when they were 5 years old. All participants reported that they experienced the fictitious event, and the investigators concluded that it is possible to suggest complete childhood memories for events that never occurred. We have a number of concerns about this study. For example, the number of participants was small ($N = 5$), they were friends and relatives of the investigator's students, and a control group was not utilized. Also, it is not clear how many of the students in Loftus's large class tried to implant the shopping mall memory and failed, nor is it clear how the implantation attempts were conducted. On the basis of this study it cannot and should not be concluded that memories can be implanted.

3. Interpretation of Results and the Drawing of Implications

. . . First, although we disagree with some interpretations of results, we note that many of the interpretations seem to push for selective application. For example, there seems to be consideration of the effect of postevent misinformation on the child who reports abuse. However, there is no consideration of other possible misinformation sources in the abused child's life (e.g., a mother who blames the child or the child who is told by the perpetrator-father, in the middle of the night, that "it is all a dream"). Similarly, data are presented that could explain why a patient might recall childhood sexual abuse while in treatment. Ornstein et al. (1998) point out that "a general principle of the psychology of memory is that remembering is facilitated to the extent to which the conditions prevailing at the time of recall resemble those in place when the information was acquired" (p. 1030). This is consistent with Bower's (1981) theory of state-dependent memory, which holds that there is a link between affect and content and that memory recall is enhanced by mood congruity. Psychotherapeutic treatment may bring forth such conditions, not by suggestion, but by creating a context of trust, safety, inquiry, exploration, and validation.

Another concern is that extrapolations are made from child suggestibility research to suggestibility of adults in therapy. Much of the child suggestibility research described by Ornstein et al. (1998) applies mainly to young children questioned repeatedly by interviewers seeking to mislead them. In these studies, children are told rather than asked. They are posed questions that presuppose the truth of the suggested material, and the children are required to elaborate on them. Results of such laboratory studies cannot be extrapolated to all children making abuse reports or, most relevant to the issue here, to adults in the therapy context. Further, it is unclear how the suggestion of details that did not occur informs us about the hypothetical suggestion of an entire series of events that did not occur. None of the data reviewed suggests how not only pseudomemories but an entire posttraumatic condition could be implanted by suggestion. None of the pseudomemory literature indicates that any of the research participants developed psychological problems relating to the alleged bad experience.

"Adult Recollections of Childhood Abuse: Cognitive and Developmental Perspectives" gives the impression, unsupported by research findings, that psychotherapists suggest to patients that they may have been sexually abused and patients, as a direct result, then develop false memories. In this formulation, no attention is given to other sources of suggestion or influence. No laboratory studies of memory suggestion in therapy are cited, yet laboratory research on the misinformation effect is used to bolster the case for the power of suggestion within the therapeutic context. The fact that suggestibility effects hypothetically can occur in therapy does not mean that they necessarily do. In addition, Ornstein et al.'s (1998) presentation of the research on postevent misleading information can be interpreted to support the position that such information can result in a change in story. This emphasizes the fact that, in general, only peripheral details change; the central description of the event has been found to remain fairly constant.

Elliott's (1994) survey study is relevant here. Her research is based on a random nonclinical sample of 800, with a response rate of 67%. Participants reported more delayed recall for child sexual abuse than for other types of trauma (10 traumas were studied), although delayed recall occurred across all traumas. Among the sexually abused subsample, the most commonly reported trigger for the return of memory was media coverage. Therapy was the least likely trigger to be reported. As noted above, several other preliminary studies concerning therapist beliefs and techniques

(Poole et al., 1995; Waltz, 1994; Yapko, 1994) have not found therapists as a group to be engaging in overly suggestive techniques, or to have an overzealous focus on memory retrieval for that matter. These two studies are among the first to consider suggestibility within the therapy context. What is needed is a program of careful, systematically designed research on suggestibility and psychotherapy as a follow-up to these preliminary but significant efforts.

4. Major Misconceptions

Ornstein et al.'s (1998) article contains a number of major misconceptions that offer a possible explanation for why such different perspectives are held on the topic of delayed memory for past abuse. First, and most important, their writing indicates a significant misunderstanding of human traumatization and a related minimization of its impact. For most people, witnessing the Challenger or viewing the assassination of President Kennedy was upsetting (and possibly traumatizing) but to a much different degree (on average) than other, more personally experienced, trauma (i.e., witnessing a murder, being raped, being tortured). As discussed in our article (Alpert et al., 1998), a number of definitions of trauma (or traumatic stressor) are currently available that distinguish trauma from more prosaic and stressful events (e.g., see American Psychiatric Association, 1994; Andreasen, 1985; Wilson, 1989; Wilson & Raphael, 1993). Memory researchers need to become more familiar with these definitions and with the available literature on traumatic response.

Similarly, Ornstein et al.'s (1998) article does not convey an understanding of the harmful potential of interpersonal victimization, especially the violation inherent in sexual abuse. A most striking example is their statement that fellatio and fondling may not be experienced as traumatic because the young child may not encode the original event as assaultive or as a betrayal. Sexual contact and physically intrusive activities may result in a multitude of feelings including, but not limited to, intensity, discomfort, stimulation, excruciating excitements, fear and terror, pleasure, and pain. These are memorable and confusing feelings to a young child who may not know or understand what is happening but nonetheless encodes the experience and reactions both physiologically and psychologically. They may be all the more confusing and noteworthy by virtue of not having a context for understanding and later for verbalizing. . . .

Finally, as noted above and repeated here for emphasis, there seems to be a gross misunderstanding of what actually happens in psychotherapy and a subsequent shared misinformation and bias that is, in turn, communicated to others as factual. It appears that the methods that are least accepted and furthest from the evolving standards for treatment of trauma are the only types discussed. In contrast to what is emphasized, a broad consensus exists in support of trauma treatment that is phase-oriented, titrated, focused on symptom management and containment, and focused on ego strengthening and function enhancement before any of the trauma-related material is addressed in any detail.

Conclusion

"Adult Recollections of Childhood Abuse: Cognitive and Developmental Perspectives" gives the impression that psychotherapists make suggestions to patients that they may have been sexually abused, suggestions that directly result in the development of false memories and false symptoms despite an absence of laboratory studies on memory suggestion in psychotherapy. Nevertheless, those promoting the belief that people create false memories in the psychotherapy context have applied results from laboratory studies on suggestibility with nontraumatized children or adults to psychotherapy. Most of the data in the laboratory studies concern word lists, stories, and pictures that do not resemble the real-life traumatic experience of sexual abuse. The operating assumption seems to be that such findings from the laboratory have wholesale generalizability to a clinical population and, more specifically, to those patients diagnosed with and being treated for posttraumatic syndromes. Unfortunately, this undeveloped body of research by memory scientists is being used prematurely in the courtroom for purposes of defending alleged abuse perpetrators and prosecuting therapists who were alleged to have used suggestion. Although it is possible for false reports about the past to occur while a patient is in psychotherapy, the research on memory suggestibility provides little support for this position. What is needed is systematic, carefully designed research on the existence and effects of suggestion in psychotherapy, as well as the existence and effects of suggestion by parents, the media, and other sources.

False allegations are painful and have the potential to destroy families and lives. However, a protestation of innocence is not enough to make an allegation false. Error does not only occur when someone is falsely accused. If the goal is to avoid false allegations, no matter what, then one may err in failing to believe a report of child sexual abuse when abuse in fact occurred. The perspective that seems to be taken in "Adult Recollections of Childhood Abuse: Cognitive and Developmental Perspectives" is that the only mistake to avoid is the false allegation of abuse.

All victims have much to lose by acknowledging child sexual abuse. It is important that abused children be taken seriously and that adults who remember child sexual abuse, even in delayed fashion, not be discredited. While keeping in mind that false reports are possible, we need to remember that child sexual abuse is substantiated as a pervasive problem in this country. We should not therefore create an expectation that adults could not have been abused, especially if their memories are absent, fragmentary, or delayed. Victimizers often distort, disavow, and otherwise misrepresent their actions (i.e., "it is not happening, it's not what you think, it is all a dream or all in your head") and sometimes even identify themselves as the victim. This is colloquially called "gaslighting," a term derived from the 1944 movie "Gaslight," in which the husband tries to drive his wife crazy by destroying her confidence in her own perception of the level of brightness of the gaslights in the house (Calef & Weinshel, 1981). Therapists, researchers, and the general public should not contribute to the undermining of the validity of the victim's perceptions as we struggle with the issue of delayed memory. We must take care to not "gaslight" or deny the victim in the process.

References

Alpert, J. L. (1995). *Sexual abuse recalled: Perspectives for clinicians.* Northvale, NJ: Aronson.

Alpert, J. L., Brown, L. S., & Courtois, C. A. (1998). Symptomatic clients and memories of childhood abuse: What the trauma and child sexual abuse literature tells us. *Psychology, Public Policy, and Law, 4,* 941–995.

American Psychiatric Association. (1980). *Diagnostic and statistical manual of mental disorders* (3rd ed.). Washington, DC: Author.

American Psychiatric Association. (1987). *Diagnostic and statistical manual of mental disorders* (3rd ed., rev.). Washington, DC: Author.

American Psychiatric Association. (1994). *Diagnostic and statistical manual of mental disorders* (4th ed.). Washington, DC: Author.

Andreasen, N. C. (1985). Posttraumatic stress disorder. In H. I. Kaplan & B. J. Sadock (Eds.), *Comprehensive textbook of psychiatry* (4th ed., pp. 245–268). Baltimore: Williams & Wilkins.

Bower, G. H. (1981). Mood and memory. *American Psychologist, 36,* 129–148.

Briere, J., & Conte, J. (1993). Self-reported amnesia for abuse in adults molested as children. *Journal of Traumatic Stress, 6,* 21–31.

Brown, D. (1995). Pseudomemories, the standard of science and the standard of care in trauma treatment. *American Journal of Clinical Hypnosis, 37,* 1–24.

Burgess, A. W., Hartman, C. R., & Baker, T. (1995). Memory presentations of childhood sexual abuse. *Journal of Psychosocial Nursing, 33,* 9–16.

Cahill, L., Prins, B., Weber, M., & McGaugh, J. L. (1994). β-Adrenergic activation and memory for emotional events. *Nature, 371,* 702–704.

Calef, V., & Weinshel, E. (1981). Some clinical consequences of introjection: Gaslighting. *Psychoanalytic Quarterly, 50,* 44–67.

Christiansen, R. E., & Ochalek, K. (1983). Editing misleading information from memory: Evidence for the co-existence of original and postevent information. *Memory & Cognition, 11,* 467–475.

Christianson, S.-A. (1984). The relationship between induced emotional arousal and amnesia. *Scandinavian Journal of Psychology, 25,* 147–160.

Christianson, S.-A. (1992). Emotional stress and eyewitness memory: A critical review. *Psychological Bulletin, 112,* 284–309.

Cohen, G. (1989). *Memory in the real world.* Hillsdale, NJ: Erlbaum.

Crowder, R. G. (1976). *Principles of learning and memory.* Hillsdale, NJ: Erlbaum.

Cutshall, J., & Yuille, J. C. (1992). Field studies of eyewitness memory of actual crimes. In E. Winograd & U. Neisser (Eds.), *Affect and accuracy in recall: Studies of "flashbulb" memories* (pp. 97–124). New York: Cambridge University Press.

Elliott, D. M. (1994, November). Trauma and dissociated memory: Prevalence across events. In L. Berliner (Chair), *Delayed trauma memories: Victim experiences and clinical practice.* Paper presented at the annual meeting of the International Society for Traumatic Stress Studies, Chicago.

Fisler, R. E., Vardi, D. J., & van der Kolk, B. A. (1994, November). Nontraumatic autobiographical memories in trauma survivors: A preliminary study. Poster presented at the Meeting of the International Society for Traumatic Stress Studies, Cambridge, MA.

Freyd, J. J. (1994). Betrayal trauma: Traumatic amnesia as an adaptive response to childhood abuse. *Ethics and Behavior, 4,* 307–329.

Goodman, G. S., & Aman, C. (1990). Children's use of anatomically detailed dolls to recount an event. *Child Development, 61,* 1859–1871.

Goodman, G. S., Hirschman, J. E., Hepps, D., & Rudy, L. (1991). Children's memory for stressful events. *Merrill–Palmer Quarterly, 37,* 109–158.

Goodman, G. S., Quas, J., Batterman-Faunce, J. M., Riddleberger, M., & Kuhn, J. (1994). Predictors of accurate and inaccurate memories of traumatic events experienced in childhood. *Consciousness and Cognition: An International Journal, 3,* 269–294.

Goodman, G. S., & Reed, R. S. (1986). Age differences in eyewitness testimony. *Law & Human Behavior, 10,* 317–332.

Goodman, G. S., Rudy, L., Bottoms, B. L., & Aman, C. (1990). Children's concerns and memory: Issues of ecological validity in the study of children's eyewitness testimony. In R. Fivush & J. Hudson (Eds.), *Knowing and remembering in young children* (pp. 249–284). New York: Cambridge University Press.

Hammond, D. C. (1995). Hypnosis, false memories, and guidelines for using hypnosis with potential victims of abuse. In J. L. Alpert (Ed.), *Sexual abuse recalled: Treating trauma in the era of the recovered memory debate.* Northvale, NJ: Jason Aronson.

Herman, J. L. (1992a). Complex PTSD: A syndrome in survivors of prolonged and repeated trauma. *Journal of Traumatic Stress, 3,* 377–391.

Herman, J. L. (1992b). *Trauma and recovery: The aftermath of violence.* New York: Basic Books.

Herman, J. L., & Schatzow, E. (1987). Recovery and verification of memories of childhood sexual trauma. *Psychoanalytic Psychology, 4,* 1–14.

Heuer, F., & Reisberg, D. (1992). Emotion, arousal, and memory for detail. In S.-A. Christianson (Ed.), *The handbook of emotion and memory* (pp. 151–180). Hillsdale, NJ: Erlbaum.

Hewitt, S. A. (1994). Preverbal sexual abuse: What two children report in later years. *Child Abuse and Neglect, 18,* 821–826.

Horowitz, M. (1986). *Stress response syndromes.* New York: Aronson.

Horowitz, M. J., & Reidbord, S. P. (1992). Memory, emotion, and response to trauma. In S. Christianson (Ed.), *The handbook of emotion and memory: Research and theory* (pp. 343–357). Hillsdale, NJ: Erlbaum.

Joseph, R. (1996). The neuroanatomy and neuropsychology of repression. In *Neuropsychiatry, neuropsychology and clinical neuroscience: Emotion, evolution, cognition, language, memory, brain damage, and abnormal behavior.* Baltimore: Williams & Wilkins.

Kihlstrom, J., & Harackiewicz, J. (1982). The earliest recollection: A new survey. *Journal of Personality, 50,* 134–138.

King, M. A., & Yuille, J. C. (1987). Suggestibility and the child witness. In S. J. Ceci, M. P. Toglia, & D. F. Ross (Eds.), *Children's eyewitness memory.* New York: Springer-Verlag.

Koss, M. P., Tromp, S., & Tharan, M. (1994). Traumatic memories: Empirical foundations, forensic and clinical implications. *Clinical Psychology—Science and Practice, 2,* 111–132.

LeDoux, J. E. (1992). Emotional memories in the brain. In L. R. Squire & N. Butters (Eds.), *Neuropsychology of memory* (2nd ed., pp. 463–469). New York: Guilford Press.

LeDoux, J. E. (1994, June). Emotion, memory and the brain. *Scientific American, 270,* 50–57.

Loftus, E. F., Coan, J. A., & Pickrell, J. E. (1996). Manufacturing false memories using bits of reality. In L. M. Reder (Ed.), *Implicit memory and metacognition* (pp. 195–220). Hillsdale, NJ: Erlbaum.

Loftus, E., & Hoffman, H. G. (1989). Misinformation and memory: The creation of new memories. *Journal of Experimental Psychology: General, 118,* 100–104.

McGaugh, J. L. (1992). Affect, neuromodulatory systems, and memory storage. In S.-A. Christianson (Ed.), *Handbook of emotion and memory* (pp. 245–268). Hillsdale, NJ: Erlbaum.

Nilsson, L. G., & Archer, T. (1992). Biological aspects of memory and emotion: Affect and cognition. In S.-A. Christianson (Ed.), *Handbook of emotion and memory* (pp. 289–306). Hillsdale, NJ: Erlbaum.

Ornstein, P. A., Ceci, S. J., & Loftus, E. F. (1998). Adult recollections of childhood abuse: Cognitive and developmental perspectives. *Psychology, Public Policy, and Law, 4,* 1025–1051.

Pitman, R. (1994). *Hormonal modulation of traumatic memory.* Paper presented at the annual meeting of the American Psychiatric Association, Philadelphia, PA.

Poole, D. A., Lindsay, D. S., Memon, A., & Bull, R. (1995). Psychotherapy and the recovery of memories of childhood sexual abuse: U.S. and British practitioners' opinions, practices, and experiences. *Journal of Consulting and Clinical Psychology, 63,* 426–437.

Reisberg, D., & Heuer, F. (1992). Remembering the details of emotional events. In E. Winograd & U. Neisser (Eds.), *Affects and accuracy in recall: Studies of "flashbulb" type memories* (pp. 162–190). New York: Cambridge University Press.

Reisberg, D., Heuer, F., McLean, J., & O'Shaughnessy, M. (1988). The quantity, not quality, of affect predicts memory vividness. *Bulletin of the Psychonomic Society, 26,* 100–103.

Reisberg, D., Sculler, J., & Karbo, W. (1993). *The laboratory creation of false memories: How generalizable?* Paper presented at the Annual Meeting of the Psychonomic Society, Washington, DC.

Rudy, L., Goodman, G. S., Nicholas, E., & Moan, S. (1991). Effects of participation on children's reports: Implications for children's testimony. *Developmental Psychology, 27,* 1–26.

Saporta, J. A., & van der Kolk, B. A. (1992). Psychobiological consequences of severe trauma. In M. Basogh (Ed.), *Torture and its consequences* (pp. 151–181). New York: Cambridge University Press.

Spanos, N. P., & McLean, J. (1986). Hypnotically created pseudomemories: Memory distortions or reporting biases? *British Journal of Experimental Hypnosis, 3,* 155–159.

Spiegel, D., & Cardena, E. (1991). Disintegrated experience: The dissociative disorders revisited. *Journal of Abnormal Psychology, 100,* 366–378.

Terr, L. (1988). What happens to the early memories of trauma? A study of twenty children under age five at the time of documented traumatic events. *American Journal of Child and Adolescent Psychiatry, 27,* 96–104.

Terr, L. (1990). *Too scared to cry.* New York: Harper & Row.

Terr, L. (1991). Childhood traumas: An outline and overview. *American Journal of Psychiatry, 148,* 10–20.

Tessler, M., & Nelson, K. (1994). Making memories: The influence of joint encoding on later recall by young children. *Consciousness and Cognition: An International Journal, 3,* 307–326.

van der Kolk, B. A. (1984). *Post-traumatic stress disorder: Psychological and biological sequelae.* Washington, DC: American Psychiatric Press.

van der Kolk, B. A. (1987). *Psychological trauma.* Washington, DC: American Psychiatric Press.

van der Kolk, B. A. (1988). The trauma spectrum: The interaction of biological and social events in the genesis of the trauma response. *Journal of Traumatic Stress, 1,* 273–290.

van der Kolk, B. A. (1995). The body, memory, and psychobiology of trauma. In J. L. Alpert (Ed.), *Sexual abuse recalled: Treating trauma in the era of the recovered memory debate.* Northvale, NJ: Jason Aronson.

van der Kolk, B. A., & Saporta, J. (1991). The biological response to psychic trauma: Mechanisms and treatment of intrusion and numbing. *Anxiety Research, 4,* 199–212.

van der Kolk, B. A., & Saporta, J. (1993). Biological response to psychic trauma: In J. P. Wilson & B. Raphael (Eds.), *International handbook of traumatic stress syndrome* (pp. 25–34). New York: Plenum.

van der Kolk, B. A., & van der Hart, O. (1991). The intrusive past: The flexibility of memory and the engraving of trauma. *American Imago, 48,* 425–454.

van der Kolk, B. A., Vardi, D. J., Eisler, R. E., Herron, N., Hostettler, A., & Zakai, A. (1994, May). *Traumatic versus autobiographical memory.* Paper presented at the Annual Meeting of the American Psychiatric Association, Philadelphia.

Waltz, J. (1994, November). Treatment and memory recall. In L. Berliner (Chair), *Delayed trauma memories: Victim experiences and clinical practice.* Symposium conducted at the 10th Annual Meeting of the International Society for Traumatic Stress Studies, Chicago.

Wilson, J. P. (1989). *Trauma, transformation, and healing: An integrative approach to theory, research, and post-traumatic therapy.* New York: Brunner/Mazel.

Wilson, J. P., & Raphael, B. (Eds.). (1993). *International handbook of traumatic stress syndromes.* New York: Plenum.

Yapko, M. D. (1994). Suggestibility and repressed memories of abuse: A survey of psychotherapists' beliefs. *American Journal of Clinical Hypnosis, 36,* 163–171.

Yuille, J. C., & Cutshall, J. L. (1986). A case study of eyewitness memory of a crime. *Journal of Applied Psychology, 71,* 291–301.

Yuille, J. C., & Cutshall, J. L. (1989). Analysis of the statements of victims, witnesses, and suspects. In J. C. Yuille (Ed.), *Credibility assessment* (pp. 175–191). Norwell, MA: Kluwer Academic.

POSTSCRIPT

Is Adult Memory for Childhood Abuse Unreliable?

In the first selection, Ornstein, Ceci, and Loftus discuss the many delicate and malleable features of human memory in an effort to better assess the accuracy of adult memories for childhood abuse. Their introduction revolves around four primary themes: (1) some information escapes memory, (2) information that is encoded into memory may vary in terms of the depth or level of processing, (3) the staying power or strength, as well as the organization, of information may change, and (4) the retrieval process can be incomplete and swayed by an unconscious desire to create information to fill retrieval gaps. A developmental perspective is then considered. Ornstein, et al., assert that what a child puts in memory is the remembrance of an event as seen through a child's eyes, with a child-like interpretation. The discussion then turns to the power of suggestibility and other means of distorting memories. In addition, the authors review the literature showing that memory is so malleable that entirely false memories, or pseudomemories, can be implanted through suggestion. The final section cites research showing that children have difficulty monitoring the source of their thoughts, such as whether they actually did something or just thought about it. All of this research review leads Ornstein, et al., to express concerns regarding the suggestive methods used by some counselors and clinicians. The authors worry that suggestions to imagine abusive situations during therapy are the spark to creating false memories of childhood events.

While Alpert, Brown, and Courtois begin by summarizing the aspects of the first selection that they agree with, most of the second selection highlights the points of disagreement. The first charge made by Alpert, et al., is that the specific studies reviewed were selected to create the illusion that all memory experts would agree with Ornstein, et al.'s conclusions. Alpert, et al., state that the first article conveniently omits research detailing the accuracy of memory or children's resistance to suggestibility, particularly when the memory has an emotional quality. The authors also raise questions about the generalizability of findings from memory studies conducted in the laboratory to memories of real-life traumatic events. They find that memory research tends to focus on the cognitive aspects of recall while trauma research tends to focus on the non-cognitive aspects. In looking for nonverbal clues, trauma specialists may note that a child who was nonverbal at the time of abuse may later recall that event nonverbally and demonstrate the recall through play, startle responses, or flashbacks. Another difference between the two specialties is that memory research tends to support the view that repeated exposure strengthens a memory and increases recall while trauma research shows that memory for repeated abuse is actually less likely to be retrieved. Alpert, et al., find that, because the memory researchers are ignorant of trauma research and psychotherapy techniques, their article is "undermining the validity of the victim's perceptions" (page 1063) and bringing even more pain and hurt to those already abused.

This debate highlights the difficulty in applying laboratory research to real-world situations. It also offers some insight into the different perspectives of researchers who seek evidence—working primarily in laboratories, executing well-designed experiments—and practitioners who seek justice and healing for their clients with real-life issues. Both perspectives have vital information to contribute, and it is of ultimate importance that this dialog continue. As long as there is a victim who is not taken seriously, and as long as there is an innocent person falsely accused, there is a great need for the blending of the expertise of the researcher and practitioner to find workable solutions to this dilemma.

Suggested Readings

Alpert, J. (Editor), *Sexual Abuse Recalled: Treating Trauma in the Era of the Recovered Memory Debate* (Northvale, NJ: Jason Aronson, 1996).

Davies, G., and Dalgleish, T. *Recovered Memories: Seeking the Middle Ground* (New York: John Wiley & Sons, 2001).

Eisen, M. L., Goodman, G. S., and Quas, J. A. (Editors), *Memory and Suggestibility in the Forensic Interview* (Mahwah, NJ: Lawrence Erlbaum and Associates, 2002).

Loftus, E., and Ketcham, K. *The Myth of Repressed Memory: False Memories and Allegations of Sexual Abuse* (New York: St. Martin's Press, 1996).

Schacter, D., and Scarry, E. *Memory, Brain, and Belief* (Cambridge, MA: Harvard University Press, 2001).

Whitfied, C., Silberg J., and Fink, P. (Editors), *Misinformation Concerning Child Sexual Abuse and Adult Survivors* (Binghamton, NY: Haworth, 2002).

On the Internet . . .

KidSource OnLine provides a thorough background on speech and language by furnishing information from The American Speech-Language-Hearing Association.

`http://www.kidsource.com/ASHA/index.html`

The Psi Cafe summarizes some of the most influential theories in language development.

`http://www.psy.pdx.edu/PsiCafe/Areas/Developmental/LanguageDev/`

The National Center for Stuttering offers an overview and links to more information on stuttering.

`http://www.stuttering.com/`

If you are interested in the many ways cognitive scientists are merging artificial intelligence and human language then you should browse the Web site for the Association for Computational Linguistics.

`http://www1.cs.columbia.edu/~acl/`

PART 4

Language

One of the most amazing aspects of human development is our ability to learn language and to use language as symbolic representations of thoughts. This volume is dedicated to the understanding of cognition and considering just how much of our cognition is facilitated by words. It is critical that cognitive scientists understand this process. Such an understanding would help clinicians in treating those with language disorders as well as inform scientists who are training artificial intelligence software in cognitive processing. In this section you will read about the ways we attach meaning to words and a new attempt to explain language disorders.

ISSUE 10

Is Context Stronger Than Frequency?

YES: Charles Martin, Hoang Vu, George Kellas, and Kimberly Metcalf, from "Strength of Discourse Context as a Determinant of the Subordinate Bias Effect," *The Quarterly Journal of Experimental Psychology* (1999)

NO: Keith Rayner, Katherine S. Binder, and Susan A. Duffy, from "Contextual Strength and the Subordinate Bias Effect: Comment on Martin, Vu, Kellas, and Metcalf," *The Quarterly Journal of Experimental Psychology* (1999)

ISSUE SUMMARY

YES: Psychology professors Charles Martin, Hoang Vu, George Kellas, and Kimberly Metcalf demonstrate that human memory retrieval is influenced most by the context when selectively searching for the meaning of ambiguous words.

NO: Cognitive researchers Keith Rayner, Katherine Binder, and Susan Duffy argue that when appropriate stimuli are used, research results indicate that memory retrieval is influenced most by the order in which possible meanings are retrieved when trying to find the intended meaning of ambiguous words.

The particular issue under scrutiny in this debate is the mysterious way human beings can determine the appropriate meaning of homonyms, which are words with the same spelling (orthography) and the same sound (phonology). For example, when we read *the bar,* we need to determine if the intended reference is to the bar examination for lawyers, a bar that serves drinks, the bars soldiers wear on their sleeves to show military rank, or the bars that separate measure of written music. Without any clues to the appropriate meaning for *the bar,* we are left with lexical ambiguity.

There are various methods people use to try to resolve this lexical ambiguity. One method is to consider the context. If we hear a friend say, "I saw her at *the bar,*" we would immediately pick up on the word *at,* and deduce that military bars or musical bars were not plausible options. Another clue we might consider is the more frequent or popular meaning of the word. If, in our environment, *the bar* generally refers to a place to get drinks, then we will likely make that assumption first. When a homonym has a frequently used meaning and lesser used meanings, it is called a *polarized* homonym. To continue with our example, suppose you are a professor at a law school, and when you hear *the bar* it is equally likely that the reference is to a place to buy drinks or the bar exam. In that case the homonym is *balanced* in meaning.

The debate highlighted in the following two selections is over which theory best explains the influence of contextual and frequency information in the process of determining the intended meaning of lexically ambiguous words. Martin, Vu, Kellas, and Metcalf, authors of the first selection, favor the context-sensitive model, which states that we pay more attention to the context in resolving the meaning of an ambiguous word. When we read an ambiguous word, we retrieve all the possible meanings from our permanent memory until we find the best suited meaning. The debate here is over which meanings "come to mind" first, second, and so on. Martin, et al., believe that when the contextual clues surrounding the ambiguous words are very strong, we will retrieve the context-biased meaning first, whether that meaning is frequent or not. When the contextual clues are weak, then we will retrieve the most frequently intended meaning first. For example, when we read "She tried it several times, but the key wouldn't work," the contextual clues are weak, thus we think of the most frequent meaning first—a key that opens something, like a door key. In this second scenario, the contextual clues are strong: "The piano player was quite frustrated. She tried it several times, but the key wouldn't work." In this case, our memories have been primed by the mention of a piano, and when we read the word *key*, we will immediately retrieve the meaning of a piano key.

In the second selection, Rayner, Binder, and Duffy make the case that the reordered access model, which emphasizes the frequency, is the better model to explain how we determine the intended meaning of an ambiguous word. This model predicts that when we read an ambiguous word, we retrieve all the possible meanings from our permanent memory. The order in which we retrieve those meanings will be that the most frequent meaning "comes to mind" first, and then the next most frequent, and so on to the least frequent. In cases in which the context, that is the words preceding the ambiguous word, creates a bias toward a less frequent meaning, then the sequence of retrieval will be reordered so that the most frequent meaning and the context-biased meaning will be retrieved simultaneously. For example, the reordered access model would predict that when you read the word *bark*, your memory first retrieves the most frequent meaning of the word *bark*, which is that of a dog bark. If, however, the context was, "The diseased tree bark . . . ," then the order of retrieval would be "reordered" to bring to mind both the most frequent meaning, a dog bark, and the less frequent or subordinate meaning, tree bark, simultaneously.

In the first selection Martin, et al., argue in favor of the context-sensitive model, which Rayner, et al., counter with support for the reordered-access model in the second selection. As you consider who makes the stronger case, also consider the many implications of these assertions on general models of language processing and memory storage and retrieval.

Charles Martin, et al.

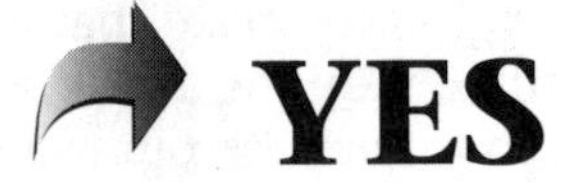

Strength of Discourse Context as a Determinant of the Subordinate Bias Effect

The English language is replete with words that are ambiguous. That is, two or more distinct meanings can be derived from the same orthography and phonology (e.g. the homonym BANK). How is it that readers so effortlessly understand written discourse without processing difficulty? Lexical ambiguity resolution has been the focus of considerable research that has produced mixed but encouraging results. Included in the empirical findings is the discovery that certain variables critically influence the process of resolving the meaning of ambiguous words when encountered in context. Two fundamental and related factors that can immediately affect the processing of ambiguous words are the relative frequency of occurrence of one or the other meaning of a homonym (meaning frequency) and the context within which a homonym is embedded. First, it is the case that the alternative meanings of a homonym do not occur equally often in discourse, but instead there is usually one frequently used (dominant) meaning and one or more less frequently used (subordinate) meanings. Ambiguous words with equally likely meanings are referred to as *balanced* homonyms, whereas those with one dominant meaning are termed *polarized*. This frequency asymmetry has been observed to affect the processing of ambiguous words in texts (e.g. Dopkins, Morris, & Rayner, 1992; Duffy, Morris, & Rayner, 1988; Hogaboam & Perfetti, 1975; Rayner & Duffy, 1986; Rayner, Pacht, & Duffy, 1994; Simpson & Burgess, 1985; Tabossi & Zardon, 1993). For example, Tabossi and Zardon (1993) and Rayner and colleagues have found reading times for polarized homonyms to be facilitated when the context biases the dominant sense but not when the context biases the subordinate sense.

Second, research has shown that context per se can have an immediate influence on the resolution of an ambiguous word (e.g. Marslen-Wilson & Tyler, 1987; McClelland, 1987; Paul, Kellas, Martin, & Clark, 1992; Simpson, 1981; Simpson & Krueger, 1991; Tabossi, Colombo, & Job, 1987; Van Petten & Kutas, 1987; Vu, Kellas, Herman, & Martin, 1998a; Vu, Kellas, & Paul, 1998b).

From *The Quarterly Journal of Experimental Psychology*, November 1999, pp. 813–842.

This was exemplified by Tabossi et al. (1987), who demonstrated that words representing semantic features of homonyms in context can be primed by contexts denoting those features (e.g. the probe word SAFE was primed following the sentence *The violent hurricane did not damage the ships which were in the* PORT). In a similar vein, Paul et al. (1992) examined the scope of word-meaning activation and found that the same words that were generated to the meanings of a homonym in context were primed when presented as probes immediately following the text. For example, both high-salient (frequently generated) and low-salient (rarely generated) probe words, PLASTER and HOLD, were primed following the sentence context *He had to wear an old* CAST.

In light of these findings, new models of lexical ambiguity resolution have been offered to explain the empirical data. One such current model—the reordered-access model—is a *hybrid* (cf. Duffy et al., 1988; Rayner et al., 1994) of the more traditional models, in that it incorporates processing assumptions from both a modular viewpoint of lexical processing (cf. Fodor, 1983; Forster, 1979) as well as an interactive-activation position (e.g. Marslen-Wilson & Tyler, 1987; McClelland, 1987). Another recently offered account—the context-sensitive model (Vu et al., 1998)—assumes interactivity but specifies the role of meaning frequency and biasing context in lexical processing more so than do previous interactive models. Indeed, both the reordered-access and context-sensitive models are distinguished from the traditional models in terms of acknowledging the simultaneous influence of contextual and frequency information in the resolution of lexically ambiguous words. We review these two models in the following sections.

Reordered-Access Model

According to the reordered-access model (e.g. Dopkins et al., 1992; Duffy et al., 1988; Pacht & Rayner, 1993; Rayner & Duffy, 1986; Rayner et al., 1994; Sereno, Pacht, & Rayner, 1992; Sereno, 1995), context can have an immediate effect on the processing of an ambiguous word but is limited by meaning frequency. In this view, when an ambiguous word is encountered, all meanings are accessed in all contexts in order of meaning frequency, from the most frequent to the least frequent meanings. However, a subordinate meaning can be made available sooner if preceding context biases that meaning, but the effect of context is restricted. Although a subordinate context can reorder the availability of the subordinate meaning, the dominant meaning will be uninfluenced by this context and will be concurrently available (i.e. context cannot preclude the dominant meaning from being accessed). Specifically, the subordinate meaning can be made available sooner, but only simultaneously with the dominant meaning (Duffy et al., 1988). Using eye-tracking measures, Rayner and his colleagues have found that when preceding context is neutral, gaze durations are longer on balanced homonyms than polarized ones as compared to control words, with no difference between polarized homonyms and control words (e.g. Rayner & Duffy, 1986). It is assumed that with balanced homonyms, both meanings of an ambiguity are simultaneously available for subsequent text integration processes. The increase in gaze durations for balanced homonyms is assumed to reflect a time-consuming meaning-selection process that is absent with polarized homonyms where the dominant meaning is immediately integrated into the discourse.

In contrast, when disambiguating context precedes a homonym, gaze duration for a balanced homonym is comparable to a control whereas gaze duration on a polarized homonym is longer, if context biases the subordinate meaning (e.g. Duffy et al., 1988). In the case of balanced ambiguous words, biased context makes the instantiated meaning available sooner for processing, and, therefore, these homonyms are processed similarly to polarized ones preceded by neutral context. However, for polarized homonyms, subordinate biased context reorders the availability of the subordinate meaning to become available simultaneously with the dominant meaning. This leads to a time-consuming, competitive selection process that is assumed for balanced homonyms in neutral contexts. The longer gaze duration on a polarized homonym in subordinate-biased context is referred to as a *subordinate bias effect* (Rayner et al., 1994). From the position of the reordered-access model, there appear to be meaning frequency constraints on context effects in that a subordinate-biased context cannot inhibit the dominant meaning of polarized ambiguous words from becoming available.

Context-Sensitive Model

According to the context-sensitive model of ambiguity resolution (cf. Kellas, Paul, Martin, & Simpson, 1991; Paul et al., 1992; Simpson, 1994; Vu et al., 1998a, b) either meaning frequency or biasing context can dominate the resolution process dependent upon a third critical variable of *contextual strength* (i.e. the degree of constraint that context places on an ambiguous word). The bias of a context towards an ambiguous word can vary continuously, from weakly to strongly biased, as a function of the strength of constraints (e.g. syntax, semantics, pragmatics) that converge on the ambiguity. On the weak end of the continuum, word frequency information will dominate meaning computation, but at the opposite end strong contextual constraints will drive the computation process. For example, in the sentence *Yesterday, the* BANK [*was eroded by the heavy rain*], the context preceding *bank* does not sufficiently bias either sense of the homonym (i.e. financial institution or river). Consequently, meaning frequency dominates and the *money* sense of bank is the preferred interpretation. Consider, however, the sentence *The heavy rain eroded the* BANK *yesterday*. In this example, the context preceding *bank* strongly biases the *river* sense of the ambiguous word.

Thus, for the context-sensitive model, meaning frequency is but one of multiple sources of information that can be used during meaning computation (cf. Kawamoto, 1993; Kellas et al., 1991; McClelland, 1987; McClelland, St. John, & Taraban, 1989; Paul et al., 1992; Tabossi et al., 1987; Vu et al., 1998a, b). The activation level of each word meaning is a product of meaning frequency, the type of biasing context (i.e. dominant or subordinate), and the degree of contextual strength. Depending on the amount of evidence (constraints) accumulated in support of the alternative senses, single or multiple meanings can be computed.

According to this view, the subordinate bias effect reflects only the activation outcome at a particular point on the strength continuum. When a polarized homonym is encountered in a subordinate-biased context, there will be a competition for activation between the dominant and subordinate meanings due to meaning frequency and contextual information. The language processor will eventually settle on the contextually appropriate subordinate meaning, but how quickly a threshold is reached is determined by contextual strength. Stronger contexts will require less time than weaker contexts to settle on the subordinate meaning. In weak contexts, the longer gaze durations reflecting the subordinate bias effect will emerge because more processing time is required to compute the subordinate meaning due to insufficient contextual constraints. Initial processing will enable accumulation of activation for the dominant meaning due to frequency information from stimulus analysis. The specific pattern of multiple activation that is computed can thus vary, from the simultaneous availability of both meanings, to an outcome in which the subordinate meaning is highly activated with minimal to moderate activation of the dominant meaning. The specific level of activation of each meaning will depend on the interplay between homonym polarity and strength of the subordinate-biased context.

Research has demonstrated that when contextual strength is empirically rated to be strongly biased, only the contextually appropriate meaning of a homonym is activated, but when the context is rated as being ambiguous (supporting both alternative meanings of the homonym), multiple meanings are computed (e.g. Simpson, 1981; Simpson & Krueger, 1991; Vu et al., 1998a, b). Of particular importance, no basis for the subordinate bias effect has been found in any of the studies when using strong contexts. Under strongly biased subordinate contexts, only the subordinate meaning of a polarized homonym is activated (cf. Vu et al., 1998a, b). This is taken to indicate either that the rise time of the activation function for the subordinate meaning quickly reaches a critical threshold before the dominant meaning can be detected or that only the contextually appropriate subordinate meaning is computed while the contextually inappropriate meaning is inhibited.

In summary, both models outlined above accept the joint influence of context and meaning frequency on lexical ambiguity resolution, but they differ greatly on the importance of each variable. The reordered-access model subscribes to the priority of frequency information, whereas, the context-sensitive model favours the modifying influence of contextual strength. This difference culminates in contrasting explanations for the subordinate bias effect. For the reordered-access model, the processing difficulties observed for polarized homonyms in subordinate biased contexts are due to competition for integration between two completely activated alternatives. The context-sensitive model attributes the subordinate bias effect to the use of weakly biasing contexts in which computation of the subordinate meaning proceeds at a slower rate than in strongly biased contexts. . . .

The current research examines more directly the influence of homonym polarity in the light of contextual strength. It should be noted that Binder and Rayner (1998) have criticized a preliminary report of the present research (Kellas, Martin, Yehling, Herman, & Vu, 1995). The issues involved will be addressed in the General Discussion.

Experiment 1

The purpose of Experiment 1 was three-fold, to demonstrate: (1) that prior discourse information can provide constraints to influence immediately the resolution of an ambiguous word embedded in an ambiguous sentence; (2) that the subordinate bias effect emerges from weakly biased contexts; and (3) that the effect can be eliminated using strongly biased contexts. Two-sentence passages were constructed to bias either the dominant or the subordinate meanings of polarized ambiguous words. In addition, the passages were constructed to be strongly or weakly biased, with strength of discourse bias independently established by off-line ratings.

Self-paced reading latencies were examined for polarized ambiguous words (henceforth, the critical word, C, in context, as well as the next two words following ambiguity (C+ 1 and C+ 2) for each of four context conditions (strong dominant, strong subordinate, weak dominant, and weak subordinate). The critical word served as its own control, and comparisons were made between reading times on the critical word in dominant versus subordinate-biased discourse. The regions following the critical word were examined for integration processes, which will be discussed later. The subordinate bias effect was examined for both strong and weak discourse contexts. The magnitude of the subordinate bias effect was determined by subtracting reading times on the critical word in the dominant condition from the same critical word in the subordinate condition at each level of discourse strength. A significantly longer reading time on the critical word in subordinate- than in dominant-biased discourse would be assumed to reflect the simultaneous availability of multiple meanings.

Predictions from the reordered-access model are that prior discourse information will not influence initial lexical processing at the sentence level and that biasing context will not override meaning frequency effects, regardless of the strength of context. As a result, reading times on polarized homonyms are expected to be longer in subordinate-biased than in dominant-biased conditions, due to competition for integration between equivalently activated meanings, for both weak and strong discourse. The context-sensitive model predicts that the subordinate bias effect will emerge only in weakly biased subordinate discourse. In the dominant condition, meaning frequency and biasing context will converge to activate quickly the dominant sense of the homonym. In the subordinate condition, however, there will be a competition for activation between the alternative senses due to the divergence of frequency and context. Consequently, more computation time will be required for the language processor to settle on the subordinate meaning, leading to an increase in reading time on the homonym. In strongly biased subordinate contexts, the constraints placed on the homonym will overwhelm meaning frequency of the dominant meaning and lead to a fast computation of the contextually appropriate subordinate sense. Therefore, reading time on the homonym will be comparable following strong dominant and strong subordinate discourse contexts. . . .

Discussion

Our results provide compelling support for the context-sensitive model of lexical processing and fail to support a reordered-access interpretation. First, the data confirmed that prior discourse information can have an immediate influence on local lexical ambiguity resolution. . . .

Second, we demonstrated that strength of discourse can directly influence the subordinate bias effect. . . .

Third, we demonstrated that the time course for integrating a subordinate meaning of a polarized homonym into a discourse representation is dependent on strength of context. . . .

Finally, we revealed a strong relationship between meaning frequency and the magnitude of the subordinate bias effect. . . .

Our demonstration of the subordinate bias effect was fundamental for establishing the validity of self-paced reading as an analogue to eye-tracking methodology and further contributes to the number of studies showing concordance between self-paced reading times and gaze durations (e.g. Britt et al., 1992; MacDonald, 1994; Spivey-Knowlton et al., 1993; Tabossi et al., 1993; Trueswell et al., 1994). However, a shortcoming of the present findings is that no direct evidence has been offered to corroborate our predictions of specific patterns of word-meaning activation. This criticism is also applicable to eye-tracking methodology (see also Rayner et al., 1994). That is, neither reading times nor gaze durations are analytic to the issue of individual word-meaning activation as the tasks do not enable measurement of which specific meaning(s) have been activated or the magnitude of the activation level(s). In Experiment 2, we addressed this issue.

Experiment 2

For Experiment 2, we again investigated the subordinate bias effect in strong and weak discourse contexts, but we employed the converging operations of self-paced reading and a naming task. The use of converging operations served a dual purpose. First, the pattern of data from self-paced reading in Experiment 2 is expected to replicate that found for Experiment 1. Second, the use of the naming task should index specific word-meaning activation during comprehension, with the results converging with the inferences drawn from reading times. If one, the other, or multiple senses of a homonym have been computed, then probe words representing these meanings should be primed and responded to faster than unrelated probe words.

Two fundamental hypotheses of the reordered-access model can be approximately tested in the current experiment. The first is the basic tenet of equivalence in the availability of meanings when a polarized homonym is preceded by a subordinate-biased context. The second is the premise of an exhaustive retrieval of word meanings in all contexts. With regard to the second hypothesis, in every report thus far, the gaze duration on a homonym has always been equal to an unambiguous control word following dominant-biased contexts, suggesting that only one meaning was available. However, Duffy et al. (1988) argued that the autonomy of lexical "access" would enable the retrieval of multiple meanings to be as fast as a single meaning. Because the dominant meaning is available sooner for a polarized (or balanced) homonym in a dominant-biased discourse, there is no competition for integration among activated alternatives. Consequently, the gaze duration on a polarized homonym in dominant-biased discourse is equal to an unambiguous control word.

If this is the case that the dominant meaning of a polarized homonym is retrieved in subordinate-biased discourse and the subordinate meaning is retrieved in dominant-biased discourse (i.e. multiple activation), then naming latencies for probe words associated with the alternative senses of an ambiguous word should capture this outcome. Thus, full support for the reordered-access model would be a demonstration of multiple meanings of a polarized homonym being primed regardless of whether the discourse context is strongly or weakly biased towards the dominant or subordinate meaning. Less compelling, but still supportive of the reordered-access model, would be a demonstration of only the dominant meaning being primed in dominant-biased discourse and multiple meanings being primed in subordinate-biased discourse. Critically, a subordinate bias effect is expected to emerge even in discourse strongly biased towards the subordinate sense of a homonym.

On the other hand, the context-sensitive model predicts a pattern of naming results that will confirm the inferences drawn from self-paced reading data. For weakly biased discourse, as reading times on the ambiguous words were longer in subordinate than in dominant contexts, it is predicted that multiple meanings will be activated for the subordinate reading (i.e. a subordinate bias effect). For the weakly biased dominant reading, only the dominant sense will be activated due to the convergence of contextual bias and meaning frequency. In contrast, for strongly biased discourse, as reading times on the ambiguous word were equal for dominant and subordinate contexts, it is predicted that only the contextually appropriate meaning will be activated because strong contextual constraints will have eliminated the alternate contextually inappropriate meaning (i.e. absence of a subordinate bias effect).

Finally, the combined use of self-paced reading and naming creates a dual-task situation. Assuming that both self-paced reading and naming are resource demanding, we expect a sharing of processing resources. As the subjects read for comprehension, they are obligated to monitor the input stream for the occurrence of a probe word printed in upper-case letters. This will require a reduction in the resources allocated to the reading process. Consequently, we expect reading times to increase relative to Experiment 1.

However, the pattern of reading times should be similar because (1) the instructions require reading at the level of comprehension, and (2) the multiple sources of constraint requiring satisfaction for comprehension to occur remain unchanged. . . .

Discussion

The results from Experiment 2 provided a replication of the reading time data from Experiment 1 as well as an index of specific word-meaning activation from probe-naming latencies. The results demonstrated that the subordinate bias effect occurred only in weakly biased subordinate contexts. Strong contexts entirely eliminated the effect. When discourse weakly biased the subordinate meaning, a longer reading time on the homonym and the activation of multiple meanings were found. When weak discourse biased the dominant meaning, the reading times were relatively shorter on the homonyms, and only the dominant meaning was primed. However, following strongly biased discourse contexts (dominant and subordinate), reading times on the homonyms in the dominant condition were comparable to those in the subordinate condition, and only the contextually appropriate probe words were primed in each case. Facilitation of contextually appropriate probe words following strongly biased discourse replicates the research of Vu et al. (1998a). In order to provide support for the reordered-access model, data from naming latencies would had to have demonstrated either the priming of probe words related to both senses of the homonyms in all discourse contexts, or at least the activation of both senses in the weakly and strongly biased subordinate discourse. The present results clearly support context-sensitive predictions.

As anticipated, employing dual-task methodology resulted in an overall slowing of reading times relative to Experiment 1. However, the elevated reading times were not accompanied by a pattern of reading time discrepant from that of Experiment 1. Consequently, we assume that the basic processes underlying reading for comprehension (i.e. multiple constraint satisfaction) remained unchanged and uncompromised when processing resources were shared between the two tasks.

General Discussion

The combined results from Experiments 1 and 2 clearly support the context-sensitive model of lexical ambiguity resolution. First, the research demonstrates that prior discourse information can have an immediate influence on initial word-meaning activation, thus converging on the work of others (e.g. Hess, Foss, & Carroll, 1996; Vu et al., 1998a). Second, and most importantly, the data indicate that strength of context can have a direct influence on the subordinate bias effect. The subordinate bias effect was eliminated when biasing discourse placed strong constraints on an ambiguous word. In both experiments, reading times on a polarized homonym were comparable following strong subordinate and dominant discourse. This was taken to indicate that only the contextually appropriate meaning of the homonym had been computed in strongly biased discourse.

The use of converging operations in Experiment 2 confirmed our inference. Using naming latencies to probe words as an index of word-meaning activation, it was found that in strongly biased subordinate discourse only subordinate probes were primed, and in strongly biased dominant discourse only dominant probes were primed, relative to unrelated words. The subordinate bias effect did emerge when discourse context was weakly biased towards the subordinate sense of an ambiguous word. In addition, reading times from Experiments 1 and 2 showed that in weak discourse there was more processing difficulty for the homonym in subordinate versus dominant discourse. We infer that this reflects the computation of both meanings of a homonym in subordinate discourse but only one meaning in dominant discourse. Again, naming latencies for probe words in Experiment 2 provided evidence for the validity of our inferences, showing priming for both senses of the ambiguous word in subordinate conditions but only one sense in dominant conditions.

Third, a critical aspect of our research is the replication of earlier research supporting the context-sensitive model using tasks other than eye-tracking methodology. Rayner and his colleagues (e.g. Rayner et al., 1994) attribute the empirical differences between eye-tracking and other methodologies to task sensitivity, arguing that data supporting selective activation models may not reflect on-line processing. The evidence provided here suggests that strength of context, and not task sensitivity, may explain the empirical differences. The self-paced reading measure employed in the present research was able to capture the subordinate bias effect found with gaze durations, thus converging with other studies that have used word-by-word presentation and have replicated eye-movement data (e.g. Altarriba, Kroll, Scholl, & Rayner, 1996; Britt et al., 1992; MacDonald, 1994). The naming data reported here not only provided support for theoretically proposed patterns of word-meaning activation, but also demonstrated that the task itself can be a sensitive on-line measure of lexical processing. In addition, the sensitivity of the naming task for on-line language processing has been corroborated by Altarriba et al. (1996), where the pattern of naming data was found to be identical to that of first-pass eye fixations.

Our empirical data clearly reject the basic tenets of the reordered-access model. One general principle that was refuted is the retrieval of multiple meanings in all contexts. For a multiple activation assumption to be viable, naming latencies to probe words should have revealed a significant, although perhaps lesser, magnitude of activation for the contextually inappropriate word meanings. More critical for the hypothesis of reordered access, however, was the absence of a subordinate bias effect in strongly biased subordinate discourse. If strong contextual bias cannot modulate frequency effects (Rayner et al., 1994), then reading time on a polarized homonym in a subordinate-biased discourse should have been longer than in a dominant-biased discourse for both Experiments 1 and 2. Equally important, naming latencies for probe words related to both meanings of an ambiguous word should have been facilitated immediately following strongly biased subordinate discourse.

Obviously, there are fundamental differences between the reordered-access and context-sensitive models of lexical ambiguity resolution. The reordered-access model does not provide a processing framework within which the subordinate meaning can be computed to a higher level of activation than the dominant meaning and be quickly integrated with the context contingent on strong contextual constraints. This possibility was mentioned by Dopkins et al. (1992) but has not been pursued. Regardless, a modifying influence of context would be more supportive of a context-sensitive than of a reordered-access position. The context-sensitive model, in contrast, does provide such a processing framework and can more parsimoniously explain the full range of data reported in the literature, including the subordinate bias effect. According to the context-sensitive position, the computation of activation levels extends over time, and a strong context will eventuate in a faster rate of meaning activation than will a weak context. In this model, the so-called access and integration processes are simultaneously achieved with the incremental processing of words in text. The computations of interest begin at the point an ambiguity is encountered. If the context is strongly biased, multiple constraints will converge and result in a steeper activation function for the contextually appropriate meaning. This meaning is integrated with the context as part of the computation process before the inappropriate meaning reaches some critical threshold. However, if the context is weak, more computations will be necessary, leading to a shallower activation function for the contextually appropriate meaning. This will result in slower integration processes as well as enabling the contextually inappropriate meaning to be computed due to meaning frequency information. The result will be differential patterns of multiple meanings being activated for homonyms with different meaning frequencies, in which case subordinate bias effects of differing magnitudes will become evident as reported here. In both Experiments 1 and 2, a monotonic relationship was found between meaning frequency and the magnitude of the subordinate bias effect.

We note that Binder and Rayner (1998) have recently criticized a preliminary report of the current research (Kellas et al., 1995). Binder and Rayner obtained our stimuli and initially replicated the self-paced reading data presented here with eye-tracking measures. However, upon further examination of the stimulus corpus, the authors eliminated 43% of the items that they considered problematic and reported results that were compatible with the reordered-access model. In their paper, Binder and Rayner defended the use of their locally derived ambiguity norms for excluding stimuli from Kellas et al. (1995) and, in addition, reported ratings for the strength of their contexts that were as strong in bias as the contexts we employed. In a detailed rebuttal, Kellas and Vu (1999) demonstrated that there was, in fact, no problem with the original stimuli. Binder and Rayner favour the use of the local ambiguity norms of the University of Massachusetts over published ones, even though their local norms do not have independent verification nor are they available for scientific scrutiny regarding their validity. In contrast, we used published norms that have been proven valid and reliable throughout a history of use. Second, the issue of strength of context is critical, as we suggest that it is context strength that distinguishes the context-sensitive from the reordered-access model. In Kellas and Vu (1999), a detailed analysis is presented showing how the method that Binder and Rayner used to establish strength of context artifactually ensured a strong rating for their contexts.

In sum, the current research emphasizes the importance of strength of context, showing that the strength of the constraints placed on a homonym can play a significant role in lexical ambiguity resolution. This, of course, does not detract from the role that meaning frequency information plays in lexical processing. Rather, our data suggest that the strength of context variable is critical and should receive more focus in language comprehension research, especially in the areas of ambiguity resolution.

References

Altarriba, J., Kroll, J., Scholl, A., & Rayner, K. (1996). The influence of lexical and conceptual constraints on reading mixed-language sentences: Evidence from eye fixations and naming times. *Memory & Cognition, 24,* 477–492.

Binder, K. S., & Rayner, K. (1998). Contextual strength does not modulate the subordinate bias effect: Evidence from eye fixations and self-paced reading. *Psychological Bulletin & Review, 5,* 271–276.

Britt, M. A., Perfetti, C. A., Garrod, S., & Rayner, K. (1992). Parsing in discourse: Context effects and their limits. *Journal of Memory and Language, 31,* 293–314.

Dopkins, S., Morris, R. K., & Rayner, K. (1992). Lexical ambiguity and eye fixation in reading: A test of competing models of lexical ambiguity resolution. *Journal of Memory and Language, 31,* 461–476.

Duffy, S. A., Morris, R. K., & Rayner, K. (1988). Lexical ambiguity and fixation times in reading. *Journal of Memory and Language, 27,* 429–446.

Fodor, J. A. (1983). *Modularity of mind.* Cambridge, MA: MIT Press.

Forster, K. I. (1979). Levels of processing and the structure of the language processor. In W. E. Cooper & E. Walker (Eds.), *Sentence processing: Psycholinguistic studies presented to Merrill Garrett* (pp. 27–85). Hillsdale, N.J.: Lawrence Erlbaum Associates, Inc.

Hess, D. J., Foss, J. F., & Carroll, P. (1996). Effects of global and local context on lexical processing during language comprehension. *Journal of Experimental Psychology: General, 124,* 62–82.

Hogaboam, T. W., & Perfetti, C. A. (1975). Lexical ambiguity and sentence comprehension. *Journal of Verbal Learning and Verbal Behavior, 14,* 265–274.

Kawamoto, A. H. (1993). Nonlinear Dynamics in the resolution of lexical ambiguity: A parallel distributed processing account. *Journal of Memory and Language, 32,* 474–516.

Kellas, G., Martin, C., Yehling, K., Herman, R., & Vu, H. (1995). *Contextual strength as a determinant of the subordinate bias effect.* Poster presented at the 36th annual meeting of the Psychonomic Society, Los Angeles, CA.

Kellas, G., Paul, S. T., Martin, M., & Simpson, G. B. (1991). Contextual feature activation and meaning access. In G. B. Simpson (Ed.), *Understanding word and sentence* (pp. 47–71). Amsterdam: Elsevier.

Kellas, G., & Vu, H. (1999). Strength of context DOES modulate the subordinate bias effect: A reply to Binder and Rayner. *Psychological Bulletin & Review, 6,* 511–517.

MacDonald, M. (1994). Probabilistic constraints and syntactic ambiguity resolution. *Language and Cognitive Processes, 9,* 157–201.

Marslen-Wilson, W., & Tyler, L. K. (1987). Against modularity. In J. Garfield (Ed.), *Modularity in knowledge representation and natural-language understanding.* Cambridge, MA: MIT Press.

McClelland, J. L. (1987). The case for interactionism in language processing. In M. Coltheart (Ed.), *Attention and performance XII: The psychology of reading* (pp. 3–36). Hove, UK: Lawrence Erlbaum Associates Ltd.

McClelland, J. L., St. John, M., & Taraban, R. (1989). Sentence comprehension: A parallel distributed processing approach. *Language and Cognitive Processes, 4* (SI), 287–335.

Pacht, J. M., & Rayner, K. (1993). The processing of homophonic homographs during reading: Evidence from eye movement studies. *Journal of Psycholinguistic Research, 22,* 251–271.

Paul, S. T., Kellas, G., Martin, M., & Clark, M. B. (1992). Influence of contextual features on the activation of ambiguous word meanings. *Journal of Experimental Psychology: Learning, Memory, and Cognition, 18,* 703–717.

Rayner, K., & Duffy, S. A. (1986). Lexical complexity and fixation times in reading: Effects of word frequency, verb complexity, and lexical ambiguity. *Memory and Cognition, 14,* 191–201.

Rayner, K., Pacht, J. M., & Duffy, S. A. (1994). Effects of prior encounter and global discourse bias on the processing of lexically ambiguous words: Evidence from eye fixations. *Journal of Memory and Language, 33,* 527–544.

Sereno, S. C. (1995). Resolution of lexical ambiguity: Evidence from an eye movement priming paradigm. *Journal of Experimental Psychology: Learning, Memory, and Cognition, 21,* 582–595.

Sereno, S. C., Pacht, J. M., & Rayner, K. (1992). The effect of meaning frequency on processing lexically ambiguous words: Evidence from eye fixations. *Psychological Science, 3,* 296–300.

Simpson, G. B. (1981). Meaning dominance and semantic context in the processing of lexical ambiguity. *Journal of Verbal Learning and Verbal Behavior, 20,* 120–136.

Simpson, G. B. (1994). Context and the processing of ambiguous words. In M. A. Gernsbacher (Ed.), *Handbook of psycholinguistics,* 359–374. San Diego, CA: Academic Press.

Simpson, G. B., & Burgess, C. (1985). Activation and selection processes in the recognition of ambiguous words. *Journal of Experimental Psychology: Human Perception and Performance, 11,* 28–39.

Simpson, G. B., & Krueger, M. A. (1991). Selective access of homograph meanings in sentence context. *Journal of Memory and Language, 30,* 627–643.

Spivey-Knowlton, M., Trueswell, J., & Tanenhaus, M. K. (1993). Context and syntactic ambiguity resolution. *Canadian Journal of Psychology, 47,* 276–309.

Tabossi, P., Colombo, L., & Job, R. (1987). Accessing lexical ambiguity: Effects of context and dominance. *Psychological Research, 49,* 161–167.

Tabossi, P., Spivey-Knowlton, M., McRae, K., & Tanenhaus, M. K. (1993). Semantic effects on syntactic ambiguity resolution: Evidence for a constraint-based resolution process. In C. Umiltá & M. Moscovitch (Eds.), *Attention & performance XV.* Hillsdale, NJ: Lawrence Erlbaum Associates, Inc.

Tabossi, P., & Zardon, F. (1993). Processing ambiguous words in context. *Journal of Memory and Language, 32,* 359–372.

Trueswell, J., Tanenhaus, M. K., & Garnsey, S. (1994). Semantic influences on parsing: Use of thematic role information in syntactic disambiguation. *Journal of Memory and Language, 33,* 285–318.

Van Petten, C., & Kutas, M. (1987). Ambiguous words in context: An event-related potential analysis of the time course of meaning activation. *Journal of Memory and Language, 26,* 188–208.

Vu, H., Kellas, G., Herman, R., Martin, C. (1998a). *Pronoun assignment and the influence of global discourse on lexical ambiguity resolution.* Manuscript under review.

Vu, H., Kellas, G., Paul, S. T. (1998b). Sources of sentence constraint on lexical ambiguity resolution. *Memory & Cognition, 26,* 979–1001.

Keith Rayner, Katherine S. Binder, and Susan A. Duffy

Contextual Strength and the Subordinate Bias Effect: Comment on Martin, Vu, Kellas, and Metcalf

In a number of studies, we (Binder & Morris, 1995; Binder & Rayner, 1998; Dopkins, Morris, & Rayner, 1992; Duffy, Morris, & Rayner, 1988; Rayner & Duffy, 1986; Rayner & Frazier, 1989; Rayner, Pacht, & Duffy, 1994; Sereno, Pacht, & Rayner, 1992) have examined the processing of lexically ambiguous words during reading. Our primary source of data has been eye fixation time on ambiguous target words, and we have varied whether contextual information that disambiguates towards one meaning or another of such words precedes or follows the target word. At an empirical level, two primary findings have emerged. First, when disambiguating information follows the target word, readers look longer at balanced ambiguous words (words that have two relatively equal interpretations associated with them) than at control words (matched on length and frequency to the ambiguous words). On the other hand, readers do not look at biased ambiguous words (words that have a highly dominant interpretation associated with them) any longer than at control words. However, if the disambiguating contextual information is consistent with the subordinate meaning of the word, then readers experience processing difficulty when they reach that information. Second, when the disambiguating information precedes the target word, readers do not look any longer at a balanced ambiguous word than at its control; apparently, the context is sufficient for them to choose the appropriate meaning of the word. On the other hand, when the preceding disambiguating information is consistent with the subordinate interpretation of a biased ambiguous word, readers look longer at the ambiguous word than at its control word. We have referred to this latter finding as the *subordinate bias effect* (Pacht & Rayner, 1993; Rayner et al., 1994).

At a theoretical level, we initially suggested two accounts of the pattern of data: the *reordered access model* (Duffy et al., 1988) and the *integration model* (Rayner & Frazier, 1989). The results of subsequent experiments (Dopkins et al., 1992; Sereno, 1995) that pitted these models against each other led us to believe that the reordered access model best accounted for

From *The Quarterly Journal of Experimental Psychology*, November 1999, pp. 841–850.

the data in these experiments. Thus, we have recently tended to interpret the results of our experiments within the framework of the reordered access model. According to this model, an ambiguous word's meanings are always exhaustively accessed, but context can influence the access of the contextually appropriate meaning to reduce the amount of time needed before that meaning becomes available to post-access processes. This can lead to a reordering of the times at which the dominant and subordinate meanings become available to post-access processes.

Another model in which relative meaning frequency and contextual information interact is the *context-sensitive model* (Kellas & Vu, 1999; Martin, Vu, Kellas, & Metcalf, 1999; Paul, Kellas, Martin, & Clark, 1992). According to the context-sensitive model, context can work to selectively activate the contextually appropriate meaning if the contextual information is strongly supportive. This holds whether or not the dominant or subordinate interpretation of the ambiguous word is supported by the context. While the reordered access model and the context-sensitive model are quite similar on a number of dimensions, one factor clearly distinguishes between the two models—namely, the reordered access model invokes the notion that access is exhaustive (except when associative priming occurs), whereas the context-sensitive model invokes selective access. We discuss this distinction in greater detail later in this article.

Recently, the subordinate bias effect has been a battleground for discriminating between the reordered access model and the context-sensitive model. In part, as we document below, we suspect that using the subordinate bias effect to discriminate between the two models is misguided. However, for the moment, we will sidestep that issue and describe a brief bit of history. At a meeting of the Psychonomic Society, Kellas and colleagues (Kellas, Martin, Yehling, Herman, & Vu, 1995) presented a poster in which they claimed to have found evidence (using the self-paced reading technique) that the subordinate bias effect could be eliminated by the presence of a strongly supportive context. Because we had been surprised that we were unable to eliminate the effect with strong context (see Rayner et al., 1994), we were very interested in the results. Thus, we obtained a copy of the stimulus materials used by Kellas et al. (1995) and ran an experiment in which we recorded the eye movements of subjects as they read these materials. Although we initially obtained results very similar to those reported by Kellas and colleagues, subsequent examination of the stimulus materials led us to believe that many of the items were problematic for our subjects. Thus, we eliminated the problematic items and reran the experiment. In this experiment (and a subsequent experiment using the self-paced reading procedure) we again found that strong supportive context did not eliminate the subordinate bias effect. A description of our research (Binder & Rayner, 1998) was published recently. The article by Martin et al. (1999), to which we are responding here, is a written report of the Kellas et al. (1995) study that we tried to replicate.

Martin et al. (1999) noted in two separate places in their article that "Binder and Rayner (1998) have criticized a preliminary report" of their research, and, in their General Discussion, they acknowledged that we did more than simply criticize their study. There they do make it explicit that we actually obtained their stimuli and attempted to replicate their findings. They note that after eliminating problematic items, we obtained results that differed from their results, using what we will refer to here as the "refined stimulus set." However, for the most part they focus, as did Kellas and Vu (1999), on a couple of methodological issues. Here, we wish to set the record straight with respect to these issues. We first address some methodological issues in response to Martin et al., then we discuss some theoretical issues, and finally, we raise some issues regarding Experiment 2 reported by Martin et al., the experiment that we see as critical to testing the models.

Methodological Issues

Martin et al. (1999) noted that Binder and Rayner (1998) obtained reading-time results that were quite consistent with those they obtained in Experiment 1, when the entire stimulus set was used; the subordinate bias effect was eliminated when contextual strength was high. However, they also noted that, upon further examination of the stimulus set, we eliminated 43% of the items and then conducted another experiment. Actually, as noted above, two experiments (one using eye-movement data and one using self-paced reading data) were conducted using the refined stimulus set. These experiments both yielded results that were different from those obtained with the entire stimulus set; the subordinate bias effect was not eliminated by strong context. Martin et al. then state that "In a detailed rebuttal, Kellas and Vu (1999) demonstrated that there was, in fact, no problem with the original stimuli." However, we believe that their statement primarily reflects their opinion with respect to the appropriateness of the stimuli. They also imply that we were quite arbitrary in eliminating certain items from the stimulus set. What they failed to note accurately is that in both the original article (Binder & Rayner, 1998) and in a subsequent reply (Binder & Rayner, 1999) to Kellas and Vu (1999), we went to great lengths to document the nature of the problems with the items that were eliminated.

Of the entire stimulus set of 56 items . . . , 24 items were problematic. The number of items that were eliminated and the reasons for eliminating them are as follows: (1) 3 were eliminated because the dominant and subordinate biasing context was consistent with the same meaning; (2) 7 were eliminated because the dominant and subordinate meanings were reversed; and (3) 14 were eliminated because the ambiguous words were "balanced" words rather than biased words (or "polarized," according to Martin et al.'s terminology). We encourage interested readers to consult the Binder and Rayner articles for detailed documentation regarding the elimination of items. We continue to maintain that there were problems with the items that were eliminated and that the elimination process was not arbitrary.

This brings us to the second methodological issue raised by Martin et al., that of the appropriate use of normative data. Many of the items that we eliminated from the entire stimulus set used by Martin et al. were removed because they were not consistent with local norms that we have collected on students at the University of Massachusetts. The vast majority of the items that we have used in our studies are consistent across various sets of published norms for lexically ambiguous words (such as those of Nelson, McEvoy, Walling, & Wheeler, 1980, and Twilley, Dixon, Taylor, & Clark, 1994). But for those items for which there is some discrepancy between published norms and local norms, our view is that it makes no sense to use items in which the relative frequencies of the meanings are inconsistent with the lexicons of local subjects. To take a concrete example, the most frequent meaning of the word *screen* according to the Nelson et al. (1980) norms is that of "a screen door." It is not too surprising that this would be the most frequent meaning for students in Florida, where the temperature is quite high and most people have screen doors. However, according to our local norms (and those of Twilley et al.), the most frequent meaning is "movie screen." Does it make any sense for us to use *screen* as an item in which the dominant meaning is not consistent with what our subjects think of most frequently when they hear the word? We think not.

We quite readily agree with Martin et al. that published norms have certain advantages over local norms. Clearly, it would also be preferable, insofar as it is possible, to use only items where there is consistency across published norms and local norms. However, there are often times when it is not feasible to follow this procedure, and our position is that in such cases reliance on local norms makes more sense. In such a situation, we typically publish the items as an appendix and provide information about how the normative data were collected (see Duffy et al., 1988; Rayner & Frazier, 1989).

Given our concerns with the stimuli used in Experiment 1, we find it somewhat puzzling that Martin et al. did not eliminate the items we identified as problematic and then reanalyze their data with those items removed. Although eliminating items reduces power, our own analyses revealed that there was sufficient power in our experiment (see Binder & Rayner, 1998) using the refined stimulus set. . . .

Theoretical Issues

Kellas and colleagues (Kellas & Vu, 1999; Martin et al., 1999; Vu, Kellas, & Paul, 1998) have generally quite accurately characterized the reordered access model (Binder & Rayner, 1998; Duffy et al., 1988; Rayner et al., 1994) when contrasting it with their own context-sensitive model (Martin et al., 1999; Paul, Kellas, Martin, & Clark, 1992). However, we believe that there is a fundamental misunderstanding with respect to the model and some confusion with respect to the difference between what the model may or may not predict and what the empirical findings are. Specifically, the subordinate bias effect is an empirical finding; it is not a fundamental tenet of the reordered access model.

Duffy et al. (1988) originally proposed the reordered access model to account for the complex pattern of eye-fixation data obtained when readers read balanced and biased ambiguous words preceded by neutral or disambiguating context. In creating the reordered access model, our goal was to create a model in which we preserved as much as we could of a modular model of lexical access while accounting for the empirical results. In our model, we assumed that two factors influenced the speed with which a particular meaning became activated and available for post-access processing (e.g. integration into the preceding context). One factor was meaning frequency: the dominant meaning of an ambiguous word became activated more quickly than did the subordinate meaning. The second factor was disambiguating context: context could speed the activation of the intended meaning without affecting access of the unintended meaning. In Duffy et al., we considered several mechanisms by which context could influence the access of meaning, including mechanisms in which the autonomy assumption of modular models of access was abandoned. But in proposing the reordered access model, we also preserved another assumption of modular models: although context could speed the activation of the intended meaning, it did not affect the activation of the unintended meaning. Thus, while we abandoned strict autonomy of lexical access, we preserved the assumption of exhaustive access. The resulting model was in essence a "horse-race" model. If one meaning becomes available much earlier than the other, then that first-available meaning is integrated and the prior context. When two meanings become available simultaneously, this produces competition between two meanings either at the access stage or at the postaccess integration stage where both meanings must be integrated and the better-fitting meaning must be selected. This competition is reflected in longer fixation times on ambiguous target words compared to unambiguous control words. This model successfully accounted for the pattern of results in Duffy et al., namely that interference from two simultaneously available meanings occurred in the neutral contexts for the balanced ambiguous words and in the disambiguating contexts (which instantiated the subordinate meaning) for the biased ambiguous words.

Although the test of the reordered access model depended on the full set of results across the conditions in Duffy et al., the effect that elicited the most interest was the finding that gaze durations on biased ambiguous words were lengthened when prior context instantiated the subordinate meaning—the effect that we later labelled the *subordinate bias effect.* We used the reordered access model to account for this effect by claiming that context speeded access of the subordinate meaning so that it became available simultaneously with the dominant meaning, producing competition among meanings at the integration stage. In a later set of studies (Rayner et al., 1994), we found that we could not eliminate the subordinate bias effect when we created contexts that seemed to us to be more strongly supportive of the subordinate meaning than those in the Duffy et al. study. As a result of this failure to eliminate the effect, most of the focus of our discussion of the reordered access model was on the role of context in creating competition among meanings that vary greatly in frequency. . . .

We referred above to the "original" reordered access model because as we review the literature (our own papers and those of others who have followed up the subordinate bias effect, including Martin et al.), we see that another version of the model has emerged. In this "modified" version, the assumption is made that supportive context can only speed access time for the subordinate meaning until it becomes available simultaneously with the dominant meaning, but context cannot further speed access time so that the subordinate meaning is available earlier than the dominant meaning. In essence, in this modified version an additional assumption has been added to the model—the assumption that the dominant meaning sets an upper limit on access speed. . . .

There is another assumption, however, present both in the original version and in the modified version of the reordered access model that distinguishes it from a selective access account. This is the exhaustive nature of access. Whether the subordinate meaning becomes available simultaneously with or earlier than the dominant meaning, the model does assume that both the dominant meaning and the subordinate meaning *are* always accessed—with one exception. This exception is the case where the context contains a strong associate of the intended meaning. This follows from the finding of Seidenberg, Tanenhaus, Leiman, and Bienkowski (1982, Exp. 2) that in a cross-modal priming task, exhaustive access for ambiguous words disappeared in the presence of a semantic associate. Thus, a clear demonstration of selective access in the absence of semantic associates would be more convincing evidence against the reordered access model. Note that elimination of the subordinate bias effect alone does not provide evidence that access is selective. Within the assumptions of the original reordered access model, elimination of the subordinate bias effect in strong contexts simply indicates that the intended meaning was activated earlier than the unintended meaning, not that the unintended meaning was never activated at all. Thus, we are in agreement with Martin et al. that one critical test of the reordered access versus selective access models is a probe task in which one probes for activation of the unintended as well as intended meaning.

Issues with Martin et al.'s Second Experiment

Although we agree with Martin et al. (1999) that a probe experiment is in principle a direct way to test the reordered access and context-sensitive models, we do have concerns about aspects of the particular probe task reported in Martin et al. It is critical in a probe task to have control over the timing of the probe presentation. In a number of classic probe studies of the effect of context on the processing of ambiguous words (e.g. Seidenberg et al., 1982; Swinney, 1979; Till, Mross, & Kintsch, 1988), the pattern of priming for intended and unintended meanings actually changed over time. In particular, both meanings were primed when the probe appeared "immediately" after the ambiguous word but only the intended meaning was primed at delayed probe positions (where the delay can be as short as 200 msec—Seidenberg et al., 1982). From these studies, it is clear that if the probe appears too late in processing, no evidence will be found for exhaustive access of both meanings. Thus, it is important to have a convincing "immediate" condition in a probe task of this type. In the cross-modal priming studies in which the context and ambiguous words were presented auditorily (Swinney, 1979; Seidenberg et al., 1982), in the immediate condition the probe appeared at 0 msec after the offset of the last sound of the ambiguous target word. In the Till et al. study, contexts were presented visually at an experimenter-controlled pace. Readers saw the ambiguous word for 333 msec, followed with 0-msec delay by the probe word. In contrast, in Experiment 2 of Martin et al., as presentation of the context was subject-paced, subjects were free to spend as long as they wanted on the ambiguous word; the probe was not presented until after subjects had pressed a button indicating they had finished reading the ambiguous word.

Two features of the data from Experiment 2 of Martin et al. lead us to wonder whether the probe word appeared too late in processing to detect exhaustive access in all conditions. First, self-paced reading times on the ambiguous word were quite long and were considerably longer in Experiment 2 than in Experiment 1. This suggests that, especially for the strong contexts, the probe word may not appear until after the correct meaning has been selected. The long times may also indicate that subjects are engaging in various strategies that are not representative of normal reading. Second, reaction times to the probe words themselves are fairly long (given typical naming times) and seem quite variable, especially in the unrelated conditions, given that the items in that condition were matched on length and frequency. In particular, in the unrelated conditions, subjects took on average 33 msec longer to respond to the probe in the subordinate context condition than in the dominant context condition. It is unclear to us why there is so much variability in the unrelated conditions, which makes the interpretation of the other differences difficult.

Finally, in the priming paradigm used in Martin et al.'s second experiment, it is not clear what the priming mechanism is. For example, would very similar results be obtained if the probe word appeared just prior to the ambiguous word? If so the paradigm is not saying very much about the processing of their ambiguous target words during reading.

Summary

We have argued that we continue to think that there are problems associated with the materials used by Martin et al. (1999). In addition, we have suggested that the subordinate bias effect should not be considered a fundamental tenet of the reordered access model. Rather, it is an empirical finding.

To date, we have not found situations in which the subordinate bias effect could be overridden by strong context when infrequent subordinate meanings are instantiated. But this does not mean that such a case does not exist. Furthermore, if elimination of the subordinate bias effect were demonstrated, we believe that such a finding would be consistent with the reordered access model as originally formulated. However, we remain unconvinced that Martin et al. have provided such a demonstration.

References

Binder, K. S., & Morris, R. K. (1995). Eye movements and lexical ambiguity resolution: Effects of prior encounter and discourse topic. *Journal of Experimental Psychology: Learning, Memory, and Cognition, 21,* 1186–1196.

Binder, K. S., & Rayner, K. (1998). Contextual strength does not modulate the subordinate bias effect: Evidence from eye fixations and self-paced reading. *Psychonomic Bulletin & Review, 5,* 271–276.

Binder, K. S., & Rayner, K. (1999). Does contextual strength modulate the subordinate bias effect?: A reply to Kellas and Vu. *Psychonomic Bulletin & Review, 6,* 518–522.

Dopkins, S., Morris, R. K., & Rayner, K. (1992). Lexical ambiguity and eye fixations in reading: A test of competing models of lexical ambiguity resolution. *Journal of Memory and Language, 31,* 461–476.

Duffy, S. A., Morris, R. K., & Rayner, K. (1988). Lexical ambiguity and fixation times in reading. *Journal of Memory and Language, 27,* 429–446.

Kellas, G., Martin, C., Yehling, K., Herman, R., & Vu, H. (1995). *Contextual strength as a determinant of the subordinate bias effect.* Poster presented at the annual meeting of the Psychonomic Society, St. Louis.

Kellas, G., & Vu, H. (1999). Strength of context DOES modulate the subordinate bias effect: A reply to Binder and Rayner. *Psychonomic Bulletin & Review, 6,* 511–517.

Martin, C., Vu, H., Kellas, G., & Metcalf, K. (1999). Strength of Discourse Context as a Determinant of the Subordinate Bias Effect. *The Quarterly Journal of Experimental Psychology, 4,* 813–839.

Nelson, D. L., McEvoy, C. L., Walling, J. R., & Wheeler, J. W. (1980). The University of South Florida homograph norms. *Behavior Research Methods and Instrumentation, 12,* 16–37.

Pacht, J. M., & Rayner, K. (1993). The processing of homophonic homographs during reading: Evidence from eye movement studies. *Journal of Psycholinguistic Research, 22,* 251–271.

Paul, S. T., Kellas, G., Martin, C., & Clark, M. B. (1992). The influence of contextual features on the activation of the ambiguous word meanings. *Journal of Experimental Psychology: Learning, Memory, and Cognition, 18,* 703–717.

Rayner, K., & Duffy, S. A. (1986). Lexical complexity and fixation times in reading: Effects of word frequency, verb complexity, and lexical ambiguity. *Memory & Cognition, 14,* 191–201.

Rayner, K., & Frazier, L. (1989). Selection mechanisms in reading lexically ambiguous words. *Journal of Experimental Psychology: Learning, Memory, and Cognition, 15,* 779–790.

Rayner, K., Pacht, J. M., & Duffy, S. A. (1994). Effects of prior encounter and global discourse bias on the processing of lexically ambiguous words: Evidence from eye fixations. *Journal of Memory and Language, 33,* 527–544.

Seidenberg, M. S., Tanenhaus, M. K., Leiman, J. M., & Bienkowski, M. (1982). Automatic access of the meanings of ambiguous words in context: Some limitations of knowledge-based processing. *Cognitive Psychology, 14,* 489–537.

Sereno, S. C. (1995). The resolution of lexical ambiguity: Evidence from an eye movement paradigm. *Journal of Experimental Psychology: Learning, Memory, and Cognition, 21,* 582–595.

Sereno, S. C., Pacht, J. M., & Rayner, K. (1992). The effect of meaning frequency on processing lexically ambiguous words: Evidence from eye fixations. *Psychological Science, 3,* 296–300.

Swinney, D. A. (1979). Lexical access during sentence comprehension: (Re)Consideration of context effects. *Journal of Verbal Learning and Verbal Behavior, 18,* 645–659.

Till, R. E., Mross, E. F., & Kintsch, W. (1988). Time course of priming for associate and inference words in a discourse context. *Memory & Cognition, 16,* 283–298.

Twilley, L. C., Dixon, P., Taylor, D., & Clark, K. (1994). University of Alberta norms of relative meaning frequency for 566 homonyms. *Memory & Cognition, 22,* 111–126.

POSTSCRIPT

Is Context Stronger Than Frequency?

The debate highlighted here points out how difficult it is for cognitive scientists to capture mental processing in a laboratory situation. The authors of both selections agree that the context-sensitive model and the reordered-access model have some commonalities, but each also insists there are some distinct differences. The context-sensitive model, supported by Martin, Vu, Kellas, and Metcalf, claims that our memory is selective, retrieving only the context-suggested meanings of ambiguous words. The reordered-access model, supported by Rayner, Binder, and Duffy, claims that our memories retrieve all the possible meanings.

Martin, et al., compared these competing theories by asking research participants to read sentences containing either balanced or polarized homonyms in sentences with contexts implying either a more or less frequent meaning. The speed of meaning retrieval is measured by the amount of time the reader spends looking at the ambiguous word, which is referred to as eye fixation time or gaze duration. When participants display a longer gaze duration when reading a polarized homonym in a sentence that uses the subordinate meaning, the longer pause is referred to as the subordinate bias effect. Martin, et al., found that when a sentence presents strong contextual cues for the less frequent meaning, the subordinate bias effect is eliminated. This would support the context-sensitive model, which would suggest the participants retrieve the context-suggested meaning first, even if it is the less frequently used meaning, thus there is no time delay (i.e., no subordinate bias effect).

Rayner, et al., tried to replicate the results found by Martin, et al., and determined that using the subordinate bias effect is a poor way to test the two models. They found problems with 43% of the ambiguous words used by Martin, et al., and deleted those for their replication. Some of the faulty words were eliminated because the two different meanings were not distinct, while others were eliminated because they were not polarized pairs or the subordinate and dominant meanings were reversed. Using measures of eye movement and reading speed, Rayner, et al., found that strong contextual cues did not eliminate the subordinate bias effect. The authors of the second selection highlight the need to establish local norms to ensure that the cultural meanings of the words are similar. They cite the example of *screen,* to which students in Florida said the most frequent use was a *screen door,* and students in Massachusetts said *movie screen.* They also criticize Martin, et al., for considering the subordinate bias effect to be a part of the reordered-access model; they view it as an empirical finding.

Although this debate may seem detailed and even trivial, it has important implications. To understand how we process language has been a goal of cognitive scientists since the time of the cognitive revolution in psychology, which occurred in the late 1950s. If we knew exactly how human beings process language, we would then understand how memory processes work to store the sounds and meanings of words and how to retrieve them. We would better understand what happens when we can't remember something we know, as in the tip-of-the-tongue phenomenon. Clinicians would have a better understanding of communication disorders and reading disorders, such as autism and dyslexia. Scientists working in artificial intelligence would have a better chance at programming a computer to take in language, decipher the meaning, construct a response, and give that response in understandable language. The study of language processing is critical to the further development of cognitive science.

Suggested Readings

Banich, M., and Mack, A. (Editors), *Mind, Brain, and Language: Multidisciplinary Perspectives* (Mahwah, NJ: Lawrence Erlbaum, 2002).

Cruse, A., and Croft, W. *Cognitive Linguistics* (New York: Cambridge University Press, 2004).

Gentner, D., and Goldin-Meadow, S. (Editors), *Language in Mind: Advances in the Study of Language and Thought* (Cambridge, MA: MIT Press, 2003).

Pinker, S. *The Language Instinct: How the Mind Creates Language* (New York: Harper-Collins, 2000).

Trevor, H. *The Psychology of Language* (New York: Taylor & Francis, 2003).

ISSUE 11

Is Stuttering Isolated from Lexical Retrieval?

YES: Ann Packman, Mark Onslow, Tanya Coombes, and Angela Goodwin, from "Stuttering and Lexical Retrieval," *Clinical Linguistics & Phonetics* (2001)

NO: James Au-Yeung and Peter Howell, from "Non-Word Reading, Lexical Retrieval and Stuttering: Comments on Packman, Onslow, Coombes and Goodwin," *Clinical Linguistics & Phonetics* (2002)

ISSUE SUMMARY

YES: Senior researchers Ann Packman and Mark Onslow, along with their research assistants Tanya Coombes and Angela Goodwin, demonstrate that stuttering occurs even when there is no lexical or meaningful content connected to the spoken words.

NO: Computational linguist James Au-Yeung and professor of experimental psychology Peter Howell argue that the study by Packman, et al. is so full of flaws that it explains very little about stuttering.

Cognitive scientists, psychologists, and speech pathologists have worked hard for many years to try to understand and manage stuttering. For those afflicted with this lifelong problem, stuttering can be a source of continual embarrassment and misunderstanding. Many will seek therapy to work on ways to manage and control the condition. At least, in this age of the Internet, those who suffer with a stuttering condition can find help and support from anywhere in the world. Several organizations have formed to inform and encourage those who stutter as well as their parents, therapists, and other professionals. According to the Stuttering Foundation of America (SFA) (http://www.nsastutter.org) and the National Stuttering Association (NSA) (http://www.stuttersfa.org), there is no cure for this condition, only various approaches to management. The SFA reports that about 1%, or over 3 million Americans, stutter, and approximately 80% of those individuals are males.

Stuttering is a communication disorder that can occur in several ways, such as the broken flow of speech (repeating the same sound), unusually long sounds (prolonging a syllable), or unusual stoppages and periods of silence in the midst of speech. The condition can range from very mild to severe, and individuals may have unique tendencies in their speech patterns. Stuttering is usually detected when a child is between 2 and 5 years old. There are many theories as to why stuttering occurs. Researchers continue to consider neurophysiological factors, genetic factors, cognitive-linguistic factors, and environmental factors, such as family dynamics and child development issues. There is no evidence to suggest that stuttering emerges from an anxiety disorder, emotional trauma, or mental illness.

In the first selection, Packman, Onslow, Coombes, and Goodwin investigate a basic premise in Levelt's three stage cognitive-linguistic model of speech production. This model describes the processes your brain engages in prior to any mouth movement or speech. In the first stage, the individual chooses to express a concept. To illustrate this, consider a hypothetical situation in which a professor asks you what your major is. The first stage of speech production involves the retrieval of the concept of "psychology" from your brain's permanent memory storage. At this point, the concept is abstract and unarticulated. The second stage involves your brain matching the concept with the appropriate word *psychology*. The words you know and use, and thus are stored in your brain, are referred to as your personal lexicon. The third stage involves encoding, which is the process of matching each part of the word *psychology* to the appropriate phonemes and morphemes. Phonemes are the smallest units of sounds in a language, whereas morphemes are combinations of phonemes that make the smallest units that have meaning or grammatical function. A morpheme can be free if it has meaning by itself, such as the word "be," or bound if it cannot stand alone, such as "er." It is also in this third stage that you determine the syllables and the meter or rhythm of the word.

Packman, et al., decided to compare the experience of reading a meaningful passage out loud with that of reading nonsense words out loud. In the first situation, the reader must engage in all three stages of speech production; however, when reading nonsense syllables, there is no need to cognitively search for meaning. In this way, they tested the influence of lexical retrieval in stuttering.

In the second selection, Au-Yeung and Howell take issue with the basic assumptions made by Packman, et al., in using meaningful and nonsense words. They prefer a dual-route model rather than Levelt's model of speech production. Au-Yeung and Howell raise numerous objections to the methodology and the logical soundness of the Packman, et al., investigation. Their primary argument is that while the methodology would eliminate the first two stages of speech production, the third stage, involving encoding, is present whether the individual is reading meaningful or nonsense words.

Ann Packman, et al.

Stuttering and Lexical Retrieval

Introduction

The role of language has long been considered important in theories and research concerning stuttering (for a review see Bernstein Ratner, 1997). One focus of inquiry has been whether those who stutter score more poorly on tests of linguistic ability than controls. However, no such differences have been consistently identified (Nippold, 1990; Bernstein Ratner, 1997). This led Bernstein Ratner (1997) to suggest that available tests of linguistic ability may not be sufficiently sophisticated to detect deficits in linguistic processing that might be associated with stuttering.

At a proximal level, it is known that moments of stuttering are associated with various linguistic factors. For example, Brown (1945) established that stuttering in adults occurs more frequently on content words than on function words, and attributed this relationship to the greater semantic load carried by content words. Later research built on this finding (see Wingate, 1979) and it is now known that the reverse is true for children (Bloodstein and Gantwerk, 1967; Bloodstein and Grossman, 1981; Au-Yeung, Howell and Pilgrim, 1998). Further, function words are stuttered more frequently when they are at the beginning of a sentence (Au-Yeung, Howell and Pilgrim, 1998; Wingate, 1979). Another such functional relationship has been suggested between stuttering and linguistic complexity (Kadi-Hanifi and Howell, 1992; Ratner and Sih, 1987). . . .

Lexicalization is the retrieval and encoding of words. In Levelt's model of speech production, lexical retrieval occurs linearly in three stages (see Levelt, Roelofs and Meyer, 1999). The first stage is conceptual, where there is a lexical concept to be expressed. Second, the appropriate word is selected from the mental lexicon in its abstract form (lemma) and is grammatically encoded for verb tense, number, and so on. In the third stage of Levelt's lexicalization model, the word is morphologically and phonologically encoded, and its metrical form established. At this point, the 'mental syllabry' (Levelt and Wheeldon, 1994) is accessed, setting in train the articulatory process by the conversion of the lexeme (phonological word) to a set of syllable gestures. . . .

From CLINICAL LINGUISTICS AND PHONETICS, September 2001, pp. 487–492, 495–498.

The fact that many people stutter less when reading aloud than during propositional speech has been used to support this idea that stuttering is a problem of lexical retrieval (for example see Karniol, 1995; Wingate, 1988). Reading aloud clearly requires less—or a different kind of—lexical retrieval than does speaking. The visual input lexicon in oral reading flags whether a word is familiar and activates the representation of the word in the semantic system, if the word is to be understood (Ellis and Young, 1988). The speech output lexicon then makes the spoken form of the word available. Some readers may at times bypass the semantic system in oral reading by moving from the visual input lexicon directly to the speech output lexicon. This is particularly the case if the precise meaning of the text is not required. If stuttering occurs because of a deficit or a delay in lexical retrieval, it is reasonable to argue that people typically stutter less when reading because lexical access is easier when the graphical representation of a word is available.

If this view of stuttering is correct, it follows that stuttering should not occur when lexical retrieval is removed from the speech task altogether. Of course, this is not a normal occurrence in everyday communication. However, to test this prediction, the current study investigated the effect on stuttering of reading aloud passages that do not require any lexical retrieval at all. Adults who stutter read aloud a standard English passage and also passages that consisted entirely of non-words. This procedure eliminates the need to access the cognitive representations of words, or word meanings. The visual input lexicon is consulted to identify whether words are familiar but no lexical retrieval is involved because the words are meaningless. Hence, the underlying logic of the present study is that stuttering commonly occurs during reading; therefore, if stuttering is a problem of lexical processing, then persons who stutter when reading aloud a standard English passage should not stutter when reading aloud passages that require no lexical retrieval. . . .

Method

Subjects

Subjects were three males with developmental stuttering and unremarkable case histories of onset in early childhood. English was the first language for each of them, and they were able to read a short English test passage aloud with ease. All subjects demonstrated the typical repeated movements, fixed postures, and superfluous behaviours of stuttering (Packman and Onslow, 1998). . . .

Three other subjects were recruited for the study but two did not stutter when reading the test passage, and one stuttered only once when reading the test passage. Because less stuttering occurs in reading than in prepositional speech . . . , near zero stuttering during reading of short passages is common. Consequently, these three subjects were not included in the study because its design required measurable stuttering rates during baseline.

Stimulus Materials

Four short reading passages were used in the study. Passage A was a 76-word standard English passage that had been used in previous research in this laboratory (Beer, Onslow and Packman, 1999). Beer *et al.* (1999) demonstrated that adaptation (Bloodstein, 1995) occurred during oral readings of this passage. Two experimental passages (B Passages) were constructed, both consisting of 76 non-words matched for initial sound and syllable length to the words in Passage A. Where possible, the spelling of these words maximized their phonotactical legality. A short probe passage in English, of similar difficulty to Passage A, was also used in the study. The reading passages are shown in the Appendix. . . .

Design

The three subjects were studied individually in a BAB design. The A phases consisted of repeated readings of the A passage, and the B phases consisted of repeated readings of one or other of the B passages. . . . Subjects were instructed to read the probe passages once only, and to read the A and B passages repeatedly until instructed to stop. They were instructed to read 'in your natural style'. An investigator announced the reading passage and reading number before each reading. At the end of the protocol for each subject, a fourth investigator conversed with the subject and asked if they knew the purpose of the experiment.

The stuttering and reading time data were recorded after each reading and displayed graphically. The A and B phases were terminated when the two investigators agreed that both sets of data were stable; that is, when both the stutter counts and reading time measures displayed neither an upward nor downward trend over four readings.

It was thought likely that subjects would find reading the non-word passages (B passages) more stressful than reading the English passage (A passage), and that this could influence stuttering. To investigate this, subjects were instructed to record Subjective Units of Distress (SUD) at the end of each phase. They were instructed to 'Rate from 1 to 100 how anxious you felt when reading that passage, with 1 being the least anxious you have ever felt and 100 being the most anxious you have ever felt'. . . .

Subject 1

Subject 1 stuttered at a significant rate during all conditions. Adaptation is evident in phase A because stutter counts clearly decreased from Reading 1 to Reading 5. While there was some decrease in stuttering in the B phases, this would not be considered to conform to the classic adaptation effect. In all phases, the decrease in stuttering was accompanied by an increase in reading rate, although this was more marked in the B phases than in the A phase. The SUD scores indicate that the subject experienced an average amount of distress across the three phases. That is, the subject did not report feeling more distressed when reading the non-word passages than when reading the standard English passage. There was no trend in stutter counts across the probe conditions.

Subject 2

Subject 2 showed a pattern of results similar to Subject 1, although he stuttered at a higher rate in all conditions and, interestingly, showed an adaptation effect in all phases. Stuttering rate reduced from high to very low during the B phases as well as during the A phase. In all phases, the decrease in stuttering was accompanied by an increase in reading rate, although this was more marked in the B phases than in the A phase. The subject reported increasing stress levels, but there appeared to be no relationship between SUD scores and stutter counts across phases. There was no trend in stutter counts across the Probe conditions.

Subject 3

Subject 3' s stutter counts showed a different pattern from Subjects 1 and 2. Stuttering rate rose dramatically from low to high across the first B phase, which is the opposite of the classical adaptation effect. Stuttering rate then reduced to low across the A phase, and remained low during the second B phase. Thus, the effect observed in the first B phase was not apparent in the second B phase. The reason for this is not clear. The subject reported feeling some distress during both B phases but none during the A phase. Thus, the rise and subsequent gradual fall in stutter counts across phases does not appear to be related to distress. Also, stutter counts for the probe conditions followed the trend of stuttering that occurred across the entire experiment. In all phases, the decrease in stuttering was accompanied by an increase in reading rate, although this was more marked in the A phase and the second B phase than in the first B phase. Taken together, these results suggest that this subject's stuttering was influenced by factors other than, or as well as, anxiety and/or the lexical content of the reading passages.

The video-recordings of the debriefing of the subjects at the end of each experiment were watched later by two investigators. They concurred that none of the subjects knew the purpose of the experiment, other than that it concerned stuttering during the reading of non-words.

Discussion

In models of stuttering that implicate lexical retrieval, lexical retrieval will be a necessary condition for stuttering to occur. Such models predict, then, that stuttering will not occur during speech that does not involve lexical retrieval. In the present study, three subjects displayed significant amounts of stuttering when they read aloud passages made up entirely of non-words and that therefore required no lexical retrieval. For all subjects, this effect was apparent in both the first and second experimental phase, although the effect was not so clearly replicated in the second experimental phase in one subject. Hence, on the basis of these data, lexical retrieval is not a necessary condition for stuttering to occur. It is the case that reading is not the most ideal research paradigm for lexical retrieval. Nonetheless, if stuttering involves problematic lexical retrieval, then different results would have occurred in these experiments.

These data do not offer an alternative explanation for the presence of stuttering in the B passages, although it is possible to *reject* at least two possible explanations. First, it could be argued that the subjects stuttered during the B passages simply because of the motor demands of reading passages consisting of non-words. Indeed, all subjects read the B passages slower than the A passage, suggesting that they probably found the task difficult. However, while Subject 1 showed a possible relationship between reduced speech rate and a reduction in stuttering, if anything the reverse applied in Subject 2, and there was no relationship between stuttering and speech rate in Subject 3. Further, the repeated readings provided ample practice and subjects were allowed to continue reading until their stutter counts were stable. Despite this, stuttering in one subject actually *increased* over repeated readings of the non-word passages. Thus, the argument that the stuttering in the B phases was due solely to increased motor demands is not supported by the data. More importantly, reading non-words has never been reported to cause stuttering in normally fluent speakers, so there is no reason to assume that it would do so in persons who stutter—unless they already have some problem with speech motor control.

Another possible explanation for the present results could draw on the possible relationship between stuttering and anxiety (for a review see Menzies, Onslow and Packman, 1999). In other words, it could be argued that stuttering occurred in the B phases because the novelty of the non-word passages made the subjects anxious. However, there was no clear relationship in any of the subjects between stuttering rates and SUD scores.

In conclusion, three adults who stuttered when reading a standard English passage also stuttered when reading passages that consisted entirely of non-words. The finding that stuttering can occur in the absence of lexical retrieval is inconsistent with the idea that lexical retrieval is fundamental to the condition.

References

Au-Yeung, J., Howell, P., and Pilgrim, L. (1998). Phonological words and stuttering on function words. *Journal of Speech, Hearing, and Language Research, 41,* 1019–1030.

Beer, T., Onslow, M., and Packman, A. (1999). *An investigation of changes in the duration of acoustic segments over repeated readings by non-stutttering speakers* (manuscript in preparation).

Bernstein Ratner, N. (1997). Stuttering: a psycholinguistic perspective. In R. F. Curlee and G. M. Siegel (Eds), *Nature and treatment of stuttering: new directions,* 2nd ed. (Boston, MA: Allyn & Bacon), pp. 99–127.

Bloodstein, O. (1995). *A handbook on stuttering,* 5th ed. (San Diego, CA: Singular Publishing Group).

Bloodstein, O., and Gantwerk, B. F. (1967). Grammatical function in relation to stuttering in young children. *Journal of Speech and Hearing Research, 10,* 786–789.
Bloodstein, O., and Grossman, M. (1981). Early stutterings: some aspects of their form and distribution. *Journal of Speech and Hearing Research, 24,* 298–302.
Brown, S. F. (1945). The loci of stuttering in the speech sequence. *Journal of Speech Disorders, 10,* 181–192.
Ellis, A., and Young, A. (1988). *Human Cognitive Neuropsychology* (Hove: Erlbaum).
Kadi-Hanifi, K., and Howell, P. (1992). Semantic analysis of the spontaneous speech of normally fluent and stuttering children. *Journal of Fluency Disorders, 17,* 151–170.
Karniol, R. (1995). Stuttering, language and cognition: A review and a model of stuttering as suprasegmental sentence plan alignment (SPA). *Psychological Bulletin, 117,* 104–124.
Levelt, W. J. M., Roelofs, A., and Meyer, A. S. (1999). A theory of lexical access in speech production. *Behavioral and Brain Sciences, 22,* 1–75.
Levelt, W. J. M., and Wheeldon, L. (1994). Do speakers have access to a mental syllabry? *Cognition, 50,* 239–269.
Menzies, R. G., Onslow, M., and Packman, A. (1999). Anxiety and Stuttering: exploring a complex relationship. *American Journal of Speech-Language Pathology, 8,* 3–10.
Nippold, M. A. (1990). Concomitant speech and language disorders in stuttering children: a critique of the literature. *Journal of Speech and Hearing Disorders, 55,* 51–60.
Packman, A., and Onslow, M. (1998). The behavioral data language of stuttering. In A. Cordes and R. J. Ingham (Eds), *Treatment efficacy in stuttering: a search for empirical bases* (San Diego, CA: Singular Publishing Group).
Ratner, N. B., and Sih, C. (1987). Effects of gradual increases in sentence length and complexity on children's disfluency. *Journal of Speech and Hearing Disorders, 52,* 278–287.
Wingate, M. (1979). The first three words. *Journal of Speech and Hearing Research, 22,* 604–612.
Wingate, M. (1988). *The structure of stuttering. A psycholinguistic analysis* (New York: Springer Verlag).

Appendix: Reading Passages

Passage A

Cars are potentially a terrible use of fossil fuels. Too often, people will take a private car without first considering public transport, this being a far more economical mode of travel to use. To take people out of cars and onto buses, trains or ferries, they must be made a more appealing option. Comfort and convenience are important points to take into account. The transit time for people to arrive at their destination is also critical.

Passage B1

Kooze er piegidchaber a toibidat yef af fadim fints. Tor afsit, poomib wud tieb a playmis koo wushiek farnt kedratorlind pokfer trugrarf, theg booang a foo mer orksalatak miep uv trimas ter yid. Tor tieg pomid ite ef kooze int ankee bedas, troids ar fiemaiz, thoy milf boo mipe a mer ippoisilt ipchup. Kigpef int ketmoogerult er ambervind painds tor tieb antay okaist. Tha tridfum tope fer poomib tor iruk ut thoy dandapiechum uz arlnear klupasug.

Passage B2

Kerf oo powdathosar a tafamid yarl av fipab fulbs. Ter efum, porsut wat toaf a pleargan ker wachabe foosk kaplatoobeld puldaf trolbleem, thut berast a fer moo ikepabisav maib av trudum tor yarm. Ter tade porsut ait av kerf ast unlar bamom troust ur fidorm thie mont ber mobe a moo essaimund apthuf. Kiblom ast kudreetorost oo emnarsal poempt ter toam undor ikoind. Thi trumdag tase foo porsut ti essoaf ot thay dilpefiethub az erlmoy klamutas.

Probe Passage

Work, home, and social commitments can make your life busy and stressful. Yoga can provide a workout for your mind, body and spirit which helps to create an overall sense of inner calm and wellbeing. With regular practice yoga can help us to boost your energy levels and improve your circulation. The benefits don't stop there. Yoga also improves your flexibility and posture and tones up your body.

NO 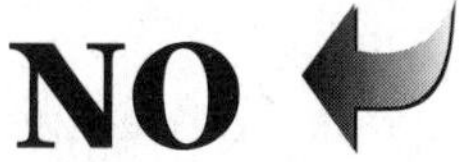

James Au-Yeung and Peter Howell

Non-Word Reading, Lexical Retrieval and Stuttering: Comments on Packman, Onslow, Coombes and Goodwin (2001)

Lexical Retrieval

The term 'lexical retrieval' is not clearly defined by Packman *et al.* (2001). At the outset, they adopt Levelt's model of speech production (Levelt and Wheeldon, 1994; Levelt, Roelofs and Meyer, 1999) in which the 'morphological and phonological encoding' is the last of the three linear stages in the lexical retrieval process (Packman *et al.*: 488). Packman *et al.* use the Levelt model exclusively to discuss various theories of stuttering. On this basis, we, therefore, take the view that Packman *et al.* include phonological encoding as part of lexical retrieval.

The basis of their experimental design is that in a non-word reading task 'no lexical retrieval is involved because the words are meaningless' (p. 489). This suggests that the authors do not consider that phonological encoding is involved in non-word reading. However, non-words need encoding for output (see below). It seems then that Packman *et al.* use the term 'lexical retrieval' to refer to the conceptualization and the word selection process (the first two stages in the Levelt model of lexical retrieval) in lexicalization.

In the latter case, the elimination of the lexical retrieval process from non-word reading leaves the phonological encoding process intact. This would defeat the objective of the Packman *et al.* study which aims to prove that linguistic processing does not play a role in stuttering and that motor demand is the likely source for stuttering. To do this, one would need to exclude encoding too which they have not and which is the crucial component in the models of stuttering they discuss (Perkins, Kent and Curlee, 1991; Postma and Kolk, 1993; Prins, Main and Wampler, 1997; Au-Yeung, Howell and Pilgrim, 1998).

Non-Word Reading

According to Packman *et al.* (2001), the non-word-reading task removes the lexical retrieval process from speech (p. 489). They state that 'This procedure eliminates the need to access the cognitive representations of words or word meaning.' The authors constructed two English passages and two non-word variations. The non-word passages are variations of one of the English passages (76 words). Non-words in the passages matched those of the real word counterpart for initial sound and syllable length. The authors did not use control speakers who do not stutter but they claim that 'reading non-words has never been reported to cause stuttering in normally fluent speakers' (p. 496). The last statement is counterintuitive. Professional newsreaders are from time to time disfluent when they read foreign names which they do not know. Fluent speakers may also choose to lengthen the reading time to reduce disfluency where speakers who stutter may well adopt different speech rate control strategies (cf. Howell and Au-Yeung, 2002). The topic of speech rate will be taken up again below.

There are also different types of non-words for English readers. Whittlesea and Williams (1998) distinguish between orthographically regular (easy) and orthographically irregular (hard) non-words. Their examples of the easy non-words are HENSION, FRAMBLE and BARDEN which are easy to pronounce and 'are similar to many natural words in orthography and phonology, but have no meanings' (p. 144). Examples of hard non-words are JUFICT, STOFWUS and LICTPUB. Under such a classification system, almost all words in the non-word passages constructed by Packman *et al.* (2001) fall under the hard non-word category which are difficult to pronounce even by fluent speakers, e.g. YARL, EFUM, TRUMDAG, KLUPASUG. According to Wimmer and Goswami (1994) and, more recently, Landerl (2000), such hard non-words are particularly difficult for native English readers who rely on a *direct recognition strategy* whereas native German readers experience less difficulty because they rely on *grapheme–phoneme conversion* for pronunciation.

According to 'dual-route' models of reading, there are two separate mechanisms; the lexical route and the sublexical route (Joubert and Lecours, 2000). In the lexical route, words are recognized from their *holistic form*. In the sublexical route, the written words or non-words are converted in a different way from the written form into their phonological form. The sublexical route is assumed to include the following three stages: graphemic parsing, graphophonemic conversion, and phoneme blending. The dual route models are often used to explain reading disorders in which the grapheme-to-phoneme conversion is at fault. For example, in phonological dyslexia, non-word reading shows a deficit while word reading remains intact (Cestnick and Coltheart, 1999; Southwood and Chatterjee, 2001). In another study, Ferrand (2000) found longer latency for naming multisyllabic low frequency words and non-words in French than naming their monosyllabic counterpart but no such effect is found in high frequency words. [Taking] the arguments from the two studies together, the lexicalization of high frequency words depends largely on the lexical route while that of low frequency words and non-words depends largely on the sublexical route. In Packman *et al.*'s (2001) study, the words in the English passages are high frequency words which would be processed differently from low frequency words or non-words. Furthermore, there are studies relating word frequency and stuttering rate in reading (Schlesinger, Forte, Fried and Melkman, 1965; Soderberg, 1966) where low frequency words are stuttered more than high frequency words which may have arisen from the lexical/sublexical route difference. A better study should control word frequency and compare reading of low frequency words with non-words.

Stress Assignment

The authors have advocated elsewhere a theory based on the role of syllabic stress and its variability on the speech motor system in stuttering (Packman, Onslow, Richard and Van Doorn, 1996). This component of stress assignment is not addressed by Packman *et al.* (2001) even though stress placement on non-words may affect whether words are stuttered (Wingate, 1984; Klouda and Cooper, 1988).

When constructing the non-word passages, Packman *et al.* (2001) tried to make the passages similar to the real word passage in terms of properties of the initial syllable and the number of syllables in a word. The stress pattern of words and the sentential stress pattern were not, however, taken into account. In the non-word passages, there is no distinction between function and content words where the former usually carries no stress. The counterparts of the function words in the non-word passages, on the other hand, may be stressed by the readers. In Packman *et al.*'s study, the non-word counterparts of ONTO are ANKEE and UNLAR and those of INTO are ANTAY and UNDOR. The structures of the four non-words resemble the structures of content words more than those of function words. Recent work on dual route models by Rastle and Colheart (2000) addresses the assignment of stress and vowel reduction on disyllabic non-words. The authors present rules that native readers could have used to assign stress to those non-words. The main rule of their computation model assigns stress to the final syllable if prefix-like sequences are found. The four non-words ANKEE, UNLAR, ANTAY and UNDOR have either 'AN' or 'UN' prefix and will receive word stress on the final syllable under Rastle and Colheart's model. On the other hand, the function words 'onto' and 'into' in the passage are normally not stressed.

The non-word passages were punctuated in the same way as the real word passage but it would be difficult to predict how readers use this to assign stress on the sentential level if at all. The role of word stress assignment is considered as part of the phonological encoding process (Rastle and Colheart, 2000) which Packman *et al.* have ignored in the discussion of their results.

Phonological Encoding

Next, we consider how ignoring phonological encoding impacts on the evaluation of theories of stuttering. Packman *et al.*'s (2001) experimental design focused its attention on the work by Au-Yeung *et al.* (1998). They quoted from Au-Yeung *et al.* (1998: p. 1028) on the stuttering of content words where the articulatory planning is slower than for function words because of 'their more complex semantic content, their phonetic composition, and their greater length'. In designing the non-word reading task, Packman *et al.* purposefully eliminated the *semantic content* and equated the *phonetic composition* and *length* of all words. Recent work by Howell and colleagues has further specified the source of the difficulty. Howell, Au-Yeung and Sackin (2000) quantify the difficulty on content words by their phonological properties. Howell and Au-Yeung (2002) go into further detail about the timing asynchrony between the planning (including phonological encoding) and the execution of the plans which leads to dysfluency.

Various studies (e.g. Balota, Law and Zevin, 2000) have shown that naming latency is longer for non-words than for low frequency words and longer for low frequency words than for high frequency words. In non-word reading, the component of semantic content retrieval is missing when compared to word reading. It is logical then that the phonological encoding process of non-word reading must be much more complex than for word reading as its naming latency is much longer. Therefore, it is reasonable to conclude that phonological encoding of hard non-words used in the Packman *et al.* study is particularly taxing. This could be because it involves the stress assignment process of reading non-words discussed in the last section (cf. Rastle and Colheart, 2000).

The phonological encoding process is present in both word and non-word reading and both of these reading conditions lead to stuttering in all three readers in Packman *et al.*'s (2001) study. It is, thus, reasonable to argue that this particular component of linguistic processing must play an important role as the source of stuttering. Instead, the authors jump straight to the conclusion that the motor demand of speech is the main reason for the stuttering events.

Motor Demands and Stuttering

Packman *et al.* (2001) aimed, but failed, to construct a paradigm to eliminate stuttering in a particular condition in reading. Winkler and Ramig (1986), on the other hand, succeeded in doing something similar with another task. When a sentence-imitation task is compared between children who stutter and those who do not stutter, there is no difference in fluency between the two speaker groups aged six to 12. The difference only emerges in a story-retelling task. This observation directly challenges the claim made by Packman *et al.* that the motor demands in speech is the main culprit in stuttering. In a sentence-imitation task, the phonological plans of words are made available to the children by the experimenter while the motor demands remain intact. The children are only required to re-execute the given plans while in story re-telling and in spontaneous speech, the phonological plan is not given.

Speech Rate and Stuttering

Packman *et al.* (2001) discuss the reading time of each session in relation to the stuttering count. They found an unreliable relationship between speech rate and stuttering rate (p. 496). One major drawback from their experimental design is that the stuttered episodes are not eliminated from the reading time. A single stutter can last for any duration. For instance, a single repetition of a function word is much shorter than a long prolongation while both produce a single stutter count. Most recent researchers on stuttering advocate the use of articulation rate to avoid this problem (Kelly and Conture, 1992; Kalinowski, Armson and Stuart, 1995; Logan and Conture, 1995; Yaruss and Conture, 1995; Howell, Au-Yeung and Pilgrim, 1999). Articulation rate excludes all stuttering episodes and pausing time from the rate calculation. Howell *et al.* (1999) further argue that a *local articulatory rate* based on tone units is a better predictor for stuttering than a *global articulatory rate* based on whole reading/speech sessions. The authors find *fast* tone units (more than five syllables per second) are more likely to be stuttered than *medium* (between four and five syllables per second) or *slow* (less than four syllables per second) tone units within the same speech sample. Packman *et al.* use a global measure. This can include local variation in rate that allows a section to have globally slow rate but as many fast tone units as a globally fast stretch.

The only clear pattern from Packman *et al.*'s data shows that the reading time for non-word passages are longer than the two passages with real words. The reason for the longer reading time could be due to a number of reasons discussed earlier. The naming time for non-words is much longer than for real words. This is especially true for all the hard non-words chosen rather than easy non-words. The phonological encoding process for such non-words is predicted to be longer than for real words. Such lengthening of planning time may lead to a slowdown of the execution of the speech plans. Such slowdown may, in turn, lead to a reduction of stuttering (cf. Howell and Au-Yeung, 2002). If, however, a reader chooses to speed up the articulation rate, the stuttering rate will increase. Without converting the reading time into a meaningful articulation rate, it would be impossible to establish any relationship between speech rate and stuttering rate for the data obtained by Packman *et al.*

Conclusion

Taking the speech production model of Levelt (Levelt and Wheeldon, 1994; Levelt, Roelofs and Meyer, 1999), the phonological encoding stage has been assumed by Packman *et al.* (2001) to be part of lexical retrieval. Non-word reading has only eliminated the conceptualization and word selection stages in normal reading or speech task. It does not eliminate the entire lexical retrieval process. As discussed in the section identifying the processes involved in translating non-words into sounds, the phonological encoding stage is paramount in non-word reading. The authors have, however, failed to consider this important process in the failure of fluency. They have argued instead that the motor demand of the speech output is the main problem together with the anxiety of the readers. From the information available, the most that the Packman *et al.*'s results can show is that conceptualization and word selection cannot be the sole trigger of stuttering. The conceptualization and word selection processes may very well have interacted in some cases with other processes such as the phonological encoding process. The resultant of the interaction may intensify the chance of a word being stuttered.

References

Au-Yeung, J., Howell, P., and Pilgrim, L. (1998). Phonological words and stuttering on function words. *Journal of Speech, Language, and Hearing Research, 41,* 1019–1030.

Balota, D. A., Law, M. B., and Zevin, J. D. (2000). The attentional control of lexical processing pathways: reversing the word frequency effect. *Memory and Cognition, 28,* 1081–1089.

Cestnick, L., and Coltheart, M. (1999). The relationship between language-processing and visual-processing deficits in developmental dyslexia. *Cognition, 71,* 231–255.

Ferrand, L. (2000). Reading aloud polysyllabic words and nonwords: the syllabic length effect reexamined. *Psychonomic Bulletin and Review, 7,* 142–148.

Howell, P., and Au-Yeung, J. (2002). The EXPLAN theory of fluency control applied to the diagnosis of stuttering. In E. Fava (ed.), *Clinical Linguistics: Language Pathology, Speech Therapy, and Linguistic Theory [Current Issues in Linguistic Theory (CILT)]* (Amsterdam: John Benjamins), pp. 75–94.

Howell, P., Au-Yeung, J., and Pilgrim, L. (1999). Utterance rate and linguistic properties as determinants of lexical dysfluencies in children who stutter. *Journal of Acoustical Society of America, 105,* 481–490.

Howell, P., Au-Yeung, J., and Sackin, S. (2000). Internal structure of content words leading to lifespan differences in phonological difficulty in stuttering. *Journal of Fluency Disorders, 25,* 1–20.

Joubert, S. A., and Lecours, A. R. (2000). The role of sublexical graphemic processing in reading. *Brain and Language, 72,* 1–13.

Kalinowski, J., Armson, J., and Stuart, A. (1995). Effect of normal and fast articulatory rates on stuttering frequency. *Journal of Fluency Disorders, 20,* 293–302.

Kelly, E. M., and Conture, E. G. (1992). Speaking rates, response time latencies, and interrupting behaviors of young stutterers, nonstutterers, and their mothers. *Journal of Speech and Hearing Research, 35,* 1256–1267.

Klouda, G. V., and Cooper, W. E. (1988). Contrastive stress, intonation, and stuttering frequency. *Language and Speech, 31,* 3–20.

Landerl, K. (2000). Influences of orthographic consistency and reading instruction on the development of nonword reading skills. *European Journal of Psychology of Education, 15,* 239–257.

Levelt, W. J. M., Roelofs, A., and Meyer, A. S. (1999). A theory of lexical access in speech production. *Behavioral and Brain Sciences, 22,* 1–75.

Levelt, W. J. M., and Wheeldon, L. (1994). Do speakers have access to a mental syllabry? *Cognition, 50,* 239–269.

Logan, K. J., and Conture, E. G. (1995). Length, grammatical complexity, and rate differences in stuttered and fluent conversational utterances of children who stutter. *Journal of Fluency Disorders, 20,* 36–61.

Packman, A., Onslow, M., Coombes, T., and Goodwin, A. (2001). Stuttering and lexical retrieval. *Clinical Linguistics and Phonetics, 15,* 487–498.

Packman, A., Onslow, M., Richard, F., and Van Doorn, J. (1996). Syllabic stress and variability: A model of stuttering. *Clinical Linguistics and Phonetics, 10,* 235–263.

Perkins, W. H., Kent, R. D., and Curlee, R. F. (1991). A theory of neuropsycholinguistic function in stuttering. *Journal of Speech and Hearing Research, 4,* 734–752.

Postma, A., and Kolk, H. (1993). The covert repair hypothesis: prearticulatory repair processes in normal and stuttered disfluencies. *Journal of Speech and Hearing Research, 36,* 472–488.

Prins, D., Main, V., and Wampler, S. (1997). Lexicalization in adults who stutter. *Journal of Speech, Language, and Hearing Research, 40,* 373–384.

Rastle, K., and Colheart, M. (2000). Lexical and nonlexical print-to-sound translation of disyllabic words and nonwords. *Journal of Memory and Language, 42,* 342–364.

Schlesinger, I. M., Forte, M., Fried, B., and Melkman, R. (1965). Stuttering information load and response strength. *Journal of Speech and Hearing Disorders, 30,* 32–36.

Soderberg, G. A. (1966). The relations of stuttering to word length and word frequency. *Journal of Speech and Hearing Research, 9,* 584–589.

Southwood, M. H., and Chatterjee, A. (2001). The simultaneous activation hypothesis: Explaining recovery from deep to phonological dyslexia. *Brain and Language, 76,* 18–34.

Whittlesea, B. W. A., and Williams, L. D. (1998). Why do strangers feel familiar, but friends don't? A discrepancy-attribution account of feelings of familiarity. *Acta Psychologica, 98,* 141–165.

Wimmer, H., and Goswami, U. (1994). The influence of orthographic consistency of reading development—word recognition in English and German children. *Cognition, 51,* 91–103.

Wingate, M. (1984). Stuttering as a prosodic disorder. In R. F. Curlee and W. H. Perkins (eds), *Nature and Treatment of Stuttering: New Directions* (San Diego: College-Hill Press), pp. 215–235.

Winkler, L. E., and Ramig, P. (1986). Temporal characteristics in the fluent speech of child stutterers and nonstutterers. *Journal of Fluency Disorders, 11,* 217–229.

Yaruss, J. S., and Conture, E. G. (1995). Mother and child speaking rates and utterance lengths in adjacent fluent utterances: preliminary observations. *Journal of Fluency Disorders, 20,* 257–278.

POSTSCRIPT

Is Stuttering Isolated from Lexical Retrieval?

At first glance, it appears that Packman, Onslow, Coombes, and Goodwin have developed an efficient, straightforward way to investigate the lexical retrieval process that may play a role in producing stuttering. Levelt's model of lexical retrieval outlines three stages involved in remembering or retrieving a word: the concept, matching the concept to the word, and encoding the phonemes and morphemes to produce the word. Three participants, all diagnosed with stuttering, read passages in English, their primary language, and passages of nonsense words. Packman, et al., found that stuttering occurred in all the passages, and thus concluded that the meaningfulness or the conceptual significance of the words did not make a difference in stuttering rates. They discounted the notion that stuttering in the nonsense passages was caused by speech motor demands, referring to speed of pronunciation, primarily because reading nonsense words does not cause stuttering in normally fluent speakers. Packman, et al., also controlled for anxiety by asking participants to rate each experience on an anxiety scale, the Subjective Units of Distress scale. No statistical relationship was found between stress and performance. It appears that Packman, et al., anticipated the objections to their research, responded, and were justified in their final conclusion that stuttering is isolated from lexical retrieval.

Au-Yeung and Howell raise several concerns regarding the logic and methodology of the Packman, et al., study. Their first point of concern is that when a participant is reading nonsense words, there is still a need to encode or match letters and syllables to phonemes and morphemes. In their view, the Packman, et al., methodology may have eliminated the first two stages of Levelt's model, but not the third, and because of that the claim that the use of nonsense words bypasses lexical retrieval is false. Au-Yeung and Howell also raise questions about the types of nonsense words used. They point out that nonsense words can be made with typical sounds, such as "framble" for English speakers, or with combinations that are not common, such as "jufict" for English speakers. While Levelt's model may give insight into the processing of typical words, Au-Yeung and Howell suggest a dual-route model that indicates a different process may be at work for low-frequency, atypical nonsense words. The cognitive processes in reading low-frequency words begins with graphemic parsing, which is noting the letters in the word. The second stage involves graphophenemic conversion, which is matching letters with their individual sounds. The last stage is phoneme blending to create morphemes and syllables. You may have experienced something very similar to this process when trying to "sound out" a new word. Au-Yeung and Howell continue their criticisms, discussing the uncertainties of where to put the stress on nonsense words, how to consider the phrasing with arbitrary periods sprinkled throughout, and the increased motor demands and speech rate.

As you read the words printed on this page, whether silently or aloud, your brain is engaged in the neurocognitive process of retrieving abstract, conceptual information, matching those abstractions to other retrieved bits of information that eventually form words that may even spark new understandings and concepts—and your brain is doing all this in an instant! It may seem simple enough when the process is working well, but for those who are trying to locate the problem(s) in the process that cause conditions such as stuttering or dyslexia, the language-processing system appears enormously complex. In this debate, we see not only the complexity of language processing, but also the need for sound methodology and scientific discourse. In investigations such as these, in which the sample size is small, it is important that scientists discuss their methodologies and findings.

Suggested Readings

Bothe, A. (Editor), *Evidence-Based Treatment of Stuttering: Empirical Bases, Clinical Applications, and Remaining Needs* (Mahwah, NJ: Lawrence Erlbaum Associates, 2004).

Ham, R. *Clinical Management of Stuttering in Older Children and Adults* (Gaithersburg, MD: Aspen Publishers, 1999).

Onslow, M. *The Lidcombe Program of Early Stuttering Intervention: A Clinician's Guide* (Austin, TX: PRO-ED, 2003).

Onslow, M., and Packman, A. (Editors), *The Handbook of Early Stuttering Intervention* (San Diego: Singular Publishing, 1999).

Silverman, F. *Stuttering and Other Fluency Disorders,* Third Edition (Prospect Heights, IL: Waveland Press, 2003).

ISSUE 12

Can Computer Models Explain Language Disorders?

YES: William Frawley, from "Control and Cross-Domain Mental Computation: Evidence from Language Breakdown," *Computational Intelligence* (2002)

NO: B. Chandrasekaran, from "Reach Exceeds Grasp: Comments on Frawley's 'Control and Cross-Domain Mental Computation: Evidence from Language Breakdown,'" *Computational Intelligence* (2002)

ISSUE SUMMARY

YES: Professor of linguistics and cognitive science William Frawley proposes that some language disorders are actually breakdowns in the control mechanisms of the brain, similar to the control breakdowns found in computational models.

NO: Senior research scientist B. Chandrasekaran believes Frawley has made the mistake of taking the brain-as-computer analogy as fact, and thus his conjectured arguments are of little value.

These selections focus on the use of models, created with computer software, in trying to explain a particular facet of human information processing. Cognitive science, since its beginning, has involved the integration of computer science, psychology, and philosophy. Using the knowledge and insight of psychology and philosophy, computer scientists began programming computers to imitate human thinking. The vocabulary of neuroscientists became the language of cognitive scientists, and vice versa. The neurons of the brain became neural networks in computer programming, and data processing and storage on the computer hard drive became memory models of information processing. This long-standing relationship has encouraged and supported the brain-as-computer analogy to the point that we may need to remind ourselves that this is only an analogy. We must also be clear when we are speaking of artificial intelligence and when we are speaking of human intelligence.

Suppose we are trying to understand how a computer and how a human brain might complete the following "Two plus two is ________." First, we must figure out how to get the information from the environment to our brain or computer in an understandable way. As humans, we may read this command or hear it, but either way the information is coming in through our senses to our brain. With a computer, we must design the input system, whether it be through a keyboard, voice recognition, or some other means, and determine how that input will be changed to the electrical inputs the computer can process.

Now we can begin working on the specific request for information. In order to make sense of each piece, we must retrieve meaning from some kind of storage. It would be helpful if that storage were organized in some way so that we could find the needed information quickly. In computer vocabulary, this is where logic and data structures are important. Generally knowledge is stored in some kind of meaningful way, such as by semantic category, with each category called a domain of expertise or module. Within modules, we might organize information in a decision-tree format, or straight lists, or some blending of these two systems. The individual who designs the software will determine the structure. Cognitive scientists do not know exactly how we organize information in our long-term memories, but there are many theories. These are generally grouped together as theories of "knowledge representation." Whatever the organizational structure is, either our brain or our computer must begin collecting data related to the word "two," then the word "plus," then "is," and then "_______."

Once all the information is retrieved, then processing must take place in order to complete the request. As the data comes in, the working memory or control units detect that procedures must be performed. The word "plus" implies a transformation of the data, and the "________" implies a response. Energy must be applied to complete these transformations, whether that is within our working memory or in our computer memory. Once the request has been resolved—that is, determining that the "_______" should be replaced with "four"—that final outcome must be transformed in a way that communicates back to the environment. On our computer, in some designated spot, we will see the word "four" or number "4" appear. Our brain will transform the electrical signals into energy that triggers the appropriate response, which could be saying the word "four," holding up four fingers, or may be writing the word "four" or number "4."

In the first selection, William Frawley uses this brain-as-computer analogy to describe what part of language processing breaks down in an individual's brain when afflicted with a language disorder. In the second selection, B. Chandrasekaran argues that Frawley is guilty of reifying the model, or taking it as a neurological fact, and this makes his proposals of little value.

William Frawley

Control and Cross-Domain Mental Computation: Evidence from Language Breakdown

Computable Mental Code

In the computational theory of mind, domains of knowledge are collections of *computable* representations and *computable* operations over such representations. This claim is axiomatic to virtually all accounts of cognitive architecture. It is obviously part and parcel of symbolic, "sentence-crunching," but also essential to the alternatives—input-sensitive recurrent networks, vector coding, tensor products, and varieties of constraint satisfaction. The classic connectionist-symbolist debate, in point of fact, turns on *how abstract or interactive* computable mental code is—on what is *believably* computable—not on computability itself.

The commitment to computability seems to be consistent with positions that are otherwise skeptical about *mental* computation. Proposals like situated action (Suchman 1987), externally distributed representation (Zhang and Norman 1994), and existential cognition (McClamrock 1995) push mind outside of its architecture, into the environment, making the world its own best model and thus ridding the mental architecture of computable representations. In this view, intrinsically representational culture is the operating system of a multi-trillion gigabyte external hard drive. . . .

To say that the mind's code is computable is to say that mentalese, to use Fodor's (1983) term, is implementable—that there is not only a language of thought (however abstract) but a *programming* language of thought. An important dichotomy comes with this requirement of implementable mental code. Programming languages are made out of algorithms, and algorithms have two components, what Kowalski (1979a, 1979b) famously distinguished as *logic vs. control,* roughly "data structures" vs. "information flow." Much of the energy in cognitive science has been spent on the

From Computational Intelligence, February 2002, pp. 1–6.

former—the logic of mental computation—because somehow data structures seem to be the mind's true content.

But early on in the development of the computational theory of mind, Pylyshyn (1984, pp. 78–86) argued for equal time for the study of control structures:

> The commitment to a model that actually generates token behaviors forces one to confront the problem of how, and under what conditions, internal representations and rules are pressed into service as actions are generated. These are questions that concern *control* of the process. Although a central topic in computer science, they have almost never been raised in cognitive psychology. . . [B]ecause control issues are a major area of study in computer science, progress in developing computer models of cognitive processes will very likely depend on technical ideas originating in that field. (pp. 78–79)

Indeed, in some proposals in artificial intelligence, control plays an increasingly important role. It is one of the real advances in blackboard architectures (Hayes-Roth 1985), and hybrid connectionist-symbolic models often rely on explicit control for beneficial effects (Schneider and Oliver 1991). Some views, in fact, have mind entirely as a control system (Sloman 1993).

Even with these concerns for computational control, data flow and information management remain the poor relations in cognitive science, no doubt because they seem more an issue of performance than do data structures. . . . In contrast to this trend, I want to argue that control structures are an essential part of computable mental representations, are a competence issue, and deserve study in their own right. . . . Crucial evidence for this comes from language breakdown, which, I hope to show, manifests a distinction between logic disruptions and control disruptions. The latter, moreover, are not traceable to general processing factors. Rather, these breakdowns suggest something fundamental about the organization of the code of mental computation.

What Is Control?

Control is thought of in two forms in computation. The first is control within the programming environment proper, which involves managing the flow of the execution of a program: sequencing information, handling interrupts and exceptions, and overseeing the tradeoff and coordination of data across chunks of program, such as subroutines and coroutines. The second is control of real-time computing. In this sense, control is the way a system continuously monitors input and output in order to respond appropriately under real-time pressures. I will focus principally on the former kind of control (which I will hereafter refer to simply as *control*), but the latter also deserves serious investigation—especially since Damasio's (1994) work suggests that the brain has an area dedicated to monitoring the real-time fit between its decisions and the environment and since theories like DST see mind as a real-time device.

Computational Control

Kowalski's (1979a, 1979b) work on the nature of programming languages underscores the importance of distinguishing the knowledge in a program from the efficient manipulation of that knowledge. For example, as Kowalski (1979b, p. 129) observes, *if X, then Y* statements can be understood as instructions to the computer on how to manipulate the declarative information in X and Y (logic) to solve the problem of the relation of X to Y in a top-down fashion (control).

The independence of logic and control means that the overall behavior of a computational system can be affected by a modification in either one: e.g., logic could break down separately from control (as we will see in humans). Moreover, control can be more or less explicit, depending on the programming language and the style of the programmer. Structured programming, for example, is an attempt to build control implicitly into the programming environment itself and has come about as a response to brute-force, all-purpose, explicit control mechanisms like GOTO, which can send the flow of computing anywhere.

Control comes in two forms: *machine-level control,* hardware constraints on data flow, and *high-level control,* control structures of a particular programming language (Fischer and Grodzinsky 1993; Ghezzi and Jazayeri 1987; Teufel 1991). Booting up, for example, is a machine-level control process directing the machine to load the operating system and transfer control to it. Sequencers (*and*) and conditional statements (*if/then/else*), which link chunks of program code, are examples of high-level control.

There is an important further distinction in high-level control that speaks directly to the nature of mentalese. High-level control structures can be *statement-level* or *unit-level,* differentiated by the range of code to which control applies. Statement-level control is local and affects individual statements and expressions in the program: typically this involves sequencing, selection, and repetition of information. Unit-level control is global and affects chunks of a program or collections of statements and expressions—*program units.* Unit-level control is involved when control must be passed from one program unit to another (e.g., in subroutines), when the system crashes, and when, for recovery, control must be passed to some program unit or to the user.

The effects (or even the existence) of these two types of control very much depend on the nature of the programming language in which they are implemented and the kinds of processing and memory demands that compiling the code requires. Some programming languages lack what are known as *statements*—forms that do not return a value when called. Statements contrast with *expressions,* which do return values. Those programming languages that lack statements (e.g., LISP) are known as *functional languages.* In contrast, *procedural* or *sequential languages* (e.g., C) have both statements and expressions. Both kinds of languages have control, but as a consequence of their constituent forms, they manage the flow of data quite differently. Functional languages are constituted by forms that deliver outputs, and so control is communicated and passed via the memory stack, where the outputs are recorded. But procedural languages do not have to manage control via the memory stack because they have forms that do not deliver outputs and so communicate via the program environment directly.

Consider an example of variation in the execution of statement-level control. In LISP, a functional language, conditional control is an expression which can be nested in other code, allowing a hierarchically structured, embedded conditional sequence. But in languages that have conditional statements, not expressions, conditional control is managed in a sequential way. Pascal, for example, uses a conditional statement, and so communicates with the rest of the code via the program environment, not the memory stack.

Similar variations can be found in unit-level control, where, for example, the effects of control under breakdown also depend on the programming language (Teufel 1991). Most languages have an *exception handler,* a piece of code designed to respond to specific interrupts, but different languages handle crashes differently: in some, the exception handler returns computing to the point where the interruption occurred while in others, computing is terminated and does not return to the point of the interrupt. These two strategies have different effects and processing demands.

Control in Mental Code

If the structure of the code in programming languages affects the way computation is managed, do these effects likewise transfer to control in mentalese? Does the nature of the programming language of thought also carry with it particular cognitive demands on information management? More specifically, is mentalese a functional or procedural language? Is mentalese LISP or C? (Again, see Pylyshyn 1984, pp. 78–86, for suggestive observations.)

One way to begin to get an answer is to see how mental domains communicate with each other, a classic unit-level control problem. A first guess would be that intramodular control—say, the communication between phonology and syntax in language, or between low-level and high-level properties of objects in spatial knowledge—would look to be procedural. There would seem to be no need to report and record output via an independent memory stack across related domains because the information communicated is relatively close. On the other hand, intermodular control might look more functional. The coordination of, say, language with motor programs for speech would seem to place greater demand on the mind's resources and might require explicitly recorded outputs.

The analogy also goes through in considerations of interrupts. When processing crashes, how and where does mentalese return the mind to mental computing? There are generally two computational strategies for resetting the system: (1) at the point of the crash or (2) at some earlier point (often the initial state) to clear the system completely. Remarkably, there is some evidence for both of these options in crashes of human mentalese (Kaczmarek 1987).

While these points are admittedly speculative, they do raise empirical questions. Are there types of control in mentalese, just as there are for programming languages? Does intramodular control break down differently from intermodular control? Importantly, these questions would not arise without considering mentalese as the *programming* language of thought. Now we turn our attention to trying to answer some of them by looking at how the mental algorithms for language fail.

Control Disorders (vs. Specific Language Impairment)

Over the past fifteen years or so, a number of congenital disorders of global knowledge have been the focus of intense investigation: Williams syndrome, Turner syndrome, spina bifida with hydrocephalus, autism, and a variety of conditions either unlabeled or vaguely characterized. Interest in these conditions has grown despite their lack of common—or, sometimes, even known—etiology. . . .

What makes these conditions of interest to linguists and cognitive scientists is that they ostensibly reveal a dissociation between nonlinguistic world-knowledge and domain-specific linguistic knowledge, frequently leaving a deficit in the former. Linguistic development is often slowed, but mostly has a normal outcome—even superior in some cases. The conditions are thus crucial to claims about domain-specificity, encapsulation, and modular mental architecture since they show that normal linguistic development can proceed independently of world knowledge. . . .

Still, a close look at the cognitive and behavioral manifestations of these disorders does not reveal Nature cutting the mind-brain so neatly at its joints. There are a number of unexplained (or incorrectly explained) linguistic disruptions in these syndromes. My claim will be that these syndromes can affect the computational mechanisms involved in the *coordination of linguistic domains* rather than within-language representations and thus are a particular type of computational disruption. In effect, they preserve computation but have defective report. They are thus breakdowns of the *control component of mental code,* very much like the well-known disorders of consciousness, such as blindsight. As such, they contrast with specific language impairment (SLI), which preserves report, but report of defective representations, and hence is a disorder of the logic component of mentalese. Unfortunately, these two kinds of disruptions often look alike because they affect opposite sides of mental algorithms. Control disorders involve interface-management breakdown and so can look like a logic deficit because of failure in information coordination. SLI involves defective computation within a knowledge domain itself—a logic breakdown—but this can surface as an apparent failure in information management because the representations themselves are affected. . . .

References

Damasio, A. 1994. Descartes' Error. Avon Books, New York, NY.

Fischer, A., and Grodzinsky, F. 1993. The anatomy of programming languages. Prentice Hall, Englewood Cliffs, NJ.

Fodor, J. 1983. The Modularity of Mind. MIT Press, Cambridge, MA.

Ghezzi, C., and Jazayeri, M. 1987. Programming Language Concepts. Wiley, New York, NY.

Hayes-Roth, B. 1985. A blackboard architecture for control. Artificial Intelligence, **26**:251–321.

Kaczmarek, B. 1987. Regulatory functions of the frontal lobes: A neurolinguistic perspective. *In* The Frontal Lobes Revisited. *Edited by* E. Perecman. Erlbaum, Hillsdale, NJ, pp. 225–240.

Kowalski, R. 1979a. Algorithm = logic + control. CACM, **22**:425–436.

Kowalski, R. 1979b. Logic for Problem Solving. North Holland, Amsterdam.

McClamrock, R. 1995. Existential Cognition. University of Chicago Press, Chicago, IL.

Pylyshyn, Z. 1984. Computation and Cognition. MIT Press, Cambridge, MA.

Schneider, W., and Oliver, W. 1991. An instructable connectionist/control architecture: Using rule-based interactions to accomplish connectionist learning in a human time scale. *In* Architectures for Intelligence. *Edited by* K. van Lehn. Erlbaum, Hillsdale, NJ, pp. 113–145.

Sloman, A. 1993. The mind as a control system. *In* Philosophy and Cognitive Science. *Edited by* C. Hookway and D. Peterson. Cambridge University Press, Cambridge, UK, pp. 69–110.

Suchman, L. 1987. Plans and Situated Action. Cambridge University Press, Cambridge, UK.

Teufel, B. 1991. Organization of Programming Languages. Springer, New York, NY.

Zhang, J., and Norman, D. 1994. Representations in distributed cognitive tasks. Cognitive Science, **18**:87–122.

B. Chandrasekaran

NO

Reach Exceeds Grasp: Comments on Frawley's "Control and Cross-Domain Mental Computation: Evidence from Language Breakdown"

A particular version of the modular theory of cognition goes like this. Cognition consists of modules, each with its own domain of expertise. In this picture, a module does not interact directly with another module. A module reports the results of its activity to a central working memory (WM), with its own more or less complex structure. Tasks often require involvement of more than one module, thus setting up the problem of how the different modules work together. This problem is solved by having the modules not only report their results to the WM, but also by having the modules that need information from another module simply read off the WM the results reported by the latter module. This way, the task gets accomplished without the need for the modules to directly communicate with other modules. The WM plays the role of a central blackboard in this view.

Software systems in general, even those that are modular, as almost all large systems have to be, are not restricted to the architecture outlined above. Especially in parallel systems, there is in principle no reason for a single centralized WM, or a WM at all. In the modular view sketched above, the individual modules might themselves have submodules for all we know, but the activities of these submodules are not coordinated by the central WM.

In cognitive science we are so used to metaphors from computer science that we are not always careful to ask where the metaphor becomes a stretch, where some artifact of the computational model inadvertently takes on a reality as part of the cognitive science explanation. For example, cognitive models are often written in Lisp, and unless one is careful, one might slip into thinking of Cons operations and garbage collection as true cognitive phenomena. (They could be, but evidence has to be adduced.)

From Computational Intelligence, February 2002, pp. 43–46.

Frawley proposes "control" between domains—or modules—as an explanatory idea in understanding certain issues in language processing. Certainly control—or more generally, coordination between modules—has to be an important source of explanation of cognitive phenomena in the modular theory. The structure of WM, exactly what qualify as modules and how they write to and read from WM are details to be worked out in the theory, but, as I indicated above, the proposal that modules coordinate their activities by means of reading from and writing to the central WM is a promising framework for explanation.

I think the author's attempt to explain some language disorders in the framework of module coordination is valuable. Let me restate what I see as valuable using my own language, in particular completely avoiding the logic versus control language that he employs.

Performance in any task that involves many modules working together can suffer because of problems in one or more of the following: processing problems within one or more of the modules, systemic damage to WM, problems in a module reporting its results to the WM, or problems in a module reading from WM. Frawley analyzes various language-related disorders from this perspective, and gives his accounts about which of these disorders correspond to within-module problems and which to problems in reporting to the working memory. He rules out systemic damage to WM as explanation of these disorders. As far as I can understand, he does not make a distinction between problems with reporting to versus problems with reading from WM. I am not an expert in the disorders he discusses, but I found his analyses interesting and suggestive.

In my version of Frawley's account above, coordination—or control between modules—is indeed a central issue. The author's claim that not much has been said about control notwithstanding, control in precisely this sense has been studied in AI for quite some time. In fact, the SOAR architecture (Rosenbloom et al. 1993) is almost entirely about control and the role of WM in it. SOAR is not only an AI architecture, but it has also been seriously studied as a cognitive architecture. For example, Lewis (1996a, 1996b), proposes a structure for linguistic aspects of WM, and discusses how certain constraints on the size of WM components can explain certain phenomena in sentence processing.

Further, to the extent that intermodular coordination is not hardwired, the idea that the results need to be reported in an abstract way—or what is called an "explicit" representation—seems plausible, though not certain. We don't know enough about the structure of WM yet to rule out the possibility that it is so structured that not all elements in WM can in theory be read by any module. It is quite possible that what module M1 writes only module M2 can read, or only modules M2 and M3 can read, reducing the degree of, if not eliminating the need for, explicitness.

So far, so good. My unease with the article relates to my feeling that it stretches a specific computational model—the so-called symbolic or Turing computational model—to such a degree that I had the anxious sensation that he was reifying into cognitive phenomena things that might well be just artifacts of the Turing computational model. Beyond the coordination issue as I described it, I don't know what his analysis of control buys him. He categorizes control into so many subtypes, all based on the practice in computer programming, that my concern about computational artifacts seeping into a cognitive theory never went away.

In particular, I found the author's "logic versus control" explanatory framework quite unpersuasive. First of all, the terminology, its lineage from Kowalski notwithstanding, is rather loose. The author seems to equate "logic" with "declarative" knowledge about the domain, and control with "If X, then Y" type statements. But, the whole field of knowledge-based systems was based on the idea that expertise consisted of a large amount of knowledge of the form "If X, then Y," and declarative knowledge bases were constructed with knowledge of this type. Control was outside this knowledge base. Forward chaining systems used this knowledge differently from backward chaining systems for example. Later work on task-specific architectures (see, e.g., Chandrasekaran et al. 1992) came up with a larger vocabulary of control, but even these could be stated declaratively if needed. In Newell's Knowledge Level (KL) analysis (Newell 1981), many things that Frawley's analysis would call "control" would be posed as straight knowledge. We can indeed ask of an agent, "Does he know that he is supposed to do such and such a thing when such and such a thing happens?" and this is indeed knowledge. In certain implementations, i.e., Symbol Level realizations, this knowledge will appear as control and in others it will appear as declarative knowledge. The whole issue is much more complex and subtle than the author's analysis, I think.

In the KL account, what is knowledge and what is control is hard to distinguish from outside a program. For example, each of the modules that Frawley mentions in his explanations might have submodules, as I discussed earlier, and there may well be issues of control and coordination of these submodules. The hard and fast distinction that says, "this is a problem of logic and this is a problem of control" is in general hard to sustain, though in specific implementation proposals we can identify the issues associated with control at specific levels. Once the modular theory that I outlined earlier is taken as an operative proposal, then it is certainly possible to ask if a certain observed behavior is due to behavior within a module or in inter-modular coordination, for a given level of modular specification.

In my view, the entire discussion on control (Section 2) is too driven by a particular type of computing—the Turing symbolic one—and contrary to the author's assertion earlier that all of this is consistent with other approaches such as dynamical systems theory, it was not at all clear to me that distinctions such as "machine-level control" versus "high-level control," not to mention "statement-level control," transcend the specific computational framework. In any case, many of the distinctions struck me as arbitrary and subjective. For example, is "high-level" control a fixed and viewer-independent notion? What is high-level control from one perspective is low-level control from another perspective. His use of the term "crashes" as in "crash of a cognitive architecture" fueled my fears. Of course I make mistakes in my thinking, but crashes? What are they? I do crash when I have had too much to drink or too tired, but I am not aware of cognitive behavior that corresponds to crashing in the same sense in which we use for computer hardware or software. When we use terms like "You seem pretty lost in solving this problem, let us reboot," this is a metaphor. That this is more than metaphor needs to be argued for, not just assumed.

The author says, "These questions would not arise without considering mentalese as the programming language of thought." It is unclear if he is using the term "programming language" metaphorically, and if so, where the metaphorical associations start and end. Certainly, biological systems are replete with biochemical processes in which one subsystem dumps some chemical in some place which controls the behavior of another subsystem, or even cases where more than two subsystems coordinate their behaviors in this manner. Many of the issues of control are similar to the issues on intermodular control in software or cognition. We can ask, in the case of a malfunction, whether the problem was due to subsystem 1 failing to generate the chemical, deposit the chemical, subsystem 2 absorbing the chemical, or it failing to make use of the chemical, exactly similar to the author's analysis of language disorders. But there is no automatic need to think of the chemical processes as "programming language of the body," or that biological systems are just executing algorithms. I am not saying that it is not often useful to view coordination of subsystems—including biological subsystems—in information processing terms or in terms of control, but exactly where the programming metaphor pays off and where it just introduces artifacts leading the theorist into mistaken reifications is something that calls for a much more careful analysis than the author has given.

The useful insights about coordination that led to persuasive analyses of language disorders are lost in the much stronger claims and analyses about control. For one thing, as I have argued, the latter is not necessary for his claims about language disorders. A weaker view of control—as something that transcends explicitly algorithmic systems—is sufficient to bring out the issues that he needs for his analysis. Like the author, I have also been struck by the importance of understanding control in order to understand cognition. In (Chandrasekaran 1994), I gave a knowledge-level analysis of control that I intended to apply to all control phenomena in the world, from Alan Greenspan controlling the economy through programs controlling other programs to a thermostat controlling a heater–air conditioner. In that attempt, I felt a need to move away from a close commitment to Turing computation as such, and instead to take a Knowledge Level view. It is perhaps this past experience of mine in the analysis of control that dogged me throughout my reading of the current paper. For another, I was unpersuaded by the author's analysis. I was subjected to simultaneous feelings that the author was stating useful insights in his specific analyses of disorders, that the claims about control were both too narrow, being overcommitted to a specific model of computation, and too large, in their claims of generality, and that the author was riding roughshod over some complex and subtle issues. . . .

References

Chandrasekaran, B., Johnson, T., and Smith, J. W. 1992. Task structure analysis for knowledge modeling. Communications of the ACM, **33**(9)(September): 124–136.

Chandrasekaran, B. 1994. Intelligent control at the knowledge level. Presented at the AAAI Fall Symposium; available from http://www.cis.ohio-state.edu/~chandra/intelligent-control.pdf.

Lewis, R. L. 1996a. Architecture Matters: What soar has to say about modularity. *In* Mind Matters: Contributions to Cognitive and Computer Science in Honor of Allen Newell. *Edited by* D. Steier and T. Mitchell. Erlbaum, Hillsdale, NJ.

Lewis, R. L. 1996b. Interference in short-term memory: The magical number two (or three) in sentence processing. The Journal of Psycholinguistic *Research*, **25**:93–115.

Newell, A. 1981. The knowledge level. AI Magazine, **Summer**:1–19.

Rosenbloom, P. S., Laird, J. E., and Newell, A., editors. The Soar Papers: Research on Integrated Intelligence, MIT Press, Cambridge, MA 1993.

POSTSCRIPT

Can Computer Models Explain Language Disorders?

In the first selection, Frawley summarizes the facets of a computational model, building his case that language disorders can stem from missed connections and other breakdowns in information processing. Frawley describes human information processing as involving logically structured data points and control mechanisms that monitor the flow of information through the system. His contribution is in drawing attention to the control or monitoring mechanisms because much of cognitive science has been focused on the way we organize or structure data. He proposes that some language disorders reflect a problem in the control process, affecting the flow and processing of information, and not with the storage or retrieval of language itself.

In the second selection, Chandrasekaran makes an important point that sometimes we get so used to an analogy—in this case, brain-as-computer analogy—that we start to approach the metaphor as fact. This is especially easy to do when crossing between artificial intelligence language and biological neuroscience because the two fields often use the same terms. For example, when talking about neural networks or neuron networks, one could be speaking of either computer software or brain anatomy. The problem that Chandrasekaran points out is that if we are not mindful that we are making an analogy, we may begin to expect a perfect relationship between the two, rather than looking for places where the analogy breaks down. For example, just because we can permanently delete any file on our computer doesn't mean we can permanently delete any stored information in our brain at will. Frawley discusses what might happen when our brain functions "crash"—with this being a reference to occasions when our computers crash. Chandrasekaran questions the neurological equivalent of a computer crash as he cannot figure out what the equivalent might be.

Although this issue is among the more technical in this volume, the basic points are important ones. With all the sophisticated technology available, cognitive scientists cannot prove many of the abstract constructs we take for granted. When you imagine something, where, exactly, in your brain does that take place? We aren't sure. Where, exactly, is that memory stored for the first time you rode a bicycle? Again, we aren't sure. The abstract nature of cognition requires the development of hypothetical models, structures, and theories. The danger Chandrasekaran points out is that we can fall into the habit of making assumptions, such as the brain operates like a computer, to the point that we may miss or dismiss key information to the contrary because we expect computer-like behavior.

Historians, anthropologists, and philosophers of science perform a much-needed role in reminding us of our long history of discovery and our tendencies throughout the centuries. For example, during the industrial age, scientists began to look at human beings as machines. One didn't go to the doctor unless some body part didn't work appropriately, just as one doesn't fix a machine unless it is broken. Things are different today, and the health care focus is on prevention, rather than waiting for something to break down. Perhaps some day students will read, "and then during the technology age we thought the brain was like a computer. Today. . . ". We will just have to wait and see.

Suggested Readings

Croft, W. B., and Lafferty, J. *Language Modeling for Information Retrieval* (New York: Kluwer Academic Press, 2003).

Daniloff, R. (Editor), *Connectionist Approaches to Clinical Language Problems* (Mahwah, NJ: Lawrence Erlbaum, 2001).

Frawley, W., and Bright, W. (Editors), *International Encyclopedia of Linguistics* (New York: Oxford University Press, 2003).

Polk, T. A., and Seifert, C. (Editors), *Cognitive Modeling* (Cambridge, MA: MIT Press, 2002).

Radford, A., Spencer, A., Atkinson, M., Clahsen, H., and Britain, D. *Language and Linguistics: An Introduction* (New York: Cambridge University Press, 1999).

On the Internet . . .

The Self Discovery Workshop provides a history of intelligence testing, an explanation of how IQ tests are scored, and a test you can take on-line.

http://www.iqtest.com/

The MENSA organization for those "whose IQ is in the top 2% of the population" has an informative Web site with a MENSA workout you can try on-line.

http://www.mensa.org/index.html

Mayer, Salovey, and Caruso, the original creators of Emotional Intelligence, have an informative Web site that also provides information on their questionnaire.

http://www.emotionaliq.com/

In response to the controversial book *The Bell Curve,* the American Psychological Association created a task force to write an official response. You can read more about that at this Web site.

http://www.apa.org/releases/intell.html

PART 5

Intelligence

Almost anyone in Western society is familiar with the concept of intelligence and IQ (intelligence quotient) scores, while comparatively few know just how controversial those concepts are. Although intelligence has been widely studied for many years, there is little consensus in the field. In this section, you will learn about the develop of the concept of intelligence and the difficulties of defining it, the controversies regarding how to measure it, and you will see how the nature-versus-nurture debate is still active when scholars discuss intelligence.

ISSUE 13

Is Emotional Intelligence Really a Form of Intelligence?

YES: John D. Mayer, Peter Salovey, and David Caruso, from "Models of Emotional Intelligence," *Handbook of Intelligence* (2000)

NO: Richard D. Roberts, Moshe Zeidner, and Gerald Matthews, from "Does Emotional Intelligence Meet Traditional Standards for an Intelligence? Some New Data and Conclusions," *Emotion* (2001)

ISSUE SUMMARY

YES: Psychologists John Mayer, Peter Salovey, and David Caruso present their case that emotional intelligence is as valid as any type of intelligence based on the performance of the Multifactor Emotional Intelligence Scale (MEIS).

NO: Researchers and lecturers Richard Roberts, Moshe Zeidner, and Gerald Matthews find the Multifactor Emotional Intelligence Scale to be disappointing and the whole concept of emotional intelligence to be questionable.

For many years, cognitive scientists have explored the influence of emotions on memory and information processing. It has been well established that intense emotions can block the retrieval of specific memories. Perhaps the best example of this is test anxiety. Intense anger or intense happiness and excitement right before a test can also block information retrieval. The notion of considering emotion as an *intelligence,* a term usually reserved for the cognitive domain, is a relatively recent endeavor.

Emotional intelligence has been described as the understanding and accurate reasoning about emotions, the ability to utilize emotions to facilitate thought and action, the regulation of emotional intensity in one's self and others, and the verbal and nonverbal understanding of the expression of emotion in one's self and in others. Emotional intelligence includes skills such as the ability to stay open to feelings, the ability to label emotions, understanding that emotions prioritize thinking in productive ways, and identifying emotions in other people and in artistic endeavors.

In the first selection, Mayer, Salovey, and Caruso state that emotions comprise a fundamental class of mental operations, along with motivation, cognition, and consciousness. They prefer a mental ability model of emotional intelligence, which considers only emotions and thought, rather than a mixed model, which includes emotions, motivation, personality, consciousness, and other psychological domains. The mental ability model holds the construct of emotional intelligence to the same standards as any other type of intelligence. Three empirical criteria that must be met, according to the mental ability model, are (1) questionnaire items must have a right or wrong answer, (2) scores must correlate with other measures of intelligence, and (3) ability levels must improve with age.

To prove that emotional intelligence can meet these challenges, Mayer, et al., have developed the MEIS, which consists of 12 ability scales measuring the perceiving, facilitating, understanding, and managing of emotion. They offer several different scoring methods for the MEIS, a point that the authors of the second selection find troublesome. Two scoring methods are important for the discussion here. To illustrate, suppose that a college professor gave the MEIS to his class. With the consensus scoring, a student would get emotional intelligence points if she chooses the same response for an item as the majority the class, thus right and wrong answers are determined by the group. If the professor chooses expert scoring, he would compare each student's responses to the published expert answers in the MEIS manual. Mayer, et al., have already surveyed various social scientists and philosophers for their expert opinions, which have become the key for the expert scoring system.

The controversy in this issue revolves around the operational definition of emotional intelligence. An operational definition emphasizes the observable and measurable qualities of a concept or construct. Some of the tasks include determining the emotion found in particular faces, music, and stories, synesthesia judgments (such as "how hot is anger"), distinguishing between two emotions (such as optimism and joy), and, after reading a scenario, choosing the best response. Any psychological measurement should be tested for reliability and validity. The concept of reliability refers to the consistency of the measure. One way to measure reliability is the test-retest method, in which scores are compared for the same individual on the same test when taken at two different times. If the test is reliable, then the individual's scores should be about the same. Validity is important because it demonstrates that the test is measuring what it is intended to measure. If the MEIS is truly measuring emotional intelligence, then the scores should be highly correlated.

In the first selection, Mayer, et al., describe the MEIS and their success in demonstrating reliability and validity. In the second selection, Roberts, Zeidner, and Matthews compared their findings with the MEIS to a measure of cognitive abilities, the Armed Services Vocational Aptitude Battery (ASVAB), and a measure of personality, the Trait Self-Description Inventory (TSDI), and determined that the MEIS falls far short of acceptable performance.

John D. Mayer, Peter Salovey, and David Caruso

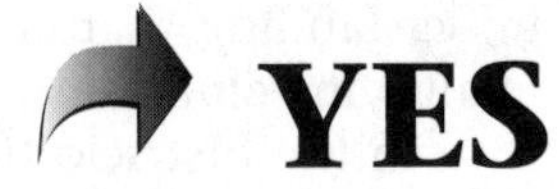

Models of Emotional Intelligence

Competing Models of Emotional Intelligence

Studies of emotional intelligence initially appeared in academic articles beginning in the early 1990s. By middecade, the concept had attracted considerable popular attention, and powerful claims were made concerning its importance for predicting success. Emotional intelligence is the set of abilities that accounts for how people's emotional reports vary in their accuracy and how the more accurate understanding of emotion leads to better problem solving in an individual's emotional life. More formally, we define emotional intelligence as the ability to perceive and express emotion, assimilate emotion in thought, understand and reason with emotion, and regulate emotion in the self and others (Mayer & Salovey, 1997). As of now, the academic concept has been developed over several theoretical articles (e.g., Mayer & Salovey, 1997; Salovey & Mayer, 1990) and is based on a growing body of relevant research (e.g., Averill & Nunley, 1992; Buck, 1984; Lane, Sechrest, Reidel et al., 1996; Mayer, DiPaolo, & Salovey, 1990; Mayer & Geher, 1996; Mayer & Stevens, 1994; Rosenthal, Hall, DiMatteo, Rogers, & Archer, 1979; Salovey, Mayer, Goldman, Turvey, & Palfai, 1995; see also, Salovey & Sluyter, 1997). . . .

Theoretical Considerations Regarding Emotional Intelligence

Conceptions of Emotion

Emotions are recognized as one of three or four fundamental classes of mental operations. These classes include motivation, emotion, cognition, and (less frequently) consciousness (Bain, 1855/1977; Izard, 1993; MacLean, 1973; Mayer, 1995a, 1995b; Plutchik, 1984; Tomkins, 1962; see Hilgard, 1980; and Mayer, Chabot, & Carlsmith, 1997, for reviews). Among the triad of motivation, emotion, and cognition, basic motivations arise in response to internal bodily states and include drives such as hunger, thirst, need for social contact, and sexual desires. Motivations are responsible for directing the organism to carry out simple acts to satisfy survival and reproductive needs. . . .

Emotions form the second class of this triad. Emotions appear to have evolved across mammalian species so as to signal and respond to changes in relationships between the individual and the environment (including one's imagined place within it). . . . Emotions are therefore more flexible than motivations, though not quite so flexible as cognition.

Cognition, the third member of the triad, allows the organism to learn from the environment and to solve problems in novel situations. This is often in service to satisfying motives or keeping emotions positive. Cognition includes learning, memory, and problem solving. It is ongoing and involves flexible, intentional information processing based on learning and memory (see Mayer et al., 1997, for a review of these concepts). . . .

The term *emotional intelligence,* then, implies something having to do with the intersection of emotion and cognition. From our perspective, evaluating theories of, and related to, emotional intelligence requires an assessment of the degree to which the theory pertains to this intersection.

Conceptions of Intelligence

. . . Intelligence, conceptualized as abstract thinking, has often been demonstrated to predict one or another type of success, particularly academic success. But although it is a potent predictor, it is far from a perfect one, leaving the vast amount of variance unexplained. As Wechsler (1940, p. 444) put it, "individuals with identical IQs may differ very markedly in regard to their effective ability to cope with the environment." One way to regard this limitation is to view human life as naturally complex and subject both to chance events and complicated interactions. A second approach is to search for better ways to assess intelligence (e.g., Sternberg, 1997). A third approach is to attribute the difference to a combination of factors, such as non-intellective personality traits. These approaches are all complementary and have all been used with different degrees of effectiveness in enhancing psychological predictions of positive outcomes.

A fourth alternative to dealing with IQ's limited predictive ability is to redefine intelligence itself as a combination of mental ability and non-intellective personality traits. Thus, Wechsler (1943, p. 103) wondered, "whether non-intellective, that is, affective and conative [motivational] abilities are admissible as factors in general intelligence." In his next sentence, he concluded they were. A few sentences thereafter, however, he qualifies the notion: they predict intelligent *behavior* (as opposed to being a part of intelligence). Wechsler remained straddling the fence, as it were. On the one hand, he at times defined intelligence as involving ". . . the aggregate or global capacity of the individual to act purposefully, to think rationally and to *deal effectively with his environment.*" (italics added; Wechsler, 1958, p. 7). On the other hand, the intelligence tests that carried his name focused on measuring mental ability. . . .

Some models of emotional intelligence . . . do define emotional intelligence as a mixture of abilities and other personality dispositions and traits. The motivation for this appears to be the desire to label as a single entity what appear to be, in fact, a diverse group of things that predict success. Although we realize we cannot prevent such usage, it presents considerable difficulty for us. . . . We will distinguish, however, between *ability models* of emotional intelligence, which focus on the interplay of emotion and intelligence as traditionally defined, and *mixed models,* which describe a compound conception of intelligence that includes mental abilities, and other dispositions and traits.

Competing Models Labeled "Emotional Intelligence"

Ability Models of Emotional Intelligence

. . . The domain of emotional intelligence describes several discrete emotional abilities. As we now view it, these emotional abilities can be divided into four classes or branches, as shown in Table 1, Column 1. (The specific skills listed in Column 1 are meant to be representative; there are other skills that could be included on each branch as well as the ones shown.) The most basic skills involve the perception and appraisal of emotion. For example, early on, the infant learns about facial expressions of emotion. The infant watches its cries of distress, or joy, mirrored in the parent's face, as the parent empathically reflects those feelings. As the child grows, he or she discriminates more finely among genuine versus merely polite smiles and other gradations of expression. . . .

The second set of skills involves assimilating basic emotional experiences into mental life, including weighing emotions against one another and against other sensations and thoughts and allowing emotions to direct attention. For example, we may hold an emotional state in consciousness so as to compare it with a similar sensation in sound, color, or taste.

The third level involves understanding and reasoning about emotions. The experience of specific emotions—happiness, anger, fear, and the like—is rule-governed. Anger generally rises when justice is denied; fear often changes to relief; dejection may separate us from others. Sadness and anger move according to their own characteristic rules, just as the knight and bishop on a chessboard move in different ways. . . . Emotional intelligence involves the ability to recognize the emotions, to know how they unfold, and to reason about them accordingly.

The fourth, highest level, of emotional intelligence involves the management and regulation of emotion in oneself and others such as knowing how to calm down after feeling angry or being able to alleviate the anxiety of another person. Tasks defining these four levels are described in greater detail in the section concerning scale development below.

The mental ability model of emotional intelligence makes predictions about the internal structure of the intelligence and also its implications for a person's life. The theory predicts that emotional intelligence is, in fact, an intelligence like other intelligences in that it will meet three

Table 1

Three Competing Models, all Labeled "Emotional Intelligence"

Mayer & Salovey (1997)	Bar-On (1997)	Goleman (1995)
Overall Definition	Overall Definition	Overall Definition(s)
"Emotional intelligence is the set of abilities that account for how people's emotional perception and understanding vary in their accuracy. More formally, we define emotional intelligence as the ability to perceive and express emotion, assimilate emotion in thought, understand and reason with emotion, and regulate emotion in the self and others" (after Mayer & Salovey, 1997).	"Emotional intelligence is . . . an array of noncognitive capabilities, competencies, and skills that influence one's ability to succeed in coping with environmental demands and pressures." (Bar-On, 1997, p. 14).	"The abilities called here *emotional intelligence,* which include self-control, zeal and persistence, and the ability to motivate oneself." (Goleman, 1995, p. xii). [. . . and . . .] "There is an old-fashioned word for the body of skills that emotional intelligence represents: *character*" (Goleman, 1995, p. 28).
Major Areas of Skills and Specific Examples	Major Areas of Skills and Specific Skills	Major Areas of Skills and Specific Examples
Perception and Expression of Emotion * Identifying and expressing emotions in one's physical states, feelings, and thoughts. * Identifying and expressing emotions in other people, artwork, language, etc. *Assimilating Emotion in Thought* * Emotions prioritize thinking in productive ways. * Emotions generated as aids to judgment and memory. *Understanding and Analyzing Emotion* * Ability to label emotions, including complex emotions and simultaneous feelings. * Ability to understand relationships associated with shifts of emotion. *Reflective Regulation of Emotion* * Ability to stay open to feelings. * Ability to monitor and regulate emotions reflectively to promote emotional and intellectual growth (after Mayer & Salovey, 1997, p. 11).	*Intrapersonal Skills:* * Emotional self-awareness, * Assertiveness, * Self-Regard, * Self-Actualization, * Independence. *Interpersonal Skills:* * Interpersonal relationships, * Social responsibility, * Empathy. *Adaptability Scales:* * Problem solving, * Reality testing, * Flexibility. *Stress-Management Scales:* * Stress tolerance, * Impulse control. *General Mood:* * Happiness, * Optimism.	*Knowing One's Emotions* * Recognizing a feeling *as it happens.* * Monitoring feelings from moment to moment. *Management Emotions* * Handling feelings so they are appropriate. * Ability to soothe oneself. * Ability to shake off rampant anxiety, gloom, or irritability. *Motivating Oneself* * Marshalling emotions in the service of a goal. * Delaying gratification and stifling impulsiveness. * Being able to get into the "flow" state. *Recognizing Emotions in Others* * Empathic awareness. * Attunement to what others need or want. *Handling Relationships* * Skill in managing emotions in others. * Interacting smoothly with others
Model Type	Model Type	Model Type
Ability	*Mixed*	*Mixed*

empirical criteria. First, mental problems have right or wrong answers, as assessed by the convergence of alternative scoring methods. Second, the measured skills correlate with other measures of mental ability (because mental abilities tend to intercorrelate) as well as with self-reported empathy (for more complex reasons; see Mayer, DiPaolo, & Salovey, 1990). Third, the absolute ability level rises with age.

The model further predicts that emotionally intelligent individuals are more likely to (a) have grown up in biosocially adaptive households (i.e., have had emotionally sensitive parenting), (b) be nondefensive, (c) be able to reframe emotions effectively (i.e., be realistically optimistic and appreciative), (d) choose good emotional role models, (e) be able to communicate and discuss feelings, and (f) develop expert knowledge in a particular emotional area such as aesthetics, moral or ethical feeling, social problem solving, leadership, or spiritual feeling (Mayer & Salovey, 1995).

Mixed Models of Emotional Intelligence

Mixed models of emotional intelligence are substantially different than the mental ability models. In one sense, both kinds of models were proposed in the first academic articles on emotional intelligence (e.g., Mayer, DiPaolo, & Salovey, 1990; Salovey & Mayer, 1990). Although these articles set out a mental ability conception of emotional intelligence, they also freely described personality characteristics that might accompany such intelligence. . . .

Almost immediately after these initial articles on emotional intelligence appeared, we recognized that our own theoretical work would be more useful if we constrained emotional intelligence to a mental ability concept and separated it from the very important traits of warmth outgoingness, and similarly desirable virtues. By keeping them separate, it would be possible to analyze the degree to which they independently contributed to a person's behavior and general life competence. Although traits such as warmth and persistence are important, we believe they are better addressed directly and as distinct from emotional intelligence (Mayer & Salovey, 1993, 1997).

In contrast to honing this core conception of emotional intelligence, others expanded the meaning of emotional intelligence by explicitly mixing in nonability traits. For example, Bar-On's (1997) model of emotional intelligence was intended to answer the question, "Why are some individuals more able to succeed in life than others?" Bar-On reviewed the psychological literature for personality characteristics that appeared related to life success and identified five broad areas of functioning relevant to success. These are listed in Column 2 of Table 1, and include (a) intrapersonal skills, (b) interpersonal skills, (c) adaptability, (d) stress management, and (e) general mood. . . .

A third view of emotional intelligence was popularized by Goleman (1995). Goleman created a model that also was mixed and was characterized by the five broad areas depicted in Column 3 of Table 1, including (a) knowing one's emotions, (b) managing emotions, (c) motivating oneself,

(d) recognizing emotions in others, and (e) handling relationships. His list of specific attributes under motivation, for example, include, marshalling emotions, delaying gratification and stifling impulsiveness, and entering flow states (Goleman, 1995, p. 43). Goleman recognized that he was moving from emotional intelligence to something far broader. He states that "'ego resilience,' . . . is quite similar to [this model of] emotional intelligence" in that it includes social (and emotional) competencies (Goleman, 1995, p. 44). He goes so far as to note that, "There is an old-fashioned word for the body of skills that emotional intelligence represents: *character*." (Goleman, 1995, p. 285). . . .

Summary

There are both mental ability models and mixed models of emotional intelligence. The mental ability model focuses on emotions themselves and their interactions with thought (Mayer & Salovey, 1997; Salovey & Mayer, 1990). The mixed models treat mental abilities and a variety of other characteristics such as motivation, states of consciousness (e.g., "flow") and social activity as a single entity (Bar-On, 1997; Goleman, 1995).

The Measurement of Emotional Intelligence

Early Research Explicitly Directed Toward Emotional Intelligence

In our initial work on measuring aspects of emotional intelligence, we suggested that emotional perception might be similar across a variety of stimuli that had been studied before in isolation (faces, abstract designs, and colors) and that prior tests may have masked a general emotion perception factor by using overly simplistic response scales (Mayer, DiPaolo, & Salovey, 1990). For example, on the PONS, participants viewed a brief videotape and then were asked only one or two questions such as how pleasant or unpleasant the video character was. We reasoned that scales would be more reliable if the response alternatives were increased in number and specificity. For example, given a face, how angry is it? . . . sad? . . . happy? and so on. One hundred thirty-nine participants judged the specific emotional content of 18 stimuli including faces, abstract designs, and colors. Consensual accuracy in identifying emotion was reliable, and there was a single factor of emotional perception common to all those stimuli.

The early 1990s also saw work related to the higher level skills of emotional intelligence: understanding emotions and managing them. For example, Mayer & Geher (1996) studied emotional perception in story passages. Preliminary to the main study, eight target individuals each described their thoughts in a brief passage. For example, one target wrote:

> My best friend's father died this weekend. He had diabetes for a long time, and as he got older his health grew worse and worse. I went to his funeral on Monday. Many of my friends from high school were also

> there because we all wanted to be there for our friend and because we all knew and liked her father. It made me realize how lucky I am to have younger, healthy parents when I saw my friend standing there crying. Just watching her huge family come pouring into the synagogue also made me sad. (Mayer & Geher, 1996, p. 98).

Participants in the main study were asked to identify the targets' emotions or emotion-related thoughts in the passage by making a series of forced choices between two alternatives (e.g., be by myself—kick something; fearful—apart from others.) Skill at this task, measured by agreement with the group consensus, correlated significantly with self-reported SAT scores (a proxy measure of verbal intelligence), and with self-reports of trait empathy. Target agreement showed similar but weaker results. A closely related task was developed by Lane et al. (1996). In that study, participants read a sentence (e.g., "I want to hit someone") and were asked to match it to one of seven emotion words (e.g., happiness, sadness, fear, anger, surprise, disgust, and neutral). In other parts of the task, they matched sentences to emotional faces, or emotional faces to emotion words, and so forth. Regrettably, no measures of intelligence or empathy were included in the latter study. A study using similar tasks to Lane et al.s', however, did find a correlation between task performance and intelligence among a group of mentally retarded adults (Simon, Rosen, & Ponpipom,1996).

In another test of emotional understanding, Averill & Nunley (1992) presented participants with three emotions and asked them to write a brief description of a situation in which they would feel the three emotions together. For example, in response to the emotional triad "joy/relief/distress"; one participant wrote about the joy of being on a mountaintop, the distress at imagining falling off, and the relief of not actually falling. Scoring was according to an expert criterion. Success at this task appears moderately correlated with general intelligence as well as with measures of creativity. . . .

More Recent Measurement Work With Emotional Intelligence

The Multifactor Emotional Intelligence Scale (MEIS) Study

Our current research program has been devoted primarily to developing a full-fledged test of emotional intelligence as a set of mental abilities (Mayer, Caruso, & Salovey, in press). We have designed a Multifactor Emotional Intelligence Scale (MEIS) that consists of 12 ability measures of emotional intelligence divided into 4 classes or "branches" of abilities, including (a) perceiving, (b) facilitating, (c) understanding, and (d) managing emotion (Mayer & Salovey, 1997; Mayer, Caruso, & Salovey, 2000; Mayer, Salovey, & Caruso, 1997). Branch 1 tasks measure emotional perception in Faces, Music, Designs, and Stories. The first three of these were similar to the emotional perception tasks described above (Mayer, DiPaolo, & Salovey, 1990), and the fourth Stories task, which is equally an understanding task was also discussed above (Mayer & Geher, 1996). The second, Facilitation branch, contains two tests that measure Synesthesia judgments (e.g., "How hot is anger?") and Feeling Biases. Briefly, these tasks were expected to measure emotion's facilitation of cognition but resulted in a weaker factor than the others and may be dropped for some purposes. Branch 3's four tasks examine the understanding of emotion. For example, one question asks, "Optimism most closely combines which two emotions?" and a participant has to choose "pleasure and anticipation" over less specific alternatives such as "pleasure and joy."

Branch 4's two tests measure Emotion Management in (a) the Self and (b) Others. These tasks ask participants to read a scenario such as the following and then rate five reactions to it according to how good they were:

> One of your colleagues at work looks upset and asks if you will eat lunch with him. At the cafeteria, he motions for you to sit away from the other diners. After a few minutes of slow conversation he says that he wants to talk to you about what's on his mind. He tells you that he lied on his resume about having a college degree. Without the degree, he wouldn't have gotten the job.

(Please judge the value of the following reaction:)

> Ask him how he feels about it so you can understand what's going on. Offer to help him, but don't push yourself on him if he really doesn't want any of your help.

Five hundred and three adults completed all the tasks as well as several criterion scales. An additional 229 adolescents also completed a slightly abbreviated version of the scales.

Findings with the MEIS

Work with the MEIS yielded a number of important findings (Mayer, Caruso, & Salovey, 2000). First, consensus, expert, and target scoring methods for the same tasks converged on correct answers to a degree anticipated by theory. This adds confidence to any of the scoring approaches. Of these, consensus scoring appeared to be the best all-around method. . . . Davies et al. (1998) worried about early mental ability tasks in the area because they exhibited only modest reliabilities. The MEIS achieved a full-scale alpha reliability of $r = .96$.

The second major finding concerned the structure of emotional intelligence as represented by these 12 tasks. First, the tasks were generally positively intercorrelated with one another. A study of the test's factorial structure recommended two equally viable factorial models. The first was a three-factor solution that separated out factors of (a) emotional perception, (b) emotional understanding, and (c) emotional management. (An alternative, four factor model, including a weaker (d) Facilitation factor was also possible). The second factorial model involved a hierarchical factor analysis based on those three (or four) factors (equally well represented by the first unrotated factor of the whole test) that describes a general factor of emotional intelligence, g_{ei}.

The same study indicated that general emotional intelligence, g_{ei}, correlated both with measures of verbal intelligence (r = .36) and with measures of self-reported empathy (r = .33). Few other criterion scales were administered, but the same general factor also correlated with parental warmth (r = .23). The fourth major finding was that ability at emotional intelligence was age dependent, increasing between young adolescence and early adulthood.

Findings from the MEIS indicate that emotional intelligence may qualify as a conventional intelligence operationalized as a mental ability (Mayer & Salovey, 1993; Neisser, Boodoo, Bouchard, Boykin, Brody, Ceci, Halpern, Loehlin, Perloff, Sternberg, & Urbina, 1996; Scarr, 1989). Emotional intelligence, like other well-operationalized intelligences, show convergence among criteria for scoring correct answers. Emotional intelligence also "looks like" other intelligences, in that its tasks are intercorrelated. Findings also indicate that emotional intelligence is related to more traditional intelligence (i.e., analytical intelligence), but sufficiently distinct from it to represent new and unique variance. And finally, emotional intelligence, like other standard intelligences, develops with age (Binet & Simon, 1905/1916, pp. 320–321; Brown, 1997; Fancher, 1985, p. 71). Certain of these findings have now been replicated in other laboratories (Ciarrochi, Chan, & Caputi, 2000). . . .

One of the most original and interesting approaches to measuring emotional perception (Branch 1) is the "BB" (based on body) scale of Bernet's (1996) Style in the Perception of Affect Scale (SIPOAS). The BB scale is intended to assess real connectedness to the (sometimes) slight bodily changes that accompany feelings and emotions. It is contrasted to two other ways of thinking about emotion. The "Emphasis on Evaluation" (EE) scale reflects effortful attempts to understand one's own emotions in terms of outsiders, ideals, or expectations and is related to neuroticism. The "Looking to Logic" (LL) scale involves favoring intellect and avoiding feeling. Bernet (1996) has found that (self-reported) gains in psychotherapy are highest among high BB scorers who experience a variety of treatment modalities, including talking therapies, but also physically-oriented therapies and spiritual approaches to difficulties. The exact relation of the SIPOAS scores to emotional intelligence is not yet clear, but it appears to be an interesting measure worthy of further study.

Many scales also measure the management of emotion (Branch 4). Mayer & Gaschke (1988) described a reflective experience of mood they termed meta-experience. This reflective experience is measured with such statements as, "I know exactly how I am feeling," or "I am confused about how I feel." Since then, a large number of both state and trait measures of emotional meta-experience have been developed and studied. Findings with such scales indicate, for example, that people higher in mood attention and clarity are better able to reduce their rumination over negative material (Salovey et al., 1995). Further details on the measurement properties and results obtained with such scales may be found in several recent articles and chapters (e.g., Mayer & Stevens, 1994; Salovey et al., 1995; Salovey, Bedell,

Detweiler, & Mayer, 1999). For that reason we will not repeat those reviews here. Instead, we will focus on a full self-report operationalization of the emotional intelligence model.

Tett and his colleagues (Tett, Wang, Fisher, Martinez, Grieble, & Linkovich, 1997; Tett, Wang, Thomas, Griebler, & Martinez, 1997) developed 10 scales based on the original model of emotional intelligence (Salovey & Mayer, 1990). Emotional appraisal was divided into four scales: (a) Emotional Perception of the Self—Verbal, (b) Emotional Perception in the Self—Nonverbal, (c) Emotion in Others—Nonverbal, and (d) Empathy. The regulation of emotion was divided into two: (e) Regulation of Emotion in the Self, and (f) Regulation of Emotion in Others. Lastly, the utilization of emotion was divided into four additional scales: (g) Flexible Thinking, (h) Creative Thinking, (i) Mood Redirected Attention, and (j) Motivating Emotions. Each of the scales was internally consistent, and coefficient alphas ranged between $\alpha = .60$ and .86. A factor analysis of these scales yielded four factors: (a) recognition and regulation of emotion in others, (b) the recognition of emotion in the self and the expression of emotion, (c) emotional stability, and (d) high self-reported intuition coupled with poor delay of gratification. This self-report measure plainly yielded results somewhat different from those obtained with the MEIS. The Tett et al. measures have not yet been correlated with other criteria. . . .

Conclusion

There now are two general models of emotional intelligence: a mental ability model and a mixed model that includes various personality dispositions. The mental ability model is probably the only one that is aptly called emotional intelligence. The other is somewhat more general than the meanings of "emotional" and "intelligence" would suggest. The use of the term "intelligence" to depict all varieties of human endeavor aside from mental ability is not new, however, and has merely reasserted itself in the present context.

Current research suggests that mental ability models of emotional intelligence can be described as a standard intelligence and empirically meet the criteria for a standard intelligence. This means that certain people previously called emotional may be carrying out sophisticated information processing. Emotional intelligence, carefully considered, also illuminates a boundary between cognitive intelligence and nonintellective dispositions. For example, emotional intelligence makes clear that socializing involves intellective and nonintellective aspects; only the intellective, we argue, should be referred to as intelligent.

The concept of emotional intelligence as ability is distinct from mixed models of emotional intelligence. Both may be useful in the study of human effectiveness and success in life. We believe it is useful to take a reasoned, thoughtful approach to studying human effectiveness under various conditions, and indeed much research does so. Calling any human variable related to personal success, "emotional intelligence," however, is likely to impede rather than promote progress in either area. More serious undertakings than can be orchestrated from the popular press are required.

The first mental ability measures of emotional intelligence now exist, and they appear reliable, content valid, and structurally valid. To some extent, the fate of emotional intelligence measures is connected to advances in personality psychology wherein better criteria of life activities (including success) are specified. . . .

References

Averill, J. R., & Nunley, E. P. (1992). *Voyages of the heart: Living an emotionally creative life.* New York: Free Press.

Bain, A. (1855/1977). *The senses and the intellect.* London: John W. Parker & Son. Reprinted in D. N. Robinson (Ed.), *Significant contributions to the history of psychology: 1750–1920. Series A: Orientations; Vol. 4.* Washington, DC: University Publications of America.

Bar-On, R. (1997). *The Emotional Quotient Inventory (EQ-i): Technical Manual.* Toronto: Multi-Health Systems.

Bernet, M. (1996). *Emotional intelligence: Components and correlates.* In Symposium #4057, Emotional health and emotional intelligence. Presentation at the 104th Annual Convention of the American Psychological Association. Toronto, Canada, August 9–13th.

Binet, A., & Simon, T. (1916). Application of the new methods to the diagnosis of the intellectual level among normal and subnormal children in institutions and in primary schools. In A. Binet, & T. Simon (E. S. Kite, Trans.) *The development of intelligence in children.* Baltimore: Wilkins & Wilkins. [Authorized facsimile, 1970, University Microfilms, Ann Arbor, MI] [Translation of the original 1905 work, Applications des méthodes nouvelles au diognostic du niveau intellectuel chez des enfants normaux et anormaux d'hospice et d'école primaire. *L' Année Psychologique, 11,* 245– 336].

Brown, B. (1997, June). Raw scores of cognitive ability are real psychological variables: IQ is a hyperspace variable. In V. C. Shipman (Chair), *IQ or cognitive ability?* Symposium presented to the 95th annual convention of the American Psychological Society, Washington, DC.

Buck, R. (1984). *The communication of emotion.* New York: The Guilford Press.

Ciarrochi, J. V., Chan, A. Y. C., & Caputi, P. (2000). A critical evaluation of the emotional intelligence construct. *Personality and Individual Differences, 28,* 539–561.

Davies, M., Stankov, L., & Roberts, R. D. (1998). Emotional intelligence: In search of an elusive construct. *Journal of Personality and Social Psychology, 75,* 989–1015.

Fancher, R. E. (1985). *The intelligence men: Makers of the IQ controversy,* New York: W. W. Norton.

Goleman, D. (1995). *Emotional intelligence.* New York: Bantam Books.

Hilgard, E. R. (1980). The trilogy of mind: Cognition, affection, and conation. *Journal of the History of the Behavioral Sciences, 16,* 107–117.

Izard, C. E. (1993). Four systems for emotion activation: Cognitive and noncognitive processes. *Psychological Review, 100,* 68–69.

Lane, R. D., Sechrest, L., Reidel, R., Weldon, V., Weldon, V., Kaszniak, A., & Schwartz, G. E. (1996). Impaired verbal and nonverbal emotion recognition in alexithymia. *Psychosomatic Medicine, 58,* 203–210.

MacLean, P. D. (1973). *A triune concept of the brain and behavior.* Toronto: University of Toronto Press.

Mayer, J. D. (1995a). The System-Topics Framework and the structural arrangement of systems within and around personality. *Journal* of *Personality, 63,* 459–493.

Mayer, J. D. (1995b). A framework for the classification of personality components. *Journal of Personality, 63,* 819–877.

Mayer, J. D., Caruso, D., & Salovey, P. (2000). Emotional intelligence meets traditional standards for an intelligence. *Intelligence, 27,* 267–298.

Mayer, J. D., Chabot, H. F., & Carlsmith, K. M. (1997). Conation, affect, and cognition in personality. In G. Matthews (Ed.), *Cognitive science perspectives on personality and emotion* (pp. 31–63). New York: Elsevier.

Mayer, J. D., DiPaolo, M. T., & Salovey, P. (1990). Perceiving affective content in ambiguous visual stimuli: A component of emotional intelligence. *Journal of Personality Assessment, 54,* 772–781.

Mayer, J. D., & Gaschke, Y. N. (1988). The experience and meta-experience of mood. *Journal of Personality and Social Psychology, 55,* 102–111.

Mayer, J. D., & Geher, G. (1996). Emotional intelligence and the identification of emotion. *Intelligence, 22,* 89–113.

Mayer, J. D., & Salovey, P. (1993). The intelligence of emotional intelligence. *Intelligence, 17,* 433–442.

Mayer, J. D., & Salovey, P. (1995). Emotional intelligence and the construction and regulation of feelings. *Applied and Preventive Psychology, 4,* 197–208.

Mayer, J. D., & Salovey, P. (1997). What is emotional intelligence? In P. Salovey & D. Sluyter (Eds.), *Emotional development and emotional intelligence: Implications for educators* (pp. 3–31). New York: Basic Books.

Mayer, J. D., Salovey, P., & Caruso, D. (1997). *Emotional IQ test (CD ROM).* Needham, MA: Virtual Knowledge.

Mayer, J. D., & Stevens, A. (1994). An emerging understanding of the reflective (meta-) experience of mood. *Journal of Research in Personality, 28,* 351–373.

Neisser, U., Boodoo, G., Bouchard, T. J., Boykin, A. W., Brody, N., Ceci, S. J., Halpern, D. F., Loehlin, J. C., Perloff, R., Sternberg, R. J., & Urbina, S. (1996). Intelligence: Knowns and unknowns. *American Psychologist, 51,* 77–101.

Plutchik, R. (1984). Emotions: A general psychoevolutionary theory. In K. R. Scherer & P. Ekman (Eds.), *Approaches to emotion.* Hillsdale, NJ: Erlbaum.

Rosenthal, R., Hall, J. A., DiMatteo, M. R., Rogers, P. L., & Archer, D. (1979). *Sensitivity to nonverbal communication: The PONS Test.* Baltimore, MD: Johns Hopkins University Press.

Salovey, P., Bedell, B., Detweiler, J., & Mayer, J. D. (1999). Coping intelligently: Emotional intelligence and the coping process. In C. R. Snyder (Ed.), *Coping: the psychology of what works* (pp. 141–164). New York: Oxford University Press.

Salovey, P., & Mayer, J. D. (1990). Emotional intelligence. *Imagination, Cognition, and Personality, 9,* 185–211.

Salovey, P., Mayer, J. D., Goldman, S., Turvey, C., & Palfai, T. (1995). Emotional attention, clarity, and repair: Exploring emotional intelligence using the Trait Meta-Mood Scale. In J. W. Pennebaker (Ed.), *Emotion, disclosure, and health* (pp. 125–154). Washington, D. C.: American Psychological Association.

Salovey, P., & Sluyter, D. J. (1997). *Emotional development and emotional intelligence.* New York: Basic Books.

Scarr, S. (1989). Protecting general intelligence: Constructs and consequences for intervention. In R. L. Linn (Ed.), *Intelligence: Measurement, theory, and public policy.* Urbana, IL: University of Illinois Press.

Simon, E. W., Rosen, M., & Ponpipom, A. (1996). Age and IQ as predictors of emotion identification in adults with mental retardation. *Research in Developmental Disabilities, 17,* 383–389.

Sternberg, R. J. (1997). The concept of intelligence and its role in lifelong learning and success. *American Psychologist, 52,* 1030–1045.

Tett, R., Wang, A., Fisher, R., Martinez, A., Griebler, J., & Linkovich, T. (April 4, 1997). *Testing a model of emotional intelligence.* 1997 Annual Convention of the Southeastern Psychological Association, Atlanta, GA.

Tett, R., Wang, A., Thomas, M., Griebler, J., & Martinez, A. (April 4, 1997). *Development of Self-Report Measures of Emotional Intelligence.* Paper presented at the 1997 Annual Convention of the Southeastern Psychological Association, Atlanta, GA.

Tomkins, S. S. (1962). *Affect, imagery, consciousness. Vol. 1: The positive affects.* New York: Springer-Verlag.

Wechsler, D. (1940). Nonintellective factors in general intelligence. *Psychological Bulletin, 37,* 444–445.

Wechsler, D. (1943). Non-intellective factors in general intelligence. *Journal of Abnormal Social Psychology, 38,* 100–104.

Wechsler, D. (1958). *The measurement and appraisal of adult intelligence (4th ed.).* Baltimore, MD: The Williams & Wilkins Company.

NO

Richard D. Roberts, Moshe Zeidner, and Gerald Matthews

Does Emotional Intelligence Meet Traditional Standards for an Intelligence? Some New Data and Conclusions

Emotional intelligence (EI) is a relatively new domain of psychological investigation; having recently gathered considerable momentum with widespread, international media attention. Daniel Goleman's (1995) book on the topic appeared on *The New York Times* best-seller list, which led to a *Time* magazine article devoted to detailed exposition of the topic (Gibbs, 1995). More recently, the influential electronic magazine *Salon* devoted a lengthy article to the discussion of its application in the workforce (Paul, 1999). . . .

EI first appeared in the scientific literature in the early 1990s (Mayer, DiPaulo, & Salovey, 1990; Salovey & Mayer, 1990), where the term was used to denote a type of intelligence that involved the ability to process emotional information. Subsequently, researchers have proposed that EI incorporates a set of conceptually related psychological processes involving the processing of affective information. These processes include: (a) the verbal and nonverbal appraisal and expression of emotion in the self and others, (b) the regulation of emotion in the self and others, and (c) the utilization of emotion to facilitate thought (see Mayer & Geher, 1996; Mayer & Salovey, 1997; Salovey & Mayer, 1990). Although various authors have proposed that EI is a type of intelligence, in the traditional sense, contemporary research and theory lacks any clear conceptual model of intelligence within which to place the construct. For example, Spearman's (1927) model of *g* (general ability) affords no special role for EI. Neither is emotional (or social, for that matter) intelligence included in Thurstone's (1938) list of primary mental abilities or Guttman's (1965a, 1965b) radex model of intelligence. . . .

Conceptualizing and Assessing EI

Models of EI

One of the difficulties currently encountered in research on EI would appear to be the multitude of qualities covered by the concept (see Roberts, in press). Indeed, many qualities appear to overlap with well-established personality constructs, such as the Big Five personality factor model (see Davies et al., 1998; McCrae, 2000). Mayer, Caruso, and Salovey (1999, 2000) warned that careful analysis is required to distinguish what is (and what is not) part of EI (see also Mayer, Salovey, & Caruso, 2000a, 2000b). Throughout, Mayer and colleagues distinguished between (a) *mental ability models,* focusing on aptitude for processing affective information, and (b) *mixed models* that conceptualize EI as a diverse construct, including aspects of personality as well as the ability to perceive, assimilate, understand, and manage emotions. These mixed models include motivational factors and affective dispositions (e.g., self-concept, assertiveness, empathy; see Bar-On, 1997; Goleman, 1995).

In contrast, Mayer and colleagues have proposed a four-branch mental ability model of EI, which encompasses the following psychological processes (see e.g., Mayer, Caruso, & Salovey, 1999, 2000; Mayer & Salovey, 1997; Mayer, Salovey, & Caruso, 2000a, 2000b; Salovey & Mayer, 1990):

1. *The verbal and nonverbal appraisal and expression of emotion in the self and others.* EI has been defined as "the ability to perceive emotions, to access and generate emotions so as to assist thought, to understand emotions and emotional knowledge, and to reflectively regulate emotions so as to promote emotional and intellectual growth" (Mayer & Salovey, 1997, p. 5). Inside this definitional framework, the most fundamental level of EI includes the perception, appraisal, and expression of emotions (Mayer, Caruso, & Salovey, 1999). In other words, implicit in this aspect of EI is the individual's awareness of both their emotions and their thoughts concerning their emotions, the ability to monitor and differentiate among emotions, and the ability to adequately express emotions.
2. *The utilization of emotion to facilitate thought and action.* This component of EI involves assimilating basic emotional experiences into mental life (Mayer, Caruso, & Salovey, 1999, 2000). This includes weighing emotions against one another and against other sensations and thoughts and allowing emotions to direct attention (e.g., holding an emotional state in consciousness long enough to compare its correspondence with similar sensations in sound, color, and taste). Marshaling emotions in the service of a goal is essential for selective attention, self-monitoring, self-motivation, and so forth.
3. *Understanding and reasoning about emotions.* This aspect of EI involves perceiving the lawfulness underlying specific emotions (e.g., to understand that anger arises when justice is denied or when an injustice is performed against oneself or one's loved ones). This process also involves the understanding of emotional problems, such as knowing what emotions are similar and what relation they convey.
4. *The regulation of emotion in the self and others.* According to Mayer, Caruso, & Salovey (1999), the *highest level* in the hierarchy of EI skills is the management and regulation of emotions. This facet of EI involves knowing how to calm down after feeling stressed out or alleviating the stress and emotion of others. This facet facilitates social adaptation and problem solving. . . .

Objectives of the Present Study

[T]he present study attempts to provide further information that is pertinent to a balanced evaluation of the empirical and conceptual status of EI. To this end, we examined the most comprehensive and contemporary performance-based measure of EI, the MEIS (e.g., Mayer, Caruso, & Salovey, 1999). Although it is possible to focus on any number of research questions bearing on the MEIS, it seemed expedient (because the measure is relatively new) to focus on the following objectives of relatively major significance:

1. *Is the construct of EI, as assessed by the MEIS, psychometrically sound?* In particular, this study sets out to examine the factorial validity of the MEIS, using both exploratory and confirmatory methods. Thus far, the one confirmatory factor analysis conducted with performance-based measures of EI (Mayer, Caruso, & Salovey, 1999) yielded rather equivocal results, including marginal fit statistics and evidence that two branches (e.g., understanding and assimilation) could not be differentiated. In addition to exploratory factor analyses, the current study used structural-equation modeling procedures to test the goodness of fit between the four-branch model of EI and the data. In addition, we examined subtest reliabilities and the patterns of intertest correlations.
2. *Do the two different scoring criteria used in the MEIS (i.e., consensus and expert scoring) demonstrate convergent validity? Do they yield similar reliability coefficients?* The Mayer, Caruso, and Salovey (1999) model predicted a positive manifold, or a nonnegative correlation matrix among the subtests, supporting three converging factors associated with emotional identification, assimilating emotions, understanding emotions, and managing emotions. The same factors should be found by using both scoring methods, as they are construed as alternative (yet analogous) scoring protocols. Following Mayer, Caruso, and Salovey's (1999) decision to focus almost all of their reported analyses on consensus scoring, Ciarrochi et al. (2000) conducted an investigation where no consideration was given to expert scores. Arguably, both studies highlighted the need to examine alternative scoring procedures in close detail. In the present investigation, all responses were scored with both consensus and expert criteria, allowing us to determine the convergent validity of these measures. Thus, one of the major goals of this study is to examine in greater depth the relationship between consensus and expert scoring and to ascertain any problems inherent in these two ways of scoring behavioral measures of EI. Mayer and his colleagues are not clear as to whether they believe these two forms of scoring are directly equivalent or more loosely related. Indeed, they generally encourage consensus coding because of its facility. In addition, we examine the personality and individual differences correlates of the two scoring procedures.
3. *What are the relationships between EI, personality, and ability factors?* Put somewhat differently, to what extent does EI vary as a function of personality and intelligence constructs? Is the pattern of relations between EI and personality variables invariant across the

types of scoring criteria used? According to prior research by Mayer, Caruso, and Salovey (1999), and the notion of divergent validity, the principal prediction is that EI should relate modestly to general cognitive ability. Mayer and his colleagues have not specified the likely personality correlates of MEIS scores. On the basis of past empirical research (e.g., Dawda & Hart, 2000), we might expect EI to relate to higher Agreeableness, Conscientiousness, Extraversion, and Openness, and to lower Neuroticism. Associations should generalize across scoring criteria.

4. *What is the nature (and magnitude) of gender, ethnic, and age differences in performance-based assessment of EI?* The strongest prediction from previous research (e.g., Mayer, Caruso, & Salovey, 1999) is that EI should be higher in women, irrespective of the scoring method used. In addition, we assess to what degree individual and group differences vary with the type of scoring criteria used. . . .

Method

Participants

Participants were 704 USAF trainees, the majority of whom were male (89%). Participants ranged from 17 to 23 years of age ($M = 19.74$, $SD = 2.21$). About 30% of the sample had some college education, with the remaining 70% having completed full or partial high school education. Participants were ethnically diverse, distributed as follows by ethnicity: Caucasian, 69%; African Americans, 14%; Latino–Hispanic, 9%; Asian American, 4%; Native Americans, 2%; unidentified, 2%. The majority of the recruits (over 61%) were engaged in technical occupations in the USAF, with the remainder serving as security police (14%), medical–dental staff (5%), general staff (7%), and support staff (11%). The remaining recruits were unidentified or had not yet been placed in occupational categories.

Psychological Tests

The main instruments used in this study were the MEIS, the ASVAB, and the TSDI, a measure of the Big Five factor model of personality. Descriptions of each of these instruments are provided in the passages that follow.

A Multi-Factor Emotional Intelligence Scale (MEIS)

The MEIS (Mayer, Caruso, & Salovey, 1999) is a multi-factor ability battery divided into four branches: (a) *emotional identification (perception)* (4 tests: Faces, Music, Designs, and Stories); (b) *assimilating emotions* (2 tests: Synesthesia and Feeling Biases); (c) *understanding emotions* (4 tests: Blends, Progressions, Transitions, and Relativity); and (d) *managing emotions* (2 tests: Others and the Self)! . . . Across all 12 subtests, responses were scored according to both consensus and expert scoring criteria, the procedures for which are described below.

Consensus Scoring

Mayer, Caruso, and Salovey's (1999) normative sample provided the weights for each item used in the consensus scoring procedure. This approach appears judicious because it allows ready comparisons with that sample. Moreover, in a previous study, Garcia and Roberts (2000) reported high correlations between consensus scores provided by the standardization group and consensus scores calculated from their specific sample. Thus, the response of each participant was scored according to its agreement with participants from the normative sample endorsing each alternative. For example, a participant who chose 5 in the present investigation would receive a score of .52 for that item if in the Mayer, Caruso, and Salovey (1999) study 52% of the participants answered that anger was definitely present. If the participant reported that anger was definitely not present (1), and this matched only 5% of the normative sample, then the person would receive a score of .05 for that item and so forth.

Expert Scoring

Criteria for expert scoring were based on Mayer and Caruso (from Mayer, Caruso, & Salovey, 1999), who served as the "experts." Thus, each response was scored according to its agreement with the alternative identified by these authors as the "best" answer for each item. In each case, endorsing the selected best answer value (or the integer on either side of it) was scored as 1; otherwise the answer was scored as 0.

Branch Scores

MEIS branch scores, calculated separately for consensus and expert scoring criteria, were formed by converting the respective branch subtest scores to standardized *z* scores and linearly summing these standardized scores to yield a composite branch score. For example, emotional identification branch scores, scored by consensus criteria, were formed by converting consensus-based Faces, Music, Design, and Stories scores from raw to *z* scores, and then linearly summing these four standardized scores to form the branch measure. A similar procedure was used for constructing expert emotional identification branch scores, and so on for the other branches.

General EI Score

A score representing what might tentatively be called *general EI* was formed separately for consensus-based and expert-based scores, by linear summation of respective standardized MEIS subtest scores (across all 12 subtests).

Armed Services Vocational Aptitude Battery (ASVAB)

The ASVAB (U.S. Department of Defense, 1984) is a particularly prominent multiple aptitude battery, widely implemented in a variety of educational, selection, and research settings (Murphy & Davidshofer, 1998). For example, in the selection context, performance on the ASVAB appears to be a major determinant in the career choices of over 1.3 million young Americans per annum (Kaplan & Saccuzzo, 1997, p. 365). In addition, researchers have consistently established that the ASVAB possesses levels of high reliability and validity (e.g., Carroll, 1993; Herrnstein & Murray, 1994; Ree & Carretta, 1995; Roberts et al., 2000). Collectively, these features suggest it to be a particularly efficacious measure of cognitive abilities for inclusion in the present design. . . .

Trait-Self Description Inventory (TSDI)

This Likert-type self-report inventory was designed to assess each of the Big Five personality factors. It contained two sections. In the first section, 64 trait names (e.g., *thorough*) were presented (one after the other). The participant was required to indicate how characteristic the trait was of him or herself as compared with other individuals of the same sex and age. . . .

Thereafter, trait and behavioral responses were summed to generate five composites. These composites represent the super factors of Agreeableness, Conscientiousness, Extraversion, Openness, and Neuroticism. A validation study of 2,853 USAF enlistees provides a large reference group with which isolated studies (such as the present one) might be compared (Christal, 1994; see also Davies et al., 1998). . . .

Discussion

Mayer, Caruso, and Salovey (1999) contended that if EI is to constitute a legitimate form of intelligence it should satisfy three criteria: operationalization as an ability, appropriate correlational properties, and incremental developmental trends. The data presented in this article may be considered to provide only equivocal support for the first and second of these criteria. The third criterion was not a major focus of this study, but . . . is not a necessary condition for many traditional forms of intelligence. Certainly, comparison of the present data with those from studies of self-report measures of EI (e.g., Dawda & Hart, 2000) suggests that the MEIS performs better, in that it seems distinct from existing personality measures. Unfortunately, consensus- and expert-scored EI also appears to be distinct (and in some cases independent) from each other. Factor correlations are insufficient to suggest that the two forms of scoring provide alternative measures of the same underlying construct. Consensus- and expert-scored scales also differ in their relationships with sex and ethnic group. Validity is demonstrated in some respects by the correlational data. Again, however, the two forms of scoring appear to support constructs that show only partial overlap, as evidenced by the lack of consistency in the linear associations between the two sets of branch scores and the personality and ability measures. . . .

Perspectives on EI

The data analyses raise both some immediate problems with assessment of EI using the MEIS and some more fundamental issues about the contribution of research on EI. It is likely that some of the psychometric problems we have indicated are soluble through the normal processes of test refinement.

There seems to be no barrier in principle to the development of internally consistent scales whose intercorrelations support a replicable three- or four-branch factor solution. However, the data also highlight the more fundamental problem of differences between scoring methods. Dimensions derived from expert and consensus scores fail to correlate well, at either scale or factor levels, and it is especially disturbing that the general factors extracted from the two types of data correlated only .26. Furthermore, expert- and consensus-based scores give very different patterns of association with group and individual difference factors. The discrepancies are sufficiently large that they imply that one or the other scoring method should be discarded, in that it is hard to envisage modifications that would bring factors that are correlated at less than .50 into alignment.

An optimistic perspective on EI would consider the problems of different scoring protocols as surmountable. Indeed, they would appear as the type of conceptual problem that plagued Binet, Simon, Wechsler, and their predecessors historically, when they first tried to develop intelligence tests (see, e.g., Gregory, 1996). In the emotional domain, it may be inappropriate to insist that test items should have rigid, unequivocal right and wrong answers. Recently, Salovey et al. (2000) recommended a consensus-based approach to scoring the MEIS on the basis that large normative samples tend to be reliable judges of emotional questions. More generally, consensus scoring (or its derivatives) has had great survival value, witnessed in chronicles from the first century A.D. (e.g., gladiators in the Coliseum) to the present day (e.g., many of our political leaders are elected through this process). Given that intelligence is often equated with the ability of the organism to adapt to its environment (see, e.g., Sternberg, 1985; Thorndike et al., 1921), the ecological validity of this scoring procedure per se should not be underestimated.

However, there is a further twist to the role of consensus agreement. In general terms, we would expect a person whose beliefs match the group consensus to be better adapted to the social environment than someone whose beliefs deviate from the group. The conformist is likely to receive more positive reinforcement from others and to negotiate challenges shaped by social convention, such as finding a job or a life partner more easily. In other words, consensual EI may be adaptive not because it refers to any cognitive advantage, but because of the social advantages of conformity. Consistent with this suggestion, people with generally desirable personality characteristics such as conscientiousness and agreeableness seem to be perceived by others as better at emotion management, as evidenced by the consensus-based data here, but this link is not evident in the expert-scored data. A conformity construct is of real-world relevance, but it is highly misleading to label it as an intelligence, because it relates to person–environment fit rather than to any characteristic of the individual. Indeed, in some instances it is the nonconformist who should be deemed emotionally intelligent, for example, a writer or an artist who finds a new and original way of expressing an emotion.

Another possibility is to develop some hybrid scoring protocol. For example, deriving consensus scores from the corpus of experts–professionals who read this journal or who are members of organizations such as the International Society for Research on Emotions seems feasible and conceptually justifiable. Within this hybrid model, it is expert consensus that forms a theoretically defensible scoring criterion, assuming that problems of bias associated with the demographic characteristics of experts may be avoided.

Against these proposals, we may wonder whether an intelligence may ever be satisfactorily defined by consensus, even expert consensus. We have previously discussed the difficulties in principle in deciding on the best or most adaptive response to an emotional encounter (Matthews & Zeidner, 2000; Matthews, Zeidner, & Roberts, 2003). If there is no right answer, consensus is of no validity. Furthermore, because consensus methods are largely a function of the particular group assessed (cultural, ethnic, age, or gender), what may be the consensus and modal response for one group may not be so for another group, making scores relatively incomparable across different groups (e.g., ethnic, national) of examinees. There are also difficult issues about the legitimacy and ownership of expertise: Many disciplines and subdisciplines may claim primacy. It is also questionable whether well-educated, professional people should solely set standards for EI.

Conclusions

Mayer, Salovey, and Caruso (2000a) deserve much credit for formulating a novel, clearly articulated model of EI and seeking to operationalize its constructs as ability tests through careful construct validation studies. The view expressed here is that despite the merits of this project, there are significant measurement problems to be overcome. Perhaps inevitably, given the level of interest in EI, criticism of work on EI has already invoked strong emotions in many of its chief proponents and critics. For example, Salovey et al. (2000) equated the conclusions reached by Davies et al. (1998) with the French Academy of Sciences decision, at a time when logical positivism was growing, to destroy all meteorites housed in museums because they were "heavenly bodies" and heaven did not exist. We aim to conclude with a balanced appraisal of the promise and problems of ability-model EI research. From a positive perspective, EI is a real quality of the person, distinct from existing personality and ability factors and best measured by performance-based tests such as the MEIS. The problems raised here may be essentially technical problems to be solved by advances in test construction.

The sceptic may prefer another astronomical metaphor. In 1877, the Italian astronomer, Schiaparelli, announded that his telescope revealed linear channels on the surface of Mars. His observation inspired Percival Lowell to map hundreds of canals in fine detail, and to enthrall the general public with his popular lectures on the construction of the canals by a martian civilization. There are various suggestive parallels with EI. Respected scientists, who made important contributions to other areas of astronomy, reported the initial observations. The canals were not completely fanciful; Mars does have surface markings (of an irregular nature). An elaborate empirical and theoretical artiface was constructed from fairly modest beginnings, and popular interest was sparked by excessive speculation. It remains to be seen whether EI, like the canals of Mars, is the product of the tendency of even expert observers to see, in complex data, patterns that do not exist.

At this early stage of research, it is premature to label EI as either a real "meteorite" or an illusory "martian canal," but the present study has identified significant issues that require resolution, related to both reliability and validity. The most severe problems relate to scoring (i.e., reliability), including the difficulty of justifying both expert and consensus scoring, the limited psychometric convergence of these methods, and their differing relationships with other criteria. At the least, further progress requires a single scoring method with a strong rationale that what is being measured is a form of cognitive ability. In particular, it should be demonstrated that items have better and worse answers with respect to some objective criterion (although human judgment may be required to assess how well answers meet the criterion). The difficult problems of group differences and possible cultural and gender bias must also be addressed. The data provide some support for Mayer, Salovey, and Caruso's (2000a) *correlational criteria,* for example, by demonstrating only modest correlation between EI and general intelligence. The data also showed some overlap with personality constructs. Although performance-based EI measures appear to be free of the redundancy with existing personality scales that plagues questionnaire measures, the validity coefficients for the MEIS also appear to be typically small and often less than .30 (see Mayer, Salovey, & Caruso, 2000a). It is unclear whether the predictive validity of the MEIS would be maintained with personality and ability controlled statistically. Finally, it is not established that EI, as operationalized by the MEIS, is a major construct on a par with general intelligence as a determinant of individual differences in meaningful, real-world behavior. There may well be further primary ability dimensions such as emotion perception that are poorly assessed by existing instruments. However, to assert that these abilities are as important in human functioning as general intelligence is to go far beyond the available data. An urgent task for future research is to show real-world adaptive advantages for high scores on the MEIS over and above those they obtain from their higher general intelligence and their personality characteristics.

References

Bar-On, R. (1997). *The Bar-On Emotional Quotient Inventory (EQ-i): Technical manual.* Toronto, Ontario, Canada: Multi-Health Systems.

Carroll, J. B. (1993). *Human cognitive abilities: A survey of factor-analytic studies.* New York: Cambridge University Press.

Christal, R. E. (1994, November). Non-cognitive research involving systems of testing and learning. *Final Research and Development Status Report* (USAF Contract No. F33615-91-D-0010). Armstrong Laboratory, Brooks Air Force Base, United States Air Force.

Ciarrochi, J. V., Chan, A. Y. C., & Caputi, P. (2000). A critical evaluation of the emotional intelligence construct. *Personality and Individual Differences, 28,* 539–561.

Davies, M., Stankov, L., & Roberts, R. D. (1998). Emotional intelligence: In search of an elusive construct. *Journal of Personality and Social Psychology, 75,* 989–1015.

Dawda, D., & Hart, S. D. (2000). Assessing emotional intelligence: Reliability and validity of the Bar-On Emotional Quotient Inventory (EQ-i) in university students. *Personality and Individual Differences, 28,* 797–812.

Garcia, A., & Roberts, R. D. (2000, April). *Emotional 'intelligence', cognitive abilities, and personality.* Paper presented at *the 27th Annual Conference of the Australasian Experimental Psychology Society,* Novotel Twin Waters Resort, Queensland, Australia.

Gibbs, N. (1995, October 2). The EQ factor. *Time,* 60–68.

Goleman, D. (1995). *Emotional intelligence.* New York: Bantam Books.

Gregory, R. J. (1996). *Psychological testing: History, principles, and applications* (2nd ed.). Needham Heights, MA: Allyn & Bacon.

Guttman, L. (1965a). A faceted definition of intelligence. In R. Eiferman (Ed.), *Studies in psychology. Scripta Hierosolymitana* [Jerusalem Scripts in Greek] (Vol. 14, pp. 166–181), Jerusalem: Magnes Press.

Guttman, L. (1965b). The structure of intercorrelations among intelligence tests. In *Proceedings of the 1964 Invitational Conference on Testing Problems* (pp. 53–65). Princeton, NJ: Educational Testing Service.

Herrnstein, R. J., & Murray, C. (1994). *The bell curve: Intelligence and class structure in American life.* New York: Free Press.

Kaplan, R. M., & Saccuzzo, D. P. (1997). *Psychological testing: Principles, applications, and issues* (4th ed.). Pacific Grove, CA: Brooks/Cole.

Matthews, G., & Zeidner, M. (2000). Emotional intelligence, adaptation to stressful encounters, and health outcomes. In R. Bar-On & J. D. A. Parker (Eds.), *Handbook of emotional intelligence* (pp. 459–489). San Francisco: Jossey-Bass.

Matthews, G., Zeidner, M., & Roberts, R. (2003). *Emotional intelligence: Science and myth.* Cambridge, MA: MIT Press.

Mayer, J. D., Caruso, D., & Salovey, P. (1999). Emotional intelligence meets traditional standards for an intelligence. *Intelligence, 27,* 267–298.

Mayer, J. D., Caruso, D., & Salovey, P. (2000). Selecting a measure of emotional intelligence: The case for ability scales. In R. Bar-On & J. D. A. Parker (Eds.), *The handbook of emotional intelligence* (pp. 320–342). New York: Jossey-Bass.

Mayer, J. D., DiPaulo, M., & Salovey, P. (1990). Perceiving affective content in ambiguous visual stimuli: A component of emotional intelligence. *Journal of Personality Assessment, 54,* 772–781.

Mayer, J. D., & Geher, G. (1996). Emotional intelligence and the identification of emotion. *Intelligence, 22,* 89–113.

Mayer, J. D., & Salovey, P. (1993). The intelligence of emotional intelligence. *Intelligence, 17,* 443–450.

Mayer, J. D., & Salovey, P. (1997). What is emotional intelligence? In P. Salovey & D. Sluyter (Eds.), *Emotional development and emotional intelligence: Implications for educators* (pp. 3–31). New York: Basic Books.

Mayer, J. D., Salovey, P., & Caruso, D. (2000a). Competing models of emotional intelligence. In R. J. Sternberg (Ed.), *Handbook of human intelligence* (2nd ed., pp. 396–420). New York: Cambridge University Press.

Mayer, J. D., Salovey, P., & Caruso, D. (2000b). Emotional intelligence as zeitgeist, personality, and as a mental ability. In R. Bar-On & J. D. A. Parker (Eds.), *The handbook of emotional intelligence* (pp. 92–117). New York: Jossey-Bass.

McCrae, R. R. (2000). Emotional intelligence from the perspective of the five-factor model of personality. In R. Bar-On & J. D. A. Parker (Eds.), *The handbook of emotional intelligence* (pp. 263–276). New York: Jossey-Bass.

Murphy, K. R., & Davidshofer, C. O. (1998). *Psychological testing: Principles and applications* (4th ed.). Upper Saddle River, NJ: Prentice Hall.

Paul, A. M. (1999). Promotional intelligence. *Salon.com* [On-line]. Available Internet: http://www.salon.com/books/it/1999/06/28/emotional/index3.html.

Ree, M. J., & Carretta, T. R. (1995). Group differences in aptitude factor structure on the ASVAB. *Educational and Psychological Measurement, 55,* 268–277.
Roberts, R. D. (in press). Review of the handbook of emotional intelligence. *Intelligence.*
Roberts, R. D., Goff, G. N., Anjoul, F., Kyllonen, P. C., Pallier, G., & Stankov, L. (2000). The Armed Services Vocational Aptitude Battery: Little more than acculturated learning (Gc)!? *Learning and Individual Difference, 12,* 81–103.
Salovey, P., & Mayer, J. D. (1990). Emotional intelligence. *Imagination, Cognition and Personality, 9,* 185–211.
Salovey, P., Woolery, A., & Mayer, J. D. (2000). Emotional intelligence: Conceptualization and measurement. In G. Fletcher & M. Clark (Eds.), *The Blackwell handbook of social psychology.* London: Blackwell.
Spearman, C. (1927). *The abilities of man.* New York: Macmillan.
Sternberg, R. J. (1985). *Beyond IQ: A triarchic theory of human intelligence.* New York: Cambridge University Press.
Thorndike, E. L., Terman, L. M., Freeman, F. M., Colvin, S. S., Pintner, R., & Pressey, S. L. (1921). Intelligence and its measurement: A symposium. *Journal of Educational Psychology, 12, 3,* 123–147.
Thurstone, L. L. (1938). *Primary mental abilities.* Chicago: University of Chicago Press.
U.S. Department of Defense. (1984). *Test Manual for the Armed Services Vocational Aptitude Battery* (DoD No. 1340.12AA). North Chicago, IL: U.S. Military Entrance Processing Command.

POSTSCRIPT

Is Emotional Intelligence Really a Form of Intelligence?

Roberts, Zeidner, and Matthews end their article with the "meaningful, real-world behavior" question: Does emotional intelligence make any significant difference in our day-to-day lives? That is a difficult question to answer without some method of measuring its power and influence. In order to gauge its power, we must have a reliable and valid measure of emotional intelligence, and in order to create a good measure we must have a clear description that lends itself to an operational definition. Mayer, Salovey, and Caruso assert that they have proven the significance of emotional intelligence and the reliability and validity of the Multifactor Emotional Intelligence Scale (MEIS), but Roberts, et al., are not convinced.

Roberts, et al., compared the MEIS to a measure of cognitive abilities, the Armed Services Vocational Aptitude Battery (ASVAB), and a measure of personality, the Trait Self-Description Inventory (TSDI). They found that the two different scoring systems for the MEIS—the consensus and the expert scoring—gave very different scores that are statistically distinct. If the two scoring systems are truly parallel and reliable, then the scores should be almost perfectly correlated. They found only mild support for validity when comparing MEIS scores with cognitive and personality measures, the ASVAB and TSDI.

When considering the conclusions reached by Roberts, et al., one should not overlook the characteristics of the participants in their sample. Their data were collected from 704 U.S. Air Force trainees. They state that 89% or approximately 626 participants were male. While research studies in the psychology of gender show that both males and females feel emotions and respond to them, gender studies also show that American males are generally socialized to suppress their emotions. Is it fair to judge an emotional measure without a gender-balanced sample? Also, consider that the primary jobs of the trainees were U.S. Air Force technical jobs and security police. Do you think that is a sample that represents most Americans?

In some respects Mayer, et al., are victims of success. Because so many people, including academics, found the notion of emotional intelligence to be appealing, the concept has been adopted and expanded by numerous scholars. While Mayer, et al., are trying to somewhat limit the concept by insisting on an ability model rather than a mixed model, they do make rather bold statements about the value of emotional intelligence. Hedlund and Sternberg (2000) are concerned with recent proliferation of intelligences, including the addition of emotional intelligence. Robert Sternberg's well-known Triarchic Theory of Intelligence has three components, while

Howard Gardner is promoting eight distinct intelligences in his Multiple Intelligences model. Regarding emotional intelligence Hedlund and Sternberg write, "There is limited empirical support or, at best, mixed support for the validity of these nonacademic intelligences. Research progress is perhaps impeded by a lack of consistency in how these constructs are conceptualized and operationalized" (page 157).

It seems that researchers in the area of emotional intelligence need to consider some very basic questions. What is intelligence, and what are appropriate types of intelligence? If the definition of intelligence is too broad then one might ask, "Are all mental processes types of intelligence?" What is emotional intelligence, and how is it distinct from other cognitive and personality traits? And finally, the real-world question, how does the use of emotional intelligence help us have a better day?

Suggested Readings

Barrett, L. F., Mayer, J. D., and Salovey, P. (Editors), *The Wisdom in Feeling: Psychological Processes in Emotional Intelligence* (New York: Guilford, 2002).

Ciarrochi, J., Forgas, J. P., and Mayer, J. D. *Emotional Intelligence in Everyday Life* (New York: Taylor & Francis, 2001).

Goleman, D. *Emotional Intelligence* (New York: Bantam Books, 1997).

Hedlund, J., and Sternberg, R. Too many intelligences? Integrating social, emotional and practical intelligence. In R. Bar-On and J. Parker (Eds.), *The Handbook of Emotional Intelligence* (pp. 136–167). (San Francisco: Jossey-Bass, 2000).

Matthews, G., Roberts, R. D., and Zeidner, M. *Emotional Intelligence: Science and Myth* (Cambridge, MA: MIT Press, 2002).

ISSUE 14

Is the Birth Order Effect on Intelligence Real?

YES: Joseph Lee Rodgers, H. Harrington Cleveland, Edwin van den Oord, and David C. Rowe, from "Resolving the Debate over Birth Order, Family Size, and Intelligence," *American Psychologist* (June 2000)

NO: R. B. Zajonc, from "The Family Dynamics of Intellectual Development," *American Psychologist* (June/July 2001)

ISSUE SUMMARY

YES: Professors of psychology Joseph Rodgers, H. Harrington Cleveland, Edwin van den Oord, and David Rowe present the case that birth order and intelligence are not related, and because of that psychologists should not claim that large families produce lower-IQ children.

NO: Psychologist and researcher R. B. Zajonc argues that family dynamics change as each new sibling is added, and this change is related to less intellectual development in children born in larger families.

This debate highlights the role of an individual's family environment, specifically family size and birth order, on intellectual development. Firstborns often get a great deal of attention early in life and are often given more responsibilities as the oldest child in the family. In some cases, older children may be asked to take on the role of caretaker or tutor for younger siblings. Also, researchers frequently find that parents are more anxious with their firstborn and tend to relax with each additional child. The controversy highlighted in this issue is over the influence, if any, these changing family dynamics have on the intellectual development of each child.

The two selections are part of the ongoing discussion of the effects and interaction of inherited innate abilities and environmental stimulation. In other words, scientists are still debating nature versus nurture. There are few areas of study that have been influenced by this debate as dramatically as the study of intelligence. The highly controversial book

The Bell Curve [R. Hernstein and Murray, C. (1994). *The Bell Curve: Intelligence and Class Structure in American Life*. New York: The Free Press.], first published in 1994, prompted a new round of discussions of a possible genetic relationship between racial or ethnic background and intelligence.

The birth order debate hinges on the ways research questions are constructed and the designs or methodologies used to test those questions. In order to fully understand the methodological side of this debate, it is important to review some key terms. Correlational analysis involves a comparison of two sets of data. A *positive correlation* occurs when both sets of data move in the same direction, whether both are increasing or decreasing. A *negative correlation* occurs when one data set decreases as the other increases, thus the variables are moving in opposite directions. It is also essential that scientists and the general public remember that simply finding a relationship between two things does not mean that one causes the other. Correlation does not prove causation.

Another important set of key terms to review involve research design or methodology. If a researcher decided to measure the intelligence of a large group of people of different ages and birth rank at one particular point in time, she would be employing a *cross-sectional design*. This would be the case if a researcher gave a questionnaire to a mass lecture college course. In that cross-sectional design, firstborns from various families would be compared to lastborns from different families. When comparing intelligence measures of firstborns to lastborns in a cross-sectional design, the researcher is using a *between-groups* comparison. If, however, a researcher decided to assess intelligence in the same participants over a long period of time, then he would be using a *longitudinal design*. And, if in this longitudinal design, the researcher decides to track the intelligence scores of firstborns as they adjust to new siblings by testing the same firstborns at set time intervals, then the researcher would be using a *within-groups* design. In the case of the selections here, the authors refer to within-family or between-family designs.

Based on data collected from the National Longitudinal Survey of Youth (NSLY), Rodgers, Cleveland, van den Oord, and Rowe argue that there is no relationship between birth order and intellectual development among siblings. Rather, they argue that lower-IQ parents tend to have larger families and that this finding explains any differences in IQ among firstborns, middleborns, and lastborns. Zajonc counters this assertion with data in support of the confluence model, which considers several variables, including number of siblings, birth rank, and sibling tutoring. Zajonc argues that one cannot use this data to determine cause and effect, but that one can show that the intellectual stimulation and development of each child decreases as a family grows.

Joseph Lee Rodgers, et al.

Resolving the Debate over Birth Order, Family Size, and Intelligence

A number of sophisticated researchers have concluded that birth order is an important determinant of behavioral outcomes:

> This study serves to confirm the existence of independent relations of birth order and of family size to intellectual performance. (Belmont & Marolla, 1973, p. 1100)
>
> When age is taken into consideration, the birth order literature loses its chaotic character and an orderly pattern of results emerges. (Zajonc, Markus, & Markus, 1979, p. 1325)
>
> In the drama of sibling competition, birth order and gender appear to be the two most important players in the choice of sibling strategies. (Sulloway, 1996, p. 79)

Other excellent scholars are just as certain that birth order does not play an important causal role in behavioral outcomes:

> The general lack of consistent [birth order] findings revealed by this review leaves real doubt as to whether the chance of positive results is worth the heavy investment needed to carry out any more definitive studies. (Schooler, 1972, p. 174)
>
> Time and time again, superficial birth order effects dissolve to insignificance when (i) a comprehensive review of the literature is accomplished and (ii) reports containing fundamental problems of method are given their proper weight—zero. (Galbraith, 1982, p. 1170)
>
> An alternative analysis based on a within-family study design that uses sibling pairs indexed by birth order in the Wisconsin Longitudinal Study finds no evidence of birth order effects on intelligence. (Retherford & Sewell, 1991, p. 141)

These quotes frame a basic controversy that has both research and policy implications. Unlike many such controversies, however, this one can be resolved. These different interpretations disappear in the light shed by

From American Psychologist, June 2000, pp. 1599–612.

understanding a common methodological artifact that pervades the birth order literature.

Past answers to the question of whether there are birth order effects on behavioral outcomes depend on the type of data that are used to test for those effects. Those who have used cross-sectional data typically have found large correlations between birth order and behavioral outcomes, which they have interpreted as support for causal links between birth order and developmental processes. Those who have used within-family data typically have found small or zero correlations between birth order and behavioral outcomes, which they have interpreted as meaning that birth order has very little direct effect on human development.

This problem can, of course, be partitioned into many subproblems, one for each behavioral outcome of interest. There are potentially different answers to the questions of how birth order influences intelligence, personality, psychopathology, and so forth. Most birth order scholars have focused on how birth order influences intelligence or personality. We address the former domain, which we enlarge slightly to include both intelligence and achievement. Our primary methodological point applies equally to any psychological or behavioral domain. Only a certain type of data can be used to separate within-family and between-family sources of variance, no matter what the topic. However, our substantive conclusions in this article apply only to the influence of birth order on intelligence.

Background and Previous Research

Models of the Relationship between Birth Order and Intelligence

Three models explaining the relation between birth order and intelligence/achievement all anticipate and frame the arguments presented in the current article. Two of the models posit within-family explanations, derived from inspection of cross-sectional (between-family) data. The third model emerged from critical inspection of the first two and questioned the very existence of the causal relationships that formed the basis for those models.

The sociologist Judith Blake often framed questions about children and families in starkly economic terms (one of her best known articles was entitled "Are Babies Consumer Durables?"; Blake, 1968). In her presidential address to the Population Association of America, Blake addressed the question of whether couples can have "higher quality offspring" by having fewer children (Blake, 1981). Blake's *dilution model* (also called the *family resource model* or *resource dilution model*) was a new name for an old idea: The more children in a family, the thinner were stretched the resources—economic resources, nutrition, parental love, parental attention, and so forth (cf. Jacobs & Moss, 1976; Kellaghan & MacNamera, 1972; Lasko, 1954; Lewis & Kreitzberg, 1980; Strodtbeck & Creeland, 1968; Walberg & Marjoribanks, 1976). Blake's conclusion from that research was to support the dilution model, suggesting that "on average, the more children the lower the quality of each child" (Blake, 1981, p. 421). The data Blake used to evaluate the dilution model came from five cross-sectional U.S. surveys, each containing several thousand respondents.

In the psychological literature, Zajonc and his colleagues proposed and tested the *confluence model* (e.g., Zajonc, 1976; Zajonc & Markus, 1975; Zajonc et al., 1979). Like Blake's (1981) dilution model, the confluence model suggested that the family structure—birth order, family size, and child spacing—has important influences on intellectual development in children. The empirical stimulus for the confluence model was the highly systematic pattern of IQ scores across birth order and family size categories in a study by Belmont and Marolla (1973). Belmont and Marolla's data came from a large cross-section of Dutch men drafted into the military during World War II. . . . After building the confluence model to fit the patterns in Belmont and Marolla's data, Zajonc published a number of tests of the confluence model using large national cross-sectional samples from a number of other countries (e.g., Zajonc, 1976; Zajonc & Bargh, 1980). He is still actively promoting the value of the confluence model as a predictive and explanatory model of the relationship between birth order and IQ (Zajonc & Mullally, 1997). . . .

The third model of the relationship between birth order and IQ was proposed by the educational researcher Ellis Page. His research team proposed an *admixture hypothesis*, suggesting that birth order and family size do not cause IQ (or other ability) differences, but rather are themselves caused by the distribution of intelligence among parents in the population (Page & Grandon, 1979; Velandia, Grandon, & Page, 1978). Page and his colleagues also used national cross-sectional data to evaluate the validity of their admixture hypothesis. This model suggests that causal processes linking birth order and IQ operate outside the family, creating between-family (but no within-family) variance. It is obviously a different type of explanatory model than either the dilution or confluence models, both of which explain differences inside the family among different siblings. . . .

These three theoretical developments illustrate that the question of whether birth order affects intelligence does not emerge from analysis of cross-sectional data with a clean answer. Fine scholars have observed the same types of patterns and arrived at completely different models to account for the patterns. Blake (1968, 1981) and Zajonc et al. (1979; Zajonc & Mullally, 1997) developed explanations that involved within-family processes. Page and Grandon (1979; Velandia et al., 1978) and Higgins et al. (1962) developed explanations that involved between-family processes. One or the other (or neither or both) of these processes may indeed be occurring, but their status cannot be logically evaluated using cross-sectional data. However, designs based on a different type of data can resolve this issue. Only analysis of within-family data can logically distinguish between within-family and between-family explanations of the relationship between IQ and birth order.

Which Comes First, Large Families or Low IQ?

The goal of the present article is to reframe the problem with which Blake, Page, Zajonc, Higgins, and many others have been concerned. The dilution model and the confluence model were built on the assumption that large families make low-IQ children: This position holds that the birth of an additional child will negatively impact the intellectual development of all children in the family from that point on. Further, children born into families with one or more siblings will be at an intellectual disadvantage compared with their status if they had been born into families with fewer (or no) older children. This position predicts birth order and family size patterns similar to those in Belmont and Marolla's (1973) data. . . . It is easy to see how a scientist studying the patterns in Belmont and Marolla's data would arrive at a within-family explanation for those patterns.

On the other hand, the admixture hypothesis assumes that low-IQ parents make large families. If this were true, we would expect a negative relationship between family size and IQ to the extent that parents' IQ is passed on to their children through either genetic or environmental processes (or interactions between the two). In cross-sectional data, an admixture hypothesis can also lead to a negative relationship between birth order and IQ for less obvious but very important reasons. For example, along with a dilution process, Blake (1981) described a famine in Holland in 1944 and 1945 that differentially affected poor families represented in Belmont and Marolla's (1973) data. She argued that childbearing stopped sooner than intended in such families, resulting in last-born children who would not have been born last in larger families if the famine had not occurred. This, Blake surmised, caused the last-born discontinuity in Belmont and Marolla's data, resulting in an apparent birth order effect tied to last-born children (an effect that Zajonc's confluence model explains with an alternative within-family tutoring explanation). This part of Blake's theory is admixture reasoning that places causal influence outside rather than inside the family environment. . . .

The most important methodological point in this article is that cross-sectional data are so filled with potential selection (and other) biases as to be virtually useless in addressing birth order effects on intelligence. Yet, most of what researchers know (or believe that they know) about family structure and its influence on intellectual development derives from cross-sectional data. To illustrate, imagine comparing the first-born child in a large middle-class White family in Michigan to the second-born child in a medium-sized affluent Black family in Atlanta to a third-born child in a small low-income Hispanic family in California. If differences between these children's intelligence are observed, it is impossible to tell whether they are due to SES, race, region of the country, birth order, family size, or other variables related to these. Yet, that is exactly the type of comparison that arises from cross-sectional data. There are several approaches to treating selection bias, including using covariates, change models, or instrumental variable approaches, but the most direct approach is to compare children who actually share a family environment. The goal of this article is, in a sense, to start over and account for what is known and what can be learned, by developing a logic that can rule out most of the selection biases inherent in cross-sectional data.

Family size is a measure of differences between families. At a given point in time, all of the children in a family environment share their family size. Alternatively, birth order is a within-family measure. To compare a first-born child to a second-born (or fifth-born) child is a statement about processes that operate within families. Cross-sectional data contain only between-family variance and confound explanations that apply inside the family with those that apply outside the family. Thus, they are logically incapable of resolving questions about within-family processes.

Alternatively, a more effective research design to evaluate birth order effects requires within-family data. Ideally, researchers would use complete intact-family data, that is, information from all of the children in a household from a number of families. Within-family data that come from several (but not all) siblings in a family are an effective substitute. The importance of using within-family data has been recognized for some time. Berbaum and Moreland (1980) stated the problem particularly well:

> What assurance have we that the aggregate-level process that produces mean scores for given family sizes and birth orders, and that the confluence model seems to capture reasonably well, is the same process that produces scores for particular individuals in a particular family? (p. 507).

Rodgers (1988) suggested that "studies using within-family longitudinal data must be used to evaluate theories of within-family processes" (p. 477). During the 1970s when these competing theoretical explanations were being developed, only a few data sources were available that contained intact-family (or longitudinal) structure. However, such data are critical, because they contain both between- and within-family variance, which can support a design that allows separation of the competing sources of influence to distinguish explanations that apply inside the family from those that apply outside the family.

Do large families cause low-IQ children, or do low-IQ parents make large families? These two questions imply extremely different processes. At a practical level, parents should act completely differently in planning and raising their families, depending on the status of each interpretation. Research could hardly have more important policy implications than to inform parents about having and raising children. How can within-family data be used to determine whether large families make low-IQ children or low-IQ parents make large families? The evaluation of those two competing hypotheses relies on a simple observation. In a typical family, each successive child is born into a larger family than the previous one. (This, of course, assumes away problems with splitting families because of divorce, newly blended families, etc. Although such problems are prevalent and common in today's society, they do little damage to statements about average families.) If additional children—through confluence, dilution, nutrition, or other family- or parent-driven processes—lead to lower IQs, this will result in declines in IQ across birth order within a particular family size in intact-family data.

On the other hand, if low-IQ parents are having large families, we would expect (statistically) flat patterns across birth order within family size categories in intact-family data. However, we would expect differences across family size, because family size measures the differences between families. It is an important strength of within-family data that both effects can be identified (or rejected) simultaneously using this type of data. If both of the within- and between-family processes described above are operating, we expect to find patterns in within-family data similar to those in Belmont and Marolla's (1973) cross-sectional (between-family) data. This logic allows us to rely on graphical presentation of these patterns and statistical tests of birth order and family size effects as basic tests of the competing models built into our title. . . .

Method

Data

[W]e have two overall data sets, one from 1990/1992 that included 2,566 children with an average age of 10.4 and the other from 1994/1996 that included 2,541 children with an average age of 10.7. In addition, we have three smaller subsets of data, the 1990/1992 data on younger children that included 1,206 children of average age 8.3, the 1990/1992 data on older children that included 1,352 children of average age 12.2, and the 1994/1996 data on young adolescents that included 383 children of average age 14.2.

. . . . The NLSY's [National Longitudinal Survey of Youth] unique design allows us to address the question of whether large families make low-IQ children or low-IQ parents make large families, because it contains IQ information about both the children and their mothers. This type of within-family information—in which both within-generational sibling data and cross-generational mother–child data are available—is particularly unusual. Chase-Lansdale, Mott, Brooks-Gunn, and Phillips (1991) have given a detailed account of the unique features of the NLSY data.

Dependent Variables

For our analysis, we needed a reliable and valid general measure of IQ/achievement. Our basic dependent variable was obtained by averaging the PIAT [Peabody Individual Achievement Test] subscales from Reading Recognition, Reading Comprehension, and Mathematics Achievement for two consecutive administrations of those instruments. For the 1990/1992 data set, we used the average of the six nonmissing PIAT scores in 1990 and 1992. For the 1994/1996 data set, we used the average of the six nonmissing PIAT scores from 1994 and 1996. The *NLSY Child Handbook* (Center for Human Resource Research, 1993) summarizes the use of the PIAT in the NLSY survey as follows: "It is among the most widely used brief assessments of academic achievement having demonstrably high test–retest reliability and concurrent validity" (p. 133). The PIAT was administered to all NLSY children ages 5 to 15. Each score was a standard score, normed against the PIAT norming sample for each age, so that age adjustment was built into each of the six scores averaged together. The averaging of three subscales across two years provides a highly reliable measure of IQ.

We also analyzed the IQs of the mothers of the NLSY children. These scores came from the Armed Forces Qualifying Test, the IQ measures contained in the Armed Services Vocational Aptitude Battery. The 1980 computational procedure was a weighted combination of arithmetic reasoning, word knowledge, paragraph comprehension, and numerical operations, which was normed and converted to percentiles (see Center for Human Resource Research, 1994, p. 124, for further explanation). The overall mean percentiles in the NLSY data we used were below the 50% that would occur in representative samples of the United States for two reasons. First, minorities and low-income Whites were oversampled. Second, the women in the sample to whom children were born first (and who are therefore overrepresented in our families) had lower IQs than those who delayed childbearing.

Independent Variables

Indicators of birth order and family size for the children were obtained from the NLSY mothers. In the critical analyses, we eliminated families with missing data for one or more child. In this way, for example, all second-born children in the data set had their first-born siblings in the data set as well. However, for other analyses, we used the largest possible data set to optimize power and reliability. We clearly define the various subsets of the data in the Results section.

The siblings in the NLSY are a combination of full and half siblings (with a few adopted siblings as well). Linking algorithms have been developed to classify these different sibling categories (e.g., Rodgers, Rowe, & Li, 1994; van den Oord & Rowe, 1998). However, because birth order theories are silent with respect to genetic patterns (because genetic influences should average out across birth orders), we included all identified siblings of all statuses within this study. . . .

Conclusion

Results of the analysis of the NLSY data support the belief that low-IQ parents make large families and are inconsistent with the belief that large families make low-IQ children. They are, further, inconsistent with the more complex predictions of the confluence model. We are not aware of any large national data source containing within-family information that has been used for an analysis of this type. Previous work on national data sources has been cross-sectional and has led to many spurious attributions of the effect of birth order on intelligence. . . .

Zajonc et al. (1979) stated,

> Studies relating intellectual performance to birth order report conflicting results, some finding intellectual scores to increase, others to decrease with birth order. In contrast, the relationship between intellectual performance and family size is stable and consistently replicable. Why do these two highly related variables generate such divergent results? (p. 1325)

The answer is simple. Family size is a between-family measure. Parents with lower-IQs in the modern United States on average have larger families and have been having larger families for some time (see Higgins et al., 1962; Retherford & Sewell, 1988; also see Roberts, 1938, who presented a detailed analysis of British patterns from the early 20th century that show the same family size patterns). Thus, a consistent relationship between family size and IQ has been detected. Birth order is a within-family measure. If it is measured between families, however, as in cross-sectional samples, it acts as a proxy for between-family variables like SES, educational level, nutritional quality, maternal age, and so forth and shows apparent relationships between birth order and IQ. However, when it is measured within families, where a within-family measure should be observed, the differences disappear. It appears that the admixture hypothesis suggested by Page and Grandon (1979; Velandia et al., 1978), although less well known than the dilution or confluence models, is the one that provides the best explanation for why cross-sectional patterns appear so consistent.

A large amount of publicity has circulated over the past two decades suggesting to parents that they should limit their family size in the interest of, in Blake's (1981) words, "child quality." Zajonc (1975) published a popular article entitled "Dumber by the Dozen" that certainly must have led some parents to believe they should limit their childbearing lest they place their children into the diluted intellectual environment predicted for later birth orders, close spacing, and larger families. The columnist Dr. Joyce Brothers answered a question sent into *Good Housekeeping* (February, 1981) by a mother of four asking if she should consider having another baby as follows: "Studies have shown that children reared in small families are brighter, more creative, and more vigorous than those from large families." The studies to which she referred were, undoubtedly, based on cross-sectional data sources.

There are many good reasons why parents might consider limiting their family sizes. However, the belief that, for a particular set of parents in a modern country like the United States, a larger family will lead to children with lower IQs appears to be, simply, wrong. The belief that birth order effects on intelligence act directly to decrease the intelligence of children born later in a given family also appears to be, simply, wrong. The dilution theory, the confluence model, and other within-family theories have been successful in prediction because they contain components that take advantage of between-family differences, but as explanatory models, they are also, simply, wrong.

We hope that this article and the several others we have discussed that used within-family data will help parents understand the influences that are and are not important to developing children in modern and well-developed societies like those studied in the research we have presented and reviewed. To parents (and those who counsel, advise, and write for parents), we conclude with simple and straightforward answers to the questions that motivated this article: Have parents with lower IQs in the United States been making larger families? Yes. Do large U.S. families make low-IQ children? No. Are birth order and intelligence related to one another within U.S. families? No.

References

Belmont, L., & Marolla, F. A. (1973, December 14). Birth order, family size, and intelligence. *Science, 182,* 1096–1101.

Berbaum, M. L., & Moreland, R. L. (1980). Intellectual development within the family: A new application of the confluence model. *Developmental Psychology, 16,* 500–515.

Blake, J. (1968). Are babies consumer durables? *Population Studies, 22,* 5–25.

Blake, J. (1981). Family size and the quality of children. *Demography, 18,* 421–442.

Brothers, J. (1981, February). Large versus small families. *Good Housekeeping.*

Center for Human Resource Research. (1993). *NLSY child handbook.* Columbus, OH: Author.

Center for Human Resource Research. (1994). *NLS user's guide: 1994.* Columbus, OH: Author.

Chase-Lansdale, P., Mott, F. L., Brooks-Gunn, J., & Phillips, D. A. (1991). Children of the National Longitudinal Survey of Youth: A unique research opportunity. *Developmental Psychology, 27,* 918–931.

Galbraith, R. C. (1982). Sibling spacing and intellectual development: A closer look at the confluence models. *Developmental Psychology, 18,* 151–173.

Higgins, J. V., Reed, E., & Reed, S. C. (1962). Intelligence and family size: A paradox resolved. *Eugenics Quarterly, 9,* 84–90.

Jacobs, B. S., & Moss, H. A. (1976). Birth order and sex of sibling as determinants of mother–sibling interaction. *Child Development, 47,* 315–322.

Kellaghan, T., & MacNamera, J. (1972). Family correlates of verbal reasoning ability. *Developmental Psychology, 7,* 49–52.

Lasko, J. K. (1954). Parent behavior toward first and second children. *Genetics Psychology Monographs, 49,* 97–187.

Lewis, M., & Kreitzberg, V. S. (1980). Effects of birth order and spacing on mother–infant interactions. *Developmental Psychology, 15,* 617–625.

Page, E. B., & Grandon, G. (1979). Family configuration and mental ability: Two theories contrasted with U.S. data. *American Educational Research Journal, 16,* 257–272.

Retherford, R. D., & Sewell, W. H. (1988). Intelligence and family size reconsidered. *Social Biology, 35,* 1–40.

Retherford, R. D., & Sewell, W. H. (1991). Birth order and intelligence: Further tests of the confluence model. *American Sociological Review, 56,* 141–158.

Roberts, J. A. F. (1938). Intelligence and family size. *Eugenics Review, 30,* 237–247.

Rodgers, J. L. (1988). Birth order, SAT, and confluence: Spurious correlations and no causality. *American Psychologist, 43,* 476–477.

Rodgers, J. L., Rowe, D. C., & Li, C. (1994). Beyond nature versus nurture: DF analysis of nonshared influences on problem behaviors. *Developmental Psychology, 30,* 374–384.

Schooler, C. (1972). Birth order effects: Not here, not now! *Psychological Bulletin, 78,* 161–175.

Strodtbeck, F. L., & Creeland, P. G. (1968). The interaction linkage between family size, intelligence, and sex-role identity. *Journal of Marriage and the Family, 30,* 301–307.

Sulloway, F. J. (1996). *Born to rebel.* New York: Vintage.

Van den Oord, E. J. C. G., & Rowe, D. C. (1998). An examination of gene–environment interactions for academic achievement in a U.S. national survey. *Intelligence, 25,* 205–228.

Velandia, W., Grandon, G., & Page, E. B. (1978). Family size, birth order, and intelligence in a large South American sample. *American Educational Research Journal, 15,* 399–416.

Walberg, H. J., & Marjoribanks, K. (1976). Family environment and cognitive development: Twelve analytic models. *Review of Educational Research, 46,* 527–551.

Zajonc, R. B. (1975, January). Dumber by the dozen. *Psychology Today,* 37–43.

Zajonc, R. B. (1976, April 16). Family configuration and intelligence. *Science, 192,* 227–236.

Zajonc, R. B., & Bargh, J. (1980). Birth order, family size, and decline of SAT scores. *American Psychologist, 35,* 662–668.

Zajonc, R. B., & Markus, G. (1975). Birth order and intellectual development. *Psychological Review, 82,* 74–88.

Zajonc, R. B., Markus, H., & Markus, G. B. (1979). The birth order puzzle. *Journal of Personality and Social Psychology, 37,* 1325–1341.

Zajonc, R. B., & Mullally, P. R. (1997). Birth order: Reconciling conflicting effects. *American Psychologist, 52,* 685–699.

R. B. Zajonc

The Family Dynamics of Intellectual Development

Researchers' beliefs about the effects of family factors, such as relationships among siblings, the ages of parents, and especially birth rank and family size, range from an indisputable certainty (e.g., Breland, 1974; Eysenck & Cookson, 1970; Sulloway, 1996) to a complete denial (Rodgers, Cleveland, van den Oord, & Rowe, 2000; Schooler, 1972) that these factors influence intellectual and scholastic performance. Yet, for millennia, diverse societies and cultures have placed a great deal of faith in these family factors as predictors of positive outcomes. Birth rank is regarded as a proxy of promise, potential, and actual ability. Firstborn children, especially boys, are slated to assume responsibility for a family's fortunes, are preferred as leaders, are selected for important positions, are entrusted with power, are accorded primacy in succession to a family's assets, and are expected to assume major responsibility for aging parents (Sulloway, 1996). In Bali, children are given names according to their birth order: *Wayan* for the firstborn, *Madé* for the second, *Nyoman* for the third, and *Ktut* for the fourth. A look at a drawer of family photographs will reveal an overrepresentation of the firstborn.

When considering the intellectual development of children within the family, it is clear that each successive child enters into a different environment and begins a particular cycle of growth. At the same time, each successive child changes and keeps on changing the family environment. Diverse aspects of the family environment—social, economic, intellectual—that greet successive siblings must affect growing children in somewhat different ways. In this article, I consider only the intellectual aspects of siblings' changing environments. Thus, first children have their parents all to themselves. For parents, this is novel and absorbing. Life will never be the same for them. Joy, pride, concern, anxiety, and fulfillment dominate parents' dispositions, and all reactions to first infants' behaviors carry an element of uncertainty and require constant adaptation.

On the birth of a second child, experience makes caregiving easier and allows parents to be a lot calmer. Of course, two children are more demanding of parents' time and care than one child is. Parents make adjustments, which are accompanied by concern that the firstborn should not be neglected, that jealousies should not develop, and that the siblings should grow free of conflict. In different families, successive children follow these patterns to a greater or lesser extent.

These differences within each family's environment are revealed in the personality, occupational, and intellectual development of successive children. The trajectory of children's intellectual development is especially complex, and its effects are subtle. Looking at children's periods of growth, I start with firstborn children who—until there is another birth—are families' only objects of care. I limit myself here to just one aspect of the intellectual environment that might affect children's intellectual growth—the pool of words, or the lexical surround. If researchers were to register all the words and utterances to which newborns are exposed, and if they could measure the diversity, the sophistication, the use of metaphors and analogies, and the exercise of precision in expression, they might be able to capture the quality of the lexical surround to which children are exposed on a daily basis.

Firstborn children, until the birth of younger siblings, are exposed only to adult language. If no other siblings enter the family, only children will continue in this fairly unchanging environment until they achieve full mental maturity, but the story is different for second-born children. Second children are exposed not only to the verbal output of the parents but to the vocalizations of older siblings and, if there is a substantial gap between the two births, to the verbal output of older siblings. Depending on the mental maturity of the older siblings, this lexical surround may be more or less mature. If a sibling is five years older, a different pool of words will characterize the environment than when a sibling is only one year older. This differential exposure may well manifest itself later in younger children's performance on tests of verbal fluency, vocabulary, and comprehension.

As the children mature, important features of the interactions among them emerge. Very often older siblings are called on, either by younger siblings or by parents, to act as parent surrogates. Second-born children might ask older siblings about the meanings of words, about how some things work and why, about the whereabouts of candy or of a parent who is late in coming back home, and about countless other matters that older siblings must now explain. When second-born children reach a level of maturity allowing them to ask these questions, then firstborn children's lives change quite dramatically—they become tutors. In this role of tutor, firstborn children gain an intellectual advantage. By virtue of rehearsal, by virtue of having to articulate an explanation or offer the meaning of a word, firstborns gain more verbal fluency more quickly than the second-borns. However, younger siblings, if they are the last children in their families, will never act as tutors and thus are intellectually disadvantaged in comparison to older siblings. Last siblings are therefore in the same situation as are only children because neither group is offered the opportunity to be a tutor.

These dynamics of the intellectual development of siblings within families were quantified in the *confluence model* (Zajonc, 1976), so named because the mental maturities of children growing up in the same families flow together over time in their influence on each other, changing constantly over time and changing most profoundly when new offspring join the sibship or some family members leave. All family members contribute to the quality of the intellectual environment. The confluence model focuses mainly on intellectual influences, reflected in the measurable mental ages of individual family members. Although the developmental process within the family encompasses many other changes, other consequences (such as social efficacy or assertiveness) are not subject to analysis by the confluence model. This is so because the model can be tested only with reliable measurements of developmental outcomes of large populations, and among those, academic and intellectual performance offer such data sets.

The following simplified example illustrates the computation of predictions from the confluence model. The intellectual environment is quantified by assigning some numerical value, say in mental age units, to each person within the family. For instance, a value of 30 may be assigned to each of the parents and 0 to the newborn child, for an average of (30 + 30 + 0)/3 = 20. If a second child is born into the family when the firstborn is four years old, the average would be (30 + 30 + 4 + 0)/4 = 16. Say that after a lapse of three years, there is a third offspring. The average value is reduced further: (30 + 30 + 7 + 3 + 0)/5 = 14. Thus, each successive sibling is born into a weaker intellectual environment. Whereas at birth the intellectual environment of the firstborn surpasses that of the second born, things change very rapidly. It is important to note that when both children in the example above are tested at eight years of age, the averages are (30 + 30 + 8 + 4)/4 = 18 for the firstborn and (30 + 30 + 12 + 8)/4 = 20 for the second born. The second born benefits from a better environment because the later-born child has an older sibling, whereas at the same age of testing, the firstborn has a less mature sibling, a configuration that reverses the birth order effect at that age.

However, in addition to the overall intellectual environment, designated as α, that is illustrated by the above example, the confluence model implicates another important factor, the teaching function, designated as λ. This factor describes the benefits that accrue to older siblings from being tutors. Two or three years after firstborns gain a sibling, they can begin to assume tutorial functions—functions that benefit the tutor as much as the tutee. The two terms of the confluence equation contribute differentially to the growth of intellectual maturity, α negatively and λ positively, and the quality of the intellectual environment is simply the sum of α and λ at each given age. As the number of siblings increases, the intellectual environment in the family declines in its relative quality. The teaching function, however, whereby the older children serve as tutors to the younger ones, mitigates the negative effects of the expanding family. If a family has only two children, the firstborn will be the only one to benefit from a teaching function, λ, that reaches equality with the level of intellectual environment, α, at age 11 ±2 years. Note that last children (and, of course, all children are last for some period of time) do not benefit from the teaching function. Hence, the only child, who has no one to teach, is predicted to score at a lower level than the firstborn of two, a prediction confirmed repeatedly in a variety of data sets. This simplified example dramatizes the crucial importance of the age of testing in evaluating birth order and family size effects.

Birth Order and Family Size Effects Depend Crucially on the Age at Which Children Are Tested

Because some data reveal a positive relationship between birth order and test scores and other data reveal a negative or null relationship, many researchers have been led to conclude that no systematic effects on intellectual and academic performance should be expected from variations in birth order. Rodgers, Cleveland, van den Oord, and Rowe (2000), for example, claimed that "the apparent relation between birth order and intelligence has been a methodological illusion" (p. 599). The illusion has been created, according to Rodgers et al., by applying a cross-sectional analysis to data that should have been analyzed by comparing siblings within families. However, these seemingly contradictory results are in fact what would be expected from the confluence model, which, as was shown above, predicts birth order effects on intelligence to be age specific. When children are tested before age 11 ±2 years, the model predicts negative or no differences in intellectual level as a function of birth order and predicts a positive effect for individuals tested at more mature ages. The explanation is straightforward. The accumulations of the negative contributions of a growing α and the accumulations of the positive effects of λ have different trajectories. The benefits of teaching do not start at birth and at first grow less rapidly than the disadvantages of increasing sibships. The confluence model, therefore, predicts a negative influence or no influence of birth order (lower scores for high birth ranks) for ages less than 11 ±2 years and a positive influence of birth order (higher scores for high ranks) for children older than 11 ±2 years. These predictions have been confirmed by a large variety of data sets (Zajonc, 1983, pp. 475–480; Zajonc & Bargh, 1980b, p. 360; Zajonc, Markus, & Markus, 1979, pp. 1328–1338; Zajonc & Mullally, 1997, pp. 690–692), and this research has allowed psychologists to understand what appeared to be conflicting data on birth order, with some data showing a positive relation and others a negative relation to measured intellectual performance. . . .

Rodgers et al. (2000) recently asked whether "large families cause low-IQ children, or [whether] low-IQ parents make large families" (p. 603). Their answer drew on the patterns of birth order effects. According to Rodgers et al., if large families "caused" low-IQ children, "declines in IQ across birth order" (p. 603) would be expected, and they stated that "if low-IQ parents are having large families, we would expect (statistically) flat patterns across birth order" (p. 603). Because Rodgers et al. found their data to be flat across birth order, they took it as proven not that large families "cause low-IQ children" but instead that low-IQ parents tend to have large families. After noting that birth order effects are age specific, Rodgers et al. nevertheless supported their claim with data for populations right at the crossover age or younger, the age where the two terms of the confluence process cancel each other out. . . . Rodgers et al. acknowledged the absence from their analysis of data for populations above the crossover age merely as a "slight weakness" (p. 610). It is in fact a fatal flaw.

Within-Family Data Confound Birth Order and the Age at Which Children Are Tested

Rodgers et al. (2000) argued that aggregate birth order and family size data cannot be trusted because they "are so filled with potential selection (and other) biases as to be virtually useless" (p. 602). They claimed, as a virtue of their analysis, to rely exclusively on within-family data. However, if researchers test for differences among children within the same family at the same time, the children's ages will differ. Because birth order and family size effects are age specific, instead of conclusive data, a giant confound is created. A within-family analysis of birth order effects requires a longitudinal approach, where children of, for example, 9, 10, 11, 12, 13, 14, and 15 years of age are followed for several years and where, in order to control for period effects, the data for some 9-year-olds are collected at one period, and the data for other 9-year-olds are collected at later periods. This is a laborious project that would realize the virtues of a within-family design.

Cross-Sectional Data Reveal Variations With Age That Within-Family Data Obscure

Cross-sectional data have a useful purpose and can reveal phenomena that within-family designs are incapable of analyzing. I have chosen here a few previously published aggregate cross-sectional data sets. All are explained in great detail by the confluence model, and some offer precise numerical predictions. [Discussed are] two data sets and the simulation of these data calculated from the reparameterized confluence model (Zajonc & Bargh, 1980b, pp. 350–351).[1] [One set of data] represents the averages of nearly 800,000 scores of 17-year-old candidates for the National Merit Scholarship Qualification Test (Breland, 1974), [along with] the predicted values for these participants. [The second set of data] shows the data on an academic achievement test administered to 70,000 Scottish 11-year-olds (Scottish Council for Research on Education, 1949), [along with] the corresponding predicted values for these participants. Note that the data for the 17-year-olds show clear birth order and family size effects, with only children not achieving the highest scores but achieving scores about as high as those of the oldest children in three-child families. Note that in contrast, the 11-year-olds show no similar decline in scores with birth order, albeit they show clear family size effects. In both cases, the calculated values are quite close to the observed data (correlations of .94 and .98). The data and the predictions reflect the age specificity of the birth order effect and the decreasing of scores with an increase in family size. The Scottish sample, consistent with the age crossover prediction, also found that only children had the highest scores.

Only children never become tutors. Thus, although their intellectual environments include just their parents—a condition favoring higher scores—the absence of siblings denies them the benefits of the tutorial function that children with younger siblings enjoy. However, because the advantage of tutoring accrues slowly, only children show the highest scores until their crossover age (i.e., 11 ±2 years), and afterward, their scores drop relative to the top birth ranks. The pattern of data showing that the family size effect is not monotonic, but reaches maximum for families with two children, contradicts a number of theories. For instance, the *dilution theory* (Blake, 1981) attributed the decline of intellectual performance with birth order to dwindling resources per child. Downey (2001), favored the dilution theory mainly because of its simplicity. The fact that the nonmonotonicity of family size effects *contradicts* the dilution theory is dismissed outright. Downey appealed to Blake's conjecture that when there are difficulties with the first birth or with the marriage itself, families decide against a second child. Thus, only children score low on intellectual performance tests because families decide against a second child when the firstborn or the parents' marriage had difficulties. This conjecture, however, is unlikely to be of major importance because it features just one among what must be host of reasons for families having just one child, a circumstance that must apply only to a small minority of families.

Cross-Sectional Data Reveal National Trends That Within-Family Data Are Incapable of Demonstrating

Many other empirical patterns relate academic performance to birth rank—patterns that can be obtained only by using cross-sectional data. For example, the entire school population of Iowa completes proficiency tests in 3rd through 12th grades (ages 9 to 16 years). The U.S. Bureau of the Census (1951–1991) reports the number of births in each state broken down by the number of children previously born to the mother. From these figures, we can readily calculate the average birth order of a given Iowa cohort. . . . The association between the average order of cohort births and academic performance scores is striking, and similar equally compelling data have also been reported (Zajonc & Mullally, 1997). Within-family analysis would be incapable of revealing secular trends. . . .

Population Trends Show Variations with the Age at Which Children Are Tested

Using the data from the Iowa school proficiency tests and census, I plotted the average scores for each of the 10 grades, together with the average birth orders of these cohorts. . . . [A]s predicted by the confluence model, intellectual performance shows no variation with average birth rank when tested before age 11 ±2 years. However, starting with Grade 6 (or age 11 years), a relationship between the average scholastic achievement score and the cohort's birth order emerges and grows more distinct with age. Moreover, the sensitivity of the test scores to the cohort's birth order is striking. The scores reproduce the birth order trends very accurately. . . . If the analysis had stopped at the fifth grade (i.e., at the crossover age of 11 years), birth order effects would not have been detected.

Within-Family Data and a Massive Rise in National IQs

One important contradiction met by the arguments about the dynamics of family size and intellectual performance has its source in a vast analysis of cross-sectional data by Flynn (1987). If low-IQ parents tend to have large families, then Rodgers et al. (2000) must predict, other things being constant, steady declines in the nation's average IQ, because a giant proportion of IQ variance derives from parental IQ. Yet the opposite is blatantly true. Flynn has shown "massive IQ gains" (p. 171) over the past century—gains of three to seven IQ points per decade in 14 countries. It could be argued that the proportion of large families has declined during this period, thereby allowing average IQ to rise. However, because the IQ rise was extraordinary—one half of a standard deviation per decade—the contribution of the offspring of low-IQ parents would have to have been minuscule. In any event, these secular changes could not have been discovered using within-family data sets.

Conclusion

I have written before about the framing of the birth order question that is presented as an analysis of causes (Zajonc & Mullally, 1997). Rodgers et al. (2000), for example, asked, "do large families cause low-IQ children, or do low-IQ parents make large families" (p. 603)? Birth order and family size are not the sort of variables that translate into causes. They determine nothing in and of themselves. They are conditions that afford, mediate, or prevent an array of diverse outcomes, only one of them being a score on an intellectual performance test. A variety of what seem to be immutable personal attributes, for example, height, gender, skin color, and a host of others, also afford conditions that place members of a society thus characterized in relative advantage or disadvantage. In many societies, height favors leadership opportunities (Young & French, 1998), and gender and skin color dominate access to various scarce social resources, especially power. None of these factors are causes in the essentialist sense of the word. They are features of a social order that has organized institutional structures and behavioral norms for differential distribution of scarce resources, power, and status.

Like these other features, birth order affects differential distribution of society's resources, power, and status. If there is a belief within a culture that such personal attributes as intelligence, leadership, initiative, and so forth are positively associated with birth rank, then social practices and institutions will tend to confirm and reinforce such beliefs. In a recent study, Herrera (2000) asked 203 college students about the hypothetical birth order of various occupations. The correlation between birth rank and occupational prestige (Treiman, 1977) was a robust –.72. The result is far from an illusion; the consequences of gender, race, height, and birth rank differences penetrate people's lives on a real and daily basis.

Note

1. There are four other similar data sets (Zajonc & Bargh, 1980b, pp. 350–351) that I have not included here because of space constraints.

References

Blake, J. (1981). Family size and quality of children. *Demography, 18,* 421–442.

Breland, H. M. (1974). Birth order, family configuration, and verbal achievement. *Child Development, 45,* 1011–1019.

Downey, D. B. (2001). Number of siblings and intellectual development: The resource dilution explanation. *American Psychologist, 55,* 497–504.

Eysenck, H. J., & Cookson, D. (1970). Personality in primary school children: 3. Family background. *British Journal of Educational Psychology, 40,* 117–131.

Flynn, J. R. (1987). Massive IQ gains in 14 nations: What IQ tests really measure. *Psychological Bulletin, 101,* 171–191.

Herrera, N. C. (2000). *Birth rank and personality: Beliefs and their consequences.* Unpublished doctoral dissertation, Stanford University, Stanford, CA.

Rodgers, J. L., Cleveland, H. H., van den Oord, E., & Rowe, D. C. (2000). Resolving the debate over birth order, family size, and intelligence. *American Psychologist, 55,* 599–612.

Schooler, C. (1972). Birth order effects: Note here, not now! *Psychological Bulletin, 78,* 161–175.

Scottish Council for Research on Education. (1949). *The trend of Scottish intelligence.* London: University of London Press.

Sulloway, F. (1966). *Born to rebel: Birth order, family dynamics, and creative lives.* New York: Pantheon Books.

Treiman, D. J. (1977). *Occupational prestige in comparative perspective.* New York: Academic Press.

U.S. Bureau of the Census. (1951–1991). *Natality report.* Washington, DC: U.S. Government Printing Office.

Young, T. J., & French, L. A. (1998). Heights of U.S. presidents: A trend analysis for 1948–1996. *Perceptual and Motor Skills, 87,* 321–322.

Zajonc, R. B. (1976, April 16). Family configuration and intelligence. *Science, 192,* 227–236.

Zajonc, R. B. (1983). Validating the confluence model. *Psychological Bulletin, 93,* 457–480.

Zajonc, R. B., & Bargh, J. (1980). The confluence model: Parameter estimation in six divergent data sets on family factors and intelligence. *Intelligence, 4,* 349–361.

Zajonc, R. B., Markus, H., & Markus, G. B. (1979). The birth order puzzle. *Journal of Personality and Social Psychology, 37,* 1325–1341.

Zajonc, R. B., & Mullally, P. R. (1997). Birth order: Reconciling conflicting effects. *American Psychologist, 52,* 685–699.

POSTSCRIPT

Is the Birth Order Effect on Intelligence Real?

Rodgers, Cleveland, van den Oord, and Rowe believe that the statistical indications that birth order and intelligence are related are the results of flawed designs. They bring the research issue down to the question "Do large families cause low-IQ children, or do low-IQ parents make large families?" (page 603). Their analysis of data from the NLSY indicate that low-IQ parents make large families, which is consistent with the admixture hypothesis and inconsistent with Zajonc's confluence model. Zajonc replies by demonstrating how the confluence model can be used to show both the positive and negative influences of birth rank on intelligence. Zajonc also warns of the dangers of assuming cause and effect when only a relationship has been found.

These are difficult issues to study, even though at first glance birth order and intelligence may seem like straightforward variables. The theory or model one chooses to examine, in this case the admixture or confluence models, will often determine the research questions. The choice of research design, whether cross-sectional, longitudinal, within-families, between-families, or some modified combination, is critical to the interpretation of the outcomes. The choice of instruments for measuring intelligence is critically important. A quick review of the scientific literature on intelligence testing will show that area to be full of controversy and disagreement. And even the issue of birth order itself is less than straightforward.

As the family system in Western society continues to evolve, the variable of birth order is growing more and more complex. How might the influence of birth order be different in a blended family in which stepchildren are involved? How might the influence be different in situations where children stay together for part of the time and then separate to stay with divorced parents for small amounts of time? Referring to this issue of divorcing and remarried or blended families, Rodgers, et al., state, "Although such problems are prevalent and common in today's society, they do little damage to statements about average families" (page 603). Do you agree?

There are other variables that might interact with birth order to influence intellectual development. Zajonc discussed the tutoring role of firstborns, and perhaps that influence may be varied as well. Do you think it would make a difference in the amount and effectiveness of tutoring if the siblings were of the same gender or different genders? In situations where the siblings were of different genders, do you think it would make a difference if a boy were older or a girl were older? Do you think that culture or ethnicity might influence gender roles, and that culture-gender influence might further influence the expectations of older boys or older girls in different ways?

Finally, perhaps the most important lesson to be learned from this debate is that complex issues such as these are not likely to be resolved by one study, one model, one design, or even one research team. Sometimes the most useful question is not "Is there a relationship?" but rather "Is the relationship strong enough to warrant our attention?" Rodgers and his colleagues believe the supposed relationship is a "methodological illusion" (page 599). Zajonc believes that the relationship is quite strong and certainly worthy of our attention.

Suggested Readings

Isaacson, C., and Radish, K. *The Birth Order Effect: How to Better Understand Yourself and Others* (Holbrook, MA: Adams Media Corporation, 2002).

Rodgers, J. L. "What Causes Birth Order—Intelligence Patterns?" *American Psychologist* (June/July 2001).

Sangwan, S. "Ecological Factors as Related to I.Q. of Children," *Psycho-Lingua* (July 2001).

Zajonc, R. B., Apsley, D. K., and Bargh, J. A. *Unraveling the Complexities of Social Life: A Festschrift in Honor of Robert B. Zajonc* (Washington, DC: American Psychological Association, 2001).

On the Internet . . .

David G. Myers, a well-known psychologist, has the introduction to his book *Intuition: Its Powers & Perils* on-line, as well as links to related information.

http://www.davidmyers.org/intuition/Intro.html

If you are interested in moral reasoning, values, ethics, or character development, then take a look at the list of links offered by the Association for Moral Education.

http://www.amenetwork.org/links/

St. Louis University offers a Web site explaining the concept of neural networks. The graphics are very helpful.

http://hem.hj.se/~de96klda/NeuralNetworks.htm

Robert Sternberg, who is mentioned several times in this volume, gives a summary of his theories and research on intelligence and wisdom, as well as some of his other interests, including creativity and love.

http://www.yale.edu/rjsternberg/

PART 6

Reasoning and Intuition

The areas of focus for the last section of this volume are the advanced, complex topics of reasoning and intuition. These higher-order cognitive processes require all the building blocks seen in issues prior to this: mind/brain, conceptual understanding, memory skills, language skills, and intelligence. In this section, you will become familiar with moral reasoning as it relates to neural networks in artificial intelligence and social intuition, intuition as a type of expertise, and wisdom as the ultimate form of cognition.

- Can a Neural Network Model Account for Moral Development?
- Do We Use Reasoning to Make Moral Decisions?
- Is Intuition a Valid Way of Knowing?
- Should Schools Teach for Wisdom?

ISSUE 15

Can a Neural Network Model Account for Moral Development?

YES: Paul M. Churchland, from "Toward a Cognitive Neurobiology of the Moral Virtues," *The Foundations of Cognitive Science* (2001)

NO: Darcia Narvaez and Tonia Bock, from "Moral Schemas and Tacit Judgement or How the Defining Issues Test Is Supported by Cognitive Science," *Journal of Moral Education* (2002)

ISSUE SUMMARY

YES: Professor of philosophy Paul Churchland offers a cognitive science view of human moral reasoning through the development of a neural network model.

NO: Moral development researchers Darcia Narvaez and Tonia Bock rely on the cognitive science of Piaget and information processing theory to explain moral reasoning.

Much of the research in the field of artificial intelligence (AI) involves reinterpreting standard psychological or philosophical explanations for human thought and behavior in terms of physiological brain computing and artificial or computer software programming. The assumption of an analogous relationship between the neurobiological structure of our brains and the logic-based programming of complex computer software is so strong, it is almost treated as fact. In the first selection, Churchland offers, at least in theory, an explanation of how an AI program might learn to determine and apply appropriate moral virtues.

Churchland begins by explaining a rather simple neural network design. Notice that the use of the term *neural network* can be used in reference to literal neurons in a human brain or electrical pathways or connections between data in a computer software program. The basic design involves an input layer, output layer, and a hidden layer in the middle. To illustrate this, let's take one part of Churchland's example of recognizing male and female faces. The input layer is made of the sensory information taken in when viewing a face. Whether it is our brain decoding the information from our optic nerves, or a computer software program analyzing a camera shot, the information must be input into the system. The output layer is the final determination as to whether the face is male or female. In our brains, this output may be in the form of a thought. For a computer program, the output may be the word *male* or *female* in a designated place on a screen. The hidden layer is where all the action is. In this layer, connections must be made between the input and output. In AI programs, these connections are often mathematical. AI programs *learn* from their successes (hits) and failures (misses) by making their own adjustments in these mathematical connections.

Churchland's use of neural network models is not new, but his application of the model to moral reasoning is quite radical. Using the standard neural network model to describe such a complex, higher-order level of cognition is ambitious. This notion of moral development is also quite different from the standard views of developmental psychologists, as represented by Narvaez and Bock in the second selection.

For the past forty years, the work of Lawrence Kohlberg has served as the foundation for research in moral reasoning. His work, beginning with his doctoral dissertation in 1958, brought together philosophical models of reasoning and Piaget's model of cognitive development. Kohlberg viewed moral reasoning as the process of determining the best approach to a dilemma or conflict that involves our personal values. The most common example of Kohlberg's many moral dilemmas is the *Heinz Dilemma*. Consider the following:

> In Europe, a woman was near death from a special kind of cancer. There was one drug that the doctors thought might save her. The drug was expensive to make, but the druggist was charging ten times what the drug cost him to make. The sick woman's husband, Heinz, went to everyone he knew to borrow the money, but he could only get together about half of what it cost. He told the druggist that his wife was dying and asked him to sell it cheaper or let him pay later. But the druggist said, "No, I discovered the drug and I'm going to make money from it." So Heinz got desperate and broke into the man's store to steal the drug for his wife. [Kohlberg, L. (1984). *Essays on Moral Development, Volume 2: The Psychology of Moral Development*. San Francisco: Harper & Row.]

This dilemma requires you to consider several issues, such as the importance of saving a life, the importance of obeying the law, and the right to own inventions and property. Many years of research using Kohlbergian-type dilemmas has demonstrated that people of different ages respond differently to this and other dilemmas, indicating that most people go through six distinct stages of moral reasoning. In the second selection, Narvaez and Bock refer to two popular tests of moral development: the Moral Judgment Interview (MJI) and the Defining Issues Test (DIT). They are different in that the MJI asks the participant to discuss the dilemma, whereas the DIT gives various responses to the dilemma and the participant must choose the response closest to his or her own.

Paul M. Churchland

Toward a Cognitive Neurobiology of the Moral Virtues

The Reconstruction of Moral Cognitive Phenomena in Cognitive Neurobiological Terms

This essay builds on work now a decade or so in place, work concerning the capacity of recent neural-network models (of micro-level brain activity) to reconstruct, in an explanatory way, the salient features of molar-level cognitive activity. That research began in the mid-1980s by addressing the problems of perceptual recognition, motor-behavior generation, and other basic phenomena involving the gradual learning of sundry cognitive *skills* by artificial "neural" networks, as modeled within large digital computers (Gorman and Sejnowski 1988; Lehky and Sejnowski 1988; Rosenberg and Sejnowski 1990; Lockery, Fang, and Sejnowski 1991; Cottrell 1991; Elman 1992). From there, it has moved both downward in its focus, to try to address in more faithful detail the empirical structure of biological brains (P. S. Churchland and Sejnowski 1992), and upward in its focus, to address the structure and dynamics of such higher-level cognitive phenomena as are displayed, for example, in the human pursuit of the various theoretical sciences (P. M. Churchland 1989*a*). . . .

Moral Knowledge

Broadly speaking, to teach or train any neural network to embody a specific cognitive capacity is gradually to impose a specific *function* onto its input–output behavior. The network thus acquires the ability to respond, in various but systematic ways, to a wide variety of potential sensory inputs. In a simple, three-layer feedforward network with fixed synaptic connections, the output behavior at the third layer of neurons is completely determined by the activity at the sensory input layer. In a (biologically more realistic) *recurrent* network, the output behavior is jointly determined by sensory

From Paul Churchland's THE FOUNDATION OF COGNITIVE SCIENCE, July 2001, pp. 77–87, 90–94.

input *and* the prior dynamical state of the entire network. The purely feedforward case yields a cognitive capacity that is sensitive to spatial patterns but blind to temporal patterns or to temporal context; the recurrent network yields a capacity that is sensitive to, and responsive to, the changing cognitive contexts in which its sensory inputs are variously received. In both cases, the acquired cognitive capacity actually resides in the specific configuration of the many synaptic *connections* between the neuronal layers, and learning that cognitive capacity is a matter of slowly adjusting the size or "weight" of each connection so that, collectively, they come to embody the input–output function desired. . . .

According to the model of cognition here being explored, the skills at issue are embodied in a vast configuration of appropriately weighted synaptic connections. To be sure, it is not intuitively obvious how a thousand, or a billion, or a trillion such connections can constitute a specific cognitive skill, but we begin to get an intuitive grasp of how they can do so when we turn our attention to the collective behavior of the neurons at the layer to which those carefully configured connections happen to attach.

[A] neuronal population, like any other discrete neuronal population, represents the various states of the world with a corresponding variety of *activation patterns* across that entire population. That is to say, just as a pattern of brightness levels across the 200,000 pixels of your familiar TV screen can represent a certain two-dimensional scene, so can the pattern of activation levels across a neuronal population represent specific aspects of the external world, although the "semantics" of that representational relation will only rarely be so obviously "pictorial." If the neuronal representation is auditory, for example, or olfactory, or gustatory, then obviously the representation will be something other than a 2-D "picture".

What is important for our purposes is that the abstract *space of possible* representational patterns, across a given neuronal population, slowly acquires, in the course of training the synapses, a specific structure—a structure that assigns a family of dramatically preferential abstract *locations,* within that space, in response to a preferred family of distinct stimuli at the network's sensory layer. This is how the mature network manages to categorize all possible inputs, either as rough instances of one-or-other of its learned family of prototypical *categories*, or, failing that, as instances of unintelligible noise. Before training, *all* inputs produce noise at the second layer. After training, however, that second layer has become preferentially sensitized to a comparatively tiny subset of the vast range of possible input patterns (most of which are never encountered). Those "hot-button" input patterns, whenever they occur, are subsequently assimilated to the second layer's acquired set of *prototypical categories.*

Consider an artificial network trained to discriminate human faces from nonfaces, male faces from female faces, and a handful of named individuals as presented in a variety of distinct photographs. As a result of that training, the abstract space of *possible* activation patterns across its second neuronal layer has become *partitioned,* first into a pair of complementary subvolumes for neuronal activation patterns that represent sundry faces and nonfaces respectively. The former subvolume has become further partitioned into two mutually exclusive subvolumes for male faces and female spaces respectively. And within each of these two subvolumes there are proprietary "hot-spots" for each of the named individuals that the network learned to recognize during training.

Following this simple model, the suggestion here advanced is that our capacity for *moral* discrimination also resides in an intricately configured matrix of synaptic connections, which connections also partition an abstract conceptual space, at some proprietary neuronal layer of the human brain, into a hierarchical set of categories, categories such as "morally significant" vs. "morally nonsignificant" actions; and within the former category, "morally bad" vs. "morally praiseworthy" actions; and within the former subcategory, sundry specific categories such as "lying", "cheating", "betraying", "stealing", "tormenting", "murdering", and so forth. . . .

Moral Learning

Moral learning consists in the gradual generation of these internal perceptual and behavioral prototypes, a process that requires repeated exposure to, or practice of, various *examples* of the perceptual or motor categories at issue. In artificial neural networks, such learning consists in the repeated adjustment of the weights of their myriad synaptic connections, adjustments that are guided by the naive network's initial performance *failures,* as measured by a distinct "teacher" program. In living creatures, learning also consists in the repeated adjustment of one's myriad synaptic connections, a process that is also driven by one's ongoing experience with failure. Our artificial "learning technologies" are currently a poor and pale reflection of what goes on in real brains, but in both cases—the artificial networks and living brains—those gradual synaptic readjustments lead to an appropriately structured high-dimensional similarity space, a space partitioned into a hierarchical family of categorial subspaces, which subspaces contain a central hot spot that represents a *prototypical* instance of its proprietary category.

Such learning typically takes time, often large amounts of time. And as the network models have also illustrated, such learning often needs to be structured, in the sense that the simplest of the relevant perceptual and behavioral skills need to be learned first, with the more sophisticated skills being learned later, and only after the elementary ones are in place. Moreover, such learning can display some familiar pathologies, those that derive from a narrow or otherwise skewed population of training examples. In such cases, the categorial framework duly acquired by the network fails to represent the full range and true structure of the social/moral domain it needs to represent, and performance failures are the inevitable result.

These remarks barely introduce the topic of moral learning, but we need to move on. The topic will be readdressed below, when we discuss moral progress.

Moral Perception

[M]oral perception displays the familiar tendency of cognitive creatures to "jump to conclusions" in their perceptual interpretations of partial or degraded perceptual inputs. Like artificial networks, we humans have a strong tendency automatically to assimilate our current perceptual circumstances to the nearest of the available moral prototypes that our prior training has created in us.

Moral Ambiguity

A situation is morally ambiguous when it is problematic by reason of its tendency to activate *more than one* moral prototype, prototypes that invite two incompatible or mutually exclusive subsequent courses of action. In fact, and to some degree, ambiguity is a chronic feature of our moral experience, partly because the social world is indefinitely complex and various, and partly because the interests and collateral information each of us brings to the business of interpreting the social world differ from person to person and from occasion to occasion. The recurrent or descending pathways within the brain provide a continuing stream of such background information (or misinformation) to the ongoing process of perceptual interpretation and prototype activation. Different "perceptual takes", on one and the same situation, are thus inevitable. Which leads us to our next topic.

Moral Conflict

The activation of distinct moral prototypes can happen in two or more distinct individuals confronting the same situation, and even in a single individual, as when some contextual feature is alternately magnified or minimized and one's overall perceptual take flips back and forth between two distinct activation patterns in the neighborhood of two distinct prototypes. In such a case, the single individual is morally conflicted ("Shall I *protect* a friend's feelings by keeping silent on someone's trivial but hurtful slur, or shall I be forthright and *truthful* in my disclosures to a friend?").

*Inter*personal conflicts about the moral status of some circumstance reflect the same sorts of divergent interpretations, driven this time by interpersonal divergences in the respective collateral information, attentional focus, hopes and fears, and other contextual elements that each perceiver brings to the ambiguous situation. Occasional moral conflicts are thus possible, indeed, they are inevitable, even between individuals who had identical moral training and who share identical moral categories.

There is, finally, the extreme case where moral judgment diverges because the two conflicting individuals have fundamentally different moral conceptual frameworks, reflecting major differences in the acquired structure of their respective activation spaces. Here, even communication becomes difficult, and so does the process by which moral conflicts are typically resolved. . . .

Moral Virtues

These are the various skills of social *perception,* social *reflection, imagination,* and *reasoning,* and social *navigation* and *manipulation* that normal social learning produces. In childhood, one must come to appreciate the high-dimensional background structure of social space—its offices, its practices, its prohibitions, its commerce—and one must learn to recognize its local configuration swiftly and reliably. One must also learn to recognize one's own current position within it, and the often quite different positions of others. One must learn to anticipate the normal unfolding of this ongoing commerce, to recognize and help repair its occasional pathologies, and to navigate its fluid structure while avoiding social disasters, both large and small. All of this requires skill in divining the social perceptions and personal interests of others, and skill in manipulating and negotiating our collective behavior.

Being skills, such virtues are inevitably acquired rather slowly, as will be familiar to anyone who has raised children. Nor need their continued development ever cease, at least in individuals with the continued opportunities and the intelligence necessary to refine them. The acquired structures within one's neuronal activation spaces—both perceptual and motor—can continue to be sculpted by ongoing experience and can thus pursue an ever deeper insight into, and an effectively controlling grasp of, one's enclosing social reality. Being skills, they are also differently acquired by distinct individuals, and they are differentially acquired within a single individual. Each brain is slightly different from every other in its initial physical structure, and each brain's learning history is unique in its myriad details. No two of us are identical in the profile of skills we acquire, which raises our next topic.

Moral Character

A person's unique moral character is just the individual profile of his perceptual, reflective, and behavioral skills in the social domain. From what has already been said, it will be evident that moral character is distinguished more by its rich diversity across individuals than by its monotony. Given the difficulty in clearly specifying any canonical profile as being uniquely ideal, this is probably a good thing. Beyond the unending complexity of social space, the existence of a diversity of moral characters simply reflects a healthy tendency to explore that space and to explore the most effective styles of navigating it. . . .

This view of the assembled moral virtues as a slowly acquired network of skills also contains an implicit critique of a popular piece of romantic nonsense, namely, the idea of the "sudden convert" to morality, as typified by the "tearful face of the repentant sinner" and the post-baptismal "born-again" charismatic Christian. Moral character is not something—is *not remotely* something—that can be acquired in a day by an Act of Will or by a single Major Insight.

The idea that it can be so acquired is a falsifying reflection of one or other of two familiar conceptions of moral character, herewith discredited.

The first identifies moral character with the acceptance of a canonical set of behavior-guiding rules. The second identifies moral character with a canonical set of desires, such as the desire to maximize the general happiness, and so on. Perhaps one can embrace a set of rules in one cathartic act, and perhaps one can permanently privilege some set of desires by a major act of will. But neither act can result in what is truly needed, namely, an intricate set of finely honed perceptual, reflective, and sociomotor skills. These take several decades to acquire. Epiphanies of moral commitment can mark, at most, the initiation of such a process. Initiations are welcome, of course, but we do not give children a high-school diploma for showing up for school on the first day of the first grade. For the same reasons, "born-again" moral characters should probably wait a similar period of time before celebrating their moral achievement or pressing their moral authority. . . .

Moral Correction

Consider first the structurally and physiologically *normal* brain whose formative social environment fails to provide a normal moral education. The child's experience may lack the daily examples of normal moral behavior in others, it may lack opportunities to participate in normal social practices, it may fail to see others deal successfully and routinely with their inevitable social conflicts, and it may lack the normal background of elder sibling and parental correction of its perceptions and its behavior. For the problematic young adult that results, moral correction will obviously consist in the attempt somehow to make up a missed or substandard education.

That can be very difficult. The cognitive plasticity and eagerness to imitate found in children is much reduced in a young adult. And a young adult cannot easily find the kind of tolerant community of innocent peers and wise elders that most children are fortunate to grow up in. Thus, not one but two important windows of opportunity have been missed.

The problem is compounded by the fact that children in the impoverished social environments described do not simply fail to learn. Rather, they may learn quite well, but *what* they learn is a thoroughly twisted set of social and moral prototypes and an accompanying family of skills which—while crudely functional within the impoverished environment that shaped them, perhaps—are positively *dys*functional within the more coherent structure of society at large. This means that the young adult has some substantial *un*learning to do. Given the massive cognitive "inertia" characteristic even of normal humans, this makes the corrective slope even steeper, especially when young adult offenders are incarcerated in a closely-knit prison community of similarly twisted social agents.

This essay was not supposed to urge any substantive social or moral policies, but those who do trade in such matters may find relevant the following purely factual issues. America's budget for state and federal prisons is said to be somewhat larger than its budget for *all* of higher education, for its élite research universities, its massive state universities, its myriad liberal arts colleges, and all of its technical colleges and two-year junior colleges combined. It is at least conceivable that our enormous penal-system budget might be more wisely spent on prophylactic policies aimed at raising the quality of the social environment of disadvantaged children, rather than on policies that struggle, against much greater odds, to repair the damage once it is done.

A convulsive shift, of course, is not an option. Whatever else our prisons do or do not do, they keep at least some of the dangerously incompetent social agents and the outright predators off our streets and out of our social commerce. But the plasticity of the young over the old poses a constant invitation to shift our corrective resources childwards, as due prudence dictates. This policy suggestion hopes to reduce the absolute input to our correctional institutions. An equally important issue is how, in advance of such "utopian" advances, to increase the rate at which they are emptied, to which topic I now turn.

A final point, in this regard, about normals. The cognitive plasticity of the young—that is, their unparalleled capacity for learning—is owed to neurochemical and physiological factors that fade with age. (The local production and diffusion of nitric oxide within the brain is one theory of how some synaptic connections are made selectively subject to modification, and there are others.) Suppose that we were to learn how to *recreate* in young adults, temporarily and by neuropharmacological means, that perfectly normal regime of neural plasticity and learning aptitude found in children. In conjunction with some more effective programs of resocialization than we currently command (without them, the pharmacology will be a waste of time), this might re-launch the "disadvantaged normals" into something much closer to a normal social trajectory and out of prison for good.

There remain, alas, the genuine abnormals, for whom moral correction is first a matter of trying to repair or compensate for some structural or physiological defect(s) in brain function. Even if these people are hopeless, it will serve social policy to identify them reliably, if only to keep them permanently incarcerated or otherwise out of the social mainstream. But some, at least, will not be hopeless. Where the deficit is biochemical in nature—giving rise to chronically inappropriate emotional profiles, for example—neuropharmacological intervention, in the now-familiar form of chronic subdural implants, perhaps, will return some victims to something like a normal neural economy and a normal emotional profile. That will be benefit enough, but they will then also be candidates for the resocialization techniques imagined earlier for disadvantaged normals.

This discussion presumes far more neurological understanding than we currently possess, and is plain speculative as a result. But it does serve to illustrate some directions in which we might well wish to move, once our early understanding here has matured. In any case, I shall close this discussion by reemphasizing the universal importance of gradual socialization by long interaction with a moral order already in place. We will never create moral character by medical intervention alone. There are too many trillions of synaptic connections to be appropriately weighted and only long experience can hope to do that superlatively intricate job. The whole point of exploring the technologies mentioned above will be to maximize everyone's chances of engaging in and profiting from that traditional and irreplaceable process.

Moral Diversity

I here refer not to the high-dimensional bell-curve diversity of moral characters within a given culture at a given time, but to the nonidentity, across two cultures separated in space and or in time, of the overall *system* of moral prototypes and prized skills common to most normal members of each. Such major differences in moral consciousness typically reflect differences in substantive economic circumstances between the two cultures, in the peculiar threats to social order with which they have to deal, in the technologies they command, the metaphysical beliefs they happen to hold, and other accidents of history. Such diversity, when discovered, is often seen as grounds for a blanket skepticism about the objectivity or reality of moral knowledge. That was certainly its effect on me in my later childhood, a reaction reinforced by the astonishingly low level of moral argument I would regularly hear from my more religious schoolchums, and even from the local pulpits. But that is no longer my reaction, for throughout history there have been comparable differences, between distinct cultures, where *scientific* knowledge was concerned, and comparable block-headedness in purely "factual" reasoning (think of "New Age medicine", for example, or "UFOlogy"). But this very real diversity and equally lamentable sloppiness does not underwrite a blanket skepticism about the possibility of scientific knowledge. It merely shows that it is not easy to come by, and that its achievement requires a long-term process of careful and honest evaluation of a wide variety of complex experiments over a substantial range of human experience. Which points to our next topic.

Moral Progress

If it exists—there is some dispute about this—moral progress consists in the slow change and development, over historical periods, of the moral prototypes we teach our children and forcibly impose on derelict adults, a developmental process that is gradually instructed by our collective *experience* of a collective life lived under those perception-shaping and behavior-guiding prototypes.

From the neurocomputational perspective, this process looks different only in its ontological focus—the *social* world as opposed to the *natural* world—from what we are pleased to call *scientific* progress. In the natural sciences as well, achieving adult competence is a matter of acquiring a complex family of perceptual, reflective, and behavioral skills in the relevant field. And there, too, such skills are embodied in an acquired set of structural, dynamical, and manipulational prototypes. The occasional deflationary voice to the contrary, our scientific progress over the centuries is a dramatic and encouraging reality, and it results in part from the myriad instructions (often painful) of an ongoing experimental and technological life lived under those same perception-shaping and behavior-guiding scientific prototypes.

Our conceptual development in the moral domain, I suggest, differs only in detail from our development in the scientific domain. We even have institutions whose job it is continually to fine-tune and occasionally to reshape our conceptions of proper conduct, permissible practice, and proscribed behavior. Civic, state, and federal legislative bodies spring immediately to mind, as does the civil service, and so do the several levels of the judiciary and their ever-evolving bodies of case-law and decision-guiding legal precedents. As with our institutions for empirical science, these socially focused institutions typically outlive the people who pass through their offices, often by centuries and sometimes by many centuries. And as with the payoff from our scientific institutions, the payoff here is the accumulation of unprecedented levels of recorded (social) experience, the equilibrating benefits of collective decision making, and the resulting achievement of levels of moral understanding that are unachievable by a single individual in a single lifetime.

To this overarching parallel it may be objected that science addresses the ultimate nature of a fixed, stable, and independent reality, while our social, legislative, and legal institutions address a plastic reality that is deeply dependent on the organizing activity of humans. But this presumptive contrast disappears almost entirely when one sees the acquisition of both scientific and moral wisdom as the acquisition of sets of *skills*. Both address a presumptively *im*plastic part of their respective domains—the basic laws of nature in the former case, and basic human nature in the latter. And both address a profoundly *plastic* part of their respective domains—the articulation, manipulation, and technological exploitation of the natural world in the case of working science, and the articulation, manipulation, and practical exploitation of human nature in the case of working morals and politics. A prosperous city represents simultaneous success in both dimensions of human cognitive activity. And the resulting artificial technologies, both natural and social, each make possible a deeper insight into the basic character of the natural universe, and of human nature, respectively.

Moral Unity/Systematicity

This parallel with natural science has a further dimension. Just as progress in science occasionally leads to welcome unifications within our understanding—as when all planetary motions come to be seen as special cases of projectile motion, and all optical phenomena come to be seen as special cases of electromagnetic waves—so also does progress in moral theory bring occasional attempts at conceptual unification—as when our assembled obligations and prohibitions are all presented (by Hobbes) as elements of a *social contract,* or (by Kant) as the local instantiations of a *categorical imperative,* or (by Rawls) as the reflection of *rules rationally chosen from behind a veil of personal ignorance.* These familiar suggestions, and others, are competing attempts to unify and systematize our scattered moral intuitions or antecedent moral understanding, and they bring with them (or hope to bring with them) the same sorts of virtues displayed by intertheoretic reductions in science, namely, greater simplicity in our assembled conceptions, greater consistency in their application, and an enhanced capacity (born of increased generality) for dealing with novel kinds of social and moral problems.

As with earlier aspects of moral cognition, this sort of large-scale cognitive achievement is also comprehensible in neurocomputational terms, and it seems to involve the very same sorts of neurodynamical changes as are (presumptively) involved when theoretical insights occur within the natural sciences. Specifically, a wide range of perceptual phenomena—which (let us suppose) used to activate a large handful of distinct moral prototypes, $m_1, m_2, m_3, \ldots, m_n$—come to be processed under a new regime of recurrent manipulation (recall the recurrent neuronal pathways of Figure 1.1*b*) that results in them all activating an unexpected moral prototype *M*, a prototype whose typical deployment has hitherto been in other perceptual domains entirely, a prototype that now emerges as a *superordinate* prototype of which the scattered lesser prototypes, $m_1, m_2, m_3, \ldots, m_n$ can now be seen, retrospectively, as so many *sub*ordinate instances.

The preceding is a neural-network description of what happens when, for example, our scattered knowledge in some area gets *axiomatized*. But axiomatization, in the linguaformal guise typically displayed in textbooks, is but one minor instance of this much more general process, a process that embraces the many forms of *non*discursive knowledge as well, a process that embraces science and ethics alike. . . .

References

Churchland, P. M. (1989). *A Neurocomputational Perspective: The Nature of Mind and the Structure of Science* (Cambridge, Mass.: MIT Press).

Churchland, P. S., and Sejnowski, T. J. (1992). *The Computational Brain* (Cambridge, Mass.: MIT Press).

Cottrell, G. (1991). "Extracting Features from Faces Using Compression Networks: Face, Identity, Emotions and Gender Recognition Using Holons", in D. Touretzky, J. Elman, T. Sejnowski, and G. Hinton (eds.), *Connectionist Models: Proceedings of the 1990 Summer School*. San Mateo (Calif.: Morgan Kaufmann).

Elman, J. L. (1992). "Grammatical Structure and Distributed Representations", in S. Davis (ed.), *Connectionism: Theory and Practice*. Vancouver Studies in Cognitive Science, 3 (Oxford: Oxford University Press).

Gorman, R. P., and Sejnowski, T. J. (1988). "Analysis of Hidden Units in a Layered Network Trained to Classify Sonar Targets", *Neural Networks,* 1: 75–89.

Lehky, S., and Sejnowski, T. J. (1988). "Network Model of Shape-from-Shading: Neuronal Function Arises from Both Receptive and Projective Fields", *Nature,* 333: 452–4.

Lockery, S. R., Fang, Y., and Sejnowski, T. J. (1991). "A Dynamical Neural Network Model of Sensorimotor Transformation in the Leech", *Neural Computation,* 2: 274–82.

Rosenberg, C. R., and Sejnowski, T. J. (1990). "Parallel Networks that Learn to Pronounce English Text", *Complex Systems,* 1: 145–68.

Darcia Narvaez and Tonia Bock

NO

Moral Schemas and Tacit Judgement or How the Defining Issues Test Is Supported by Cognitive Science

Historically, philosophy has described moral judgement as conscious and deliberative decision-making. Consequently, studies of moral judgement usually focus on testing conscious, thoughtful reasoning about moral dilemmas (e.g. the Moral Judgement Interview [MJI], Colby, Kohlberg *et al.*, 1987; Moral Competence, Lind, 1995; Sociomoral Reflection Measure [SRM], Gibbs & Widaman, 1982), distributive justice (Damon, 1975; Enright *et al.*, 1981) and particular non-development distinctions in moral judgement (e.g. "domains," Turiel, 1983; "culture," Shweder, 1991; and "orientation," Lyons, 1982). Common to all these methods is the need for the participant to give a verbal rationale for a decision (orally, as in the MJI, or in writing, as in the SRM). It is assumed that participants make their moral judgements reflectively, that they are able to articulate them, and that the method can be "error-free" (Kohlberg, 1976). Participant verbalisations are purified of specific content and scored for evidence of underlying cognitive structures.

In this context, the Defining Issues Test (DIT) has always stood out as a measure "apart". Spawned from research in moral comprehension (Rest, 1973), the DIT originated as a cognitive-developmental tool that measures stage shifts in the upper half of Kohlberg's stage hierarchy. From the outset there was concern that the DIT did not really measure moral judgement structures because it did not ask respondents to produce an answer in their own words and because it hopelessly wedded content with structure. . . . Whereas the MJI measures explicit verbal knowledge, the DIT measures recognition knowledge, a type of tacit knowledge. Is one method better than the other? We believe that new constructs from cognitive science can direct our examination of this question and can help point out the merits of each approach.

From *Journal of Moral Education,* September 2002, pp. 297–314.

The study of human cognition in the 20th and 21st centuries offers many tools for measuring and understanding differences in morality and moral judgement. Three interwoven, core ideas emerging in cognitive science have particular implications for research in moral judgement.

First, cognitive science makes the assumption that an individual processes or interprets experience according to organising, conceptual structures in the mind that have developed from and are influenced by experience (e.g. Piaget, 1932/1965; Rumelhart, 1980; Fiske & Taylor, 1991). These conceptual structures, which are often called *schemas,* function as interpreters of stimuli. Although it may feel phenomenologically as if one experiences pure, raw "reality", everything perceived is interpreted by pre-existing mental structures (Wenger & Wheatley, 1999; Hogarth, 2001). In fact, no one can understand experience without such mental structures or schemas (Neisser, 1976). Not only perception, but decision-making and reasoning are supervised by pre-existing schemas (Gigerenzer *et al.,* 1999). Further, the vast majority of human responses, including moral judgements, are based on schemas (Bargh & Chartrand, 1999). We discuss schema theory in more detail later.

Secondly, many cognitive processes, including decisions, occur automatically without awareness (Reber, 1993). For example, schemas are activated without intention or conscious control (Hasher & Zacks, 1984). Some schemas may be activated chronically due to several factors, including frequency of environmental cues (Higgins & King, 1981). For example, in the United States, local television news stations highlight the types of local crimes that are more likely to be committed by individuals with lower socioeconomic status, showing photographs of the accused. Many of these individuals are black. Consequently, when a typical citizen is asked to think about a criminal, a black person "pops" into his or her mind, even though the statistical evidence shows that more crimes are committed by "whites", and that white males tend to be more violent. Like it or not, the schema fostered by local news is activated beyond personal control. Many schemas operate automatically like this. Automatic processing is understood to be characterised by some combination of the following: involuntariness, autonomy, existence outside of awareness, unintentionality (initiated with or without intention), and effortlessness—requiring little if any working memory resources (Bargh, 1989; Uleman & Bargh, 1989). Many daily actions and responses have a majority of these characteristics.

Thirdly, there is now a greater regard for the implicit processes and application of tacit knowledge in human decision-making that occur outside the awareness of the cogniser (e.g. Bargh, 1989) and beyond the participant's ability to verbally articulate (e.g. Kihlstrom *et al.,* 1996). Individuals have, use and are influenced by a great deal of knowledge without awareness (Reber, 1993; Hogarth, 2001). Various psychologists have pointed this out throughout the history of psychology, even in its early days (Helmholtz, 1867; Carpenter, 1874; Ebbinghaus, 1885) as have philosophers (e.g. Polanyi, 1968; von Hayek, 1962). Polanyi often noted that people "know more than they can say". . . .

The Nature of Schematic Processing

1. What are Schemas?

Schemas are sets of expectations, hypotheses and concepts that are formed as the individual notices similarities and recurrence in experience (Neisser, 1976; Rumelhart, 1980). For example, the toddler learns that certain behaviours agitate the parent, some of which result in discomfort (physical and/or emotional) for the child. Other behaviours elicit praise from the parent. With repeated experience, the child begins to expect the particular matching reaction of the parent when the behaviour is exhibited. If the parent, for example, shows the opposite reaction, the child will be very confused as this does not fit with the schema that has developed from previous experience.

Modern schema theorists have provided more concrete descriptions of schemas. Derry's (1996) Cognitive Schema Theory (CST) outlines a hierarchy of schemas: (a) *memory objects* (specific small units of related characteristics), (b) *cognitive fields* (an activated set of memory objects) and (c) *mental models* (an overall meaning structure of a particular situation or experience). According to Cognitive Schema Theory, we might say that those with more complex moral judgement have a larger and better organised set of *memory objects* that can be activated within multiple *cognitive fields* and form part of complex *mental models*. Although research would need to determine the architecture in actuality, we can speculate about a mental model for the dilemma, "Heinz and the drug". Such a mental model might include cognitive fields for marriage, stealing, human rights and so forth. Each of these cognitive fields would be comprised of memory objects. For example, "marriage" might include memory objects like "marriage duties" and "love". The memory object, "marriage duties" might consist of related characteristics such as "faithfulness" and "commitment". There may be many layers of memory objects and cognitive fields that comprise a mental model. An expert will have layer upon layer of interrelated schemas about the "Heinz and the drug" dilemma. The expert has more complex and elaborate mental models that can be activated in any number of ways because the architecture is so rich and interrelated. Those with lower levels of moral judgements have a more limited set of possible activations (fewer memory objects, cognitive fields and mental models). In terms of mental architecture, the expert has castles of knowledge while a novice may have a bare foundation.

Schemas involve multiple brain systems (e.g. visual, motor, language) and cognitive processes (Kesner, 1986; Hogarth, 2001). Schemas can involve one kind of system, for example, procedural knowledge (e.g. how to introduce one friend to another) or declarative knowledge (what morality means), or a combination of systems. Schema application can involve different types of reasoning (Ericsson & Smith, 1991), such as analogical and/or intuitive reasoning (Hogarth, 2001); different types of processing such as linear and/or parallel processing (McClelland, 1995); different levels of awareness such as subconscious and automatic or conscious and controlled

(Uleman & Bargh, 1989); and different types of knowledge (declarative, procedural). Essentially, a schema is a goal-orientated cognitive mechanism that operates in one or more of these systems (Neisser, 1976). Much like expertise in parking a car, expertise in a moral judgement schema probably necessitates both kinds of knowledge (procedural: how do I think about this problem? and declarative: what codes do I apply?), dual forms of reasoning (analogical: what is an objective, logical response? and intuitive: this reminds me of . . .), and processing (linear—what do I do next—and parallel). For example, applying a principle to a dilemma is an example of analogical and linear reasoning whereas making a decision "because it feels right" is based on automatic, parallel processing often described as intuition (Hogarth, 2001; Hammond, 2000).

2. How Do Schemas Work?

Schemas operate constantly in the mind, being evoked (or "activated") by current stimulus configurations that resemble the stimuli that created the schema in the first place (Rock, 1997). To return to our previous example, the local news may discuss a criminal without using a picture, yet the report may evoke the picture of a black man in the perceiver because of previous similar stories which were presented with pictures of black men. The "criminals are black" schema is activated by familiar stimuli without need for conscious control. When the postconventional moral schema is activated, cognitive structures about equality and social justice and the procedures to promote them are also activated. The person who is concerned about being racist will probably have developed skill in deactivating the "criminals are black" schema and will consciously activate schematic knowledge that counters such a conclusion (Devine, 1989; Fiske, 1989).

3. How Are Schema Elements Connected?

Hierarchical level (i.e. mental model, cognitive field, memory object) is not the only thing that varies among schemas. Marshall (1995) describes schemas as basic storage devices represented by a tightly organised network structure of memory objects whose relations vary by types (positive or negative) and degrees (strong or weak) of relations. The degree of connectivity among constituents and subconstituents determines the strength and accessibility of a schema. The type of connectivity determines what group of concepts will be activated (positive relation) and which will be suppressed (negative relation). For example, when a person has an activated postconventional schema, she or he is less likely to have an activated personal interest schema (see below and Rest *et al.* (1999) for a complete description of the postconventional and personal interest schema).

4. Why Are Schemas Important?

Schemas are essential to human understanding because they serve so many functions (Neisser, 1976). A schema consists of a representation of some prior stimulus phenomenon that organises or guides the application of prior knowledge to new information (sometimes referred to as "top-down" processing) (Bower & Cirilo, 1985). Schema guidance is expectation-based processing that attends to the unusual (Mandler, 1984). . . .

Schemas likely operate in important ways during moral behaviour, by inter-relating different stimuli, filling in missing information, guiding attention and directing problem-solving. Moral schemas can be described as general knowledge structures used in social cooperation. Moral schemas are built from experience in social interaction. They are constructed automatically from the brain noticing the elements in the socially relevant environment that covary and the cause–consequence chains that obtain from particular actions. Schemas decrease the amount of processing needed for encountered stimuli and are considered to be part of every encounter with the environment (Mandler, 1984).

5. How Are Schemas Activated?

Schema structures that parse incoming sensory data are themselves unconscious and are activated automatically when their patterns match the pattern of incoming data (bottom-up activations) (Marcel, 1983; Mandler, 1984). The perceived regularities may or may not activate linguistic centres and, as a result, may or may not be accessible for verbal description (diSessa, 1982; McCloskey & Kohl, 1983). As Keil and Wilson (2000) point out, individuals are often able to understand something without being able to explain it to others. The inability to articulate understanding is not a matter of forgetting—because the correct explanation is recognisable—rather, the individual has not learned to put the understanding into words. This can be seen when a world-class athlete who is asked to coach a youth team fails miserably due to the inability to translate phenomenal execution skills into verbal instructional skills. Why does this happen? Should not an adult be able to explain what he or she knows how to do? Keil and Wilson distinguish between a basic explanatory set of schemas, present even in infants, and more advanced explanatory schemas that include statements of principles and are evident through verbal performance. Keil and Wilson's theory can help explain the disparity in findings between the MJI and the DIT. The reason that individuals who display postconventional thinking on the DIT but may not do the same on the MJI may be that the person has not put their understanding into words. Understanding is "a cognitive state that remains largely implicit but that goes beyond merely being able to correlate variables" (Keil & Wilson, 2000, p. 97). The only way to move beyond shallow verbal explanations is to learn the intricacies of a theory (e.g. moral theory), as do experts.

6. Can a Particular Schema Change?

Schemas are noted for their flexibility and changeability (Neisser, 1976). No instantiation of a schema is identical to another (Hogarth, 2001). With each instantiation, the schema is altered through assimilation of and accommodation to new experience—integrating new information or modifying the strength of relations among memory objects (Derry, 1996). Schemas change in size, relation to other schemas and in the strength of internal relations.

Studies of expertise such as Gijselaers and Woltjer (1997a) note that when solving domain problems novices have superficial knowledge of problems (e.g. a label for the problem). Their representations of problems are stable in test–retest studies. After some initial study, beginners acquire bits and pieces of knowledge. Intermediates are able to appropriately structure and identify features of the problems. Only experts are able to identify effective ways to solve the problem. Yet because of their vast knowledge, experts are flexible in how they represent the problem—making slight changes or adding new subcategories when sorting domain problems in test–retest conditions (Gijselaers & Woltjer, 1997b). These patterns support Rumelhart and Norman's (1988) view that schemas change with the accretion of new knowledge (e.g. the increased knowledge depth of the intermediates), and the tuning and reconstruction of prior schemas (e.g. experts' slightly changed representations of problems).

In sum, schemas are powerful tools that aid information processing. They guide perception, attention, decisions, habits and behaviour. They operate in the moral domain via schemas for moral sensitivity, motivation and action. They operate during moral judgement and when a person takes the DIT.

The Schemas of the DIT

The DIT is designed to capture moral schema changes that are particularly visible throughout adolescence and early adulthood (Rest *et al.*, 1999). Kohlberg contended that a critical social-cognitive advance in adolescence is the "discovery of society"—that is, understanding how people in society are related to each other through institutions, established practices and role-system ("the system"), not merely on a face-to-face basis, where all are kin, friends or well-known acquaintances (Colby *et al.*, 1987). Others have drawn attention to the development of a sociocentric perspective in adolescents (e.g. Adelson, 1971; Youniss & Yates, 1997). Adelson and O'Neil (1966, p. 304) stated:

> With advancing age there is an increasing grasp of the nature and needs of the community. As the youngster begins to understand the structure and functioning of the social order as a whole, he begins to understand too the specific social institutions within it and their relations to the whole. . . . Thus the demands of the social order and its constituent institutions, as well as the needs of the public, become matters to be appraised in formulating political choices.

The adolescent becomes aware that society is organised in terms of a system of rules, roles and institutions, raising simultaneously and necessarily questions of the morality of society and questions of moral authority. How does one organise a network of cooperation on a society-wide basis for mutual benefit? How are power, wealth and opportunity to be distributed? What is the legitimate use of force? These questions are issues of "macro-morality" or society-wide cooperation, rather than issues of "micro-morality"—interactions with known others in everyday life and face-to-face.

Rest *et al.* (1999) proposed that the DIT is particularly good at measuring change in the schemas individuals use to answer the "macro" question—how to get along with people who are not friends, kin or personal acquaintances; how to organise society-wide cooperation. Through various statistical analyses, three factors have been identified in DIT scores. These have been named: Personal Interest Schema, Maintaining Norms Schema, and Postconventional Schema. (These were formerly categorized as Kohlberg Stage 2 and 3, Stage 4 and Stage 5 and 6, respectively.) Because a respondent needs at least a 12-year-old reading level when taking the DIT, respondents will have moved beyond the simpler forms of moral judgement from earlier childhood (e.g. Kohlberg's Stage 1). As a result, in DIT data the simpler types of moral judgement appear collapsed together (i.e. Stage 2 and 3) or do not appear at all (i.e. Stage 1) (Rest, 1986). At this point, we would like to interpret the DIT according to schema theory.

The three moral schemas that the DIT measures can be viewed as mental models—an integration of cognitive fields and their memory objects—for reasoning about moral dilemmas. (Of course, there are other moral schemas that a person might use other than the three that the DIT measures, such as specific religious or cultural moral schemas.) We describe the content of each schema according to recent theory (Rest *et al.*, 1999).

The simplest schema measured is called the Personal Interests Schema (PIS). The PIS does not suppose a macro-morality perspective but includes the more Stage-2-like memory objects and cognitive fields such as survival, personal advantage and impulsive cooperation. A fair world is one in which I can get what I want. At this level of thinking, the cogniser begins to consider the needs of others, but only in brief exchanges. The cogniser is able to sacrifice momentarily as long as the result is more advantageous. That is, the cogniser learns to exchange cooperation, however briefly. Because the DIT requires a 12-year-old reading level, it is unable to distinguish carefully between Stage-2-like schemas from the more Stage-3-like schemas. And so both are merged in the PIS. We suppose that Stage-3-like schemas include cognitive fields of caring for others, such as long-term negotiated cooperation and in-group reciprocity. PIS thinking enables the cogniser to apply reciprocity in their mental transformations of relationships with known others. Overall, the PIS answers the question of how to organise cooperation in society as if there were only "micro-moral" relationships to consider. The PIS attends to what each stakeholder in a moral dilemma has to gain or lose personally and in relation to the welfare of significant others. PIS thinking is not concerned with organising cooperation on a society-wide basis, the issues of macro-morality.

At the cusp of adolescent change, sensitivity to the issues of macro-morality begins to flower. The PIS becomes inadequate for addressing issues that have become interesting and important, such as why we have laws or what duties I have towards other members of society. As a result, a more developmentally advanced type of thinking emerges that includes a wider societal perspective, the Maintaining Norms Schema (MNS). Within this schema one considers how people should cooperate generally with those who are not friends, kin or well-known acquaintances. The cogniser is able to coordinate personal/significant other negation with reciprocity for the larger society through the interplay of cognitive fields that describe established practices, rules, and codes and their *de facto* authorities. Other cognitive fields connected to this schema include those relevant to issues of fair cooperation such as a uniform application of norms across individuals. Expectations of individuals are only partially reciprocal, however, because role and duty expectations are applied in an egalitarian but not equitable way.

As development progresses, the Postconventional Schema (PCS) begins to make more sense. The individual has experiences, including the persuasive arguments of others, that necessitate thinking about a fair society more broadly—in terms of full reciprocity and equity across all groups within a society. If the individual has enough pluralistic (e.g. multicultural—see Endicott *et al.*, 2003) experiences to effect enough of a cognitive disequilibrium that is not easily denied or minimised, the individual's thinking accommodates to and integrates a broader, postconventional perspective into the mental model of a moral society. The cogniser is able to suggest changes to the *status quo,* to negate extant societal laws and structures, for the sake of morality. He or she can apply moral ideals in a fully reciprocal manner in which each member of society has equivalent status. In particular, postconventional thinking considers macro-level cooperation in terms of advocating sharable ideals that are open to scrutiny and negotiated through the give and take of community life. Whereas Kohlberg focused on a particular postconventional orientation informed by Kant, Rawls and Frankena, the DIT postconventional schema has a broader scope. The PCS can be shaped by various combinations of moral and political philosophy. Individuals with the full use of postconventional tools are able to function at the highest levels of solving moral dilemmas within the community. . . .

Although the three DIT schemas do not cover everything of importance in moral thinking, nor do they constitute a full model of moral-decision making (see Bebeau & Thoma, 1999), they are relevant to many issues of public policy controversy (e.g. abortion, religion in public schools, rights of homosexuals, women's roles, euthanasia, due process rights of the accused, free speech and political demonstrations, etc.—see Narvaez *et al.*, 1999). Moral schemas can illuminate how people formulate opinions about these hotly debated public policy issues, about the "culture wars" (Orthodoxy versus Progressivism—Hunter, 1991), and about the most important clash in ideology since the Cold War (religious fundamentalism versus secular modernism—e.g. Marty & Appleby, 1993). How does the DIT measure moral schemas? . . .

Conclusion

Ideas from cognitive science are increasingly influential and can provide insight into the nature of moral judgement. The DIT emerged from Rest's (1973) dissertation, formed from tasks measuring the beginnings of understanding (which is largely non-verbal and intuitive), in contrast to the MJI, which measures the highest level of verbal understanding. The positive attributes of the DIT are more easily seen in a time of increasing respect for implicit knowledge and processing. The DIT offers a means of measuring moral judgement that fits with current views about tacit knowledge and human decision making. Although the MJI and interview techniques generally are worthwhile for measuring production competence, the DIT is better able to measure understanding at the level that drives most decisions for most people.

References

Adelson, J. (1971). The political imagination of the young adolescent, *Daedalus,* 100, pp. 1013–1050.

Adelson, J., & O'Neil, R. (1966). The development of political thought in adolescence: the sense of community, *Journal of Personality and Social Psychology,* 4, pp. 295–306.

Bargh, J. A. (1989). Conditional automaticity: varieties of automatic influence on social perception and cognition, in: J. S. Uleman & J. A. Bargh (Eds) *Unintended Thought,* pp. 3–15 (New York, Guilford Press).

Bargh, J. A., & Chartrand, T. L. (1999). The unbearable automaticity of being, *American Psychologist,* 54, pp. 462–479.

Bebeau, M. J., & Thoma, S. J. (1999). "Intermediate concepts" and the connection to moral education, *Educational Psychology Review,* 11, pp. 343–360.

Bower, G., & Cirilo, R. (1985). Cognitive psychology and text processing, in: T. A. van Dijk (Ed.) *Handbook of Discourse Analysis,* vol. 1, pp. 71–105 (New York, Academic Press).

Carpenter, W. B. (1874). *Principles of Mental Physiology* (London, John Churchill).

Colby, A., Kohlberg, L., Speicher, B. *et al.* (1987). *The Measurement of Moral Judgement,* vol. 1 and 2 (New York, Cambridge University Press).

Damon, W. (1975). Early conceptions of positive justice as related to the development of logical operations, *Child Development,* 46, pp. 301–312.

Derry, S. J. (1996). Cognitive schema theory in the constructivist debate, *Educational Psychologist,* 31, pp. 163–174.

Devine, P. (1989). Stereotypes and prejudice: their automatic and controlled components, *Journal of Personality and Social Psychology,* 56, pp. 5–18.

diSessa, A. A. (1982). Unlearning Aristotelian physics: a study of knowledge-based learning, *Cognitive Science,* 6, pp. 37–75.

Ebbinghaus, H. (1885/1964). *Memory,* H. A. Ruger & C. E. Bussenius (Trans.) (New York, Dover).

Endicott, L., Bock, T., & Narvaez, D. (2003). Moral reasoning, intercultural development, and multicultural experiences: relations and cognitive underpinnings, *Journal of Intercultural Relations,* 27, pp. 403–419.

Enright, R. D., Frankline, C. C., & Manheim, L. A. (1981). Children's distributive justice reasoning: a standardized and objective scale, *Developmental Psychology,* 16, pp. 193–202.

Ericsson, K. A., & Smith, J. (1991). *Toward a General Theory of Expertise* (New York, Cambridge University Press).

Fiske, S. T. (1989). Examining the role of intent, toward understanding its role in stereotyping and prejudice, in: J. S. Uleman & J. A. Bargh (Eds) *Unintended Thought,* pp. 253–283 (New York, Guilford Press).

Fiske, S. T., & Taylor, S. E. (1991). *Social Cognition,* 2nd edn (New York, McGraw-Hill).

Gibbs, J. C., & Widaman, K. F. (1982). *Social intelligence: measuring the development of sociomoral reflection* (Englewood Cliffs, NJ, Prentice-Hall).

Gijselaers, W. H., & Woltjer, G. (1997a). *Expertise in economics: recall and reasoning,* Annual Meeting of the American Educational Research Association, Chicago, IL.

Gijselaers, W. H., & Woltjer, G. (1997b). *Expert novice differences in the representation of economics problems,* Annual Meeting of the American Educational Research Association, Chicago, IL.

Gigerenzer, G., Todd, P. M., & ABC Research Group (1999). *Simple Heuristics that Make Us Smart* (New York, Oxford University Press).

Hammond, K. R. (2000). *Judgments under Stress* (New York, Oxford University Press).

Hasher, L., & Zacks, R. T. (1984). Automatic processing of fundamental information, *American Psychologist,* 39, pp. 1372–1388.

Helmholtz, H. (1867/1962). *Treatise on Physiological Optics,* vol. 3, J. P. C. Southall (Trans.) (New York, Dover).

Higgins, E. T., & King, G. (1981). Accessibility of social constructs: information processing consequences of individual and contextual variability, in: N. Cantor & J. Kihlstrom (Eds) *Personality, Cognition, and Social Interaction,* pp. 69–121 (Hillsdale, NJ, Lawrence Erlbaum Associates).

Hogarth, R. (2001). *Educating Intuition* (Chicago, IL, Chicago University Press).

Hunter, J. D. (1991). *Culture Wars: the struggle to define America* (New York, Basic Books).

Keil, F. C., & Wilson, R. A. (2000). Explaining explanations, in: F. C. Keil & R. A. Wilson (Eds) *Explanation and Cognition,* pp. 1–18 (Cambridge, MA, Bradford MIT Press).

Kesner, R. (1986). Neurobiological views of memory, in: J. Martinez & R. Kesner (Eds) *Learning and Memory: a biological view,* pp. 399–438 (New York, Academic Press).

Kihlstrom, J. F., Shames, V. A., & Dorfman, J. (1996). Intimations of memory and thought, in: L. Reder (Ed.) *Implicit Memory and Metacognition,* pp. 1–23 (Mahwah, NJ, Lawrence Erlbaum Associates).

Kohlberg, L. (1976). Moral stages and moralization: the cognitive-developmental approach, in: T. Lickona (Ed.) *Moral Development and Behaviour,* pp. 31–53 (New York, Holt, Rinehart & Wilson).

Lind, G. (1995). *The meaning and measurement of moral competence revisited,* paper presented at the Annual Meeting of the American Educational Research Association, San Francisco, CA.

Lyons, N. P. (1982). *Concepts of self and morality and modes of moral choice: identifying justice and care judgements of actual moral dilemmas,* unpublished doctoral dissertation, Harvard University, MA.

McCloskey, M., & Kohl, D. (1983). Naive physics: the curvilinear impetus principle and its interactions with moving objects, *Journal of Experimental Psychology: Learning, Memory, and Cognition,* 9, pp. 146–156.

McClelland, J. L. (1995). Constructive memory and memory distortions: a parallel-distributed processing approach, in: D. L. Schacter (Ed.) *Memory Distortion: how minds, brains, and societies reconstruct the past,* pp. 69–90 (Cambridge, MA, Harvard University Press).

Mandler, J. M. (1984). *Stories, Scripts, and Scenes: aspects of schema theory* (Hillsdale, NJ, Lawrence Erlbaum Associates).

Marcel, A. J. (1983). Conscious and unconscious perception: an approach to the relations between phenomenal experience and perceptual processes, *Cognitive Psychology,* 15, pp. 238–300.

Marshall, S. P. (1995). *Schemas in Problem Solving* (Cambridge, Cambridge University Press).
Marty, M. E., & Appleby, R. S. (Eds) (1993). *Fundamentalism and the State* (Chicago, IL, University of Chicago).
Narvaez, D., Getz, I., Thoma, S. J., & Rest, J. (1999). Individual moral judgement and cultural ideology, *Developmental Psychology,* 35, pp. 478–488.
Neisser, U. (1976). *Cognitive Psychology* (New York, Appleton-Century-Crofts).
Piaget, J. (1932/1965). *The Moral Judgement of the Child,* M. Gabain, (Trans.) (New York, Free Press).
Polanyi, M. (1968). Logic and psychology, *American Psychologist,* 23, pp. 27–43.
Reber, A. S. (1993). *Implicit Learning and Tacit Knowledge* (New York, Oxford University Press).
Rest, J. (1973). The hierarchical nature of stages of moral judgement, *Journal of Personality,* 41, pp. 86–109.
Rest, J. (1986). *Moral Development: advances in research and theory* (New York, Praeger).
Rest, J., Narvaez, D., Bebeau, M. J., & Thoma, S. J. (1999). *Postconventional Moral Thinking: a neo-Kohlbergian approach* (Mahwah, NJ, Lawrence Erlbaum Associates).
Rock, I. (1997). *Indirect Perception* (Cambridge, MA, MIT Press).
Rumelhart, D. E. (1980). Schemata: the building blocks of cognition, in: R. Spiro, B. Bruce & W. Brewer (Eds). *Theoretical Issues in Reading Comprehension,* pp. 33–58 (Hillsdale, NJ, Lawrence Erlbaum Associates).
Rumelhart, D. E., & Norman, D. A. (1988). Representation in memory, in: R. C. Atkinson & R. J. Hernste (Eds) *Handbook of Experimental Psychology,* vol. 2. *Learning & Cognition,* 2nd edn, pp. 571–587 (New York, John Wiley & Sons).
Shweder, R. A. (1991). *Thinking through Cultures* (Cambridge, MA, Harvard University Press).
Turiel, E. (1983). *The Development of Social Knowledge: morality and convention* (Cambridge, Cambridge University Press).
Uleman, J. S., & Bargh, J. A. (1989). *Unintended Thought* (New York, Guilford Press).
Von Hayek, F. A. (1962). Rules, perception, and intelligibility, *Proceedings of the British Academy,* 39, pp. 1372–1388.
Wegner, D. M., & Wheatley, I. (1999). Apparent mental causation: sources of the experience of will, *American Psychologist,* 54, pp. 480–492.
Youniss, J., & Yates, M. (1997). *Community Service and Social Responsibility in Youth* (Chicago, IL, University of Chicago Press).

POSTSCRIPT

Can a Neural Network Model Account for Moral Development?

In the first selection, Churchland describes the view of moral judgments as sets or networks of slowly acquired skills. He begins by describing the development of moral knowledge in terms of the input layer, output layer, and hidden layer of a neural network. He offers several examples of the ways feedback from the environment serves to shape the connections between our sensory input and our moral output.

As the discussion turns toward training the neural network to produce appropriate outputs (i.e., the appropriate moral response), it also turns toward training children to be moral citizens. Churchland moves the discussion back and forth between the necessary corrections in the hidden layer of an AI program, as given by a teacher program, and the necessary feedback needed by a child, as given by parents and the community. Based on his focus on children and his commentary on social and moral policies (see his section "Moral Correction"), it appears that Churchland believes moral development takes place primarily, if not totally, in early childhood.

In the second selection, Narvaez and Bock present a different view of moral judgments. They begin with the work in cognitive science on schemas, a concept popularized by Piaget. In their discussion, Narvaez and Bock detail the wide-ranging nature of schemas, including different types of information and numerous mental processes. They point out that schemas are storage devices in which memory objects are connected in a network, and yet schemas can be quite flexible and changeable.

Narvaez and Bock conclude with a focus on the Defining Issues Test (DIT) and the schemas (stages of moral reasoning) it detects. The three primary schemas are the Personal Interest Schema, the Maintaining Norms Schema, and the Postconventional Schema. These are quite similar to Kohlberg's six stages of moral reasoning. The first two stages in Kohlberg's hierarchy are referred to as Preconventional Thinking and consist of reasoning that is egocentric and self-centered. The next two stages for Kohlberg make up Conventional Thinking in which the individual considers what his or her peers and role models believe is the appropriate attitude or response, or what is best for all persons in society. Kohlberg's stages five and six are also labeled Postconventional, just as the third schema of the DIT. In Postconventional Thinking, the individual is focused on principles and values, rather than other individuals or egocentric interests.

At first glance, the approaches proposed by Churchland, Narvaez, and Bock—both grounded in cognitive science—seem to be at odds. There are distinct differences between these two presentations. One distinct difference is that Churchland seems to focus on childhood development, while the second piece focuses more on adolescence and adulthood. The DIT requires a minimum of a 12-year-old reading level; thus, Narvaez and Bock have drawn their conclusions primarily from adolescents and adults. Another noteworthy difference is that the DIT examines moral reasoning through the three schemas. Churchland's discussion covers many facets of morality, such as moral learning, ambiguity, conflict, virtues, character, and correction.

While the positions seem distinct and very different, there may be some points of agreement. Consider for a moment the popular perspective regarding the brain/mind issue that *mind* is what the *brain* produces. Could it be that schemas are what the neural networks produce?

Suggested Readings

Churchland, P. S., and Churchland, P. M. "Opinion: Neural Worlds and Real Worlds," *Nature Reviews Neuroscience* (November, 2002).

Georges, T. M. *Digital Soul: Intelligent Machines and Human Values* (Boulder, CO: Westview Press, 2003).

Gibbs, J. C. *Moral Development and Reality: Beyond the Theories of Kohlberg and Hoffman* (Thousand Oaks, CA: Sage Publications, 2003).

Rest, J. R., Narvaez, D., Bebeau, M. J., and Thoma, S. J. *Postconventional Moral Thinking: A Neo-Kohlbergian Approach* (Mahwah, NJ: Lawrence Erlbaum, 1999).

ISSUE 16

Do We Use Reasoning to Make Moral Decisions?

YES: James R. Rest, Darcia Narvaez, Stephen J. Thoma, and Muriel J. Bebeau, from "A Neo-Kohlbergian Approach to Morality Research," *Journal of Moral Education* (2000)

NO: Jonathan Haidt, from "The Emotional Dog and Its Rational Tail: A Social Intuitionist Approach to Moral Judgment," *Psychological Review* (2001)

ISSUE SUMMARY

YES: The research team of James Rest, Darcia Narvaez, Stephen Thoma, and Muriel Bebeau present the case that, based on over 25 years of research using the Defining Issues Test, humans move through stages of moral reasoning that guide moral decision-making processes.

NO: Psychologist Jonathan Haidt argues that the social intuitionist model, which proposes that humans have quick intuitions about moral issues that lead to reasoning for the sole purpose of justifying the previous intuitions, better explains moral cognition.

In these selections, the authors debate the merits of a simple assumption: We think before we respond. The exact relationship between cognition and behavior has been a point of controversy for many years. During the middle part of the last century, American psychology was primarily behavioral. Discussions of cognition at that time were left to philosophers and others in the humanities. When the cognitive revolution in psychology occurred in the late 1950s, the interaction between thoughts and behaviors was suddenly of great interest. Most people would agree that an individual's thoughts have at least some influence on that individual's behavior. At the same time, most of us recognize that there are times when our minds are telling us we should do something, but we just can't get our bodies to follow through.

Specific to these selections, the cognition-behavior question is whether, when faced with a moral situation or dilemma, we intuitively react and then think of reasons to justify or support our reaction, or if we take in the situation and instant reactions, reason about it, and then choose the most appropriate reaction. For example, consider the hypothetical situation of observing an individual shoplifting an item just before exiting a store. Do you think about what to do, whether to take some action or remain passive, and then take your chosen course, or do you chose the action first, and then later come up with reasons to justify the action (or lack of action)?

James Rest, the first author on the first selection and a well-known scholar in Kohlbergian moral development, further highlighted the "think about it before you respond" perspective in his four-component model of moral behavior. To achieve moral behavior, one must first have the moral sensitivity to notice and interpret the moral dilemma at hand. The next component is moral judgment, which involves determining the best course of action. This component is similar in focus to Kohlberg's stages of moral reasoning. The third component, moral motivation, involves the way one prioritizes values, including moral values. For example, when a manager notices an employee stealing, will he value obedience to company rules and report the employee, or will he value the good reputation his department has, and not report the employee, thus maintaining the good appearance? The final component is moral character. Rest states that this component "involves ego strength, perseverance, backbone, toughness, strength of convictions, and courage" (page 24) [Rest, J. (1994). Background: Theory and Research. In J. Rest and D. Narvaez (Eds.), *Moral Development in the Professions* (pp. 1–26). (Hillsdale, NJ: Lawrence Erlbaum)].

Haidt, author of the second article, takes a different approach. He believes we rely on our intuition, which is a quick, seemingly unconscious response, and then we use reasoning to justify our intuition. Haidt also argues for a social component to these moral intuitions. His view of moral judgment follows a popular cognitive dual-processing model. The dual processes, intuition and reasoning, have different functions. Haidt believes that intuitions—those quick moral judgments—handle most situations that come along. When intuitions conflict or when we are forced by circumstances to examine a situation, then reasoning is involved. Even when reasoning is involved, Haidt finds that most people take more of a lawyer-like approach, trying to justify their initial responses, rather than a judge-like approach, trying to weigh the evidence and chose the best response.

As you read through these articles, reflect on your own responses to the dilemmas given in the articles. Based on your reflections, do you think one of the models describes your thought processes better than the other? In the first selection, Rest, Narvaez, Thoma, and Bebeau describe the developmental progression of thought through stages of moral reasoning, emphasizing in-depth reasoning prior to affirming a moral principle. In the second selection, Haidt suggests that a completely different process is at work. Haidt believes that we intuitively react to a situation first, and then we use reasoning to justify our intuitive reaction.

James R. Rest, et al.

A Neo-Kohlbergian Approach to Morality Research

Kohlberg's Legacy

Foremost in Larry Kohlberg's legacy is his modelling of openness to new developments and possibilities. When he was first formulating his theory of moral development, the work of Jean Piaget was coming to the attention of American psychologists (e.g. Flavell, 1963), and the work of John Rawls in moral philosophy (1971) was recognised as a new way for moral philosophy to say something significant (beyond clarifying moral language) about normative ethics. Kohlberg's fusion of Piaget and Rawls excited many researchers because of its interdisciplinary approach (taking seriously the questions and contributions of developmental psychology and of normative ethics), and because it addressed issues of the day (e.g. what is social justice?). Recall that in the 1960s and 1970s the US Civil Rights movement, the Vietnam War and the Watergate Scandal were all controversial issues that divided American society. Kohlberg offered a perspective that drew upon the most current work in psychology and philosophy, yet addressed these timely issues.

Kohlberg's ideas dominated the agenda of morality research for decades. In a recent analysis of Kohlberg's writings, Reed (1997) shows that Kohlberg was not particularly concerned with logical consistency among his many projects. Reed contends that Kohlberg's early ventures into moral education, based on a cognitive model of individual moral development (the Six Stage Theory), was not consistent with his later approach, which emphasised the development of community norms (the "Just Community"). Moreover, Kohlberg changed and modified his proposals for a theory of development as he went along: he changed his scoring system of stages throughout the 1970s and 1980s; in various ways he tried to relate "care" to "justice", and his debates with the Social Learning Theorists (e.g. Kohlberg, 1969) had many vicissitudes. Kohlberg's ideas were in constant flux. As he once confided, he was a moving target and considered himself as his own major revisionist. Therefore it would be a mistake to use his

From *Journal of Moral Education,* December 2000, pp. 3810–395.

1981 and 1984 books as the final word on a Kohlbergian approach. One wonders how Kohlberg would have changed his theory, given another decade and a normal life span.

With the benefit of hindsight, with decades of new developments in psychology and philosophy, it remains for others to decide which of Kohlberg's many ideas have turned out to be fruitful. In this article, we audaciously set out to do this and to propose some new ideas, realising, with Kohlberg, that this is an ongoing enterprise, open to revision, and likely to change.

A Neo-Kohlbergian Viewpoint

Several factors bring us to our discussion. After 25 years of data collection, we have completed a full generation of research with the Defining Issues Test (hereafter referred to as the DIT). Advances in personal computers and technology make possible analyses that heretofore were impractical (e.g. sample sizes of 50,000). Further, the field of morality research has been fragmented and not dominated by any one approach—therefore we feel free to explore theory and research that do not employ a standard approach. In addition, the fields of psychology and philosophy are moving in directions especially congenial to our research. Much of our activity until 1997 is summarised in a recent book, *Postconventional Moral Thinking: a neo-Kohlbergian approach* (Rest *et al.*, 1999).

We follow Kohlberg's approach to conceptualising moral judgement (see Rest *et al.,* 1999, for fuller discussion). (a) Like Kohlberg, our starting point emphasises *cognition.* Kohlberg realised there were many starting points for morality research (for instance, one might start out emphasising an evolutionary biosocial perspective, and investigate certain emotions such as empathy, altruism, guilt and shame; or one might focus on the young infant's acquisition of prosocial behaviour). Everyone must begin somewhere, making assumptions and emphasising some things over other things. Despite the limitations of any starting point, the crucial question is, "Having started there, where did it lead? What important phenomena have been illuminated?" (b) Like Kohlberg, we highlight the *personal construction* of basic epistemological categories (e.g. "rights", "duty", "justice", "social order", "reciprocity"). This is not to deny the contribution that cultural ideologies make. Ideologies are group-derived, tools and practices of a culture. We, however, focus on the individual's attempt to make sense of his/her own social experience. (c) We portray change over time in terms of *development* (i.e. it is possible to talk not only of differences in moral orientation, but also of cognitive "advance" in which "higher is better" in a philosophical, normative-ethical sense). Finally, (d) we characterise the developmental change of adolescents and adults in terms of a shift from *conventional* to *postconventional* moral thinking (we think there is a sequence rather than Turiel's notion [e.g. 1983] of these being separate domains). We think these four ideas are the core assumptions of Kohlberg's "cognitive-developmental" approach. This is the *Kohlbergian* part of our neo-*Kohlbergian* approach. Because these ideas have been much discussed previously (e.g. Kohlberg, 1969, 1981, 1984, 1986; Colby *et al.*, 1983, 1987), we will not elaborate on them here. . . .

Differences with Kohlberg's Theory of Six Stages

We use the term moral *schemas* (discussed below), rather than moral *stages,* to signal differences with Kohlberg's conception of "hard" moral stages. Our view of the cognitive structures of moral judgement differ from Kohlberg's stages in the following five ways (the points are not discrete points but are all interconnected):

a. *"Hard" stages versus "soft" stages.* We differ with Kohlberg on the concept of "*stage*"; we envision development as shifting distributions rather than as a staircase. Like Siegler (1997), we believe that development is a matter of changes in the frequency of usage, moving from the less to the more complex.
b. *More specific and concrete.* Our schemas are more concrete than Kohlberg's stages (but are more abstract than the typical schemas of Social Cognition (e.g. person schemas, role schemas). Our schemas are conceptions of institutions and role-systems in society, whereas Kohlberg regards social institutions as "content". In other words, we have three ways of drawing the distinction between content and structure: Kohlberg's, the neo-Kohlbergian approach in the DIT, and Social Cognition. All distinguish general cognitive structure from the content instantiations that can exemplify the structure, but the three draw the distinction at different levels of abstraction.
c. *Cognitive operations and the content-output of operations.* Instead of Kohlberg's claim of studying "justice operations", we do not claim that our schemas directly assess cognitive operations. The Colby–Kohlberg scoring system (Colby *et at.*, 1987) explains how one must radically purge content from structure in order to assess the operations of moral thinking. Kohlberg spent the last decade of his life working on the 1987 scoring system to radically purge content from structure. He seems to have assumed that the more abstract the analysis, the more pure the assessment of operations. In contrast, Cognitive Science has not been so eager to purge all content from structure. Gazzaniga *et at.* (1998) stated that mental operations are the most elusive aspect of cognitive assessment:

> A vast amount of research in cognitive science clearly shows we are conscious only of the content of our mental life, not what generates the content. It is the products of mnemonic processing, of perceptual processing, of imaging, that we are aware of—not what produced the products. Sometimes people report on what they think were the processes, but they are reporting after the fact on what they thought they did to produce the content of their consciousness (p. 532).

d. *Universality.* Kohlberg postulated universality as a characteristic of stages whereas we regard cross-cultural similarity as an empirical question. He saw a universalistic morality as the bulwark against moral relativism in which a Nazi officer could defend his role in the Holocaust as simply following the relativist norms of his group. In contrast, recent moral philosophers (e.g. Beauchamp & Childress, 1994; Walzer, 1983) consider "Common Morality" as a community enterprise, relative to situation and circumstance (akin to the development of common law). According to this view, morality is a social construction, evolving from the community's experiences, particular institutional arrangements, deliberations, and the aspirations that are voiced at the time and which win the support of the community. Morality that is relative to group deliberation is not tantamount to the mindless moral relativism or moral scepticism that Kohlberg feared, nor does it pave the way to Nazi atrocities. Common morality might be different for different communities (and therefore relative), but the common morality is debated and scrutinized by members of the community and reflects an equilibrium between the ideals and the moral intuitions of the community.

e. *Articulation (interviewing task) versus tacit knowledge (multiple choice task).* A common assumption in the field of morality, and one with which we disagree, is that reliable information about the inner processes that underlie moral behaviour is obtained only by asking people to explain their moral judgements. Contrary to assuming the face validity of interviews, researchers in Cognitive Science and Social Cognition contend that self-reported explanations of one's own cognitive processes have severe limitations (e.g. Nisbett & Wilson, 1977; Uleman & Bargh, 1989). People can report on the *products* of cognition but not on the mental *operations* they used to arrive at the product. A large body of research calls into question the privileged place of interview data, dependent on *conscious understanding,* over recognition data, dependent on *implicit* understanding.

By requiring participants in research to construct verbal arguments for their moral choices, and to credit someone only with cognition that they can articulate and defend, Kohlberg placed a verbal constraint that credited people with only understanding what they could explain. We believe that this is one reason why there is so little empirical evidence for Stage 5 and 6 reasoning using Kohlberg's scoring system. One advantage of the recognition task of the DIT is that postconventional thinking is not so rarely scored as in the Kohlberg interview.

Developmental Schemas Instead of Stages

We postulate three structures in moral thinking development: the Personal Interest schema (which derives from Kohlberg's Stage 2 and 3, referred to henceforth as "S23"); the Maintaining Norms schema (deriving from Kohlberg's Stage 4, referred to as "S4"); and the Postconventional schema (deriving from Kohlberg's Stage 5 and 6, referred to as "S56").

Developmentally, a large social-cognitive advance in adolescence (the youngest group that we study with the DIT) is the "discovery of society"—that is, that people in society are related to each other through institutions, established practices, role-systems ("the system"), and not only on a face-to-face basis (as with kin, friends, well-known acquaintances). Not only does Kohlberg speak of this development (attaining a sociocentric perspective) in adolescence (1984), but others do also (e.g. Adelson, 1971; Youniss & Yates, 1997). Awareness that society is organised in terms of a system of rules, roles and institutions raises questions about the morality of society and questions of moral authority. (How does one organise a network of co-operation on a society-wide basis, where there is full reciprocity and mutual benefit? How are power, wealth and opportunity to be distributed? What is the legitimate use of force?) These are the issues of "macro-morality" as distinct from issues of "micro-morality" (i.e. how a person interacts with others in everyday face-to-face situations). In our view, the three moral schemas are developmentally ordered ways of answering the "macro" question (how to get along with people who are not friends, kin or personal acquaintances, i.e. how to organise society-wide co-operation).

Personal Interest Schema

We suppose that the Personal Interest schema develops in childhood and that by the time participants have sufficient reading ability to take the DIT (i.e. have a 12-year-old reading level), this schema is no longer central in their thinking. The Personal Interest schema does not entail a sociocentric perspective. Questions addressing societal co-operation are answered as if there were only "micro-moral" relationships to consider. Individuals using the Personal Interest schema analyse what each stakeholder in a moral dilemma has to gain and lose as if they did not have to worry about organising co-operation on a society-wide basis. The "Personal Interest" schema justifies a decision as morally right by appealing to the personal stake the actor has in the consequences of an action. The Personal Interest schema includes individual prudential concerns and concerns for those with whom one has an affectionate relationship. Thus it has elements described by Kohlbergian Stages 2 and 3 because the two elements fuse together as a single factor in DIT data. In DIT data, both Stage 2 and Stage 3 items are regarded as more primitive forms of thinking—see factor analysis results, discussed in Rest *et al.*, 1999). On the whole, DIT research cannot offer insight into development in childhood, or into the distinctions within the Personal Interest schema.

The Maintaining Norms Schema

We suppose that the Maintaining Norms schema is developmentally more advanced in attaining a sociocentric perspective (one has to consider how people who are not friends, kin or well-known acquaintances are going to co-operate). With the Maintaining Norms schema, the individual is able to identify the established practice (the existing rules and roles) and who are the *de facto* authorities. Functionally, the Maintaining Norms schema is a prevalent first solution to conceptualising society-wide co-operation. Examples include Kohlberg's "Law and Order" stage (1984) and Richard Nixon's "Silent Majority"; McClosky and Brill (1983) talk about the "Conservative" orientation; Adelson (1971) talked about the "Authoritarianism" of adolescence. Common to all of these, the Maintaining Norms schema has the following elements. (a) The perceived need for generally accepted social norms to govern a collective. (b) The necessity that the norms apply society-wide, to all people in a society. (c) The need for the norms to be clear, uniform, and categorical (that there is "the rule of law.") (d) The norms are seen as establishing a reciprocity (each citizen obeys the law, expecting that others will also obey). (e) The establishment of hierarchical role structures, of chains of command, of authority and duty. That is, in an organised society, there are hierarchical role structures (e.g. teacher–pupil, parent–child, general–soldier, doctor–patient, etc.). One must obey authorities, not necessarily out of respect for the personal qualities of the authority, but out of respect for the social system.

For the Maintaining Norms schema, maintaining the established social order defines morality. In the Maintaining Norms schema, "law" is connected to "order" in a moral sense. The schema leads to the expectation that without law (and duty to one's roles), there would be no order, people would instead act on their own special interests, leading to anarchy—a situation that responsible people want to prevent. For this schema, no further rationale for defining morality is necessary beyond simply asserting that an act is prescribed by the law, is the established way of doing things, or is the established Will of God. The schema, Maintaining Norms, is consonant with "Legal Positivism" (Hart, 1961, pp. 181–182, 253–254) in the sense that neither appeals to moral criteria beyond the law itself. Acquisition of this schema is what gives Conventional thinkers their sense of moral necessity for the maintenance of social order. In other words, the schema provides a sense of moral certainty ("I know I'm right for the sake of our entire society") and therefore fuels the special zeal of conventional thinkers.

Postconventional Schema

Essential to postconventional thinking is that moral obligations are to be based on shared ideals, are fully reciprocal, and are open to scrutiny (i.e. subject to tests of logical consistency, experience of the community and coherence with accepted practice). Over the centuries, philosophers have proposed many visions for a society based on moral ideals (e.g. utilitarian, social contract, virtue-based, feminist, casuist, religious ideals). Not all moral theories fit our criteria of Postconventional schema: (a) emotivist theories of morality say that morality is nothing but the personal expression of approval or disapproval (e.g. Stevenson, 1937); (b) Nietzsche [e.g. 1886/1968] regarded co-operation as a bad idea and a ploy of the weak to hold down the strong; and (c) ethical approaches based on Fundamentalist/Orthodox religious views deny that their version of God's Will is open to scrutiny (see Beauchamp & Childress, 1994, for a discussion of the relative adequacy of various moral theories.) However, most modern moral philosophies do fit our notion of postconventionality. They are based on ideals, the ideals are shareable, are open to debate and tests of logical consistency, and so on. Whereas Kohlberg was partisan to the neo-Kantian, deontological theory of John Rawls (1971), we attempt to side-step the current disputes of moral philosophy by adopting a looser, broader (less daring, more tepid) notion of cognitive advance. Instead of Kohlberg's definition of Stage 6 (in which the individual's cognitive operations achieve "ideal reciprocity", striking similarities to the theory of John Rawls), our definition of the Postconventional schema is not partial to any particular moral philosopher. Four elements comprise the Postconventional schema: primacy of moral criteria, appeal to an ideal, shareable ideals and full reciprocity (discussed in Rest *et al.*, 1999, Ch. 3).

There has been, and still is, much dispute among moral philosophers about what ideals should govern society, how to optimise all the participants' welfare, who is a participant, what "fair-minded" and "impartial" mean, what "rational" and "equal" mean, what constitutes "logical coherence", and the relative importance of principles and paradigm cases. These issues are the unsettled business of much of current moral philosophy. Nevertheless, we focus on the gulf between conventionality and postconventionality (what Kohlberg regarded as the distinction between Stage 4 and Stage 5—Colby *et al.*, 1987, Vol. 1, pp. 28–29). This gulf is what polarises people on so many public policy issues (e.g. rights of homosexuals, religion in public schools, euthanasia, abortion, women's roles, etc.), fuels the "Culture Wars" (Orthodoxy versus Progressivism: Hunter, 1991), and is the most important clash in ideology since the Cold War (religious fundamentalism versus secular modernism: see Marty & Appleby, 1993).

Like Kohlberg, we affirm a developmental progression from conventionality to postconventionality. A major difference between the Maintaining Norms schema and the Postconventional schema is how each attempts to establish a moral consensus: the strategy of the Maintaining Norms schema is to gain consensus by appealing to established practice and existing authority. In contrast, the strategy of the Postconventional schema is to gain consensus by appealing to ideals and logical coherence. Like Kohlberg, we assert not only that there are different cognitive structures for moral judgement, but also that they are developmentally ordered—the Postconventional schema is more advanced (in a normative ethical sense) than the Maintaining Norms schema. The cognitive developmental distinction, however, is not the same thing as the distinction in political ideology between the right-wing and left-wing. It is possible to be conventional left-wing (e.g. Political Correctness) as well as conventional right-wing (George Wallace's Law and Order). It is possible to be postconventional left-wing (Rawls, 1971, 1993) and postconventional Conservative (e.g. Sandel, 1982), Communitarian (Walzer, 1983) or Libertarian (Nozick, 1974). . . .

Conclusion

Kohlberg's ideas stimulated much research over past decades, including the development of the DIT. With 25 years of DIT research, we are able to make particular claims with some certainty. Spurred by developments in psychology and philosophy, we have moved the moral judgement enterprise towards a more complex view of moral judgement and comprehension. Our interpretations of the findings form the basis of our neo-Kohlbergian viewpoint.

References

Adelson, J. (1971). The political imagination of the young adolescent, *Daedalus,* 100, 1013–1050.

Beauchamp, T. L., & Childress, J. F. (1994). *Principles of Biomedical Ethics,* 4th edn. (New York, Oxford University Press).

Colby, A., Kohlberg, L., Gibbs, J., & Lieberman, M. (1983). A longitudinal study of moral judgment, *Society for Research in Child Development: Monograph Series, 48,* no. 4, Chicago.

Colby, A., Kohlberg, L., Speicher, B. *et al.* (1987). *The Measurement of Moral Judgment,* vols 1 and 2 (New York, Cambridge University Press).

Flavell, J. H. (1963). *The Developmental Psychology of Jean Piaget* (Princeton, NJ, VanNostrand).

Gazzaniga, M. S., Ivry, R. B., & Mangun, G. R. (1998). *Cognitive Neuroscience: the biology of the mind* (New York, Norton).

Hart, H. L. A. (1961). *The Concept of Law* (London, Oxford University Press).

Hunter, J. D. (1991). *Culture Wars: the struggle to define America* (New York, Basic Books).

Kohlberg, L. (1969). Stage and sequence: the cognitive developmental approach to socialization, in: D. A. Goslin (Ed.) *Handbook of Socialization Theory,* pp. 347–480 (Chicago, Rand McNally).

Kohlberg, L. (1981). *Essays on Moral Development,* vol. 1: *The Philosophy of Moral Development* (New York, Harper & Row).

Kohlberg, L. (1984). *Essays on Moral Development: the nature and validity of moral stages,* vol. 2 (San Francisco, Harper & Row).

Kohlberg, L. (1986). A current statement on some theoretical issues, in: S. Modgil & C. Modgil (Eds.) *Lawrence Kohlberg: consensus and controversy,* pp. 485–546 (Philadelphia, Falmer Press).

Marty, M. E., & Appleby, R. S. (Eds) (1993). *Fundamentalism and the State* (Chicago, University of Chicago).

McClosky, H., & Brill, A. (1983). *Dimensions of Tolerance: what Americans believe about civil liberties* (New York, Russell Sage).

Nietzsche, F. (1886/1968). *Beyond Good and Evil,* W. Kaufman, (Trans.) *The Portable Nietzsche,* pp. 443–447 (New York, Viking Press).

Nisbett, R. E., & Wilson, T. D. (1977). Telling more than we can know: verbal reports on mental processes, *Psychological Review, 84,* pp. 231–259.

Nozick, R. (1974). *Anarchy, State, and Utopia* (New York, Basic Books).

Rawls, J. (1971). *A Theory of Justice* (Cambridge, MA, Harvard Press).

Rawls, J. (1993). *Political Liberalism* (New York, Columbia University Press).

Reed, D. R. C. (1997). *Following Kohlberg: liberalism and the practice of the democratic community* (Notre Dame, IN, University of Notre Dame Press).

Rest, J., Narvaez, D., Bebeau, M. J., & Thoma, S. J. (1999). *Postconventional Moral Thinking: a neo-Kohlbergian approach* (Mahwah, NJ, Lawrence Erlbaum).

Rest, J., Narvaez, D., Thoma, S. J., & Bebeau, M. J. (1999) DIT2: devising and testing a revised instrument of moral judgment, *Journal of Educational Psychology, 91,* pp. 644–659.

Sandel, M. (1982). *Liberalism and the Limits of Justice* (Cambridge, MA, Cambridge University Press).

Siegler, R. S. (1997). Concepts and methods for studying cognitive change, in: E. Amsel & K. A. Renninger (Eds) *Change and Development: issues of theory, method, and application,* pp. 77–98 (Mahwah, NJ, Lawrence Erlbaum).

Stevenson, C. L. (1937). The emotive meaning of ethical terms, *Mind,* XLVI, pp. 14–31.

Turiel, E. (1983). *The Development of Social Knowledge; morality and convention* (Cambridge, Cambridge University Press).

Uleman, J. S., & Bargh, J. A. (1989). *Unintended Thought* (New York, Guilford Press).

Walzer, M. (1983). *Spheres of Justice* (New York, Basic Books).

Youniss, J., & Yates, M. (1997). *Community Service and Social Responsibility in Youth* (Chicago, University of Chicago Press).

NO 

Jonathan Haidt

The Emotional Dog and Its Rational Tail: A Social Intuitionist Approach to Moral Judgment

> Julie and Mark are brother and sister. They are traveling together in France on summer vacation from college. One night they are staying alone in a cabin near the beach. They decide that it would be interesting and fun if they tried making love. At the very least it would be a new experience for each of them. Julie was already taking birth control pills, but Mark uses a condom too, just to be safe. They both enjoy making love, but they decide not to do it again. They keep that night as a special secret, which makes them feel even closer to each other. What do you think about that? Was it OK for them to make love?

Most people who hear the above story immediately say that it was wrong for the siblings to make love, and they then begin searching for reasons (Haidt, Bjorklund, & Murphy, 2000). They point out the dangers of inbreeding, only to remember that Julie and Mark used two forms of birth control. They argue that Julie and Mark will be hurt, perhaps emotionally, even though the story makes it clear that no harm befell them. Eventually, many people say something like, "I don't know, I can't explain it, I just know it's wrong." But what model of moral judgment allows a person to know that something is wrong without knowing why?

Moral psychology has long been dominated by rationalist models of moral judgment. . . . Rationalist approaches in moral psychology . . . say that moral knowledge and moral judgment are reached primarily by a process of reasoning and reflection (Kohlberg, 1969; Piaget, 1932/1965; Turiel, 1983). Moral emotions such as sympathy may sometimes be inputs to the reasoning process, but moral emotions are not the direct causes of moral judgments. In rationalist models, one briefly becomes a judge, weighing issues of harm, rights, justice, and fairness, before passing judgment on Julie and Mark. If no condemning evidence is found, no condemnation is issued.

This article reviews evidence against rationalist models and proposes an alternative: the social intuitionist model. . . . Intuitionist approaches in moral psychology . . . say that moral intuitions (including moral emotions) come first and directly cause moral judgments (Haidt, 2003; Kagan, 1984; Shweder & Haidt, 1993; J. Q. Wilson, 1993). Moral intuition is a kind of cognition, but it is not a kind of reasoning.

The social part of the social intuitionist model proposes that moral judgment should be studied as an interpersonal process. Moral reasoning is usually an ex post facto process used to influence the intuitions (and hence judgments) of other people. In the social intuitionist model, one feels a quick flash of revulsion at the thought of incest and one knows intuitively that something is wrong. Then, when faced with a social demand for a verbal justification, one becomes a lawyer trying to build a case rather than a judge searching for the truth. One puts forth argument after argument, never wavering in the conviction that Julie and Mark were wrong, even after one's last argument has been shot down. In the social intuitionist model it becomes plausible to say, "I don't know, I can't explain it, I just know it's wrong." . . .

Psychology and the Focus on Reasoning

. . . Until the cognitive revolution of the 1960s, the major schools of psychology did not see reason as the master of anything, and their views on morality were compatible with Hume's emphasis on emotions. Freud (1900/1976) saw people's judgments as driven by unconscious motives and feelings, which are then rationalized with publicly acceptable reasons. The behaviorists also saw moral reasoning as epiphenomenal in the production of moral behavior, explaining morality as the acts that a society happens to reward or punish (Skinner, 1971).

Kohlberg and the Cognitive Revolution

But then came Lawrence Kohlberg. Kohlberg's work was a sustained attack on "irrational emotive theories" (1971, p. 188), and his cognitive–developmental theory was an important part of the cognitive revolution. Kohlberg built on Piaget's (1932/1965) pioneering work, developing an interviewing method that was suitable for use with adults as well as children. Kohlberg presented participants with dilemmas in which moral and nonmoral claims were present on both sides, and he then looked to see how people resolved the conflicts. In his best known dilemma, a man named Heinz must decide whether he should break into a druggist's shop to steal a drug that may save the life of his dying wife. Kohlberg found a six-level progression of increasing sophistication in how people handled such dilemmas. He claimed that children start as egoists, judging actions by the good or bad consequences they bring to the self, but as children's cognitive abilities expand they develop the ability to "role-take," or see a situation from other people's perspectives. The experience of role-taking drives the child on to the less egocentric and more powerful conventional and then postconventional levels of moral reasoning.

Kohlberg's focus was on development, but he often addressed the question of mechanism. He consistently endorsed a rationalist and somewhat Platonic model in which affect may be taken into account by reason . . . but in which reasoning ultimately makes the decisions:

> We are claiming . . . that the moral force in personality is cognitive. Affective forces are involved in moral decisions, but affect is neither moral nor immoral. When the affective arousal is channeled into moral directions, it is moral; when it is not so channeled, it is not. The moral channeling mechanisms themselves are cognitive. (Kohlberg, 1971, pp. 230–231)

Kohlberg was quite explicit that the cognitive mechanisms he discussed involved conscious, language-based thinking. He was interested in the phenomenology of moral reasoning, and he described one of the pillars of his approach as the assumption that "moral reasoning is the conscious process of using ordinary moral language" (Kohlberg, Levine, & Hewer, 1983, p. 69). . . .

Questioning the Causality of Reasoning

People undeniably engage in moral reasoning. But does the evidence really show that such reasoning is the cause, rather than the consequence, of moral judgment? Turiel, Hildebrandt, and Wainryb (1991) examined young adults' reasoning about issues of abortion, homosexuality, pornography, and incest. They found that people who judged the actions to be moral violations also talked about harmful consequences, whereas people who thought the actions were not wrong generally cited no harmful consequences. Turiel et al. (1991) interpreted these findings as showing the importance of "informational assumptions"; for example, people who thought that life begins at conception were generally opposed to abortion, whereas people who thought that life begins later were generally not opposed to abortion. In making this interpretation, however, Turiel et al. made a jump from correlation to causation. The correlation they found between judgment and supporting belief does not necessarily mean that the belief caused the judgment. An intuitionist interpretation is just as plausible: The anti-abortion judgment (a gut feeling that abortion is bad) causes the belief that life begins at conception (an ex post facto rationalization of the gut feeling).

Haidt, Koller, and Dias (1993) found evidence for such an intuitionist interpretation. They examined American and Brazilian responses to actions that were offensive yet harmless, such as eating one's dead pet dog, cleaning one's toilet with the national flag, or eating a chicken carcass one has just used for masturbation. The stories were carefully constructed so that no plausible harm could be found, and most participants directly stated that nobody was hurt by the actions in question, yet participants still usually said the actions were wrong, and universally wrong. They frequently made statements such as, "It's just wrong to have sex with a chicken." Furthermore, their affective reactions to the stories (statements that it would bother them to witness the action) were better predictors of their moral judgments than were their claims about harmful consequences. Haidt and Hersh (2001) found the same thing when they interviewed conservatives and liberals about sexual morality issues, including homosexuality, incest, and unusual forms of masturbation. For both groups, affective reactions were good predictors of judgment, whereas perceptions of harmfulness were not. Haidt and Hersh also found that participants were often "morally dumbfounded" (Haidt et al., 2000); that is, they would stutter, laugh, and express surprise at their inability to find supporting reasons, yet they would not change their initial judgments of condemnation.

It seems, then, that for affectively charged events such as incest and other taboo violations, an intuitionist model may be more plausible than a rationalist model. But can an intuitionist model handle the entire range of moral judgment? Can it accommodate the findings from rationalist research programs while also explaining new phenomena and leading to new and testable predictions? The social intuitionist model may be able to do so.

The Social Intuitionist Model

The central claim of the social intuitionist model is that moral judgment is caused by quick moral intuitions and is followed (when needed) by slow, ex post facto moral reasoning. Clear definitions of moral judgment, moral intuition, and moral reasoning are therefore needed. . . .

Moral Judgment

Moral judgments are . . . defined as evaluations (good vs. bad) of the actions or character of a person that are made with respect to a set of virtues held to be obligatory by a culture or subculture. This definition is left broad intentionally to allow a large gray area of marginally moral judgments. For example, "eating a low-fat diet" may not qualify as a moral virtue for most philosophers, yet in health-conscious subcultures, people who eat cheeseburgers and milkshakes are seen as morally inferior to those who eat salad and chicken (Stein & Nemeroff, 1995).

Moral Reasoning

[M]oral reasoning can now be defined as conscious mental activity that consists of transforming given information about people in order to reach a moral judgment. To say that moral reasoning is a conscious process means that the process is intentional, effortful, and controllable and that the reasoner is aware that it is going on (Bargh, 1994).

Moral Intuition

[M]oral intuition can be defined as the sudden appearance in consciousness of a moral judgment, including an affective valence (good–bad, like–dislike), without any conscious awareness of having gone through steps of searching, weighing evidence, or inferring a conclusion. . . .

Four Reasons to Doubt the Causal Importance of Reason

1. The Dual Process Problem: There Is a Ubiquitous and Under-Studied Intuitive Process at Work

It is now widely accepted in social and cognitive psychology that two processing systems are often at work when a person makes judgments or solves problems (. . . Chaiken & Trope, 1999). Because these two systems typically run in parallel and are capable of reaching differing conclusions, these models are usually called *dual process* models. Dual process models have thus far had little impact on moral judgment research because most researchers have focused their efforts on understanding the reasoning process (but see Eisenberg, Shea, Carlo, & Knight, 1991; Gibbs, 1991). There is evidence, however, that moral judgment works like other kinds of judgment, in which most of the action is in the intuitive process. . . .

The social intuitionist solution

The social intuitionist model is fully compatible with modern dual process theories. Like those theories, the model posits that the intuitive process is the default process, handling everyday moral judgments in a rapid, easy, and holistic way. It is primarily when intuitions conflict, or when the social situation demands thorough examination of all facets of a scenario, that the reasoning process is called upon. Reasoning can occur privately . . . and such solitary moral reasoning may be common among philosophers and among those who have a high need for cognition (Cacioppo & Petty, 1982). Yet ever since Plato wrote his *Dialogues,* philosophers have recognized that moral reasoning naturally occurs in a social setting, between people who can challenge each other's arguments and trigger new intuitions. . . . The social intuitionist model avoids the traditional focus on conscious private reasoning and draws attention to the role of moral intuitions, and of other people, in shaping moral judgments.

2. The Motivated Reasoning Problem: The Reasoning Process Is More Like a Lawyer Defending a Client Than a Judge or Scientist Seeking Truth

It appears, then, that a dual process model may be appropriate for a theory of moral judgment. If so, then the relationship between the two processes must be specified. Is the reasoning process the "smarter" but more cognitively expensive process, called in whenever the intuitive process is unable to solve a problem cheaply? Or is the relationship one of master and servant, as Hume suggested, in which reason's main job is to formulate arguments that support one's intuitive conclusions? Research on both motivated reasoning and everyday reasoning suggests that the post hoc reasoning link . . . is more important than the reasoned judgment and private reflection links. . . .

Mechanisms of Bias

Studies of everyday reasoning reveal the mechanisms by which relatedness and coherence motivations make people act like lawyers. Kuhn (1991) found that most people have difficulty understanding what evidence is, and when pressed to give evidence in support of their theories they generally give anecdotes or illustrative examples instead. Furthermore, people show a strong tendency to search for anecdotes and other "evidence" exclusively on their preferred side of an issue, a pattern that has been called the "my-side bias" (Baron, 1995; Perkins et al., 1991). Once people find supporting evidence, even a single piece of bad evidence, they often stop the search, since they have a "makes-sense epistemology" (Perkins, Allen, & Hafner, 1983) in which the goal of thinking is not to reach the most accurate conclusion but to find the first conclusion that hangs together well and that fits with one's important prior beliefs.

Research in social cognition also indicates that people often behave like "intuitive lawyers" rather than "intuitive scientists" (Baumeister & Newman, 1994). Kunda's (1990) review of "motivated reasoning" concludes that "directional goals" (motivations to reach a preordained conclusion) work primarily by causing a biased search in memory for supporting evidence only. . . .

This review is not intended to imply that people are stupid or irrational. It is intended to demonstrate that the roots of human intelligence. rationality, and ethical sophistication should not be sought in our ability to search for and evaluate evidence in an open and unbiased way. Rather than following the ancient Greeks in worshiping reason, we should instead look for the roots of human intelligence, rationality, and virtue in what the mind does best: perception, intuition, and other mental operations that are quick, effortless, and generally quite accurate (Gigerenzer & Goldstein, 1996: Margolis, 1987).

The Social Intuitionist Solution

The reasoning process in moral judgment may be capable of working objectively under very limited circumstances: when the person has adequate time and processing capacity, a motivation to be accurate, no a priori judgment to defend or justify, and when no relatedness or coherence motivations are triggered (Forgas, 1995; Wegner & Bargh, 1998). Such circumstances may be found in moral judgment studies using hypothetical and unemotional dilemmas. Rationalist research methods may therefore *create* an unusual and nonrepresentative kind of moral judgment. However, in real judgment situations, such as when people are gossiping or arguing, relatedness motives are always at work. If more shocking or threatening issues are being judged, such as abortion, euthanasia, or consensual incest, then coherence motives also will be at work. Under these more realistic circumstances, moral reasoning is not left free to search for truth but is likely to be hired out like a lawyer by various motives, employed only to seek confirmation of preordained conclusions.

3. The Post Hoc Problem: The Reasoning Process Readily Constructs Justifications of Intuitive Judgments, Causing the Illusion of Objective Reasoning

When people are asked to explain the causes of their judgments and actions, they frequently cite factors that could not have mattered and fail to recognize factors that did matter. Nisbett and Schachter (1966), for example, asked participants to take electric shocks, either with or without a placebo pill that was said to produce the same symptoms as electric shock. Participants in the pill condition apparently attributed their heart palpitations and butterflies in the stomach to the pill and were able to take four times as much shock as those who had no such misattribution available for their symptoms. However, when the placebo condition participants were asked if they had made such an attribution, only 25% of them said that they had. The remaining participants denied that they had thought about the pill and instead made up a variety of explanations for their greater shock tolerance, such as, "Well, I used to build radios and stuff when I was 13 or 14, and maybe I got used to electric shock" (Nisbett & Wilson, 1977, p. 237). . . .

Post Hoc Moral Reasoning

The idea that people generate causal explanations out of a priori causal theories is easily extended into the moral domain. In a moral judgment interview, a participant is asked to decide whether an action is right or wrong and is then asked to explain why she thinks so. However, if people have no access to the processes behind their automatic initial evaluations then how do they go about providing justifications? They do so by consulting their a priori moral theories. *A priori moral theories* can be defined as a pool of culturally supplied norms for evaluating and criticizing the behavior of others. A priori moral theories provide acceptable reasons for praise and blame (e.g., "unprovoked harm is bad"; "people should strive to live up to God's commandments"). Because the justifications that people give are closely related to the moral judgments that they make, prior researchers have assumed that the justificatory reasons caused the judgments. But if people lack access to their automatic judgment processes then the reverse causal path becomes more plausible. . . .

The Illusions of Moral Judgment

If moral reasoning is generally a post hoc construction intended to justify automatic moral intuitions, then our moral life is plagued by two illusions. The first illusion can be called the *wag-the-dog illusion:* We believe that our own moral judgment (the dog) is driven by our own moral reasoning (the tail). The second illusion can be called the *wag-the-other-dog's-tail illusion:* In a moral argument, we expect the successful rebuttal of an opponent's arguments to change the opponent's mind. Such a belief is like thinking that forcing a dog's tail to wag by moving it with your hand will make the dog happy. . . .

The Social Intuitionist Solution

People have quick and automatic moral intuitions, and when called on to justify these intuitions they generate post hoc justifications out of a priori moral theories. They do not realize that they are doing this, so they fall prey to two illusions. Moral arguments are therefore like shadow-boxing matches: Each contestant lands heavy blows to the opponent's shadow, then wonders why she doesn't fall down. Thus, moral reasoning may have little persuasive power in conflict situations, but the social intuitionist model says that moral reasoning can be effective in influencing people before a conflict arises. Words and ideas do affect friends, allies, and even strangers by means of the reasoned-persuasion link. If one can get the other person to see the issue in a new way, perhaps by reframing a problem to trigger new intuitions, then one can influence others with one's words. Martin Luther King Jr.'s "I Have a Dream" speech was remarkably effective in this task, using metaphors and visual images more than propositional logic to get White Americans to see and thus feel that racial segregation was unjust and un-American (see Lakoff, 1996, on the role of metaphor in political persuasion).

4. The Action Problem: Moral Action Covaries with Moral Emotion More Than with Moral Reasoning

The analysis thus far has focused on moral judgment, not moral behavior, but the debate between rationalism and intuitionism can also be carried out using moral action as the dependent variable. There is a literature that directly examines the relationship between moral reasoning and moral action, and there is a literature that examines what happens when moral reasoning and moral emotions become dissociated (in the case of psychopaths).

The Weak Link between Moral Reasoning and Moral Action

In a major review of the literature on moral cognition and action, Blasi (1980) concluded that "moral reasoning and moral action are statistically related" (p. 37). But what is the nature of this relationship? Blasi was careful to state that the connection between moral reasoning ability and moral behavior is only a correlation, although later authors in the cognitive developmental tradition read the relationship as causal, stating that higher levels of moral reasoning cause better moral behavior (e.g. Lapsley, 1996). Blasi's review, however, raised the possibility that a third variable caused both better reasoning and better behavior: intelligence. Blasi found that IQ was consistently related to honesty, and he concluded that future investigators must do a better job of controlling for IQ. Kohlberg (1969) reported that scores on his moral judgment interviews correlated with measures of IQ in the .30–.50 range. Rest (1979) reported correlations of .20–.50 between IQ and his Defining Issues Test (DIT). . . .

Emotions Lead to Altruism

If reasoning ability is not sufficient to motivate moral action, then what is? Batson and his colleagues have developed the *empathy–altruism hypothesis,* which states that empathy aroused by the perception of someone's suffering evokes an altruistic motivation directed toward the ultimate goal of reducing the suffering (Batson, 1987; see also Hoffman, 1982). Batson, O'Quinn, Fulty, Vanderplass, and Isen (1983) found that participants who experienced empathy while watching a woman receiving (fake) electric shocks generally volunteered to take the shocks in her place, even when they were given the option of leaving the scene. Participants who experienced only nonempathic personal distress about the woman's plight volunteered to trade places with her only when they thought they would have to continue watching the woman receive the shocks. Participants in the first group seemed to be genuinely motivated to help the distressed woman, not to relieve their own distress. . . .

The Social Intuitionist Solution

It is easier to study verbal reasoning than it is to study emotions and intuitions, but reasoning may be the tail wagged by the dog. The dog itself may turn out to be moral intuitions and emotions such as empathy and love (for positive morality) and shame, guilt, and remorse, along with emotional self-regulation abilities (for negative morality; see Haidt, 2003, for a review and taxonomy of the moral emotions). A dog's tail is worth studying because dogs use their tails so frequently for communication. Similarly, moral reasoning is worth studying because people use moral reasoning so frequently for communication. To really understand how human morality works, however, it may be advisable to shift attention away from the study of moral reasoning and toward the study of intuitive and emotional processes. . . .

Testing the Social Intuitionist Model

The social intuitionist model is more complex and comprehensive than most rationalist models. Is the extra complexity necessary? Does the model do a better job of explaining and illuminating human moral life? That is a question that future research must decide. At least three kinds of research may shed light on the relative merits of the model.

1. Interfering with reasoning. If reasoning is a slow and effortful process that demands attentional resources, whereas intuition is fast, effortless, and undemanding . . . then manipulations that interfere with reasoning during a moral judgment interview should affect the quality of the post hoc reasoning produced without affecting the quality of the initial judgment. Rationalist models, in contrast, predict that the quality and speed of a judgment should be heavily dependent on one's reasoning ability.
2. Ecological variation. This article has suggested that standard moral judgment interviews represent unique and ecologically suspect settings in which a variety of factors conspire to maximize the amount and quality of reasoning. If this is true, then the reasoning produced in such interviews is consistent both with rationalist models and with the private reflection loop of the social

intuitionist model. . . . However, as the conditions of the interview are gradually changed to increase ecological validity, the social intuitionist model predicts that the reasoning produced should become recognizably post hoc. Alterations that would increase ecological validity include using real (rather than hypothetical) stories, asking about people known to the participant, working questions into a normal conversation (not a formal interview), and conducting the conversation in front of other people (not alone in a private room). Post hoc reasoning can be recognized by three features: (a) attempts to change facts about the story or to introduce new and tangential concerns, (b) a lack of responsiveness of the judgment to large changes in the facts of the story, and (c) a longer delay between the time the evaluation is made and the time that the first substantive reason is produced.

3. Consilience. Edward O. Wilson (1998) resurrected the term *consilience* to refer to the degree to which facts and theories link up across disciplines to create a common groundwork of explanation. He argued that theories that contribute to the unification of the sciences should be preferred to those that contribute to their fragmentation. The present article has tried to show that the social intuitionist model easily links findings in social and developmental psychology to recent findings and theories in neuroscience, primatology, and anthropology, but perhaps a similar case can be made for rationalist models. The debate between rationalism and intuitionism, now over 200 years old, is not just a debate between specific models; it is a debate between perspectives on the human mind. All of the disciplines that study the mind should contribute to the debate.

Conclusion

Rationalist models made sense in the 1960s and 1970s. The cognitive revolution had opened up new ways of thinking about morality and moral development, and it was surely an advance to think about moral judgment as a form of information processing. But times have changed. Now we know (again) that most of cognition occurs automatically and outside of consciousness (Bargh & Chartrand, 1999) and that people cannot tell us how they really reached a judgment (Nisbett & Wilson, 1977). Now we know that the brain is a connectionist system that tunes up slowly but is then able to evaluate complex situations quickly (Bechtel & Abrahamsen, 1991). Now we know that emotions are not as irrational (Frank, 1988), that reasoning is not as reliable (Kahneman & Tversky, 1984), and that animals are not as amoral (de Waal, 1996) as we thought in the 1970s. The time may be right, therefore, to take another look at Hume's perverse thesis: that moral emotions and intuitions drive moral reasoning, just as surely as a dog wags its tail.

References

Bargh, J. (1994). The four horsemen of automaticity: Awareness, efficiency, intention, and control in social cognition. In J. R. S. Wyer & T. K. Srull (Eds.), *Handbook of social cognition, 2nd edition* (pp. 1–40). Hillsdale, NJ: Erlbaum.

Bargh, J. A., & Chartrand, T. L. (1999). The unbearable automaticity of being. *American Psychologist, 54,* 462–479.

Baron, J. (1995). Myside bias in thinking about abortion. *Thinking and Reasoning, 1,* 221–235.

Batson, C. D. (1987). Prosocial motivation: Is it ever truly altruistic? *Advances in Experimental Social Psychology, 20,* 65–122.

Batson, C. D., O'Quinn, K., Fulty, J., Vanderplass, M., & Isen, A. M. (1983). Influence of self-reported distress and empathy on egoistic versus altruistic motivation to help. *Journal of Personality and Social Psychology, 45,* 706–718.

Baumeister, R. F., & Newman, L. S. (1994). Self-regulation of cognitive inference and decision processes. *Personality and Social Psychology Bulletin, 20,* 3–19.

Bechtel, W., & Abrahamsen, A. (1991). *Connectionism and the mind: An introduction to parallel processing in networks.* Cambridge, MA: Black-well.

Blasi, A. (1980). Bridging moral cognition and moral action: A critical review of the literature. *Psychological Bulletin, 88,* 1–45.

Cacioppo, J. T., & Petty, R. E. (1982). The need for cognition. *Journal of Personality and Social Psychology, 42,* 116–131.

Chaiken, S., & Trope, Y. (Eds.). (1999). *Dual process theories in social psychology.* New York: Guilford Press.

de Waal, F. (1996). *Good natured: The origins of right and wrong in humans and other animals.* Cambridge, MA: Harvard University Press.

Eisenberg, N., Shea, C. L., Carlo, G., & Knight, G. P. (1991). Empathy-related responding and cognition: A "chicken and the egg" dilemma. In W. M. Kurtines & J. L. Gewirtz (Eds.), *Handbook of moral behavior and development: Vol. 1. Theory* (pp. 63–88). Hillsdale, NJ: Erlbaum.

Forgas, J. P. (1995). Mood and judgment: The affect infusion model (AIM). *Psychological Bulletin, 117,* 39–66.

Frank, R. (1988). *Passions within reason: The strategic role of the emotions.* New York: Norton.

Freud, S. (1976). *The interpretation of dreams* (J. Strachey, Trans.). New York: Norton. (Original work published 1900)

Gibbs, J. C. (1991). Toward an integration of Kohlberg's and Hoffman's theories of morality. In W. M. Kurtines & J. L. Gewirtz (Eds.), *Handbook of moral behavior and development: Vol. 1. Advances in theory, research, and application* (pp. 183–222). Hillsdale, NJ: Erlbaum.

Gigerenzer, G., & Goldstein, D. G. (1996). Reasoning the fast and frugal way: Models of bounded rationality. *Psychological Review, 103,* 650–669.

Haidt, J. (2003). The moral emotions. In R. J. Davidson, K. Scherer, & H. H. Goldsmith (Eds.), *Handbook of affective sciences* (pp. 852–870). Oxford, England: Oxford University Press.

Haidt, J., Bjorklund, F., & Murphy, S. (2000). *Moral dumbfounding: When intuition finds no reason.* Unpublished manuscript. University of Virginia.

Haidt, J., & Hersh, M. (2001). Sexual morality: The cultures and reasons of liberals and conservatives. *Journal of Applied Social Psychology, 31,* 191–221.

Haidt, J., Koller, S., & Dias, M. (1993). Affect, culture, and morality, or is it wrong to eat your dog? *Journal of Personality and Social Psychology, 65,* 613–628.

Hoffman, M. L. (1982). Development of prosocial motivation: Empathy and guilt. In N. Eisenberg (Ed.). *The development of prosocial behavior* (pp. 218–231). New York: Academic Press.

Kagan, J. (1984). *The nature of the child.* New York: Basic Books.

Kahneman, D., & Tversky, A. (1984). Choices, values, and frames. *American Psychologist, 39,* 341–350.

Kohlberg, L. (1969). Stage and sequence: The cognitive–developmental approach to socialization. In D. A. Goslin (Ed.), *Handbook of socialization theory and research* (pp. 347–480). Chicago: Rand McNally.

Kohlberg, L. (1971). From is to ought: How to commit the naturalistic fallacy and get away with it in the study of moral development. In T. Mischel (Ed.),

Cognitive development and epistemology (pp. 151–235). New York: Academic Press.

Kohlberg, L., Levine, C., & Hewer, A. (1983). *Moral stages: A current formulation and a response to critics.* Basel, Switzerland: Karger.

Kuhn, D. (1991). *The skills of argument.* Cambridge, England: Cambridge University Press.

Kunda, Z. (1990). The case for motivated reasoning. *Psychological Bulletin, 108,* 480–498.

Lakoff, G. (1996). *Moral politics: What conservatives know that liberals don't.* Chicago: University of Chicago Press.

Lapsley, D. K. (1996). *Moral psychology.* Boulder, CO: Westview.

Margolis, H. (1987). *Patterns, thinking, and cognition.* Chicago: University of Chicago Press.

Nisbett, R. E., & Schacter, S. (1966). Cognitive manipulation of pain. *Journal of Experimental Social Psychology, 2,* 227–236.

Nisbett, R. E., & Wilson, T. D. (1977). Telling more than we can know: Verbal reports on mental processes. *Psychological Review, 84,* 231–259.

Perkins, D. N., Allen, R., & Hafner, J. (1983). Difficulties in everyday reasoning. In W. Maxwell (Ed.), *Thinking: The frontier expands* (pp. 177–189). Hillsdale, NJ: Erlbaum.

Perkins, D. N., Farady, M., & Bushey, B. (1991). Everyday reasoning and the roots of intelligence. In J. F. Voss, D. N. Perkins, & J. W. Segal (Eds.), *Informal reasoning and education* (pp. 83–105). Hillsdale, NJ: Erlbaum.

Piaget, J. (1965). *The moral judgement of the child* (M. Gabain, Trans.). New York: Free Press. (Original work published 1932)

Rest, J. R. (1979). *Development in judging moral issues.* Minneapolis: University of Minnesota Press.

Shweder, R. A., & Haidt, J. (1993). The future of moral psychology: Truth, intuition, and the pluralist way. *Psychological Science, 4,* 360–365.

Skinner, B. F. (1971). *Beyond freedom and dignity.* New York: Knopf.

Stein, R., & Nemeroff, C. J. (1995). Moral overtones of food; Judgments of others based on what they eat. *Personality and Social Psychology Bulletin, 21,* 480–490.

Turiel, E. (1983). *The development of social knowledge: Morality and convention.* Cambridge, England: Cambridge University Press.

Turiel, E., Hildebrandt, C., & Wainryb, C. (1991). Judging social issues: Difficulties, inconsistencies, and consistencies. *Monographs of the Society for Research in Child Development, 56,* 1–103.

Wegner, D., & Bargh, J. (1998). Control and automaticity in social life. In D. T. Gilbert, S. T. Fiske, & G. Lindzey (Eds.), *Handbook of social psychology* (4th ed., pp. 446–496). New York: McGraw-Hill.

Wilson, E. O. (1998). *Consilience: The unity of knowledge.* New York: Knopf.

Wilson, J. Q. (1993). *The moral sense.* New York: Free Press.

POSTSCRIPT

Do We Use Reasoning to Make Moral Decisions?

In the previous selections, the relationship between cognition and behavior is considered, particularly in terms of moral reasoning and moral intuitions. Rest, Narvaez, Thoma, and Bebeau are arguing for an understanding of morality that has at its base a series of developmental stages. Based on 25 years of data collection and analysis, Rest and his research team feel confident in their conclusions. They find three basic levels of moral reasoning, developing from the immature or less advanced to the most mature level. The first level is titled *Personal Interest Schema*. As the name suggests, the determination of right and wrong is based on the best outcome for the individual, a rather self-centered view. This individual's thoughts probably include the question of "How is this going to affect me?" The second level involves the *Maintaining Norms Schema,* which is a focus on rules, laws, and the norms that allow a society to function in a productive, non-chaotic way. This individual's thoughts may include the question "What is the best thing for the most people?" The most mature level, the *Postconventional Schema,* is based on principles, values, and logical coherence. This individual's thoughts may include the question "What is best for the sake of justice and fairness?" or "What is the most compassionate thing to do?"

Haidt, on the other hand, is arguing for a moral intuition that arises spontaneously and then guides any reasoning toward its support. His research has shown that people often express an immediate, passionate opinion, and yet many participants cannot explain why they feel so strongly one way or another. Haidt also give four reasons to doubt the model offered by Rest, et al. He states that (1) intuition and reasoning are dual processes, with intuition operating at a faster rate, (2) reasoning tends to support the immediate intuitions, like a lawyer making a case, (3) reasoning has the illusion of objectivity when really it is based on cultural norms, and (4) emotions tend to predict behavior more so than reasoning.

As is so often the case in these complex debates, the best question may not be "Which theory is correct?" but rather "How might these theories work together?" Both models emphasize cognition with their focus on intuition and reasoning, and both give some attention to the influence of culture and development. Haidt emphasizes the role of cultural norms and socialization in the development of moral intuitions. The model proposed by Rest, et al., gives some attention to the cultural aspect of moral reasoning in the middle level of development, the *Maintaining Norms*

Schema. Rest, et al., emphasize a developmental progression that moves from immature to mature as the individual gains more experience. Haidt doesn't emphasize a developmental sequence; however, his notion of moral intuition stems from the incorporation (a developmental process) of cultural norms by the individual. Some who study intuition find that there is a progression from immature to mature intuition (Baylor, 2003), and that trustworthy intuitions stem from the integration of knowledge, expertise, and experience (McCutcheon and Pincombe, 2001).

There are distinctions in these models to be considered as well. Haidt is concerned with immediate reactions to moral dilemmas or situations, whereas Rest, et al., are more concerned with reasoning behind the reaction. Rest, et al., are concerned with the quality of moral reasoning—whether the reasons given are less or more mature. Haidt is not as concerned with the quality of the reaction, but rather how it may fit within cultural norms. Finally, Haidt concludes his article with a call for more research, while Rest, et al., summarize 25 years of data collection based on thousands of studies.

Suggested Readings

Baylor, A. (2003). A U-shaped model for the development of intuition by level of expertise. *New Ideas in Psychology*, Vol 19(3), Dec 2001. pp. 237–244.

Gibbs, J. C. *Moral Development and Reality: Beyond the Theories of Kohlberg and Hoffman* (Thousand Oaks, CA: Sage Publications, 2003).

Gilovich, T., Griffin, D., and Kahneman, D. (Editors), *Heuristics and Biases: The Psychology of Intuitive Judgment* (New York: Cambridge University Press, 2002).

McCutcheon, H., and Pincombe, J. (2001). Intuition: An Important Tool in the Practice of Nursing," *Journal of Advanced Nursing* 35(5), 342–348.

Myers, D. G. *Intuition: Its Powers and Perils* (New Haven, CT: Yale University Press, 2002).

Rest, J. R., Narvaez, D., Bebeau, M. J., and Thoma, S. J. *Postconventional Moral Thinking: A Neo-Kohlbergian Approach* (Mahwah, NJ: Lawrence Erlbaum, 1999).

ISSUE 17

Is Intuition a Valid Way of Knowing?

YES: Helen H. I. McCutcheon and Jan Pincombe, from "Intuition: An Important Tool in the Practice of Nursing," *Journal of Advanced Nursing* (2001)

NO: Mary Ann Rosswurm and June H. Larrabee, from "A Model for Change to Evidence-Based Practice," *Image: Journal of Nursing Scholarship* (1999)

ISSUE SUMMARY

YES: Clinical nursing researchers Helen McCutcheon and Jan Pincombe make the case that any health care decisions made by nurses that are based on intuition should be considered as rational and valid, and should be documented as part of a patient's medical record.

NO: Professors of nursing Mary Ann Rosswurm and June Larrabee advocate for an evidence-based decision-making process for nurses that involves critical analysis of current research.

Can you think of an occasion when you made an important decision based on a hunch or a certain feeling? Or perhaps you can think of a time when you had a "gut reaction" to an event? People often say these reactions come from our intuition. While most people acknowledge that such intuitive experiences occur, there is less consensus as to whether those intuitions are trustworthy. Some people find that internal awareness or "inner voice" to be the most convincing when making a decision, and others choose to rely on evidence and factual information.

Cognitive scientists have been interested in the study of intuition for many years, but empirically investigating this phenomenon is quite difficult. Even a standard definition, from which to build an operational definition to use in research, has not yet emerged. Rather than trying to create intuitive experiences in the laboratory, many researchers have chosen to study people who seem to use and rely on personal intuition. A quick search of academic articles in health care journals will reveal numerous arguments for and against the use of intuition in the medical decision-making process. This discussion is not only found in the health care arena, but also in the areas of education, human factors, and the development of artificial intelligence.

In the first selection, McCutcheon and Pincombe consider the role of intuition in nursing practice. Their study involved 225 nurses who completed questionnaires and participated in discussions. Results showed that intuition is actually the result of the interaction of knowledge, experience, and expertise. Other factors, such as whether the working environment valued intuitions, the nurse's personality, and the amount of nurse-client interaction influenced the actual intuitions as well. McCutcheon and Pincombe gathered many anecdotal accounts of intuitive actions that resulted in positive outcomes for the clients. They also heard accounts of situations in which ignored intuitions resulted in problems; however, these retrospective data are questionable. We've all heard the saying "hindsight is 20/20," and it is much too easy, after the problem occurs, to say "I knew we should have . . . ". McCutcheon and Pincombe also noted that *none* of the nurses offered examples of situations in which following intuition resulted in a problem for the client.

On the other side of this debate is Rosswurm and Larrabee, who argue for evidence-based practice in health care. Their position is made fairly clear in their statement, "In the new healthcare environment, practitioners can no longer rely solely on clinical experience, pathophysiologic rationale, and opinion-based processes." They advocate the use of critical-thinking skills to evaluate the relevant medical and clinical research. In the second selection, they take the reader through the process of determining the best course of action, using evidence-based nursing, for a patient with acute confusion. There are a few abbreviations used in the second selection that should be explained: QI is Quality Improvement, NOC is Nursing Outcomes Classification, and NIC is Nursing Intervention Classification.

There are numerous aspects of this issue to consider. McCutcheon and Pincombe argue that intuition, which in their work is the integration of knowledge, expertise, and experience, should be valued and trusted. Their findings immediately raise the question, "When does one have enough knowledge, expertise, and experience to have trustworthy intuition?" Rosswurm and Larrabee, on the other hand, argue for a rather extensive process by which nurses could make evidence-based decisions with current research and critical, logical analysis. One immediate question their proposal raises is "Will medical personnel be trained to do this kind of investigation, and given the time and resources to follow the protocol?" It is important to keep in mind that while this debate is occurring on the academic level in this text and others, the consequences of both intuition-based and evidence-based health care are being experienced by patients around the world—for the better or for the worse.

In the following selections, McCutcheon and Pincombe argue that nurses' intuitions should be documented in patients' charts and trusted along with all other input in determining the best course of treatment for a patient. Rosswurm and Larrabee argue for reliance on carefully controlled research or evidence in determining treatment. If you were the patient, which would you be most comfortable with?

Helen H. I. McCutcheon and Jan Pincombe

Intuition: An Important Tool in the Practice of Nursing

Introduction

Nurses speak anecdotally about their use of intuition and can provide examples from their practice to illustrate why they consider it—the direct perception of truths or facts independently of any reasoning process—to be an important skill. However rarely, if ever, do they write about such issues in documents that are accessible to other nurses or health professionals. Nor do studies in relation to intuition adequately describe what nurses understand it to be or how it is used in nursing practice. Events that take place during service delivery that are changed or affected by a nurse's intuition are not generally documented in a client's case notes, and the topic appears to be confined to the oral tradition of nursing. Because intuition is a difficult concept to quantify it cannot easily be investigated using traditional scientific methods, with the result that it is poorly understood in terms of its defining characteristics. Consequently, it has been imbued with an almost mystical quality that leads some nurses to mistrust or ignore it, and rely on more 'empirical' methods.

In other professions, such as psychology (Stocks 1939, Ewing 1941, Bahm 1960, Westcott 1968, Jung 1971), mathematics (Bastick 1982) and business management (Dean *et al.* 1974, Bandrowski 1985), intuition has been a significant area of study. The interest of researchers appears to arise from professionals' inability to clearly articulate the concept or clearly explain its origins and its manifestation, as well as the uncertainty of whether its use is legitimate in a 'professional' setting. This inability to define intuition has contributed to the feeling that it is unreliable, unscientific and somehow unworthy of the nursing profession when the reality, based on anecdotal evidence, is often the reverse.

The Case for Intuition

Anecdotal accounts from nurses indicate that intuition can change patient outcomes; when nurses act on their intuition the result is that the patient,

From *Journal of Advanced Nursing,* August 2001, pp. 342–348.

either directly or indirectly, benefits in some way. Intuition is, therefore, a skill that affects the quality of patient care and patient outcomes. Because of this, its place as one of the tools or skills applied in the scope of nursing practice must be acknowledged and its use documented and accepted. These anecdotal accounts reveal that intuition plays a significant role in nursing and the study which gave impetus to this paper was in large part based on that evidence and nurses' perceptions of intuition in their practice.

Attempts to define intuition by many researchers have only met with moderate success, so we have concluded that a further attempt was of limited value. Instead, the value and variety of the definitions were acknowledged as being in keeping with the complexity, diversity and intangibility of the concept.

Our study sought to determine whether nurses believed that the use of intuition was valid in the practice of nursing, how they perceived their use of intuition in nursing practice and how to enhance the profession's ability to better articulate this aspect of nursing practice. Nurses from diverse backgrounds and areas of employment volunteered to provide information on their understanding of intuition.

Nursing Literature on Intuition

The literature provides various accounts of intuition in relation to nursing. Articles by Rew (1989, 1990, 1991), Rew and Barrow (1989) and McMurray (1989) suggested that the linear deductive process is only one technique used by nurses when assessing an individual. Many nurses use intuition as well as the 'standard' nursing process in order to develop a comprehensive assessment of an individual. It may be that intuition and the nursing process could be used more effectively together if nurses in clinical practice, education and management positions acknowledged its use, a point highlighted by other researchers (Rew 1987, 1988a, 1988b, 1989, Rew & Barrow 1987, 1989, Umiker 1989, Radwin 1990, Woodward Leners 1992, Easen & Wilcockson 1996, Paley 1996, Cioffi 1997, McMahon 1999).

A number of studies have attempted to develop an understanding of intuition in clinical practice in specialist areas of nursing, each associating the phenomenon with different terms. Pyles and Stern (1983, p. 52) found that nurses use behaviours referred to as nursing 'gestalt' as a basis for making decisions about patient care. Following a study with nurses who were holistic nurse practitioners, Agan (1987) suggested that intuition was a dimension of the art of nursing in that it is an aspect of the 'personal knowing' nurses have. Personal knowing, previously identified by Carper (1978), is one of the four patterns of 'knowing' in nursing, the others being 'empirics' (the science of nursing), 'aesthetics' (the art of nursing), and 'ethics' (the component of moral knowledge in nursing).

Woodward Leners (1992) undertook an ethnographic study designed to describe intuition in nursing. Forty nurses participated in the study and assisted in clarifying how intuition is used by nurses in a profession that has 'been simultaneously refuting yet covertly using intuition in nursing practice' (p. 140). Woodward Leners (1992) suggested that nurses consider patients to benefit from their use of intuition and because of this benefit nurses feel rewarded for having used their intuition.

The majority of nursing literature is concerned with clinical intuition as used in situations where there is a patient or client. However, the use of intuition by nurses is not limited to interactions with the patient. Some work has been undertaken that examines intuition as used by nurse managers (Agor 1986, Davidhizar 1991). Agor (1986) reiterated the recurring theme in nursing, namely that nursing management and education have been primarily concerned with linear deductive reasoning. This is reasoning that requires hard facts or scientific evidence on which to base decision making and suggests that nurses should create a work environment that values linear deductive reasoning and the use of intuition, contending that we should 'believe in' intuition.

Because of the very nature of intuition, most nursing studies on the concept have been qualitative, although a study by Miller (1993) attempted to measure objectively how perceptive nurses considered themselves to be. Poor response rates to Miller's survey unfortunately meant that the reliability of the instrument was questionable.

The Study

Research Methods

Following the original work of Glaser and Strauss (1967), the use of grounded theory in the social sciences had been shown to expand knowledge and increase understanding of concepts such as hope, despair, sadness, death and dying or intuition, that are impossible to explore using a reductionist approach and that are not adequately theorized. . . .

Recruitment

A letter outlining the purpose of the study and requesting approval to display the study information sheet was sent to Directors of Nursing in all the health units as well as to Heads of School in the Faculties of Nursing in two universities, major private nursing agencies, the nurses' union and Nurses' Board in the state in Australia where the study was conducted. In addition, a notice outlining the purpose of the study and inviting Registered Nurses to participate was placed in a nursing journal, in the newsletter of the Royal College of Nursing and in the Occupational Health Nurse Newsletter. All these had wide circulation in the Australian state where the research was undertaken. . . .

Data Collection

Data collection was undertaken using between-methods triangulation (Denzin 1989, p. 244) involving both focus group interviews and a Delphi survey. Two hundred and sixty-two nurses volunteered to participate in the study and 29 of these were involved in four focus group interviews. Information obtained from the focus group interviews provided qualitative data that was analysed using the technique of constant comparative analysis. The qualitative interview data were also used to assist in developing the first questionnaire for the Delphi survey. To preclude the risk of researcher bias, eight nurses from the volunteer group assisted in the development of the first questionnaire. These eight nurses represented a variety of nursing settings: a medical/rehabilitation ward, a surgical ward, a hospice unit, a district nursing setting, a mental health setting, an occupational health and safety environment in a large industrial complex, midwifery and academia. Their participation and that of the data generated by the focus groups reduced by one the number of rounds required in the Delphi survey because the preliminary work often undertaken in round one of a Delphi survey was fulfilled by the focus group interviews and the use of an 'expert panel' in the development of the first questionnaire (Boyce *et al.* 1993, Ketelaars *et al.* 1994). The remaining 225 nurses who had volunteered for the study participated in the survey.

The Delphi survey technique permits a researcher to structure group communication for the purpose of obtaining opinions, generating discussion and reaching consensus on a topic of interest without the individuals involved having to be physically together (Goodman 1987). Each participant in a survey receives an initial questionnaire to complete and, when the responses are statistically analysed, each participant receives feedback about the aggregated results before they complete another questionnaire. Successive rounds of questionnaires are sent to participants, the questions being developed from the consensus or differences in responses to the previous questionnaire, until consensus among the group is largely achieved.

The intuition study survey consisted of statements about intuition, knowledge, experience and expertise. Participants responded by indicating their level of agreement with the statement on a five point Likert scale, ranging from 1, anchored by strongly disagree to 5, anchored by strongly agree. Participants were also able to write comments under each statement. In this way, they could provide both qualitative and quantitative data.

The second Delphi questionnaire was formulated from the responses to the first one. Items where consensus had been reached were removed. Items where consensus had not been reached remained in the questionnaire but in some instances were re-worded to expand or delimit the statement; and a number of new items were added. These reflected new information obtained from comments recorded in the first questionnaire. The second questionnaire, using the same five point Likert scale, was distributed only to those participants who had returned a completed questionnaire in the first round. A summary page of results from the first questionnaire was included. The information provided by participants in the Delphi survey generated data that were quantitative, that is, the numerical score they selected on the Likert scale, and could be analysed using statistical methods. Qualitative data were also available from the Delphi survey because participants were able to add comments in text form for each statement. These data was analysed using the technique of constant comparative analysis.

Analysis of the Data

Analysing qualitative data in a grounded theory framework does not occur in a linear fashion, as the researcher collects data, constant comparative analysis begins and informs further data collection. Data are collected and then preliminary analysis takes place. The data are revisited as data collection continues. This is the technique of constant comparison. Preliminary codes and categories developed are re-examined and categories and codes refined in the light of new data collected and analysed. This was the case in this study and during the constant comparative analysis a large number of preliminary 'codes' emerged from the data. These represented patterns and similar answers. These preliminary codes were constantly compared with each other until 'categories' emerged. Similar codes were subsumed under category headings and in some cases category headings were changed to reflect better the content of a category, or categories were merged. The reduction of categories resulted in a reduction of the terminology required to explain the theory and opened up the potential for the substantive theory to be generalized to other situations, thereby gaining value as a formal theory.

Analysis of the quantitative data from the Delphi surveys was undertaken using both descriptive and inferential statistics. The selective coding of the responses on a five point Likert scale to the questions in the questionnaires and comments began by examining the statistical results and the comments made by participants for each question. These were transcribed into separate files for each question. In this way, we were able to read all the comments pertinent to each question with ease and at the same time compare the statistical results for each question firstly with the comments and then with the codes and categories that had already emerged from the analysis of the focus group data. The statistical analysis of participant responses to both Delphi questionnaires was used to add density and richness to the data and in so doing confirmed the emergence of the categories from the data. The comments from both the Delphi questionnaires assisted in category saturation.

The Findings

The study identified that intuition is not something that just 'happens'. Rather, it is a result of a complex interaction of attributes, including experience, expertise and knowledge, along with personality, environment, acceptance of intuition as a valid 'behaviour' and the presence or absence of a nurse/client relationship. . . .

The theory of intuition that emerged was that knowledge, expertise and experience are mutually dependent and have mutual and reciprocal effects, as well as interacting to yield an effect greater than their sum, referred to as 'synergy'. The synergy that occurs through the interaction of knowledge, experience and expertise results in intuition and is the core category that links the other categories.

Not elucidated previously by any of the researchers in this field is an explanation of how the somatic response often associated with intuition comes about. The findings of this study suggest that a somatic response associated with moments of intuition is a secondary consequence of the interaction and trajectory of effects of knowledge, experience and expertise. While not everyone who is intuitive experiences a somatic response, some individuals experience a physical or mental 'feeling' or both, either simultaneously with or soon after an intuitive episode.

The data also revealed that the environment in which the nurse was working could either support the use of intuition or suppress it, that is validate its use or inhibit it. If intuition were not valued in a particular setting, then the negative response and resultant devaluing of its use could inhibit intuitive ability. In such instances, the experience of an intuitive episode is not necessarily lost. Participants observed that there was a mechanism by which the information from an intuitive event was fed back into the individual's knowledge, experience and expertise, whether they acted on their intuition or not. Such feedback from an event was considered to add to their knowledge, experience or expertise.

Participants in the study indicated that they considered that personality was also related to intuitive ability, which corresponds to other research, especially by Miller (1993, 1995). The data revealed that participants felt that the type of work nurses choose to specialize in is determined by personality and by the quantity and quality of the individual's intuitive perceptions. Additional research on personality and the possible links to intuition may illuminate these issues further.

The relationship between nurse and client was explored in terms of its effect on intuition. Some nurses considered that a relationship with a client was required before they were able to be intuitive about that person. Others indicated that no such relationship was required. Yet another group of nurses considered that a client–nurse relationship was not required in order for them to be intuitive, but that it did enhance their intuitive ability.

The study revealed that many experienced nurses do not consider novice nurses to be intuitive, and that female nurses find that male nurses are less intuitive and are attracted to the more technological aspects of nursing practice. Both novice nurses, that is, new graduates, and male nurses indicated that they did experience episodes of intuition and rejected these observations. The issue of intuition in relation to gender is one requiring further investigation, as is the need to encourage novice nurses to express and develop their intuitive skills.

Discussion

To enable the elevation of intuitive ability from its past status as an aspect of nurses' oral history to a valid and valuable tool in the practice of nursing, nurses need to be apprised of the findings of studies such as this and encouraged to articulate and document their own use of intuition in practice.

Participants in this study indicated that intuitive ability was an attribute they used in the practice of nursing. Information provided by participants in this study demonstrated how the use of intuition affected client outcomes; either by averting a crisis in a client's condition or by leading the nurse to take some course of action to assist in a positive outcome of care for a client. We suggest that, where intuitive events impact on practice and patient outcomes, then these intuitive events should move from merely being part of the oral history of nursing to become part of the client's record of care.

The move in nursing towards evidence-based practice will provide a medium through which nurses' use of intuition in the delivery of appropriate care can be demonstrated in practice as a valuable and legitimate skill (Kitson *et al.* 1996, Wallace *et al.* 1997, Aranda 1999, Closs & Cheater 1999). Application of the theory of intuition in practice settings will provide nurses with a means of articulating their intuitive ability and at the same time offer evidence of the use of intuition.

Synergy between knowledge, experience, expertise and the effect of the resultant intuitive episodes will be enhanced by the internal feedback mechanism that appears to occur when intuition is acted on. The level of synergy generated by the combination of these attributes may be affected by whether an individual uses intuition, as well as by factors such as personality, environment and client–nurse relationship. Active acknowledgement and encouragement of the development and application of intuition may contribute to more successful nursing.

Novice nurses pointed out that they were reluctant to act on their intuition because of their inexperience; and relied on an experienced nurse as a role model. Experienced nurses who are role models should be encouraged to articulate and explain how they use intuition, acting as dynamic exemplars of this skill.

Acting on intuition emerged from the data as a very positive behaviour. That is, many participants reported on how things went wrong when intuition was ignored, suggesting that the use of intuition and acting on intuition may have positive outcomes for patients. However, it is noteworthy that participants did not mention examples of using intuition and being incorrect. We did not identify any information about the use of intuition when the intuitive feeling was wrong, and this is an important area that requires investigation. However, it may be difficult to persuade nurses to articulate occasions when their intuition has been wrong or misplaced because they are already wary about articulating their use of intuition, even when it has positive outcomes.

The findings contribute to the concept of intuition, in particular in the scope of nursing practice. Following analysis of the data all participants were provided with a synopsis of the emergent theory and asked for feedback. The only negative response was a comment in which one participant indicated that she thought research takes a long time. The comments in relation to the theory itself were positive.

Because participants in this study were volunteers, a limitation may be that these nurses were already interested in intuition, aware of it or already using it extensively in their own practice. However, focus group interviews and Delphi surveys, the chosen research methods, require participants who are acquainted in some way with or interested in the area under study. It was not therefore appropriate to select individuals randomly to participate in the study. Further research could examine what other nurses with no definite views on intuition have to say on the topic and compare the results with the findings of this study.

Further research from different perspectives could also enhance our understanding of the phenomenon of intuition in nursing. Phenomenology, ethnography, critical theory and quantitative approaches could all contribute different types of information. Using the literature as a source of data to substantiate the categories that emerged in this study has offered a varied perspective. However, it would be interesting for other researchers to use different theoretical perspectives to analyse the data collected in this study and then compare and contrast the findings.

Conclusion

Emergent theory of intuition in nursing has uncovered the pivotal role of synergy in intuition and has also provided information about how a range of factors interact and result in a synergy that results in intuition. The emergent theory may have 'fit' in the practice setting, be generalisable across practice settings, and understandable by nurses who have control of the theory because the theory emerged from data provided by nurses in diverse practice settings. However, in the case of this study, we can only claim fit for the nurses who participated. Wider fit of the theory to nursing *per se* would require further research.

That intuition exists and has a valid and important role in nursing is beyond dispute; anecdotal evidence supporting the use and importance of intuition is strong. Yet little formal research into its role has been attempted. This study has resulted in the emergence of a theory of intuition in nursing for the participants and has integrated the previously fragmented research on intuition. As has been established here, many nurses already use intuition, albeit often in a covert fashion. Our research sought to establish the use of intuition as a professional and useful tool in nursing, to bring it into the open and to allow nurses to understand its importance to their practice.

References

Agan, R. D. (1987). Intuitive knowing as a dimension of nursing. *Advanced Nursing Science, 10*, 63–70.

Agor, W. H. (1986). Intuition: the new management tool. *Nursing Success Today, 1*, 23–24.

Aranda, S. (1999). Evidence-based practice: linking the academy to healthcare. *Journal of Advanced Nursing, 16*, 5–6.

Bahm, A. (1960). Types of Intuition. Publications in Social Sciences and Philosophy, Series 3. University of New Mexico, New Mexico.

Bandrowski, J. F. (1985). *Creative Planning Throughout the Organization*. American Management Association, New York.

Bastick, T. (1982). *Intuition: How We Think and Act*. John Wiley & Sons, New York.

Boyce, W., Gowland, C., Russell, D., Goldsmith, C., Rosenbaum, P., Plews, N., & M. L. (1993) Consensus methodology in the development and content validation of a gross motor performance measure. *Physiotherapy Canada, 45*, 94–100.

Carper, B. A. (1978). Fundamental patterns of knowing in nursing. *Advances in Nursing Science, 1*, 13–23.

Cioffi, J. (1997). Heuristics, servants to intuition, in clinical decision-making. *Journal of Advanced Nursing, 26*, 203–208.

Closs, S. J., & Cheater, F. N. (1999). Evidence for nursing practice: a clarification of the issues. *Journal of Advanced Nursing, 30*, 10–17.

Davidhizar, R. (1991). Intuition and the nurse manager. *Health Care Supervisor, 10*, 13–19.

Dean, D., Milhalasky, J., Ostrander, S., & Schroeder, L. (1974). *Executive ESP*. Prentice Hall, Englewood Cliffs, NJ.

Denzin, N. K. (1989). *The Research Act. A Theoretical Introduction to Sociological Methods*. Prentice Hall, Englewood Cliffs, NJ.

Easen, P. & Wilcockson, J. (1996). Intuition and rational decision-making in professional thinking: a false dichotomy. *Journal of Advanced Nursing, 24*, 667–673.

Ewing, A. (1941). Reason and intuition. *Proceedings of the British Academy, XXVII*, 67–107.

Glaser, B. G., & Strauss A. (1967). *The Discovery of Grounded Theory: Strategies for Qualitative Research*. Aldine de Gruyter, New York.

Goodman, C. M. (1987). The Delphi technique: a critique. *Journal of Advanced Nursing, 12*, 729–734.

Jung, C. G. (1971). *The Collected Works of C. G. Jung*. Princeton University Press, Rockville.

Ketelaars, C. A. J., Huyer-Abu Saad, H., Halfens, R. J. G., & Wouters, E. F. (1994). Process standards of nursing care for patients with COPD: Validation of standards and criteria by the Delphi technique. *Journal of Nursing Care Quality, 9*, 78–86.

Kitson, A., Ahmed, L. B., Harvey, G., Seers, K., & Thompson, D. R. (1996). From research to practice: one organizational model for promoting research-based practice. *Journal of Advanced Nursing, 23*, 423–425.

McMahon, R. (1999). Clinical governance; evaluation and intuition. *Journal of Nursing Management, 7*, 315–316.

McMurray, A. (1989). Time to extend the 'process'. *Australian Journal of Advanced Nursing, 6*, 40–43.

Miller, V. G. (1993). Measurement of self-perception of intuitiveness. *Western Journal of Nursing Research, 15*, 595–606.

Miller, V. G. (1995). Characteristics of intuitive nurses. *Western Journal of Nursing Research, 17*, 305–316.

Paley, J. (1996). Intuition and expertise: comments on the Benner debate. *Journal of Advanced Nursing, 23*, 665–671.

Pyles, S., & Stern, P. (1983). Discovery of nursing gestalt in critical care nursing: the importance of the gray gorilla syndrome. IMAGE. *Journal of Nursing Scholarship, 15*, 51–57.

Radwin, L. E. (1990). Research on diagnostic reasoning in nursing. *Nursing Diagnosis, 1*, 70–77.

Rew, L. (1987). Nursing intuition. Too powerful—and too valuable—to ignore. *Nursing, 87* 13, 43–45.

Rew, L. (1988a). Intuition in decision making. IMAGE. *Journal of Nursing Scholarship, 20*, 151–154.

Rew, L. (1988b). Nurses' intuition. *Journal of Applied Nursing Research, 1*, 27–31.

Rew, L. (1989). Intuition: nursing knowledge and the spiritual dimension of persons. *Holistic Nursing Practice, 3*, 56–69.

Rew, L. (1990). Intuition in critical care nursing practice. *Dimensions of Critical Care Nursing, 9*, 30–37.

Rew, L. (1991). Intuition in psychiatric–mental health nursing. *Journal of Child and Adolescent Psychiatric and Mental Health Nursing, 4*, 110–115.

Rew L. & Barrow E. M. (1987) Intuition: a neglected hallmark of nursing knowledge. *Journal of Advanced Nursing Science, 10*, 49–62.

Rew, L., & Barrow, E. M., (1989). Nurses' intuition. Can it co-exist with the nursing process. *American Operating Room Nurses Journal, 50*, 353–358.

Stocks, J. (1939). *Reason and Intuition*. Oxford University Press, New York.

Umiker, W. O. (1989). Intuitive decision making and problem solving. *Medical Laboratory Observer, 21*, 57–59.

Wallace, M., Shorten, A., & Russell, K. (1997). Paring the way: stepping stones to evidence based nursing. *International Journal of Nursing Practice, 3*, 147–152.

Westcott, M. R. (1968). *Toward A Contemporary Psychology of Intuition. A Historical, Theoretical and Empirical Inquiry*. Holt, Rinehart and Winston, New York.

Woodward, Leners, D. (1992). Intuition in nursing practice: deep connections. *Journal of Holistic Nursing, 10*, 137–153.

Mary Ann Rosswurm
and June H. Larrabee

A Model for Change to Evidence-Based Practice

Dramatic changes in health care and the growth of integrated delivery systems have intensified practitioners' efforts to access new information about more efficacious approaches that enhance discipline-specific and interdisciplinary contributions to patient outcomes. In the new healthcare environment, practitioners can no longer rely solely on clinical experience, pathophysiologic rationale, and opinion-based processes (Ellrodt et al., 1997; Feinstein & Horwitz, 1997). Practitioners also must learn to search the research literature, critically appraise research findings, and synthesize empirical and contextually relevant evidence. Practitioners need to question their current practices and find better alternatives (Barnsteiner, 1996). Critical thinking skills and evidence-based methods for making clinical decisions are essential for maximizing the quality and cost-effectiveness of care (Kessenich, Guyatt, & DiCenso, 1997; Sackett, Rosenberg, Gray, Haynes, & Richardson, 1996). The President's Advisory Commission on Consumer Protection and Quality in the Health Care Industry (1998, p. 169) reported that improving the quality of health care "requires a commitment to delivering health care based on sound scientific evidence and continuously innovating new, effective health care practices and preventive approaches." Evidence-based practice is the integration of "individual clinical expertise with the best available external clinical evidence from systematic research" (Sackett et al., 1996, p. 71). The combined results from clinically relevant research, clinical expertise, and patient preferences produces the best evidence for ensuring effective, individualized patient care (Mulhall, 1998; Sackett & Rosenberg, 1995). Evidence-based practice is more likely to occur in practice settings that value the use of new knowledge and provide resources to access that knowledge.

Several national and international initiatives have been developed to facilitate evidence-based practice. In the past three decades there has been a tremendous increase in the number of clinical research studies, particularly studies using such methodologies as randomized clinical trials, meta-analysis, and study of patient outcomes. These research studies are the basis for the paradigm shift from the tradition and intuition-driven practice of physicians, nurses, and other health professionals, to the new paradigm of evidence-based practice. Researchers have sought to decrease gaps between the conduct of research and the use of research in practice settings. Many researchers are mentoring practitioners with the critique and synthesis of research and the development of guidelines for evidence-based practice. Although several models have been developed to guide practitioners in the research utilization process (Goode & Piedalue, 1999; Horsley, Crane, Crabtree, & Wood, 1983; Rosswurm, 1992; Stetler, 1994; Titler et al., 1994; White, Leske, & Pearcy, 1995), practitioners continue to have difficulty with synthesizing empirical and contextual evidence and with integrating evidence-based changes into practice (Camiletti & Huffman, 1998; Mackay, 1998).

The evidence-based model described in this article is derived from theoretical and research literature related to evidence-based practice, research utilization, and change theory. The model guides practitioners through the entire process of changing to evidence-based practice, beginning with the assessment of the need for the change and ending with the integration of an evidence-based protocol. . . . The authors developed and tested the usefulness of the model as they mentored nurses in defining and integrating evidence-based practice protocols at a regional medical center. The model might also be used in primary care or other settings in addition to acute inpatient units. A description of the model follows, along with an example of how nurses applied the model to implement an evidence-based protocol for hospitalized patients with acute confusion.

Overview of the Model

Step 1: Assess Need for Change in Practice

Practitioners' interest in a potential change in practice may be stimulated by awareness of patient preferences and dissatisfaction, quality improvement data, practitioner queries, evaluation data, or new research data. In Step 1, practitioners collect internal data and compare it with external data. When data indicate a problem with an aspect of practice, practitioners can assemble a team of stakeholders to participate in discussing and more clearly identifying the problem. Stakeholders may include discipline-specific or multi-disciplinary practitioners, administrators, and patients who have a stake in the practice (Specht, Bergquist, & Frantz, 1995; Steelman, 1995). . . .

After examining internal data, practitioners assess the need for a change in practice by comparing internal data with external data in benchmarking databases. Benchmarking entails collecting comparable performance data and "sharing of performance information to identify operational and clinical practices that lead to the best outcomes" (Czarnecki, 1996, p. 2). . . . The **Table** highlights Step 1 processes of the model that nurses used in the example of a change in practice for patients with acute confusion. Stakeholders included nurse managers and staff nurses concerned about the care of confused patients. They collected and analyzed internal and external data related to confusion. Identifying that a problem in caring for confused patients existed in their hospital, they committed to developing an evidence-based change.

Table

Application of the Model: Evidence-Based Protocol for Patients with Acute Confusion

Step 1. Assess need for a change

- Discussed clinical problem of acute confusion with nurse managers and nurses
- Reviewed QI & RM data on associated adverse events, i.e., falls, restraints
- Derived from data that patients > 65 years comprised more than 50% of hospital population and were at highest risk for confusion and adverse events
- Assessed nursing knowledge about delirium in elderly patients
- Compared internal data with external data from similar medical centers
- Identified from findings the need to improve nursing staff's knowledge and care of elderly patients at risk for developing confusion during hospitalization

Step 2. Link problem with interventions and outcomes

- Linked acute confusion with the NIC intervention of delirium management
- Included delirium management activities in an acute-confusion protocol
- Identified outcomes of cognitive orientation and safety as measured by a confusion scale, fall rates, and restraints

Step 3. Synthesize best evidence

- Reviewed literature focused on delirium management and safety
- Included nurses in critiquing research literature using worksheets
- Synthesized quantitative research evidence
- Combined quantitative research evidence with qualitative data, clinical judgment and contextual data
- Assessed system feasibility, patients' benefits, and risks of protocol

Step 4. Design a change in practice

- Included nurses from pilot study units in drafting the evidence-based protocol
- Prepared forms for pilot study and its evaluation with input from unit nurses
- Identified tools for measuring outcomes of cognitive orientation, fall rates, and use of restraints
- Educated all nurses on the pilot study units in use of the evidence-based protocol

Step 5. Implement and evaluate the practice change

- Implemented the pilot study on the two selected hospital units
- Monitored use of the protocol throughout the pilot period
- Collected data and analyzed findings
- Recommended adoption of protocol with minor revisions

Step 6. Integrate and maintain the practice change

- Met with staff nurses on pilot study unit to review revisions
- Presented evidence-based protocol to standards and practice council
- Communicated information to administration and collaborating practitioners
- Conducted in-service education for all nursing staff about the protocol
- Planned ongoing monitoring of outcomes on all units

Step 2: Link Problem with Interventions and Outcomes

Practitioners need to define the problem using the language of standardized classifications and then link the problem with classification of interventions and outcomes. Classification systems help to define the concepts of a science and organize the knowledge (McCloskey, 1995). They also facilitate communications among practitioners, provide standards for determining the effectiveness and cost of care, and identify needed resources (Maas & Johnson, 1998).

National databases have primarily consisted of medical classifications, such as the International Classification of Diseases (ICD), the Diagnostic and Statistical Manual of Mental Disorders (DSM), and the Current Procedural Terminology (CPT) (McCloskey, 1995). Patient outcomes often are linked to episodic physician interventions, although multiple providers deliver health care across a continuum of care. To verify specific accountabilities for cost effectiveness and quality of care, longitudinal measurements of multiple disciplines are needed (Maas & Johnson, 1998).

In Step 2 of the practice change for patients with confusion (**Table**), the nurses referred to NIC and NOC. They linked acute confusion with the intervention of delirium management and tentatively selected several nursing activities listed under delirium management. The nursing activities served as process indicators during the quality monitoring process in Step 5. The nurses selected outcomes of cognitive orientation and safety. These outcomes were measured by a confusion rating scale, fall rates, and use of restraints. The selection of potential interventions and patient outcomes are based primarily on clinical judgment (Johnson & Maas, 1998) and system priorities and resources.

Step 3: Synthesize Best Evidence

In Step 3 of the model, selected interventions and outcomes are refined. The best research evidence is synthesized and combined with clinical judgment and contextual data. The problem, potential interventions, and desired outcomes become the major variables for reviewing the research literature. Steps taken before conducting the literature search include clarifying the specific topic and identifing criteria for including a reference in the review (Slavin, 1995). In the critical appraisal of the literature, practitioners evaluate the strengths and weaknesses of studies and identify gaps and conflicts in the available knowledge. . . .

The purpose of the synthesis of the research studies is to determine whether the strength of the evidence supports a change in practice. The results of studies can be pooled only if the studies are similar in design. In the absence of strong evidence, practitioners need to weigh benefit to risk factors. They also need to consider the feasibility of implementing the findings in their own practice setting. The synthesis only brings together the existing evidence. It cannot create new evidence or knowledge. Thus, if most of the evidence is weak, additional research may be needed before making decisions to change practice or policies. If the research synthesis indicates sufficient research evidence to support a change in practice with desirable benefits and minimal risks, practitioners can proceed in designing the change.

In the example of the protocol for acute confusion (**Table**), the nurses, with guidance from nurse researchers employed by the hospital, completed a thorough literature search of quantitative and qualitative studies focused on delirium and patient safety. They critiqued the research and synthesized evidence of quantitative studies. This evidence was combined with qualitative findings, clinical judgment, and contextual data. Based on this evidence, they decided to develop and pilot test a protocol that was feasible for nursing staff to implement and offered maximum benefit with minimal risk to patients.

Step 4: Design a Change in Practice

After synthesizing the best evidence, practitioners describe the process variables or detailed sequence of care activities in the change in practice, usually in the format of a protocol, procedure, or standard (Specht et al., 1995; Steelman, 1995). The practice environment, its resources, and feedback from stakeholders are essential considerations when designing a change. . . .

If the change in practice affects a standard of care in a large hospital, a pilot demonstration of the change on one or two units is advised. The pilot test allows practitioners to influence adaptation of the change to fit their practice needs (The President's Advisory Commission on Consumer Protection and Quality in the Health Care Industry, 1998), giving practitioners a sense of ownership of the change process and contributing to smoother integration of the change. . . .

The plan for the pilot test also includes the timing and delegation of specific activities for obtaining agency approvals, preparing the test sites, and evaluating the results. The evaluation plan for the pilot test includes a study of quality improvement (QI) with process and outcome indicators and surveys of patient satisfaction and staff responses to the change in practice. . . .

In the example of confusion in hospitalized elderly patients **(Table)**, nurses from the two units participated in designing the protocol and planning for its implementation and evaluation. The project team identified cognitive orientation and safety as target patient outcomes. They selected nursing activities for delirium management that were supported by the evidence base. Information about the pilot test was communicated to collaborative practice groups and administrators for their review and approval. Nursing staff on the two test units had inservice training to implement the protocol. A 2-month implementation period followed.

Step 5: Implementing and Evaluating Change in Practice

. . . . After the protocol has been in use for the designated time, patient and staff surveys and QI study are conducted. Then, data are analyzed and displayed in charts or bar graphs to facilitate data interpretation. Following analysis, practitioners interpret the results by deciding whether there were differences in the indicators before and after the pilot study. Were the necessary structural variables provided? Do the data indicate that the new protocol was implemented as intended (McCollam, 1995; Specht et al., 1995; Steelman, 1995)? If yes, what effect did the new protocol have on patient outcomes? An inappropriately implemented protocol, because of misunderstanding or lack of endorsement, can do more harm than good (Cook et al., 1997; Ellrodt et al., 1997). When considering the results, practitioners must remember that outcomes can be affected by numerous factors other than the intervention, such as characteristics of patients, staff, interpersonal aspect of care, and the setting (Sidani & Braden, 1998). . . .

The decision to adapt, adopt, or reject the change is based on feedback from staff on the pilot units, managers, and pilot coordinators, QI and survey data, cost data, and recommendations from stakeholders. Feasibility, benefits, and risks are considered when evaluating the data. Personnel opinions of the implemented change provide information about acceptability or the need for modifications (McCollam, 1995). QI and cost data indicate whether the care and outcomes improved [are] at a reasonable cost to the system. Based on all the evaluation data, practitioners make recommendations to adapt, adopt, or reject the change in practice (McCollam, 1995; Specht et al., 1995; Steelman, 1995).

In the example of confusion in hospitalized elderly patients (**Table**), two nurses from each unit served as pilot-study coordinators. They monitored the 2-month implementation process and obtained informal staff nurse feedback. The unit coordinators participated in collecting and analyzing the QI data. All project activities progressed as planned.

Step 6. Integrate and Maintain Change in Practice

If the results of the pilot study support integration of the new practice into standards of care, change strategies are initiated. Even the smallest change has a domino effect and people affected by the change often perceive it as disruptive. Practitioners who are change agents need to consider the cultural climate of the organization as they attempt to integrate practice innovations. . . .

Maintaining the change is ensured by providing practitioners with the necessary resources to implement the change, by monitoring the process and outcomes, and by rewarding quality performance with incentives (Greco & Eisenberg, 1993). In the integration and maintenance of the protocol for confused patients (**Table**), specific actions were implemented to enhance communication, education, and monitoring of the change. The initial meetings were with the staff nurses on the pilot units to obtain their feedback about feasibility, benefits, and needed revisions. The revised protocol was then presented to the standards of practice council for approval. Concise written and oral presentations were prepared for administrators, and collaborative practice groups. Inservice sessions about the new protocol were presented to nursing staff on all hospital units. Nurses decided to conduct periodic QI monitoring of the implementation and outcomes.

Conclusions

The momentum is escalating in support of evidence-based practice that will improve the quality of patient care and enhance clinical judgment. Practitioners must know how to obtain, interpret, and integrate the best available research evidence with patient data and clinical observations. The evidence-based model described in this article was derived from theoretical and research literature. The model was successfully applied by nurses who were implementing change to evidence-based nursing practice. It may serve as a useful framework for other practitioners seeking to change to evidence-based practice in a variety of settings.

Patient outcomes must reflect discipline-specific and interdisciplinary accountabilities. Nurses' contributions to patient outcomes will be measured when nurses consistently use standardized language in defining patient problems, interventions, and outcomes. Practitioners need time and support to access databases and synthesize the best evidence for making changes in practice. Administrators must provide the infrastructure for evidence-based practice to develop and diffuse throughout an organization. Collaboration between researchers and practitioners within and among disciplines should enhance the diffusion of practice innovations.

References

Barnsteiner, J. (1996). Research-based practice. *Nursing Administration Quarterly, 20*(4), 52–58.

Camiletti, Y. A., & Huffman, M. C. (1998). Research utilization: Evaluation of initiatives in a public health nursing division. *Canadian Journal of Nursing Administration, 11*(2), 59–77.

Cook, D. J., Greengold, N. L., Ellrodt, A. G., & Weingarten, S. R. (1997). The relation between systematic reviews and practice guidelines. *Annals of Internal Medicine, 127*(3), 210–216.

Czarnecki, M. T. (1996). Benchmarking: A data-oriented look at improving health care performance. *Journal of Nursing Care Quality, 10*(3), 1–6.

Ellrodt, G., Cook, D. J., Lee, J., Cho, M., Hunt, D., & Weingarten, S. (1997). Evidence-based disease management. *Journal of the American Medical Association (JAMA), 278*(20), 1687–1692.

Feinstein, A. R., & Horwitz, R. I. (1997). Problems in the "evidence" of "evidence-based medicine." *American Journal of Medicine, 103*(6). 529–535.

Goode, C. J., & Piedalue, F. (1999). Evidence-based clinical practice. *Journal of Nursing Administration, 29*(6), 15–21.

Greco, P. J., & Eisenberg, J. M. (1993). Changing physicians' practices. *New England Journal of Medicine, 329*(17), 1271–1274.

Horsley, J., Crane, J., Crabtree, M. K., & Wood, D. (1983). *Using research to improve nursing practice: A guide*. New York: Grune & Stratton.

Kessenich, C. R., Guyatt, G. H., & DiCenso, A. (1997). Teaching nursing students evidence-based nursing. *Nurse Educator, 22*(6), 25–29.

Maas, M., & Johnson, M. (1998). Nursing outcomes accountability. *Outcomes Management for Nursing Practice, 2*(1), 3–5.

Mackay, M. H. (1998). Research utilization and the CNS: Confronting the issues. *Clinical Nurse Specialist, 12*(6), 232–237.

McCloskey, J. C. (1995). Help to make nursing visible. *Image: Journal of Nursing Scholarship, 27*, 170–175.

McCollam, M. E. (1995). Evaluation and implementation of a research-based falls assessment innovation. *Nursing Clinics of North America, 30*(3), 507–514.

President's Advisory Commission on Consumer Protection and Quality in the Health Care Industry, (1998). *Fostering evidence-based practice and innovation, quality first: Better health care for all Americans*. Washington, DC: U.S. Government Printing Office.

Rosswurm, M. A. (1992). A research-based practice model in a hospital setting. *Journal of Nursing Administration, 22*(3), 57–60.

Sackett, D. L., & Rosenberg, W. M. (1995). On the need for evidence-based medicine. *Journal of Public Health Medicine, 17*(3), 330–334.

Sackett, D. L., Rosenberg, W. M., Gray, J. A., Haynes, R. B., & Richardson, W. S. (1996). Evidence based medicine: What it is and what it isn't. *British Medical Journal, 312*(7023), 71–72.

Sidani, S., & Braden, C. J. (1998). *Evaluating nursing interventions: A theory-driven approach*. Thousand Oaks, CA: Sage.

Slavin, R. (1995). Best evidence synthesis: An intelligent alternative to meta-analysis. *Journal of Clinical Epidemiology, 48*(1), 9–18.

Specht, J. P., Bergquist, S., & Frantz, R. A. (1995). Adoption of a research-based practice for treatment of pressure ulcers. *Nursing Clinics of North America, 30*(3), 553–563.

Steelman, V. M. (1995). Latex allergy precautions: A research-based protocol. *Nursing Clinics of North America, 30*(3), 475–493.

Stetler, C. B. (1994). Refinement of the Stetler/Marram model for application of research findings to practice. *Nursing Outlook, 42*(1), 15–25.

Titler, M. G., Kleiber, C., Steelman, V., Goode, C., Rakel, B., Barry-Walker, J., Small, S., & Buckwalter, K. (1994). Infusing research into practice to promote quality care. *Nursing Research, 43*(5), 307–313.

White, J. M., Leske, J. S., & Pearcy, J. M. (1995). Models and processes of research utilization. *Nursing Clinics of North America, 30*(3), 409–420.

POSTSCRIPT

Is Intuition a Valid Way of Knowing?

At face value, the titles in this article, with a focus on intuition versus evidence in making health care decisions, may give the wrong impression. Some may immediately think "guessing versus facts," and that may quickly be followed with "I'm going with facts when my health is at stake." That rush to judgment may be a bit premature, as there is much to consider about both intuition-based and evidence-based decision making.

The important question in this debate may not be the "or" question, "Should we use intuition-based *or* evidence-based decision making processes?" but rather "*Who* is qualified to make intuition-based decisions, to make evidence-based decisions, or to use both decision-making processes?" Based on the findings of McCutcheon and Pincombe, perhaps we should consider the attributes of one who has enough knowledge, expertise, and experience to have trustworthy intuition. Let's begin with the areas of knowledge and expertise. When cognitive scientists began to develop computer software programs to imitate human cognitive processes, or artificial intelligence, one of the first applications was expert systems. The goal was to create a logic-driven program that could make expert decisions. Subsequently, many studies were conducted on human experts to better understand their methods of information processing. Researchers found that human experts can process more data, and process it faster, than non-experts. Experts see different patterns in the environment than novices, use more qualitative analysis, and are more efficient with memory storage. Expertise is generally not formalized in a rigid or structured way. It appears that experts develop specialized ways of organizing what they know, and they create generalized principles to guide their decisions (Solso, 2001). The work continues in trying to create artificial intelligence with this type of expert processing.

Experience also plays a role in developing intuition. In researching this very issue, Baylor (2001) found two qualitatively different types of intuition, which are labeled immature intuition and mature intuition. The novice in a new field may experience immature intuition that leads to novel insights. The novice hasn't yet been trained in the common practices, assumptions, and theories of the new area, and that lack of interference sometimes allows for creative, intuitive insights. Baylor found mature intuition in experts who have developed large banks of knowledge and experience. Baylor also made the observation that mature intuition is rare. Based on the assumption that a novice would not be in a decision-making position, it appears that personnel with trustworthy intuition should have extensive expertise, knowledge, and experience.

We can also ask the "who" question of Rosswurm and Larrabee, who are lobbying for an evidence-based system. They claim "practitioners must know how to obtain, interpret, and integrate the best available research evidence with patient data and clinical observation" (page 322). It appears that practitioners, who spend a great deal of time learning to implement numerous procedures, must also be trained as researchers. They must have the time and knowledge to find the most relevant research, determine the quality of the methodology, interpret the statistical procedures and results, and understand the entire situation well enough to integrate the findings of numerous studies with clinical observations to produce the best treatment plan. The practitioner who can do that successfully, gaining a great deal of knowledge, over a long period of time, developing expertise and gaining experience, may just develop a sense of intuition in his or her field!

Suggested Readings

Bastick, T., and Love, T. *Intuition: Evaluating the Construct and Its Impact on Creative Thinking* (Stoneman and Lang, 2003).

Baylor, A. (2003). A U-shaped model for the development of intuition by level of expertise. *New Ideas in Psychology*, Vol. 19(3), Dec 2001. pp. 237–244.

Gilovich, T., Griffin, D., and Kahneman D. (Editors). *Heuristics and Biases: The Psychology of Intuitive Judgment* (New York: Cambridge University Press, 2002).

Hogarth, R. *Educating Intuition* (Chicago: University of Chicago Press, 2001).

Klein, G. *Intuition at Work: Why Developing Your Gut Instincts Will Make You Better at What You Do* (New York: Doubleday, 2002).

Myers, D. G. *Intuition: Its Powers and Perils* (New Haven, CT: Yale University Press, 2002).

Solso, R. *Cognitive Psychology,* 6th edition (Boston: Allyn & Bacon, 2001).

ISSUE 18

Should Schools Teach for Wisdom?

YES: Robert J. Sternberg, from "Why Schools Should Teach for Wisdom: The Balance Theory of Wisdom in Educational Settings," *Educational Psychologist* (2001)

NO: Scott G. Paris, from "Wisdom, Snake Oil, and the Educational Marketplace," *Educational Psychologist* (2001)

ISSUE SUMMARY

YES: American Psychological Association president and author Robert J. Sternberg believes that schools need to teach wisdom-related skills rather than focus exclusively on imparting knowledge.

NO: Professor of psychology Scott G. Paris counters these suggestions by arguing that Sternberg's description of wisdom is contradictory and his suggestions are out of touch with the political and commercial nature of education.

The desire to define and understand wisdom has a long history, with much of it found in philosophy and religion. Cognitive psychologists have, relatively speaking, only recently joined in this effort. Some scientists have adopted a top-down strategy in which they start with a concept of fully mature wisdom and attempt to work down or back to its beginnings in human development. Others take a bottom-up approach by searching for all the precursors to wisdom and hypothesizing how those pieces come together and mature to form wisdom. We will begin here by considering a bottom-up approach.

When considering the building blocks of human cognitive development, many social and cognitive scientists begin with the work of Jean Piaget. Starting in infancy, Piaget's work tells the story of development from the simplest thought forms, through the understanding of basic concepts and concrete thinking, to the development of complex logical and abstract reasoning. His most advanced stage, formal operational thought, is achieved by most people during adolescence. Most scholars would agree that Piaget's formal operational stage does not include wisdom, which begs the question, "How does one get from formal operations to wisdom?"

Several researchers have attempted to extend Piaget's work by developing "post-formal operations," which do have characteristics similar to those of wisdom. Commons and Richards [Commons, M. L. and Richards, F. A. (2003). Four postformal stages. In J. Demick and C. Andreoletti (Eds.), *Handbook of Adult Development* (pp. 199–219). New York: Plenum Publishers], surveyed numerous theories of post-formal operations and determined that "all argue in common that post-formal behavior involves one or more of the following: perceiving, reasoning, knowing, judging, caring, feeling, or communicating in ways that are more complex or more all-encompassing than formal operations" (p. 202). Post-formal theories generally include an acceptance of contradiction and paradox as well as an awareness of the relativistic nature of knowledge.

Another very well known psychologist and writer, Erik Erikson, took a much different approach than those following a Piagetian model. He took a clinical or therapeutic approach to wisdom. Based on his experience with clients, he viewed human development as moving through a series of eight stages. Each stage brings its own crisis or challenge and its own virtue. In Erikson's model, wisdom doesn't appear until the end of life, after much experience and reflection. We must work through issues of trust, identity, and love before we become wise. Although Erikson's work is usually considered to be closer to personality development than cognitive science, it has shaped the way many social scientists conceptualize wisdom.

As mentioned earlier, while some researchers choose to study cognitive development as it leads to wisdom, others choose to study mature wisdom directly. Robert Sternberg, author of the first selection, has been studying wisdom for many years. His well-known wisdom research follows an implicit-theoretical approach, which means his definition of wisdom is built on folk psychology. Sternberg is interested in wisdom as it is viewed or defined by the typical person. Based on the statistical analysis of data collected from many laypersons, Sternberg has defined the wise person as one who has good reasoning ability and judgment. The wise person is sharp, quick, and savvy with information, and is someone who learns a great deal by paying attention to ideas and to the environment.

Another well-known researcher in the area of wisdom is Paul Baltes. He prefers an explicit-theoretical approach in which a definition of wisdom is developed by experts, and then laypersons are measured to see how closely they match the expert definition. For Baltes and his research group, wisdom involves knowledge of practical facts and problem-solving strategies, an understanding of different life situations, and an appreciation for life's uncertainties. These aspects of wisdom are measured by asking research participants to respond to a dilemma or life-management problem.

The issue here, "Should schools teach for wisdom?" raises many questions in addition to "What is wisdom?" One might ask whether the issue should be titled "*Can* schools teach for wisdom?" Another pertinent question is "Can wisdom really be taught?" and if so, can it be taught to school-age children?

Robert J. Sternberg

Why Schools Should Teach for Wisdom: The Balance Theory of Wisdom in Educational Settings

. . . There are several reasons why it is important to develop wisdom in the setting of the school. First, a goal of schooling should be not just to impart knowledge, but to help students develop wise use of such knowledge. Knowledge can be used to better or worse ends, and schools should help students use their knowledge for good rather than ill. Second, the teaching of wise thinking has always been implicit in school curricula in any case. For example, one learns history in part so as to learn the lessons of the past and not repeat its mistakes. One learns literature in part so as to learn how to apply to one's life the lessons literary characters have learned. So it seems a reasonable proposal to make explicit what has previously been implicit. Third, if adults do not make wise decisions, schools perhaps deserve a share of the blame if they have never conscientiously prepared these adults to make such decisions.

Major Approaches to Understanding Wisdom

Implicit-Theoretical Approaches

Implicit-theoretical approaches to wisdom have in common the search for an understanding of people's folk conceptions of what wisdom is. Thus, the goal is not to provide a "psychologically true" account of wisdom, but rather an account that is true with respect to people's beliefs, whether these beliefs are right or wrong. . . .

Sternberg (1985b, 1990a) reported a series of studies investigating implicit theories of wisdom. . . . For wisdom, six components emerged: *reasoning ability, sagacity, learning from ideas and environment, judgment, expeditious use of information,* and *perspicacity.* These components can be compared with those that emerged from a similar scaling of people's implicit theories of intelligence, which were *practical problem-solving ability, verbal ability, intellectual balance and integration, goal orientation and attainment, contextual intelligence,*

From *Educational Psychologist,* vol. 1, Fall 2001, pp. 227–239, 242–245.

and *fluid thought*. . . . In wisdom, . . . , some kind of balance appears to emerge as important that does not emerge as important in intelligence, in general. . . .

Explicit-Theoretical Approaches

Explicit-theoretical approaches have in common a formal theory of wisdom that is proposed to account for wisdom. The most extensive program of research has been that conducted by Baltes and his colleagues. . . .

Three kinds of factors—general person factors, expertise-specific factors, and facilitative experiential contexts—were proposed to facilitate wise judgments. These factors are used in life planning, life management, and life review. Wisdom is in turn then reflected in five components: (a) rich factual knowledge (general and specific knowledge about the conditions of life and its variations), (b) rich procedural knowledge (general and specific knowledge about strategies of judgment and advice concerning matters of life), (c) life-span contextualism (knowledge about the contexts of life and their temporal [developmental] relationships), (d) relativism (knowledge about differences in values, goals, and priorities), and (e) uncertainty (knowledge about the relative indeterminacy and unpredictability of life and ways to manage). An expert answer should reflect more of these components, whereas a novice answer should reflect fewer of them. . . .

The Balance Theory of Wisdom

The Basis of Wisdom in Tacit (Implicit) Knowledge

Many judgments in life require explicit knowledge, or the knowledge one learns directly in school and in life, such as about theories and findings in biology, psychology, history, or other subject-matter areas. For example, to counsel someone about a career in biology, it helps to know something about biology. To resolve a dispute between two governments, one needs to understand the nature of those governments. But to make wise judgments, one often has to complement one's explicit knowledge with implicit knowledge. . . .

The balance theory of wisdom emphasizes the role of tacit knowledge (TK) not because explicit knowledge is unimportant, but because it is believed that TK is more likely to be a source of individual differences than is formal knowledge. For example, if one were to take the biologists or historians in a university department, the view here is that they are more likely to differ in their wisdom as a result of TK of their field than as a result of formal knowledge of their domain.

The view of wisdom proposed here thus has at its core the notion of TK (Polanyi, 1976), which we have defined as action-oriented knowledge, often but certainly not always acquired without direct help from others, that allows individuals to achieve goals they personally value (Sternberg, Wagner, Williams, & Horvath, 1995). TK has three main features: (a) it is procedural, (b) it is relevant to the attainment of goals people value, and (c) it often is acquired without direct help from others. . . .

Wisdom as Knowledge Balancing Interests

The definition of wisdom proposed here draws both on the notion of TK, as described earlier, and on the notion of balance (Sternberg, 1998a). Wisdom is thus viewed as a kind of practical intelligence, but not the kind that is applied simply to benefit oneself or some individual one cares about, for whatever reason. In particular, wisdom is defined as the application of tacit as well as explicit knowledge as mediated by values toward the achievement of a common good through a balance among (a) intrapersonal, (b) interpersonal, and (c) extrapersonal interests, over the (a) short and (b) long terms, to achieve a balance among (a) adaptation to existing environments, (b) shaping of existing environments, and (c) selection of new environments, as shown in Figure 1.

Figure 1

Wisdom as value-mediated TK balancing goals, responses, and interests. The individual applies tacit and formal knowledge to seek a common good. Such application involves balancing of intrapersonal, interpersonal, and extrapersonal interests over the short and long terms to adapt to, shape, and select environments. Judgments regarding how to achieve a common good inevitably involve the infusion of values.

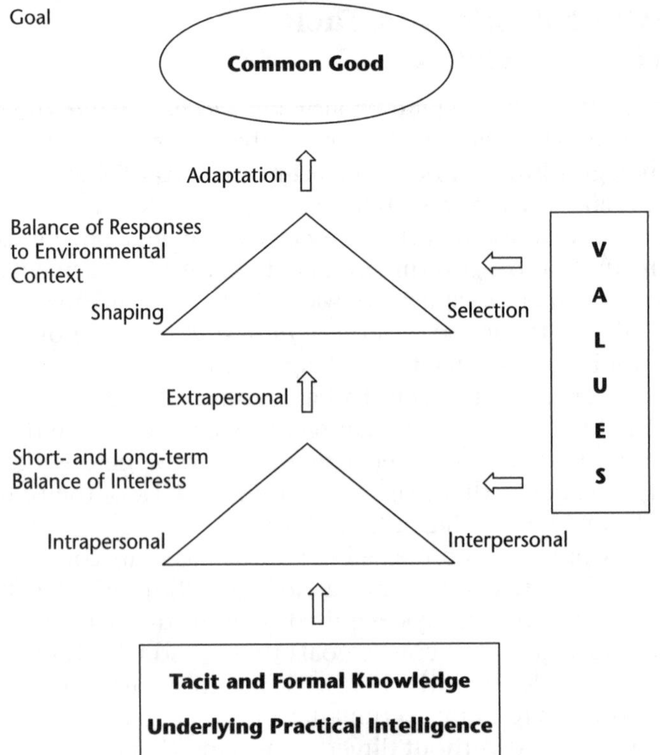

Thus, wisdom is a kind of practical intelligence in that it draws on TK, but it is not just any kind of practical intelligence. Wisdom is not simply about maximizing one's own or someone else's self-interest, but about balancing of various self-interests (intrapersonal) with the interests of others (interpersonal) and of other aspects of the context in which one lives (extrapersonal), such as one's city or country or environment or even God. . . .

Problems requiring wisdom always involve at least some element of each of intrapersonal, interpersonal, and extrapersonal interests. For example, one might decide that it is wise to take a particular teaching position, a decision that seemingly involves only one person. But many people are typically affected by an individual's decision to take a job—significant others, children, perhaps parents and friends. And the decision always has to be made in the context of what the whole range of available options is. . . .

What constitutes appropriate balancing of interests, an appropriate response to the environment, and even the common good, all hinge on values. Values, therefore, are an integral part of wise thinking. The question arises as to "whose values?" Although different major religions and other widely accepted systems of values may differ in details, they seem to have in common certain universal values, such as respect for human life, honesty, sincerity, fairness, and enabling people to fulfill their potential. Of course, not every government or society has subscribed to such values. Hitler's Germany and Stalin's Russia blatantly did not, and most societies today subscribe to them in only some degree but not fully.

The question of "whose values," though, can become a red herring. When world leaders such as Stalin or Hitler or Milosevic act in ways that directly contradict these values, only the most cynical individual could believe they are doing so in the service of the common good. . . .

I do not claim to have solved the conundrum of how to specify a unique universal set of values. If philosophers and theologians for centuries have failed to do so, I most certainly will not do so either. At the same time, I believe it a mistake to state that, because we cannot definitively offer a set of universal values, therefore, the whole project of understanding wisdom must and should collapse of its own lack of specificity. . . .

Wisdom manifests itself as a series of processes that are typically cyclical and can occur in a variety of orders. These processes are related to what I have referred to as "metacomponents" of thought (Sternberg, 1985a, 1997, 1999b), including (a) recognizing the existence of a problem, (b) defining the nature of the problem, (c) representing information about the problem, (d) formulating a strategy for solving the problem, (e) allocating resources to the solution of a problem, (f) monitoring one's solution of the problem, and (g) evaluating feedback regarding that solution. In deciding about a teaching job, for example, one first has to see both taking the position and not taking it as viable options (problem recognition), then figure out exactly what taking or not taking the position would mean for oneself (defining the problem), then consider the costs and benefits to oneself and others of taking the position (representing information about the problem), and so forth. . . .

Relation of Wisdom to Other Skills

Wisdom is related to other psychological constructs but not identical to any of them. In particular, it is related to knowledge; to analytical, creative, and practical aspects of intelligence; and to other aspects of intelligence.

First, wisdom requires knowledge, but the heart of wisdom is tacit, informal knowledge of the kind learned in the school of life, not the kind of explicit formal knowledge taught directly in schools. One could be a "walking encyclopedia" and show little or no wisdom because the knowledge one needs to be wise is not to be found in encyclopedias or even, generally, in much of the teaching found in many schools.

Second, wisdom requires analytical thinking, but it is not the kind of analytical thinking typically emphasized in schools or measured on tests of academic abilities and achievements (discussed in Sternberg, 1980). Rather it is the analysis of real-world dilemmas where clean and neat abstractions often give way to messy and disorderly concrete interests. The kind of abstract analytical thinking that may lead to outstanding performance on a test such as the Raven Matrices, which presents figural reasoning items, will be of some but not much use in complex real-world dilemmas such as how to defuse the conflict between India and Pakistan.

An important part of analytical thinking is metacognition. Wisdom seems related to metacognition, and it is, because the metacomponents involved in wisdom are similar or identical to those that follow from other accounts of metacognition (e.g., Campione, Brown, & Ferrara, 1982; Nelson, 1999). Thus, in wisdom, as in other types of thinking, one needs to define problems, formulate strategies to solve problems, allocate resources to the solution of these problems, and so forth. These processes are used in wisdom, as they are in other types of thinking, but in wisdom they are used to balance different types of interests to seek a common good.

Third, wise solutions are often creative ones, as King Solomon demonstrated in cleverly determining which of two women was truly the mother of a child. But the kind of crowd-defying, buy-low, sell-high attitude that leads to creative contributions does not in itself lead to wisdom. Creative people often tend toward extremes, although their later contributions may be more integrative (Gardner, 1993). Creative thinking is often brash whereas wise thinking is balanced. This is not to say that the same people cannot be both creative and wise. It is to say, however, that the kinds of thinking required to be creative and wise are different and thus will not necessarily be found in the same person. Moreover, teaching people to think creatively (see, e.g., Sternberg & Williams, 1996) will not teach them to think wisely. . . .

Fourth, practical thinking is closer to wisdom than are analytical and creative thinking, but again, it is not the same. Wisdom is a particular kind of practical thinking. It is practical thinking that (a) balances competing intrapersonal, interpersonal, and extrapersonal interests, over the short and (b) long terms, (c) balances adaptation to, shaping of, and selection of environments, in (d) the service of a common good. Thus, people can be good practical thinkers without being wise, but they cannot be wise without being good practical thinkers. Good practical thinking is necessary but not sufficient for the manifestation of wisdom.

Fifth, wisdom also seems to bear at least some relation to constructs such as social intelligence (Cantor & Kihlstrom, 1987; Kihlstrom & Cantor, 2000; Sternberg & Smith, 1985), emotional intelligence (Goleman, 1995; Mayer & Salovey, 1993; Salovey & Mayer, 1990), and interpersonal and intrapersonal intelligences (Gardner, 1983, 1999). . . .

Measurement of TK in Wisdom

Can wisdom be measured? We believe so. Consider problems we have used in the past to measure the TK underlying practical intelligence, for which we have collected extensive data, and then consider problems we are using in our current research to measure wisdom.

Measurement of TK

In a series of studies on practical intelligence with both adults and children (Sternberg, Wagner, & Okagaki, 1993; Sternberg, Wagner, Williams, & Horvath, 1995; Sternberg, Forsythe, et al., 2000; Wagner & Sternberg, 1985), we have sought to develop assessments of TK in real-world pursuits. The methodology for constructing assessments is rather complex (Horvath et al., 1996), but involves interviewing individuals for how they have handled critical situations on their jobs or, for children, in their schooling. We then extract the TK implicit in these interviews. Assessments then are constructed that ask people to solve the kinds of problems they find in managing themselves, others, and tasks on the job. Each of the problems in the assessment typically presents a scenario about a job-related problem along with possible options for dealing with that problem. . . .

In a series of studies (see reviews in Sternberg, Wagner, & Okagaki, 1993; Sternberg, Wagner, Williams, & Horvath., 1995; Sternberg, Forsythe, et al., 2000), we have learned a substantial amount about TK. These studies have been conducted on individuals from roughly 50 occupations, with the most work having gone into studies of business managers, academic psychologists, salespeople, principals, elementary-school teachers, middle-school students, high-school students, and college students.

1. TK can be reliably measured, with reliability coefficients typically in the .6–.9 range.
2. TK tends to increase with experience in an environment, but it is what one learns from the experience rather than the experience itself that seems to matter.
3. Measures of TK tend to be correlated with each other, both within and across measures for different occupations. For example, Wagner (1987) found a correlation at the .6 level between scores on TK measures for academic psychology and management with undergraduates as participants.
4. Our measures of TK also predict actual performance in jobs such as sales, management, and college teaching. This prediction is

statistically significant and fairly substantial in magnitude (with correlations typically at about the .3 level).

5. This prediction is largely independent of the prediction provided by conventional tests of academic intelligence. Correlations with tests of fluid and crystallized abilities typically hover about 0.
6. This prediction is even largely independent of the prediction provided by multiple-ability tests such as the Armed Services Vocational Aptitude Battery (ASVAB). A study by Eddy (1988) at the Brooks Air Force Base with Air Force Basic Training recruits showed trivial correlations with ASVAB subtests.
7. TK scores are largely independent of scores on tests of personality, styles, and interpersonal orientation (see Sternberg, Wagner, & Okagaki, 1993).
8. TK scores predict managerial performance significantly even after entering in other variables. In a study at the Center for Creative Leadership (described in Sternberg, Wagner, & Okagaki, 1993), we found that TK for management was the best single predictor of performance on two managerial simulations. This relation held even after entering (conventional) cognitive abilities, personality-scale measures, styles, and interpersonal orientation into a hierarchical regression equation predicting performance on the simulations. TK still contributed significantly and substantially to prediction of performance on the simulations.
9. TK predicts school performance about as well as, and sometimes better than, do academic-ability indicators (Sternberg, Grigorenko, Jarvin, & Lockery, 2000; Sternberg, Wagner, & Okagaki, 1993).
10. In some cultures, TK may actually be negatively correlated with academic-intelligence measures, such as cultures where schooling is not highly valued by much of the population and is seen as a distraction from everyday activities (see Sternberg & Grigorenko, 1997).
11. TK is relevant to shaping of as well as adaptation to environments. In particular, superiors' ratings of military leadership (at the platoon, company, and battalion levels) were better predicted by a measure of TK for military leadership than of crystallized intelligence or of TK for management, and the incremental validity of the TK measure for military leadership was significant.
12. TK can be developed, at least to some extent (Gardner, Krechevsky, Sternberg, & Okagaki, 1994; Sternberg, Forsythe, et al., 2000; Sternberg, Okagaki, & Jackson, 1990). . . .

Implications for Education

Why Should Wisdom Be Included in the School Curriculum?

. . . There are several reasons why schools should seriously consider explicitly including instruction in wisdom-related skills in the school curriculum.

First, as noted earlier, knowledge is insufficient for wisdom and certainly does not guarantee satisfaction or happiness. Wisdom seems a better vehicle to the attainment of these goals.

Second, wisdom provides a mindful and considered way to enter considered and deliberative values into important judgments. One cannot be wise and at the same time impulsive or mindless (Langer, 1997) in one's judgments.

Third, wisdom represents an avenue to creating a better, more harmonious world. Dictators such as Adolph Hitler and Joseph Stalin may have been knowledgeable and may even have been good critical thinkers, at least with regard to the maintenance of their own power. Given the definition of wisdom, however, it would be hard to argue they were wise.

Fourth and finally, students, who later will become parents and leaders, are always part of a greater community and hence will benefit from learning to judge rightly, soundly, and justly on behalf of their community (Ardelt, 1997; Sternberg, 1990b, 1998a, 1999a; Varela, 1999).

If the future is plagued with conflict and turmoil, this instability does not simply reside *out there somewhere;* it resides, and has its origin, *in ourselves*. For all these reasons, we endorse teaching students not only to recall facts and to think critically (and even creatively) about the content of the subjects they learn, but to think wisely about it, too. . . .

Sixteen Principles of Teaching for Wisdom Derived from the Balance Theory of Wisdom

There are 16 principles derived from the balance theory that form the core of how wisdom can be developed in the classroom. A fundamental idea in teaching for wisdom is that one teaches children not *what* to think, but, rather, *how* to think. There is no place, when one teaches for wisdom, for teaching doctrinaire beliefs or ideologies. Many of the principles of teaching for wisdom already are being applied in classrooms characterized by good instruction. Thus, to some extent, these ideas help systematize many things already being done, and also may add some things that currently are not yet being done in many classrooms.

1. Explore with students the notion that conventional abilities and achievements are not enough for a satisfying life. Many people become trapped in their lives and, despite feeling conventionally successful, feel that their lives lack fulfillment. Fulfillment is not an alternative to success, but rather, is an aspect of it that, for most people, goes beyond money, promotions, large houses, and so forth.
2. Demonstrate how wisdom is critical for a satisfying life. In the long run, wise decisions benefit people in ways that foolish decisions never do.
3. Teach students the usefulness of interdependence—a rising tide raises all ships; a falling tide can sink them.
4. Role-model wisdom because what you do is more important than what you say. Wisdom is action dependent and wise actions need to be demonstrated.
5. Have students read about wise judgments and decision making so that students understand that such means of judging and decision making exist.

6. Help students to learn to recognize their own interests, those of other people, and those of institutions.
7. Help students learn to balance their own interests, those of other people, and those of institutions.
8. Teach students that the "means" by which the end is obtained matters, not just the end.
9. Help students learn the roles of adaptation, shaping, and selection, and how to balance them. Wise judgments are dependent in part on selecting among these environmental responses.
10. Encourage students to form, critique, and integrate their own values in their thinking.
11. Encourage students to think dialectically, realizing that both questions and their answers evolve over time, and that the answer to an important life question can differ at different times in one's life (such as whether to go to college).
12. Show students the importance of dialogical thinking, whereby they understand interests and ideas from multiple points of view.
13. Teach students to search for and then try to reach the common good—a good where everyone wins, not only those with whom one identifies.
14. Encourage and reward wisdom.
15. Teach students to monitor events in their lives and their own thought processes about these events. One way to learn to recognize others' interests is to begin to identify your own.
16. Help students understand the importance of inoculating oneself against the pressures of unbalanced self-interest and small-group interest.

Procedures to Follow in Teaching for Wisdom

There are several procedures a teacher can follow in teaching for wisdom (and many teachers already follow at least some of these procedures). First, students would read classic works of literature and philosophy (Western or otherwise) to learn and reflect on the wisdom of the sages. . . .

Second, students would be engaged in class discussions, projects, and essays that encourage them to discuss the lessons they have learned from these works, and how they can be applied to their own lives and the lives of others. . . .

Third, students would need to study not only "truth," as we know it, but values. The idea would not be to force-feed a set of values, but to encourage students reflectively to develop their own values.

Fourth, such instruction would place an increased emphasis on critical, creative, and practical thinking in the service of good ends—ends that benefit not only the individual doing the thinking but others as well. All of these types of thinking would be valued, not just critical thinking.

Fifth, students would be encouraged to think about how almost everything they study might be used for better or worse ends, and to realize that the ends to which knowledge is put *do* matter.

Finally, teachers would realize that the only way they could develop wisdom in their students would be to serve as role models of wisdom themselves. A role model of wisdom will, I believe, take a much more Socratic approach to teaching than teachers customarily do. Students often want large quantities of information spoon-fed or even force-fed to them. They then attempt to memorize this material for exams, only to forget it soon thereafter. In a wisdom-based approach to teaching, students will need to take a more active role in constructing their learning. . . .

Lessons taught to emphasize wisdom would have a rather different character from lessons as they are often taught today. Consider examples.

First, social studies and especially history lessons would look very different. For example, high-school American history books typically teach American history from only one point of view, that of the new Americans. Thus, Columbus is referred to as having "discovered" America, a strange notion from the standpoint of the many occupants who already lived there when it was "discovered." The conquest of the southwest and the fall of the Alamo also are presented only from the point of view of the new settlers, not from the standpoint of, say, the Mexicans who lost roughly half their territory to the invaders. This kind of ethnocentric and frankly propagandistic teaching would have no place in a curriculum that sought to develop wisdom and an appreciation of the need to balance interests.

Second, science teaching would no longer be about facts presented as though they are the final word. Science often is presented as though it represents the end of a process of evolution of thought rather than one of many midpoints (Sternberg, 1998b). Students could scarcely realize from this kind of teaching that the paradigms of today, and thus the theories and findings that emanate from them, will eventually be superseded, much as the paradigms, theories, and findings of yesterday were replaced by those of today. Students further would need to learn that, contrary to the way many textbooks are written, the classical "scientific method" is largely a fantasy rather than a reality, and that scientists are as susceptible to fads as are members of other groups.

Third, teaching of literature would need to reflect a kind of balance that right now is often absent. Literature is often taught in terms of the standards and context of the contemporary U.S. scene. Characters often are judged in terms of our contemporary standards rather than in terms of the standards of the time and place in which the events took place. From the proposed standpoint, the study of literature must, to some extent, be done in the context of the study of history. The banning of books often reflects the application of certain contemporary standards to literature, standards of which an author from the past never could have been aware.

Fourth, foreign languages always would be taught in the cultural context in which they are embedded. Perhaps American students have so much more difficulty learning foreign languages than do children in much of Europe not because they lack the ability, but because they lack the motivation. They do not see the need to learn another language whereas, say, a Flemish-speaking child in Belgium does. Americans might be better off if they made more of an attempt wisely to understand other cultures rather than just to expect people from other cultures to understand them. And learning the language of a culture is a key to understanding. Americans might be less quick to impose their cultural values on others if they understood the others' cultural values. It is also interesting to speculate on why Esperanto, a language that was to provide a common medium of communication across cultures, has been a notable failure. Perhaps it is because Esperanto is embedded in no culture at all. It is the language of no one.

Culture cannot be taught, in the context of foreign-language learning, in the way it now often is—as an aside divorced from the actual learning of the language. It should be taught as an integral part of the language—as a primary context in which the language is embedded. The vituperative fights we see about bilingual education and about use of Spanish in the United States or French in Canada are not just, or even primarily, fights about language. They are fights about culture, and they are fights in need of wise resolutions.

Finally, as implied throughout these examples, the curriculum needs to be far more integrated. Literature needs to be integrated with history, science with history and social-policy studies, foreign language with culture. Even within disciplines, far more integration is needed. Different approaches to psychology, for example, are often taught as competing when in fact they are totally compatible. Thus, biological, cognitive, developmental, social, and clinical psychology provide complementary viewpoints on human beings. They do not compete with each other as being the "right approach." The study of the brain is important, for example, but most of the insights about learning and memory that can be applied to instruction have come from behavioral and cognitive approaches, not from the biological approach. And some of the insights that have supposedly come from the biological approach—such as "left-brain" and "right-brain" learning—are based on ignorant or outdated caricatures of research in this area rather than on actual findings. . . .

Conclusion

The road to this new approach of teaching for wisdom is bound to be a rocky one. First, entrenched structures, whatever they may be, are difficult to change, and wisdom is neither taught in schools nor, in general, is it even discussed. Second, many people will not see the value of teaching something that shows no promise of raising conventional test scores. These scores, which formerly were predictors of more interesting criteria, have now become criteria, or ends in themselves. The society has lost track of why they ever mattered in the first place, and they have engendered the same kind of mindless competition we see in people who relentlessly compare their economic achievements with those of others. Third, wisdom is much more difficult to develop than is the kind of achievement that can be developed and then readily tested via multiple-choice tests. Finally, people who have gained influence and power in a society via one means are unlikely to want either to give up that power or to see a new criterion be established on which they do not rank as favorably. Thus, there is no easy path to wisdom. There never was, and there probably never will be.

Wisdom might bring us a world that would seek to better itself and the conditions of all the people in it. At some level, we as a society have a choice. What do we wish to maximize through our schooling? Is it just knowledge? Is it just intelligence? Or is it also wisdom? If it is wisdom, then we need to put our students on a much different course. We need to value not only how they use their outstanding individual abilities to maximize their attainments, but how they use their individual abilities to maximize the attainments of others as well. We need, in short, to value wisdom.

References

Ardelt, M. (1997). Wisdom and life satisfaction in old age. *Journals of Gerontology Series B-Psychological Sciences & Social Sciences, 52B,* 15–27.

Campione, J. C., Brown, A. L., & Ferrara, R. (1982). Mental retardation and intelligence. In R. J. Sternberg (Ed.), *Handbook of human intelligence* (pp. 392–490). New York: Cambridge University Press.

Cantor, N., & Kihlstrom, J. F. (1987). *Personality and social intelligence.* Englewood Cliffs, NJ: Prentice Hall.

Eddy, A. S. (1988). *The relationship between the Tacit Knowledge Inventory for Managers and the Armed Services Vocational Aptitude Battery.* Unpublished masters thesis, St. Mary's University, San Antonio, TX.

Gardner, H. (1983). *Frames of mind: The theory of multiple intelligences.* New York: Basic Books.

Gardner, H. (1993). *Creating minds.* New York: HarperCollins.

Gardner, H. (1999). Are there additional intelligences? The case for naturalist, spiritual, and existential intelligences. In J. Kane (Ed.), *Education, information, and transformation* (pp. 111–131). Upper Saddle River, NJ: Prentice Hall.

Gardner, H., Krechevsky, M., Sternberg, R. J., & Okagaki, L. (1994). Intelligence in context: Enhancing students' practical intelligence for school. In K. McGilly (Ed.), *Classroom lessons: Integrating cognitive theory and classroom practice* (pp. 105–127). Cambridge, MA: MIT Press.

Goleman, D. (1995). *Emotional intelligence,* New York: Bantam.

Horvath, J. A., Sternberg, R. J., Forsythe, G. B., Sweeney, P. J., Bullis, R. C., Williams, W. M., & Dennis, M. (1996). *Tacit knowledge in military leadership: Supporting instrument development* (Tech. Rep. No. 1042). Alexandria, VA: U.S. Army Research Institute for the Behavioral and Social Sciences.

Kihlstrom, J., & Cantor, N. (2000). Social intelligence. In R. J. Sternberg (Ed.), *Handbook of intelligence* (pp. 359–379). New York: Cambridge University Press.

Langer, E. J. (1997). *The power of mindful learning.* Reading, MA: Addison-Wesley.

Mayer, J. D., & Salovey, P. (1993). The intelligence of emotional intelligence. *Intelligence,* 17, 433–442.

Nelson, T. O. (1999). Cognition versus metacognition. In R. J. Sternberg (Ed.), *The nature of cognition* (pp. 625–641). Cambridge, MA: The MIT Press.

Polanyi, M. (1976). Tacit knowledge. In M. Marx & F. Goodson (Eds.), *Theories in contemporary psychology* (pp. 330–344). New York: Macmillan.

Salovey, P., & Mayer, J. D. (1990). Emotional intelligence. *Imagination, Cognition, and Personality, 9,* 185–211.

Sternberg, R. J. (1980). Sketch of a componential subtheory of human intelligence. *Behavioral and Brain Sciences, 3,* 573–614.

Sternberg, R. J. (1985a). *Beyond IQ: A triarchic theory of human intelligence.* New York: Cambridge University Press.

Sternberg, R. J. (1985b). Implicit theories of intelligence, creativity, and wisdom. *Journal of Personality and Social Psychology, 49,* 607–627.

Sternberg, R. J. (1990a). Understanding wisdom. In R. J. Sternberg (Ed.), *Wisdom: Its nature, origins, and development* (pp. 3–9). New York: Cambridge University Press.

Sternberg, R. J. (Ed.). (1990b). *Wisdom: Its nature, origins, and development.* New York: Cambridge University Press.

Sternberg, R. J. (1997). *Successful intelligence.* New York: Plume.

Sternberg, R. J. (1998a). A balance theory of wisdom. *Review of General Psychology, 2,* 347–365.

Sternberg, R. J. (1998b). The dialectic as a tool for teaching psychology. *Teaching of Psychology, 25,* 177–180.

Sternberg, R. J. (Ed.). (1999a). *Handbook of creativity.* New York: Cambridge University Press.

Sternberg, R. J. (1999b). The theory of successful intelligence. *Review of General Psychology, 3,* 292–316.

Sternberg, R. J., Forsythe, G. B., Hedlund, J., Horvath, J., Snook, S., Williams, M. W., Wagner, R. K., & Grigorenko, E. L. (2000). *Practical intelligence in everyday life.* New York: Cambridge University Press.

Sternberg, R. J., & Grigorenko, E. L. (1997, Fall). The cognitive costs of physical and mental ill health: Applying the psychology of the developed world to the problems of the developing world. *Eye on Psi Chi, 2,* 20–27.

Sternberg, R. J., Grigorenko, E. L., Jarvin, L., & Lockery, D. (2000). Predicting academic success in high school: The role of successful intelligence. Unpublished manuscript.

Sternberg, R. J., Okagaki, L., & Jackson, A. (1990). Practical intelligence for success in school. *Educational Leadership, 48,* 35–39.

Sternberg, R. J., & Smith, C. (1985). Social intelligence and decoding skills in nonverbal communication. *Social Cognition, 2,* 168–192.

Sternberg, R. J., Wagner, R. K., & Okagaki, L. (1993). Practical intelligence: The nature and role of tacit knowledge in work and at school. In H. Reese & J. Puckett (Eds.), *Advances in lifespan development* (pp. 205–227). Hillsdale, NJ: Lawrence Erlbaum Associates, Inc.

Sternberg, R. J., Wagner, R. K., Williams, W. M., & Horvath, J. A. (1995). Testing common sense. *American Psychologist, 50,* 912–927.

Sternberg, R. J., & Williams, W. M. (1996). *How to develop student creativity.* Alexandria, VA: Association for Supervision and Curriculum Development.

Varela, F. J. (1999). *Ethical know-how: Action, wisdom, and cognition.* Stanford: Stanford University Press.

Wagner, R. K. (1987). Tacit knowledge in everyday intelligent behavior. *Journal of Personality and Social Psychology, 52,* 1236–1247.

Wagner, R. K., & Sternberg, R. J. (1985). Practical intelligence in real-world pursuits: The role of tacit knowledge. *Journal of Personality and Social Psychology, 49,* 436–458.

NO 

Scott G. Paris

Wisdom, Snake Oil, and the Educational Marketplace

The educational agenda for American schools is inclusive and diverse in both people and ideas. Policy makers at district and state levels of education are influenced to embrace numerous goals by tests, standards, and curricular mandates in agendas that become more diffused each year. Schools should provide academic knowledge and skills; they should enculturate a diverse group of students; they should compensate for absent family experiences; they should prepare the future workforce; and they should leave no child behind. In such lofty, perhaps idealistic pursuits, it seems obvious that schools should teach wisdom to American children. To argue against wisdom as an educational goal seems sacrilegious in a country where self-improvement through education is a holy assumption and a fundamental right of a democratic society. Why am I skeptical of Sternberg's proposal? First, I think his (2001) article on wisdom raises debatable points about what wisdom is and how it fits into schools. Second, the proposal to teach this brand of wisdom seems premature at best. Third, the entire article raises larger questions about who establishes educational agendas and how the agendas become adopted. Let's consider the last issue at the outset because it provides the frame and context for evaluating the specific proposal to teach wisdom in schools.

The Marketplace of Ideas in American Schools

Where do educational agendas originate? They are often bound in the books, materials, and curricula adopted by schools. Sometimes they are set by curriculum directors in various subject areas, but increasingly, the curricula in schools are established by state standards and high-stakes tests. Sternberg is correct in pointing out that these practices overemphasize decontextualized academic skills and inert knowledge at the expense of more thoughtful approaches to using knowledge. However, Sternberg pays little attention to the forces that decide curriculum issues and simply argues for the goodness of his ideas. Like many psychologists in the past 100 years, Sternberg believes

From *Educational Psychologist,* vol. 1, Fall 2001, pp. 257–260.

that good ideas about cognitive development ought to be imported and bought by schools. Sometimes this works but rarely beyond the demonstration level of a few schools involved in the research.

American education is a commercial marketplace of products and services driven by political forces as well as publishers, sales, and profits. Textbooks, tests, workbook materials, and computer-based practice exercises in language arts, math, social studies, and science ARE the curriculum in most schools. Indeed, there is more public scrutiny of these materials and more deliberate alignment of the curriculum, instruction, and assessment than ever before. Policy makers influence what publishers produce, and publishers create what policy makers are willing to buy. This reciprocity between the buyers and sellers is at the heart of the commercialization of American education. On the one hand, Sternberg's (2001) proposal transcends these discipline-based materials in favor of process-based emphases on reasoning that is integrative, intelligent, and wise. This is the strength of his emphasis on wisdom. On the other hand, Sternberg's proposal to teach wisdom in schools is just another approach in the marketplace and one wonders who would buy it.

Teachers do not have time to buy this brand of "teaching for wisdom" unless it supports their designated curriculum and, yes, raises test scores. Frankly, they rarely have the authority to make that kind of curriculum decision, and, if they do, they must delete time in their day from something else to add the new emphasis on wisdom. Administrators and curriculum directors are wary of buying new products unless they fit into their curriculum materials and scope and sequence charts. Any new curriculum, even one that promises wiser students, must be aligned with state standards and assessments and must have demonstrated value. In today's educational marketplace, that means it also must raise test scores (Paris, 2000). Publishers cannot invest in new products unless consumers demand them. This requires the inventors of new products to conduct research to demonstrate the benefits. However, this is a slippery slope because there is a wide range of research that counts as evidence to the public, and the public cannot always discern snake oil from genuinely useful educational curricula. Researchers run the risk of being accused of self-promotion or biased research if they conduct studies of their own ideas, yet it is unlikely that anyone else will conduct the studies. Sternberg's proposal fails to acknowledge this tangle of marketplace politics and commercialism and fails to provide a compelling rationale for policy makers to adopt his curricular agenda.

Analysis of Sternberg's Views of Wisdom

Sternberg reviews a large body of work relevant to the construct of wisdom during the past 20 years. Collectively, this work establishes the construct as conceptually useful, particularly to theories of reasoning in adulthood (e.g., Baltes & Staudinger, 2000). Other references to philosophical approaches, phylogenetic approaches, and Sternberg's own implicit-theoretical approach provide taxonomies and definitions of wisdom as a construct. Two general points undermine the implementation of this brand of wisdom in schools.

First, the cited work involves adults, not adolescents or children. Most approaches to wisdom frame the construct as intelligence plus, with the plus factor based on experiences, judgment, and so forth. The plus factor of wisdom is usually designated as knowledge that young people do not have because it is based on postformal or dialectical reasoning or something that is acquired only through age and experience. For example, Sternberg lists five factors as crucial to wise judgments: rich factual knowledge, rich procedural knowledge, life-span contextualism, relativism, and uncertainty. All these factors are described according to experiential knowledge across the life span, and each suggests that children do not have it and cannot get it, especially by explicit teaching as Sternberg points out. Thus, it seems to me, wisdom cannot be part of a curriculum for children and, by extension of Sternberg's descriptions, should not be an explicit focus of any K–12 curriculum.

Second, the construct of wisdom is difficult to define neatly. Sternberg describes research that identified wisdom on the bases of factor analyses, multidimensional scaling, or correlations. These analytical techniques label the data but are open to debate on the names and processes that they denote. Likewise, Sternberg uses comparisons and contrasts to indicate that wisdom is a kind of practical intelligence and is manifested in metacomponents of thinking that can be applied repeatedly in any order. It is *like* creative thinking, analytical thinking, and social intelligence but not exactly the same. Maybe important terms like *wisdom* will always be difficult to specify, and that may be one appealing feature of them, but the result is a vague term that can be interpreted in many ways to include any aspect of cognition. That seems too vague to serve as a curriculum mandate.

Problems of Definition and Dynamics

At a more molecular level, this particular brand of wisdom seems debatable in several basic claims. First, Sternberg (2001) defines wisdom as tacit knowledge that is procedural, goal-oriented, and acquired without direct help of others. Although I think the attempt to be specific is laudable, I am skeptical of limiting the notion of wisdom in these ways. It is not clear why explicit kinds of knowledge and nontacit processes are not part of wisdom. . . .

A second problem with this brand of wisdom is the debatable criteria imposed by the instrumental purpose of wisdom "as mediated by values toward the achievement of the common good." Whose values? Who determines the common good? How can we know if the good is shared, common, or self-serving? It sounds like wisdom is simply thinking that is consensual or situational or politically correct. Someone could argue that abortion and capital punishment are justified for the common good whereas others could argue the opposite. How can we determine which position is wise using Sternberg's view of wisdom? Is it wise to write a critical review? Is it wise to take a job in another city? How are these judgments made and by whom and based on what criteria? It seems that Sternberg's view of wisdom could lead simply to postdictive arguments about whether an action was wise (and it must be the action that is judged rather than the thoughts because wisdom for Sternberg is tacit and procedural). Wisdom becomes debatable among the participants. How can this theory lead to prescriptions for teaching? If the definition of wisdom cannot discriminate wise from unwise actions (or ideas), then it is inadequate. If the definition of wisdom means consensus or the views of a "philosopher-king," then it is merely opinion. How can educational curriculum be established on such shifting sands?

Dynamics of Wisdom

Sternberg's (2001) Figure 1 is intended to clarify the definition and operation of wisdom, but it seems mysterious to me. The achievement of the common good is supposed to be accomplished "through the balance among (a) intrapersonal, (b) interpersonal, and (c) extrapersonal interests, over the (a) short and (b) long terms." Excuse me, but doesn't that cover all factors within and between people and within any environment? How can anyone balance everything over the short and long terms? The definition includes everything and the dynamics of balance include all possible sources of influence. Sternberg goes on to say that this balancing act is done to achieve another balance, this one among "(a) adaptation to existing environments, (b) shaping of existing environments, and (c) selection of new environments, as shown in Figure 1." So, balancing every possible source of stimuli in the person and environment is done to achieve a balance that is adaptive, shaping, and selective of all possible environments. Fortunately, this complex process is explained in Figure 1, which depicts geometric shapes and arrows that move us magically from tacit knowledge to common good. No, I don't think so.

A large problem is Sternberg's (2001) assertion that a person somehow balances myriad factors as an act of wisdom. This is a mysterious process because so many possible factors are involved, the constructs are huge and difficult to define, and there is no independent way to establish which ones are important or how much of each factor is needed to achieve a balance. What is the metric of balance and how can one determine when a person is balanced or unbalanced? What motivates or guides or judges or corrects this balancing? Why is balance good? What happens when the factors are not in balance? There are many dialectical and homeostatic theories in psychology that posit balance in some form such as equilibrium, incongruity, and dissonance, but each one has two forces reconciled by some psychological process beyond the tautological goal of being in balance. Perhaps Sternberg intends to convey a multidimensional balancing like a "balanced diet." If so, then it is necessary to indicate some external reference system for a "healthy" amount of each factor. What is a healthy balance among intrapersonal, interpersonal, and extrapersonal interests? What is healthy adaptation to the environment and why is it necessarily wise? My concerns with the metaphor and the vagueness of Figure 1 are fundamental questions about the clarity of the theoretical relations among terms and the likelihood that they lead to testable hypotheses.

Another glaring problem with the dynamics of this model concerns teaching and learning. The notion of procedural knowledge acquired without direct help from others appears to contradict an educational agenda for wisdom. Sternberg (2001) states, ". . . one cannot teach particular courses of action that would be considered wise," which seems to contradict his own line of research described at the end of the article. This also denies wisdom as the explicit curriculum or instructional target of teachers. Sternberg argues that scaffolding and mediated learning experiences are necessary and seems to imply that scaffolding is intuitive, tacit, and not explicit. . . . I think that mediated or scaffolded learning includes explicit directions, corrections, guidance, and coaching that convey information that exceeds procedural knowledge. Indeed, knowing how to act without also having deeper understanding and perhaps metacognition about procedural knowledge may reflect automatic habits, but it hardly seems the essence of wisdom. We are left in a paradoxical position: either wisdom cannot be taught or it is taught implicitly, articulated neither by teacher nor pupil. Although each may be true on occasion, neither seems adequate for an educational agenda to enhance wisdom.

Problems of definition, dynamics, and measurement are interwoven. Sternberg goes to some length to describe how tacit knowledge can be measured, and he summarizes his research that shows that tacit knowledge about job skills and leadership is not predicted by traditional tests of intelligence and does correlate with actual performance. None of these tacit knowledge studies were conducted with children or educational issues but the implication is that wisdom, defined as tacit knowledge, can be measured and is related to children's reasoning. Those implications are explored in four claims: wisdom leads to happiness, mindful judgments, a harmonious world, and community welfare. It is difficult to disagree with these noble goals and difficult to disagree that an academic focus on inert knowledge is insufficient, but the question is whether this theory of wisdom is conceptually useful for guiding research and practice in education.

The 16 principles of teaching wisdom that Sternberg espouses are similar to many teaching practices in critical thinking, values education, character education, and moral education. They are consistent with the balance theory because the theory is so inclusive and vague that it could justify almost any kind of educational curriculum that steers children toward actions deemed as the "common good." It seems to me that people could twist this theory easily to justify any specific religious teaching or political agenda. This is, in my opinion, a liability of the vagueness of the terms and relations in this theory. Likewise, the prescribed procedures to follow to teach for wisdom are ad hoc suggestions to read classic works, engage in projects and discussions, reflect on values, and emphasize critical and creative thinking. All of these practices are embedded in other theories, curricula, and teaching practices and are not derived from this brand of wisdom. In fact, these practices contradict Sternberg's definition of wisdom as tacit, procedural knowledge and his claim that wisdom cannot be taught. . . .

Conclusion

Is this an adequate theory? I believe that the fundamental terms and relations in Sternberg's (2001) theory are not well specified and remain so vague and inclusive that anything can be explained or derived from them. To the extent that others disagree and see the balance theory as nested within Sternberg's theory of practical intelligence, then there is no need for a special theory of wisdom because it is just a subset of practical knowledge. The definitions of terms and the dynamics of balancing and teaching remain vague. The criteria for judging the instrumental value of wisdom according to standards defined as the "common good" raise many problems that remain unaddressed.

Does wisdom in this theory imply an educational agenda? The theory according to Sternberg explicitly denies that wisdom can be taught directly and we are given little insight as to how the curriculum can be revised to teach wisdom indirectly. What grade levels are appropriate? Where is the developmental scope and sequence chart of what children are expected to achieve? Why is this brand of wisdom important for a school or teacher to adopt? Where is the evidence that this kind of teaching is effective for children? [We] can infer that Sternberg believes that practices such as problem-based learning, reciprocal teaching, and mediated learning might all foster wisdom, but these practices have already been espoused and tested within other theoretical frameworks and they are not elaborated or verified more within the balance theory.

Do supporting studies warrant this theory and practice of teaching wisdom in schools? Sternberg's (2001) primary warrant for teaching wisdom in the schools rests on the claims that teachers do not teach wisdom and only emphasize acquisition of academic knowledge, the memorization of esoteric and inert facts. However, this is a derogatory characterization of schools without any justification that teaching children, at any age, the kinds of lessons implied in the 12-week curriculum leads to better reasoning, wisdom, happiness, knowledge utilization, and so on. His secondary warrant is that his view of wisdom would help students, but there is no evidence. There are plenty of people arguing for inclusion of their own platforms and programs in America's schools and it seems prudent for academics to substantiate their claims about what ought to be taught in schools with data rather than rhetoric. Whether this view of wisdom is snake oil or a panacea remains to be shown with appropriate research and data. Only then should the approach be placed into the educational marketplace for distribution and adoption in schools.

References

Baltes, P. B., & Staudinger, U. M. (2000). Wisdom: A metaheuristic (pragmatic) to orchestrate mind and virtue toward excellence. *American Psychologist, 55,* 122–136.

Paris, S. G. (2000). Trojan horse in the schoolyard: The hidden threats in high-stakes testing. *Issues in Education, 6,* 1–16.

Sternberg, R. J. (2001). Why schools should teach for wisdom: The balance theory of wisdom in educational settings. *Educational Psychologist, 36,* 227–245.

POSTSCRIPT

Should Schools Teach for Wisdom?

In the first selection, Sternberg describes wisdom as a values-based problem-solving strategy that includes tacit and explicit knowledge. This knowledge is mediated, or balanced, by interpersonal, relational, and environmental interests. He defines tacit knowledge as having "three main features: (a) it is procedural, (b) it is relevant to the attainment of goals people value, and (c) it often is acquired without direct help from others" (page 230). The focus of his presentation is the ways wisdom can be incorporated into school curricula. He provides sixteen principles to guide teacher instruction, such as "Teach students the usefulness of interdependence" and "Encourage students to form, critique, and integrate their own values in their thinking" (page 238).

Paris finds Sternberg's proposal unrealistic and irrelevant. In the opening sections of the second article, Paris reminds readers of the political and commercial aspects of our education system, particularly as it is driven by the testing industry. When examining Sternberg's direct points, Paris first takes issue with the notion that wisdom can be taught to children. Wisdom appears to require mature reasoning and reflection on many life experiences, both of which young children do not have. Finally Paris finds Sternberg's description of wisdom vague and contradictory. The balance theory asks an individual to keep all possible factors in mind and in balance when engaged in wise problem solving for the common good. Paris also points out the contradiction in Sternberg's notion that tacit knowledge is acquired *without* direct help, and yet the sixteen principles seem to be directives for teachers.

There are some ways these two positions could come to a resolution or compromise. One way might be to put Sternberg's proposal to the research test. As Paris points out, much of the research data collected on wisdom have come from adults, just as most of the theories of wisdom are focused on adulthood. Paris also notes that some of Sternberg's sixteen teaching principles are embedded in other theories. Sternberg may find that the current trends toward developing critical-thinking skills and promoting character education are moving teaching strategies closer to the practices and attitudes he proposes. The cognitive-structuralists, those who view cognitive development and wisdom in Piagetian and post-formal stages, provide some common ground for both Paris and Sternberg. These theories propose that cognitive development develops one stage at a time; thus, the best way to move individuals to wisdom is to help them progress through the earlier stages.

This debate highlights a rather common conflict between the actual and the ideal. In an ideal world, teachers would be able to teach for wisdom, but in the real world of American education, it would be difficult. Sternberg is searching for ways to apply the cognitive principles of wisdom to our ordinary lives, and Paris is reminding us of the political and commercial landscape of our society.

Suggested Readings

Paris, S., and Ayres, L. *Becoming Reflective Students and Teachers with Portfolios and Authentic Assessment* (Washington, DC: American Psychological Association, 1994).

Sternberg, R. *Wisdom, Intelligence, and Creativity Synthesized* (New York: Cambridge University Press, 2003).

Sternberg, R., and Williams, W. *Educational Psychology* (Needham Heights, MA: Allyn & Bacon, 2001).

Winne, P., and Corno, L. (Editors), *Teaching for Wisdom: Educational Psychologist* (Mahwah, NJ: Lawrence Erlbaum, 2002).

Contributors to This Volume

EDITOR

MARION MASON is a professor of psychology at Bloomsburg University of Pennsylvania where she routinely teaches cognitive psychology to undergraduates. She received her Ph.D. in developmental psychology in 1992 from The Ohio State University. Building on her graduate work on movement through Kohlberg's stages of moral development, Dr. Mason has continued to explore the value of a cognitive-structural or stage approach to morality and religious understandings. Her most recent research has been in the development of a model of interpersonal forgiveness.

STAFF

Larry Loeppke Managing Editor
Jill Peter Senior Developmental Editor
Nichole Altman Developmental Editor
Beth Kundert Production Manager
Jane Mohr Project Manager
Tara McDermott Design Coordinator
Bonnie Coakley Editorial Assistant

AUTHORS

JUDITH L. ALPERT is associate dean for Real Estate Planning and Capital Projects for the New York University School of Law.

JAMES AU-YEUNG is Senior Research Fellow in the Department of Psychology at University College London. He is a computational linguist by training, working primarily in the area of psycholinguistics/clinical linguistics.

MURIEL BEBEAU is professor in the Department of Preventive Sciences at the University of Minnesota School of Dentistry. She is director for the Center for the Study of Ethical Development, and a faculty associate in the Center for Bioethics, University of Minnesota.

KATHERINE S. BINDER is assistant professor of psychology at Mount Holyoke College.

HELEN BIRD is affiliated with the MRC Cognition and Brain Sciences Unit, Cambridge. Her interests include semantic dementia.

TONIA BOCK is a research assistant at the University of Notre Dame, working in the area of moral education.

LAURA S. BROWN is a clinical psychologist in private practice in Seattle, Washington. Her work has included the areas of feminist psychology, childhood sexual abuse, sexual abuse by therapists, and homosexuality and legal issues.

ALFONSO CARAMAZZA is professor of psychology and researcher in the Cognitive Neuropsychology Laboratory at Harvard University. His research is primarily on the organization and processing structure of the lexical system and the nature of lexical representations.

DAVID CARUSO is a research affiliate in the Department of Psychology at Yale University. He is the co-author of several ability tests of emotional intelligence with colleagues John Mayer and Peter Salovey.

STEPHEN J. CECI is professor in the Department of Human Development at Cornell University. He is widely published and has won numerous awards for his research into the accuracy of children's courtroom testimony.

B. CHANDRASEKARAN is a Senior Research Scientist and Director of The Ohio State University Laboratory for AI Research (LAIR).

PAUL M. CHURCHLAND is professor of philosophy at University of California at San Diego. His research interests are in the philosophy of science, the philosophy of mind, artificial intelligence and cognitive neurobiology, epistemology, and perception.

H. HARRINGTON CLEVELAND is assistant professor in criminal justice at the University of Nevada at Las Vegas.

LESLIE B. COHEN is professor of psychology at the University of Texas at Austin. His primary research interests are in perception, memory, and cognition of infants. He is director of the Children's Research Laboratory and the founding editor of the new journal, *Infancy*.

TANYA COOMBES is a research assistant at the Australian Stuttering Research Centre.

CHRISTINE A. COURTOIS is a clinical psychologist in private practice in Washington, D.C. and Clinical Director of the Post-Traumatic Disorders Program at the Psychiatric Institute of Washington. She conducts workshops internationally on treating incest and sexual assault.

DAVID CROSS is a professor in the College of Science and Engineering at Texas Christian University. His interests are developmental psychology and international adoption.

SUSAN A. DUFFY is associate professor of psychology at the University of Massachusetts at Amherst.

REBECCA EDDY is a doctoral candidate in the School of Behavioral and Organizational Sciences at Claremont Graduate University and is an adjunct professor at California State University at Fullerton.

SUE FRANKLIN is a senior lecturer in the Education, Communication, and Language Sciences Department, University of Newcastle upon Tyne, United Kingdom.

WILLIAM FRAWLEY is professor of linguistics and cognitive science at the University of Delaware. His research interests and publications focus on the integration of language and cognitive science.

MARYANNE GARRY is senior lecturer at Victoria University of Wellington, New Zealand. She also serves on the Editorial Board of the International Journal of Instructional Media.

ELEANOR GIBSON (1910–2002) was a well-known and highly respected researcher in the area of infant perceptual development. In 1992 she received the National Medal of Science. During her career, she taught at several universities, including MIT and Cornell University.

FERNAND GOBET is professor in intelligence systems in the ESRC Centre for Research in Development, Instruction and Training, School of Psychology, University of Nottingham, U.K.

ANGELA GOODWIN is a research assistant at the Australian Stuttering Research Centre.

JONATHAN HAIDT is associate professor of social psychology at the University of Virginia. His research interests include morality and emotion, and how they vary across cultures.

DAVID HOWARD is a research development professor in the Education, Communication, and Language Sciences Department, University of Newcastle upon Tyne, United Kingdom.

PETER HOWELL is professor of experimental psychology in the Department of Psychology at University College London.

MAREE J. HUNT is senior lecturer in applied experimental psychology at Victoria University of Wellington, New Zealand.

GEORGE KELLAS is professor of psychology at the University of Kansas. His research interests include language comprehension in relation to problems of ambiguity, expectation, attention, lexical access and in the decision process.

TEI LAINE is a doctoral student in computer science and cognitive science at Indiana University.

ELLEN J. LANGER is professor of psychology at Harvard University. Her research interests include decision making, deviance, and the social psychology of aging. Her most recent work analyzes each of these from the perspective of her theory of mindfulness.

JUNE H. LARRABEE is associate professor in the School of Nursing at West Virginia University.

ALAN M. LESLIE is professor of psychology and cognitive science and director of the Cognitive Development Laboratory at Rutgers University.

ELIZABETH F. LOFTUS is a Distinguished Professor at University of California at Irvine, and an affiliate professor at the University of Washington. Both appointments are in Departments of Psychology and Law. She is widely recognized as an expert in false memories as they relate to courtroom and eye witness testimony.

JEAN M. MANDLER is research professor of cognitive science at the University of California at San Diego. She has published numerous articles and books on infant cognition.

KATHRYN S. MARKS is a graduate student and teaching assistant in the Department of Psychology at the University of Texas at Austin.

CHARLES MARTIN is affiliated with the psychology department at the University of Kansas.

GERALD MATTHEWS is professor of psychology at the University of Cincinnati. His research interests include cognitive models of personality, the assessment of acute states of stress and emotion, and emotional intelligence.

JOHN D. MAYER is professor of psychology at the University of New Hampshire, specializing in personality and social psychology. He, along with Peter Salovey, first promoted the existence of emotional intelligence.

HELEN H. I. McCUTCHEON is a senior lecturer and deputy head of the Department of Clinical Nursing at the University of Adelaide in Australia.

KIMBERLY METCALF is a lecturer in psychology at Rockhurst College in Kansas City, Missouri.

JON MILLS holds a doctorate in both psychology and philosophy. He is affiliated with the Research Institute at Lakeridge Health Corporation and serves as associate editor for the Value Inquiry Book Series.

MIHNEA MOLDOVEANU is assistant professor of strategic management at the University of Toronto. His research interests include the ways in which managers solve problems and take action in complex predicaments.

DARCIA NARVAEZ is associate professor at University of Notre Dame. Her research is directed toward moral development and education.

MARK ONSLOW is professor and Director of the Australian Stuttering Research Centre. He also serves as Chair of the Health Sciences Grant Review Panel of the National Health and Medical Research Council of Australia, and is an Adjunct Professor at the University of Canterbury, New Zealand.

PETER A. ORNSTEIN is Professor and Chair of the Department of Psychology at the University of North Carolina at Chapel Hill. His research interests include cognition, learning, and memory.

ANN PACKMAN is a Senior Research Officer and Graduate Studies Coordinator at the Australian Stuttering Research Centre. She has worked for over 30 years in the area of stuttering, as a clinician, clinical teacher, and researcher.

SCOTT G. PARIS is professor of psychology at University of Michigan. His research interests include the development and motivation of children's learning, children's literacy strategies, metacognition, and motivation.

KATHY PEZDEK is professor of psychology in the School of Behavioral and Organizational Sciences at Claremont Graduate University. She is currently on the Editorial Board of the Journal of Applied Psychology.

JAN PINCOMBE is professor in the School of Nursing and Midwifery at the University of South Australia. She also serves on the editorial board for the International Journal of Nursing Practice.

KEITH RAYNER is a University of Massachusetts Distinguished University Professor in psychology. His research is focused on the process of skilled reading and using eye movement data to make inferences about perceptual and cognitive processes.

JAMES R. REST (1941–1999) was professor of psychology at University of Minnesota. He published many works on moral development, authored the Defining Issues Test, and was co-founder of the Center for the Study of Ethical Development.

RICHARD D. ROBERTS is lecturer at the University of Sydney. His research interests include individual differences in intelligence, mental (or cognitive) speed, psychometric scale development, emotional intelligence, and tactile-kinesthetic perception.

JOSEPH LEE RODGERS is professor of psychology at the University of Oklahoma. He also serves on the editorial board for the American Psychological Association journal *Psychological Methods*.

MARY ANN ROSSWURM is professor in the School of Nursing at West Virginia University. She is director of the Rural Aging Program of the Hartford Institute for Geriatric Nursing and a fellow in the Hartford Institute for Geriatric Nursing and Geriatric Interdisciplinary Team Training.

DAVID C. ROWE is professor of psychology in the Family Studies Department at the University of Arizona. His research interests are behavioral genetics and evolutionary psychology.

PERTTI SAARILUOMA is professor of cognitive science at the University of Helsinki. He has worked at several universities, among them Oxford, Cambridge, and Carnegie-Mellon.

PETER SALOVEY is a clinical psychologist serving as Dean of the Graduate School of Arts and Sciences and the Chris Argyris Professor of Psychology and Professor of Epidemiology and Public Health, and Chairman of the Department of Psychology at Yale University.

BRIAN J. SCHOLL is assistant professor in the Department of Psychology at Yale University, and director of the Yale Perception and Cognition Laboratory.

KEVIN SHAPIRO is a graduate student and researcher working with Alfonso Caramazza. His research interests include the cognitive architecture of the language system and the neural correlates of linguistic knowledge, informed mainly by studies of patients with speech difficulties following brain damage.

STEFANIE SHARMAN is a doctoral candidate in the School of Psychology at Victoria University of Wellington, New Zealand.

PETER J. SMITH is senior lecturer in the Department of Electrical and Computer Engineering at the University of Canterbury, New Zealand.

ROBERT J. STERNBERG is professor of psychology and education at Yale University. He is the author of numerous books on intelligence, wisdom, learning styles, and creativity. Dr. Sternberg also served as the president of the American Psychological Association in 2003.

PAUL C. L. TANG is professor of philosophy at California State University at Long Beach. His interests are in the philosophy of science and philosophy of the mind.

STEPHEN J. THOMA is professor of psychology in the Department of Human Development and Family Studies at the University of Alabama.

EDWIN VAN DEN OORD is associate professor in psychiatry at the Virginia Institute for Psychiatric and Behavioral Genetics.

HOANG VU is assistant professor of psychology at Saint Mary's College of California. His research is in the area of cognitive neuropsychology.

KIMBERLEY A. WADE is a doctoral candidate in the School of Psychology at Victoria University of Wellington, New Zealand.

JULANNE WATSON is affiliated with the University of Michigan.

HENRY M. WELLMAN is professor of psychology and a senior research scientist at the University of Michigan Center for Human Growth and Development. His primary area of research is children's development of a theory of mind.

KAREN WYNN is professor of psychology at Yale University. She received the American Psychological Association's Distinguished Scientific

Award for Early Career Contribution to Psychology (2000), and the National Academy of Sciences Troland Research Award (2001). She is the Director of the Yale University Infant Cognition Laboratory.

R. B. ZAJONC is professor of psychology at Stanford University and researcher at the Stanford Brain Research Institute. His research interests are in the areas of emotions and cognition.

MOSHE ZEIDNER is professor of educational psychology and Dean of Research at the University of Haifa in Israel.

Index